Costa Rica
a travel survival kit

Rob Rachowiecki

Costa Rica – a travel survival kit

2nd edition

Published by
Lonely Planet Publications
Head Office: PO Box 617, Hawthorn, Vic 3122, Australia
Branches: PO Box 2001A, Berkeley, CA 94702, USA
12 Barley Mow Passage, Chiswick, London W4 4PH, UK

Printed by
Colorcraft Ltd, Hong Kong
Printed in China

Photographs by
Amos Bien (AB), Randy Galati (RG), Robert Harrison (RH), Richard Laval (RL),
Michael Medill (MM), Rob Rachowiecki (RR), Ronald Todd (RT)

Front cover: Orange-fronted parakeet (RR)

First Published
September 1991

This Edition
January 1994

Although the authors and publisher have tried to make the information as
accurate as possible, they accept no responsibility for any loss, injury or
inconvenience sustained by any person using this book.

National Library of Australia Cataloguing in Publication Data

Rachowiecki, Rob
Costa Rica – a travel survival kit.

2nd ed.
Includes index.
ISBN 0 86442 205 9.

1. Costa Rica – Guidebooks.
I. Title. (Series: Lonely Planet travel survival kit).

917.286045

text & maps © Lonely Planet 1994
photos © photographers as indicated 1994
climate charts compiled from information supplied by Patrick J Tyson, © Patrick J Tyson, 1994

Rob Rachowiecki

Rob was born in London and became an avid traveller while still a teenager. He spent most of the 1980s in Latin America, travelling, teaching English, visiting National Parks, and working for *Wilderness Travel*, an adventure travel company. His first visits to Costa Rica in 1980-81 led to his co-authorship, with Hilary Bradt, of *Backpacking in Mexico & Central America*, Bradt Publications. He is the author of Lonely Planet's travel survival kits for *Ecuador* and *Peru* and he has contributed to Lonely Planet's shoestring guides to *South America* and *Central America*. Rob found Costa Rica to be an ideal country for combining his particular interests of bird-watching and natural history, visiting wilderness areas, and conservation. Rob has a Masters Degree in Biology from the University of Arizona. When not travelling, he lives in Arizona with his American wife, Cathy, and three small children: Julia Begulia, Ali Punelli, and The Baby Dey (aka 'Boobieman').

Dedication

This book is for my A L I S O N, who is learning to write her name and wants to write books like her daddy.

From the Author

Many people in Costa Rica helped me see the country through their eyes – their conversations, suggestions, hospitality and help were greatly appreciated. I was very fortunate to meet Randy Galati, road-traveller extraordinaire, during his peregrinations around the country – he provided me with a huge amount of insider traveller information.

Michael Kaye of Costa Rica Expeditions spent much time discussing responsible tourism issues with me – the staff of Costa Rica expeditions were also very helpful, especially biologist/guide Marcos Soto, driver and gentleman Ronald Sequeira Soto, and office staff Natalie Ewing, Alex Herrera, Annie Simpson de Gamboa, and Brenda Hannu. Hospitality and information was generously given by Susan and Mike Kalmbach of La Paloma Jungle Lodge in

Drake, Michael Medill of Rainbow Adventures near Golfito, Jaime Hamilton of the Tilajari Hotel in Muelle, Paul Vigneault of the Hotel Jaguar in Cahuita, Heidi Cruz B and Criss and Laurie Coberly of Los Ranchos in Jacó, and Ronald Esquivel and Marisela Rozados of Travelair.

I enjoyed useful and memorable talks with Jack and Diane Ewing of Hacienda Barú, Mauricio Salazar of ATEC in Puerto Viejo de Talmanca, Gordon Frankie of Amigos de Lomas Barbudal, Giovanni Bassey, marine biologist at Cuajiniquil, Jan Dankers of Jacó, Mary Messenger of Drake, Ligia of The Bookstore in San José, Amos Bien of Rara Avis, John Aspinall of Costa Rica Sun Tours, Luis Wachong of Hotel del Cerro in Golfito, Bob Hara of the Sol y Mar in Zancudo, and various national park rangers and staff to whom I apologise for not getting their names.

I also had a pleasant chat with the irrepressible columnist for the *The Tico Times*, Gypsy Cole, and thank that publication's excellent journalists whom I did not meet, but who provided me with many valuable insights within their columns. Some of my best information came from other travellers I met around the country.

During the writing of this book I was greatly aided by many of the above, who continued to fax/write/phone me information to make this book as up to date as possible. I also thank Val Merriman for cheerfully receiving and forwarding my many faxes, the absolutely angelic Andrea Webster for efficiently expressing travel info from the UK, and my wonderful mother-in-law, Pat Payson, for clipping every piece of Costa Rican information she came across during her voluminous reading. My dear wife and children tolerated with equanimity my time-consuming love/hate relationship with the word processor – thank you all.

From the Publisher

At Lonely Planet this edition was edited by David Meagher. Thanks also to Jeff Williams and James Lyon for their editorial contributions. Proofing and indexing was done by Frith Pike who saw the book through production.

Michelle Stamp was responsible for design and cartography; with Margaret Jung, for cover design; and, with Ann Jeffree and Chris Lee Ack, for illustrations.

Warning & Request

Things change – prices go up, schedules change, good places go bad and bad places go bankrupt – nothing stays the same. So if you find things better or worse, recently opened or long since closed, please write and tell us and help make the next edition better.

Your letters will be used to help update future editions and, where possible, important changes will also be included in a Stop Press section in reprints.

We greatly appreciate all information that is sent to us by travellers. Back at Lonely Planet we employ a hard-working readers' letters team to sort through the many letters we receive. The best ones will be rewarded with a free copy of the next edition or another Lonely Planet guide if you prefer. We give away lots of books, but, unfortunately, not every letter/postcard receives one.

Contents

Map Legend

BOUNDARIES

International Boundary
Internal Boundary
National Park or Reserve
The Equator
The Tropics

SYMBOLS

◉	NATIONAL	National Capital
●	PROVINCIAL	Provincial or State Capital
●	Major	Major Town
●	Minor	Minor Town
■		Places to Stay
▼		Places to Eat
✉		Post Office
✈		Airport
i		Tourist Information
⊖		Bus Station or Terminal
66		Highway Route Number
☾ ✝ 🕆 ♛		Mosque, Church, Cathedral
∴		Temple or Ruin
✚		Hospital
※		Lookout
▲		Camping Area
⊓		Picnic Area
⌂		Hut or Chalet
▲		Mountain or Hill
		Railway Station
		Road Bridge
		Railway Bridge
⇒ ⇐		Road Tunnel
→) (←		Railway Tunnel
		Escarpment or Cliff
⌣		Pass
⊓⊔⊓⊔		Ancient or Historic Wall

ROUTES

Major Road or Highway
Unsealed Major Road
Sealed Road
Unsealed Road or Track
City Street
Railway
Subway
Walking Track
Ferry Route
Cable Car or Chair Lift

HYDROGRAPHIC FEATURES

River or Creek
Intermittent Stream
Lake, Intermittent Lake
Coast Line
Spring
Waterfall
Swamp

Salt Lake or Reef

Glacier

OTHER FEATURES

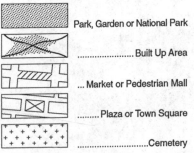

Park, Garden or National Park

Built Up Area

Market or Pedestrian Mall

Plaza or Town Square

Cemetery

Note: not all symbols displayed above appear in this book

Introduction

Travellers today are turning increasingly towards the tropics as an exciting, adventurous and exotic destination. Of the many attractive tropical countries to choose from, Costa Rica stands out as one of the most delightful in the world. There are not only tropical rainforests and beautiful beaches but also some surprises – active volcanoes and windswept mountain tops. So although Costa Rica is a small country, a large variety of tropical habitats is found within it – and they are protected by the best developed conservation program in Latin America.

Costa Rica is famous for its enlightened approach to conservation. About 27% of the country is protected in one form or another and over 11% is found in the national park system. This means that the traveller who wishes to do so can experience the tropics in a natural way. The variety and density of wildlife in the preserved areas attracts people whose dream is to see monkeys, sloths, caimans, sea turtles, and exotic birds in their natural habitat. And see them they will! Many other animals can be seen and, with a lot of luck, such rare and elusive animals as jaguars, tapirs, and harpy eagles may be glimpsed.

With both a Pacific and Caribbean coast, there is no shortage of beaches in Costa Rica. Some have been developed for tourism while others are remote and rarely visited. For a relaxing seaside vacation, you can stay in a luxurious hotel or you can camp – the choice is yours. And wherever you stay, you are likely to find a preserved area within driving distance where you will find monkeys in the trees by the ocean's edge.

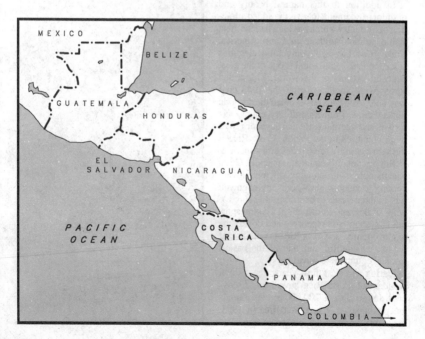

An active volcano is surely one of the most dramatic natural sights, and few visitors to Costa Rica can resist the opportunity to peer into the crater of a smoking giant. Whether you want to take a guided bus tour to a volcanic summit or hike up through the rainforest and camp out amid a landscape of boiling mud pools and steaming vents, you will find the information you need within the pages of this book.

Apart from hiking and camping in rainforests, mountains, and beaches, the adventurous traveller will find the opportunity to snorkel on tropical reefs, surf the best waves in Central America, or raft some of the most thrilling white water in the tropics. Pristine rivers tumble down the lower slopes of the mountains and the river banks are clothed with curtains of rainforest – a truly unique whitewater experience. Those liking to fish will find the rivers and lakes offer a beautiful setting for their sport, and the ocean fishing is definitely world class.

In addition to this natural beauty and outdoor excitement, there is the added attraction of a country which has long had the most stable political climate in Latin America. Costa Rica has had democratic elections since the 19th century and is one of the most peaceful nations in the world. The armed forces were abolished after the 1948 civil war, and Costa Rica has avoided the despotic dictatorships, frequent military coups, terrorism, and internal strife that have torn apart other countries in the region. Costa Rica is the safest country to visit in Latin America.

But it is not only safe – it is friendly. Costa Ricans delight in showing off their lovely country to visitors and wherever you go you will find the locals to be a constant source of help, smiles, and information. The transportation system is inexpensive and covers the whole country, so Costa Rica is both one of the most beautiful and one of the easiest tropical countries to travel in.

During the past few years, the natural wonders of Costa Rica have been discovered, and so close to 700,000 foreign tourists are predicted to visit Costa Rica in 1993, twice the number of five years ago. The

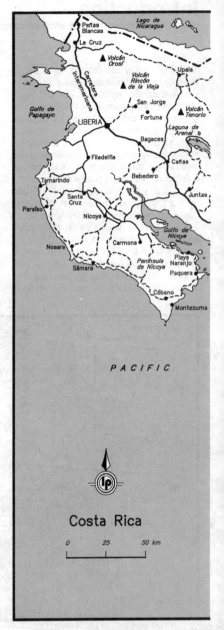

Costa Rica

0   25   50 km

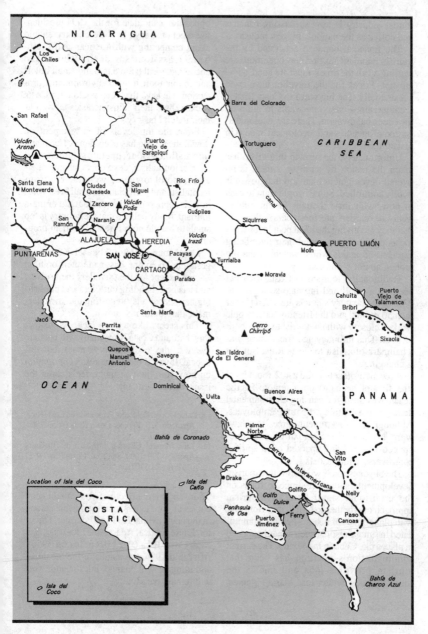

tourist industry is now surpassing bananas and coffee as the nation's biggest industry.

The financial bonanza generated by the tourism boom means that new operations are starting up all the time – most are good, a few are not. Prices for the traveller have risen substantially. The big word in Costa Rica is 'ecotourism' – everyone wants to jump on the Green bandwagon. There are 'ecological' car rental agencies and 'ecological' menus in restaurants!

Unfortunately, the growth in tourism has taken the nation by surprise – there is no overall development plan and the growth is poorly controlled. Some people want to cash in now, with little thought for the future. Many developers are foreigners – they say that they are giving the local people jobs, but locals don't want to spend their lives being waiters and maids whilst watching the big money go out of the country.

Traditionally, tourism in Costa Rica has been on a small and intimate scale. About 93% of the country's hotels are small (fewer than 50 rooms) and the friendly local people worked closely with the tourist to the benefit of both. This intimacy and friendliness was a hallmark of a visit to Costa Rica. But this is changing.

A recent project to build a 402-room hotel (the first of a chain) on a remote Pacific beach was sued for causing environmental damage and unfairly treating employees. Although the government agrees that laws were broken, the Spanish-owned hotel opened in 1992 and sparked off a spirited controversy within Costa Rica.

The big question is whether future tourism developments should continue to focus on the traditional small hotel, ecotourism approach or whether to turn to mass tourism, with plane-loads of visitors being accommodated in 'mega-resorts' such as has happened in places like Cancún in Mexico. The current administration's position has been that tourism provides jobs and boosts the economy; meanwhile, José María Figueres,

opposition candidate for the 1994 presidential elections, says that the country should avoid competing with Mexican and Caribbean mass-tourism destinations, and encourage local people to build small hotels and to link tourism with environmental protection. He says that this would help Costa Ricans share their idiosyncrasies as well as their natural history.

From the top levels of government on down, the debate has been fierce. Local and international tour operators and travel agents, journalists, developers, airline operators, hotel owners, writers, environmentalists and politicians have all been vocal in their support of either ecotourism or mass tourism. Many believe that the country is too small to handle both forms of tourism properly.

Local tour operator Michael Kaye suggests that everyone has made their opinion known except for the travellers themselves, and has been handing out fliers and publishing newspaper ads suggesting that travellers make their opinions known.

This seems like a good idea. As visitors travel around Costa Rica, many will become aware of the 'ecotourism vs mass tourism' debate. If you'd like to express your opinion on how you, the consumer, feels about the issue, call or write to:

Lic Rafael Angel Calderón, Presidente de Costa Rica, Apartado 520, Zapote, Costa Rica (☎ 53 7569, fax 53 9676).

Ing Luis Manuel Chacón, Ministro de Turismo, Apartado 777-1000, San José, Costa Rica (☎ 22 6152, fax 23 5107).

To make letters effective, you should send copies of your letters to a responsible person in the news media: Rodrigo Fournier, Director, La Républica, Apartado 2130-1000, San José, Costa Rica (☎ 23 0266, fax 55 3950). After mid-1994, the names of the president and minister will change, but the addresses will remain the same.

Facts about the Country

HISTORY
Pre-Conquest

Of all the Central American countries, Costa Rica is the one which has been most influenced by the Spanish conquest, and there are relatively few signs of pre-Columbian cultures. The well-known Mexican and northern Central American civilisations, such as the Aztecs, Olmecs and Mayas, did not reach as far south as Costa Rica. Those peoples who did exist in Costa Rica were few in number and relatively poorly organised. They offered little resistance to the Spanish, left us little in the way of ancient archaeological monuments, and had no written language. Many indigenous populations were wiped out by diseases after the arrival of Europeans.

This is not to say that Costa Rica's pre-Columbian peoples were uncivilised. A visit to San José's Museo de Jade (Jade Museum) or Museo de Oro Pre-Colombino (Pre-Colombian Gold Museum) will awe the visitor. The Museo Jade has the world's largest collection of pre-Columbian jade – and most of it comes from the Costa Rican area. The Museo de Oro has approximately 2000 pieces on display. Unfortunately, not a great deal is known about the cultures which produced these treasures.

The Greater Nicoya Area (consisting of Costa Rica's Península de Nicoya and reaching north along the Pacific coast into Nicaragua) has recently been the focus of archaeological study. This area, still noteworthy today for its pottery, has left workers

Pre-Columbian stone corn grinding table

with a wealth of ceramics, stonework and jade which have provided excellent insights into the pre-Columbian peoples who lived here. Although it is almost certain that people were living in Central America prior to 20,000 BC, the first definite evidence (in the form of ceramics) is dated to about 2000 BC, which corresponds to what is called Period III by archaeologists.

Period IV (from 1000 BC to 500 AD) was characterised by the establishment of villages and of social hierarchies, and the development of jade production. Ceramics and jade from Mayan areas indicate the influence of other peoples through trade. Skill in making pottery improved during Period V (500-1000 AD), and by Period VI (1000-1520 AD) society had developed into a number of settlements, some with populations of about 20,000 and ruled over by a chief. Most of these were quickly destroyed by the conquest and its aftermath. Today, the few remaining Indian groups are often known by the name of their last chief, as noted by the Spanish chroniclers. Particularly important in the Greater Nicoya area are the Chorotegas.

The Nicoya area had a dry and wet season – this led to a greater development in ceramics than on the Caribbean side, where water was rarely difficult to obtain and rarely had to be stored or transported long distances. In addition, the many bays and safe anchorages of the Península de Nicoya area led to trading in that area. Thus it is not surprising that the Greater Nicoya area has left archaeologists with more artefacts than has the Caribbean coast.

The major archaeological site in Costa Rica is the Monumento Nacional Guayabo, which is about 85 km east of the capital at San José. Guayabo is currently under investigation and is thought to have been inhabited from about 500 BC to 1400 AD. Streets, aqueducts and causeways may be seen, though most of the buildings have collapsed and have not yet been restored. Gold and stone artefacts have been discovered there. Archaeologists believe Guayabo was an important religious and cultural centre, although minor compared to Aztec, Inca or Maya sites.

But of all the existing remnants of pre-Columbian culture, none are more mysterious than the stone spheres of the Diquis region. This region covers the southern half of Costa Rica. Dotted throughout the area are perfectly shaped spheres of granite, some as large as a tall person and others as small as a grapefruit. They can be seen in the Museo Nacional and various parks and gardens in San José, as well as throughout the Diquis region. Some have been found, undisturbed for centuries, on the Isla del Caño, 20 km west of the southern Pacific coast. Who carved these enigmatic orbs? What was their purpose? How did they get to Isla del Caño?

No one has the answers to these questions. The puzzling granite spheres of southern Costa Rica serve to underscore how little we know and understand of the pre-Columbian cultures of the region.

Spanish Conquest

Because of the lack of a large and rich Indian empire at the time of the arrival of the Spaniards, the conquest of Costa Rica is euphemistically called a 'settlement' by some writers. In reality, the Spanish arrival was accompanied by diseases to which the Indians had no resistance, and they died of sickness as much as by the sword. Although the Indians did try to fight the Spanish, the small numbers of natives were unable to stop the ever larger groups of Spaniards who arrived every few years attempting to colonise the land.

The first arrival was Christopher Columbus himself, who landed near present-day Puerto Limón on 18 September 1502 during his fourth (and last) voyage to the Americas. He was treated well by the coastal Indians during his stay of 17 days and he noted that some of the natives wore gold decorations. Because of this, the area was dubbed 'costa rica' (the rich coast) by the Spaniards who imagined that there must be a rich empire lying further inland.

Spanish king Ferdinand appointed Diego

de Nicuesa as governor of the region and sent him to colonise it in 1506. This time the Indians did not provide a friendly welcome – perhaps they had become aware of the deadly diseases which accompanied the Europeans. The colonisers were hampered by the jungle, tropical diseases and the small bands of Indians who used guerrilla tactics to fight off the invaders. About half the colonisers died and the rest returned home, unsuccessful.

Further expeditions followed. The most successful, from the Spaniards' point of view, was a 1522 expedition to the Golfo de Nicoya area led by Gil González Dávila. Although the expedition claimed to have converted tens of thousands of Indians to Catholicism and returned home with a hoard of gold and other treasures, it was unable to form a permanent colony and many expedition members died of hunger and disease.

By the 1560s, the Spanish had unsuccessfully attempted colonisation several more times. By this time the Indian resistance, such as it was, had been worn down. Many Indians had died or were dying of disease and others had simply moved on to more inhospitable terrain.

In 1562 Juan Vásquez de Coronado arrived as governor and decided that the best place to found a colony was in the central highlands. This was an unusual move because the Spanish were a seafaring people and had naturally tried to colonise the coastal areas where they could build ports and maintain a contact with Spain. This proved problematical because the coastal areas were more prone to disease. When Coronado founded Cartago in 1563, his followers found a healthy climate and fertile volcanic soil and thus the colony survived.

Cartago was quite different from Spanish colonies in other parts of the New World. There were few Indians and so the Spanish did not have a huge workforce available, nor were they able to intermarry with the Indians to form the *mestizo* culture prevalent in many other parts of Latin America. The imagined riches of Costa Rica turned out to be very little and were soon plundered. The small

highland colony soon became removed from the mainstream of Spanish influence.

For the next century and a half the colony remained a forgotten backwater, isolated from the coast and major trading routes. It survived only by dint of hard work and the generosity and friendliness which have become the hallmarks of the contemporary Costa Rican character.

Eventually, in the 1700s, the colony began to spread and change. Settlements became established throughout the fertile plains of the central highlands (now known as the *meseta central*). Heredia was founded in 1717, San José in 1737, and Alajuela in 1782, although at the time of their founding the cities had different names. Much of Cartago was destroyed in an eruption of Volcán Irazú in 1723, but the survivors rebuilt the town. This expansion reflected slow growth from within Costa Rica, but the colony remained one of the poorest and most isolated in the Spanish empire.

Independence

Central America became independent from Spain on 15 September 1821, although Costa Rica was not aware of this situation until at least a month later. It briefly became part of the Mexican empire, then a state within the Central American United Provinces. The first elected head of state was Juan Mora Fernández, who governed from 1824 to 1833. During his time in office, coffee (introduced in 1808 from Cuba) began to be exported in modest amounts.

The rest of the 19th century saw a steady increase in coffee exports and this turned Costa Rica from an extremely poor and struggling country to a more successful and worldly one. Inevitably, some of the coffee growers became relatively rich and a class structure began to emerge. In 1849, a successful coffee grower, Juan Rafael Mora, became president and governed for 10 years.

Mora's presidency is remembered both for economic and cultural growth, and for a somewhat bizarre military incident which has earned a place in every Costa Rican child's history books. In June 1855, the US filibuster William Walker arrived in Nicaragua with the aim of conquering Central America and converting it into slaving territory, then using the slaves to build a Nicaraguan canal to join the Atlantic and Pacific. Walker defeated the Nicaraguans and marched for Costa Rica, which he entered more or less unopposed, reaching a hacienda at Santa Rosa (now a national park in north-western Costa Rica).

Costa Rica had no army, and so Mora organised 9000 civilians to gather what arms they could and march north in February 1856. In a short but determined battle, the Costa Ricans defeated Walker who retreated to Rivas in Nicaragua, followed by the victorious Costa Ricans. Walker and his soldiers made a stand in a wooden fort, and Juan Santamaría, a drummer boy from Alajuela, volunteered to torch the building, thus forcing Walker to flee. Santamaría was killed in this action and is now remembered as one of Costa Rica's favourite national heroes.

Despite his defeat, Walker returned unsuccessfully to Central America several more times before finally being shot in Honduras in 1860. Meanwhile, Mora lost favour in his country – he and his army were thought to have brought back cholera which caused a massive epidemic in Costa Rica. He was deposed in 1859, led a coup in 1860, failed, and was executed in the same year as Walker.

Democracy

The next three decades were characterised by power struggles among members of the coffee-growing elite. In 1869, a free and compulsory elementary education system was established – though, inevitably, families in more remote areas were not able to send children to schools. In 1889, the first democratic elections were held, with the poor *campesinos* (small farmer) as well as the rich coffee growers able to vote, although women and Blacks had not yet received that right.

Democracy has been a hallmark of Costa Rican politics since then, and there have been few lapses. One was between 1917 and 1919 when the Minister of War, Frederico

Tinoco, overthrew the democratically elected president and formed a dictatorship. This ended in Tinoco's exile after opposition from both the rest of Costa Rica and the US government.

In 1940, Rafael Angel Calderón Guardia became president. His presidency was marked by reforms which were supported by the poor but criticised by the rich. These reforms included workers' rights to organise, minimum wages and social security. To further widen his power base, Calderón allied himself, strangely, with both the Catholic church and the communist party to form a Christian Socialist group. This further alienated him from the conservatives, the intellectuals and the upper classes.

Calderón was succeeded in 1944 by the Christian Socialist Teodoro Picado who was a supporter of Calderón's policies, but the conservative opposition claimed the elections were a fraud. In 1948, Calderón again ran for the presidency against Otilio Ulate. The election was won by Ulate but Calderón claimed fraud because some of the ballots had been destroyed. Picado's government did not recognise Ulate's victory and the tense situation escalated into civil war.

Calderón and Picado were opposed by José (Don Pepe) Figueres Ferrer. After several weeks of civil warfare over 2000 people had been killed, and Figueres emerged victorious. He took over an interim government and in 1949 handed over the presidency to Otilio Ulate.

That year marked the formation of the Costa Rican constitution, which is still in effect. Women and Blacks received the vote, presidents were not allowed to run for successive terms, and a neutral electoral tribunal was established to guarantee free and fair elections. All citizens over the age of 18 are required to vote in elections held every four years. But the constitutional dissolution of the armed forces is the act which has had the most long-lasting impact on the nation. Today, almost half a century later, Costa Rica is known as 'the country which doesn't have an army.'

Although there are over a dozen political

parties, since 1949 the Partido Liberación Nacional (PLN – National Liberation Party), formed by Don Pepe Figueres has dominated, usually being elected every other four years. Figueres continued to be popular, and was returned to two more terms of office (in 1953 and 1970). He died in 1990. Another famous PLN president was Oscar Arias, who governed from 1986 to 1990. For his work in attempting to spread peace from Costa Rica to all of Central America, Arias received the Nobel Peace Prize in 1987.

In recent years the Christian Socialists have continued to be the favoured party of the poor and working classes and Calderón's son, Rafael Angel Calderón Fournier, has played a large role in that party, running for president three times. After two losses, he was finally elected president in 1990, succeeding Oscar Arias.

The next presidential elections are due in 1994. During 1993, six PLN politicians vied for their party's candidacy for the forthcoming presidential elections. These included Margarita Penon, who was the first woman to have reached such an advanced position in a presidential race in Costa Rica. Penon is the wife of ex-president Oscar Arias. The

Oscar Arias

winner of the PLN candidacy, however, was José María Figueres, son of Don Pepe.

PLN's Figueres will be opposed by the Partido Unidad Social Cristiana (PUSC – Social Christian Unity Party). The PUSC pre-candidates for the 1994 presidential elections included Juan José Trejos, the son of ex-president José Juaquin Trejos (1966-70), and economist Miguel Angel Rodriguez who emerged the winner.

Clearly, the history of politics in Costa Rica is strongly influenced by a handful of families, as shown by the father-son, husband-wife associations mentioned. In fact, 75% of the 44 presidents of Costa Rica prior to 1970 were descended from just three original colonisers.

GEOGRAPHY

Costa Rica is bordered to the north by Nicaragua, to the north-east by the Caribbean Sea, to the south-east by Panama, and to the west and south-west by the Pacific Ocean. It lies completely within the tropics between latitudes 11°13'N and 8°N, and longitudes 82°33'W and 85°58'W. In addition, Costa Rica claims the Isla del Coco (25 sq km) at about 5°30'N and 87°05'W.

Geographically, Costa Rica is an extremely varied country despite its tiny size, which at 51,100 sq km is almost half the size of the state of Kentucky in the USA, two-thirds the size of Scotland, or three-quarters the size of Tasmania in Australia.

A series of volcanic mountain chains runs from the Nicaraguan border in the north-west to the Panamanian border in the south-east, thus splitting the country in two. The most north-westerly range is the Cordillera de Guanacaste, consisting of a spectacular chain of volcanoes which can be appreciated by the traveller heading south from the Nicaraguan border along the Carretera Interamericana (Interamerican Highway). These include Volcán Orosí (1487 metres) in the Parque Nacional Guanacaste, Volcán Rincón de la Vieja (1895 metres) and Volcán Santa María (1916 metres), both in the Parque Nacional Rincón de la Vieja, as well as Volcán Miravalles

Provinces of Costa Rica

(2026 metres) and Volcán Tenorio (1916 metres).

Further to the south-east is the Cordillera de Tilarán which includes the renowned cloud forest preserve at Monteverde and, just north of the main massif, the continually exploding Volcán Arenal (1633 metres), the most active volcano in Costa Rica.

The Cordillera de Tilarán runs into the Cordillera Central, which includes the famous Volcán Poás (2704 metres) and Volcán Irazú (3432 metres) both of which are active volcanoes lying at the centre of national parks named after them, and Volcán Barva (2906 metres) which is in Parque Nacional Braulio Carrillo.

The most south-easterly mountains are associated with the Cordillera de Talamanca which is higher, geologically older and more remote and more rugged than the other ranges. About 16 separate peaks reach in excess of 3000 metres, the highest being Cerro Chirripó (3820 metres). Changing altitudes play an important part in determining geographical, climatic and ecological variation. Many different ecological habitats are found, corresponding with altitudinal changes up the mountains.

In the centre of the highlands lies the meseta central, which is surrounded by mountains (the Cordillera Central to the north and east, the Cordillera de Talamanca to the south). It is this central plain, between about 1000 and 1500 metres above sea level, which contains four of Costa Rica's five largest cities, including San José, the capital. Over half of the population lives on this plain, which contains fertile volcanic soils.

On either side of the volcanic central highlands lie coastal lowlands which differ greatly in character. The smooth Caribbean coastline is 212 km long and is characterised by year-round rain, mangroves, swamps, an intracoastal waterway, sandy beaches and small tides.

The Pacific coast is much more rugged and rocky. The tortuous coastline is 1016 km long, with various gulfs and peninsulas. It is bordered by tropical dry forests, which receive almost no rain for several months each year, as well as by mangroves, swamps and beaches. Tidal variation is quite large and there are many offshore islands.

The two most important peninsulas are the Nicoya, separated from the mainland by a gulf of the same name, and the Osa, separated from the mainland by the Golfo Dulce. The Península de Nicoya is hilly, dry and dusty. It is known for its cattle farming and also its beach resorts. The Península de Osa contains the Parque Nacional Corcovado which is one of Costa Rica's protected rainforests.

CLIMATE

Like many tropical countries, Costa Rica experiences two seasons, the wet and the dry, rather than the four seasons temperate regions are used to. The dry season is generally from about late December to April and this is called *verano* (or summer) by Costa Ricans. The rest of the year tends to be wet, and is called *invierno* (or winter).

The Caribbean coastal region tends to be wet all the year round. The dry season is characterised by fewer rainy days and spells of fine weather sometimes lasting a week or more. In the highlands, the dry season really is dry, with only one or two rainy days per month. It can, however, rain for up to 20 days per month in the wet season. The north and central Pacific coastal regions have similar rain patterns to the highlands, whilst the southern Pacific coast can experience rain year round, though less so in the dry season.

Temperature varies little from season to season and the main influencing factor is altitude. San José, at 1150 metres, has a climate which the locals refer to as 'eternal spring'. Lows average a mild 15°C year round whilst highs are a pleasant 26°C. The coasts are much hotter with the Caribbean

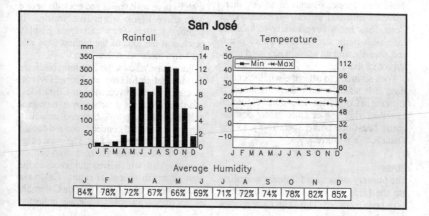

averaging 21°C at night and over 30°C during the day; the Pacific is 2°C or 3°C warmer. People used to a more temperate climate can find the high heat and humidity of the coastal areas oppressive – but mostly adjust to the conditions after a few days.

FLORA & FAUNA

Costa Rica is a small country, but its range of habitats gives it an incredibly rich diversity of flora and fauna. This biodiversity attracts nature lovers from all over the world.

Life Zones

Ecologists use a system called Holdridge Life Zones, presented by L R Holdridge in 1947, which classifies the type of vegetation to be found in a given area by analysing climatic data such as temperature, rainfall and its variation throughout the year. This data is combined with latitudinal regions and altitudinal belts to give approximately 116 'life zones' on earth. Twelve tropical life zones are found in Costa Rica, and are named according to forest type and altitude. Thus there are dry, moist, wet and rain forests in tropical, premontane, lower montane, montane and subalpine areas.

Within a life zone several types of habitat may occur. Much of Parque Nacional Santa Rosa, for example, is tropical dry forest, but types of vegetation within this zone include deciduous forest, evergreen forest, mangrove swamp and littoral woodland. Thus Costa Rica has a huge variety of habitats, each with particular associations of plants and animals, and an attempt has been made to protect them all.

With so much to offer the wildlife enthusiast, it is small wonder that ecotourism is growing in Costa Rica. Two-thirds of foreign travellers visit one or more nature destinations; one-third come specifically to see Costa Rica's wildlife.

Birds

The primary attractions for many naturalists are the birds, of which some 850 species have been recorded. This is far more species than found in any one of the continents of North America, Australia or Europe.

It is not only the biodiversity which makes Costa Rica attractive to the birder (birdwatcher). The birds are spectacular, and, if you know where to go, surprisingly easy to see. A favourite destination of birders is the Monteverde Cloud Forest. Here, based in comfortable hotel accommodation, you can see birds such as the resplendent quetzal, perhaps one of the most dazzling birds of the tropical rainforest.

A member of the trogon family, the male resplendent quetzal lives up to its name with a glittering green plumage set off by a crimson belly, and white tail feathers contrasting with bright green tail coverts streaming over 60 cm beyond the bird's body. The head feathers stick out in a spiky green helmet through which the yellow bill peeks coyly. The male tries to impress the female by almost vertical display flights during which the long tail coverts flutter sensuously. A glimpse of this bird is the highlight of many a birder's trip to Costa Rica.

A walk through the cloud forest is often made eerie by the penetrating whistles and ventriloqual 'bonk!' calls of the three-wattled bellbird, a member of the cotinga family. The haunting notes sound so loud that they can easily be heard half a km away. Spotting this large, chestnut-brown bird, with its pure white head and neck decorated with three black worm-like wattles, is another matter. They call from display perches at the tops of the highest trees and are heard more often than seen.

For many visitors the hummingbirds are the most delightful birds to observe. Over 50 species have been recorded in Costa Rica, and their beauty is matched by extravagant names, such as purple-throated mountain gem, white-crested coquette, and red-footed plumeleteer, to name a few. The most enigmatic of these birds is the indigo-capped hummingbird, which lives and breeds in the high mountain valleys of central Colombia and has never been found outside Colombia except once – a single female was collected high on Volcán Miravalles in the Cordillera de Guanacaste, in 1895! So if you happen to see an indigo-capped hummingbird, be sure to tell someone.

Hummingbirds can beat their wings up to 80 times a second, thus producing the typical hum for which they are named. This exceptionally rapid beat also enables them to hover in place when feeding on nectar, or even to fly backwards. The energy needed to keep these tiny birds flying is high, and species living in the mountains have evolved an amazing strategy to survive a cold night. They go into a state of torpor, which is like a nightly hibernation, by lowering their body temperature by between 17°C and 28°C, depending on the species, thus lowering their metabolism drastically.

Other exciting birds include brightly coloured scarlet macaws and 15 other parrot species; six different toucans, with their incredibly large and hollow bills; the huge and very rare harpy eagle, which is capable of snatching monkeys and sloths off branches as it flies past; and a large array of other tropical birds such as flycatchers (75

Hummingbird

species), tanagers (45 species), antbirds (29 species) and cotingas (19 species).

Costa Rica's national bird is the clay-coloured robin, locally called the *yigüirro*. This bird rarely sings, except during the breeding season. This coincides with the onset of the rainy season, and early colonisers used to say that the yig rro song brought the rains – the most important event of the agricultural year. The bird is relatively drab-looking but the popular folk-tale of 'rain-bringing' led to the clay-coloured robin's standing as the national bird.

Mammals

Mammals, too, are fairly well represented, with over 200 species recorded in the country. Visitors to national parks and other protected areas are likely to see one or more of the four monkeys found in Costa Rica – the howler, spider, white-faced capuchin and squirrel monkeys.

The male howler monkeys are heard as often as they are seen; their eerie vocalisations carry long distances and have been likened to a baby crying or the wind moaning through the trees. Many visitors are unable to believe they are hearing a monkey when they first hear the mournful sound.

Blue and Gold Macaw

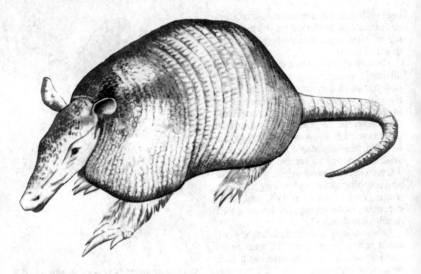

Nine-banded armadillo

Other tropical specialities include two species of sloths. The three-toed is quite often sighted because it is diurnal, whereas the two-toed sloth is nocturnal and is therefore rarely seen. Sloths are often found hanging motionless from tree limbs, or seen progressing at a painfully slow speed along a branch towards a particularly succulent bunch of leaves, which are their primary food source. Leaf digestion takes several days and sloths defecate about once a week.

Sloths are most fastidious with their toilet habits, always climbing down from their tree to deposit their weekly bowel movement on the ground. Biologists do not know why sloths do this; one suggested hypothesis is that by consistently defecating at the base of a particular tree, the sloths provide a natural fertiliser which increases the quality of the leaves of that tree, thus improving the sloth's diet.

There are three anteater species, of which the tamandua is the most commonly seen by visitors, while the giant and silky anteaters are glimpsed only occasionally.

Other likely mammal sightings include armadillos, agoutis (large rodents), peccaries (wild pigs), kinkajous, raccoons, skunks, otters, foxes, squirrels and bats. Other exotic mammals such as ocelots, jaguars and tapirs are rarely seen, but the chance of seeing one of these rare species in the wild makes any trip to a national park an exciting one.

Insects

At least 35,000 species of insects have been recorded in Costa Rica, and many thousands remain undiscovered. Among the first insects that the visitor to the tropics notices are the butterflies. One source claims that Costa Rica has 10% of all the butterfly species in the world; another states that hundreds of butterfly species remain to be discovered here; a third reports that over 3000 species of butterflies and moths are recorded from one national park alone (Santa Rosa).

Perhaps the most dazzling butterflies are the morphos. With their 15 cm wingspans and electric-blue upper wings, they lazily flap and glide along tropical rivers in a shimmering display. When they land, however, their wings close and only the brown underwings are visible. In an instant they have changed from outrageous display to modest camouflage.

Camouflage plays an important part in the lives of many insects. Some resting butterflies look exactly like green or brown leaves, while others look like the scaly bark of the tree on which they are resting. Caterpillars are often masters of disguise. Some species mimic twigs, another is capable of constricting certain muscles to make itself look like the head of a viper, and yet another species looks so much like a bird dropping that it rarely gets attacked by predators.

Any walk through a tropical forest will almost invariably allow the observer to study several different types of ants. Among my favourites are the *Atta* leaf-cutter ants, which can be seen marching in columns along the forest floor, carrying pieces of leaves like little parasols above their heads. The leaf segments are taken into the underground colony and there they are allowed to rot down into a mulch. The ants tend their mulch gardens carefully, and allow a certain species of fungus to grow there. The bodies of the fungus are then used to feed the colony, which can exceed a million ants.

Other insects are so tiny as to be barely visible, yet their lifestyles are no less esoteric. The hummingbird flower mites are barely half a mm in length, and live in flowers visited by hummingbirds. When the flowers are visited by the hummers, the mites scuttle up into the bird's nostrils and use this novel form of air transport to disperse themselves to other plants. Smaller still are mites which live on the proboscis of the morpho butterflies.

From the largest to the smallest insects, there is a world of wonder in the tropical forests.

Other Animals

Amphibians and reptiles form a fascinating part of the Costa Rican fauna. The approximately 150 species of amphibians include

Tree frog

species such as a type of tree frog which spends it entire life cycle in trees. These remarkable creatures have solved the problem of where to lay their eggs by doing so into the water trapped in cup-like plants called bromeliads, which live high up in the forest canopy.

Dendrobatids, better known by their colloquial name of poison-arrow frogs, have also been well studied. They are among the most brightly coloured of frogs; some are bright red with black dots, others red with blue legs, and still others are bright green with black markings. Several Costa Rican species have skin glands exuding toxins which can cause paralysis and death in many animals and also humans. It is well known that dendrobatids have long been used by Latin American forest Indians to provide a poison with which to dip the tips of their hunting arrows. It should be mentioned that the toxins are most effective when introduced into the bloodstream (as with arrows) but have little effect when a frog is casually touched.

A toad which many people see is the so-called marine toad, which is actually found both on the coast and inland up to a height of

2000 metres. It is frequently seen in the evenings around human habitations in rural areas and is unmistakable because of its size. It is the largest lowland toad in tropical America and specimens reaching 20 cm long and weighing up to 1.2 kg have been recorded – that is one big toad!

Snakes make up over half of the 200-plus species of reptiles found in Costa Rica. They are much talked about but seldom seen – they usually slither away into the undergrowth when people approach, and only a lucky few visitors are able to catch sight of one. Perhaps the most feared is the fer-de-lance, which is very poisonous and sometimes fatal to humans. It often lives in overgrown, brushy fields. Agricultural workers clearing these fields are the most frequent victims; tourists get bitten very rarely.

More frequently seen reptiles include the common *Ameiva* lizards, which have a white stripe running down their backs. Also common, the bright green basilisk lizards are seen on or near water and the males are noted for the huge crests running the length of their head, body and tail, giving them the appearance of a small dinosaur. They can reach almost a metre in length and are nicknamed

Jesus Christ lizards for their ability to literally run across water when they are disturbed.

Larger reptiles which attract visitors to coastal national parks such as Tortuguero on the Caribbean or Santa Rosa on the Pacific include turtles and crocodiles (or caymans). There are 14 species of turtles, some of which are marine and others freshwater.

Marine turtles reproduce by climbing up sandy beaches to lay their eggs, and this can be a spectacular sight. The largest marine turtle is the leatherback, which has a carapace (shell) up to 1.6 metres long and an average weight of a stunning 360 kg. Watching this giant come lumbering out of the sea is a memorable experience. The olive ridleys are much smaller, but practise synchronous nesting when tens of thousands of females may emerge out of the sea on a single night – another unforgettable sight.

Other sea creatures are found by snorkellers and divers visiting offshore islands and coral reefs. Spectacularly coloured tropical fish, starfish, sea urchins, sea anemones and other species await those travellers willing to venture below the surface of the sea.

Basilik Lizard

Plants

The floral biodiversity is also high; some 10,000 species of vascular plants have been described, and more are being added to the list every year. Orchids alone account for some 1200 species, of which the most famous is the March-blooming *Cattleya skinneri* which is Costa Rica's national flower. Its local name is *guaria morada*.

The tropical forest is very different from the temperate forests that many North Americans or Europeans may be used to. Temperate forests, such as the coniferous forests of the far north or the deciduous woodlands of milder regions, tend to have little variety. They are pines, pines and more pines, or endless tracts of oaks, beech and birch.

Tropical forests, on the other hand, have great variety; about 1400 tree species have been recorded in Costa Rica. If you stand in one spot and look around, you'll see scores of different species of trees, but often have to walk several hundred metres to find another example of any particular species.

This incredible variety generates biodiversity in the animals which live within the forests. There are several dozen species of fig trees in Costa Rica, for example, and the fruit of each species is the home of one particular wasp species. The wasp benefits by obtaining food and protection; when it flies to another fig tree, the fig benefits because the wasp carries pollen on its body. Many trees and plants of the forest provide fruit, seeds or nectar for insects, birds and bats. They rely upon these visitors to carry pollen across several hundred metres of forest to fertilise another member of the appropriate plant species.

These complex interrelationships and high biodiversity are among the reasons why biologists and conservationists are calling for a halt to the destruction of tropical forests. It is a sobering thought that three-quarters of Costa Rica was forested in the late 1940s; by the early 1990s, less than a quarter of the country remained covered by forest. To try and control this deforestation and protect its wildlife, Costa Rica has instigated the most progressive national parks system in Latin America.

NATIONAL PARKS

The national parks system began in the 1960s and now there are about three dozen national parks, wildlife refuges, biological reserves, monuments and recreation areas in Costa Rica. These comprise almost 12% of the total land area, and more are being planned, notably in the Volcán Arenal area. In addition there are various buffer zones such as forest reserves and Indian reservations which boost the total area of 'protected' land to about 27%. These buffer zones still allow farming, logging and other exploitation, however, so the environment is not totally protected within them.

As well as the national parks system there are about two dozen privately-owned lodges, reserves and haciendas which have been set up to protect the land, and these are well worth visiting.

There is a slowly moving project to link geographically close groups of national

Orchids

National Parks & Protected Areas

parks and reserves, private preserves, and national forests into regional conservation units (RCUs). Carefully managed agricultural land will help create buffer zones to protect the more critical areas. Wildlife corridors will be used to enable wildlife to range over larger areas. These areas have been dubbed 'megaparks' by local conservationists, and it is has been suggested that they will eventually cover about a quarter of Costa Rica's land area.

The result will have two major implications. First, larger areas of wildlife habitats will be protected in blocks, allowing greater numbers of species and individuals to exist. Second, the administration of the national parks will be delegated to regional offices, allowing a more appropriate management approach for each particular area. This is happening to a certain extent, although many regional offices play what appear to be obscure bureaucratic roles rather than providing necessary management and guidance.

Up-to-date information about the national parks can be obtained from the public information office of the Servicio de Parques Nacionales (SPN) (☎ 57 0922) at Calle 25,

1	Refugio Nacional de Fauna Silvestre Isla Bolaños	26	Reserva Indígena Zapatón
2	Parque Nacional Santa Rosa	27	Parque Nacional Manuel Antonio
3	Parque Nacional Guanacaste	28	Parque Nacional Volcán Irazú
4	Estación Experimental Horizontes	29	Monumento Nacional Guayabo
5	Parque Nacional Rincón de la Vieja	30	Reserva Indígena Barbilla
6	Refugio Nacional de Vida Silvestre Caño Negro	31	Reserva Indígena Alto y Bajo Chirripó
7	Reserva Indígena Guatuso	32	Parque Nacional Chirripó
8	Parque Nacional Marino Las Baulas de Guanacaste	33	Reserva de la Biosfera La Amistad
9	Refugio Nacional de Fauna Silvestre Ostional	34	Reserva Indígena Tayní
10	Reserva Indígena Matambú	35	Reserva Biológica Hitoy-Cerere
11	Parque Nacional Barra Honda	36	Reserva Indígena Telire
12	Reserva Biológica Lomas Barbudal	37	Reserva Indígena Talamanca
13	Parque Nacional Palo Verde	38	Reserva Indígena Bribrí & Cabécar
14	Reserva Biológica Bosque Nuboso Monteverde	39	Parque Nacional Cahuita
15	Refugio Silvestre Peñas Blancas	40	Reserva Indígena Cocles/KéköLdi
16	Reservas Biológicas de Guayabo, Negritos y de los Pájaros	41	Refugio Nacional de Vida Silvestre Gandoca-Manzanillo
17	Refugio Nacional de Vida Silvestre Curú	42	Reserva Indígena Ujarrás
18	Reserva Natural Absoluta Cabo Blanco	43	Reserva Indígena Salitre
19	Refugio Nacional de Fauna Silvestre Barra del Colorado	44	Reserva Indígena Cabagra
20	Parque Nacional Tortuguero	45	Parque Nacional Marino Ballena
21	Parque Nacional Volcán Poás	46	Reserva Indígena Térraba
22	Estación Biológica La Selva	47	Reserva Indígena Boruca
23	Parque Nacional Braulio Carrillo	48	Reserva Indígena Curré
24	Reserva Indígena Quitirrisí	49	Reserva Indígena Coto Brus
25	Reserva Biológica Carara	50	Reserva Biológica Isla del Caño
		51	Parque Nacional Corcovado
		52	Reserva Indígena Osa
		53	Refugio Nacional de Fauna Silvestre Golfito
		54	Reserva Indígena Abrojo-Montezuma
		55	Reserva Indígena Conte Burica
		56	Parque Nacional Isla del Coco

Avenida 8 & 10 in San José. Office hours are 8 am to 4 pm Monday to Friday. The SPN headquarters (☎ 33 4118, 33 4246, fax 23 6963; Apartado 10104-1000, San José) is at the same address.

The SPN radio communications office (☎ 33 4160) maintains radio contact with many national parks which do not have a regular telephone service. If you speak Spanish, you can call to arrange for overnight accommodation, meals, and other services provided by the rangers in many parks. Some parks have telephones – their numbers are given in the appropriate sections.

Most national parks can be entered without permits, but a few of the biological reserves do require a permit which can be obtained by applying to the public information office. The entrance fee to most parks is US$1.50, and a further US$2.25 is charged if you intend to camp overnight.

These entrance fees are remarkably low when compared to the fees charged to enter the national parks of other countries in which tourism is economically important. Unfortunately, the SPN doesn't have enough funding to staff the national parks adequately, and illegal poaching, logging and other activities are endangering remote areas of the parks. It would make sense to raise the park fees and use the increased revenue to improve the national parks infrastructure. The current entry fee is about what you'd pay for a *gallo pinto* (rice and beans) breakfast – these magnificent national parks are certainly worth more than a handful of rice and beans.

Many national parks are in remote areas and are rarely visited – they suffer from a lack of rangers and protection. Others are extremely (and deservedly) popular for their world-class scenic and natural beauty as well as their wildlife. In the idyllic Parque Nacional Manuel Antonio, a tiny park on the Pacific coast, the number of visitors often reaches 1000 per day in the high season. Annual visitation has rocketed from about 36,000 visitors in 1982 to over 150,000 by 1991. This number of visitors threatens to ruin the area by driving away the wildlife, polluting the beaches and replacing wilderness by hotel development. Over the past couple of years there have been serious discussions about limiting park visitation to certain days or limiting numbers of visitors. Implementing such a plan would require rangers, public information and monitoring – but the money is not available for this.

Costa Rica has a world-famous reputation for the excellence and far-sightedness of its national park system – but lack of funds, sometimes fuzzy leadership and concentrated visitor use have shown that there are problems in paradise.

Volunteering

Each year, several hundred people work as volunteers for the park system, and almost half of the volunteers are foreigners. Work ranges from building trails to organising surveys to office work. Attempts are made to match volunteers' skills and desires with the work available. Foreign volunteers pay about US$5 to US$7 per day towards food, housing and administrative costs. Some volunteers stay with park rangers in remote and relatively primitive ranger stations – amenities such as hot water and electricity may not be available. Other volunteers may work in a parks office in a town and live in an apartment.

If you are interested, you need to make a commitment of a minimum of two months. For an application, write or fax Stanley Arguedas at the SPN address above or go in person for an interview if you are already in Costa Rica.

Conservation

The loss of key habitats, particularly tropical forests, is a problem which has become significantly more pressing in recent years. Deforestation is happening at such a rate that most of Costa Rica's (and the world's) tropical forests will have disappeared by early in the 21st century; loss of other habitats is a less publicised but equally pressing concern. With this in mind, two important questions arise: why are habitats such as the tropical rainforests so important, and what can be done to prevent their loss?

Much of Costa Rica's remaining natural vegetation is tropical forest and there are many reasons why this particular habitat is important. Almost a million of the known species on earth live in tropical rainforests such as that found in the Parque Nacional Corcovado. Scientists predict that millions more plant and animal species remain to be discovered, principally in the world's remaining rainforests, which have the greatest biodiversity of all the habitats known on the planet. This incredible array of plants and animals cannot exist unless the rainforest that they inhabit is protected – deforestation will result not only in the loss of the rainforest but in countless extinctions as well.

The value of tropical plants is more than in simply providing habitat and food for animals; it is more than the aesthetic value of the plants themselves. Many types of medicines have been extracted from forest trees, shrubs and flowers. These range from anaesthetics to antibiotics, from contraceptives to cures for heart diseases, malaria and various other illnesses. Many medicinal uses of plants are known only to the indigenous inhabitants of the forest. Other pharmaceutical treasures remain locked up in tropical forests, unknown to anybody. They may never be discovered if the forests are destroyed.

Costa Rica's Instituto Nacional de Biodiversidad (INBio) has recently signed contracts with pharmaceutical companies (such as Merck & Company of the USA, the world's largest pharmaceutical company). Funding from the companies is used to support INBio's efforts to protect the rainforests by training local campesinos to make plant and animal collections in the field and to make detailed inventories. Simple preliminary studies are carried out to identify those species which may have potential in medicine. Thus local people are involved at a grass-roots level and pharmaceutical companies receive selections of species which may lead to vital medical breakthroughs. The deal doesn't stop there, however. Part of the contract earmarks a percentage of the potential profits for conservation and preservation efforts. Although this innovative plan is still in its fledgling stages, it is hoped that it will prove to be a success not only in Costa Rica, but in other countries too.

A number of Costa Rica's crops are monocultures which suffer from a lack of genetic diversity. In other words, all the plants are almost identical because agriculturalists have bred strains which are high yielding, easy to harvest, good tasting etc. If these monocultures are attacked by a new disease or pest epidemic they could be wiped out because the resistant strains may have been bred out of the population. Plants such as bananas (an important part of Costa Rica's economy) are found in the wild in tropical forests, so in the event of an epidemic scientists could look for disease-resistant wild strains to breed into the commercially raised crops. Deforestation leads not only to species extinction, but also to loss of the genetic diversity which could help species adapt to a changing world.

Whilst biodiversity for aesthetic, medicinal and genetic reasons may be important to us, it is even more important to the local indigenous peoples who still survive in tropical rainforests. In Costa Rica there are Bribri Indian groups still living in the rainforest in a more or less traditional manner. A few remaining Cabecar Indians still practise shifting agriculture, hunting and gathering. Over 60% of Costa Rica's remaining Indian

people are protected in the new Reserva de La Biosfera La Amistad which comprises two national parks and a host of indigenous and biological reserves in the Talamanca region on the Costa Rica-Panama border. Various international agencies, notably Conservation International, are working with the Costa Rican authorities to protect this area and the cultural and anthropological treasures within.

Rainforests are important on a global scale because they moderate global climatic patterns. Scientists have recently determined that the destruction of the rainforests is a major contributing factor to global warming which would lead to disastrous changes to our world. These changes include melting of ice caps causing rising ocean levels and flooding of major coastal cities, many of which are only a scant few metres above present sea level. Global warming would also make many of the world's 'breadbasket' regions unsuitable for crop production.

All these are good reasons why the rainforest and other habitats should be preserved and protected, but the reality of the economic importance of forest exploitation by the developing nations which own tropical forests must also be considered. It is undeniably true that the clearing of the rainforest provides resources in the way of timber, pasture and possible mineral wealth, but this is a short-sighted view.

The long-term importance of the rainforest both from a global view and as a resource of biodiversity, genetic variation and pharmaceutical wealth is becoming recognised by the countries that contain forest as well as the other nations of the world which will be affected by the destruction of these rainforests. Efforts are now underway to show that the economic value of the standing rainforest is greater than the wealth realised by deforestation.

One important way of making the tropical forest an economically productive resource without cutting it down is by protecting it in national parks and preserves and making it accessible to visitors. This type of ecotourism has become extremely important for the economy of Costa Rica and other nations with similar natural resources. More people are likely to visit Costa Rica to see monkeys in the forest than to see cows on pasture. The visitors spend money on hotels, transport, tours, food and souvenirs. In addition, many people who spend time in the tropics gain a better understanding of the natural beauty within the forests, and the importance of preserving them. The result is that when the visitors return home they become goodwill ambassadors for tropical forests.

The fundamental concepts of ecotourism are excellent and it has been very successful – so successful that there have been inevitable abuses. Taking advantage of Costa Rica's 'green' image, some developers are trying to promote mass tourism and are building large hotels with accompanying environmental problems. Apart from the obvious impact such as cutting down vegetation, diverting or damming rivers and driving away wildlife, there are secondary impacts such as erosion, lack of adequate waste treatment facilities for a huge hotel in an area away from sewerage lines, and the building of socially, environmentally and economically inadequate 'shanty towns' to house the maids, waiters, cooks, cleaners and many other employees needed. I recommend that you stay in smaller hotels that have a positive attitude about the environment rather than the large, mass-tourism destinations.

Apart from ecotourism, other innovative projects for sustainable development of tropical forests are being developed. Many of these developments are occurring on private reserves such as Monteverde and Rara Avis. Here individuals not connected with the government are showing how forests can be preserved and yield a higher economic return than if they were cut down for a one-time sale of lumber and then the land turned into low-yield pasture.

Monteverde is particularly interested in educating children worldwide. It has created the Children's Rainforest program which preserves rainforest and promotes education of children in Costa Rica and throughout the world. It has also begun the Monteverde

Conservation League (MCL) which works towards protecting existing forest by promoting environmentally responsible use of surrounding lands. The MCL works with farmers to increase their productivity and thereby remove pressures on further farm expansion into forested areas. It promotes reforestation in regions where it is possible to plant seedlings as a future economic resource and for prevention of soil erosion.

Rara Avis is a private preserve with two lodges set in pristine rainforest with superb bird-watching. In addition to ecotourism, Rara Avis is developing sustainable use of the surrounding rainforest by harvesting seeds from valuable ornamental plants growing in the area, by harvesting aerial roots of philodendron plants for use as wicker in local furniture manufacture, and by developing a butterfly research station and farm.

Hacienda Barú is on a private reserve on the southern Pacific coast of Costa Rica. Their main focus is, simply, tourism – but a form of tourism with several significant implications. Most importantly, they advise and encourage local people to set up other environmentally and socially sensitive tourism projects.

Instead of trying to take it all for themselves, they strictly limit the number of tourists that they allow onto their reserve and are very active in promoting their neighbours' small tourism projects. This is an excellent approach to involving local people in conserving their environment through carefully managed ecotourism.

Some SPN-managed parks and reserves have privately funded support groups which work at the grass-roots level to educate and involve local people in the conservation process. These small non-government organisations often play a crucial role of instigating environmental awareness into the campesino neighbours of the national parks – a role which bureaucratically-hampered political appointees to the park system may not always be able to carry out. A good example is the Amigos de Lomas Barbudal (Friends of the Lomas Barbudal Biological

Reserve) who have developed in-depth educational programs for local people who are now, in their turn, involved in educating reserve visitors in the visitor centre. Another excellent example of community involvement is the Asociación Talamanqueña de Ecoturismo y Conservación (ATEC) based in Puerto Viejo de Talamanca on the southern Caribbean coast. ATEC teaches and encourages local people to provide tourist facilities which include staying in small local lodges, learning about the environment and discovering the local culture.

On a governmental and international level, Costa Rica is considered a leader in conservation. The national parks system is the best-developed in Latin America, although it was set up only just in time. Had the system not been implemented, Costa Rica would undoubtedly have lost all its tropical forests by the end of the century. The Fundación de Parques Nacionales and the Fundación Neotropica work hand-in-hand to preserve the national parks.

The Costa Rican authorities have been particularly progressive in working towards conservation of natural areas. Various international agencies such as Conservation International, The Nature Conservancy and the Worldwide Fund for Nature (WWF) have provided much needed expertise and economic support. They have also developed programs such as the 'debt for nature' swaps whereby parts of Costa Rica's national debt are paid off in return for preserving crucial habitat areas.

These large organisations have been criticised because they spend a good proportion of their money on government-level projects, with more funds going into intangibles like bureaucracy and not enough trickling down to the local people. This is undeniably true – Costa Rica has its fair share of desk conservationists who don't really seem to *do* anything apart from pull a pay cheque.

However, it is also true that it is important to support organisations which use part of their funds in political ways – this leads to an environmental awareness at the governmen-tal level which is an essential background to successful conservation at all levels. At the opposite end of the spectrum are small grass-roots organisations working with local people to educate and involve them in conservation work.

This is also essential – local people *must* be involved if conservation projects are to succeed in the long term. On the other hand, grass-roots organisations are sometimes viewed as upstarts with little respect for the status quo and bureaucratically mired governmental policies. So who is right? Clearly, both are.

Most of these organisations, whether well-known large charities or obscure grass-roots level groups, rely on support from the public. Even large entities such as the WWF receive the bulk of their income not from government agencies or corporate contributions, but from individual members.

In 1992, for example, fully 57% of the WWF's revenue came from its individual members worldwide. The Nature Conservancy reports that 62% of its 1992 revenue came from individual members. The vital work of these and other agencies requires every assistance possible.

If you visit Costa Rica and want to conserve it, think about volunteering for one of the following organisations (it helps if you speak Spanish) or sending a cheque. Some of these donations are tax deductible (especially if sent to the country in which you pay taxes). The price of a dinner in a fine restaurant will help ensure that future generations will be able to enjoy the Costa Rica that you see now.

Amigos de Las Aves
  Apartado 32-4001, Río Segundo, Alajuela
  (☎ 41 2658)
  Breeds (non-wild) macaws for release in the wild; needs volunteers, donations and pet/zoo macaws
Amigos de Lomas Barbudal
  Bagaces, Guanacaste (☎ 67 1029, fax 67 1203)
  Friends of Lomas Barbudal, 691 Colusa Ave, Berkeley, CA 94707-1517, USA
  (☎ (510) 526 4115, fax (510) 528 0346)
  Grass-roots organisation dedicated to conservation of tropical dry forest

APREFLORAS
Apartado 917-2150, Moravia, San José
(☎ 40 6087)
Patrols wilderness areas; needs Spanish-speaking volunteers

Arbofilia
Apartado 512-1100, Tibas, San José
(☎ 35 5470, fax 40 8832)
Has innovative reforestation projects in the Carara area

ASCONA
Apartado 8-3790-1000, San José
(☎ 22 2296, 22 2288)
One of the first environmental watchdog groups in Costa Rica; needs volunteers with scientific backgrounds

Caribbean Conservation Corporation (CCC)
Apartado 246-2050, San Pedro, San José
(☎ 25 7516, fax 34 1061)
PO Box 2866, Gainesville, FL 32602, USA
(☎ (904) 373 6441, fax (904) 375 2449)
Especially concerned with sea-turtle conservation and accept volunteers with biology backgrounds. Involved in the Paseo Pantera project to conserve the coast and lowlands of Central America

CEDARENA
Apartado 134-2050, San Pedro, San José
(☎ 25 1019)
An environmental law group which supports conservation organisations – donations and Spanish-speaking volunteers with a legal background are needed

Conservation International
1015 18th St NW, Suite 1000, Washington DC 20036, USA (☎ (202) 429 5660, fax (202) 887 5188)
Works worldwide in conservation projects and is particularly involved with La Reserva de la Biosfera La Amistad in Costa Rica

Cultural Survival
Apartado 246-2050, San Pedro, San José
(☎ 24 9215, fax 34 1061 – shares office with CCC)
53A Church St, Cambridge, MA 02138, USA
(☎ 617 495 2562, fax 617 495 1396)
An advocacy and self-help organisation for indigenous groups worldwide. Works with Bribri and other coastal Indians

FECON
Apartado 1948-1002, Paseo de los Estudiantes, San José (☎ 22 5977)
Coordinates and raises funds for many of Costa Rica's conservation organisations

Fundación de Parques Nacionales
Apartado 1008-1002, Paseo de los Estudiantes, San José (☎ 20 1744, fax 20 0939)

Fundación Neotropica
Apartado 236-1002, Paseo de los Estudiantes, San José (☎ 53 2130)
Works on sustainable development in communities near protected areas and aids the national park system

Monteverde Conservation League
Apartado 10165-1000, San José
(☎ 61 2953, fax 61 1104)
Works on several conservation projects in the Monteverde area, including the Children's Rainforest

The Nature Conservancy – Latin America Division
1815 North Lynn St, Arlington, VA 22209, USA
(☎ 703 841 5300)
Is involved in many projects and accepts contributions designated for the Fundación Neotropica, Monteverde Conservation League, Costa Rica Marine Parks Fund and CEDARENA

Rainforest Alliance
270 Lafayette St, Suite 512, New York, NY 10012, USA (☎ 212 941 1900)
Works to save rainforests worldwide

Worldwide Fund for Nature
1250 24th St, NW, Washington DC 20037, USA
(☎ 202 293 4800)
Works to save endangered wildlife everywhere and accepts contributions designated for ASCONA
90 Eglinton Ave E, Suite 504, Toronto, Ontario M4P2Z7, Canada
Accepts contributions designated for the Monteverde Conservation League

There is an Environmental Hotline (☎ 21 8484) open 24 hours a day for reports of abuses to Costa Rica's environment.

GOVERNMENT

Government is based on the Constitution of 7 November 1949 (see the History section). The president, who is both the head of government and head of state, wields executive power, assisted by two vice-presidents and a cabinet of 18 ministers. Elections are held every four years, and an incumbent cannot be re-elected.

The country is divided into the seven provinces of San José, Alajuela, Cartago, Heredia, Guanacaste, Puntarenas, and Limón. Each province has a governor who is appointed by the president. The provinces are divided into 81 *cantons* (counties) and subdivided into 429 districts. For about every 30,000 people in each province, a *diputado/a* (congressman/woman) is elected every four years to the Legislative Assembly, or Congress, which totals 57 diputados in all. This is where much of the power of government lies. Incumbents cannot serve successive terms.

The Legislative Assembly appoints 22 Supreme Court magistrates for minimum terms of eight years, and these judges select judges for the lower courts. The idea behind these three power structures is to prevent any one person or group from having too much control, thus ensuring a real democracy. There is also an Electoral Tribunal which is responsible for supervising elections and ensuring that the electoral process is fair and democratic. Known as the 'fourth power', the Electoral Tribunal consists of three magistrates (and six substitutes) who are independent of the government.

There is no army in Costa Rica. Instead, there is a 5000-strong Civil Guard, which is a form of police force. There are also rural and municipal police forces.

Although there are about a dozen political parties, only two groups have been in power since 1949; the National Liberation Party or a Christian Socialist party. Since 1990, the Social Christian Unity Party has been in power under the presidency of Rafael Angel Calderón Fournier.

The next elections will be held in February of 1994. The vote is mandatory for all citizens aged over 18 years. An up-to-date and validated electoral card must be carried by all Costa Ricans as identification and is needed for anything from opening a bank account to getting a job. During the 1990 elections, about 82% of eligible voters cast a ballot. Election day is very upbeat in Costa Rica – everyone treats it like a patriotic holiday, with flag waving, car-horn honking and general euphoria.

ECONOMY

Until the middle of the 19th century, Costa Rica was a very poor country with an economy based on subsistence agriculture. Then the introduction of coffee began to provide a product suitable for export. This was followed by bananas, and today these two crops continue to be the most important in the country. During 1990, banana exports brought Costa Rica US$317 million and coffee brought in US$245 million. Other important traditional exports included beef (US$46 million) and sugar (US$34 million). In 1992 and 1993, however, a drop in world coffee prices and a European Economic Community quota system for banana imports threatened to decrease the value of these traditionally foremost foreign money earners.

Recent economic news shows that, as Costa Rica enters the 1990s, non-traditional export items such as ornamental plants and flowers, fish, pineapples, pharmaceutical products, textiles and clothing, tires, furniture and many other products are beginning to rival the traditional exports. In 1990, for the first time, non-traditional exports combined edged out the traditional products as dollar earners with US$710 million com-

Coffee harvesting

pared to US$667 million. The European Economic Community bought 47% of the traditional and 12% of the non-traditional exports; the USA bought 37% and 41% respectively.

Imports for 1990 reached US$2026 million. Raw materials and capital goods for industry accounted for 54.5 of the imports, and the USA was the main supplier of imports (41%). In 1991, the gap between exports and imports closed to US$1598 million in exports and US$1877 million in imports.

Meanwhile, tourism was experiencing an unprecedented boom in Costa Rica. Numbers of foreign tourists visiting the country rose from 376,000 in 1989 to 610,000 in 1992. The value of revenues from tourism in 1992 was US$421 million, making tourism a contender for the position of the single most important earner of foreign currency. This boom has led to much controversy over which way this rapidly growing industry should develop. There are those who want to bring in mass tourism and build huge hotels – a sort of cut-rate Cancún. Critics of this approach point out that Costa Rica is simply not capable of handling any more tourists and that mass tourism would lead to severe environmental and cultural degradation, spoiling the Costa Rica which people were flocking to see. Haphazard building and development is occurring without adequate controls and the country lacks a master plan for the development of tourism. The debate continues to rage at all levels, from the president on down.

Inflation has been dropping steadily over the past few years (27.3% in 1990, 25.3% in 1991, 16.9% in 1992). This is much less than what it was in the 1980s, but is still higher than in the 1960s and 1970s. The government says that its aim is to reduce inflation to 12%. The national debt is about US$4 billion. The standard of living is the second highest in Central America (after Panama). The economic growth of the country in 1992 was 7.3%, the highest total in almost a decade. In 1992, the Gross National Product grew by 4.9% over the 1991 figure of US$1806 per inhabitant – the highest such growth in 14 years. Unemployment is between 5% and 6%. Average wages are under US$200 per month and the government claims that 22.2% of families live below the poverty level, which is a significant improvement over past years.

POPULATION

As of July 1992 the population of Costa Rica was 3,160,405, of which just over 50.5% were male. About 60% of the people live in the highlands. The annual population growth rate is 2.5%, and infant mortality has dropped steadily, reaching 13.2 per 1000 in 1992. Almost 37% of the population is under 15. Life expectancy is 75.2 years. Literacy is over 90% – among the best in Latin America.

The population density is about 62 people per sq km, the third highest in Central America, after El Salvador and Guatemala. This is about 25% of the population density of the UK, but over twice as high as that of the USA.

PEOPLE

The vast majority of the people are White, mainly of Spanish descent. Less than 2% of the population is Black, except in the thinly populated Caribbean province of Limón. Here, about 33% of the inhabitants trace their ancestry to either the early days of slavery in Costa Rica or to the immigration of labour forces from Jamaica to build the railways and work the banana plantations in the late 1800s. As with other Caribbean Blacks, many of them speak a lively dialect of English. They were actively discriminated against in the early 1900s, not even being allowed to spend a night in the highlands, but since the 1949 constitution they have had equal rights.

A small number of Indians remain, making up less than 1% of the population. (Note that the literal translation of Indian is *indio* which is an insulting term to Costa Rica's indigenous inhabitants. They prefer the term *indígena* which means native inhabitant.) Estimates of the Indian population vary from 5,000 to 30,000 – the higher end is the most likely if one includes non pure-blooded Indians. Many of these have integrated to the extent that they are more or less indistinguishable from other Costa Ricans. Small populations of culturally distinct tribes include the Bribri from the Talamanca area near the south-eastern coast and Panamanian border, the Borucas in the southern Pacific coastal areas and the Guayami straddling the Panamanian border. Other groups – the Chorotegas, Cabecares, Terrabas and others – have been either assimilated into the Costa Rican way of life or wiped out soon after the conquest.

There are 22 Indian reservations in Costa Rica but, for the most part, these are of little interest to travellers who often may not even know they are within a reservation. A few reservations discourage visitation and a few have perhaps a store selling some local crafts (along with the usual country-store items like cans of sardines and bottles of soft drinks).

The Costa Rican people call themselves *ticos* or *ticas* (male and female). This supposedly stems from their love of the use of diminutives such as *chico* (small) becoming *chiquito* and *chiquitito* or *chiqitico*. You don't hear the *tico* ending as much as you used to, though one of my last memories of my most recent trip was of the waiter at the airport café telling me he'd be with me in a *momentico*.

I find them to be the most friendly, polite and helpful people I have met. Visitors are constantly surprised at the warmth of the Costa Rican people. This is still a very family-oriented society, however, and the friendliness and politeness tends to form somewhat of a shell over their true personalities. It is easy to make friends with a tico, but it is much more difficult to form deeper relationships.

CULTURE

Because of the overwhelmingly European population, there is very little indigenous cultural influence. And because the country was a poor subsistence-agriculture nation until the middle of the 19th century, cultural activities have only really blossomed in the last 100 years.

Costa Rica is famous for its natural beauty and friendly people, rather than its culture. Ticos consider San José to be the cultural centre of the country, and it is here that the most important museums are found. It is also the centre of a thriving acting community, and theatre is one of the favourite cultural activities in Costa Rica.

The most famous theatre in the country is the Teatro Nacional, built between 1890 and 1897. The story goes that a noted European opera company featuring the talented singer Adelina Patti was on a Latin American tour but declined to perform in Costa Rica for lack of a suitable hall. Immediately, the coffee elite put a special cultural tax on coffee exports to enable a world-class theatre to be built.

The Teatro Nacional in the heart of San José is now the venue for plays, opera, performances by the National Symphony, ballet, poetry readings and other cultural events. It also is an architectural work in its own right and is a landmark in any city tour of San José.

RELIGION

This can be summed up in one word, Catholicism. About 81% of the population is Roman Catholic, at least in principle. In practice, many people tend to go to church only at the time of birth, marriage and death, but they consider themselves Catholics nevertheless. Religious processions on holy days are generally less fervent or colourful than those found in other Latin American countries. Holy Week (the week before Easter) is a national holiday; everything, including buses, stops operating at lunch time on Maundy Thursday and doesn't start up till Holy Saturday.

Other religious views are permitted – after all, Costa Rica is Latin America's most democratic country. The Blacks on the Caribbean coast tend to be Protestants, and most other denominations have a church in or around San José. There is a small Jewish community with a B'Nai Israel church and a synagogue, and there's a sprinkling of people holding Oriental or Asian beliefs.

LANGUAGE

Spanish is the official language and is the main language for the traveller. English is understood in the better hotels, airline offices and tourist agencies, as well as along much of the Caribbean coast.

Indian languages are spoken in isolated areas, primarily Bribri which is estimated to be understood by about 10,000 people living on both sides of the Cordillera Talamanca. In 1993 an illustrated Bribri alphabet book was published by the Education Committee of the CCCU (Comisión Costarricense de Cooperación con La UNESCO (☎ 24 4320, Calle 33, Avenida 3, San José). It is planned to use the book in elementary schools of the Talamanca area.

If you don't speak Spanish, take heart. It is an easy language to learn. Courses are available in San José (see under the San José section) or you can study books, records and tapes before your trip. These study aids are often available free from many public libraries, or you might want to consider taking an evening or college course. Once you have learned the basics, you'll find it possible to travel all over Latin America because, apart from Brazil which is Portuguese-speaking, most of the countries use Spanish.

Spanish is easy to learn for several reasons. First, it uses Roman script, and secondly, with few exceptions, it is spoken as it is written, and vice versa. Imagine trying to explain to someone learning English that there are seven different ways of pronouncing 'ough'. This isn't a problem in Spanish. Thirdly, many words are similar enough to English that you can figure them out by guesswork. Instituto Geográfico Nacional means the National Geographical Institute, for example.

Even if you don't have time to take a course, at least bring a phrasebook and dictionary. Don't dispense with the dictionary, because the phrasebook limits you to asking where the bus station is and won't help you translate the local newspaper. My favourite

dictionary is the University of Chicago's paperback *Spanish-English, English-Spanish Dictionary*. It's small enough to travel with, yet has many more entries than most pocket dictionaries and also contains words used in Latin America but not in Spain. Some readers complain, however, that the print is too small and hard to read in the University of Chicago dictionary and prefer the Collins *Gem*.

Although the Spanish alphabet looks like the English one, it is in fact different. '*Ch*' is considered a separate letter, for example, so *champú* (which simply means 'shampoo') will be listed in a dictionary after all the words beginning with just '*c*'. Similarly, '*ll*' is a separate letter, so *llave* (key) is listed after all the words beginning with a single '*l*'. The letter '*ñ*' is listed after the ordinary '*n*'. Vowels with an accent are accented for stress and are not considered separate letters.

Pronunciation is generally more straightforward than it is in English, and if you say a word the way it looks like it should be said, the chances are that it will be close enough to be understood. You will get better with practice of course. A few notable exceptions are '*ll*' which is always pronounced 'y' as in 'yacht', the '*j*' which is pronounced 'h' as in 'happy', and the '*h*' which isn't pronounced at all. Thus the phrase *hojas en la calle* (leaves in the street) would be pronounced 'o-has en la ka-yea'. Finally, the letter '*ñ*' is pronounced as the 'ny' sound in 'canyon'.

Grammar

Articles, adjectives and demonstrative pronouns must agree with the noun in both gender and number. Nouns ending in 'a' are generally feminine and the corresponding articles are *la* (singular) and *las* (plural). Those ending in 'o' are usually masculine and require the articles *el* (singular) and *los* (plural).

There are, however, hundreds of exceptions to these guidelines which can only be memorised or deduced by the meaning of the word. Plurals are formed by adding *s* to words ending in a vowel and *es* to those ending in a consonant.

In addition to using all the familiar English tenses, Spanish also uses the imperfect tense and two subjunctive tenses (past and present). Tenses are formed either by adding a myriad of endings to the root verb or preceding the participle form by some variation of the verb *haber* (to have/to exist).

There are verb endings for first, second and third person singular and plural. Second person singular and plural are divided into formal and familiar modes. If that's not enough, there are three types of verbs – those ending in *ar*, *er* and *ir* – which are all conjugated differently. There is also a whole collection of stem-changing rules and irregularities which must be memorised. This sounds a lot more complicated than it really is – you'll be surprised how quickly you'll pick it up!

Common Courtesies

good morning	*buenos días*
good afternoon (or good evening)	*buenas tardes*
yes	*sí*
no	*no*
hello	*hola*
See you later.	*Hasta luego.*
How are you?	*Cómo estás?* (familiar) or *Cómo está?* (formal)
please	*por favor*
thank you	*gracias*
It's a pleasure.	*Con mucho gusto.*

Some Useful Phrases

Do you speak Spanish?	*Habla usted castellano?*
Where do you come from?	*De donde es usted?*
What time is it?	*Qué hora tiene?*
Don't you have smaller change?	*No tiene suelto?*
Do you understand? (casual)	*Me entiende?*
I don't understand	*No entiendo.*
Where can I change money/travellers' cheques?	*Donde se cambia dinero/cheques de viajeros?*

Where is the...?	*Donde está el/la...?*
How much is this? There are fortunately several variations on this well-worn phrase.	*A cómo? Cuanto cuesta esto? Cuanto vale esto?*
too expensive	*muy caro*
cheaper	*más barato*
I'll take it	*Lo llevo*
The bill please	*La cuenta por favor*
to the right	*a la derecha*
to the left	*a la izquierda*
continue straight ahead	*siga derecho*
more or less	*más o menos*
when?	*cuando?*
how?	*cómo?*
How's that again?	*Cómo?*
where?	*donde?*
What time does the next plane/bus/train leave for...?	*A qué hora sale el próximo avión/bús/tren para...?*
where from?	*de donde?*
around there	*por allá*
around here	*por aquí*
It's hot/cold.	*Hace calor/frío.*

Some Useful Words

airport	*aeropuerto*
bank	*banco*
block	*cuadra, cien metros*
bus station/stop	*terminal/parada de autobuses*
cathedral/church	*catedral/iglesia*
city	*ciudad*
downhill	*para abajo*
exchange house	*casa de cambio*
friend	*amigo/a*
here	*aquí*
husband/wife	*marido/esposa*
mother/father	*madre/padre*
people	*la gente*
police	*policía*
post office	*correo*
rain	*lluvia*
there	*allí, alla*
town square	*plaza* or *parque*
train station	*estación de trenes*
uphill	*para arriba*

wind	*viento*

Time & Dates

What time is it?	*Qué hora es?* or
	Qué horas son?
It is one o'clock.	*Es la una.*
It is two/three/etc. o'clock.	*Son las (dos/tres/etc).*
midnight	*medianoche*
noon	*mediodía*
in the afternoon	*de la tarde*
in the morning	*de la mañana*
at night	*de la noche*
half past two	*dos y media*
quarter past two	*dos y cuarto*
two twenty-five	*dos con veinticinco minutos*
twenty to two	*veinte para las dos*

Sunday	*domingo*
Monday	*lunes*
Tuesday	*martes*
Wednesday	*miércoles*
Thursday	*jueves*
Friday	*viernes*
Saturday	*sábado*

spring	*la primavera*
summer (the December to April dry season)	*el verano*
winter (the May to December wet season)	*el invierno*
autumn	*el otoño*

today	*hoy*
tomorrow	*mañana*
yesterday	*ayer*

Numbers

0	*cero*
1	*uno, una*
2	*dos*
3	*tres*
4	*cuatro*
5	*cinco*
6	*seis*
7	*siete*
8	*ocho*
9	*nueve*
10	*diez*
11	*once*
12	*doce*
13	*trece*
14	*catorce*
15	*quince*
16	*dieciseis*
17	*diecisiete*
18	*dieciocho*
19	*diecinueve*
20	*veinte*
21	*veintiuno*
30	*treinta*
40	*cuarenta*
50	*cincuenta*
60	*sesenta*
70	*setenta*
80	*ochenta*
90	*noventa*
100	*cien(to)*
101	*ciento uno*
200	*doscientos*
201	*doscientos uno*
300	*trescientos*
400	*cuatrocientos*
500	*quinientos*
600	*seiscientos*
700	*setecientos*
800	*ochocientos*
900	*novecientos*
1000	*mil*
100,000	*cien mil*
1,000,000	*un millón*

Costa Rican Terms

The following colloquialisms and slang are mainly used only in Costa Rica.

Adios!	Hi! (used when passing a friend in the street, or anyone in remote rural areas; also means 'farewell' but only when leaving for a long time)
bomba	petrol (gas) station
buena nota	OK, excellent (literally 'good note')
Hay campo?	Is there space? (on a bus)
cien metros	one city block
maje	buddy

mi amor	my love (used as a friendly form of address)	*soda*	café or lunch counter
pulpería	corner grocery store	*Upe!*	Anybody home? (used mainly in rural areas at people's houses, instead of knocking)
pura vida	super, (literally 'pure life', also an expression of approval or even a greeting)		
salado	too bad, tough luck	*vos*	you (informal, the same as *tu*)

Facts for the Visitor

VISAS & EMBASSIES

Citizens of all nations require at least a passport to enter Costa Rica. There are three entry levels for passport holders. The first level requires passport only and allows entry for 90 days; the second level requires passport only and allows entry for 30 days; the third level requires both a passport and a visa and allows entry for 30 days.

Passport-carrying nationals of the following countries are allowed 90 days' stay with no visa: Most western European countries, Argentina, Canada, Colombia, Israel, Japan, Panama, Romania, South Korea, UK, USA, Uruguay.

Passport-carrying nationals of the following countries are allowed 30 days' stay with no visa: most eastern European countries, Australia, Belgium, Brazil, Ecuador, Eire (Ireland), El Salvador, France, Guatemala, Honduras, Iceland, Liechtenstein, Mexico, Monaco, New Zealand, Sweden, Switzerland, Vatican City and Venezuela.

Most other nationalities require a visa, which can be obtained from a Costa Rican consulate for US$20. Some nationalities are restricted by so-called political problems and may have difficulty in obtaining a visa for tourism. These have included Nicaragua and most communist countries, but with the 1990 election of Violeta Chamorro in Nicaragua and the general political upheaval in eastern Europe, this has been changing dramatically. Recent reports indicate that travellers arriving from Nicaragua need to have malaria tablets with them.

Costa Rican entry requirements change frequently and so it is worth checking at a consulate before your trip, especially if you want to stay more than 30 days. Travellers officially need an exit ticket out of the country before they are allowed to enter, although this is not often asked for at the airport in San José because most airlines will not let you board their planes unless you have a return or onward ticket, or an MCO.

Travellers arriving by land are more likely to need an exit ticket. The easiest way for overland travellers to solve the onward ticket requirement is by buying a ticket from the TICA bus company which has offices in both Managua (Nicaragua) and Panama City. (Ask other travellers if you get the chance – they can beat any guide book for up-to-the-minute information.) Sometimes a show of cash is required, US$300 to US$400 per month should be sufficient. Costa Ricans are sensitive to appearances; putting on your most presentable clothes and avoiding unusual fashions will make entrance procedures easier.

During your stay, the law requires that you carry your passport or tourist card at all times. A photocopy of the pages bearing your photo, passport number and entry stamp will suffice when walking around town, but the passport should at least be in the hotel you are staying at, and not locked up in San José.

Visa Extensions

Extending your stay beyond the authorised 30 or 90 days is a time-consuming hassle. It is easier to simply leave the country for 72 hours or more and then re-enter. If you cannot or do not wish to do this, then go to the Migración office in San José. A better alternative is to ask a travel agent to do the paperwork for you – many will do so for a small fee.

In the past, requirements for extending your stay include presenting three passport-size photos, a ticket out of the country, sufficient funds to support yourself, and maybe even a blood test (to prove you don't have AIDS). Allow several working days for all this. Requirements change – it really is easiest to try and get 90 days on entry and then leave for Nicaragua or Panama for a couple of days. Check with Migración before you decide whether to stay, leave or visit another country for 72 hours.

If you overstay your 30 or 90 day stay

without obtaining an extension, you will not be allowed to leave the country without an exit visa, and these are available from Migración. They require the usual exit ticket, as well as a statement from the Tribunales de Justicia on Calle 17, between avenidas 6 & 8 in San José, stating that you aren't leaving any dependents in the country. You pay a fine of US$4 per month of overstay, plus a US$12 fee if you leave by air, US$40 if you leave by land. In addition, exit-visa holders departing by air must pay a US$40 airport departure tax. The exit visa is valid for 30 days, so you can legally stay that long on top of whatever time you've already been there.

Children (under 18 years) of all nationalities are special cases. They are not allowed to stay for more than 30 days unless *both* parents request permission from the National Child Protection Agency (Patronato Nacional de la Infancia, on Calle 19 at Avenida 6 in San José). Permission will not be granted to just one parent or guardian. If a child is planning a stay of more than 30 days and will not be travelling with both parents, it is necessary for the non-accompanying parent (or parents) to get a notarised permit from the Costa Rican consulate in the child's home country. I recently received a letter from a married couple who had different last names. In addition, these were second marriages and so their children's names were different from the father's. When they tried to obtain visa extensions, they ran into the worst kind of stupid bureaucracy.

All this talk of red tape and bureaucracy may have put you off the idea of travelling in Costa Rica entirely. Remember, however, that if you stay less than 30 days there is no problem at all. If you stay from 30 to 90 days and are entitled to do so, there is no problem either. And if you want to stay longer, a few days in Panama or Nicaragua may be easier than dealing with extensions. Finally, good travel agents are used to dealing with the red tape and will help you obtain the necessary extensions for a fee.

Working Holidays

It is difficult, but not impossible, to find work in Costa Rica. The most likely source of paid employment is as an English teacher in language institutes in San José, and which advertise courses in the local newspapers. By word of mouth from other travellers is another way of finding out about this kind of work.

Writers can occasionally sell work to the English-language weekly, *The Tico Times*. Naturalists or river guides may be able to find work with the private lodges or adventure travel operators. Don't expect to make more than survival wages from these jobs, and don't arrive in Costa Rica expecting to get a job easily and immediately.

Getting a bona fide job requires a work permit which, as you can gather from the preceding section on extending your stay, is a bureaucratic, time-consuming, and difficult process.

Full-time US students who are over 18 years can apply to work in Costa Rica between 1 June and 1 October by writing to the Council on International Educational Exchange, Work Abroad Program, 205 East 42nd Street, New York, NY 10017 (☎ (212) 661 1414 ext 1130). You should apply as early as possible – at least one month in advance. There is a US$125 application fee and you should be able to speak some Spanish. Although you won't get rich, your wages should cover the cost of your trip and give you an insider's perspective on the country.

Volunteer work in nature preserves or national parks is sometimes possible. Volunteers usually provide their own transport to Costa Rica, and pay roughly US$5 per day for living expenses. Volunteers live with park rangers in ranger stations and help with a variety of work ranging from providing visitor information to constructing trails or buildings to office work or surveys.

Some volunteers are needed in the San José headquarters as well as in remote areas – efforts are made to match volunteers' interests and skills with the projects available. A minimum commitment of 60 days is requested, and volunteers work six days a week. Several hundred volunteers are used each year; almost half of them are foreign and the rest are Costa Rican.

If you are interested in working in the national parks, try writing to the Asociación Voluntarias de Parques Nacionales, Apartado 10104-1000, San José, for more information and an application. Allow several months. Many people apply, but few actually end up volunteering. If you are already in Costa Rica, you could apply in person at the Servicio Parques Nacionales (☎ 57 0922), Calle 25, Avenida 8 & 10, San José.

Other Visas

Nicaragua Australians and New Zealanders travelling to Nicaragua require visas, as do many Europeans except those from the UK and a few western European nations. Regulations change often, so check with the Nicaraguan consulate before you go. Visas reportedly require at least 48 hours to process. Canadians and US citizens do not require Nicaraguan visas.

Panama Travellers to Panama require visas if they hold passports from the USA, Japan, Canada, Australia, New Zealand and many European nations except the UK and a few others. Check with the Panamanian consulate for current requirements.

Visas cost anything up to US$20, depending on your nationality. Go to the consulate in San José if you need a visa and don't have one, as visas are not normally obtainable at the border-crossing points. Regulations and lists of countries requiring visas can and do change frequently.

Foreign Embassies in Costa Rica

The following countries have embassies or consulates in the San José area. Addresses change frequently, particularly those of the smallest embassies, so call ahead to confirm locations and get directions. Local landmark directions (see Orientation in the San José chapter) are also given. The Instituto Costarricense de Turismo (ICT) in San José can help you get an up-to-date address if the addresses given below are changed. Embassies tend to be open in the mornings more often than in the afternoons.

Argentina
    Avenida 6, Calle 21 & 25, (☎ 21 3438, 21 6869)
Austria
    Avenida 4, Calle 36 & 38, (☎ 55 3007)
Belgium
    Avenida 3, Calle 35 & 37; Cuatra entrada de Los Yoses (☎ 25 6255, 25 6633)
Belize
    25 metres west, 75 metres south of Plaza Mayor, Rohrmoser (☎ 31 7766, 32 6637)
Bolivia
    Avenida 2, Calle 19 & 21 (☎ 33 6244, 33 4994)
Brazil
    Avenida 2, Calle 20 & 22 (☎ 33 1544)
Canada
    Calle 3, Avenida Central & 1; Edificio Cronos, 6th floor (☎ 55 3522, 28 5154; fax 23 2395)
Chile
    50 metres east, 225 metres north of Automercado Los Yoses (☎ 24 4243; fax 53 7016)
Colombia
    Calle 29, Avenida 1 (☎ 21 0725, 55 0937)
Denmark
    Paseo Colón, Calle 38 & 40, Edificio Centro Colón (☎ 57 2695, 57 2696)
Ecuador
    Sabana Sur, 100 metres east, 125 metres south of Colegio Medicos (☎ 32 1503, 31 1899)
El Salvador
    Avenida 10, Calle 33 & 35; final de Avenida 10, Los Yoses (☎ 24 9034)
Finland
    Paseo Colón, Calle 38 & 40, Edificio Centro Colón (☎ 57 0210)
France
    200 metres south, 25 metres west of the Indoor Club, Carretera a Curridabat (☎ 25 0733)
Germany
    200 metres north, 75 metres east of the Oscar Arias residence, Rohrmoser (☎ 32 5533)
Guatemala
    (☎ 31 6645, 31 6654)
Holland
    Avenida 8, Calle 37, 100 metres south of La Secunda Entrada de Los Yoses (☎ 34 0949)
Honduras
    300 metres east, 200 metres north of ITAN, Los Yoses Sur (☎ 34 9502)
Israel
    Calle 2, Avenida 2 & 4 (☎ 21 6011, 21 6444)
Italy
    Calle 33, Avenida 8 & 10, Los Yoses (☎ 25 6574, 34 2326)

Japan
    400 metres west, 100 metres north of La Nunciatura, Rohrmoser (☎ 32 1255, 31 3140)
Mexico
    Avenida 7, Calle 13 & 15, north side of Fábrica Nacional de Licores (☎ 22 5528, 22 5485)
Nicaragua
    Avenida Central, Calle 25 & 27 (☎ 33 3479)
Norway
    Paseo Colón, Calle 38 & 40, Edificio Centro Colón (☎ 57 1414)
Panama
    600 metres south of El Antiguo Higueron, San Pedro (☎ 25 3401, 25 0667)
Peru
    200 metres south, 50 metres west of the Automercado, Los Yoses (☎ 25 9145)
Spain
    Calle 32, Paseo Colón & Avenida 2 (☎ 22 1933, fax 21 2908)
Switzerland
    Paseo Colón, Calle 38 & 40, Edificio Centro Colón (☎ 33 0052, 21 4829, fax 55 2831)
UK
    Paseo Colón, Calle 38 & 40, Edificio Centro Colón (☎ 21 5566, 21 5816, fax 33 9938)
USA
    Carretera Pavas frente de Centro Commercial (☎ 20 3939, fax 20 2305)
Venezuela
    Los Yoses (☎ 25 8810, 25 1335, fax 53 8710)

Embassies of other countries open and close sporadically. Among these are the following, ask locally if you need them: Bulgaria, China, Dominican Republic, Greece, Haiti, Holy See (Vatican), Hungary, Jamaica, Korea, Malta, Paraguay, Poland, Romania, Russia, Taiwan and Uruguay.

Costa Rican Embassies

The following is a list of Costa Rican embassies in other countries:

Canada
    135 York St No 208, Ottawa K1N 5T4 (☎ (613) 562 2855)
    Also in Calgary (Alberta), Montreal (Quebec), Toronto (Ontario), Vancouver (BC)
France
    74 avenue Paul-Doumer, 75016 Paris (☎ (1) 45 04 50 93)
Germany
    5300 Bonn 1, Borsigallee 2 (☎ (0228) 252940)

Guatemala
    Avenida La Reforma 8-60, Zona 9, Edificio Galerías Reforma No 902, 01009 Guatemala City (☎ (02) 319604)
Honduras
    Blvd Morazán, Costado Oeste de Reasa, Apartado 512, Tegucigalpa (☎ 32 1768)
Israel
    13 Diskin St No 1, Jerusalem 91012 (☎ (02) 666197)
Nicaragua
    Centro Comercial Camino de Oriente, contiguo a AeroNica, Managua JR
Panama
    Edificio Regency No 2, Apartado 8963, Panama (☎ 642980)
Spain
    Paseo de la Castellana 166, No 5 28046, Madrid (☎ 2509398)
UK
    36 Upper Brook St, London W1 Y 1PE (☎ (071) 495 3985)
USA
    1825 Connecticut Ave, NW, No 211, Washington DC 20009 (☎ (202) 234 2945, 234 2947)
    Also in Chicago, Houston, Los Angeles, Miami, New Orleans and New York City

Other countries with Costa Rican embassies or consulates include the following: Argentina, Barbados, Belgium, Belize, Bolivia, Brazil, Canada, Chile, Colombia, Denmark, Dominican Republic, El Salvador, Hungary, Italy, Jamaica, Japan, Kenya, Mexico, Norway, Paraguay, Poland, Portugal, Romania, Russia, South Korea, Switzerland, Taiwan, Uruguay, Vatican City, Venezuela.

CUSTOMS

From the point of view of importing duty-free items like alcohol and tobacco, Costa Rica is less restrictive than many countries. You are allowed 500 cigarettes or 500 grams of tobacco, and three litres of wine or spirits.

Camera gear, binoculars and camping, snorkelling or other sporting equipment are readily allowed into the country. Officially, you are limited to six rolls of film but this is rarely checked or enforced – I routinely carry 20 or 30 rolls of film into Costa Rica. Generally, if you are bringing in items for personal use, there's no problem. If you are trying to bring in new items which you want to sell, you may be asked to pay duty. Don't ask me how they know the difference.

MONEY
Currency
The Costa Rican currency is the *colón*, plural *colones*, named after Cristóbal Colón, which is the Spanish version of Christopher Columbus. Colones are normally written c\c.

Bills come in 10, 20, 50, 100, 500, 1000 and 5000 colones, though the 10 and 20 colones bills are being phased out. A 10,000 colones bill is planned. Coins come in 1, 2, 5, 10 and 20 colones. The colón is subdivided into 100 céntimos, and coins of 25 and 50 céntimos are occasionally encountered.

Exchange Rates
The value of the colón has been dropping steadily against the US dollar for years. Sometimes the exchange rate will remain stable for some months, at other times there is a gradual downward increase, and at other times there is a fairly sudden drop in value. Once in a while, however, the value of the colón will rise sharply against the dollar, as happened in 1992 when the dollar fell in value from 140 colones in February to 120 colones in June. During the second half of 1992, the dollar rose slowly and by early 1993 was worth about 136 colones. After about five months of stability, the colón is once again falling against the US dollar, with July 1993 rates at just over 140 colones to the US dollar.

Prices in this book are quoted in US dollar terms. The table below is the exchange as of mid 1993.

US$1	=	143 colones
UK£1	=	211 colones
A$1	=	97 colones
C$1	=	109 colones
NZ$1	=	78 colones
1 FFr	=	24 colones
1 DM	=	82 colones
1 SFr	=	94 colones

Changing Money
It is easiest to change US dollars in Costa Rica. You can change some other major currencies in the capital, but rates are poor. Out of San José, US dollars are the only way to go. Travellers' cheques are usually exchanged at one or two colones lower than the rate for cash, so plan accordingly.

There are three places to change money: in the better hotels and travel agencies; in banks and exchange houses; and on the street.

Hotels & Travel Agencies Hotels and travel agencies often give the same rate as the banks, and are much faster and more convenient. One drawback to using these is that usually only guests and customers can use their services, although some places will serve outsiders – it's worth trying. Another drawback is that they have limited cash resources and sometimes don't have enough colones. Some hotels charge a 'commission' – though they should give you the official rate.

Banks & Exchange Houses Banks tend to be slow in changing money and the process can take an hour or more. Often you have to stand in one line to have your transaction approved, then in a second line to actually get your money. Some banks won't take travellers' cheques, others will take only certain kinds.

Banking hours are from 9 am to 3 pm, Monday to Friday, though in San José the banks often open by 8.30 am and may remain open till 4 pm. The main offices of the Banco Nacional and Banco de Costa Rica in San José are often open for longer hours for foreign exchange (Banco Nacional, Avenida 3, between Calle 2 & 4; Banco de Costa Rica, Avenida Central, between Calles 4 & 6; Avenida 1 at Calle 7). However, the national banks tend to be slower than the private banks. For faster service, try Banco Lyon, Banex or Banco Mercantil.

The San José airport bank is open from 6.30 am to 5 pm Monday to Friday and from 7 am to 1 pm on weekends and holidays. This bank is often the most efficient place to change money.

Always carry your passport when changing money. Several travellers have reported that they have been asked for proof of purchase of travellers' cheques when exchanging. This has never happened to me, but you might want to carry a copy of your receipt.

There are virtually no *casas de cambio* or exchange houses in Costa Rica. The only one I found was Valorinsa in San José which had good rates. There may be a few others.

Note that if you buy colones in advance in your home country, you will receive a very poor exchange rate – one traveller reports buying 112 colones for a US dollar at Miami airport and discovering that the exchange rate was 135 colones when he arrived. If you arrive at the airport after the bank closes, you can pay the cab driver to your hotel in US dollars (have some small bills handy – it's a US$10 fare) and then have the hotel help you.

On the Streets Changing money on the streets is technically illegal, but there are so many people doing it that obviously the authorities are turning a blind eye at present. The area to find street changers is around the Banco Central at Avenida Central and Calle 2 in San José. Currently, street changers were giving rates only 1 or 2% better than the bank, though in the past, street changers have given rates as high as 5 to 10% better. Street rates depend on whether you have travellers' cheques or cash, how much you want to change, and how well you can bargain. US dollars are the only currency that street changers are seriously interested in.

Bear in mind that street changing is illegal, and the present blind eye may not be in effect when you arrive – ask other travellers. Also remember that street changing may result in your getting cheated, so always count your money carefully before handing over your dollars. Also remember that there are plenty of thieves on the streets and scams abound. A favourite scam is for the changer to say that the police are coming, and giving you back your dollars – except that the dollars are counterfeit. Many travellers prefer to change

money legally at a slightly lower rate in a bank to avoid any hassle – I recommend avoiding street changers unless you are sure you're street smart.

Outside San José, money changing in major hotels is OK, but only banks in main towns and moneychangers at the land borders can be relied upon to change money. If visiting small towns, always change plenty of money beforehand. Also bring small bills, as changing large colones bills can be difficult in rural area.

It is possible to change excess colones back into dollars (up to US$50) at the main banks and at the airport, but you may need to show your passport, ticket out of the country, and the original exchange receipts.

In May 1993, police broke up a counterfeiting ring which made false 5000 colones bills, but there are believed to be millions of colones worth of false 5000s out there. Police say the false 5000s can be identified by the absence of a watermark above the 5000 to the right of the official signature – the watermark can be seen in normal light. Also, counterfeits lack the fine gridlines in the blue section and the fake blue is brighter than the normal blue.

Credit Cards
Holders of credit cards can buy colones (but not US dollars) in banks, although this is subject to change as dollars have been available in the past.

Credit cards can also be used at the more expensive hotels, restaurants, travel and car rental agencies, and stores. Visa and MasterCard are both widely accepted, you are charged at the normal bank rates, and commissions are low.

American Express cardholders can buy American Express travellers' cheques in US dollars. The office is in the TAM travel agency at Calle 1, between Avenidas Central & 1, in San José.

Telephone numbers for credit card offices in San José are given in that chapter. I suggest that credit card holders call the customer service of their credit card company at home, before leaving for Costa Rica, to find out the most current numbers to dial in the case of loss or other problems with their credit cards in Costa Rica.

Transferring Money

If you need money sent to you from home, you'll find the main branches of several banks in San José will accept cash transfers but charge a commission. Shop around for the best deal. The Banco Anglo-Costarricense has been recommended. Allow several days for a bank transfer – it is generally recommended to try and bring what you need with you.

Costs

Costa Rica is not as cheap as many other Central or South American countries, although budget travellers will find that it is much cheaper than, say, the USA or Europe. Generally speaking, San José and the most popular tourist areas (Monteverde, Jacó, Manuel Antonio, Guanacaste beaches) are more expensive than the rest of the country, the dry season (from December to April) is the high season and thus more expensive, and imported goods are expensive.

Travellers on a tight budget will find the cheapest hotels start at about US$3 per person for a box with a bed. Fairly decent but still quite basic rooms with private bathroom, hot water and maybe air-conditioning start at around US$10 per person. First class hotels are well over US$100 for a single room but there are plenty of good ones for about US$50 and up.

Meals cost from about US$2 to US$20, depending on the quality of the restaurant. Budget travellers should stick to the cheaper set lunches offered in many restaurants, which usually cost about US$2. Cafés or lunch counters, called *sodas*, are cheap places for meals. Beer costs from US$0.70 to US$2.50 depending on how fancy the restaurant or bar is. Cinemas charge about US$2.50.

Public transport is quite cheap, with the longest bus journeys from San José (to the Panamanian or Nicaraguan borders) costing about US$7. Internal air fares are also rela-

tively cheap, ranging from US$30 to US$70 round trip with SANSA or US$60 to US$114 with Travelair. (Chartered flights are more expensive.) A taxi, particularly when you're in a group, isn't expensive and usually costs US$1 to US$2 for short rides. Car rental is expensive – figure on US$250 per week as a minimum for the cheapest cars.

A budget traveller economising hard can get by on US$10 to US$20 per day. (Some readers have written to say that it's impossible to get by on US$10 a day – obviously their definition of budget travel is higher than rock bottom.) If you want some basic comforts, such as rooms with private baths, meals other than set meals, and occasional flights, expect to pay about US$30 to US40 per day. Travellers wanting to be very comfortable can spend from US$50 to over US$100 per day. Tours can cost upwards of US$150 per day, but you do get first class accommodation and services.

Travelling hard, eating well, staying in rooms with a private bath, writing an average of one letter each day to friends or family, buying a daily newspaper, seeing a movie once in a while, and drinking a couple of beers with dinner most nights sounds expensive – almost decadent – to the 'purist' budget traveller. I did that for several weeks while researching this book, and averaged about US$30 a day. (I also spent some time driving a rental car as well as taking an expensive tour of some of the more remote national parks, so I covered various levels of expense.)

I sometimes meet travellers who spend most of their time worrying how to make every penny stretch further. It seems to me that they spend more time looking at their finances than looking at the places they're visiting.

Of course many travellers are on a grand tour of Latin America and want to make their money last, but you can get so burned out on squalid hotels and bad food that the grand tour becomes an endurance test. I'd rather spend six months travelling comfortably and enjoyably than a full year of strain and sacrifice.

Tipping

Most restaurants automatically add 13% tax and 10% tip to the bill. Cheaper restaurants might not do this. Tipping above the included amount is not necessary (ticos rarely do), but adding a few percent for excellent service is OK. Tipping bellboys in the better hotels costs about US$0.25 or US$0.50 per bag. Tip hairdressers about 10% of the bill. Taxi drivers are not normally tipped.

On guided tours, tip the guide about US$2 per person per day (more if the group is very small, less or nothing if the guide doesn't meet your expectations).

WHEN TO GO

In general, visitors are told that the late December to mid-April dry season is the best time to visit Costa Rica. During this time beach resorts tend to be busy and often full at weekends and holidays, especially Easter week which is booked months ahead. School children take their main vacations from December to February.

From late April, when the rains start, many of the dirt roads in the backcountry require 4WD vehicles (which can be rented). However, travel in the wet season also means smaller crowds and lower hotel prices. Bring your umbrella and take advantage of it! I have travelled in Costa Rica in both seasons, and have thoroughly enjoyed myself at both times.

To travel in the least crowded months, try late April and May, and from mid October to mid December.

WHAT TO BRING

As an inveterate traveller and guidebook writer, I've naturally read many guidebooks. I always find the What to Bring section depressing, as I'm always told to bring as little as possible; I look around at my huge backpack, my two beat-up duffel bags bursting at the seams, and I wonder sadly where I went wrong. I enjoy camping, so I carry tent and sleeping bag. I'm an avid bird-watcher, and I'd feel naked without my binoculars and field guides. And of course I want to photo-graph the scenery and birds, which adds a camera, lenses, tripod and other paraphernalia. In addition, I enjoy relaxing just as much as travelling so I always have at least two books to read as well as all my indispensable guides and maps. Luckily, I'm not a music addict so I'm able to live without a guitar, a portable tape player or a shortwave radio.

It appears that I'm not the only one afflicted with the kitchen-sink disease. In Latin America alone, I've met an Australian surfer who travelled the length of the Pacific coast with his board looking for the world's longest left-handed wave; a Black man from Chicago who travelled with a pair of three-foot-high bongo drums; an Italian with a saxophone (a memorable night in San José when those two got together); a Danish journalist with a portable typewriter; a French freak with a ghetto blaster and (by my count) 32 tapes; and a woman from the USA with several hundred weavings which she was planning on selling. All of these were budget travellers staying for at least 1½ months and using public transport.

After confessing to the amount of stuff I travel with, I can't very well give the time-honoured advice of 'travel as lightly as possible.' I suggest you bring anything that is important to you; if you're interested in photography, you'll only curse every time you see a good shot if you haven't brought your telephoto lens, and if you're a musician you won't enjoy the trip if you constantly worry about how out of practice your fingers are getting.

A good idea once you're in San José is to divide your gear into two piles. One is what you need for the next section of your trip, the rest you can stash in the storage room at your hotel (most hotels have one). Costa Rica is a small country so you can use San José as a base and divide your travelling into, say, coastal, highland and jungle portions, easily returning to the capital between sections and picking up the gear you need for the next.

There's no denying, however, that travel-ling light is much less of a hassle, so don't bring things you can do without. Travelling on buses and trains is bound to make you slightly grubby, so bring one or two changes of dark clothes that don't show the dirt, rather than seven changes of smart clothes for a six-week trip. On the other hand, if you are going to spend a lot of time in the lowlands, dark clothes definitely feel hotter than light-coloured ones. Many people go overboard with changes of clothes, but one change to wash, one to wear and maybe one in reserve for emergencies is the best idea for travelling light. Of course, bring more than two or three changes of socks, underwear and tee or sports shirts. Bring clothes that wash and dry easily. (Jeans take forever to dry.)

The highlands can be cool, so bring a wind-proof jacket and a warm layer to wear underneath. A hat is indispensable; it'll keep you warm when it's cold, shade your eyes when it's sunny, and keep your head dry when it rains (a great deal!). A collapsible umbrella is great protection against sun and rain as well, particularly during the rainy season. Rainwear in tropical rainforest often makes you sweat, so an umbrella is the preferred choice of many travellers.

You can buy clothes of almost any size if you need them, but shoes in large sizes are difficult to find. I have size 12 feet (don't laugh, they're not that big!) and I can't buy footwear in Costa Rica unless I have it specially made. This is also true of most Latin countries, so bring a spare pair of shoes if you're planning a long multi-country trip. Also, if planning a trip to the rainforest, bear in mind that it will often be muddy even during the dry season, and very wet at other times, so bring a pair of shoes that you are prepared to get wet and muddy over and over again. Rubber boots are popular with the locals and are easily available in small and medium sizes in Costa Rica. Some people swear by Teva-type sandals; others love reef-walking shoes or aqua socks – it's a matter of what you are most comfortable with. Long sleeves and pants are recommended for both sun and insect protection in the tropics. Shorts and skirts are fine on the beaches but less useful in the rainforests.

I believe clothing is a personal thing and what works for one person is unsuitable for another. Therefore I don't provide an exhaustive clothing list. The following is a checklist of small items you will find useful and will probably need:

pocket torch (flashlight) with spare bulb and batteries
travel alarm clock (or watch – though I always sleep through my alarm)
Swiss Army-style pocket knife
sewing & repairs kit (dental floss makes excellent, strong and colourless emergency thread)
a few metres of cord (also useful for clothesline and spare shoelaces)
sunglasses
plastic bags (ziploc bags are very hard to find in Costa Rica)
soap and dish, shampoo, tooth brush and paste, shaving gear, towel (soap & towel are supplied in all but the cheapest hotels)
toilet paper (rarely found in cheaper hotels and restaurants)
ear plugs to aid sleeping in noisy hotels
sun block (strong blocking lotions: SPF 20 and above) are hard to find and pricey in Costa Rica – SPF 4 & 8 are the most common)
insect repellent (containing a high percentage of Deet – use with care)
address book, notebook, pens & pencils
paperback book (easily exchanged with other travellers when you've finished)
water bottle
first-aid kit (see Health section)
prescription medicines

Optional items:

camera and film (expensive in Costa Rica)
binoculars and field guides
Spanish-English dictionary
small padlock
large folding nylon bag to leave things in storage
snorkelling gear (only if you are really dedicated)
folding umbrella (rainy season – they are reasonably priced in San José)
light sleeping bag and camping mattress
cup (supplied in many hotels, but not the cheaper ones)

Tampons are available in Costa Rica but imported items are heavily taxed so you may want to bring your own supply if you like a particular brand or size. Contraceptives are available in the major cities but, again, if you use a preferred brand or method, you should bring it from home.

You need something to carry everything around in. A backpack is recommended because carrying your baggage on your back is less exhausting than carrying it in your hands. On the other hand, it's often more difficult to get at things inside a pack, so some travellers prefer a duffel bag with a full-length zip. Also, in crowded places (eg buses, busy street corners) backpacks occasionally get slit by thieves who run off with whatever falls out.

Whichever you choose, ensure that it is a good, strong piece of luggage, or you'll find that you spend much of your trip replacing zips, straps and buckles. Hard travelling is notoriously hard on your luggage, and if you bring a backpack, I suggest one with an internal frame. External frames snag on bus doors, luggage racks and airline baggage belts, and are prone to getting twisted, cracked or broken.

TOURIST OFFICES
Local Tourist Offices

In San José, the Instituto Costarricense de Turismo (ICT) answers questions (in English!) and sometimes provides maps at their public information office on the Plaza de la Cultura at Calle 5 and Avenida Central. They also have an information centre at the airport.

In other towns, there is sometimes a locally run information centre. These are mentioned in the text, where appropriate.

Representatives Abroad

Roughly 30% of all foreign visitors to Costa Rica come from the USA, and there is a Costa Rican National Tourist Bureau in the USA (☎ (305) 358 2150 or toll-free (800) 327 7033; 1101 Brickel Ave, BIV Tower, Suite 801, Miami, FL 33131). Call or write for brochures or information. Note that their information is of a very general nature – they don't have hotel prices etc.

Citizens of other countries can ask the local Costa Rican consulate for tourist information, or write to Instituto Costarricense de Turismo, Apartado 777, San José, Costa Rica.

Other

The South American Explorers Club (☎ (607) 277 0488) is at 126 Indian Creek Rd, Ithaca, NY 14850, USA. Founded in 1977, the club functions as an information centre for travellers, adventurers, scientific expeditions etc. It has club houses in Lima (Peru) and Quito (Ecuador). Although the club has focused on South America, it has recently expanded to provide information for travellers to Central America as well. It is evaluating the possibility of opening a clubhouse in Costa Rica.

The club has an extensive library of books, maps, and trip reports left by other travellers. Many maps and books are for sale. It is an entirely membership supported, nonprofit organisation. Membership costs US$30 and lasts for four quarterly issues of their excellent and informative *South American Explorer* magazine. Members can make use of the club houses (if heading on to Peru or Ecuador) as well as the extensive information facilities and books available by mail before they go.

BUSINESS HOURS & HOLIDAYS
Business Hours
Banks are open from 9 am to 3 pm Monday to Friday, with a few exceptions in San José.

Government offices are supposedly open from 8 am to 4 pm, Monday to Friday, but often close for lunch between about 11.30 am and 1 pm.

Stores are open from 8 am to 6 or 7 pm, Monday to Saturday, but a two-hour lunch break is not uncommon.

Holidays
National holidays (*días feriados*) are taken seriously in Costa Rica, and banks, public offices and many stores close. There are no buses at all on the Thursday afternoon and Friday before Easter, and many businesses are closed for the entire week before Easter. From Thursday to Easter Sunday all bars are closed and locked and alcohol sales are prohibited. Beach hotels are usually booked weeks ahead for this week, though a limited choice of rooms is often available. Public transport tends to be tight on all holidays and the days immediately preceding or following them, so book tickets ahead.

1 January
　New Year's Day
19 March
　Saint Joseph's Day (patron saint of San José)
March or April
　Holy Week (moveable, the Thursday and Friday before Easter)
11 April
　Juan Santamaría's Day (national hero at Battle of Rivas against William Walker in 1856)
1 May
　Labor Day
29 June
　Saint Peter & Saint Paul's Day
25 July
　Guanacaste Day (annexation of Guanacaste Province, formerly part of Nicaragua)
2 August
　Virgin of Los Angeles Day (patron saint of Costa Rica)
15 August
　Mothers' Day (coincides with Catholic feast of the Assumption)
15 September
　Independence Day

12 October
　Columbus Day (discovery of the Americas, locally called *Día de la Raza*)
8 December
　Immaculate Conception
25 December
　Christmas Day

In addition, various towns have celebrations for their own particular day. The week between Christmas and New Year's Day tends to be an unofficial holiday, especially in San José.

POST & TELECOMMUNICATIONS
Sending Mail
The better hotels provide stamps for your letters and postcards, otherwise go to the main post office in each town. In San José only, the Costa Rican post and telegraph system (CORTEL) has recently installed stamp-vending machines operating 24 hours a day. These are in the Correo Central (Central Post Office), Calle 2, Avenida 1 & 3; the Gran Hotel Costa Rica, Calle 3, Avenida Central & 2; the Hotel Alameda, Avenida Central, Calle 12; and the Soda Palace, Avenida 2, Calle 2. The machines operate on coins.

Airmail letters to the USA are about US$0.32 for the first 20 grams and about US$0.40 to Europe. Parcels can also be

mailed from post offices, but tend to be rather expensive.

In addresses, Apartado means PO Box; it is not a street or apartment address.

Receiving Mail

Sometimes embassies will hold mail for you, but many embassies refuse to do so and will return it to the sender. You can also have mail sent care of a hotel or travel agency, but it's liable to get lost or delayed.

The best way to receive mail is at the Correo Central of whichever town you are staying in. San José is the most efficient, and letters usually arrive within a week from North America, a little longer from more distant places. Post offices charge about US$0.10 per letter received and you need to show your passport to receive your mail – you can't pick up other people's.

If you have mail sent to the post office, remember that the mail is filed alphabetically; so if it's addressed to John Gillis Payson it could well be filed under 'G' or 'J' instead of the correct 'P'. For San José it should be addressed to (for example) John PAYSON, Lista de Correos, Correo Central, San José, Costa Rica. Ask your correspondents to clearly print your last name and avoid appending witticisms such as 'World Traveller Extraordinaire' to your name.

Avoid having parcels sent to you, as they are held in customs and cannot be retrieved until you have paid a duty usually equivalent to the value of the gift plus the value of the mailing cost combined. The process requires two visits to the customs – one to open your package and have it inspected; the second, a few days later, to pay the (usually exorbitant) customs fee assessed. This is true of even small packages.

Unfortunately, there have been many recent reports of theft and corruption in the local post office system. Try to avoid mailing valuables.

Telephones

New Telephone System Telephone numbers in Costa Rica currently consist of six digits with no area codes used. This obvi-ously limits the number of possible telephone numbers to a theoretical one million (00 0000 to 99 9999) but, in reality, less than half the numbers are usable because of tech-nical reasons. Therefore the telephone system is now running out of numbers.

A new telephone numbering system, con-sisting of seven digits, is scheduled to come into effect on 30 March 1994. (As we go to press, this date is still the scheduled one, but it may be delayed for unforeseen reasons. Check locally.) This will make the six digit telephone numbers instantly obsolete.

The first two digits of the six digit system will become three digits. The last four digits will not change. After the new system comes into effect, use the list given in the Telephone Numbers appendix at the back of this book to find the new seven digit number for all the six digit numbers given.

Local Calls There are nearly 400,000 tele-phones in Costa Rica, which is the highest per capita number of phones in any Latin American country. Public telephones are found all over Costa Rica and are signed with a telephone symbol. They accept coins of 5, 10 and 20 colones.

You can call anywhere in the country from a public booth. There are no area codes. Calls are generally inexpensive, with a three minute call anywhere never costing more than US$0.50. Of course, operator-assisted calls from hotels are more expensive – it seems that the more expensive the hotel, the more they charge for a phone call. A local call costing 5 colones often costs 100 colones in a fancy hotel.

In remote areas of the country, look for the telephone symbol in even the most unlikely places. I was heading north on the Río Sarapiquí towards the Nicaraguan border in a motorised dugout canoe when I spied a telephone symbol on a post by the river. Sure enough, there was a tiny general store and a radiotelephone. Calls could be put through to San José in a minute or two. These radio-telephones require an operator (in this case it was the store assistant) and there is a meter.

You pay whatever the meter charges for the call – it's not very expensive.

International Calls Calling internationally is quite straightforward. For collect (reverse charge) calls, dial 116 on any public phone to get an English-speaking international operator. The party you call can ring you back at many public telephones. Only countries with reciprocal agreements with Costa Rica will accept collect calls. These include the USA and many other countries.

If you want to pay for the call, however, you should use a telephone calling card or go through an operator-assisted public telephone facility or a hotel, because trying to pay for an international call with 20 colón coins can be difficult. In San José, Radiográfica on Avenida 5, between Calles 1 & 3, will put international calls through from 7 am to 10 pm daily. ICE (Instituto Costarricense de Electricidad) on Avenida 2, Calle 1, has the same type of service. There is also an international phone facility in the airport. Both these places have direct phones to operators in various foreign countries which you can use if you have the appropriate calling card. Dial the following numbers from any phone to reach operators in these foreign countries:

Canada	161
Germany	168
Italy	169
Spain	164
UK	167
USA (AT&T)	114
USA (MCI)	162
USA (Sprint)	163

After reaching the operator, you can either call collect or charge the call to your calling-card number – you can get through in less than a minute. The set-up fee and first minute are expensive. I called the USA from Costa Rica using AT&T Direct and was charged US$4.07 for the first minute and US$1.13 for each additional minute. Thus a 12 minute call cost US$16.50.

It is no cheaper to go through an operator. Costs of calls per minute from Costa Rica are approximately US$2 to US$3 to North America (depending on the area code), US$3 to US$4 to Europe, and US$5 to Australia. Cheaper rates apply from 8 pm to 7 am and during weekends.

To call Costa Rica from abroad, use the international code (506) before the six digit (seven digit after 30 March 1994) Costa Rican telephone number.

Fax, Telex & Telegraph
Main post offices usually have telegraph facilities. Radiográfica and ICE in San José also have telex and fax machines. They will also accept and hold telex and fax messages. Outside San José, the ICE office in many towns will send faxes and telexes – I sent a one page fax from the ICE in Liberia to the UK for about US$5.50.

TIME
Costa Rica is six hours behind GMT, which means that Costa Rican time is equivalent to Central Time in North America. There is no daylight saving time.

ELECTRICITY
Costa Rica's electricity supply is 110 V AC at 60 Hz. You will need a voltage converter if you want to use 240/250 V AC-powered items.

LAUNDRY
There are almost no self-service laundries in Costa Rica, although I did find a couple of expensive ones in San José which charged close to US$4 a load to wash and dry. This means that you have to find someone to wash your clothes for you or wash them yourself.

Many hotels will have someone to do your laundry; this can cost very little in the cheaper hotels (about a dollar for a full change of clothes). The major problem is that you might not see your clothes again for two or three days, particularly if it is raining and they can't be dried. Better hotels charge more but have driers.

If you wash the clothes yourself, ask the hotel staff where to do this. Some hotels have a huge cement sink (called a *pila)* and scrubbing board which is much easier to use than a bathroom washbasin. Next to the scrubbing board there may be a well-like section full of clean water. Don't dunk your clothes in this water to soak or rinse them as it is often used as an emergency water supply in the case of water failure. Use a bowl or bucket to scoop water out instead, or run water from a tap.

WEIGHTS & MEASURES

Costa Rica uses the metric system. For those travellers who still use miles, pounds, ounces, bushels, leagues, rods, roods, magnums, stones and other quaint and arcane expressions, there is a metric conversion table at the back of this book.

BOOKS

Costa Rica has changed greatly over the past few years and the tourism boom is one of the greatest changes of all. When choosing travel guidebooks, get a recent edition – older editions may be selling cheaply, but their travel information is way out of date.

Regional Travel Guides

South American Handbook (Trade & Travel Publications, Bath, England). This was first published in 1924 and has been updated every year since. In 1991, for the first time, this well known book was issued in three separate volumes, one of which was the *Mexico & Central American Handbook*. Its section on Costa Rica is limited to some 70 pages out of about 800. Nevertheless, it remains a useful source of travel information, particularly for travellers doing a grand tour of Central America.

Lonely Planet's *Central America on a Shoestring* (2nd edition due in 1994) is written for the traveller on a tight budget, and again is useful for someone visiting several Central American countries. There are many useful maps. Both this book and the Handbook have much background as well as travel information and both are recommended.

Fodor's *Costa Rica, Belize, Guatemala* (Fodor's, New York & London) is an upmarket general guide, updated every couple of years.

Frommers' *Costa Rica, Guatemala & Belize on $35 a Day '93-'94* is a nicely laid out book, but covers only the most popular spots. The fine print tells you that the $35 (US) a day is per person for double occupancy plus meals – travel expenses and entrance fees are extra. The Costa Rican section is replete with 'Worth The Extra Bucks' choices, so lone travellers in particular will have a hard time using this book to travel on a US$35-a-day budget.

Costa Rica Travel Guides

At my last count, there were eight travel guidebooks dealing exclusively with Costa Rica. All provide general background and travel information. All are OK to very good and have been well received. The editions I read are listed here but more recent editions may be available by the time you read this.

The New Key to Costa Rica by Beatrice Blake and Anne Becher (Ulysses Press, Berkeley, California, 1993) is the oldest guide and has been updated most years for over a decade. Its emphasis is on living and travelling in Costa Rica and ethical travel – an excellent book.

The Costa Rica Traveller by Ellen Searby (Windham Bay Press, Occidental, California, 3rd edition, 1991, updated 1993) has an emphasis on hotel listings.

Costa Rica by Paul Glassman (Passport Press, Champlain, New York, 1991) has an emphasis on general travel.

Costa Rica: A Natural Destination by Ree Strange Sheck (John Muir Publications, Santa Fe, New Mexico, 2nd edition, 1992) has an emphasis on visiting and staying in and near the national parks and private reserves.

Adventure Guide to Costa Rica by Harry S Pariser (Hunyer, New Jersey, USA, and Moorland, Derbyshire, UK, 1992) is a general guidebook.

Insight Guides Gosta Rica edited by Harvey Haber (APA Publications, 1992) is a general book with many stunning photographs and good background essays, but there is little hard travel information. The editor now runs a B&B in San José and writes for *The Tico Times*.

Costa Rica Traveler's Handbook (Moon Publications, California) is due out in 1994.

Costa Rica Special Interest Guides

Choose Costa Rica – A Guide to Wintering or Retirement by John Howells (Gateway Books, California 1992). This is the best of the 'how to retire in Costa Rica' books.

Pura Vida; Gay & Lesbian Costa Rica by Joseph Itiel (Orchid House, California, due late 1993). This book includes a chapter written by a woman and should be a useful source for gay and lesbian travellers.

Mapa-Guía de la Naturaleza – Costa Rica by Herrera S Wilberth (Incafo, Costa Rica, 1992). A book of maps based on the Costa Rican IGN 1:200,000 topographical series. All natural areas are highlighted and described in Spanish and English, accompanied by good colour photographs. This guide is a cross between Boza's park book and the IGN maps (both described here). Some readers complain that it is hard to use the non-overlapping 23 cm x 34 cm double-page maps, of which 27 are needed to cover the country. Also, my edition had the highlighted natural areas on map pages 18 and 22 transposed, which made those maps hard to use. Nevertheless, an attractive and useful book.

The Essential Road Guide for Costa Rica by Bill Baker (Baker, Apartado 1185-1011, San José, 1992). A useful km by km guide for driving along the major roads of the country plus good background information and maps on bus terminals, getting around and driving in Costa Rica.

People & Services is a locally produced booklet co-sponsored by AT&T and *The Tico Times* which is due to appear in late 1993. It gives a list of English-speaking services ranging from plumbers to paediatricians.

Adventure Travel

Backpacking in Mexico & Central America by Hilary Bradt & Rob Rachowiecki (Bradt Publications, Chalfont St Peter, UK, 2nd edition, 1982). Out of print and out-dated, but with useful background if you can find it at a public library.

The Rivers of Costa Rica: a Canoeing, Kayaking, and Rafting Guide by Michael W Mayfield & Rafael E Gallo (Menasha Ridge Press, Alabama, 1988). Just the ticket for river runners – but is reportedly out of print.

Costa Rica's National Parks and Preserves – a Visitor's Guide by Joseph Franke (The Mountaineers, Seattle, 1993). Despite its recent publication date, many of the details are already out of date, but it provides useful maps and background.

Nature & Wildlife

Several very useful books have been published for the many people coming to Costa Rica to observe wildlife, visit national parks, and enjoy the outdoors. All of the following are recommended.

Parques Nacionales Costa Rica by Mario Boza (Incafo, Madrid, 1992) – the author is currently Costa Rican Vice-Minister of Natural Resources. The hardbound version is a beautifully photographed coffee-table book with bilingual (Spanish-English) text describing the national parks; the softbound version is half the size but also has good photos and interesting text. Both books are readily available in San José.

Costa Rican Natural History by Daniel H Janzen with 174 contributors (University of Chicago Press, 1983) is an excellent, if weighty (almost two kg and over 800 large pages), introduction for the biologist.

Tropical Nature by Adrian Forsyth & Ken Miyata (Charles Scribner's Sons, New York, 1984). I recommend this entertaining and readable book for the layperson interested in biology, particularly of the rainforest. Forsyth is also the author of a children's book *Journey Through a Tropical Jungle* (Greey de Pencier, Toronto, 1988).

A Naturalist in Costa Rica (University of Florida Press, Gainesville, 1971) and *A Naturalist on a Tropical Farm* (University of California Press, Berkeley, 1980) both by Alexander F Skutch. They are slightly dated but still excellent – the earlier one was recently out of print. Skutch is the author of several other books about natural history in Costa Rica.

A Neotropical Companion by John C Kricher (Princeton University Press, 1989). This readable book is sub-titled 'An Introduction to the Animals, Plants, and Ecosystems of the New World Tropics' – which tells you all you need to know.

In the Rainforest by Catherine Caulfield (University of Chicago Press, 1986). Another good choice, it emphasises the problems of the loss of the rainforest.

Life Above the Jungle Floor by Donald Perry (Simon & Schuster, New York, 1986). Donald Perry, whose Automated Web for Canopy Exploration (AWCE) can be seen at Rara Avis Rainforest Preserve, is the author of this fascinating book.

The Enchanted Canopy by Andrew W Mitchell (Macmillan, New York, 1986) – another very good book.

Rainforests – A Guide to Research and Tourist Facilities at Selected Tropical Forest Sites in Central and South America by James L Castner (Feline Press, Gainesville, Florida, 1990). This is a good source book, particularly for those people wishing to visit rainforests in a variety of neotropical countries. Thirty-nine sites in seven countries are described and much useful background is referred to.

Sarapiqui Chronicle by Allen M Young (Smithsonian Institution, Washington, 1991). Subtitled 'A Naturalist in Costa Rica', the book tells the story of the invertebrate zoologist's quarter century of expeditions to the rainforests near the Río Sarapiquí. A good read.

The Quetzal and the Macaw by David Rains Wallace (Sierra Club, 1992). The sub-title tells it all: 'The Story of Costa Rica's National Parks'. A good book about the formation and development of the parks system written for the general reader.

Field Guides

A Guide to the Birds of Costa Rica by F Gary Stiles and Alexander F Skutch (Cornell University Press, 1989). Bird-watchers will need this excellent and thorough book.

Neotropical Rainforest Mammals – A Field Guide by Louise H Emmons (University of Chicago Press, 1990). An excellent, detailed and portable book, with almost 300 mammal species described and illustrated. Although some of the mammals included are found only in other neotropical countries, most of Costa Rica's mammals, and certainly all the rainforest inhabitants, are found within the book's pages.

The Butterflies of Costa Rica and Their Natural History by Philip J DeVries (Princeton University Press, 1987). A detailed guide for lepidopterists.

The Sea Turtles of Santa Rosa National Park by Stephen E Cornelius (Fundación de Parques Nacionales, San José, 1986). Descriptions of the four species found in Costa Rica – reportedly now out of print.

People & Politics

The Costa Ricans by Richard Biesanz et al (Waveland Press, Illinois, reissued 1988 with update) is a recommended book with a historical perspective on politics and social change in Costa Rica and many insights into the tico character.

Costa Rica – A Country Guide by Tom Barry (The Inter-Hemispheric Education Resource Center, Albuquerque, New Mexico, 2nd edition, 1990). A good overview for social scientists – discusses politics, security forces, the economy, society and environment, and foreign influence.

The Costa Rica Reader edited by Marc Edelman & Joanne Kenen (Grove Weidenfield, New York, 1989) is an anthology covering socio-political aspects of the country.

Costa Rica: A Geographical Interpretation in Historical Perspective by Carolyn Hall (Westview Press, Boulder, Colorado, 1985) is a valuable resource dealing also with social and environmental issues.

What Happen: A Folk History of Costa Rica's Talamanca Coast (Ecodesarollos, San José, 1977) and *Wa'apin Man* (Editorial Costa Rica, 1986). Written by former Peace Corps volunteer and sociologist, Paula Palmer, these books are about the people of the south Caribbean coast of Costa Rica. They may be available in reprints by other publishers by the time you read this.

Taking Care of Sibö's Gifts by Paula Palmer, Juanita Sánchez & Gloria Mayorga (Asociación de Desarrollo Integral de la Reserva Indígena Cocles/KéköLdi, San José, 1991). Subtitled 'An Environmental Treatise from Costa Rica's KéköLdi Indigenous Reserve', this excellent booklet discusses the traditional Bribri lifestyle from the point of view of their natural surroundings. Book profits go to indigenous conservation and educational programs.

Archaeology

Between Continents/Between Seas: Pre-Columbian Art of Costa Rica by Detroit Institute of the Arts (Harry Abrams, New York, 1981) is a large and well-illustrated book.

Ancient Treasures of Costa Rica edited by Frederick W Lange (Johnson Books, Colorado, 1990), subtitled 'Art and Archaeology of the Rich Coast', this 40-page booklet deals with the archaeology of the Nicoya region and is one of the few accessible books about pre-Columbian Costa Rica.

Costa Rican Art and Archaeology: Essays in Honor of Frederick R Mayer edited by Frederick W Lange (Johnson Books, Colorado, 1988) is a more in-depth introduction to Costa Rican archaeology.

Miscellaneous

La Loca de Gandoca by Anacristina Rossi (EDUCA, San José, 3rd edition, February 1993). This book, written by a prize-winning tica novelist, describes the struggle of a local conservationist trying to halt the development of a hotel in a protected area of the Caribbean coast, and the problems with corruption at various levels of government. Although the author claims that all the characters in her novel are imaginary and that any similarity to reality is coincidental, local cognoscenti will tell you that remarkably similar events happened here recently. It's a deplorable story, and will give you a different view of Costa Rica as a 'perfect

environmental destination'. The book is available locally and only in Spanish, but is short and simply written. Thus it makes a good choice for someone who is interested in local conservation issues, even if their Spanish is limited. The book has been a hot seller – the 3rd edition is already sold out, so grab the 4th or 5th when you see them.

Jurassic Park by Michael Crichton (Ballantine Books). Unless your interest in Hollywood blockbusters is zero, you've heard of the movie. This is the novel that gave rise to the movie, and the dino-action is based in Costa Rica. Locals don't appreciate the references to the Costa Rican Air Force (there is no military force here) and 'ticans' (should be 'ticos') but it beats *War and Peace* for those lazy moments of your trip. (With an apology to dedicated Tolstoy readers.)

The Tropical Traveller by John Hatt (Penguin Books, London, 3rd edition 1993). Useful, enjoyable and recommended source book for tropical travel worldwide – everything from animal hazards to human hazards, conversion tables to culture shock, accommodation to artificial resuscitation.

Bookshops

There is a large variety of books about Costa Rica. Many are available outside Costa Rica in good bookshops specialising in travel and wildlife. There are a few bookshops in San José which carry some titles, especially those published in Costa Rica. These bookshops are listed under San José. Note that books published outside Costa Rica are expensive – get them at home if possible. Bookshops outside San José rarely carry books of interest to the traveller.

MAPS

If you want a good map of Costa Rica before you go, the best is the very detailed map drawn by Kevin Healey, an Australian cartographer who has made the best maps of Latin America I've seen. His *Costa Rica* (1990; 2nd edition, due 1994) map is a single 1:500,000 sheet with a 1:250,000 *Environs of San José* inset, and provides road, rail, topography, national park and private reserve information. It is published by and available from International Travel Map Productions (ITM), PO Box 2290, Vancouver, British Columbia, V6B 3W5, Canada. In Europe write to Bradt Publications, 41 Nortoft Road, Chalfont St Peter, Bucks, SL9 0LA, England. ITM also publishes an excellent regional map *Traveller's Reference Map of Central America* (2nd edition, 1993) also by Kevin Healey.

Once you arrive in Costa Rica, there are several choices. The Costa Rican National Tourist Bureau has published several useful maps, all of which were free but also subject to availability. None were available when I visited in 1993 – but ask about reissues. Past maps include a 1:10,000 Centre of San José Map, a 1:200,000 San José Area Map, and a 1:1,000,000 Costa Rica Road Map.

The Instituto Geográfico Nacional de Costa Rica (IGN) publishes four kinds of maps which can be bought at the IGN in San José, or in major bookstores in the capital. There is a single sheet 1:500,000 map of Costa Rica, which is very good but not as detailed as the ITM map, and there is a nine sheet 1:200,000 map covering the country in detail. Most of the country is covered with 1:50,000 scale topographical maps (useful for hiking and backpacking), and some of the cities and urban areas are covered by a variety of 1:10,000 and 1:5000 maps. All these maps provide physical as well as political detail and are well produced.

MEDIA
Newspapers & Magazines
The best local daily newspapers are *La Nación* and *La República* – their coverage is conservative. *Esta Semana* is the best local weekly news magazine.

An English-language newspaper published every Friday is *The Tico Times*, now in its 37th year of publication. It costs about US$0.25 and is a well-recommended source of information about everything to do with Costa Rica. It publishes an annual tourism edition each October which is available in local bookstores or directly from the newspaper. Foreign subscriptions are available

for one year for US$45 (the Americas), US$70 (Europe & the Middle East), and US$80 (Africa, Asia & the Far East). Write to Apartado 4632, San José, Costa Rica (fax 33 6378). US residents can write to Dept 717, PO Box 025216, Miami, FL 33102.

A second English-language weekly, *Costa Rica Today*, was launched in 1992; publication day is Thursday. It doesn't give the news coverage of *The Tico Times* but caters to tourists and is relentlessly upbeat, though useful nonetheless. Note that the owners of the weekly also own the Bosque Puerto Carrillo teak farms – so anything they write about teak farms is not entirely without bias!

Major bookstores in San José carry some North American and other newspapers (two or three days late) as well as magazines such as *Time* or *Newsweek*.

Radio & TV
There are six local TV stations and many of the better hotels also receive cable TV from the USA. There are many AM/FM radio stations. If you have a portable shortwave radio you can listen to, among many others, the BBC World Service, Voice of America and Radio Moscow.

FILM & PHOTOGRAPHY
Definitely bring everything you'll need. Camera gear is expensive in Costa Rica and film choice is limited. Film may have been kept in hot storage cabinets and is sometimes outdated, so if you do buy any in Costa Rica, check the expiry date.

You can have film developed in Costa Rica but processing is pricey and not always very good. Don't carry around exposed film for months either – that's asking for washed-out results. If you are on an extended trip, try to send film home as soon after it's exposed as possible. You'll often meet people heading back to whichever continent you're from and they can usually be persuaded to do you the favour of carrying film home, particularly if you offer to take them out to dinner. I always buy either process-paid film or prepaid film mailers so I can place the exposed film in the mailer and not worry about the costs. The last thing you want to do on your return from a trip is worry about how you're going to find the money to develop a few dozen rolls of film. Tropical shadows are very strong and come out almost black on photographs. Often a bright but hazy day makes for better photographs than a very sunny one. Photography in open shade or using fill-in flash will help. The best time for shooting is when the sun is low – the first and last two hours of the day. If you are heading into the rainforest you will need high-speed film, flash, a tripod, or a combination of these if you want to take photographs within the jungle. The amount of light penetrating the layers of vegetation is surprisingly very low.

The Costa Rican people make wonderful subjects for photos. However, most people resent having a camera thrust in their face. Ask for permission with a smile or a joke and if this is refused (rarely) don't become offended. Be aware and sensitive of people's feelings – it is not worth upsetting someone to get a photograph.

The international airport in San José has a vicious X-ray machine. My film came home with a greyish cast to it, and two friends who were there later reported the same thing. Carry all your film on separately. I have received a report that the X-ray machine can also damage computer discs.

HEALTH

It's true that most people travelling for any length of time in Latin America are likely to have an occasional mild stomach upset. It's also true that if you take the appropriate precautions before, during and after your trip, it's unlikely that you will become seriously ill. In a decade of living and travelling in Latin America, I'm happy to report that I've picked up no major illnesses. Costa Rica has one of the highest standards of health care and hygiene in Latin America, so you are unlikely to get seriously ill.

Predeparture Preparations

Vaccinations The Costa Rican authorities do not, at present, require anyone to have an up-to-date international vaccination card to enter the country, though you should make sure that your vaccinations are up to date. However, overland travellers from Nicaragua have been asked for evidence of cholera vaccinations at the border – some travellers report that they were given shots at the border. My advice here is to bring your own needle (or buy one from a local pharmacy) as it is not unheard of for needles to be reused. Pregnant women should consult their doctor before taking any vaccinations.

Travel Insurance However fit and healthy you are, *do* take out medical insurance, preferably one with provisions for flying you home in the event of a medical emergency. Even if you don't get sick, you might be involved in an accident.

First-Aid Kit How large or small your first-aid kit should be depends on your knowledge of first-aid procedures, where and how far off the beaten track you are going, how long you will need the kit for, and how many people will be sharing it. The following is a suggested checklist which you should amend as you require.

antiseptic cream
antihistamine or other anti-itch cream for insect bites
aspirin
Lomotil and/or a non-prescription preparation such as
    Pepto Bismol for diarrhoea
antibiotics such as ampicillin and a tetracycline
throat lozenges
ear and eye drops
antacid tablets
motion-sickness medication
alcohol swabs
water purification tablets
lip salve
anti-fungal powder
thermometer in a case
surgical tape, assorted adhesive strips, gauze,
    bandages, butterfly closures
moleskin
scissors
first-aid booklet

Basic Rules

Water & Food Water is usually safe in San José and the major towns, though it is worth boiling, filtering or purifying it in out of the way places. The lowlands are the most likely places to find unsafe drinking water. Ask if in doubt. Some better hotels may be able to show you a certificate of water purity. Bottled mineral water, soft drinks and beer are readily available alternatives.

Many places have recently had problems with contaminated ice. Try to avoid ice if in doubt. Uncooked foods (such as salads and fruits) are best avoided unless they can be peeled.

Health Precautions Several things must be thought about before leaving home. If you wear prescription glasses, make sure you have a spare pair and a copy of the prescription. The tropical sun is strong, so you may want to have a prescription pair of sunglasses made.

Also buy strong sunblock lotion, as most sunblocks in Costa Rica have a sun protection factor of 4 or 8, though stronger ones are occasionally available. A minimum SPF of 15 is recommended; higher if you are fair or burn easily.

Ensure that you have an adequate supply of any prescription medicines you use regularly. If you haven't had a dental examination for a long time, you should have one rather than risk a dental problem on your trip.

Medical Problems & Treatment

Diarrhoea The drastic change in diet experienced by travellers means that they are often susceptible to minor stomach ailments, such as diarrhoea. After you've been travelling in Latin America for a while you seem to build up some sort of immunity. If this is your first trip to the area, take heart. Costa Rica is one of the healthiest countries in Latin America. Many people get minor stomach problems, but a simple non-prescription medicine such as Pepto Bismol usually takes care of the discomfort quickly.

Dysentery If your diarrhoea continues for several days and is accompanied by nausea, severe abdominal pain and fever, and you find blood in your stools, it's likely that you have contracted dysentery. Although travellers may suffer from an occasional bout of diarrhoea, dysentery is fortunately not very common. There are two types: amoebic and bacillary. It is not always obvious which kind you have. Although bacillary responds well to antibiotics, amoebic – which is rarer – involves more complex treatment. If you contract dysentery, you should seek medical advice.

Hepatitis Hepatitis A is caused by ingesting contaminated food or water. Salads, uncooked or unpeeled fruit, and unboiled drinks are the worst offenders. Infection risks are minimised by using bottled drinks except in major towns or where you know the water has been purified, washing your own salads with purified water, and paying scrupulous attention to your toilet habits.

If you get the disease you'll know it. Your skin and especially the whites of your eyes turn yellow, and you feel so tired that it literally takes all your effort to go to the toilet. There is no cure except rest. If you're lucky, you'll be on your feet in a couple of weeks; if you're not, expect to stay in bed for a couple of months.

Until recently, the usual prophylaxis was a gamma globulin shot as close to departure as possible. Although not 100% effective, your chances of getting hepatitis A are minimised. The shot should be repeated every six months, although some authorities recommend more frequent shots. Research is currently underway to find a 100% effective prophylactic; there are recent reports from the UK that a new and better vaccine is available – talk to your doctor.

The incidence of hepatitis A is low in Costa Rica, so many travellers opt not to bother with these shots.

Cholera The cholera epidemic that swept Latin America in 1992 was largely avoided in Costa Rica. Whereas hundreds of thousands of cases were reported in Latin America as a whole, with thousands of deaths resulting from the disease, Costa Rica reported only 15 cases and no deaths in the period from January 1992 to March 1993. Nicaragua has reported several hundred cases and about two dozen deaths and therefore overland travellers entering Costa Rica from Nicaragua are required to have vaccinations. Travellers arriving by air from North America and Europe are not required to have cholera shots.

Malaria Malarial mosquitoes aren't a problem in the highlands but some cases of malaria have recently been reported in the lowlands, particularly the south Caribbean coastal area near the Panamanian border. If you plan on visiting the lowlands, you should purchase anti-malarial pills in advance because they should be taken from two weeks before until six weeks after your visit. Dosage and frequency of administration varies from brand to brand, so check this carefully.

Chloroquine (known as Aralen in Costa Rica) is recommended for short-term protection. The usual dose is 500 mg once a week. Long-term use of chloroquine *may* cause side effects and travellers planning a long trip into the lowlands should discuss this risk against the value of protection with their doctor. Pregnant women are at a higher risk when taking anti-malarials. Fansidar is now known to cause sometimes fatal side effects and this drug should be used only under medical supervision.

People who are going to spend a great deal of time in tropical lowlands and prefer not to take anti-malarial pills on a semipermanent basis should remember that malarial mosquitoes bite mostly at night. You should wear long-sleeved shirts and long trousers from dusk till dawn, use frequent applications of an insect repellent, and sleep under a mosquito net. Sleeping under a fan is also effective; mosquitoes don't like wind. A woman traveller suggests that getting changed or dressed for dinner is not a good idea in mosquito-prone areas, because dusk is a particularly bad time for mosquitoes and that dressy skirt does nothing to keep the insects away. Keep the long pants and bug repellent on. Another suggestion is for small

battery-operated devices which emit a high-pitched whine which repels mosquitoes – this won't stop you getting bitten by other, non-malarial, insects.

The most effective ingredient in insect repellents is diethyl-metatoluamide, also known as 'Deet'. You should buy repellent with a high percentage of this ingredient; many brands, including those available in Costa Rica, contain less than 15%. I find that the rub-on lotions are the most effective, and sprays are good for spraying clothes, especially at the neck, wrist, waist and ankle openings. Bear in mind that Deet is strong stuff – it is toxic to children and shouldn't be used on their skin. 'Skin So Soft' made by Avon has insect repellent properties and is not toxic – get the oil, not the lotion. Deet dissolves plastic, so keep it off plastic lenses etc.

Mosquito spirals (coils) can be bought in Costa Rican pharmacies (ask for *espirales*). They work like incense sticks and are fairly effective at keeping mosquitoes away.

Insect Problems Insect repellents go a long way in preventing bites, but if you do get bitten, avoid scratching. Unfortunately this is easier said than done.

To alleviate itching, try applying hydrocortisone cream, calamine lotion, some other kind of anti-itch cream, or soaking in baking soda. Scratching will quickly open bites and cause them to become infected. Skin infections are slow to heal in the heat of the tropics and all infected bites as well as cuts and grazes should be kept scrupulously clean, treated with antiseptic creams, and covered with dressings on a daily basis.

Another insect problem is infestation with lice (including crabs) and scabies. Lice or crabs crawl around in your body hair and make you itch. To get rid of them, wash with a shampoo which contains benzene hexachloride, or shave the affected area. To avoid being re-infected, wash all your clothes and bedding in hot water and the shampoo. It's probably best to just throw away your underwear if you had body lice or crabs. Lice thrive on body warmth; these beasties lurking in clothes will die in about 72 hours if the clothing isn't worn.

Chiggers are mites which burrow into your skin and cause it to become red and itchy. The recommended prevention is to sprinkle sulphur powder on socks, shoes and lower legs when walking through grass. Liberal application of insect repellent works reasonably well.

Scorpions and spiders can give severely painful – but rarely fatal – stings or bites. A common way to get bitten is to put on your clothes and shoes in the morning without checking them first. Develop the habit of shaking out your clothing before putting it on, especially in the lowlands. Check your bedding before going to sleep. Don't walk barefoot, and look where you place your hands when reaching to a shelf or branch. It's unlikely that you will get stung, so don't worry too much about it, but take the precautions outlined above.

Fer-de-lance snake

Snakebite This is also extremely unlikely. Should you be bitten, the snake may be a non-venomous one (try to identify the offending creature). Try to prevent the circulation of any venom already inside you around your body. Do not try the slash-and-suck routine on the bite.

One of the world's deadliest snakes is the fer-de-lance, and it has an anti-coagulating agent in its venom. If you're bitten by a fer-de-lance, your blood coagulates twice as slowly as the average haemophiliac's and so slashing at the wound with a razor is a good way to help you bleed to death. The slash-and-suck routine does work in some cases, but this should be done only by someone who knows what they are doing.

The venom of most dangerous snakes does its nasty work via the lymph system, not the blood stream, so treatment aimed at reducing the flow of blood or removing venom from the bloodstream is likely to be futile. Aim to immobilise the venom in the limb's lymph system or the capillary system, preventing it from spreading to the vital organs. It is now a preferred method of treat-

ing snakebite. Tourniquets are much too dangerous and not particularly effective.

In Australia, where they have a fair amount of snake bite experience, a new method of treatment is now recommended. This is simply to immobilise the limb where the bite took place and bandage it tightly (but not like a tourniquet) and completely. Then with the minimum of disturbance, particularly of the bound limb, get the victim to medical attention as soon as possible. Keep calm and reassure the victim. Even the deadly fer-de-lance only succeeds in killing a small percentage of its victims.

Sexually Transmitted Diseases (STDs)
Prostitution is legal in Costa Rica, and female prostitutes are required to be registered and receive regular medical check-ups. Nevertheless incidence of sexually transmitted diseases (including HIV/AIDS) is increasing in Costa Rican prostitutes. There are two effective ways of avoiding contracting an STD: have a monogamous relationship with a healthy partner or abstain from sexual encounters.

Abstinence is easy to recommend but

tough to practice. Travellers who have no sexual partner and who are unwilling to abstain are strongly advised against using prostitutes. Having sex with a person other than a prostitute is somewhat safer, but still far from risk-free. The use of condoms minimises, but does not eliminate, the chances of contracting a STD. Condoms are available in Costa Rican pharmacies.

Diseases such as syphilis and gonorrhoea are marked by rashes or sores in the genital area and burning pain during urination. Women's symptoms may be less obvious than men's. These diseases can be cured relatively straightforwardly by antibiotics. If not treated they can become dormant, only to emerge in much more difficult to treat forms a few months or years later. Costa Rican doctors know how to treat most STDs – if you have a rash, discharge, or pain, see a doctor. However, there is no known cure for herpes at present but it is not fatal.

HIV, the human immunodeficiency virus, may develop into AIDS, which whilst not fatal in itself, leads to a loss of immunity to other diseases, a combination of which is fatal within a few years of contracting AIDS.

Altitude Sickness This occurs when you ascend to high altitude quickly, for example if you fly into the highlands. This is not a problem in San José (1150 metres) which is not high enough to cause altitude problems.

If you are planning on driving up one of the volcanoes such as Poás (2704 metres) or Irazú (3432 metres) you may experience some shortness of breath and headache. Overnight stays are not allowed on these volcanoes, so you will be able to descend quickly if you feel unwell. Heading south from San José on the Carretera Interamericana, the road crosses the continental divide at 3335 metres, 95 km south of the capital. Again, you will probably be going down again before you get sick.

If you are planning a climb of Chirripó (3819 metres, the highest mountain in Costa Rica and south Central America) you may experience much more severe symptoms, including vomiting, fatigue, insomnia, loss of appetite, a rapid pulse and irregular (or Cheyne-Stokes) breathing during sleep.

The best thing you can do to avoid altitude sickness is to climb gradually. Consider taking two days for the Chirripó ascent rather than one. If you feel sick, the best treatment is rest, deep breathing, an adequate fluid intake and a mild pain killer such as Tylenol to alleviate headaches. If symptoms are very severe, the only effective cure is to descend to a lower elevation.

Heat & Sun The heat and humidity of the coastal tropics make you sweat profusely and can also make you feel apathetic. It is important to maintain a high fluid intake and to ensure that your food is well salted. If fluids lost through perspiration are not replaced, heat exhaustion and cramps may result. The feeling of apathy that some people experience usually fades after a week or two.

If you're arriving in the tropics with a great desire to improve your tan, you've certainly come to the right place. The tropical sun will not only improve your tan, it will also burn you to a crisp. I know several travellers who have enjoyed themselves in the sun for an afternoon, and then spent the next couple of days with severe sunburn. An effective way of immobilising yourself is to cover yourself with suntan lotion, walk down to the beach, remove your shoes and badly burn your feet, which you forgot to put lotion on and which are especially untanned.

The power of the tropical sun cannot be overemphasised. Don't spoil your trip by trying to tan too quickly; use strong sunblock lotion frequently and put it on all exposed skin. Wearing a wide-brimmed sun hat is also a good idea.

Medical Attention

If you've taken the precautions mentioned in the previous sections you can look forward to a generally healthy trip. Should something go wrong, however, you can get good medical advice and treatment in the major cities in Costa Rica.

The social security hospitals provide free

emergency services to everyone, including foreigners. The main one in San José is the Hospital San Juan de Dios (☎ 22 0166) on Calle 14, Avenida Central. Private clinics are also available and are listed under San José and other main towns. Emergency phone numbers worth knowing are the Red Cross (Cruz Roja, ☎ 21 5818) for ambulances in the San José area, and San José Paramedics (☎ 118, no coin needed). Outside San José, call the Guardia on 127.

Most prescription drugs are available in Costa Rica; some are sold over the counter. For minor ailments and illnesses, pharmacists will often advise and prescribe for you.

Medical care is generally less expensive than it is in most Western countries, although the standards in San José are high. Costa Rica is experiencing a boom in cosmetic and plastic surgery. Foreigners come here specifically for these non-essential medical procedures at lower cost than at home. If you have insurance to cover medical emergencies, note that many doctors expect to be paid up-front – then you have to claim from the insurance company to get reimbursed.

WOMEN TRAVELLERS
Generally, women travellers find Costa Rica safe and pleasant to visit.

Women are traditionally respected in Costa Rica (Mother's Day is a national holiday) and recently women have made gains in the workplace. A woman vice-president (Victoria Garrón) was elected in 1986, another woman (Margarita Penon) ran as a presidential candidate in 1993 and women routinely occupy roles in the political, legal, scientific and medical fields – professions which used to be overpoweringly dominated by men.

This is not to say that machismo is a thing of the past. On the contrary, it is very much alive and practised. Costa Rican men generally consider *gringas* to have looser morals and to be easier 'conquests' than ticas. They will often make flirtatious comments to or stare at single women, both local and foreign. Women travelling with another woman are not exempt from this attention;

women travelling with men are less likely to receive attention.

Comments are rarely blatantly rude; the usual thing is a smiling *'Mi amor'* or an appreciative hiss. The best way to deal with this is to do what the ticas do – ignore the comments completely and not look at the man making them.

Women travellers will meet pleasant and friendly Costa Rican men. It is worth remembering, though, that gentle seduction is a sport, a challenge, even a way of life for many Costa Rican men, particularly in San José. Men may conveniently forget to mention that they are married, and declarations of undying love mean little in this Catholic society where divorce is frowned upon.

Women who firmly resist unwanted verbal advances from men are normally treated with respect. But there are always a small number of men who will insist on trying to hold hands or give a 'friendly' hug or kiss – if the feeling is not mutual, turn them down firmly and explicitly. Some women find that wearing a cheap 'wedding' ring helps – though, of course, you have to be ready to answer the inevitable 'Where is your husband?'.

There have also been recent reports of cab drivers making inappropriate advances to women – women alone may want to use cabs from a hotel rather than a cab on the street. Pirate cabs (without the insignia of a cab company) are more likely to present a problem. Lone women might avoid those, especially after dark if going for a long ride. (Nevertheless, I get the impression that cab drivers are generally OK – use your best judgement.)

Costa Ricans are generally quite conservative, and that applies to dress. Travellers are advised to follow suit to avoid calling unnecessary attention to themselves.

Neither men nor women wear shorts in the highlands – though shorts are fine in the beach resorts. This doesn't stop many gringos from wearing shorts in San José – look around and see how many locals dress that way.

DANGERS & ANNOYANCES
Thefts & Muggings

Locals and frequent visitors have noted an increase in tourist-oriented crime in recent years – the increase in tourism is a likely cause of this. Although rip-offs are a fact of life when travelling anywhere, you'll find Costa Rica is still less prone to theft than many countries. You should, nevertheless, take some simple precautions to avoid being robbed.

Armed robbery is very rare but sneak theft is more common, and you should remember that crowded places are the haunts of pickpockets – places such as badly lit bus stations or bustling streets. Crowded streets around the market and Coca-Cola bus terminal in San José, as well as along Avenida 2 around the Parque Central, are areas noted for thefts. (Also the avenidas running east of these areas for several blocks.) Muggings have been reported after dark – so keep alert. This is also the heart of the tourist area, with many budget hotels nearby and high-quality hotels on the edges. I spend many a night walking these streets and rarely have a problem.

Occasionally, a couple of women may try to physically harass a man – one tries lasciviously to gain your attention while the other tries to pull your wallet (as happened to me: a stiff-armed shove sent one woman dramatically cart-wheeling across the sidewalk yelling abusive epithets); other travellers report a number of incidents, particularly at night. Alertness helps – but if you are used to dealing with big-city hassles, you should have no great problem.

Thieves look for easy targets. Tourists who carry a wallet or passport in a hip pocket are asking for trouble. Leave your wallet at home; it's an easy mark for a pickpocket. Carrying a roll of bills loosely wadded under a handkerchief in your front pocket is as safe a way as any of carrying your daily spending money. The rest should be hidden. Always use at least an inside pocket or preferably a body pouch, money belt or leg pouch to protect your money and passport.

It is worth carrying a proportion of your money in the form of travellers' cheques or credit cards. The former can be refunded if lost or stolen; the latter can be cancelled and reissued. Some airlines will also reissue your ticket if it is lost. You have to give them details such as where and when you got it, the ticket number and which flight was involved. Sometimes a reissuing fee (about US$20) is charged, but that's much better than buying a new ticket.

It is a good idea to carry an emergency packet somewhere separate from all your other valuables. This emergency packet could be sewn into a jacket (don't lose the jacket!) or even carried in your shoe – anywhere separate from your main stash of belongings. It should contain a photocopy of the important pages of your passport in case it is lost or stolen. On the back of the photocopy you should list important numbers such as all your travellers' cheques serial numbers, airline ticket numbers and credit card or bank account numbers. Also keep one high-denomination bill in with this emergency stash. You will probably never have to use it, but it's a good idea not to put all your eggs into one basket.

Take out travellers' luggage insurance if you're carrying valuable gear such as a good camera. But don't get paranoid: Costa Rica is still a reasonably safe country.

If you are robbed, you should get a police report as soon as possible. This is a requirement for any insurance claims, although it is unlikely that the police will be able to recover the property. Police reports should be filed with the Organismo de Investigación Judicial (OIJ) (☎ 55 0122, 22 1365) in the Corte Suprema de Justicia (Supreme Court) complex at Calle 19 & 21, Avenida 6 & 8, in San José. If you don't speak Spanish and are having a hard time in making a police report, your embassy can often advise and help. In addition, travellers who have suffered crimes or price-gouging can write to the Costa Rican Tourist Board, Apartado 777-1000, San José. By Costa Rican law, the tourist board is obliged to represent foreign tourists (who are victims of tourist-related crimes) in a court case, if necessary, thus allowing the tourist to go elsewhere (like home).

Top Left: Orchids (RR)
Top Right: Hibiscus & bromeliad (RR)
Bottom Left: Torch ginger (RR)
Bottom Right: Heliconia (RR)

Top Left: Red-lored parrot (RR)
Top Right: Keel-billed toucan (RR)
Bottom Left: Resplendent quetzal (RL)
Bottom Right: Long-tailed manakin (RL)

There have been several recent reports of police corruption (see under Road Safety in the Getting Around chapter). In addition, police have been known to shake down 'suspects', removing their wallets or other valuables. If you are stopped by the police for no obvious reason, do your best to insist that any searches or investigations are done in front of other witness ('*Lo hacemos con testigos*' – 'We'll do that with witnesses'). Try and head for the nearest bar, house, hotel, restaurant or whatever. The Costa Rican authorities are aware of this problem and are working on it – you should be aware too. (There are several reports like this, but there are hundreds of thousands of visitors. It is unlikely to happen to you but, if it does, be prepared.)

Costa Rica has a long history of business-related crimes – real estate and investment scams have occurred frequently over the years. If you want to sink money into any kind of Costa Rican business, make sure you both know what you are doing and check it out really thoroughly.

Swimming Safety

The tourist brochures with their enticing photographs of tropical paradises do not mention that approximately 200 drownings a year occur on Costa Rican beaches. Of these, an estimated 80% are caused by rip-tides.

A rip-tide is a strong current which pulls the swimmer out to sea. It can occur in waist-deep water. It is most important to remember that rip-tides will pull you *out but not under*. Many deaths are caused by panicked swimmers struggling to the point of exhaustion.

If you are caught in a rip-tide, float, do not struggle. Let the rip-tide carry you out beyond the breakers. If you swim, do so parallel to the beach, not directly back in. You are very unlikely to be able to swim against a rip-tide and will only exhaust yourself. When you are carried out beyond the breakers, you will find that the rip-tide will dissipate – it won't carry you out for miles. Then you can swim back in to shore. Swim

in at a 45° angle to the shore to avoid being caught by the current again.

If you feel a rip-tide whilst you are wading, try to come back in sideways, thus offering less body surface to the current. Also remember to walk parallel to the beach if you cannot make headway, so that you can get out of the rip-tide. Some rip-tides are permanent, others come and go or move along a beach. Beaches with a reputation for rips are Playa Bonita near Limón; the area at the entrance of Parque Nacional Cahuita; Playa Doña Ana and Playa Barranca near Puntarenas; Playa Espadilla at Parque Nacional Manuel Antonio.

Earthquakes

It comes as no surprise that Costa Rica, with its mountain chains of active volcanoes, should be earthquake-prone. Recent major quakes occurred on 25 March 1990 (7.1 on the Richter Scale) and 22 April 1991 (7.4 on the Richter Scale, killing over 50 people in Costa Rica and about 30 more in Panama). The most recent serious earthquake as of this writing occurred on 10 July 1993, killing two people, injuring dozens and damaging hundreds of buildings. Small tremors are a frequent occurrence.

If you are caught in a quake, make sure you are not standing under heavy objects which could fall and injure you. The best places to take shelter if you are in a building is in a door frame or under a sturdy table. If you are in the open, don't stand near walls, telegraph poles etc which could collapse on you.

Hiking Safety

Many visitors like to hike in the national parks and wilderness areas. Hikers should be adequately prepared for this. Always carry plenty of water, even on short trips. In 1993, two German hikers going for a short 90 minute hike in Parque Nacional Barra Honda got lost and died of heat prostration and thirst. Hikers are always getting lost in rainforests. Carry maps, extra food, and let someone know where you are going to narrow the search area in the event of an emergency.

ACTIVITIES

San José is the cultural centre of Costa Rica, with good restaurants, the Teatro Nacional which puts on theatre, symphony, music and dance performances, cinemas, art galleries, museums and shopping centres. But it is away from the capital that many of Costa Rica's greatest attractions are to be found.

Without a doubt, Costa Rica's conservationist attitude and activity is still the most developed in Latin America. The wonderful array of national parks and private preserves and their attendant wildlife and scenery draw travellers from all over the world. Visitors can enjoy an intimate look at habitats and environments ranging from tropical rainforest to highland *páramo*, from beautiful beaches to active volcanoes, and from whitewater rivers to mountain ranges. The wildlife and vegetation is magnificent and accessible. No wonder that most visitors travel to at least one park or preserve, and that the primary focus of many trips is natural history, especially bird-watching, which is among the best in the world.

Outdoor enthusiasts will find much to their liking. From running some of the best whitewater in Central America to just relaxing on palm-fringed beaches; from backpacking through the rainforest to horseriding to camping on mountain tops; from record-breaking, deep-sea sportfishing to snorkelling, to world-class surfing; many adventures are possible.

The more sedentary visitor can enjoy leisurely drives through the pretty countryside, perhaps visiting a coffee *finca* (farm) or villages known for handicrafts. Luxurious lunch or dinner cruises on elegant boats in the Golfo de Nicoya on the Pacific coast are also popular activities as are day trips to peer into the crater of one of Costa Rica's many volcanoes.

ACCOMMODATION
Youth Hostels & Camping

There is a small youth hostel system, and the charge for a night in a hostel varies from about US$6 to US$35, depending on the hostel. The more expensive hostels are usually good hotels or lodges giving a discount to youth hostel members. The main hostel is in San José and it has further information about other hostels.

There are rarely campsites in the towns; the constant availability of cheap hotels makes town campsites redundant.

Cheap camping facilities are available in many of the national parks. The handful of campgrounds suitable for caravans or motorhomes are mentioned in the text.

B&Bs

Almost unknown in Costa Rica in the 1980s, the B&B phenomenon has swept San José and begun to expand over the country in the last few years. B&B places vary from middle to top end in prices and have been generally well-received and recommended by travellers. A new 'Costa Rica Bed & Breakfast Group' (CRBBG) has formed with a 'one call does it all' motto. They try and set you up with a variety of accommodation throughout the country during your stay. More details are given under Places to Stay in the San José chapter. Members of the group are denoted by CRBBG in the listings in this book.

Hotels

There is great variety and no shortage of places to stay in Costa Rica. It is rare to arrive in a town and not be able to find somewhere to sleep, but during Easter week or weekends in the dry season the beach hotels can be full. Indeed, most beach hotels are booked several weeks in advance for Easter week. Hotel accommodation can also be tight if there is a special event going on in a particular town. Private lodges and expensive hotels in remote areas should always be reserved in advance.

Some travellers prefer to make advance reservations everywhere – this is possible even in the cheapest hotels and recommended in the better places. Faxes are being used increasingly to make reservations as they are cheaper than telephones and solve the problem of language difficulties – they can be translated readily enough. Mail is slow. In the Places to Stay entries in this book, I give telephone and fax numbers for those hotels that have them, as well as street and mailing addresses (Apartado means PO Box and is not a street address). Note that most hotels will give rainy season discounts (from mid-April to mid-December). If you are already in Costa Rica, a telephone call a day or two ahead will often yield a reservation.

Sometimes it's a little difficult to find single rooms, and you may get a room with two or even three beds. In most cases, though, you will be charged the single rate, except perhaps in cheaper hotels when they are full. The single rate is rarely half of the double rate, except in a few of the cheapest hotels. In a few hotels, single and double rates are the same. If you are economising, find someone with whom to travel and share a room.

Before accepting a room, look around the hotel if possible. The same prices are often charged for rooms of widely differing quality. Even in the US$4-a-night cheapies it's worth looking around. If you get shown into a horrible airless box with just a bed and a bare light bulb, you can ask to see a better room without giving offence. You'll often be amazed at the results. I recommend that you ask to see a room before you rent it, particularly in the cheapest hotels. At the other end of the scale, hotels may want to rent you their most expensive suites – ask if they have more economical rooms if you don't want the suite.

Bathroom facilities in the cheaper hotels are rarely what you may be used to at home. The cheapest hotels don't always have hot water. Even if they do, it might not work or it may only be turned on at certain hours of the day.

An intriguing device you should know about is the electric shower. This consists of a single cold-water shower head hooked up to an electric heating element which is switched on when you want a hot (more likely tepid) shower. Don't touch anything metal while you're in the shower or you may discover what an electric shock feels like. The power is never high enough to actually throw you across the room, but it's unpleasant nevertheless – kind of like holding a nine V battery across your tongue, if you're really interested! I managed to shock myself by simply picking up the soap which I had balanced on a horizontal water pipe. Many hotels have electric showers and advertise hot water – beware that electric showers vary from just taking the chill off the water to very warm. They are never really hot and they sometimes simply don't work at all and you have to be content with a cold shower.

Flushing a toilet in the cheaper hotels creates another hazard – overflow. Putting toilet paper into the bowl seems to clog up the system, so a waste receptacle is often provided for the paper. This may not seem particularly sanitary, but it is much better than clogged bowls and water on the floor. A well-run hotel, even if it is cheap, will ensure that the receptacle is emptied and the toilet cleaned every day.

Most hotels will give you a key to lock your room, and theft from your hotel room is not as frequent as it is in some other countries. Nevertheless, carrying your own padlock is a good idea if you plan on staying in the cheaper hotels.

Once in a while you'll find that a room doesn't look very secure – perhaps there's a window that doesn't close or the wall doesn't come to the ceiling and can be climbed over. It's worth finding another room. This is another reason why it's good to look at a room before you rent it.

You should never leave valuables lying around the room; it's just too tempting for someone who makes US$3 a day for their work. Money and passport should be in a secure body pouch; other valuables can usually be kept in the hotel strongbox, although some cheaper hotels might not want to take this responsibility. In this case, keep your valuables locked in your bag and not in plain sight. Beware of local 'fishermen' – people who poke sticks with hooks on through openable windows to fish out whatever they can get.

Hotel Categories Hotels listed as 'bottom end' are certainly the cheapest, but not necessarily the worst. Although they are usually quite basic, with just a bed and four walls, they can nevertheless be well looked after, very clean, and amazing value for money. They are often good places to meet other budget travellers, both Costa Rican and foreign.

Prices in the bottom end section begin at about US$3 per person and go up to US$20 for a double room. Every town has hotels in this price range. Although you'll usually have to use communal bathrooms in the cheapest hotels, you can sometimes find rooms with a private bathroom for less than US$10 a double.

Hotels in the 'middle' category usually cost from about US$20 to US$60 for a double room, but the cheaper ones are not always better than the best hotels in the bottom price range. On the whole, however, you can find some very decent hotels here. Even if you're travelling on a budget, there may be occasions when you feel like indulging in comparative luxury for a day or two.

'Top-end' hotels are over US$60 a double and can go to over US$100 a double in San José and in the beach resorts. The prices and services compare favourably with international standards in the best places.

Hotel Tax A 14.4% tax is added to hotel prices – some hotels give prices including tax, others give prices without tax, so always clarify this point when asking about room rates. I have tried to give full prices including taxes for the 1993-94 season. Hotel prices have, however, risen dramatically with the tourism boom of the past few years, and you can expect further increases.

Staying with a Family

This is another relatively recent phenomenon in Costa Rica, especially in San José. Details are given in the San José chapter.

FOOD

If you're on a tight budget, food is the most important part of your expenses. You can stay in rock-bottom hotels, travel by bus, and never consider buying a souvenir, but you've got to eat well. This doesn't mean expensively, but it does mean that you want to avoid spending half your trip sitting on the toilet.

The worst culprits for making you sick are salads and unpeeled fruit. With the fruit, stick to bananas, oranges, pineapples and other fruit that you can peel yourself. With unpeeled fruit or salad vegetables, wash them yourself in water which you can trust (see the Health section). It can be a lot of fun getting a group of you together and heading out to the market to buy salad vegies and preparing a huge salad.

As long as you take heed of the salad warning, you'll find plenty of good things to eat at reasonable prices. You certainly don't have to eat at a fancy restaurant – their kitchen facilities may not be as clean as their white tablecloths. A good sign for any restaurant is if the locals eat there – restaurants aren't empty if the food is delicious and healthy.

If you're on a tight budget eat the set meal offered in most restaurants at lunchtime – it's usually filling and cheap. Also try the cheap luncheon counters called *sodas*. There are also reasonably priced Chinese and Italian restaurants in most towns. The sodas in the central markets of most towns are locally popular and usually very cheap. Eat at one that is frequented by ticos and you'll probably find that the food is good and clean.

Whatever your budget, I have given a good range of restaurants at all price-levels throughout this book. Remember that a combined 23% in taxes and services is added to restaurant bills in all but the cheapest sodas. Further tipping is not necessary unless you want to. Where I give an idea of prices for the restaurant meals in this book, I include the tax for a main course. Drinks and desserts, for example, are extra.

Most restaurants serve *bistek* (beef), *pollo* (chicken) and *pescado* (fish) dishes. Vegetarians should note that *carne* literally means meat, but in Costa Rica tends to refer to beef. Chicken, *puerco* (pork) and *chivo* (goat) isn't necessarily included, so be specific if you want something without any meat. Many visitors from North America, used to spicy Mexican food capable of burning out taste buds, mistakenly assume that Costa Rican food is very spicy too. Generally, it's tasty rather than spicy-hot.

Costa Rican specialities include:

Gallo Pinto
literally 'spotted rooster', a mixture of rice and black beans that is traditionally served for breakfast, sometimes with *natilla* (sour cream) or *huevos fritos/revueltos* (fried/scrambled eggs). This dish is lightly spiced with herbs and is filling and tasty.
Tortillas
either Mexican style corn pancakes or omelettes, depending on what kind of meal you're having
Casado
a set meal which is usually filling and economical. It contains *arroz* (rice), *frijoles* (black beans), *platano* (fried plantain), beef, chopped *repollo* (cabbage), and maybe an egg or an avocado.
Olla de carne
a beef and vegetable soup containing vegetables such as potatoes, plantains, corn, squash and a local tuber called *yuca*
Palmitos
hearts of palm, usually served in a salad with vinegar dressing; *pejibaye* is a rather starchy tasting palm fruit also eaten as a salad
Arroz con pollo
a basic dish of rice and chicken
Elote
corn served boiled on the cob *(elote cocinado)* or roasted on the cob *(elote asado)*

Traditional desserts *(postres)* include:

Mazamorra
a pudding made from corn starch
Queque seco
simply a pound cake
Dulce de leche
milk and sugar boiled to make a thick syrup which may be used in a layered cake called *torta chilena*
Cajeta
similar to dulce de leche, but thicker still, like a fudge
Flan
a cold caramel custard

The following are snacks, often obtained in sodas:

Arreglados
little puff pastries stuffed with beef, chicken or cheese
Enchiladas
heavier pastries stuffed with potatoes and cheese and maybe meat
Empanadas
Chilean-style turnovers stuffed with meat or cheese and raisins
Pupusas
El Salvadoran-style fried corn and cheese cakes
Gallos
tortilla sandwiches containing meat, beans or cheese
Ceviche
seafood marinated with lemon, onion, garlic, sweet red peppers and coriander or made with *corvina* (a white sea bass), or occasionally with *langostinos* (shrimps) or *conchas* (shellfish)
Patacones
a coastal speciality, especially on the Caribbean side, consisting of slices of plantain deep fried like French fried potatoes – delicious
Tamales
boiled cornmeal pasties, usually wrapped in a banana leaf (you don't eat the leaf). At Christmas they traditionally come stuffed with chicken or pork, at other times of year they may come stuffed with corn and wrapped in a corn leaf. *Tamales asado* are sweet cornmeal cakes.

Many bars traditionally serve *bocas*, also known as *boquitas*. These are little savoury side dishes such as black beans, ceviche, chicken stew, potato chips and sausages and are designed to make your drink more pleasurable – maybe you'll have another one! If you had several rounds, you could eat enough bocas to make a very light meal. Many of the cheaper bars have free bocas, some charge a small amount extra for them, and some don't have them at all.

DRINKS
Nonalcoholic Drinks
Coffee is traditionally served very strong and mixed with hot milk to taste, but increasingly fewer establishments serve it this way. As far as I am concerned, this is just as well, because the hot milk tends to form a skin which I find quite unappetising. I much

prefer it strong, tasty and black. Tea (including herb tea) is also available. Milk is pasteurised and safe to drink.

The usual brands of soft drinks are available, although many people prefer *refrescos* which are fruit drinks made either *con agua* (with water) or *con leche* (with milk). Possible fruit drinks to try are mango, papaya, *piña* (pineapple), *sandía* (water melon), *melón* (cantaloupe), *mora* (blackberry), *zanahoria* (carrot), *cebada* (barley) or *tamarindo* (a slightly tart but refreshing drink made from the fruit of the tamarind tree). Be careful where you buy these, to avoid getting sick.

Pipas are green coconuts which have a hole macheted into the top of them and a straw stuck in so you can drink the coconut 'milk' – a slightly bitter but refreshing and filling drink.

Agua dulce is simply boiled water mixed with brown sugar, and *horchata* is a cornmeal drink flavoured with cinnamon.

Alcohol

Costa Ricans like to drink, though they don't like drunks. Most restaurants serve a good variety of alcoholic drinks. Imported drinks are expensive, local ones are quite cheap.

There are five brands of local beer. Pilsen and Imperial are both good, popular beers; I prefer the Imperial. Tropical is a low-calorie 'lite' beer, not available everywhere. Bavaria has a gold foil around the cap and is a little more expensive than the first two, though I can't say it's much better. Also, a local version of Heineken is made, which costs about the same as Bavaria. Most of these are 4.0% alcohol, with the exception of Pilsen which is 4.5%. Other beers are imported and expensive.

Local beers cost about US$0.60 in the very cheapest bars to about US$1 in average bars and restaurants and well over US$2 in some of the fancy tourist lodges, restaurants, hotels and resorts.

Costa Rican wines are cheap, taste cheap, and provide a memorable hangover. Good imported wines are available but are expen-

sive. Chilean brands are your best bet for a palatable wine at an affordable price.

Sugarcane is grown in Costa Rica and so liquor made from this is cheap. The cheapest is *guaro* which is the local firewater, drunk by the shot. Also inexpensive and good is local rum, usually drunk as a *cuba libre* (rum & cola). A 750 ml bottle of local Gold Ron Rico is only US$3.

Local vodka and gin isn't bad, but whisky is not as good. Expensive imported liquors are available, as are imported liqueurs. One locally made liqueur is Café Rica which, predictably, is based on coffee and tastes rather like the better known Mexican Kahlua.

THINGS TO BUY
Coffee

Coffee is excellent and cheap; many visitors bring a kg of freshly roasted coffee beans back home. Gift stores sell expensive elegantly wrapped packages of coffee beans for export but savvy travellers will go to the market and buy coffee direct from the coffee stalls, or from ordinary grocery stores. If a kg seems like too much, you can buy as little as 250 grams without any problem.

Handicrafts

The things to buy are wood and leather items, which are very well made and inexpensive. Wood items include salad bowls, plates, carving boards and other useful kitchen utensils, jewellery boxes, and a variety of carvings and ornaments. Furniture is also made but is hard to bring home, and having it shipped is expensive. Leatherwork includes the usual wallets and purses, hand bags and brief cases, and is usually cheaper than at home.

Interesting wood/leather combinations are the rocking chairs seen in many tourist lodges and better hotels in the country. Because of their leather seats and backs, they can be folded for transport and are usually packed two to a carton. If you're not bringing too much else back, you could check a pair of them in your airline baggage.

There are plenty of excellent souvenir shops in San José. Many people, however, opt to visit a village such as Sarchí where many souvenirs are made, especially woodwork, and where you can watch artisans at work. Sarchí is the centre for making the colourfully painted replicas of the ox carts *(carretas)* that were traditionally used for hauling produce and people in the countryside – and still are in some remote regions. These ox carts are, as much as anything else, a typical souvenir peculiar to Costa Rica. They come in all sizes from table-top models to nearly life-size replicas which double as drinks cabinets. They all fold down for transport.

Ceramics and jewellery are also popular souvenirs. Some ceramics are replicas of pre-Columbian artefacts. Colourful posters and T-shirts with wildlife, national park and ecological themes are also very popular, attractive and reasonably priced. Some of the profits from these go towards conservation organisations in Costa Rica. Indian handicrafts from Guatemala and Panama are also available.

Getting There & Away

There are three ways of getting to Costa Rica: air, land and sea. However, very few people use the ocean route because it is less convenient and usually more expensive than flying.

AIR

Juan Santamaría International Airport, 17 km outside San José, is where international flights to Costa Rica arrive. The airport in Liberia, 217 km north-west of San José on the Carretera Interamericana, is the back-up international airport but is rarely used. There are plans to expand the facilities at the Liberia airport and it may begin to take more international arrivals, particularly those connected with beach charter vacations. Often, going through immigration, baggage pickup and customs at the airport is fairly straightforward and takes about 30 minutes to an hour. Once in a while, however, several international charters and regular flights will land within a few minutes of one another and the airport is simply not equipped to handle this influx. Waits of up to three hours have been reported in such situations, with Sundays during the dry season being particularly busy with many charter arrivals. If you have a choice, try to avoid arriving on Sunday. The airport is slated for expansion.

Cheap Tickets

The ordinary tourist or economy-class fare is not the most economical way to go. It is convenient, however, because it enables you to fly on the next plane out and your ticket is valid for 12 months. If you want to economise further, there are several options.

Youth & Student Fares Students with international student ID cards and anyone under 26 years of age can get discounts with most airlines. In addition, the Costa Rican carrier Lacsa gives discounts to teachers and college staff. Although youth and student fares can be arranged through most travel agents and

airlines, it is a good idea to go through agents which specialise in student travel – several are listed in the To/From sections following. Note that student fares are not only cheap, but often include free stopovers, don't require advance purchase, and may be valid for up to a year – a great deal if you are a student.

The agency which specialises in student and youth fares in Costa Rica is OTEC (☎ 22 0866, fax 33 2321), Calle 3, Avenida 3, San José. OTEC works closely with most of the student travel specialists listed below.

Airline Deals Whatever age you are, if you can purchase your ticket well in advance and stay a minimum length of time, you can buy a ticket which is usually about 30 or 40% cheaper than the full economy fare. These are often called APEX, excursion or promotional fares depending on the country you are flying from and the rules and fare structures that apply there.

Often the following restrictions apply. You must purchase your ticket at least 21 days (sometimes more) in advance and you must stay away a minimum period (about 14 days on average) and return within 180 days (sometimes less, for example passengers from the USA must return within 30 days). Individual airlines have different requirements and these change from time to time. Most of these tickets do not allow stopovers and there are extra charges if you change your dates of travel or destinations. These tickets are often sold out well in advance of departure so try to book early.

Standby fares are another possibility from some countries, such as the USA. Some airlines will let you travel at the last minute if they have available seats just before the flight. These standby tickets cost less than an economy fare but are not usually as cheap as other discounted tickets.

Bucket Shops A cheap way to go is via the

so-called bucket shops or consolidators, which are allowed to sell discounted tickets to help airlines fill their flights. These tickets are often the cheapest of all, particularly in the low season, but they may sell out fast and you may be limited to only a few available dates.

While discounted tickets, economy and student flights are available direct from the airlines or from a travel agency (there is no extra charge for any of these flights if you buy them from an agent rather than direct from the airline), discount bucket shop tickets are available only from the bucket shops themselves. Most of them are good and reputable companies. However, once in a while a fly-by-night operator comes along and takes your money for a super-cheap flight and gives you an invalid or unusable ticket, so check what you are buying carefully before handing over your money.

Bucket shops often advertise in newspapers and travel oriented magazines and are more common in the UK than the USA; there is much competition and a variety of fares and schedules are available. Fares to Latin America have traditionally been relatively expensive, but bucket shops have recently been able to offer increasingly economical fares.

Courier Flights If you are travelling with minimal luggage, you can fly to Costa Rica as a courier. Couriers are hired by companies who need to have packages delivered to international destinations. They will give the courier exceptionally cheap tickets in return for using his or her baggage allowance. You can bring carry-on luggage only. These are legitimate operations – all baggage that you are to deliver is completely legal. And it is amazing how much you can bring in your carry-on luggage. I have heard of couriers boarding an aircraft wearing two pairs of trousers and two shirts under a sweater and rain jacket and stuffing the pockets with travel essentials. Bring a folded plastic shopping bag and, once you have boarded the aircraft, you can remove the extra clothes and place them in the plastic bag! (Try not to

have metal objects in inside pockets when you go through the metal detector at the airport! Also bear in mind that most courier companies want their couriers to look reasonably neat, so you can't overdo it.) Remember, you can buy things like T-shirts, a towel and soap after you arrive at your destination, so travelling with just carry-on luggage is certainly feasible. Courier flights are more common from the USA than Europe. More details are given in the To/From the USA section.

Other Considerations Round-trip fares are always much cheaper than two one-way tickets. They are also cheaper than 'open jaws' tickets, which enable you to fly into one city (say San José) and leave via another (say Panama City).

If, because of a late flight (but not a rescheduled one) you miss a connection or are forced to stay overnight, the carrier is responsible for providing you with help in making the earliest possible connection and paying for a room in a hotel of their choice. They should also provide you with meal vouchers. If you are seriously delayed on an international flight, ask for these services.

And finally, make sure your airline ticket is for a flight to San José, Costa Rica. *The Tico Times* recently reported on a German traveller who ended up in San José, California. After checking into a hotel (which wouldn't take the colones she had obtained in advance) and spending a night, she asked a German-speaking clerk about getting a bus to Nosara. It took everyone quite a while before they all realised she was in the wrong country!

To/From the USA
Generally speaking, the USA does not have as strong a bucket shop tradition as Europe or Asia, so it's a little harder getting super-cheap flights from the USA to Latin America. Sometimes the Sunday travel sections in the major newspapers (the *Los Angeles Times* and the *New York Times*) advertise cheap fares to South America, although these are sometimes no cheaper

than the APEX fares with one of the several airlines serving Costa Rica. However, because of the relatively short distance from the USA to Costa Rica, air fares from the USA are not prohibitively expensive.

Any reputable travel agent can help you find the cheapest current fares to Costa Rica. Students and people under 26 years of age should try one of the following experts in student fares – they also deal with regular fares as well and can help with things like International Student ID cards, guidebooks, and youth hostels.

Council Travel is affiliated with the Council on International Educational Exchange (CIEE) and is a well-known and recommended company for budget travel. They have sales offices in the following cities (those with phone numbers are regional sales offices with extra phone lines and staff). Berkeley, Davis, La Jolla, Long Beach, Los Angeles, Palo Alto, San Diego, San Francisco (☎ (415) 421 3473), Santa Barbara and Sherman Oaks (all in California); Boulder, Colorado (☎ (303) 447 8101); Washington DC (☎ (202) 337 6464); Chicago (☎ (312) 951 0585) and Evanston, Illinois; Amherst, Boston (☎ (617) 266 1926) and Cambridge, Massachusetts; New York City (☎ (212) 661 1450); Austin (☎ (512) 472 4931) and Dallas, Texas; Seattle, Washington (☎ (206) 632 2448); Tempe, Arizona; New Haven, Connecticut; Miami, Florida; Atlanta, Georgia; Bloomington, Indiana; New Orleans, Louisiana; Ann Arbor, Michigan; Minneapolis, Minnesota; Durham, North Carolina; Columbus, Ohio; Portland, Oregon; Philadelphia and Pittsburgh, Pennsylvania; Providence, Rhode Island; Salt Lake City, Utah; Milwaukee, Wisconsin and other cities.

STA Travel (☎ 1 (800) 777 0112, fax (212) 682 0953) is another major source of student, youth and budget airfares, with some 120 offices around the world. Their main US sales offices are in Berkeley, California (☎ (510) 642 3000, fax (510) 649 1407); Boston, Massachusetts (☎ (617) 266 6014, fax (617) 266 5579); Cambridge, Massachusetts (☎ (617) 576 4623, fax (617) 576 2740); Los Angeles, California (☎ (310) 824 1574, fax (310) 824 2928); New York City (☎ (212) 477 7166, fax (212) 477 7348); Philadelphia, Pennsylvania (☎ (215) 382 2929, fax (215) 382 4716); San Francisco, California (☎ (415) 391 8407, fax (415) 391 4105); Santa Monica, California (☎ (310) 394 5126, fax (310) 394 4041).

Airlines are geared to providing cheap fares for visitors staying 30 days or less. Recent sample prices for round-trip tickets valid for up to 30 days are US$676 from Los Angeles, US$427 from New Orleans, Houston or Dallas, and US$330 from Miami – these flights departed Monday to Thursday; weekend departures cost about US$50 more. If you want to stay more than 30 days you end up paying about US$200 more per ticket. Student and youth fares are usually US$30 to US$100 cheaper than the fares quoted above and they don't necessarily have a 30 day limit – many are valid for a full year for travellers who want to start in Costa Rica and then go to other Central American countries before returning home.

The national Costa Rican airlines are Lacsa and Aero Costa Rica. They fly from the USA to Costa Rica and other Central American countries. The cheapest fares are often with Costa Rican and other Central American airlines such as Taca (of El Salvador), Tan/SAHSA (of Honduras – they recently required an overnight in Tegucigalpa) and Aviateca (of Guatemala).

Because Houston, New Orleans and Miami are roughly north of the Central American republics, they make good gateway cities to Costa Rica.

On one visit to Costa Rica I flew from Houston with Taca and returned with Aviateca. Southbound we stopped at Belize City and changed planes at San Salvador; northbound we stopped at Managua and changed planes at Guatemala City. It was a good opportunity to see some of Central America from the air and it was fun hopping from country to country.

The following airlines (with telephone numbers) currently serve Costa Rica from the USA:

Airline	Telephone
Aero Costa Rica	1 (800) 237 6274
Lacsa	1 (800) 225 2272
Aviateca	1 (800) 327 9832
Taca	1 (800) 535 8780
Tan/SAHSA	1 (800) 327 1225
American	1 (800) 433 7300
Continental	1 (800) 525 0280
	1 (800) 231 0856
United	1 (800) 722 5243
	1 (800) 241 6522

Miami charges an airport security tax – about US$30. When I last flew to San José, I went from Dallas and was not charged an airport tax.

Courier Flights Courier travel is another possibility. Travel Unlimited (PO Box 1058, Allston, MA 02134) publishes monthly listings of courier and cheap flights to Costa Rica and many other countries. A one-year subscription costs US$25 (US$35 foreign) or US$5 for a single issue.

Most courier flights to San José originate in Miami, but very few were offered in 1993, though they may be reinstated. It's worth calling Miami courier companies to see what they have. Another option is a courier flight to Mexico City, Guatemala City or Panama City (flights are available from Los Angeles and New York as well as Miami) and continuing by Central American bus.

Package Deals Several US companies are able to provide reasonable package fares to Costa Rica, usually in combination with hotel stays. Try to avoid a trip that involves being stuck in some large and impersonal beach hotel for several days – you won't get to see much of Costa Rica that way. For the best choices of accommodation, I recommend that you contact the following as early as possible:

American Tours & Travel
   1402 Third Ave No 1019, Seattle, WA 98101-2110 (☎ 1 (800) 553 2513, (206) 623 8850, fax (206) 467 0454) – represents a variety of small hotels and nature lodges in Costa Rica

González Travel
   4508 Academy Drive, Metairie, LA 70003 (☎ 1 (800) 688 4058, (504) 885 4058; fax (504) 469 7500)
Preferred Adventures
   1 West Water St, Suite 300, Saint Paul, MN 55107 (☎ (612) 222 8131, fax (612) 222 4221) – this recommended company specialises in customised adventure and nature travel for individuals, families and small groups and has cheap airfares with any land package
Southern Horizons Travel & Tours
   6100 Simpson Ave, N Hollywood, CA 91606 (☎ 1 (800) 333 9361, (818) 980 7011; fax (818) 980 6987) – books major hotels, tours and flights
Worldwide Holidays
   7800 Red Rd, Suite 112, South Miami, FL 33143 (☎ 1 (800) 327 9854, 1 (800) 929 7148), (305) 665 0841) – does customised itineraries using some of the best smaller hotels and lodges

To/From Canada
Canadians will find that various companies arrange cheap winter getaway charters to Costa Rica. Often these include several days of hotel accommodation in San José and/or a beach resort, but nevertheless represent good value for money if the hotels happen to be what you want. Charter companies also sell trips which include tours to national parks etc or will sell air travel only at good prices. You may be able to arrange a charter that provides a few days in San José and then some free days in the middle of your trip. It is usually best to go through a travel agent as charter companies don't always sell direct to the public. The phone numbers listed below are for information – ask for the nearest agent to you that deals with Costa Rica.

Possible companies to contact are: Fiesta Holidays (☎ (416) 498 5566) out of Toronto, Fiesta West (☎ (604) 688 1102) out of Vancouver, and Fun Sun Vacations (☎ (403) 482 2030, fax (403) 488 2212) out of Edmonton (they do charters from Vancouver, Calgary, Edmonton and Winnipeg, and arrange adventure/nature tours, homestays with local families and are planning on opening a tent camp near Gandoca-Manzanillo in 1994).

Students and people under 26 should call Travel CUTS (☎ (416) 977 3703) who are experts in discounted and budget air fares.

They have offices all over Canada – call the number above for the office nearest to you.

To/From Latin America

The Central American airlines mentioned under To/From the USA provide services between all the Central American capitals and San José. In addition, COPA (Panama) and Aeronica (Nicaragua) provide services to San José.

For South America, you'll find that Lacsa flies to and from Venezuela, Ecuador and Peru, Varig flies to and from Brazil, Avianca flies to and from Colombia and American Airlines has connections to several Latin American countries.

To/From the UK

Bucket shops generally provide the cheapest fares from Europe to Latin America. Fares from London, where the competition is fiercest, are often cheaper than from other European cities, and there are also more bucket shops there. Some Europeans find it cheaper to fly from London than from their home countries.

Bucket shops advertise in the classifieds of newspapers ranging from *The Times* to *Time Out*. I have heard consistently good reports about Journey Latin America (☎ (081) 747 3108, fax (081) 742 1312), 16 Devonshire Rd, Chiswick, London W4 2HD. They specialise in cheap fares to all Latin American countries as well as arranging itineraries for both independent and escorted travel. Look for their free magazine available outside tube stations and other places. They will make arrangements for you over the phone.

Another reputable budget travel agency is Trailfinders (☎ (071) 938 3366, fax (071) 937 9294), 42 Earl's Court Rd, London W8 6EJ (with a travel books/supplies store). They also have branches in Kensington (with an immunisation centre), Manchester and Glasgow. Their useful travel newspaper *Trailfinder* is available free from them.

Agencies specialising in student fares and youth discounts include Council Travel (☎ 071) 437 7767), 28A Poland St, Oxford Circus, London W1V 3DB; STA Travel (☎ (071) 937 9971, fax (071) 938 5321), 74 Old Brompton Rd, London SW7 3LQ and other offices elsewhere in the UK; Campus Travel (☎ (071) 730 8111), 52 Grosvenor Gardens, London SW1W 0AG and other offices around the UK.

The cheap British agencies will sell tickets to European nationals but you have to pick them up in person in London (or have them mailed to a UK address). Flights from London with some carriers may include a connecting flight from another British city at no extra cost – ask about this.

Typical round-trip fares from London are about UK£520 to UK£670. The variation in fares depends on how long you want to stay (longer stays are more expensive), which airline you choose, and when you travel. The cheapest airfare from London that I could find at the time of writing was UK£469 with Continental, stopping over in Miami – this was a low-season, midweek fare with a number of restrictions. High-season fares can be over UK£100 more. Other airlines had different fares and seasons, but usually the northern summer and around Christmas time are considered high seasons (note that the northern summer coincides with Costa Rica's low (wet) season).

Some airlines from Europe will take you to Miami, where you connect with other airlines for flights to Costa Rica. Two airlines which fly direct to San José (with stops in the Caribbean) are KLM from the Netherlands and Iberia from Spain. LTU has charter flights from Germany. Fares, routes and low/high seasons change frequently; the best information is to be had from travel professionals.

To/From Continental Europe

On the Continent you can try one of the following companies. Council Travel has several locations in Paris, as well as in the French towns of Aix-en-Provence, Lyon, Montepelier and Nice. The main office in Paris is at 31 rue St Augustin, 75002, Paris (☎ (1) 42 66 20 87). Council Travel is also in Düsseldorf (☎ (211) 32 90 88) and Munich (☎ (089) 89 50 22), Germany.

STA Travel is at Srid Reisen, Berger Strasse 118, 6000 Frankfurt 1, Germany (☎ (4969) 43 01 91, fax (4969) 43 98 58).

Other companies which deal with cheap fares and charters to Central America are Voyages Découvertes, 21 rue Cambon, Paris, France (☎ (1) 42 61 00 01); Uniclam, 63 rue Monsieur Le Prince, 75006, Paris, France; and Globetrotter Travel, Remweg, 8001 Zurich, Switzerland.

Aeroflot from Moscow also has cheap fares to Managua, Nicaragua, with a Cuban stopover – this may be worth investigating if you like your air travel to be a little out of the ordinary. From Managua there are cheap buses to Costa Rica taking just a few hours.

Courier flights are possible from Europe, although they are not yet as well known or popular as they are in the USA. Look in the classifieds of Sunday newspapers or read a book on the subject – one is the *Courier Air Travel Handbook*, by Mark Field, Spectrum, 1993.

To/From Australia & NZ

Travellers coming from Australia's east coast will usually fly to Costa Rica via the USA and Mexico. Most major airlines fly to Los Angeles, from where you can get direct connecting flights to Costa Rica. The low season in terms of fares is from February to March.

STA Travel in Australia offers an unusual route on Malaysian Airlines via Kuala Lumpur, Taipei and Los Angeles, connecting with Lacsa to San José. This is a remarkably cheap option: the low-season round-trip fare to Costa Rica from east coast cities or Adelaide is around A$1860, with one stopover. Academics, students under 30 with an international student ID, and anyone under 25 can obtain an even lower fare of A$1715. Flights from Perth cost an extra A$205.

Qantas, Air New Zealand and other trans-Pacific carriers fly to Los Angeles via Auckland, Nadi or Honolulu, usually with one stopover allowed on the round trip, and connect with various carriers onward to San

José. Fares to Los Angeles range from around A$1300 for off-season twin-share deals to A$1800 for high-season solo travellers. Add another A$800 to A$1000 to fly to and from San José from there, or consider the overland route through Mexico as a cheaper alternative.

Fares from New Zealand via the Pacific will be somewhat lower than those from east coast Australia. Routes via Asia are impractical.

Students and under 30s would do well to contact STA Travel in Australia or its affiliate STS in New Zealand. Head offices are at:

STA Travel, 1a Lee St, Sydney 2000
  (☎ (02) 212 1255)
STS, 10 O'Connell St, Auckland (☎ (09) 39 9191).

To/From Asia

There is also very little choice of direct flights between Asia and Latin America apart from Japan, and there certainly won't be any bargains there. The cheapest way is to fly to the USA west coast and connect from there.

LAND

If you live in North or Central America, it is possible to travel overland. The nearest US town to San José is Brownsville, Texas, on the Mexican border. From there it is about 4000 km by road to San José, half of which is crossing Mexico and the rest is through Guatemala, Honduras, Nicaragua and Costa Rica. It is possible to travel through El Salvador, but remember that country currently has the most violent civil and political conflicts in the region and it is considered safer to travel directly from Guatemala to Honduras.

It is possible to drive your own car, but the costs of insurance, fuel, border permits, food and accommodation will be much higher than an airline ticket. Many people opt for flying down and renting a car when they arrive in San José.

If you do drive down, think about the following. It is not recommended to drive Central American roads at night – they are narrow, rarely painted with a centre stripe (forget about lights), often pot-holed, and subject to hazards such as cattle and pedestrians in rural areas. Travelling by day, allowing for time-consuming and bureaucratic border crossings, will take about a week – definitely more if you want to enjoy some of the fantastic sights (ruins, villages, markets, volcanoes etc) en route. But it can certainly be done – my main advice here is get good insurance, be prepared for border bureaucracy and have your papers in impeccable order, and never leave your car unattended except in safely guarded parking areas. (It should go without saying that you need a reliable vehicle in excellent mechanical shape.)

The American Automobile Association (AAA) publishes a map of Mexico & Central America (free to AAA members) which highlights the Carretera Interamericana and major side roads. The AAA sells insurance for driving in Mexico, but not in Central America. For insurance in Mexico and Central America, call Sanborn's which has offices in several cities close to the USA-Mexican border including McAllen (☎ (210) 686 0711), 2009 South 10th, TX 78501, or talk to your insurance agent.

Another excellent map of the region is the Traveller's Reference Map of Central America, published by International Travel Map Productions, P O Box 2290, Vancouver, BC, V6B 3W5, Canada.

A series of public buses will take you all the way from the USA to San José (see also the San José Getting There & Away section). Bus travel is slow, cramped, but cheap (and, I think, fun). See Lonely Planet's *Central America on a Shoestring* or *The Mexico & Central American Handbook* (Trade & Travel Publications, Bath, England) for details of bus travel and places to stay en route. When you add all the costs of bus tickets plus food and hotels, even if you travel 2nd class and sleep in the cheapest hotels, you'll pay as much as the airfare. You will, however, see and experience far more – it depends on your schedule. Young travellers will often make the Central American bus trip and consider travelling as important as arriving in Costa Rica; those less young,

with families and careers, might not be able to afford to think about travelling overland – fly in, fly out and grab a quick trip; older folks may have the luxury of being able to pay for the airfare or to take the time to sit on local buses – your choice.

It is worth noting that the Carretera Interamericana continues as far south as Panama, then peters out in the Darien Gap, an area of roadless rainforest. It is not possible to drive on to South America; vehicles must be shipped or air freighted.

To/From Nicaragua

There is one major crossing point between Nicaragua and Costa Rica. This is at Peñas Blancas on the Interamericana – almost all international overland travellers enter through here, though there are other border posts.

Via Peñas Blancas This is the main border post, not a town, and so there is nowhere to stay.

The border is open from 8 am to 5 pm daily on the Costa Rican side, but only till 4 pm on the Nicaraguan side. The earlier in the day that you get there, the better. It is closed from noon to 1 pm. It is four km between the Costa Rican and Nicaraguan immigration offices – minibuses are available for about US$1 and there are taxis. The Oficina de Migraciones (☎ 66 9025) is next to the Restaurant La Frontera (☎ 66 9156, 66 9175), which has reasonable food.

There is also a Costa Rican tourist information office in the immigration building as well as a bus ticket office. Bus tickets can be bought for buses to San José and Liberia which leave about five times a day. If coming from Nicaragua, you'll find no buses and nowhere to stay after early afternoon, though a taxi could be found. Try to arrive early.

If you are entering Costa Rica, sometimes a ticket out of Costa Rica is asked for – if you don't have one you can buy a bus ticket back into Nicaragua from next to the tourist information office. This is accepted by the Costa Rican authorities, who are generally helpful as long as your documents are in order. If you are leaving Costa Rica, no special permit is required if you haven't overstayed the time allocated in your passport. If your time has expired, you need an exit visa and will be sent back to San José to get one – make sure your documents are in order before trying to leave the country.

International travellers between San José and Managua (or vice versa) on Sirca or TICA bus will find that the bus will wait for all passengers to be processed. This is time consuming, and delays of up to eight hours have been reported (though two or three hours is more likely). To avoid the crowds, you could take local buses to the border, a taxi or minibus to the other border, and then continue on another bus – but cross as early as possible. Several travellers have reported that luggage placed on the roofs of buses in Nicaragua has been pilfered, sometimes when only a bus employee has been allowed on the roof. Stolen objects are often mundane items like deodorant or clothes. If you can't lock your luggage, try wrapping it in a large sack with a lock on that. Primitive – but it deters pilferers. Carry luggage aboard the bus if possible. Note that poverty in Nicaragua is at a desperate level – thefts from buses are depressingly frequent, so watch your gear very carefully.

Exit fees are reportedly charged – US$2 to leave Nicaragua and less than US$1 to leave Costa Rica. These seem to change from year to year.

Moneychangers at the Costa Rican post give good rates for US cash dollars but travellers' cheques receive worse rates at the border bank. Both Costa Rican colones and Nicaraguan cordobas are freely available. Excess cordobas or colones can also be sold but usually at a small loss. Try to arrive with as little local money as possible. The best place to sell cordobas is with the moneychangers at the Nicaraguan border post.

The first (or last) Nicaraguan city of any size is Rivas, 37 km north of the border, and it has several cheap hotels. There are four or five buses a day from the border to Rivas – get to the border by early afternoon to make sure you get on a bus. From Rivas, you can continue to the cities of Granada and Managua by bus, or across Lago de Nicaragua by boat.

Nicaraguan visa regulations keep changing frequently, so check with the Nicaraguan embassy in San José if you plan on travelling overland into Nicaragua. Recently citizens of the USA, UK and a few western European nations were allowed to enter Nicaragua for up to 90 days with a valid passport, but citizens of Canada, Australia, New Zealand and several western European nations required a visa, which costs about US$25 and is valid for only 30 days (though extensions are possible – another US$25). Allow several days to obtain a visa and make sure it is valid from the day you want to enter Nicaragua, not from the date of issue at the embassy. Note that if you require a visa, but only wish to transit Nicaragua in order to go to Honduras or to catch a flight from Managua, a 72 hour transit visa is available for US$14.

Via Los Chiles Officially, there is a border crossing here, but travellers who are not Nicaraguan or Costa Rican rarely use this route. When I spoke to Migraciones in Los Chiles, they told me that it was possible to cross here if your papers were in order.

A very rough road (4WD essential, or walk) takes you the 14 km from Los Chiles to the Nicaraguan town of San Carlos, on the south-eastern corner of Lake Nicaragua at the beginning of the Río San Juan. Boats on the Río Frío go from Los Chiles to San Carlos every day.

San Carlos has a couple of extremely basic pensiones and regular boat service several times a week to Granada, a major Nicaraguan town on the north-western corner of Lake Nicaragua.

To/From Panama
There are two border crossings between Costa Rica and Panama. Note that Panama's time is one hour ahead of Costa Rica's.

Via Paso Canoas This crossing is on the Carretera Interamericana, and is the most frequently used entry and exit point with Panama.

Border hours have changed several times in the last few years – recently the border was open from 6 am to 10 pm with a two hour lunch break (from 11 am to 1 pm). There's not much point in arriving after dark because buses leave during daylight hours only.

If you are entering Panama, you may need a visa or tourist card. US, Canadian, New Zealand, Australian and some western European citizens require visas. Visitors from the UK and some European nations do not. Visas may be free or may cost up to about US$20, depending on your nationality.

Regulations are subject to change, so you should check at the Panamanian consulate in San José about current requirements. Visas are not obtainable at the border. Tourist cards are officially available but the immigration office on the border has been known to run out, so get your visa or tourist card in advance if you need one.

Once you are in Panama, there is a Panamanian bus terminal in front of the border-crossing post. The nearest town of any size and with decent hotels is David, about 1½ hours away by bus. There are buses every hour or two throughout the day and the last one leaves the border at 7 pm. If you want to travel on to Panama City, you can either fly or catch a bus from David – the last departure is at 5 pm and the trip takes about seven hours.

If you are entering Costa Rica, you may require a ticket out of the country, although this is not always asked for. If you don't have one, buy a TRACOPA bus ticket in David for David to Paso Canoas and return; this is acceptable to the Costa Rican authorities. Apparently, you can't buy just the Paso Canoas to David section at the border.

There is a Costa Rican consulate in David, as well as in Panama City.

People of most nationalities require only a passport and exit ticket to enter Costa Rica. See the Facts for the Visitor chapter for more details about this. The border crossing either way is generally straightforward if your documents are in order.

Via Sixaola/Guabito This crossing is on the Caribbean coast. The continuation of Sixaola on the Panamanian side is called Guabito. There are no banks, but stores in Guabito will accept colones, balboas or US dollars. The border is open from 7 to 11 am and 1 to 5 pm, but there are reports that the border guards are frequently late and may even take a day off from Friday to Sunday (though they claim that someone is there seven days a week). There are frequent minibuses from near the border crossing to Changuinola, 16 km into Panama.

In Changuinola, there is a bank and an airport, with daily flights to David. There is a hotel near the airport which charges about US$15 a double.

From Changuinola, several buses go the 30 km to Almirante, where there are cheaper hotels. There are also trains, but these are mainly freight trains – ask if passenger trains are operating. (I have read conflicting reports about train services – the 1991 earthquake closed the tracks but apparently some freight trains are running again.) From Almirante, there are cheap passenger ferries or expensive water taxis (US$10) every day (an unconfirmed report says there are no water taxis on Wednesday) to Bocas del Toro, where there are pleasant beaches and reasonable hotels. There are no roads beyond Almirante, though some are planned. Also from Almirante, there are daily boats at 7 am to Chiriquí Grande (hotels) from where there is a road to David and the rest of Panama. There is a Costa Rican consulate in David.

People who have travelled this way say that the Bocas del Toro area is attractive and worth seeing, but be prepared for delays. Almirante is the first (or last) place in Panama with a selection of reasonably priced accommodation, although the town is much less attractive than Bocas del Toro.

SEA

Several cruise lines make stops in Costa Rican ports and enable passengers to make a quick foray into the country. Most cruises are, however, geared to shipboard life and ocean travel, so passengers can expect no more than a brief glimpse of Costa Rica – perhaps a day or so. Typically, cruise ships dock at either the Pacific port of Caldera (near Puntarenas) or the Caribbean port of Moín (near Puerto Limón). Passengers at Caldera get a chance to do a day trip to San José and the Central Valley or perhaps visit the Reserva Biológica Carara. Passengers at Moín may take a trip up the canals towards Parque Nacional Tortuguero or go on a river rafting excursion. Other options are often possible.

Freighters also arrive in Costa Rica but most are for cargo only. A few may accept a small number of passengers. Private yachts cruise down the Pacific coast from North America.

TOURS

Scores of tour operators in North America and Europe run tours to Costa Rica. It is beyond the scope of this book to list them all (there are about three dozen tour operators running Costa Rica tours from California alone). Typical tours combine nature and adventure. One or several national parks and reserves are usually visited, with overnight accommodation in comfortable lodges and hotels. Apart from bird-watching and wildlife observation, and guided cloud or rainforest hikes, other activities may include river running, snorkelling, deep-sea or freshwater fishing, horse-riding, sailing, touring the countryside and plain relaxing.

Tours in Costa Rica tend to be first class and expensive, and costs for the best trips can reach US$150 to US$200 per person per day, plus airfare to San José. The best tours usually provide an experienced bilingual guide, accommodation, all transport and most meals. If you are shopping for a tour you'll obviously be interested in the itinerary. In addition you should check on what kind of guide is provided. Is the guide fluent in English? What are the guide's particular interests and qualifications? Will they accompany you throughout the trip or will there be different guides for different portions? Other questions to consider are: How big will the tour group be? How many meals

are included? What kind of accommodation is used? Can you talk to past clients?

The advantages of a tour are that you have everything taken care of from the time you arrive till the time you leave. You don't have to worry about speaking Spanish, figuring out itineraries, finding bus stations, haggling with cab drivers, locating hotels with available rooms and translating restaurant menus. Tours are often preferred by people who have a short vacation period and enough money to be able to afford being taken care of. People on tours have activities scheduled for every day of their trip and don't need to spend time figuring out what to do and how to do it once they get to San José.

Those people with more time may prefer the adventure of arranging their travels for themselves – that's what this book is for. I have travelled to Costa Rica on guided tours, with a friend on public transport, alone, and by hired car. All methods are quite feasible and only you can decide which is best for you.

Tour operators often advertise in magazines which deal with travel, natural history, the outdoors, or culture. Thumb through a few magazines in your local library to get an idea of what's available. It is best to book your tour in advance, even though there are plenty of tour operators in San José who can provide you with a variety of travel opportunities once you get there. If you book ahead, you get the best choices of hotels.

For more information on tours around Costa Rica, see the Getting Around chapter.

LEAVING COSTA RICA

There is a US$7.25 departure tax (depending on current exchange rate) on international flights from San José. This is payable in US dollars cash or colones – Costa Rican residents pay approximately US$40 airport departure tax. (As we go to press, I have received an unconfirmed report that the airport departure tax is US$11 – check locally.)

Recent (unconfirmed) reports indicate that about US$0.70 is charged to visitors leaving overland.

If you overstay your 30 or 90 days, you need to get an exit visa before leaving the country. This costs US$12 if you are leaving by air and US$30 or US$40 when leaving overland. In addition, you have to pay the Costa Rican rate for the airport departure tax. Budget travellers who want to stay longer than 30 or 90 days will save money by spending 72 hours in Panama or Nicaragua, and then returning to Costa Rica.

Getting Around

The population distribution of Costa Rica dictates how its public transport works. Roughly one quarter of the country's almost three million inhabitants live in the greater San José area, and roughly two thirds live in the Central Valley, one of the most densely populated regions in Central America. This means that there are a lot of roads and buses in the centre of the country. As you go further afield, there are generally fewer roads and less public transport.

To get to most regions you have to start from San José, which is the main centre for public transport. It is often easier to go to one region, then return to San José to find transport to another area.

The majority of Costa Ricans do not own cars. Therefore, public transport is quite well developed and you can get buses to almost any part of the country. Remote or small towns may be served by only one bus a day, but you can get there.

AIR

The two domestic airlines are SANSA (Servicios Aereos Nacionales SA) and Travelair. Don't confuse SANSA with the Honduran airline SAHSA.

SANSA flies from the domestic terminal of Juan Santamaría International Airport, 17 km from the centre of San José. Services are with small twin-engined DC3s (32 passengers) and similar aircraft. Demand for seats is high, so try to book as far in advance as possible. Because the aircraft are small, baggage allowance is limited to 12 kg. SANSA flies between San José and Quepos,

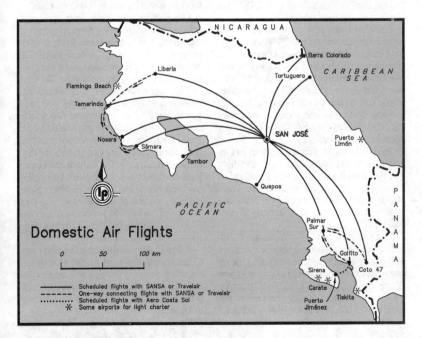

Domestic Air Flights

| 0 | 50 | 100 km |

——— Scheduled flights with SANSA or Travelair
– – – One-way connecting flights with SANSA or Travelair
·········· Scheduled flights with Aero Costa Sol
✳ Some airports for light charter

Golfito, Palmar Sur, Coto 47, Tamarindo, Nosara, Sámara and Barra Colorado.

Travelair flies from the smaller Tobías Bolaños Airport in Pavas, about five km from the centre of San José. Service is with nine-passenger Britten Islanders, 15-passenger Britten Trislanders, and similar. Again, book as far in advance as possible and remember to limit your luggage to 25 pounds (about 11.3 kg). Travelair flies between San José and Quepos, Golfito, Palmar Sur, Liberia, Tamarindo, Nosara, Carrillo, Tambor and Tortuguero.

If you have a reservation with SANSA, you must pay the fare in full to SANSA before it can be confirmed. You should also reconfirm in advance, preferably several times. SANSA is notorious for delayed, cancelled or overbooked flights.

Since Travelair began operation in December 1991, however, the passenger pressure on SANSA has decreased somewhat and the competition has increased. This has resulted in higher fares on SANSA, but also somewhat better service.

Travelair is the new domestic airline and is more expensive than SANSA. The most important differences between them are that Travelair can be booked through any reputable travel agent (you have to pay SANSA direct before they can confirm your reservation) and Travelair is working hard to provide better on-time services and fewer cancelled flights than SANSA. So far, they seem to be succeeding.

Tobías Bolaños Airport also caters to small single and twin-engined aircraft which can be chartered to just about anywhere in the country where there is an airport. Fares start at about US$250 per hour per plane and it takes the best part of an hour to fly to most coastal destinations.

You also have to pay for the return flight, unless you can co-ordinate with the company to fly you out on a day when they are picking somebody else up. If there is a group of you filling up the plane (three, five or seven passengers in most cases) the fare is not prohibitive. Luggage space is very limited.

Many towns which have an airport will have light aircraft available for charter; those which are of particular interest to the traveller are mentioned in the text.

You can arrange flights directly by going to Tobías Bolaños Airport or you can look in the Getting There & Away section of the San José chapter for the telephone numbers of several companies which charter aircraft. Many tour agencies will charter planes for you if you are taking one of their tours.

Details of SANSA and Travelair flights, fares and telephone numbers are given under the appropriate towns.

BUS

The ICT tourist office in San José has an up-to-date listing of many bus departure points and the destinations they serve. Buses depart from San José for just about anywhere in the country.

There is no central bus terminal. Some bus companies leave from what used to be the old Coca-Cola bottling plant in San José – the area is still known as 'La Coca-Cola'.

Other companies leave from their own offices. Still others leave from bus stops in the street, and others leave from a street corner without even a bus stop. The addresses or street intersections of bus companies are given under the appropriate city.

The larger companies with offices and buses going to major destinations will allow you to buy a ticket in advance. The smaller companies with just a bus stop expect you to queue for the next bus, but normally there is room for everyone. The exception is the days before and after a major holiday, especially Easter, when buses are ridiculously full. I have resorted to hitchhiking in these cases.

Friday night and Saturday morning trips out of San José can be very crowded, as can Sunday afternoon and evening return trips; try to avoid those if possible.

If this all seems a little chaotic, take heart. Costa Ricans are used to the system and know where many buses leave from – just ask. The people are known for their friendliness, and you'll soon find out what you need to know.

Fares are generally cheap, with the longest

and most expensive run out of San José costing under US$7. (The exceptions are the international buses going to Managua or Panama City from San José.)

Long-distance buses are of two types, *directo* and *normal* (or *corriente*). The direct buses are a little faster and more expensive. Travellers on a budget can save as much as a quarter of the direct bus fare by taking a normal bus which stops on demand at various intermediate points and usually takes an hour or two longer.

Roads are narrow and winding and sometimes unpaved; buses are rather old and so comfort is not one of the things that the bus journeys are known for, particularly to smaller and more remote destinations which are served by battered old Bluebird school buses. But they get you there. Trips longer than four hours have a rest stop, and no trips are scheduled to take longer than about nine hours.

Luggage space is limited, so I suggest breaking your Costa Rican stay into sections and leaving what you don't need for a certain section in San José. A small bag is certainly much easier to travel with and it is easier to keep your eye on it if you can take it aboard with you. There have been reports of checked luggage on buses getting 'lost'.

If your bag is too big to take aboard the bus with you, watch it getting loaded and keep your eyes open during any stops the bus makes to ensure that it doesn't 'accidentally' get given to the wrong passenger.

TRAIN

The railway lines in Costa Rica were severely damaged in the 1991 earthquake and have mostly been closed since then. They were running at a financial deficit before the closure, so it is unlikely that the system will be repaired in the future. This is a shame, because the run from San José to Puerto Limón on the Caribbean coast was a famous and well-loved ride.

Railway buffs do still have some train-riding possibilities. There is a short commuter train linking San José with Heredia – about 10 km away. There is also a

train which began oper links Puerto Limón wi area, about 90 minutes 1

The second alternati called 'banana train'. T carriage used by tour companies, which travels on a section of track in the banana plantations around Guápiles.

One company which has been recommended for this tour is Swiss Travel Service (☎ 31 4055) with offices in several of the major hotels. They charge about US$75 for the trip. For this they provide lunch, a bilingual guide, bus transport from San José to the train, and a visit to a banana plantation along the way.

This ride is a good way to see some of back-country Costa Rica. This section of the track is flat, going through banana plantations. Thousands of workers lost their lives to yellow fever and malaria when this section was being built in the 1870s. The entire line was completed in 1890 and created the first permanent year-round link between San José and the Caribbean coast, thus improving export facilities and expanding the economy. Today, you can get a glimpse of this history on the 'banana train' tour.

TAXI

It may come as a surprise to most people that taxis are considered to be a form of public transport outside urban areas. Taxis can be hired by the hour, the half day or the day. Meters are not used on long trips so you arrange the fare with the driver beforehand.

There are various occasions when you may want to consider using a taxi. Visiting some of the national parks is not possible by public transport. Your alternatives are to take a tour, rent a car, hitch a ride, walk, cycle or catch a taxi.

The round trip from San José to Volcán Poás, for example, is about 110 km. An all-day excursion allowing a couple of hours at the volcano and photo stops along the way costs about US$40 to US$50 depending on the taxi driver and your bargaining ability. That's not a bad deal, and actually fairly if you share your cab with other trav-s.

When you are out in the country, you may need to take a taxi to a remote destination on a bad road. During the rainy season 4WD may be required. Many taxis are 4WD jeeps and can get you almost anywhere.

CAR & MOTORBIKE

Few people drive to Costa Rica in their own vehicle, though it is certainly possible. Renting a car or motorbike upon arrival, on the other hand, is something which many travellers do for part of their trip.

Rental

There are plenty of car rental agencies in San José, but few in other cities. Many agencies also have offices at Juan Santamaría International Airport.

Car rental is popular because it gets you to places where you can't go by public transport. It also gives you the freedom to travel when you want, and to stop wherever you like. Because buses to remote areas are not very frequent, you can cover more ground in a shorter time in a car.

Realise that car rental is not very cheap. There are discounts available if you rent by the week, but expect to pay at least US$250 per week for the smallest sub-compact car with no air-conditioning or closer to US$300 if it comes with air-conditioning.

The cost includes (mandatory) insurance and unlimited mileage (or *kilometraje*, as they call it). If you plan on driving 500 km or more in a week, you should get unlimited km; less than that and you'll save by paying a daily base rate plus the per km charge.

The insurance accounts for about US$12 per day of your cost (more for larger vehicles); rental companies won't let you rent a car without it because they say that your policy at home will not be valid in Costa Rica in case of an accident or theft of the car.

A few companies may waive the insurance fee if you rent with a particular credit card – a recent report in *The Tico Times* claims that this is limited to Adobe, Budget, and National car rental companies and only if you use American Express. Note that there is usually a US$750 deductible on the insurance; if you want to be fully covered, add another US$3 per day.

If you want more than a sub-compact car without air-conditioning, expect to pay about US$350 to US$400 for a medium-size car with air-conditioning, and about US$450 to US$500 for a van or 4WD jeep. All rates are per week, including free km and insurance.

For travel during the rainy season many rental agencies insist that you rent a 4WD vehicle if you are going to places where you need to drive on dirt roads – the Península de Nicoya, for example. But the rainy season is also the low season and discounted rates may apply.

Many of the major car rental companies like Avis, Budget, Dollar, Hertz or National have offices worldwide, so you can rent a car in advance from home. Normally, you need to book a car at least 14 days in advance and I've read that the rate when booked at home is a little cheaper than it is in San José. (I did talk to one driver who booked at home and then was charged a hefty 'pick-up' fee when he arrived in San José.)

I found that when I tried to book a sub-compact with air-conditioning from home, I couldn't find anything for under US$400 a week, and there are plenty of agencies offering a similar car for around US$300 in San José. Make sure you clearly understand your agreement with the rental company before paying at home for a rental car.

To hire a car you need a valid driver's licence, a major credit card and your passport. If you don't have a major credit card some companies may allow you to make a cash deposit of about US$700. Your driver's licence from home is acceptable for up to three months if you are a tourist; you don't need an international driving permit.

The minimum age for car rental is 18 years, though most car rental companies won't rent to drivers under 25. (Ada Rent-A-Car claims to have a minimum of 18 years; Pilot claims 21 years; and Adobe 23 years.) Dozens of other companies are listed in the

San José Yellow Pages. I haven't heard too many complaints about them – most are fairly reputable. (One that I have received complaints about is U-Haul Rent a Car which, the lawyers of U-Haul International in the USA told me, is not affiliated with U-Haul International.)

When you rent a car, carefully inspect it for minor dents and scratches, missing radio antennae or hubcaps, and anything else which makes the car look less than brand new. These damages must be noted on your rental agreement, otherwise you may be charged for them when you return the car. The insurance won't cover it, because of the US$750 deductible.

Rental cars have special licence plates and it is immediately obvious to everyone that you are driving a rental car. There have been many instances of theft from rental cars. You should never leave valuables in sight when you are out of the car, and you should remove luggage from the trunk when checking into a hotel overnight. Many hotels will provide parking areas for cars. It is better to park the car in a guarded parking lot than on the street. This cannot be over-emphasised – don't leave valuables in the car.

Motorbikes can be rented in a few places in San José and along the coast – they are somewhat cheaper than cars, but not very much so; about US$200 a week is about average.

The price of petrol is currently under US$0.40 per litre of regular (about US$1.60 per US gallon), although this is down on previous years, when it was as high as US$2 per gallon. Most stations sell regular and diesel; unleaded and super are available in larger towns. Most rental cars take regular. The price of petrol is the same at all stations nation-wide.

Road Safety

San José is notorious for its narrow streets, complicated one-way system, heavy traffic and thefts from cars. I certainly would not recommend driving a rental car around San José, except to get out of the city.

Once out of San José, the roads vary from barely passable to very good. But even the good ones can suffer from landslides and thick fog, and so you should always be prepared for the unexpected. Most roads are single lane, lack hard shoulders and are very winding, so defensive driving is recommended. Always be prepared for cyclists, pedestrians, a broken-down vehicle or even an ox-cart around the next bend.

There are some roads which have a reputation for being especially dangerous. The Cerro de la Muerte area on the Carretera Interamericana between Cartago and San Isidro del General (the highest section of the Interamericana) suffers from frequent landslides and dense fog at any time of day or night. (I have several times driven this section with visibility down to under 10 metres.)

The busy San José to Puntarenas road is steep, narrow and tortuously winding, but local drivers familiar with the road drive it very fast. The section between San Ramón and Esparza is especially notorious – there is one area which suffers from permanent earth subsidence and the road goes over a chassis-breaking drop – be careful. The new road from San José to Guápiles goes through Parque Nacional Braulio Carrillo and is subject to landslides and heavy fog, especially later in the day. Similarly, the stretch of the Interamericana from Palmar Norte to Buenos Aires is subject to frequent rockfall and landslides.

Because of the relatively poor driving conditions, I wouldn't recommend driving a motorbike – though some people do it. It can be very dusty in the dry season and very wet in the rainy season.

If you should be involved in an accident you should not move the cars until the police get there. Injured people should not be taken from the scene until the Red Cross ambulance arrives. Try to make a note or sketch of what happened, and don't make statements except to authorised people.

Telephone the Red Cross (☎ 21 5818), or the transit police (☎ 22 7150 or 27 8030), or if you're away from towns call the Guardia de Asistencia Rural (☎ 127). Patrol cars can be called on 117 and emergency rescue units on 118.

Because of difficult driving conditions, there are speed limits of 80 km/h on all primary roads and 60 km/h or less on secondary roads. Traffic police use radar and speed limits are enforced with speeding tickets.

You can also get a traffic ticket for not wearing a seat belt. All rental cars have seat belts. It is not legal to enter an intersection unless you can also leave it, and it is not legal to make a right turn on a red light unless a white arrow painted on the road indicates that a turn is permitted. At unmarked intersections, yield to the car on your right. Driving in Costa Rica is on the right, and passing is allowed only on the left.

If you are given a ticket, you have to pay the fine at a bank; instructions are given on the ticket. If you are driving a rented car, the rental company can arrange your payment for you – the amount of the fine should be on the ticket.

Fines used to be ridiculously low, but a new traffic law passed in 1993 has raised the fines substantially. Some examples: US$150 for driving 40 km per hour over the speed limit, US$70 for running a red light, US$15 for not wearing a seat belt.

There has been a spate of recent incidents in which traffic police try to intimidate tourists by threatening to confiscate their cars or suggesting that the tourist pays a 'fine' (a bribe) directly to the officer. Police have no right to confiscate a car except if the driver cannot produce licence and ownership papers or if the car lacks licence plates; or if the driver is drunk or has been involved in an accident causing serious injury or death.

Police have no right to ask for money under any circumstances. You have the right to see the officer's identification and report any infraction to the Transit Police (☎ 27 2188 ext 546) between 7.30 am and 4 pm from Monday to Friday.

If you are driving and see on-coming cars flashing their lights at you it often means that there is a radar speed-trap ahead or some kind of road problem. Slow down immediately. Police cars are blue with white

doors and have a small red light on the roof – they can be small sedans or pickups. White or red police motorbikes are also in use.

Many foreign drivers complain that the roads are inadequately signposted. This is often true, so try to get hold of a decent road map and ask locals if you are not sure. They are nearly always able and willing to help.

Some signposting problems which I have encountered include having a sign five km before a turn-off, but not at the actual turn-off; having signs for a turn-off in only one direction (try and look over your shoulder at signs on the other side of the road if you are expecting one soon); and signs which are placed on the road you want to turn off on, rather than the road you are driving on.

BICYCLE

All the warnings under the Road Safety section apply here – but even more so. There are no bike lanes and traffic can be hazardous on the narrow, steep, winding roads. Cycling is a possibility, however, and long-distance cyclists report that locals tend to be very friendly towards them. It is possible to cycle all the way from the USA or you can fly your bicycle down as luggage. Check with airlines for regulations – often a bicycle will be carried free of charge if it is properly packed and doesn't exceed luggage size and weight requirements.

Those planning a bicycle trip might want to read *Latin America on a Bicycle* by J P Panet (Passport Press, Champlain, New York, 1987) which includes a chapter on cycling through Costa Rica.

Cycle touring is just beginning in Costa Rica. A division of Ríos Tropicales (☎ 33 6455, fax 55 4354) organises cycle tours; you may also rent a bike from them.

HITCHING

The frequency of buses on the main roads makes hitching less common, though it is by no means impossible. Hitchhikers are more often seen on minor rural roads.

Don't simply stand there with your thumb out. Vehicles may pass only a few times per hour and you should try and wave them down in a friendly fashion. (Watch how the locals do it.) Tell the driver where you're going, ask if there's any room, could they give you a ride as you've been waiting for ages and there's no bus or all the buses are full and you really need to get to wherever you're going... Obviously, speaking Spanish and having a relaxed and friendly attitude go a long way towards getting a ride in this way.

Sometimes hitching is the only way out of town during holiday weekends when the buses coming through are already full to overflowing. If you get a ride, offer to pay for it when you arrive: *Cuanto le debo?* (How much do I owe you?) is the standard way of doing this.

Often, your offer will be waved aside; sometimes you'll be asked to help with petrol money. If you are driving, picking up hitchhikers in the countryside is normally no problem and often gets you into some interesting conversations.

Single women do hitch sometimes and I haven't yet heard a negative story about it, in Costa Rica at least. Ticos are generally helpful and friendly. Nevertheless, discretion is urged.

Try to talk to the occupants of the car and get an idea of whether they seem OK; don't get into the car if you don't feel comfortable; try to hitch from somewhere (a petrol station, store, restaurant, police post) where you can retreat to if you don't like the look of your prospective ride. Hitching with a companion is a good idea.

BOAT

There are various passenger and car ferries in operation. Two cheap ferries operate out of Puntarenas across the Golfo de Nicoya.

One is a huge car ferry which leaves several times a day for Playa Naranjo (a 90 minute trip). The other is a small passenger ferry which crosses to Paquera two or three times a day, taking about two hours. Buses meet the ferry at Paquera to transport you onwards into the Península de Nicoya. Complete details are given under the appropriate towns.

There is also a car ferry operating across the mouth of the Río Tempisque which cuts two or three hours off the road trip to the Península de Nicoya – if you can time your ferry crossing just right. The ferry runs every hour from 6 am to 8 pm.

A daily passenger ferry links Golfito with Puerto Jiménez on the Península de Osa; a trip taking about 90 minutes. This ferry is subject to cancellation – there was no service in 1992 but it was running again when I visited in 1993. Puerto Jiménez is the nearest town of any size to Parque Nacional Corcovado.

Motorised dug-out canoes ply the Río Sarapiquí once a day on a scheduled basis and more frequently on demand. See under Puerto Viejo de Sarapiquí for more details.

Other boat trips can be made, but these are tours rather than rides on scheduled ferries. These include canal boats up the inland waterway from Moín (near Limón) to Parque Nacional Tortuguero and Refugio Nacional de Fauna Silvestre Barro del Colorado.

Dugouts can be hired at Puerto Viejo de Sarapiquí up the Río Sarapiquí to the Río San Juan, which forms much of the Costa Rica/Nicaragua border. Relations with Nicaragua have improved since the 1990 electoral defeat of the Sandinistas, and it is now possible to travel along the border down the Río San Juan as far as its mouth, and then down into the Refugio Nacional de Fauna Silvestre Barro del Colorado.

This is not a regularly scheduled trip but can be arranged – see under Puerto Viejo de Sarapiquí for further information. People staying in the Bahía Drake area usually arrive or leave via an exciting boat trip on the Río Sierpe.

For adventurous types, river running down the Ríos Pacuare, Chirripó, Reventazón, Corobici and Sarapiquí for one or more days is one option – see under Tours in this chapter for further information. Fishing trips, either on Laguna de Arenal or offshore is another.

One-day sailing trips in the Golfo de Nicoya can be booked on the yacht *Calypso* – others can be arranged with travel agents in San José.

LOCAL TRANSPORT
To/From the Airport

Taxis from Juan Santamaría International Airport will take you into San José, 17 km away, for US$10. Alajuela, five km away, can be reached by taxi for about US$3.

Buses between Alajuela and San José pass the airport several times an hour and often have room for passengers; the fare is about US$0.40. See the Getting Around section of the San José chapter for details.

Bus

Local buses serve urban and suburban areas, but services and routes can be difficult to figure out. Many towns are small enough so that getting around on foot is easy. Some local bus details are described in the Getting There & Away sections for each of the major towns.

Local people are usually very helpful, and this includes bus drivers, who will often be able to tell you where to wait for a particular bus.

Taxi

In San José, taxis have meters, called *marías*, but these might not be used, particularly for foreigners who can't speak Spanish. (It is illegal not to use the meter.) Outside San José, taxis don't have meters and so fares are agreed upon in advance; bargaining is acceptable.

Within San José, a short ride should cost a dollar or less. A ride across town will be around US$2. Rates are comparable in other parts of the country. Taxi cabs are red and have a small sticker in the windshield identifying them as a 'TAXI'.

TOURS
Travel & Tour Agencies in San José

There are scores, if not hundreds, of travel agencies in San José. I have attempted to include as wide a variety of agencies as possible and have listed the San José addresses of some of the wilderness lodges described in detail elsewhere in this book.

Many companies specialise in nature tours, with visits to the national parks and wilderness lodges. They can provide entire guided itineraries (with English-speaking guides) and private transport to any part of the country, especially the nature destinations. Many of these nature tour companies also specialise in adventure tourism such as river rafting.

Almost all agencies also provide services such as day trips around the Central Valley, San José city tours, hotel reservations, and airport transfers.

Prices vary depending on the services you require. Two people wishing to travel with a private English-speaking guide and a private vehicle will obviously pay a lot more than two people who are prepared to join a group or can understand a Spanish-speaking guide.

Among the longest running (since 1978) and biggest nature/adventure-tour companies is Costa Rica Expeditions (☎ 57 0766, fax 57 1665) at Calle Central, Avenida 3. They pioneered adventure and nature tourism in Costa Rica. Some of their guides are well-qualified naturalists or ornithologists. They specialise in natural history tours, particularly to Parque Nacional Tortuguero and Reserva Biológica Monteverde (where they have their own luxurious lodges), and Parque Nacional Corcovado (where they have a tent camp and boat); in river rafting and kayaking trips; and in fishing trips.

The standards of services are excellent (their motto is 'Legendary Service. Unforgettable Memories') and their trips are priced accordingly. The mailing address is Apartado 6941, San José, but you often can get a faster response from their USA address: Department 235, PO Box 025216, Miami, FL 33102-5216, USA.

Another recommended nature-tour company is Horizontes (☎ 22 2022, fax 55 4513, Apartado 1780-1002, San José). They have been arranging nature and adventure tours for over a decade and have built up an excellent reputation. Their street address is Calle 28, Avenida 1 & 3.

Costa Rican Sun Tours (☎ 55 3418 or 55 3518, fax 55 4410) is at Avenida 7, Calle 3 & 5. They do the normal nature tours and fishing trips and, in addition, operate the observatory at Volcán Arenal (from where fishing trips on Lago Arenal can also be undertaken) and Tiskita Lodge on a private reserve on the far southern Pacific coast. Their operation is also excellent and recommended. Sun Tours' mailing address is Apartado 1195-1250, Escazú, Costa Rica.

Several other companies specialise in nature tours and have been recommended. They include Tikal (☎ 23 2811, fax 23 1916) at Avenida 2, Calle 7 & 9, or write to Apartado 6398-1000, San José. Tikal also runs the EcoAdventure Lodge north of Lago Arenal.

Geotur (☎ 34 1867, fax 53 6338; Apartado 469 Y Griega 1011, San José) specialises in Reserva Biológica Carara and Parque Nacional Braulio Carrillo tours.

Los Caminos de la Selva (Jungle Tours) (☎ 55 3486, fax 55 2782) on Calle 38, Avenida 5 & 7, specialise in trips to Volcán Barva and will arrange (if you can get a group together) a tree-planting tour where you learn about the ecological value of native trees. You get to plant a tree of your choice. Write to them at Apartado 2413-1000, San José.

Senderos de Iberoamérica (☎/fax 55 2859), Avenida 7, Calle 5 & 7, specialises in trips to Monumento Nacional Guayabo and to their private cloud forest reserve at Los Juncos.

Companies specialising in river rafting include the following, and all are recommended. Ríos Tropicales (☎ 33 6455, fax 55 4354), Calle 32, Avenida 2 (100 metres south of Pollos Kentucky on Paseo Colón) has both river rafting and kayaking trips, and sea kayaking expeditions. Write to Apartado 472-1200, Pavas, Costa Rica.

There's also Aventuras Naturales (☎ 25 3939, fax 53 6934) at Avenida Central, Calle 33 & 35, or write to Apartado 812-2050, San Pedro, San José; or check out Costa Rica Expeditions (see earlier reference in this section).

One of the most famous boat trips is an all-day yacht cruise through the Golfo de Nicoya to Isla Tortuga – excellent food and good swimming opportunities. The longest

running of these cruises is ▮ (☎ 33 3617, fax 33 0401; A▮ 1000, San José). Bay Island ▮ 2898; Apartado 145-1007, Sai▮ does this cruise.

There are other cruises along ▮ Caribbean canals to Tortuguero. These usually involve one or two nights at lodges in either Parques Nacionales Tortuguero or Barra del Colorado, and can be combined with bus or airplane returns, wildlife watching, and fishing trips, depending on your time and budget.

Apart from Costa Rica Expeditions, companies running Caribbean canal cruises include Cotur (☎ 33 0155, fax 33 0778; Apartado 1818-1002, Paseo de Los Estudiantes, San José), Calle 38, Paseo Colón & Avenida 1; and Mitur (☎ 55 2031, fax 55 1946; Apartado 91-1150, San José), Paseo Colón, Calle 20 & 22.

The luxurious MV *Temptress* is a 53 metre vessel with 29 double and four single air-conditioned cabins with private shower and outside windows. The boat is run by Temptress Cruises (in San José ☎ 20 1679; in the USA (☎ (305) 871 2663, fax (305) 871 2657; 1600 N W LeJeune Rd, Suite 301, Miami, FL 33126). They do multi-day cruises along the Pacific coast visiting several of the national parks and reserves en route. Depending on the cruise, some of the following are visited: Palo Verde, Manuel Antonio, Corcovado, Isla del Caño, Bahía Drake (Drake Bay), Cabo Blanco, Curu. The emphasis of the cruises is natural history and there are naturalist and biologist guides aboard. Scuba diving is also possible for certified divers with their own gear – the boat has air, tanks and weights. There is an onboard photographer and dark room. Cruises leave from Puntarenas, though prices are all-inclusive from San José.

Single/double fares for two days and three nights cost US$795/1190; for three days and four nights it costs US$1000/1590 and for six nights, US$1900/2980. Children under 12 years old get big discounts.

Several agencies have been recommended for general travel and tour arrangements.

...y can arrange city tours, book you into beach resort hotels, sell you standard day trips, as well as arrange more exotic tours.

Swiss Travel (☎ 31 4055, fax 31 3030) has offices in several of the best hotels including the Corobici (main office), Amstel, Balmoral, Irazú and Sheraton. Swiss Travel introduced the 'banana train' tour. For information write to Apartado 7-1970-1000, San José.

Also recommended is TAM (☎ 23 5111, fax 22 8092), Calle Central, Avenida Central & 1. It is also the American Express agent and has been recommended for international air ticketing; write to Apartado 1864-1000, San José.

San José

For the traveller who arrives at the Costa Rican capital overland through other Central American nations, as I first did in 1980, San José comes as something of a surprise. Compared to other capitals of the region, it is more cosmopolitan, even North Americanised. There are department stores and shopping malls, fast-food chain restaurants and blue jeans. There are almost no Indians and no Indian markets, as there are in Guatemala, for example.

It takes a day or two to start getting the real tico feeling of the city. Perhaps the first sign of being in Costa Rica is the friendliness of the people. Asking someone the way will often result in a smile and a genuine attempt to help you out – a refreshing change from many other capital cities.

Although the city was founded in 1737, little remains from the colonial era. Indeed, until the Teatro Nacional was built in the 1890s, San José was a small and largely forgotten city. Today, the capital boasts several excellent museums, good restaurants, and a fine climate – these are the main attractions for visitors. Because Costa Rica's public transport and road system radiates from San José, the capital is often used as a base from which to visit the many attractions of the country.

The population of the city itself is around 280,000 but the surrounding suburbs boost the number to about 885,000. The population of the whole province is 1,140,000, or 37% of the country. Inhabitants of San José are sometimes referred to as *joséfinos*.

Orientation

The city stands at an elevation of 1150 metres and is set in a wide and fertile valley which is known throughout Costa Rica as the Valle Central.

The city centre, where many visitors spend most of their time, is arranged in a grid. All the streets are numbered in a logical fashion, and it is important to learn the

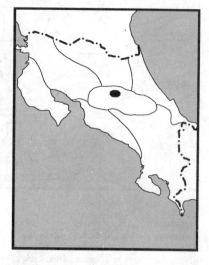

system because all street directions and addresses rely on this grid system.

The streets running east to west are *avenidas* whilst the streets running north to south are *calles*. Avenida Central runs east-west through the middle of the city; avenidas north of Avenida Central are odd-numbered, with Avenida 1 running parallel and one block north of Avenida Central, followed by Avenida 3 and so on. The avenidas south of Avenida Central are even-numbered. Similarly, Calle Central runs north-south through the heart of downtown, and calles east of Calle Central are odd-numbered and calles west of Calle Central are even-numbered.

If you ask a passer-by for directions, you'll probably be told to go seven blocks west and four blocks north (*'Siete cuadras al oeste y quatro cuadras al norte'*). Often, 100 metres is used to mean a city block, and so you may be told *'Setecientos metros al oeste y quatrocientos metros al norte'*. This does not literally mean 700 metres west and 400

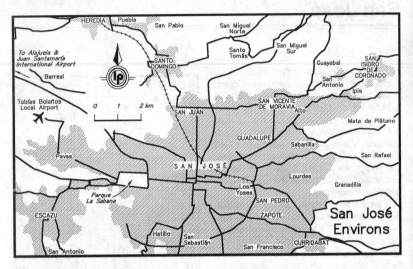

San José Environs

metres north; it refers to city blocks. *Cincuenta metros* (50 metres) means half a block. Perhaps one reason for this method of giving directions is because of the lack of street signs, especially away from downtown.

Street addresses in San José are rarely given by the building number (although building numbers do exist). Instead, the nearest street intersection is given. Thus the address of the ITC is Calle 5, Avenidas Central y 2. This means it is on Calle 5, between Avenida Central & Avenida 2 (*y* means 'and' in Spanish). This is often abbreviated in telephone directories or other literature to C5, A Ctl/2, or occasionally C5, A 0/2, with 0 replacing the Central. This system is also used in many other Costa Rican towns, so it's worth getting to know.

Note that Avenida Central becomes Paseo Colón west of Calle 14. The building on the north side of Paseo Colón, Calles 38 & 40, is known as Centro Colón and is a local landmark.

Many ticos use local landmarks to give directions, or even addresses in smaller towns. Thus an address may be 200 metres south and 150 metres east of a church, a radio station, a restaurant, or even a *pulpería* (corner grocery store). Sometimes, the landmark may no longer exist, but because it has been used for so long, its position is known by all the locals.

A good example is La Coca-Cola, which is a bus terminal in San José where a Coca-Cola bottling plant used to be for many years. Everyone knows this, except for the first time visitor! This can get confusing, but persevere. The friendly ticos will usually help you out. Note that taxi drivers especially like to know the landmark address. Drivers will sometimes say that they don't understand where you're going until you explain your destination in terms of landmarks!

Information

The friendliness of the Costa Ricans has already been mentioned – but it really is one of the outstanding features of this country. The local people can often be your best sources of information.

Tourist Office The main tourist office is known as the ICT, or Instituto Costarricense de Turismo (☎ 22 1090), and is on the east side of the Plaza de la Cultura. It is in the same building as the Museo de Oro Precolombino (Gold Museum), on Calle 5 between Avenidas Central & 2. Hours are from 9 am to 5 pm Monday to Friday, and 9 am to 1 pm on Saturday. There is normally an English-speaking person on duty.

There is also an ICT office at the airport which is open for longer hours, though I find that when I arrive loaded down with luggage and tired from a flight, I have little inclination to search for tourist information. ICT's main office is marked on some maps at Avenida 4, Calles 5 & 7, but this is an administrative office rather than an actual tourist information office.

Money Any bank will change foreign currency into colones, but US dollars are the most accepted currency. Commissions, when charged, should be small – never more than 1% of the transaction – otherwise go elsewhere. The non-national banks tend to give the fastest service.

One recommendation is Banco Lyon, a branch of Lloyds (☎ 22 7137, 21 2611), Calle 2, Avenida Central & 1. It is reasonably efficient, friendly, has some English-speaking staff, and changes travellers' cheques in Canadian dollars and major European currencies at official rates. Travellers in 1993 reported that the Banco Metropolitano (☎ 33 8111; Calle Central & Avenida 2) had English-speaking staff and was fast and efficient. Other non-national bank choices are Banex (☎ 57 0522; Calle Central, Avenida 1) and Banco de San José (☎ 21 9911; Calle Central, Avenida 3 & 5). There are many others.

The better hotels have exchange windows for their guests. Rates should be similar to those at banks, but occasionally they aren't, so check before changing large sums.

Most banks are open from 9 am to 3 pm, Monday to Friday. A few banks are open longer than normal hours. The Banco Nacional de Costa Rica at Avenida 1, Calle 7, is open from 8 am to 6 pm, Monday to Friday. The bank at the airport is open from 6.30 am to 5 pm from Monday to Friday, and from 7 am to 1 pm on weekends and holidays. The ICT office at the airport (but not downtown) can help with changing cash US dollars.

A good alternative to banks is an exchange house. One I have used frequently is Valorinsa (☎ 57 1010, 57 2002; Calle 9, Avenida Central & 2). They are open from 9 am to 5 pm, Monday to Friday, and their rates are about the same as in the banks.

Changing money on the streets gives you about a 1% or 2% advantage over the banks – rip-offs, forged currency and other scams abound and street moneychanging can't be recommended. Still, if you are desperate after hours, street moneychangers are a choice – they hang out around Avenida Central & Calle 2. Go with a friend and be very careful. There are also moneychangers at the airport.

Credit cards are widely accepted and you can use them to buy colones in banks (see the Money section in the Facts for the Visitor chapter). The American Express office is in the TAM Travel Agency at Calle 1, Avenida Central & 1 (☎ 33 0044; after hours 23 0116; in the USA, 001 (800) 528 2121, 001 801 968 8300). American Express cardholders can buy US dollars travellers' cheques. TAM will hold mail for Amex customers addressed to them c/o TAM, Apartado 1864, San José. Visa (☎ 57 1357, 22 4611, 23 2211) is in the Galería La Paz, Avenida 2, Calle 2 & 4. MasterCard (☎ 53 2155) is in San Pedro – call for directions.

Post The Correo Central (Central Post Office, or CPO) is on Calle 2, Avenida 1 & 3. Hours are from 7 am to 6 pm Monday to Friday, and from 7 am to noon on Saturday. The better hotels have mail boxes and sell stamps. Most people use the CPO to mail their letters; I couldn't find any other mail boxes in central San José.

You can receive mail addressed to you c/o Lista de Correos, Correo Central, San José, Costa Rica. They are very strict about whom they give mail to. You must produce identification (usually your passport) before they will even look for your mail. They will not give mail to friends or family members; you must get it in person. There is a US$0.10 fee per piece of mail received.

Receiving packages can be problematical because of customs requirements – try to have only letters sent to you. Mail theft has been a recent problem, so don't have valuables sent to you in the mail if you can avoid it.

Telephone You can make local calls (to anywhere in Costa Rica) from public telephone booths, which accept five, 10 and 20 colón coins. You can also make international calls from public telephone booths – see the Facts for the Visitor chapter.

To make international calls which you pay for, go to Radiográfica (☎ 87 0087; Calle 1, Avenida 5). They are open from 7 am to 10 pm daily and also provide telex and fax services. Similar hours and services are available from the ICE office at Avenida 2, Calle 1. The better hotels will put international calls through from their switchboards, but these calls are more expensive.

Telephone directories are available in hotels and at Radiográfica. There are none in the public telephone booths.

Foreign Embassies Many countries have diplomatic representation in San José. See the Facts for the Visitor chapter for a full list.

Immigration Office The 'migraciones' office for visa extensions or exit visas is opposite the Hospital Mexico, about four km north of Parque La Sabana. Any Alajuela bus will drop you nearby. Hours are from 8 am to 4 pm Monday to Friday, and waiting lines can be long. Many travel agencies will do the paperwork for you – a processing fee of US$5 is normally charged.

Servicio de Parques Nacionales The public information office (☎ 57 0922) of the Servicio de Parques Nacionales (SPN) is in the headquarters building at Calle 25, Avenida 8 & 10. Office hours are from 8 am to 4 pm Monday to Friday. You can obtain information here, as well as make reservations to stay in places like the mountain huts

on Chirripó, but I have generally found that the most accurate information is at the parks themselves. The SPN headquarters are served by (☎ 33 4118, 33 4246, fax 23 6963; Apartado 10104-1000, San José).

There is also an SPN radio communications office (☎ 33 4160) which maintains radio contact with many of the outlying national parks that do not have regular telephone service. Call to arrange for overnight accommodation, meals, and other services – all provided by the rangers in many parks. (It helps if you speak Spanish.)

Travel & Tour Agencies There are scores, if not hundreds, of travel agencies in San José. See the Getting Around chapter for full details of tours and operators.

Bookshops The following bookstores are particularly noteworthy.

The Bookshop
  (☎ 21 6847), Avenida 1, Calle 1 & 3, has the largest and best selection of books in English (including Lonely Planet guides) but charges up to twice the US price because of import taxes. There is also a good selection of magazines and newspapers in English.
Lehmann's
  Avenida Central, Calle 1 & 3, has some books, magazines, and newspapers in English and a good selection of Costa Rican maps (in the map department upstairs).
Librería Universal
  Avenida Central, Calle Central & 1, has maps and is one of the biggest bookstores in Costa Rica, but it has few books in English and tends to be crowded.
Book Traders
  (☎ 55 0508), Avenida 1, Calle 3 & 5, sells and exchanges used English books. Hours are from 9 am to 5 pm Monday to Saturday.
Librería Francesa
  Calle 3, Avenida Central & 1, sells French books.
The Travelers Store
  (☎ 57 0766), Calle Central, Avenida 3, sells souvenirs and books in English, including *Costa Rica – a Travel survival kit*.

English-language magazines, newspapers, and some books are also available in the gift shops of the international airport and several of the top-end hotels.

Left: View of San José from the Museo de Jade (RR)
Right: Market scene, San José (RG)
Bottom: Traditionally painted carreta (ox-cart) (RR)

Photographs by Rob Rachowiecki

Medical Services The most centrally located (free) hospital is Hospital San Juan de Dios (☎ 22 0166) at Paseo Colón, Calle 14.

If you can afford to pay for medical attention (costs are much cheaper than in the USA or Europe, for example) go to the well-recommended Clínica Bíblica (☎ 23 6422 or, in an emergency, 57 0466) on Avenida 14, Calle Central & 1. They have some English speaking staff and are open 24 hours for emergencies.

They will carry out laboratory tests (stool, urine, blood samples etc) and recommend specialists if necessary. They also have a full range of other medical services including a 24-hour pharmacy.

There are plenty of other pharmacies in San José. The Farmacia Rex, Calle 5, Avenida 5 & 7, has been recommended as being helpful and having English and French-speaking pharmacists.

For an ambulance, call the Red Cross (☎ 21 5818).

Your embassy is a good source of references for specialists if you need one. Embassy staff get sick too – and they usually know the best doctors, dentists etc around.

Laundry There are very few laundromats or launderettes in San José (or, indeed, in Costa Rica) though there are plenty of *lavanderías* most of which do dry cleaning only. To simply wash your own clothes go to: Lavamás (☎ 25 1645), Avenida 8, Calle 45 (next to the Los Yoses Spoon coffee shop). It's US$3 per machine load for cold and US$4 for hot water wash & dry; all is self service. Nearby is Betamatic (☎ 34 0993), Avenida 8, Calle 47, Los Yoses, open from 8 am to 12.30 pm and 1.30 to 6 pm (hours for dropping-off laundry) or from 8 am to 4.30 pm (hours for self-service) Monday to Saturday. The charge is about US$3 per machine load to wash & dry (self service) or US$1.20 a kg if you drop it off and they do it for you.

Burbujas (☎ 24 9822), 50 metres west and 25 metres south of the Mas x Menos Supermercado in San Pedro, is open from 8 am to 6.30 pm Monday to Friday and from 8.30 am to 5 pm on Saturday. They have coin-operated machines. Downtown, the Sixaola (☎ 21 2111), Avenida 2, Calle 7 & 9, charges US$4 a load (wash & dry) and has same-day service.

Another recommendation is Dona Rosa, near the gas station in front of the Tica Bus Terminal, Avenida 4, Calle 9 – they charge US$3.60 for washing and drying a large load.

Most hotels will arrange for your laundry to be washed, but beware that the top-end hotels will rip you off – they'll charge as much for a couple of items as you'll pay to get a whole load washed elsewhere.

Dangers & Annoyances There has been a noticeable increase in street crime over the past few years. That doesn't make San José as dangerous as other Latin American capitals, or many North American and European cities, but you should exercise basic precautions. Pickpockets and bag snatchers abound, so carry your money in an inside pocket and carry bags firmly attached to your body with a strap rather than let them dangle loosely over your shoulder. Keep day packs in front of you rather than on your back, where they can be unzipped and pilfered in a crowd. Don't wear expensive jewellery, watches etc downtown – they can be snatched off. The area around Avenida 2 and the Parque Central has been the scene of many pickpocketing attempts, particularly later at night, so be careful. (Nevertheless, I go to the Soda Palace on Avenida 2 and the Parque Central on a regular basis and haven't had any problems – though I'm tall and I like to think that I look like I know what I'm doing.)

Don't leave cars parked on the streets – find a guarded parking lot. Don't leave any packages inside the car (even if in a guarded lot) as they invite window-smashing and theft. Men should beware of friendly prostitutes – they pair up with you on quiet streets and will pickpocket you whilst distracting you. Prostitutes are known for their abilities to take more than you bargained for. Single women have complained of being harassed by cab drivers at night – the only advice I can offer is to firmly discourage a macho driver at the first sign of an inappropriate comment. (This does not happen very frequently.)

There have been some reports of the police stopping and searching lone tourists, especially at night. They claim they are looking for drugs but aren't supposed to do this unless you actually are committing a crime. Several tourists have reported having money stolen by policemen shaking them down. If stopped, insist that you will show them your passport in front of witnesses *(solamente con testigos)* and try to walk into a hotel, bar or restaurant.

The best way to prevent problems is to first find out (from your hotel or friends) about the area you are going to and, especially if bar-hopping at night, to go with a friend.

Spanish Courses

There are some excellent Spanish-language schools in San José, but they are not particularly cheap. Tuition is usually intensive, with class sizes varying from two to five pupils per teacher and individual tuition available. Classes are usually for several hours every week day. Most students are encouraged to stay with a Costa Rican family to immerse themselves in the language. Family homestays are arranged by the schools, as are the necessary visa extensions. Cheaper classes usually involve larger group sizes and/or fewer hours. Shorter and longer courses are available.

Most schools offer more than just language tuition. Lectures, discussions, field trips and other activities may be available – topics include the environment, women's issues, human rights, social studies, economics, political studies, agriculture, culture and travel.

Spending a month learning Spanish in Costa Rica is an excellent and recommended way of seeing and learning about the country.

Many language schools advertise in the

The Tico Times every week. If you want to arrange classes in advance, write to or call the following selection (arranged alphabetically) for details.

The first address given is the mailing address; the second address is the street or suburb where the school is, but addresses can change so telephone before heading over to a particular school. (I haven't found out about every existing school – non-inclusion does not automatically mean that the school is not good.)

Brief descriptions follow – most schools have longer or shorter programs than those I describe and will tailor a program to fit your needs.

Academia Costarricense de Lenguaje
> (☎ 21 1624, 33 8914, fax 33 8670), Apartado 336-2070, Sabanilla, San José. In the San Pedro suburb, this academy gives students a chance to learn about Costa Rican culture through (optional) lessons in music, cooking, dancing and customs.

American Institute for Language & Culture
> (☎ 25 4313, fax 24 4244), Apartado 200-1001, San José. This San Pedro suburb school offers homestay and four hours daily of instruction for individuals and small classes. Cultural and community activities are available. Rates start at US$300 per week.

Centro Cultural Costarricense-Norteamericano
> (☎ 25 9433, fax 24 1480), Apartado 1489-1000, San José. This school at Calle 37, Avenida 1 & 5, Los Yoses offers basic classes starting at US$375 for five weeks without homestays (which are also available). It also teaches English and has a large library of English books and offers other bicultural programs.

Centro Lingüístico Conversa
> (☎ 21 7649, fax 33 2418), Apartado 17-1007, Centro Colón, San José. There are two locations: Paseo Colón, Calle 38 & 40 in San José and in Santa Ana suburb. Cheap classes without homestays and for short periods are available in Paseo Colón. Classes in Santa Ana are intensive and include homestays and cultural programs – they start at US$1265 per month.

Centro Lingüístico Latinoamericano (CELL)
> (☎ 41 0261, 39 1869), Apartado 151, Alajuela. For those who don't want to stay in San José, this school is in San Antonio de Belén (near Alajuela). Individual instruction with homestay is US$900 per month – recommended by readers.

Centro Panamericano de Idiomas
(☎/fax 38 05610), Apartado 151-3007, San Joaquín, Heredia. Another out-of-but-close-to San José option, it offers four weeks of classes for US$560, or US$1000 with family homestay, all meals, and field trips. Classes average two or three students (four maximum).

Forester Instituto Internacional
(☎ 25 3155, fax 25 9236), Apartado 6945-1000, San José. About 75 metres south of the Automercado, Los Yoses. Prices start at US$600 for two weeks of classes with homestays.

ICADS – Institute for Central American Development Studies
(☎ 25 0508, fax 34 1337; or write to Dept 826, Box 025216, Miami, FL 33102-5216, USA), Apartado 3-2070, Sabanilla, San José. This school, in the suburb of San Pedro, offers 30 day intensive programs (4½ hours daily, three students maximum) for US$900, including homestay and meals. They have many extra lectures and activities devoted to environmental, women's and human rights issues and will place you in volunteer positions with local grass roots organisations. They also offer 'semester abroad' programs for college credit.

ICAI – Central American Institute for International Affairs
(☎ 33 8571, fax 21 5238), Apartado 10302, San José. In a residential area 10 minutes from the heart of San José, this program offers four week total immersion courses with homestays, lectures and field trips for US$895 and up, depending on the number of field trips.

ILISA – Instituto Latinoamericano de Idiomas
(☎ 25 2495, fax 25 4665; in the USA, 1 800 ESPANOL), Apartado 1001-2050, San Pedro. About 400 metres south and 50 metres east of the San Pedro church. They offer small groups (four students maximum), intensive studies (four to six hours a day), family homestays and a Central American history and culture program.

Instituto Britanico
(☎ 34 9054, 25 0256, fax 53 1894), Apartado 8184-1000, San José. About 75 metres south of the Subaru dealership in San Yoses. They also have a department in Liberia (☎ 66 2415). Prices start at US$325 for three weeks of classes; homestays and cultural activities are also available.

Instituto de Lengua Española
(☎ 27 7366, fax 27 0211), Apartado 100-2350, San José. In San Francisco suburb, this is a program for missionaries but lay-people are accepted if there is space available. An intensive 15 week program starts at US$750 (with discounts for missionaries).

Instituto Universal de Idiomas
(☎ 23 9662, fax 23 9917), Apartado 751-2150, Moravia. On the 2nd floor, Avenida 2, Calle 9, San José. They offer classes with six students maximum, ranging from three day crash courses (six hours a day, US$110) to economy packages (four weeks, three hours per day, homestay with meals, textbook and airport pick-up, US$680). Individual instruction is available for US$12 per hour.

Intensa
(☎ 25 6009, 24 6353, fax 53 8912), Apartado 8110-1000, San José. At Calle 33, Avenida 5 & 7, Barrio Escalante, they offer four week programs with homestay for US$775.

Lisa Tec
(☎/fax 39 2255), Apartado 228-4005, San Antonio de Belén. This school is near Cariari Country Club, 10 km north-west of downtown San José. Prices start at US$550 for two weeks including homestay, meals and field trips.

Mesoamerica Language Institute
(☎ 33 7710, 33 7112, fax 33 7221), Apartado 300-1002, San José. At Calle 13, Avenida 10 & 12 (1030) they offer a one day Spanish Survival course with six hours of instruction and lunch for US$60. A one week class (four hours per day) is US$95. Homestays can be arranged.

Dance Schools

Speak all the Spanish you need and want to meet some locals? Dance classes are offered not for tourists, but for ticos. Travellers who speak Spanish are welcomed. Classes teach Latin dancing – salsa, cha-cha-cha, merengue, bolero, tango etc, as well as the latest local dance crazes. Costs are inexpensive – around US$20 a month gives you two hours of classes per week.

Academia de Bailes Latinos
Avenida Central, Calle 25 & 27 (☎ 33 8938)
Bailes Latinos
Avenida Central, Calle 25 & 27 (☎ 21 1624)
Danza Viva
San Pedro (☎ 53 3110)
Latin Dancing Club (☎ 39 9116)
Malecón
Avenida 2, Calle 17 & 19
Merecumbe
Next to the US Embassy in Rohrmoser or in San Pedro (☎ 24 3531, 31 7496, 34 1548).

Museo de Jade

This is perhaps Costa Rica's most famous museum. It houses the world's largest collec-

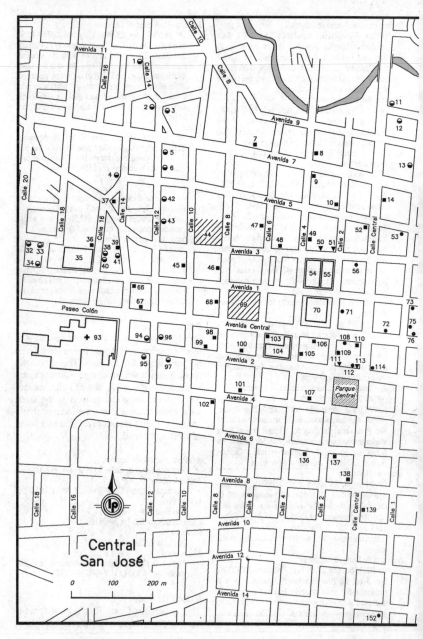

Central
San José

0   100   200 m

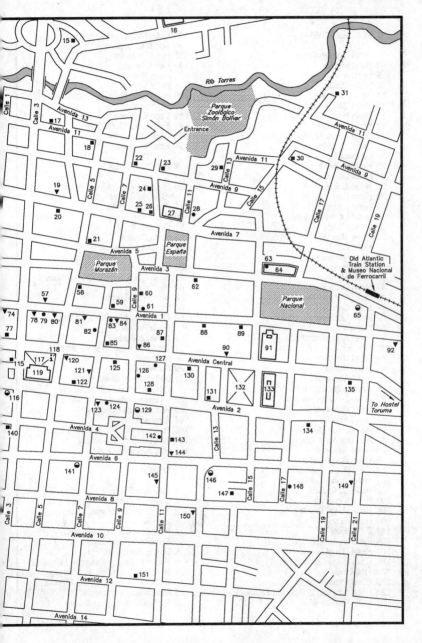

■ PLACES TO STAY

7   Hotel Garden Court
8   Hotel Marlyn
9   Hotel América
10 Hotel Rialto
14 Pensión Otoya
15 Hotel Villa Tournón
17 Hotel Hilda
18 Hotel Dunn Inn
20 Hotel Santo Tomás
21 Aurola Holiday Inn
22 La Casa Verde de Amón
23 Hemingway Inn
24 Hotel Don Carlos
25 Hotel Astoria
26 Hotel Rey
29 Hotel L'Ambiance
30 Hotel La Amistad Inn
31 D'Raya Vida
36 Hotel Musoc
37 Hotel Cocorí
39 Hotel Boruca
45 Hotel Bienvenido
46 Hotel Moderno
47 Hotel Compostela
48 Hotel Central
49 Hotel Capital
52 Hotel Europa
58 Diana's Inn
59 Hotel Amstel Morazán
60 Pensión Costa Rica Inn
62 Hotel Morazán
66 Hotel Roma
67 Hotel Alameda
68 Gran Hotel Imperial
77 Hotel La Gran Via
85 Hotel Balmoral
87 Hotel Asia
88 Pensión La Cuesta
89 Apartamentos Lamm
98 Hotel Johnson
99 Hotel Generaleño
100 Gran Hotel Centroamericano
101 Hotel Doral
102 Hotel La Aurora
103 Hotel Diplomat
105 Hotel Royal Dutch
106 Hotel Plaza
107 Park Hotel
109 Pensión Americana
110 Hotel Royal Garden
115 Gran Hotel Costa Rica
122 Tica Linda
125 Hotel Presidente
128 Hotel Avenida 2; Pensión Salamanca
130 Hotel Galilea

131 Hotel Nicaragua
134 Apartotel San José
135 Hotel Bellavista
136 Hotel Fortuna
137 Hotel Príncipe
138 Hotel Boston
139 Hotel Ritz; Pensión Centro
     Continental
140 Casa El Paso
143 Gran Hotel Doña Inés
147 Casa Ridgeway
151 Hotel La Gema

▼ PLACES TO EAT

16 El Pueblo Shopping Centre
     (Several Restaurants)
19 Restaurant Poás
50 Soda Nini
51 Lido Bar
57 Soda Central
74 Restaurant Vishnu
78 Restaurante Marisquería Omni
80 La Vasconia
81 Restaurant Goya & Chalet Suizo
84 Mr Pizza
86 Balcon de Europa
90 La Fogata
92 El Cuartel de la Boca de Monte
111 Soda Palace
113 Soda La Perla
119 Café Ruisenor (in the Teatro
     Nacional)
120 Soda B&B
121 La Hacienda Steak House,
     L'Ile de France & Restaurante Fulusu
122 La Esmeralda Bar/Restaurant
123 Restaurante Campesino
144 Tommy's Ribs
145 Restaurantes Tin-jo & Don Wang
149 La Cocina de Bordolino
150 Restaurant El Shakti

OTHER

1   Buses to Tilarán & Monteverde
2   Buses to Puerto Jiménez & Bejuco
3   Buses to Puntarenas, Guápiles,
     Río Frio
4   Buses to Nicoya, Sámana,
     Tamarindo, Coto Brus
5   Bus to Bejuco
6   Buses to Playas Panamá, Hermosa
11 Bus to Puerto Viejo de Sarapiquí
12 Buses to Cahuita, Bribri, Sixaola
13 Microbuses to Heredia
16 El Pueblo Shopping Centre

tion of American jade and hundreds of pieces are on display. Many pieces are mounted with a backlight so that the exquisite translucent quality of this gemstone can be fully appreciated. There are also archaeological exhibits of ceramics, stonework and gold, arranged by cultural regions.

The museum (☎ 23 5800, ext 2581) is on the 11th floor of the Instituto Nacional de Seguros at Calle 9, Avenida 7. It is open from 9 am to 3 pm Monday to Friday, and admission is free.

There is a good view of the city from the 11th floor vantage point – bring your camera. There's an interesting metal building to the south-west. It was designed in France and shipped over in prefabricated sections. It is now a school. With the city view, world-class jade collection and free admission, this museum is at the top of most visitors' lists of places to see.

Note that 'jade' is written the same as in English but is pronounced 'ha-day' in Spanish.

Museo Nacional

The Museo Nacional is housed in the Bellavista Fortress, the old army headquarters. The museum displays Costa Rican archaeology, some jade and gold, colonial furniture and costumes, colonial and religious art, and historical exhibits. Some pieces are labelled in English as well as Spanish. There is a small garden with cannons, and some of the walls are pockmarked with bullet holes from the 1948 civil war.

The museum (☎ 57 1433) is on Calle 17, Avenida Central & 2. Opening hours are from 9 am to 5 pm Tuesday to Sunday and admission is US$0.75; there is also a gift shop here. This is another favourite museum for visitors.

Museo del Oro Precolombino

This museum houses a dazzling collection of pre-Columbian gold pieces and is well worth seeing. There is also a small numismatic museum and a display of Costa Rican Art.

The museum (☎ 23 0528) is in the basement of the Plaza de la Cultura complex on Calle 5, Avenida Central & 2, under the tourist information office. The museum, owned by the Banco Central, is open from 10 am to 5 pm Friday to Sunday, and admission is free. Security is tight, however: you must leave your bags at the door and you may need to show your passport to get in.

Free bilingual (Spanish and English) guided tours are sometimes given – ask the doorkeeper about these. The museum was damaged in the 1991 earthquake and was temporarily closed. The current Friday to Sunday opening hours may well be extended in the future.

Museo de Arte Costarricense

This small art museum contains a collection of local paintings and sculpture from the 19th and 20th centuries. The sculptures are especially worth a look. There are also changing shows of local artists.

The museum (☎ 22 7155) is in Sabana Park, which used to be San José's airport. The collection is housed in the old control tower just off Calle 42, Paseo Colón & Avenida 2. Hours are 10 am to 5 pm Tuesday to Sunday; admission is US$0.75, but it is free on Sunday.

Galería Nacional de Arte Contemporaneo

The contemporary art gallery houses changing shows of working Costa Rican artists. It is next to the National Library on Calle 15, Avenida 3 & 5. Hours are from 10 am to 1 pm and 1.45 to 5 pm Monday to Saturday; admission is free.

Serpentario

This is a small but unusual collection of live snakes (as well as poison-arrow frogs) housed in the centre of San José. Anyone interested in reptile or amphibian identification will benefit from a visit to this live display of many of Costa Rica's exotic species.

A bilingual biologist is available to explain the collection and there is a small gift shop. The serpentarium (☎ 55 4210) is on Avenida 1, Calle 9 & 11, and is open from 10 am to 7 pm daily; admission is US$1.50.

Museo de Ciencias Naturales

The Natural History Museum is housed in the old Colegio (High School) La Salle near the south-west corner of Sabana Park. Basically it is a collection of stuffed animals and mounted butterflies, and is a resource for those wishing to identify some of the species they may see in the wild. There are also paleontology and archaeology exhibits.

The museum (☎ 32 1306) is open from 7.30 am to 3 pm on weekdays and 8 am to noon on Saturday (recent reports are that it's closed on Saturday – call ahead); admission is US$0.75 (half price for students).

Most cab drivers know the Colegio La Salle and charge less than US$2 to get there. A Sabana-Estadio or Sabana-Cementario city bus from the Parque Central will take you there for a few cents – ask the driver to let you know where the museum is.

Museo de Insectos

Also known as the Entomology Museum, this is a fine collection of insects curated by the Facultad de Agronomía at the Universidad de Costa Rica. It is claimed that this is the only insect museum of any size in Central America – I don't know if that's true but the collection is certainly extensive and many splendid and exotic insects can be seen.

Surprisingly, the museum (☎ 53 5323, 53 3253 ext 5318) is housed in the basement of the Artes Musicales building on campus. It is signposted, or you can ask for directions. Hours are from 1 to 4.45 pm on weekdays, and admission is US$0.75; ring the bell to gain admission. A cab to the University (in San Pedro) costs about US$2 or take a San Pedro bus along Avenida 2 from Calle 5.

Parque Zoológico Simón Bolívar
This small national zoo (☎ 33 6701) is in the Simón Bolívar Park, hence its name. Many of Costa Rica's animals are to be seen, along with a small sprinkling of exotics.

Unfortunately, as in many Latin American countries, the cages are too small, although not as bad as in some zoos I've seen. The zoo is popular with josefinos at weekends. The gate is at Avenida 11, Calle 7 & 9 (go north on Calle 7 and east on Avenida 11 to get there). Hours are from 8.30 am to 3.30 pm daily; admission is US$0.30.

Spirogyra Jardín de Mariposas
Not to be confused with the large butterfly farm in La Guacima, this smaller version offers close-up looks at Costa Rican butterflies in a garden setting close to downtown. The garden is 100 metres east and 150 metres south of Centro Comercial El Pueblo and can be reached on foot (about a half hour from downtown), by taxi or by buses to El Pueblo (from where there is a sign). Spirogyra (☎ 22 2937) is open daily from 9 am to 4 pm, except Tuesday; the last guided tour starts at 3.30 pm. Admission is US$4.

Museo Postal, Telegráfico y Filatélico de Costa Rica
This museum (☎ 23 9766, ext 269) is upstairs in the CPO, Calle 2, Avenida 1 & 3. Hours are 8 am to 4 pm Monday to Friday; admission is free.

Museo de Criminología
The stated objective of this museum (☎ 23 0666, ext 2378) is the prevention of crime through the presentation of exhibits of criminal acts. I plead guilty to not personally visiting this museum, which reportedly contains such niceties as limbs which have been separated from their rightful owners by machete-wielding criminals.

These displays may be high on the 'must see lists' of visitors travelling with male offspring. 'Wayyyy cool, dad!' The museum is in the Supreme Court of Justice, Calle 17, Avenida 6, open from 1 to 4 pm on Monday, Wednesday and Thursday.

Museo Nacional de Ferrocarril
Inaugurated in May 1993, this is the most recently opened of the capital's museums. Railroad buffs will want to see the first locomotive serving the San José-Limón run, as well as a model railway, old photographs and railroad paraphernalia.

The museum is appropriately housed in the old Atlantic railway station at Avenida 3, Calle 19 and is open from 9 am to 4 pm Monday to Thursday, 9 am to 3.30 pm on Friday, and 10 am to 3 pm on weekends. Admission is US$0.75.

Museo de Fotos
This privately owned collection of many thousands of photographs gives a glimpse of life in Costa Rica during the early 1900s. The museum is on Calle 7, Avenida Central & 1. It is open from 8.30 to 11.15 am and 1.30 to 5 pm Monday to Friday, and from 8.30 to 11.15 am on Saturday. Admission is US$2.25.

Teatro Nacional
The Teatro Nacional is considered San José's most impressive public building. Built in the 1890s, the Teatro Nacional is the centre of Costa Rican culture. The outside is not particularly impressive, with statues of Beethoven and Calderón de la Barca (a 17th century Spanish dramatist) flanking the entrance, and a columned façade.

Inside, there are some paintings of Costa Rica, of which the most famous is a huge canvas showing coffee harvesting and export. It was painted in Italy in the late 19th century and was reproduced on the five colón note. (This note is now out of circulation, but can sometimes be obtained in banks – or by paying 100 colones to one of the street vendors outside).

The marble staircases, gilded ceilings, and parquet floors of local hardwoods are worth seeing. Unfortunately, these were all severely damaged in the 1991 earthquake and the theatre was closed until early 1993. Repairs are still continuing in some of the rooms, though the main auditorium is now functioning.

There are regular performances in the theatre and this is the best way to see the inside of the building. I saw the highly acclaimed national symphony orchestra here, got a great seat and had a fine time. Otherwise, the theatre is open from 10 am to noon and 2 to 6 pm Monday to Friday; it costs about US$1.80 to visit. There is a pleasant coffee shop to the left of the lobby with changing shows of local artists, good coffee and a quiet atmosphere in which to write postcards – though it gets very crowded at lunchtime.

Mercado Central

This market is interesting to visit if you've never been to a Latin American market, although it is a little tame compared to the markets of many other countries. Nevertheless, it is crowded and bustling, has a variety of produce and other goods ranging from live turkeys to leatherwork for sale. Some of the cheapest meals in town are served here.

The Central Market is at Avenida Central & 1, Calle 6 & 8. A block away at Avenida 3, Calle 8 is the similar Mercado Borbón. Beware of pickpockets in these areas. The streets surrounding the markets are jam-packed with vendors.

Parque Nacional

This pleasant and shady park is between Avenida 1 & 3, Calle 15 & 19. It has two statues of note. In the centre of the park is the Monumento Nacional showing the Central American nations driving out William Walker. Opposite the south-west corner is a statue of national hero Juan Santamaría.

Important buildings surrounding the park include the Asamblea Legislativa (Legislative Assembly or Congress Building) to the south, the Biblioteca Nacional (National Library) to the north, and the Fábrica Nacio-

nal de Licores (National Liquor Factory, founded in 1856) to the north-west.

Parque España

This small park seems to have some of the tallest trees in San José. It is a riot of birdsong just before sunset, and a riot of colour on Sunday when there is an outdoor art market. The park is between Avenida 3 & 7, Calle 9 & 11.

To the north of the park is the INS building, housing the Jade Museum, and fronted by a huge statue of 'The Family'. To the west is the famous iron building (now a school); to the east is the Liquor Factory; and to the north-east is the Casa Amarilla (Yellow House), which is Costa Rica's Ministry of Foreign Affairs.

Parque Morazán

This park covers four city blocks and is graced in the centre by a dome-roofed structure, the so-called Templo de Musica. There are several other statues and monuments. The north-east quarter of the park has a small Japanese garden. Parents with small children should note there is a playground here. The park is around the intersection of Calle 7 and Avenida 3.

Plaza de la Cultura

This plaza is not particularly prepossessing in itself, but it is the site of the Teatro Nacional, Museo de Oro and ICT office. In addition, the western side of the plaza is an open-air market of arts and crafts – it gets very busy just before Christmas and around other holidays. Young people hang out here and check out what everyone else is doing – a good place to people-watch.

Every once in a while the municipal authorities ban the street vendors from the plaza – but they seem to drift back again a few weeks later.

Parque Central

This park is between Avenida 2 & 4, Calle Central & 2. These streets are very busy (especially Avenida 2) and the park is known as the place to catch many of the local city buses. To the east is the fairly modern and not very interesting Catedral Metropolitana. To the north is the well-known Teatro Melico Salazar and the Soda Palace Bar, which is a plain but very popular 24 hour soda restaurant and bar.

Tours

The following is a list of the most popular tours offered in, around, and out of San José. Approximate prices per person are given, but look around for occasional bargains such as two people for the price of one.

Day tours normally include lunch and pick up and return from your San José hotel; multi-day tours normally include overnight accommodation, meals and transport. Guides, usually bilingual in English, accompany most tours.

For a full list of tour operators, see the Getting Around chapter.

Half-day city tour – US$17 to US$20
Half-day tours to one of the following: Volcán Irazú; Volcán Poás; ox-cart factory at Sarchí; Valle de Orosi; coffee tour; butterfly farm – US$20 to US$30
Full day tours combining two of the above – US$40 to US$50
Full-day tours to one of the following: Jungle Train with Parque Nacional de Braulio Carrillo; Volcán Arenal; Volcán Barva; Reserva Biológica Carara with Playa de Jacó; Cerro de la Muerte; Refugio Nacional de Fauna Silvestre Tapantí; La Virgen del Socorro; Golfo de Nicoya cruise to Isla Tortuga; horse-riding; white-water rafting trip on one of the Reventazón, Sarapiquí or Corobicí rivers – US$50 to US$90. (Note: one-day tours from San José to Manuel Antonio, Tortuguero, Caño Negro or Monteverde are offered from about US$100. I feel these involve too much travel to be comfortable one-day trips, though by all means take one if your time is limited.)
Two days/one night river rafting and camping – US$250 to US$300
Three days/two nights at Tortuguero – per person, double occupancy, US$180 to US$265 and up depending on transport, accommodation and guides desired
Three days/two nights at Monteverde – per person, double occupancy, US$265 and up

Bungy Jumping

Yes, finally in Costa Rica...you can safely make a head-first screaming plunge off a bridge to which you are safely attached with a 60 metre elastic rope. After safely bouncing around for a while you are gently lowered into a river before you can swim to shore. Highly trained jump masters guarantee your safety.

For further information contact Tropical Bungee (☎ 33 6455) – it is affiliated with Ríos Tropicales which has several years of experience in adventure activities in Costa Rica.

Or call the German-certified Eurobungy at Saragundí Speciality Tours (☎ 55 0011, 55 2055) at Avenida 7, Calle Central & 1. If you just want to watch the jumpers from the safety of solid ground (or bridge), contact these outfits anyway. They'll provide transportation for spectators as well as jumpers.

Surfing

Surfers can obtain up-to-date wave information, and buy, sell, repair or rent surfing equipment from surf shops in San Pedro. Mango Surf Shop (☎ 25 1067) is 25 metres west of the Banco Popular in San Pedro – it also has a branch in Escazú (☎ 89 7469). Keola Surf Shop (☎ 25 6041) is 100 metres east and 100 metres south of the Banco Popular.

Places to Stay

There are well over 100 hotels of all types in San José, but accommodation may be tight during the high season (December to May) and especially in the week before and after Christmas and the week before Easter. If you want to stay in a particular hotel then, you should make reservations – as much as three months in advance for Christmas and Easter. Reservations should be prepaid, or they will sometimes be ignored. If you have no reservations, you can find rooms, but your choices are limited.

Although there is a large choice of hotels, I find that the accommodation is generally lacklustre, especially downtown. Many hotels, although clean and secure, tend to suffer from musty carpets, street noise and unappealing décor (though there are exceptions – especially the smaller hotels which are often in beautifully restored older houses).

For people staying for a while *apartotels* offer furnished rooms with kitchens at medium hotel rates; you can also look in the newspapers for apartments to rent. Those advertising in the Spanish-language *La Nación* are generally a little cheaper than those advertising in the English-language *The Tico Times*. The most luxurious hotels are good, but not many travellers want to pay US$100 or more for a room. Budget hotel rooms are usually grim and noisy little boxes, but at least they are fairly cheap. There is also a youth hostel.

Since the early 1990s, however, a large number of small bed & breakfast hotels have appeared on the scene and offer a reasonably priced alternative to the more traditional hotels. B&Bs offer more than just breakfast with your room – they also tend to provide a family-like atmosphere in a house rather than a more impersonal hotel. Many of them are in the suburbs, but buses or taxis will get you into town quite easily. A B&B group has formed and will provide referrals as well as make reservations for you all over the country.

Further information can be obtained from co-founders Debbi McMurray at D'Raya Vida (☎ 23 4168, fax 23 4157) or Pat Bliss at Park Place (☎/fax 28 9200) or write to the Costa Rica Bed & Breakfast Group (CRBBG), Apartado 1012, Escazú, Costa Rica. Members of this group are denoted by CRBBG in the listings given in this chapter and throughout the book.

Another alternative is the homestay concept. You stay with a local family (most are ticos, a few are foreign residents) who provide a room for one to three guests. Thus you or your small group will be the only guests and you receive a more in-depth look at Costa Rica, often participating in family activities and so on. Host families may or may not speak English, smoke, have children, have pets, have private showers for guests. All are unique.

One agency that has been highly recom-

mended is run by Vernon Bell (a Californian who has lived in Costa Rica for two decades) and his tica wife, Marcela. They have some 70 homes available, each of which has been personally inspected to maintain their high standards of cleanliness and wholesomeness. They'll help to match you up with a suitable host family.

Rates are US$35/53 single/double, including breakfast, or an extra US$6 with private bath. Dinners are US$6 per person. Contact Bell's Home Hospitality (☎ 25 4752, fax 24 5884, Apartado 185-1000, San José).

Another organisation offering homestays is Costa Rica Home & Host Inc (☎ 612 871 0596, fax 612 871 8853; 2445 Park Ave, Minneapolis, MN 55404, USA). They guarantee English-speaking hosts and provide cultural events and all meals – their prices are concomitantly higher.

Many of the mid-priced and all of the top-end hotels will accept reservations from outside Costa Rica by phone or mail. Some have US telephone numbers (occasionally toll free). A reservation deposit is normally required. A good travel agent will help you make reservations from home.

Local phone numbers and street addresses are given below, and, for those hotels which normally accept reservations from abroad, postal addresses (Apartados) and/or US phone numbers are also given.

If you are making mail reservations, allow several months – letters can be very slow. Phoning, faxing or using a travel agent are the best ways to make reservations.

Bottom-end hotels may not accept reservations, but the phone numbers will at least enable you to find out if they have room available.

Prices given here (and in the rest of the book) are current high-season rates, including the 14% government and tourist tax.

For San José, bottom-end hotels provide doubles for US$4.40 to about US$20, middle hotels are in the US$20 to US$60 a double range and top-end places cost from US$60 and up. The big boom in tourism will mean that price levels may change quickly.

Places to Stay – bottom end

Hotels Many cheap hotels are found west of Calle Central. There have been reports of occasional thefts and a mugging in the area around the Coca-Cola bus terminal, Mercado Central and Parque Central I've stayed in this neighbourhood several times (no, I don't always stay in dives), and haven't had any problems, but budget travellers should keep their eyes open and use taxis if arriving at night.

Many shoestring travellers head for the basic *Gran Hotel Imperial* (☎ 22 7899), Calle 8, Avenida Central & 1. Fronted by an unprepossessing chained iron door leading into a bare stairwell, this cavernous hotel provides all the bare necessities – security, reasonably clean beds, rather grungy showers that have hot water once in a while, and one of the best value cheap restaurants in town. Rooms are US$2.20 per person (though there are few singles) and the place is full of international backpackers. They'll hold a room for you until the afternoon if you call ahead.

Another place which is popular with young travellers on the 'gringo trail', is the *Tica Linda* (☎ 33 0528) at Avenida 2, Calle 5 & 7. It's next door to the La Esmeralda Bar where *mariachis* play late into the night. (Mariachis are bands of Mexican street musicians whose members dress elegantly in tight-fitting sequined suits and enormous sombreros.) The sign is just a tiny plate on the door – ring the bell to get in. Cramped rooms, which sleep four, are US$3.30 per person or you can have your own private little box for US$4.40. The place is noisy but friendly and secure. Laundry facilities are available, but its main attraction is as a place to meet other travellers.

Other basic places to try include the *Hotel Nicaragua* (☎ 23 0292), Avenida 2, Calle 13, which charges US$2.20 per person. The small hotel is family run, reasonably clean, friendly and secure. There are only cold water showers and the hotel is often full with travellers from other Central American countries.

Nearby is the basic but clean and OK *Hotel Avenida 2* (☎ 22 0260) at Avenida 2, Calle 9 & 11, which has hot showers and charges US$4.40 per person. On the same block is the more basic *Pensión Salamanca* at Avenida 2, Calle 9 & 11. The charge is US$2.20 per person in box-like rooms and there are cold showers only. The *Hotel Moderno* (☎ 21 2572), Calle 8, Avenida 1 & 3, is a basic cold water hotel charging US$2.60/3.70 single/double (one bed) or US$5.10 a double (two beds).

Another reasonable cheapie is the *Hotel Rialto* (☎ 21 7456), Calle 2, Avenida 5, which is decent, has hot water in the mornings and charges US$4.40/5.10 for a single/double, or US$6.60 with a private washbasin and toilet. The *Hotel América* (☎ 21 4116), Calle 4, Avenida 7, is clean but lacks hot water – rooms are US$7.30 a double. Another cheap place is the *Hotel Marlyn* (☎ 33 3212), Calle 4, Avenida 7 & 9, which charges US$5.50 for a small single or double with communal cold showers, or US$10 with private bath and (usually) hot water. This is very secure – the entrance is always locked and the owners let you in personally.

The basic but secure *Hotel Asia* (☎ 23 3893), Calle 11, Avenida Central & 1, charges US$5.25/7.50 single/double in small but clean rooms and has hot water in the communal showers. The *Hotel Generaleño* (☎ 33 7877), Avenida 2, Calle 8 & 10, is large, clean, but basic and has cold showers only. Spartan rooms are US$3.70 per person.

The *Hotel Boruca* (☎ 23 0016), Calle 14, Avenida 1 & 3, is convenient for buses but some rooms are somewhat noisy because of them. It is family run, friendly, secure, clean and has hot water some of the time. Rooms are small and cost US$4.40 per person. Nearby is the similarly priced *Hotel Roma* (☎ 23 2179), Calle 14, Avenida Central & 1. It is adequate, clean and secure, but spartan and has cold water only.

A less noisy (though not necessarily quiet) choice is the *Hotel Central* (☎ 22 3509, 21 2767) at Avenida 3, Calle 4 & 6. It has large clean rooms for US$11.75/15.50 single/double with private bath and tepid water.

Four people can share a room for US$20.50. The upstairs rooms are the nicest. The *Hotel Astoria* (☎ 21 2174, fax 21 8497), Avenida 7, Calle 7 & 9, has been popular for years and is often full, though it's not especially remarkable. They have a few very basic and grim rooms in the back for US$4.40 per person and some better rooms with private bath and hot water for US$17.50 a double.

The *Pensión Americana* (☎ 21 4171, 21 9799), Calle 2, Avenida Central & 2, charges US$5.10 per person in large but dark rooms, though there is a pleasant TV room and the management is friendly. The communal showers are cold. The *Hotel Boston* (☎ 21 0563), Avenida 8, Calle Central & 2, has large rooms with private baths and tepid water for US$9.50/12.50 single/double. The management is friendly, some rooms are noisy, but inside rooms are reasonably quiet.

The *Hotel Morazán* (☎ 21 9083), Avenida 3, Calle 11 & 15, has large, clean, bare rooms, and it is secure. When I went there in March (high season) I was quoted US$7.25 for a single with communal cold shower and US$14.50 a double with hot water, but a friend who visited in September (low season) was quoted about half these prices.

The *Pensión Otoya* (☎ 21 3925), Calle Central, Avenida 5 & 7 is clean, friendly, has long been popular with foreigners and is often full. Decent rooms are US$7/12 or US$10/14 single/double with private bath and hot water. The *Hotel Príncipe* (☎ 22 7983, 23 1589), Avenida 6, Calle Central & 2, is secure and has good rooms with private warm showers for US$10/15 single/double. Some readers have complained that the sheets weren't clean and there were several cockroaches. The secure *Hotel Compostela* (☎ 21 0694), Calle 6, Avenida 3 & 5, charges US$12.50 for very clean single or double rooms – each room has a private hot bath, but you have to cross the corridor to reach it. They also have small rooms for US$5.10 per person with communal cold showers. The *Hotel La Aurora* (☎ 22 1463), Calle 8, Avenida 4, is reasonably clean and has rooms with private hot showers – those on the outside suffer from street noise. Rooms with

one bed are US$10 (single/double) and rooms with two beds are US$18.50.

The *Pensión Centro Continental* (☎ 22 4103), Calle Central, Avenida 8 & 10, is run by the same folks who run the neighbouring middle-priced Hotel Ritz. It is a small but clean and friendly hotel and it is popular. There are kitchen facilities and tepid electric communal showers. Rooms are US$7/12.20 for singles/doubles and US$3.70 per extra person (up to five people).

The *Hotel Musoc* (☎ 22 9437, fax 55 0031, Apartado 1049-1000, San José), Calle 16, Avenida 1 & 3, is a large building which is very convenient for the Coca-Cola bus terminal. The hotel is clean, has English-speaking staff and accepts credit cards – but I have received criticisms of their left luggage facility. They charge US$10/16 for singles/doubles and US$12/17.50 in rooms with private hot showers. The *Hotel Cocorí* (☎ 33 0081, 33 2188), Calle 16, Avenida 3, is also near the Coca-Cola bus terminal. Clean rooms with private hot showers are US$13/17.50 for a single/double, or US$11.25/14.25 in rooms with communal cold showers.

The *Casa Leo* (☎ 22 9725), Avenida 6 bis, Calle 13 & 15, charges US$8 per person in dormitories and US$10 per person in private rooms. Bathrooms have hot showers, kitchen privileges are available, the owners are friendly and helpful with tourist information, and the place attracts budget travellers.

The *Hotel Johnson* (☎ 23 7633, 23 7827, fax 22 3683, Apartado 6638-1000, San José), Calle 8, Avenida Central & 2, accepts credit cards and reservations, has hot water in the private showers, and reasonably sized rooms with telephones and fax facilities. This makes it popular with Central Americans in town on business and is a good choice for a budget traveller needing the facilities offered (and which I used on several occasions).

This large hotel has about 60 rooms. The quiet inside rooms are a bit on the dark side and the beds have seen better days but – you can't expect the Hilton for these prices. One of my guide-book writing colleagues was much taken by the double bass decorating the 3rd floor – there's no accounting for tastes. Talking of taste – there is a mid-priced restaurant and bar on the premises, with music on Friday nights. Rates are US$13/16.25 for singles/doubles. Some rooms which take up to five people cost about US$22.

The *Hotel Bellavista* (☎ 23 0095), Avenida Central, Calle 19 & 21, is friendly and clean, and has pleasant rooms with private baths and hot water for US$30 a double, plus US$3 for additional people. The *Gran Hotel Centroamericano* (☎ 21 3362; Apartado 3072-1000, San José), Avenida 2, Calle 6 & 8, has rather small, dark rooms with private bathroom and tepid water for US$15 a single and about US$3.50 more for each extra person (up to six people). Its main attraction is its central location. The *Hotel Bienvenido* (☎ 21 1872, 33 2161; Apartado 389-2200, San José), Calle 10, Avenida 1 & 3, is secure, has helpful staff and good clean rooms with hot water sometimes. Rates are US$15/18.50 for singles/doubles.

Hostels There is one youth hostel which is associated with the IYHF. This is the *Hostel Toruma* (☎/fax 24 4085 or ☎ 53 6588; Apartado 1355-1002 PE, San José), Avenida Central, Calle 29 & 31, a little over a km east of downtown. There are bunk beds in segregated dormitories, and hot water is available at times. The charge is US$6.15 per person for IYHF members, and US$7.90 for non-members. (The hostel was remodelled in 1993 and may raise its prices.)

Inexpensive meals are available in the cafeteria. There used to be an 11 pm curfew (though exit passes were available); check this. Laundry facilities are available in the afternoons. There is a message board and it is a good place to meet other budget travellers.

The hostel is also the headquarters for the network of Costa Rican youth hostels and information and reservations for the others can be made here. (Note that the San José hostel is by far the cheapest – the others offer private rather than dormitory rooms). They are at Rincón de la Vieja, Rara Avis, Arenal,

Fortuna, Puntarenas and Chilamate de Sarapiquí; others are planned.

One reader found that a reservation she made at the Toruma for the Arenal Hostel was not properly confirmed. I suggest that you receive and carry a written copy of all confirmed reservations made at the Toruma for hostels elsewhere.

An interesting small hostel is the *Casa Ridgeway* (☎ 33 6168), Calle 15, Avenida 6 bis, 1336 (Avenida 6 bis runs between Avenida 6 & 8, west of Calle 15). This hostel was formerly known as the Peace Centre and continues to remain affiliated with and operated by Quakers. It is a useful place for information and discussion of peace issues. There is a small library and the centre is staffed mainly by volunteers. Accommodation is available for US$10 per person in one single and four double rooms (strangers may share a double room if they wish). There are basic kitchen facilities and communal hot showers.

Places to Stay – middle

Hotels The Swiss-run *Hotel Ritz* (☎ 22 4103, fax 22 8849, Apartado 6783-1000, San José), Calle Central, Avenida 8 & 10, also runs the cheaper Pensión Centro Continental next door. They are friendly and helpful. Rooms are US$12.50/19.50 single/double or US$18/24 with private bathrooms and tepid water.

The *Petit Hotel* (☎ 33 0766, fax 33 1938, Apartado 357-1007, Centro Colón, San José), Calle 24, Paseo Colón & Avenida 2 (25 metres south of the Mercedes Benz dealer on Paseo Colón – tell that to the cab driver and get tico treatment), is a friendly but not fancy hotel which allows kitchen privileges on request and has electric showers. Rooms vary substantially, so try to look at several before choosing. Rates are US$19 (single or double) with communal bathroom and US$29 to US$32 with private bathroom.

The *Pensión Costa Rica Inn* (☎ 22 5203, fax 23 8385; Apartado 10282-1000, San José); in the USA (☎ 1 (800) 637 0899, 318 263 2059; PO Box 59, Arcadia, LA 71001, USA), Calle 9, Avenida 1 & 3, is central and has hot water, but the rooms are small and some lack outside windows. The inn is popular with North Americans, perhaps because it has a toll-free number in the USA for reservations. Rooms are US$22/28 single/double.

The *Hotel Cacts* (☎ 21 2928, 21 6546, fax 21 8616; Apartado 379-1005, San José) is a little out of the way at Avenida 3 bis, Calle 28 & 30, but is quiet because of that. This is a small but popular hotel. Friendly management, clean and spacious rooms, hot water in the private baths, and breakfast is included in the price of US$31/35 single/double, or US$4 less in rooms with communal bathrooms.

The *Hotel Galilea* (☎ 33 6925, fax 23 1689), Avenida Central, Calle 11 & 13, is clean, pleasant and helpful, and is near several museums. The hotel card claims that their fax speaks English OK. The hotel is popular with biologists and researchers, and students can get a discount, as can visitors spending a week or more. Rooms with private baths and hot water are US$23/29 single/double – ask for an inside room if you like quiet.

Another clean and quiet choice is the *Hotel Fortuna* (☎ 23 5344), Avenida 6, Calle 2 & 4, which has decent rooms with good beds and private hot showers for US$20/31 single/double. Less decent is the *Park Hotel* (☎ 21 6944), Avenida 4, Calle 2 & 4, which charges US$30 for a room with hot water – men bringing in women are charged the same as singles. At least the rooms are clean.

Several other hotels are in this price range for rooms with private bathroom. All are acceptable. The *Hotel Diplomat* (☎ 21 8133, 21 8744; Apartado 6606, San José), Calle 6, Avenida Central & 2, has a good restaurant. Good rooms are US$24/33 but showers are tepid.

The *Hotel Capital* (☎ 21 8583, fax 21 8497; Apartado 6091-1000, San José), Calle 4, Avenida 3 & 5, charges US$22/26 for fairly basic singles/doubles with hot water. The *Hotel Doral* (☎ 33 0665, 33 5069, fax 33 4827; Apartado 5530-1000, San José), Avenida 4, Calle 6 & 8, has nice rooms with

TV, telephone and private hot showers for US$24/36. There is a bar and restaurant.

The *Hotel Garden Court* (☎ 55 4766, fax 55 4613; in the USA, ☎ 1 (800) 272 6654; Apartado 962-1000, San José), Avenida 7, Calle 6, is a large hotel with pool, sauna, tour information, parking, airport shuttle bus, and restaurant. Rooms are air-conditioned and have TV, telephone and hot water, and the price of US$37/47 includes breakfast. This is good value – but the neighbourhood is not the best. The *Hotel La Gema* (☎ 57 2524, fax 22 1074; Apartado 5729-1000, San José), Avenida 12, Calle 9 & 11, has pleasant rooms with fans, hot water, TV and telephone for US$32/44 and there is a restaurant on the premises. The *Hotel Alameda* (☎ 23 6333, fax 22 9673; Apartado 680-1000, San José), Avenida Central, Calle 12, has a restaurant and is quite close to the bus terminals. The staff is friendly and the rooms are clean, though noisy on the street side (a standard problem in downtown hotels). Rates are about US$38/48 and rooms with up to five beds are available. This is one of the largest hotels in this price range, with over 50 rooms all with private hot showers.

The *Hotel Plaza* (☎ 22 5533, 22 58 27, fax 22 2641; Apartado 2019-1000, San José), Avenida Central, Calle 2 & 4, charges US$40/52 for nice rooms in the heart of downtown. The *Hotel La Gran Via* (☎ 22 7737, fax 22 7205; Apartado 1433-1000, San José), Avenida Central, Calle 1 & 3, has some attractive rooms with balconies onto the street (which is a pedestrian zone, so traffic noise is minimised) and quieter inside rooms, some of which are air-conditioned. The cost is US$48/60 for singles/doubles.

The *Hotel Amstel Morazán* (☎ 22 4622, fax 33 3329; Apartado 4192-1000, San José), Avenida 1, Calle 7, is central and has comfortable air-conditioned rooms for US$50/58 or a few dollar more for 'superior' rooms – one reader complains of a lost reservation so be sure to get reservations confirmed in writing (or by fax). Apart from the central location, its main attraction is a good and popular restaurant (reservations accepted). The hotel was formerly the Hotel

Amstel, but the owners are planning on opening the top-end *Amstel Amón* in 1994 (see following).

The *Hotel Royal Garden* (☎ 57 0022 or 0023, fax 57 1517; Apartado 3493-1000, San José), Calle Central, Avenida Central & 2, charges US$52/57 for singles/doubles. It has a casino, a good Chinese restaurant (featuring Dim Sum), and quiet, pleasant rooms with air-conditioning, TV, and telephone. The *Hotel Dunn Inn* (☎ 22 3232, 22 3426, fax 21 4596; Apartado 1584-1000, San José), Calle 5, Avenida 11, is a small hotel in an attractive late 19th century house. It is owned by a North American whose name is Dunn. Unpretentious but comfortable rooms begin around US$55 a single or double. The *Hotel Royal Dutch* (☎ 24 1414, 21 4000), Calle 4, Avenida Central & 2, calls itself a 'Budget Hotel in the Heart of Town' and charges US$48/63 for singles/doubles. Rooms are large, air-conditioned and have TV and phones.

Apartotels These are a cross between an apartment building and a hotel. Rooms come fully furnished and have TV and telephone, private bathroom and a kitchen unit including utensils. There is often a separate sitting room. Apartotels are designed for people who wish to cater for themselves to some extent. Although singles and doubles are always available, rooms are also suitable for families.

Apartotels can be rented by the day (which are the prices I give) but discounts are available for stays of a week or a month. If you do not need to be in the town centre, and do not need restaurant, casino and travel agent facilities in the hotel, then these apartotels provide some of the best value accommodation in San José. You should think ahead, however, as they are often booked up during the high season.

Apartamentos Lamm (☎ 21 4920, fax 21 4720; Apartado 2729-1000, San José) is at Calle 15, Avenida 1. Rates are US$40 per day, US$265 per week, and US$965 for four weeks. There is maid service and laundry available, the place (although in an older

building) is clean and the staff are helpful. Apartments come with sitting rooms, and some have two bedrooms.

The *Apartotel San José* (☎ 22 0455, fax 33 3329; Apartado 4192-1000, San José), Calle 17, Avenida 2, is in a more modern building near the Museo Nacional. Rates are US$48/55 single/double in one-bedroom apartments and US$66/71 in two-bedroom apartments (which sleep five for US$84).

At the other end of downtown is the *Apartotel Castilla* (☎ 22 2113, ☎/fax 21 2080; Apartado 944-1007, San José), Calle 24, Avenida 2 & 4, which charges from US$37 a single to US$61 for four people and also features maid and laundry service. Monthly discounts are 20%.

All the following places are west of the centre. The *Apartotel Ramgo* (☎ 32 3823, 32 3366, fax 32 3111; Apartado 1441-1000, San José) is at Sabana Sur, a block south of the Parque La Sabana. Buses for downtown stop nearby. All apartments come with two bedrooms. Daily rates are US$52 a double, or US$63 for four people. The new *Apartotel La Sabana* (☎ 20 2422, fax 31 7386; Apartado 8446-1000, San José) is 50 metres west and 150 metres north of the Burger King on La Sabana. They have a pool, sauna, laundry service and air-conditioned apartments ranging from US$40 to US$86 depending on the size.

Further away from the centre towards the east is *Apartotel Conquistador* (☎ 25 3022; Apartado 303-2050, San Pedro, San José) in Los Yoses. They have a variety of units ranging from studios to two-bedroom apartments and there is a swimming pool available. Also in Los Yoses is the more expensive *Apartotel Los Yoses* (☎ 25 0033, 25 0044, fax 25 5595; Apartado 1597-1000, San José). They also have a pool and a variety of apartments ranging in price from US$46 to US$57 a single, from US$54 to US$65 a double, and US$84 for four people.

Just before Los Yoses is *Apartotel Don Carlos* (☎ 21 6707, fax 55 0828; Apartado 1593, 1000 San José) at Calle 29, Avenida Central (25 metres south of Pollos Kentucky). This is managed by the folks who own the top-end Hotel Don Carlos – it's a well-run place. They prefer weekly renters; rates are US$400 per week or US$1030 per month. Nearby is *Apartamentos Scotland* (☎ 23 0833 or 0033), Avenida 1, Calle 27, which caters mainly for long-stay guests. One-bedroom apartments start at US$225 a week or US$450 a month.

Another choice for long-term stays is renting a house. Paul Vigneault (of the Hotel Jaguar in Cahuita) has furnished three-bedroom, two-bathroom houses in the suburbs, two blocks from a bus route into town. Rates per house, including maid service and utilities, are US$172 a week or US$550 per month. Contact Consulta Pavi (☎ 26 3775, fax 26 4693; Apartado 7046, San José) for information.

B&Bs From a couple of places in the 1980s to dozens today – the B&B phenomenon has swept San José. See the introduction to Places to Stay above for more information. Those places listed here are middle priced – see under top end and out of town for more options.

Pensión La Cuesta (☎ 55 2896, fax 57 2272) is on a little hill cuesta behind the Asamblea Legislativa on Avenida 1, Calle 11 & 15. It is an attractive house with plenty of art work (the owner is an artist) and a pleasant living room for hanging out. Half a dozen rather plain bedrooms sharing communal baths rent for US$25/35 single/double. The *Hotel Aranjuez* (☎ 23 3559, fax 23 3528; Apartado 457-2070, San José), Calle 19, Avenida 11 & 13, has rooms with private baths and hot water for US$35 a single or double. There is plenty of parking. The *Hotel Hilda* (☎ 21 0037, fax 55 4028; Apartado 8079-1000, San José), Avenida 11, Calle 3 & 3b, is in a recently renovated and distinctive papaya-coloured house. (That's what the owners call it – I guess if you can have orange or lime green, why not papaya? It's a sort of pink colour.) Nice rooms with private bathroom and hot water are good value for US$28.50/35. Although they call it a B&B, you have to pay an extra US$2 for breakfast.

The owners are friendly, and professional massage and tour services are available.

The *Hotel La Amistad Inn* (☎ 21 1597, fax 21 1409), Avenida 11, Calle 15, has 18 rooms in a German-operated villa. Rates range from US$25 to US$35 a single, US$35 to US$45 a double, and US$60 for a suite. It's a nice place, though a little large for its B&B moniker. Slightly smaller, the 13 room *Hotel Rey* (☎ 33 3819, ☎/fax 33 1769; Apartado 7145-1000, San José; CRBBG member), Avenida 7, Calle 7 & 9, is in a refurbished, tile-floored mansion almost next door to the Museo de Jade. Nice rooms with private bath, electric showers and TV are US$40/57 single/double. Airport pick-up is available. The newly opened and recommended *Belmundo Hotel* (☎ 22 9624), Calle 20, Avenida 9, has a pool and restaurant. Rooms start at US$25/35 including breakfast buffet. It also has dormitory rooms for US$15 per person.

Out in Los Yoses, the friendly and recommended *Tres Arcos* (☎/fax 25 0271 or ☎ 34 9073; Apartado 161-1000, San José; CRBBG member) is set in pleasant gardens and has six rooms with nice views. They are at 3773 Avenida 10, Calle 37 – cab drivers will take you there if you ask for 200 metres south and 50 metres west of the Los Yoses Automercado (supermarket). The owners (Lee & Eric Warrington) are active in local theatre. Rooms are US$40 for a single or double with shared baths, US$52 with a private bath, and US$85 for a suite. Weekly (10%) and monthly (15%) discounts are available.

Diana's Inn (☎/fax 23 6542), Calle 5, Avenida 3, is an attractive clapboard house overlooking the Parque Morazán near the centre of town. Pleasant air-conditioned rooms with private bath, TV, and phone rent for US$40/52. The *Hemingway Inn* (☎ 21 1804, fax 22 5741; Apartado 1711-1002, San José), Calle 9, Avenida 9, is in a solid-looking 1930s house in the traditional Barrio Amon. About 10 slightly old-fashioned rooms are offered, each bearing the name of a 20th century writer (I found no women's names) and offering comfortable beds, ceiling fans, TV (wouldn't a wireless or wind-up gramophone have been more appropriate?) and private hot shower. Rates are US$35/57 single/double and US$75 in the Hemingway Suite. Breakfast is served in a plant-filled patio.

Places to Stay – top end

Hotels A very popular hotel in this price category is the recommended (and often full) *Hotel Don Carlos* (☎ 21 6707, fax 55 0828; Apartado 1593-1000, San José; in the USA, Department 1686, PO Box 025216, Miami FL 33102-5216) at Calle 9, Avenida 7 & 9. The hotel is in a beautifully remodelled mansion, and each of the approximately 25 rooms is different but comfortable and attractive; however, those on the street side suffer from traffic noise. Their excellent gift shop is one of the best in town, and they have a tour desk and occasionally live marimba music. Rates are from US$46 to US$57 for singles and US$57 to US$69 for doubles and include continental breakfast and a welcome cocktail. They don't take credit cards. (Along with the Santo Tomás and Don Fadrique, described next, these hotels are almost like B&Bs in that they provide personal service and breakfast. They are just a bit bigger than most B&B places, however.)

Another excellent choice is the *Hotel Santo Tomás* (☎ 55 0448, fax 22 3950), Avenida 7, Calle 3 & 5. They have 20 rooms with tiled or wood floors and high ceilings in a refurbished house. Antique pieces and Persian rugs add to the elegance. The hotel is very comfortable, with helpful and friendly management, and includes continental breakfast in its rates, which range from US$49/55 single/double for their standard rooms to US$85.50 for a single or double for their largest rooms.

Also recommended is the new *Hotel Don Fadrique* (☎ 23 3617, 25 8166, fax 24 9746; Apartado 4225-1000, San José) Calle 37, Avenida 8 in Los Yoses. This family-run hotel is decorated with Central American art and features a large plant-filled patio with a fountain. A tropical garden is being landscaped around the hotel (which opened in 1993) and should be finished by 1994. There are 20 rooms with hardwood floors and comfortable furnishings. Standard rooms are US$63/75 and deluxe rooms are US$75/86 for singles/doubles, including continental breakfast.

The *Don Paco Inn* (☎ 34 9088, fax 34 9588; in the USA ☎ 1 (800) 288 2107), Avenida 11, Calle 33, is in a more modern home dating from the 1940s. The rooms are light and cheerful, and the hotel is clean, quiet and recommended. Two smaller downstairs rooms rent for US$49/55 single/double and eight larger upstairs rooms are US$64 for one or two people and US$78/89 for three/four people. Breakfast is included.

Another delightful small hotel in a refurbished turn-of-the-century house is the *Hotel Petit Victoria* (☎ 33 1812 or 1813, fax 33 1938), Calle 24, Avenida 2. The original tiled floors are attractive. The 16 rooms are US$50/65 single/double and guests have kitchen privileges. Unfortunately, the rooms at the front are very close to the street and somewhat noisy. Continuing with small hotels in older houses, the *Gran Hotel Doña Inés* (☎ 22 7443, 22 7553, fax 23 5426; Apartado 1754-1002, San José), Calle 11, Avenida 2 & 6, charges US$56/71 for quaint rooms around a pretty inside courtyard. Most rooms are around the courtyard and off the street (quiet), but one of the rooms I looked at was a little musty – I guess they rent that one last. The other rooms seemed fine.

Yet another early 20th century mansion turned into an attractive hotel is the *Hotel Grano de Oro* (☎ 55 3322, fax 21 2782; Apartado 1157-1007, Centro Colón, San José; in the USA, PO Box 025216-36, Miami, FL 33102-5216). This hotel is at Calle 30, Avenida 2 & 4, and features 21 rooms (17 more are planned) which vary from standard (US$65/77) to somewhat larger deluxe (US$79/90) to the lovely Garden Suite with a private jacuzzi and miniature garden (US$132). All rooms are non-smoking and have TV and telephone, and are comfortably furnished. The hotel has an attractive courtyard, serves delicious meals in a sunny dining area (which attracts in-the-know locals as well as hotel guests) and is friendly and recommended.

The most luxurious and exclusive of the 'hotel in a house' places is the *Hotel L'Ambiance* (☎ 22 6702, fax 23 0481; Apartado 1040-2050, San Pedro, San José; in the USA, c/o Interlink 179, PO Box 526770, Miami FL 33152). The Spanish-style house at Calle 13, Avenida 9 & 11, is furnished with antiques and has six rooms and a presidential suite around a central courtyard. The emphasis is on service and quiet intimacy – no children. Rooms are US$80/110 single/double and the suite is US$130/170 single/double including breakfast.

The strangely named *Hotel Tennis Club* (☎ 32 1266, fax 32 3867; Apartado 4964-1000, San José) on the south side of Parque La Sabana is the place to stay if you like to keep fit whilst on vacation. There are 11 tennis courts, two pools, a gym, a sauna and other games facilities. The hotel is clean, quiet and safe. Some of the more expensive rooms have kitchenettes. Rooms are US$54/67 for singles/doubles and suites are US$84/95 plus US$20 for additional persons. Continental breakfast and complimentary coffee in the lobby is included.

The modern *Hotel Ambassador* (☎ 21 8155, 21 8089, fax 55 3396; Apartado 10186-1000, San José), Paseo Colón, Calle 26 & 28, has over 70 large, comfortable rooms for US$62/74 single/double and about US$15 more for top floor suites with good views. Group discounts are available and children under 12 years old stay free in the same room as their parents. The staff are friendly and the hotel is popular, but its restaurant is pricey.

The *Hotel Torremolinos* (☎ 22 5266, fax 55 3167; in the USA, ☎ 1 (800) 531 7036; Apartado 2029-1000, San José), Calle 40, Avenida 5 bis, has a pool and sauna, and is in a quiet neighbourhood. Smallish but very clean rooms with TV are US$52/63 for a single/double; larger suites are US$86. Across the street is *Hotel Ejecutivo Napoleon* (☎ 23 3252, 23 3282, fax 22 9487; Apartado 8-6340, San José). Modern, spacious air-conditioned rooms with TV are US$86/98, or US$12 less without air-conditioning. There is a pool and bar, and a buffet breakfast is included in the price although there is no restaurant on the premises.

About five km west of town just off the freeway to the airport is the *Hotel Irazú* (☎ 32 4811, fax 32 4549; Apartado 962-1000, San José). With over 300 rooms, this hotel is the largest in the city. There is a small shopping mall, tennis, swimming pool and sauna, a casino, discotheque, restaurant, cafeteria and bar. The hotel is popular with charter tour groups escaping the North American winter and, with the facilities available, some guests don't leave the hotel! But if you do, there is a minibus shuttle to downtown and a daily bus to a beach resort in Jacó. Rates vary depending on air-conditioning and size. Singles are US$52 to US$88, doubles US$70 to US$101, and suites US$153. Guests without reservations may be able to arrange a cheaper rate, particularly in the wet season.

The following hotels are in the downtown area. The *Gran Hotel Costa Rica* (☎ 21 4000, fax 21 3501; Apartado 527-1000, San José), Calle 3, Avenida Central & 2, dates from the 1930s and has a certain old-world charm. The rather small air-conditioned rooms are modern, however, and all have TV. The pavement cafeteria outside the lobby is an attractive and popular place for breakfast, and there is a casino and restaurant on the top floor. Rates are about US$60/80 single/double.

The *Hotel Balmoral* (☎ 22 5022, fax 21 1919; Apartado 3344-1000, San José), Avenida Central, Calle 7 & 9, is being remodelled, which is just as well. The room they showed me lacked both hot and cold water in the shower, and I've received various complaints from other people. They'll probably be OK after the renovating is done – rooms are US$76/89. One guide book claims that the hotel has 'conversational lounges on each floor.' I suppose the lounges chat about the lack of water in the showers! The *Hotel Presidente* (☎ 22 3022, fax 2 1205; Apartado 2922-1000, San José) at Avenida Central, Calle 7 & 9, has large air-conditioned rooms, a casino, a decent restaurant and a disco. Rates are US$63/75. The *Hotel Europa* (☎ 22 1222, fax 21 3976; Apartado 72-1000, San José), Calle Central, Avenida 3 & 5, has a pool, is central, and has a restaurant. Spacious air-conditioned rooms overlooking the pool cost US$57/69 single/double. Cheaper rooms overlooking the street are available, but are pretty noisy.

A new downtown hotel is the *Amstel Amón* (☎ 22 4622, fax 33 3329; Apartado 4192-1000, San José) under the same ownership as the well-known middle-priced Hotel Amstel. The Amón is due to open in 1994 with a restaurant, bar, casino, spa and travel agency. The 75 rooms will cost US$86 a single or double, the 14 suites will be US$103 and three deluxe suites will be US$137.

Similarly priced but about 750 metres north of downtown and across the Río Torres is the modern *Hotel Villa Tournón*, formerly the Hotel Bougainvillea (☎ 33 6622, fax 22 5211; Apartado 6606-1000, San José). There is a decent restaurant, pool, jacuzzi and a spacious feel, and the popular El Pueblo Shopping Centre is nearby. Cab drivers know it as 300 metres east of the *La República* newspaper office. Rooms with air-conditioning and TV range from US$57 to US$69 for singles, US$63 to US$75 for doubles.

Next we get into the modern luxury-class hotels with many facilities such as restaurants, shops, pool, gym, sauna, casino, discotheque, convention facilities, travel agents etc. These include the *Hotel Corobicí* (☎ 32 8122, fax 31 5834; Apartado 2443-1000, San José), Calle 42, 200 metres north of the Sabana Park. When I stayed here, I found that the pool was closed for maintenance (in the high season) and the desk staff were snotty. The cavernous architecture was interesting to look at, but the huge lobby area echoed loudly into the bedrooms, which wasn't conducive to sleep when the hotel accommodated a huge wedding party complete with mariachis. When rooms are US$126 to US$195 for a double, you'd like

to get some sleep. On the other hand, the air-conditioned rooms were spacious and comfortable and the restaurants, whilst very expensive, served good food.

Further out, along the road to the airport near the La Uruca suburb, is the 280 room *San José Palacio Hotel* (☎ 20 2034, fax 202036). This new and modern hotel is owned by the Barcelo group, which has been much criticised for the way it has developed its Playa Tambor megahotel (see the Península de Nicoya chapter). Rates are US$110/120 and up for a single/double.

Right downtown you'll find the *Aurola Holiday Inn* (☎ 33 7233, fax 55 1036; in the USA, 1 (800) HOLIDAY; Apartado 7802-1000, San José), Calle 5, Avenida 5. This new, luxurious, 17 storey building topped with a fancy restaurant is a San José landmark – ticos and cab drivers know it as the Hotel Aurola rather than the Holiday Inn. This is the most convenient large luxury hotel to downtown and has all the amenities you might expect. Rooms start at US$125/135 single/double and there are more expensive suites including the presidential suite which you can rent for a cool US$460 per night. Children under 12 years stay free in their parents rooms.

B&Bs There are three top-end B&Bs close to downtown. All three are CRBBG members.

The *D'Raya Vida* (☎ 23 4168, 23 4157; Apartado 495-1000, San José; in the USA, PO Box 025216-1638, Miami FL 33102) is owned by CRBBG co-founder Debbi McMurray and her husband. Tell cab drivers to go 100 metres north of Hospital Calderón Guardia on Calle 17, then 50 metres west on Avenida 11 where a sign directs you 50 metres north to the hotel. This elegant Costa Rican house is described as an 'antebellum estate'. (This is an interesting use of the word – normally it refers to the period before the American Civil War, but here it alludes to the years preceding the Costa Rican civil war. The architecture, however, is reminiscent of the USA's deep south.) The attractive bedrooms, dining and sitting areas reflect the owners' interests in art, antiques and decorating. Stained glass, hardwood floors, a patio with fountain and a fireplace make this a nice place to spend a few days. Guests have kitchen privileges on request. Four bedrooms share three bathrooms and cost US$75/97 including full breakfast and airport pick-up. Ask for weekly/monthly discounts.

Another B&B choice is the *Casa El Paso* (☎ 22 1708, fax 33 5785), 429 Calle 3, Avenida 4 & 6 which is in an older San José home close to the Plaza de la Cultura in the heart of downtown. They have five large and comfortable rooms which rent for US$57 a double with shared bath or US$86 with private bath. This is a retreat for adults only. Amenities include a lovely breakfast room (full breakfast is served) and a jacuzzi.

The *Casa Verde de Amón* (☎/fax 23 0969; Dept 1701, PO Box 025216, Miami FL 33102-5216), Calle 7, Avenida 9, is a distinctive mint-green clapboard house dating from 1910. A sitting room with a grand piano and a sauna are available for guests. There are eight rooms all with queen and king-sized beds. Rates are US$57/69 with shared bath, US$69/80 with private bath and US$103/120 for a suite, all including full breakfast. Smoking is allowed outside only.

Places to Stay – out of town

There are several outlying suburbs with middle to top-end hotels and B&Bs. People like to stay here to get out of the hustle and bustle of San José, or to be closer to the airport (17 km away), or because of the quiet, rural atmosphere. These areas are served by local buses, described in the San José Getting Around section.

Camping There is a full service campground in San Antonio de Belén, two km west of the San Antonio-Heredia intersection with the Interamericana near the Hotel Cariari. In San Antonio, there are signs for the *Belén Trailer Park* (☎ 39 0421, 39 0731, fax 39 1613). The owner is Laurie Atkinson, Apartado 143, San Antonio de Belén, Heredia, and she has run the campground for 20 years. There are full

hook-ups for camper vehicles as well as safe tenting areas for backpackers. Hot showers, laundry facilities, public phone, local information and nearby public buses to San José are all available.

Hotels There are several hotels in San Rafael de Escazú, about seven km west of downtown San José, and in San Antonio de Escazú, about 1.5 km to the south of San Rafael. The Escazú suburb has some elegant residential areas, popular with foreign residents.

The *Apartotel María Alexandra* (☎ 28 1507, fax 28 5192; Apartado 3756-1000, San José), Calle 3, Avenida 23, San Rafael de Escazú, is clean, quiet, and has a pool and laundry facilities. Their restaurant (☎ 28 4876) is medium priced and well recommended – people come up from the city to eat. This is one of the most comfortable apartotels and is usually booked up several months ahead, especially for the dry season. Apartments are about US$80 per day.

The *Mirador Pico Blanco* (☎ 28 1908, fax 89 5189; Apartado 900-1250, Escazú, San José), is a 25 room, friendly and pleasant countryside hotel in Escazú. There are balconies with views of the mountains and of San José below. Rooms with queen-sized bed, private hot shower and refrigerator rent for US$40/46. Nearby is the slightly cheaper and smaller *Posada Pegasus* (☎ 28 4196; Apartado 370-1250, Escazú, San José) which also has good views and a jacuzzi.

The *Tara* (☎ 28 6992, fax 28 9651; Apartado 1459-1250, Escazú), is in a beautiful building in the hills above Escazú. Some 30 rooms with balconies offer good views and rent for US$125 – or more for suites. There is a pool, jacuzzi, sauna and gym and the service is very good.

There are two luxury hotels near the Cariari Country Club, about nine km northwest of San José on the way to the airport. The *Hotel Cariari* (☎ 39 0022, fax 39 2803; Apartado 737-1007, Centro Colón, San José) has exceptional resort facilities (golf, pool, tennis, horse riding, gym, disco, sauna, casino, shopping mall, restaurants). Almost

200 rooms (standard, deluxe, junior and master suites) cost from US$120 to US$320 depending on facilities. Not far away is the *Hotel Herradura* (☎ 39 0033, fax 39 2292; Apartado 7-1880, San José). This place also has full convention facilities. Rooms and suites go from around US$125 to US$360.

B&Bs These have really proliferated in the suburbs of San José over the past few years, especially in the Escazú area. Your best bet is to call the B&B for directions – the owners all speak English. Most are within walking distance of a bus line or are a 15 minute cab ride from San José. The following are all CRBBG members – see above for more details.

The *Casa Amable* (☎ 28 2802, fax 28 6823; Apartado 1431-1250, San Antonio de Escazú, San José) have two rooms with mountain views sharing one bath for US$30/35 single/double. Children should be at least eight years old. The *White Horse Inn* (☎ 28 4290, 28 1895; Apartado 1012, San Antonio de Escazú) is in a new house in a quiet area. Four rooms share two bathrooms and rent for US$40 a double or US$460 per month. Both these places provide continental breakfast, and smoking is allowed outside only.

Park Place (☎ 28 1895, ☎/fax 28 9200; Apartado 1012, San Antonio de Escazú, San José) is a mountain house with city views. Four bedrooms share two bathrooms and rent for US$35/40 single/double or US$400 a month. Guests have kitchen privileges in addition to use of living and dining areas. The owner, Pat Bliss, is a co-founder of the CRBBG and also owns the *Grand View Inn* (same address as Park Place) which is a Spanish-style villa with a pool, city views and nearby forest trails. Four rooms sharing baths rent for US$46/52 single/double plus US$11.50 for additional people. A suite is US$69. Both places serve continental breakfast, allow older children (12 years and up), and allow smoking outside only. The owner's interests include diving and river rafting.

Casa de Las Tías (☎/fax 28 5517; Apartado 295-1200, Escazú, San José) is in a quiet area of San Rafael de Escazú. The tico owners provide typical breakfasts and other meals on request. The house is decorated with art and crafts from all over Latin America. Five rooms share three bathrooms and rent for US$52/63 a single/double. Smoking is allowed outside only, children are accepted with advance notice and free airport pick-up is available if you have a reservation.

Villa Escazú (☎/fax 28 9566; Apartado 1401-1250, Escazú, San José) is a Swiss chalet type of building surrounded by terraced gardens and fruit trees. A verandah is good for watching birds and eating the full American breakfast which is included in the US$35/40 single/double rent – no smoking allowed inside, no small children, and the seventh night is free. Another 'Swiss chalet' choice is the *Parvati Inn* (☎ 28 4011; Apartado 20-1250, Escazú) which has four bedrooms sharing one bathroom, opening in early 1993 (call for rates). The vegetarian owners are art collectors and teach Hathayoga and meditation. No children are allowed.

Posada del Bosque (☎ 28 1164, fax 28 6381; Apartado 669-1250, Escazú) is a country inn set in pleasant gardens. The friendly tico owners will cook for you on request and have five bedrooms sharing three bathrooms, and a fireplace. Swimming pool, tennis and horse-riding trails are nearby. Children are invited. No smoking is allowed in the bedrooms. Rates are US$40 to US$50 a single (add US$6 for each extra person) including full breakfast – several readers have recommended this place.

The *Costa Verde Inn* (☎ 31 5973; ☎/fax 28 4080; Apartado 89-1250, Escazú) is an attractive country inn with hot tub, tennis court and fireplace. Eight bedrooms, each with fan, king-sized bed and private hot shower, rent for about US$35 to US$65 including full breakfast served on an outdoor terrace. Weekly discounts are available. Smoking and children over nine years are permitted and the staff strive to provide personal service. The owner, Harvey Haber, writes about B&B in a witty and thoughtful weekly column in the *The Tico Times* and is also the editor of the richly illustrated *Insight Guide: Costa Rica.*

Casa María (☎ 28 2270, 28 0190, fax 28 0015; Apartado 123-1250, Escazú is a small hotel that includes a full breakfast in its rates, which range from US$38 to US$100 depending on the room. (Some share baths, others don't.) Lunches and dinners are available on request. There is a 'resource centre' with maps, books and travel information to help guests plan their trips. There is also a large pool with the innovative new attraction of offering scuba diving certification! Learn to dive in the pool and then head out to the coast – all gear is provided. Call the hotel for details.

A B&B that is not a CRBBG member is the *Forest Bed & Breakfast* (☎ 89 5438, tel/fax 28 0900; Apartado 5043-1000, San José). They are at Casa 78, Bello Horizonte, Escazú and offer hammock space for US$9, bunkbeds in a dormitory for US$14.25, private rooms for US$44.50 and a suite for US$74.50. There is a pool and exercise area.

Escazú is not the only place with B&Bs. The *Centro Creativo de Arte* (☎ 82 8769, 82 6556, fax 82 6959; Apartado 597, Santa Ana, San José) is in Santa Ana, about six km west of Escazú.

Four rustic rooms share three bathrooms and rent for US$15/25 a single/double including continental breakfast. The grounds are extensive.

Facilities available at this centre include a variety of art and yoga classes, massage, reflexology, colour healing, chiropractic and other alternative health care. There is also the 'Soda-Sana', which serves health food.

Roxana's B&B (☎/fax 35 4440; Apartado 1086-1100, Tibas, San José) is in the suburb of (San Juan de) Tibas, a few km north of San José. Three bedrooms share baths and rent for US$25/35 a single/double including full breakfast.

Children over 11 years are invited and smoking is permitted outside only. The owner is interested in gardening and orchid collecting.

Places to Eat

Cosmopolitan San José has a wide variety of restaurants – something to satisfy most tastes and budgets. I found Peruvian and Middle Eastern restaurants, as well as the old standbys: Italian, Chinese and French. American chain food restaurants are also popular – though I can't get too excited about them myself. And, of course, there are tico specialities.

Remember that most restaurants, apart from the very cheapest, add a 13% tax plus a 10% service to your bill. Many of the better restaurants can get quite busy so a telephoned reservation may help avoid a wait. Where I give approximate prices as a guide, bear in mind that anything with shellfish (shrimp, lobster or crab) will be more expensive.

Sodas These luncheonette-type snack bars are usually inexpensive and are a good choice for the budget traveller, particularly for breakfast or lunch, when you can have a light meal for US$1 to US$2. Most are rather featureless and certainly not fancy, but are popular with ticos looking for a cheap meal. They cater to students and working people, and hence some tend to close at weekends. There are dozens of sodas in San José, so what follows is just a selection.

An inexpensive and popular one is the *Soda Central* (☎ 21 9085), Avenida 1, Calle 3 & 5, where the empanadas are good and you can have gallo pinto con huevo (rice and beans with an egg) for just over a US$1. The *Soda B&B* (☎ 22 7316), is on the north-east corner of the Plaza de Cultura and has been discovered by and is popular with tourists – the 23% is charged and credit cards are accepted. The menu has a few tico dishes (pinto con huevos for US$2.60) and plenty of hamburgers and hot dogs, shakes and sandwiches.

The cheap *Soda Nini* (☎ 33 7771), Avenida 3, Calle 2 & 4, has both tico and Chinese food. The *Soda Magaly* at Avenida Central, Calle 23, has a good variety of cheap meals under US$2 and is close to the Toruma Youth Hostel. There are several other sodas near here. Also close to the hostel is the *Soda Pulpería La Luz* at Avenida Central, Calle 33 – this old pulpería is a local landmark. The menu is limited to cheap but tasty local snacks and meals.

On the north side of Parque Central there is the *Soda Palace* at Avenida 2, Calle 2, and the *Soda La Perla*, Avenida 2, Calle Central. Both are open 24 hours. The Palace is a very popular gathering spot with harsh lights, plenty of action, and musicians wandering in and out at night. Meals are about US$5 though the beer and boca for US$1.20 is the most frequently ordered item (at least at night – the morning coffee and pastry are also popular). The Perla is quieter though crowded at lunchtime, when ticos eat the set lunch for US$3 or other meals in the US$2 to US$7 range. Both are recommended as classic tico joints and are favourites of mine.

If you're out by Parque La Sabana, stop by the locally popular *Soda Tapia* (☎ 22 6734), Calle 42, Avenida 2.

Budget Shoestring travellers trying to economise may find San José a somewhat expensive city to eat in. Apart from the sodas, here are some suggestions. The *Mercado Central* at Avenida Central & 1, Calle 6 & 8, has a variety of cheap sodas and restaurants inside. It's a great place to eat elbow to elbow with local ticos – plenty of atmosphere. There are several other cheap places to eat near the market, especially on the Avenida 1 side. The area around the market is not dangerous, but it is a little rough: single women may prefer not to go there alone. There are pickpockets too. (Don't wander around with cameras and cash bursting out of your pockets. And leave that diamond-studded gold tennis bracelet at home. I've often wondered exactly what a tennis bracelet was – my dictionary defines it as an expensive bauble prone to getting ripped off your wrist.)

The *Restaurant Campesino* (☎ 55 1438, 22 1170), Calle 7, Avenida 2, is a pleasant place with a homey atmosphere, open from 10 am to midnight daily. It serves a few Chinese dishes or chicken roasted over a wood fire (not fried) – the latter is a real deal for US$1.50 for a quarter chicken with tortillas or fries. This is my favourite cheap chicken restaurant in town. They have take out and home delivery too. Another good chicken restaurant is *La Fogata*, Avenida Central, Calle 13, which also has a quarter chicken for US$1.50. The *La Vasconia*, Avenida 1, Calle 5, is a cheap but decent place with a largely tico clientele and a wide variety of food on the chalkboard menu. I like eating here too, when I'm saving my colones. A pinto con huevo breakfast is under US$1 and they have set *casado* (cheap meal of the day) lunches for US$1.50.

Nearby, next to the Omni Cinema, is the clean *Restaurante Marisquería Omni*, Avenida 1, Calle 3 & 5, where a good set lunch is served from 11.30 am to 1.30 pm for under US$2. Another cheap possibility is the *Lido Bar* at Calle 2, Avenida 3, which is less of a bar and more a cheap lunch place, at least during the middle of the day. Ticos like to drink (in moderation) and see nothing surprising in eating in a bar. Three or four blocks south-east of the Museo Nacional is *La Cocina de Bordolino*, Calle 21, Avenida 6 & 8, which is a hole-in-the-wall Argentinian-run empanada place serving local office workers from 8 am to 7 pm, Monday to Friday and 9 am to 6 pm on Saturdays. Delicious empanadas are less than US$1 each.

Most restaurants will offer a casado for lunch at a price well below eating à la carte. These fixed-price meals can cost from just under US$1 in the very cheapest places to US$4 or US$5 in the fancier restaurants, where the meal may be called an *almuerzo ejecutivo*.

Vegetarian Although vegetarianism isn't very big in Costa Rica, there are several reasonable vegetarian restaurants, most of them fairly inexpensive. There are three *Vishnu* restaurants: at Calle 3, Avenida Central & 1 (☎ 22 2549), Calle 14, Avenida Central & 2 (23 0294), and Avenida 1, Calle 1 & 3. The last seems the most popular and has a set lunch for about US$2.50.

À la carte menus have no prices, so you have to ask your waiter – mine didn't know the prices and kept repeating that they were 'Very cheap! Very cheap!' I felt like dragging his ass over to the Mercado Central. Vishnu has received many recommendations for vegetarian food – but if I can't get a straight answer about prices, it spoils my appetite.

Others which have been recommended are *Restaurant El Shakti*, Avenida 8, Calle 13, and *Restaurante El Eden*, Avenida 5, Calle Central & 2. For good-value lunches try *Don Sol* at Avenida 7 bis, Calle 13 & 15, two blocks east of the Museo de Jade.

Two up-market macrobiotic/vegetarian restaurants are the recommended *Restaurant Mordisco* (☎ 55 2448), Paseo Colón, Avenida 24 & 26 (with meals in the US$4 to US$8 range) and the *La Mazorca* (☎ 24 8069), 100 metres north and 25 metres west of the Banco Anglo in San Pedro.

Cafés & Coffee Shops These are very popular among Costa Ricans, who seem to have a collective sweet tooth for pastries and cakes. They are often good places for travellers to catch up on journal or letter writing. Prices are not necessarily cheap, but you don't have to buy much and can sit for hours.

A favourite place is the pavement café of the *Gran Hotel Costa Rica* at Calle 3, Avenida 2, where you get a good view of the comings and goings in the Plaza de la Cultura. Full meals are also served here. In the Plaza de la Cultura itself is the Teatro Nacional, within which you'll find the elegant *Café Ruiseñor* which has become very popular recently and is always full at lunch time – come early and people-watch. Changing art is displayed on the walls. Hours are 11 am to 6 pm, Monday to Saturday (later if there's a show on). At the other end of the elegance scale is *La Miel* (☎ 23 3193), Avenida 6, Calle 13 & 15. This homey little pastelería serves delicious and inexpensive pastries and desserts to local office workers between 7 am and 7 pm, Monday to Friday – a real boon to sweet-toothed travellers conscious of their wallets, if not their waists!

Spoon has three locations: Avenida Central, Calle 5 & 7 downtown (☎ 21 6702);

Avenida 8, Calle 45 in Los Yoses (☎ 24 0328, a local landmark); and another in Rohrmoser (☎ 31 6359) near the US embassy. They are known for a great selection of pastries and cakes, as well as light lunch items. Similar, and perhaps slightly up-market, is *Ruiseñor* (☎ 25 2562), 100 metres east of the Automercado in Los Yoses, and *Azafran* (☎ 25 5230) across the street and 150 metres east of the Los Yoses Automercado. (If using a map, you'll find them on Avenida Central near Calle 41.)

Churrería Manolo's at Avenida Central, Calle Central & 2 (☎ 21 2041), and Avenida Central, Calle 9 & 11 (☎ 23 4067), is famous for its cream-filled churros (hollow doughnut tubes) as well as a variety of other desserts and light meals. Nearby, *Panadería Schmidt* on Avenida 2, Calle 4 and Avenida Central, Calle 11 is locally popular for cakes, pastries and breads for carry-out (though there are small eat-in areas). Ice-cream eaters should look for *Pops* and *Mönpik* for the best ice creams; each chain has several locations in San José and can be found outside the capital.

Chinese Chinese restaurants are found all over the Americas from Alaska to Argentina, and San José has its fair share. Most are good and medium priced; I couldn't find any very cheap ones. Two of the best downtown are the *Restaurante Tin-jo* (☎ 21 7605) which has Szechuan and Cantonese specialities (and was selected as the best Chinese restaurant in 1989 and 1990 by the *La Nación* newspaper) and the *Restaurante Don Wang* (☎ 33 6484) which specialises in Taiwanese food. Both are on Calle 11, Avenida 6 & 8. Expect to pay about US$5 to US$8 for a meal.

A highly recommended Chinese restaurant in San Pedro is the *Nueva China* (☎ 24 4478), 100 metres east of the Banco Popular (most locals and taxi drivers know it). They have a chef from Hong Kong and the food is authentic – Chinese white wine is available and a dim-sum (a Chinese breakfast buffet with a wide variety of delicious snacks) is served on weekend mornings. This is one of the most elegant of Chinese restaurants in town. For dim-sum downtown, the restaurant in the *Hotel Royal Garden* (☎ 57 0023) Calle Central, Avenida Central has been recommended. They serve dim-sum and other Chinese dishes all week.

Other good Chinese restaurants which have been recommended include the *Restaurant Fulusu* (☎ 23 7568), Calle 7, Avenida Central & 2, for Szechuan and Mandarin food; the *Ave Fénix* (☎ 25 3362), 200 metres west of the San Pedro church for Szechuan meals; the *Flor de Loto* (☎ 32 4652) on the north side of Parque La Sabana by the ICE building, which specialises in hot and spicy Szechuan and Hunan dishes; and *Beijing City* (☎ 28 6939), one km west of the US ambassador's house in Escazú – that's what the cab-drivers know – which prepares Peking duck with 48 hours notice. There are many others.

Spanish My favourite Spanish restaurant is *La Masia de Triquell* (☎ 21 5073), Avenida 2, Calle 40. The restaurant is in an elegant mansion and the food and service are very good without being snooty. The house speciality is Catalonian style cuisine. Meals are around US$10 for the main course – it is a recommended splurge. Hours are noon to 2 pm and 7 to 11 pm from Tuesday to Saturday, and noon to 4 pm on Sunday.

Closer to downtown, there are a number of well-run and recommended Spanish restaurants. *Casino Español* (☎ 22 9440) Calle 9, Avenida Central & 1, serves both Spanish and international dishes and has been recommended for its excellent service. Main courses are about US$6 or US$7. Hours are 11 am to 3 pm and 5.30 to midnight daily. The elegant-looking *Goya* (☎ 21 3887) Avenida 1, Calle 5 & 7, has received several recommendations for its good food and service. Hours are 11 am to 2.30 pm and 5.30 to 11 pm daily except Sunday. Out in San Pedro, the *Marbella* (☎ 24 9452) in the Centro Comercial Calle Real, 75 metres east of the Banco Popular, has a Spanish chef who claims to make the best paella in Costa Rica – I'm not going to argue with him.

French There are several French restaurants in San José, most of them very expensive (at least by Costa Rican standards), and all recommended by and for lovers of French cuisine. Downtown there's the classy *L'Ile de France* (☎ 22 4241), Calle 7, Avenida Central & 2. Their daily lunch special is US$10, which gives you an idea of the prices – but the food is good. Hours are noon to 2 pm, Monday to Friday and 6.30 to 10 pm, Monday to Saturday. Out along Paseo Colón is the elegant *La Bastilla* (☎ 55 4994), Paseo Colón, Calle 22, with excellent main courses starting around US$12. It is another place which is closed on Sunday.

Le Chandelier (☎ 25 3980), is in Los Yoses and is the best French restaurant in town – and also closed on Sundays. Tell the cab driver to go to the Los Yoses ICE building and then 100 metres west and 100 metres south. The restaurant is lovely, with dining in a choice of outdoor patios, indoor areas next to a fireplace, or larger and smaller private rooms. Main courses are in the US$10 to US$40 range.

If you yearn for French cooking but can't afford the best part of US$100 for a complete meal, try the more moderately priced *Le Bistrot* (☎ 53 8062), 100 metres east and 25 metres north of the San Pedro church. This one is open on Sunday – but closed Monday.

Italian One of San José's most popular restaurants is the *Balcón de Europa* (☎ 21 4841), Calle 9, just north of Avenida Central. The restaurant has been in San José (though not always in the same location) supposedly since 1909 and claims to be the oldest eatery in Costa Rica. The place is usually packed with both ticos and visitors.

Chef/owner Franco Piatti has been running the Balcón for over a decade and is much in evidence (he puts his photo in *The Tico Times* ads almost every week). Some people claim he serves the best Italian food in town. The first time I went I was disappointed – the lasagne I ordered was not as good as my wife's (and Cathy claims neither Italian heritage nor culinary kudos). The next time I tried a sampler plate with three types of pasta and found it much more acceptable.

Certainly, this one restaurant has generated more

letters from readers than any other eatery in Costa Rica, and their opinions were richly diverse: 'Charming Italian restaurant with serenading guitarist'; 'The owner visits with guests but doesn't see that service is very slow'; 'Turn of the century black & white photographs decorating the walls are most interesting'; 'The pasta is mushy, tasteless and unappetizing'; 'Heavenly cheeses and desserts'.

OK, readers, it looks like there's a restaurant critic lurking within many of you – let me hear more about this place (and others) for the next edition! Meals cost about US$5 to US$10 and are served from noon to 10 pm daily except Saturday. No credit cards or personal cheques accepted – cash is OK, or maybe just bring your dishcloth.

Out on Paseo Colón you'll find the pleasant *Restaurante Ana* (☎ 22 6153) with main courses in the US$4.50 to US$12 range. Further out on Paseo Colón near Calle 40 is the more expensive *La Piazetta* (☎ 22 7869) with a mouth-watering menu of creative Italian food served on silver platters – locals call this the most elegant Italian restaurant in San José. Another fancy and pricey restaurant vying for the title of 'best Italian' is *Il Tulá* (☎ 28 0053) in San Rafael de Escazú.

At the other end of town, in San Pedro, another elegant Italian place is *Il Ponte Vecchio* (☎ 25 9399), 150 metres east of La Fuente de Hispanidad (or 200 metres west of the San Pedro church) and 10 metres north. (I love these addresses – so much more fun than 123 Main St). Their chef survived 18 years of preparing Italian food in New York and his work is recommended. Hours are noon to 2.30 pm and 6 to 10.30 pm except Sunday (noon to 6.30 pm) and Wednesday (closed).

Also recommended is the slightly out of the way *Miro's Bistro* (☎ 53 4242), next to the railway tracks 300 metres north and 25 metres east of Pulpería La Luz in Barrio Escalante, Calle 33, Avenida 1 & 5, on the east side of the street. This is a cozy, intimate (dare I say small?) place with good food; closed on Sunday.

A recommended pizza restaurant is *Mr Pizza* (☎ 23 1221), Avenida 1, Calle 7 & 9, which is reputedly the nation's oldest pizzería – it opened in 1972 and is still going strong, so it must be doing something right. Along with the reasonably priced pizza (from about US$1.50 for individual pizzas to about US$6 for a loaded large pizza) you can get a glass of acceptable house wine for about US$1.30 – a good deal in a nation which imports most of its wine. They are closed on Monday.

Another decent pizza choice is the *San Remo* (☎ 21 8145) at Calle 2, Avenida 3 & 5. They also serve other reasonably priced Italian and tico food. There is also a *Pizza Hut* chain: two locations are Calle 4, Avenida Central & 2; and Paseo Colón, Calle 28.

Continental Several restaurants serve food with a European flair. *La Galería* (☎ 34 0850), 125 metres west of the ICE building in Los Yoses (behind Apartotel Los Yoses) has long been popular for its well-prepared and reasonably priced food served in a classical setting. The cuisine has a strong German influence and most main courses are well under US$10. Hours are from noon to 2.30 pm Monday to Friday and 7 to 11 pm Monday to Saturday.

A recommended downtown restaurant is *Chalet Suizo* (☎ 22 3118), Avenida 1, Calle 5 & 7, which serves, as you may guess, Swiss dishes such as fondue and a variety of other European dishes. Their US$5 set lunch is very popular, and about US$10 buys you a meal à la carte. Hours are 11.30 am to 2 pm and 6 to 11.30 pm daily. A fancier and more expensive place for fondues and other Swiss delights is *Zermatt* (☎ 22 0604), Avenida 11, Calle 23 (100 metres north of the Santa Teresita church). They are closed on Sundays.

Out in the south-eastern suburb of Curridabat, 100 metres south of Pops Ice Cream restaurant, is the expensive but recommended *Marcois* (☎ 24 9838) which serves a variety of light Danish meals, as well as dishes with a more French or Italian influence. Another choice with French/Italian cuisine is *Emilia Romagna* (☎ 33 2843), Paseo Colón, Calle 32 & 34. This is definitely a high-class place with attentive service and haute cuisine – it also features live jazz from 9 pm onwards. This is one of the most expensive restaurants in town for a special night out or to impress your friends. They are closed on Sunday.

Bromelias (☎ 22 3535), Calle 23, Avenida 3, (100 metres north of the Cine Magaly) is hard to define. A tropical cuisine prepared by a French chef results in a variety of intriguing and enjoyable dishes. They are open daily and have live music in their cocktail lounge from Tuesday to Saturday. Another restaurant serving good and varied food with a French influence is *Arlene* (☎ 28 0370), almost opposite the country club in Escazú. Arlene is a well-known local character who hosts her own cooking show on Costa Rican TV. Hours are noon to 2 pm and 6.30 to 11 pm daily except Sunday (noon to 5 pm).

Fast Food These US-style restaurants serve food which is similar in taste and price to what you get in the USA (about US$3 for a medium-sized meal). They are popular among ticos, especially the younger ones.

McDonald's at Calle 4, Avenida Central & 1, and on the north side of the Plaza de la Cultura at Avenida Central, Calle 3 & 5, and elsewhere have been recommended for their clean bathrooms. Also on the north side of the Plaza de la Cultura is *Archi's*, a Costa Rican version of US fast food serving both hamburgers and chicken.

Kentucky Fried Chicken (Pollo Kentucky) has two downtown locations: Avenida 2, Calle 6; and Avenida 3, Calle 1 & 3. For some reason, Pollo Kentucky at Paseo Colón, Calle 32 & 34, and in Los Yoses at Avenida Central, Calle 31, have both become local landmarks. Tell a cab driver that you want to go 125 metres north of the Pollo Kentucky on Paseo Colón and you'll be taken there directly and probably charged exactly the same fare as a local! (This is actually the address of the Machu Pichu restaurant, described further on.)

Other fast food restaurants include *Hardee's*, Calle 1, Avenida Central, for hamburgers; and *Don Taco*, Avenida 1, Calle 2, for instant burritos and tacos.

Steak & Seafood Some of these restaurants are for dedicated carnivores: side salads are usually available but otherwise the meals are very meaty. Many have a good selection of both meat and seafood dishes, whilst others tend to have seafood only.

For mainly meat, *La Hacienda* (☎ 23 5493) at Calle 7, Avenida Central & 2, is quiet and unpretentious, and has very good steaks for under US$10. I'd eat here again... and again.

Other steak houses are away from the centre. *Los Ranchos* (☎ 32 7757) on the north side of the Sabana Park, behind the ICE building (most cab drivers know it), is about the same price as La Hacienda and also recommended. *El Chicote* (☎ 32 0936, 32 3777) is another good steak house on the north side of La Sabana, 400 metres west of the ICE building, and includes seafood on its menu. You can get to the north side of the Sabana Park on the Sabana Estadio bus which goes out along the Paseo Colón.

Out on the road to Escazú is the well known *Los Anonos BBQ* (☎ 28 0180) which has served barbecued steaks and other food for three decades. Prices are very reasonable – a huge one pound steak is about US$7.50. They are closed on Mondays. Also in Escazú is another long-time favourite, *Barbecue La Cascada* (☎ 28 0906, 28 9393), with a good selection of seafoods as well as grilled steaks.

Lancers Steak House (☎ 22 5938) is in the El Pueblo Shopping Centre, about 1.5 km north of downtown. Steaks are about US$6 to US$8 and there is a good selection of seafood as well. Also in El Pueblo (which is recommended for a good variety of restaurants, bars and nightspots, as well as shops) is the upscale *Rias Bajas* (☎ 21 7123) which serves excellent seafood, as well as meat dishes. It is closed on Sundays.

For barbecued ribs, *Tommy's Ribs* (☎ 23 2957), Avenida 6, Calle 11 & 13, is probably your best bet downtown. Popularly known as 'TR', this place is stylish yet not too expensive – ribs range from US$7 to US$14 and there is a variety of other items. Another popular similarly priced choice is *JR House of Ribs* (☎ 25 5918), which is in the north-eastern suburb of Guadalupe – cab drivers know it.

An elegant seafood restaurant with a good variety of meat dishes is *Lobster's Inn* (☎ 23 8954) at Paseo Colón, Calle 24. Main courses (fish) are about US$8 to US$10, but shrimp and lobster are about two or three times that much.

A restaurant specialising in seafood is the moderately priced *La Fuente de Mariscos* (☎ 31 0631), in the shopping centre next to the Hotel Irazú, a few km north-west of downtown. They have another location in San Pedro, at the Centro Comercial Plaza de Sol (☎ 34 1931). Also moderately priced, *La Princesa Marina* (☎ 32 0481) is open daily from 11.30 am to 10.30 pm on the west side of La Sabana (150 metres south of Canal 7 TV station). A full fried fish dinner is around US$4 to US$5.

Costa Rican As much as anything else, national specialities include steak and seafood, and most of the restaurants in the previous section could be thought of as Costa Rican. There isn't a very strong typical culinary tradition in Costa Rica, but a few restaurants serve what could be considered tico country cooking, and the food is very good.

The best-known one is the *La Cocina de Leña* (☎ 23 3704, 55 1360) in the El Pueblo Shopping Centre. The restaurant's name literally means 'the wood stove' and the atmosphere attempts to be country kitchen and homey. They have had so much success in recent years, however, that they have moved to bigger premises which detracts from the homey feel somewhat and their prices are no longer 'country kitchen'. Still, it's a nice enough place, the food is well prepared and they continue their charming tradition of printing their menu on a brown paper bag. A selection of their typical dishes includes corn soup with pork; black bean soup with eggs; tamales (US$5); beef casado; gallo pinto with meat and eggs; stuffed peppers; ox tail served with yucca and plantain (US$8.50), and, of course, steak

and fish (US$9 to US$11). They also serve local desserts and alcoholic concoctions, including the tico firewater, guaro.

Another upmarket place (price wise) with good Costa Rican food in a rustic setting is *Tiquicia* (☎ 89 5839). Located in a farmhouse up in the hills of Escazú, this restaurant gives diners great views and sometimes has live local music. Their hours are erratic – call first and ask for directions.

Also try *El Cuartel de la Boca del Monte* (☎ 21 0327), Avenida 1, Calle 21 & 23, which is a coffee house and restaurant during the day serving some Costa Rican dishes – casually elegant and moderately priced. Eat during the day – it's mainly a bar at night, loud with young people and live bands. Another possibility is the *Restaurant Poás* (☎ 21 7802), Avenida 7, Calle 3 & 5, which advertises 'dine in a jungle' – the place is dark and chock-a-block full of plants. It can be an urban jungle as well and the music can get overpoweringly loud at times, but the 'native cuisine platter' for US$4.50 has been recommended. They also serve some dishes from other Central American countries. They are open from 8 am until 2 pm and have a dance floor.

A cheap place selling tico food in rustic surroundings is *Chosa del Indio* which is in the north-eastern suburb of Sabanilla, 100 metres east of the church. For typical Costa Rican desserts, fruit juices and snacks, stop by *Pipo's* on Avenida Central, Calle 9 & 11.

If you come right down to it, as good a way as any of eating Costa Rican food is to head down to the Mercado Central and get a plate of pinto with sour cream or a couple of banana-leaf-wrapped tamales – it'll be your cheapest option.

Other Cuisines There is a host of other international restaurants with food from many countries. One of my favourites is the *Machu Pichu* (☎ 22 7384), Calle 32, Avenida 1 & 3, 125 metres north of the Pollo Kentucky. They serve authentic Peruvian cuisine, especially seafood, at moderate prices – about US$4 to US$8 gets you a decent meal. Hours are noon to 3 pm and 6 to 10 pm Monday to Saturday. Nearby is the *Beirut* (☎ 57 1808) at Calle 32, Avenida 1, which serves good Middle Eastern food at slightly higher prices. Hours are noon to 3 pm and 6 to 11 pm from Tuesday to Saturday, noon to 5 pm on Sunday.

Sus Antojos (☎ 22 9086), Paseo Colón, Calles 24 & 26, serves inexpensive to moderately priced Mexican food (US$3 to US$9, most around US$5), and may have mariachis on Friday nights.

Arirang (☎ 23 2838) at Paseo Colón, Calle 38 & 40, serves moderately priced Korean food; about US$5 to US$10 buys a good meal. Hours are 11.30 am to 2.30 pm from Monday to Friday and 5.30 to 9.30 pm from Monday to Saturday.

Hotels Many of the better hotels have good restaurants. The *Hotel Amstel* has a well-recommended grill room and the *Hotel Tournon* has an excellent restaurant as well. The *Hotel Diplomat* serves pretty fancy fixed lunches for moderate prices. The *Hotel L'Ambiance* (☎ 22 6702) serves fancy vegetarian meals as well as other dishes – call for reservations.

Further afield is the *Sakura* (☎ 39 0033) in the Hotel Herradura. They serve excellent and authentic Japanese food – but it's not cheap. It is closed on Monday. Another good Japanese restaurant is the *Fuji* (☎ 32 8122) in the Hotel Corobicí. They are closed on Sunday. The *Maria Alexandra* in the apartotel of the same name in Escazú has a small and locally recommended restaurant – they are also closed on Sunday.

See under Places to Stay for more information.

Entertainment
Bars & Discotheques Try and get hold of the weekly leaflet *Info-Spectacles* which comes out on Tuesdays and gives information on live music and nightclub acts for the next week. The leaflet is available at some of the places listed below and in the ICT information centre.

Local bands and musicians which are currently popular (or as current as I can be in the fast-moving music business) include Liver-

pool, Hora Zero Group, Baby Rasta Band, Abracadabra (rock/blues/reggae); Marfil, La Pandylla, Los Hicsos, La Maffia, Jacque Mate Group (Latin rhythm); Oveja Negra, Luis Angel Castro (nueva trova – modern Latin folk music, often with a political, anti-establishment, human rights, etc theme). There are many others.

El Cuartel de la Boca del Monte (☎ 21 0327), Avenida 1, Calle 21 & 23, is a restaurant by day but at night is transformed into one of the capital's busiest and most popular nightspots for young people. The music is sometimes recorded and sometimes live (Wednesday is a good night for live bands), but always loud, and it's elbow room only in the back room where there is a small dance floor. In front it's rather less frenzied but still crowded. It's a good place to meet young ticos.

Contravía (☎ 53 6989), 100 metres south of the Banco Popular in San Pedro, is popular with university students and politically aware young ticos for its Nueva Trova music and *peñas* (a generic term for folk music, particularly popular in South America). *Baleares* (☎ 53 4577), 100 metres west of the Mas x Menos Supermercado in San Pedro, features Latin music some nights. The *Akelare* (☎ 23 0345), Calle 21, Avenida 2 & 6, is in a huge mansion and has a variety of live bands playing two or three nights a week. *Catastrofe Bar* (☎ 25 1043), Avenida Central and Calle 35 at the beginning of Los Yoses, has mainly rock music and, so locals tell me, can get pretty wild and obnoxious. It was quiet when I stopped by – but then, I have this wonderfully calming influence on everybody...

Many a visitor to San José checks out the well-known *La Esmeralda* (☎ 21 0530), Avenida 2, Calle 5 & 7. It's open all day and all night (except Sunday) and is the centre of the city's mariachi tradition. You can get a meal (from US$3 to US$6) any time, but the action begins later at night when there are dozens of strolling musicians around.

A few blocks west are the bare fluorescent lights of *Soda Palace*, Avenida 2, Calle 2 – another 24 hour joint. The beers here come with free bocas, and the place is usually crowded with locals and a sprinkling of travellers. It is open to the street and people come to watch the street action, see who comes in, or eat a moderately priced meal (US$3 and up). Musicians wander in later on in the evening – practising mariachis, lone guitarists, Caribbean Black bands, the occasional lady of the night and street urchins wander in and out and it stays pretty lively.

Key Largo, Calle 7, Avenida 3, is a somewhat expensive bar housed in a beautiful mansion built in colonial style. It is busy, popular and fun, and has a casino, live music and dancing. It also has a slightly raffish atmosphere with attractively dressed ladies discreetly working at the world's oldest profession. (Women may prefer not to go there alone, although it's the sort of place where you could take your mother-in-law – I did. On the other hand, one reader called it a 'notorious house of ill-repute'. One thing is for sure – you won't find many places in San José with more expensive beers – I don't know about other costs).

The El Pueblo Shopping Centre has a good variety of restaurants and nightspots – most rather pricey. Wander around on Friday or Saturday night and take your pick; some spots are cheaper than others. The *Bar Tango Che Molinari* is an Argentine bar featuring live tango for a small cover charge. Nearby, *Bar Los Balcones* is a small bar with folk or acoustic musicians and no cover charge. I heard a good Bolivian folk singer here.

Other bars feature jazz or reggae; others still are just quiet places to have a drink without any music. There is less selection of live music midweek, but there's usually something going on. There are several discotheques which charge as much as US$4 to get in – and then may ask you to buy at least US$4 worth of drinks. Three of the better known discos here are the *Cocoloco*, *Infinito* and *La Plaza*.

Discotheques downtown include *El Tunel de Tiempo*, Avenida Central, Calle 7 & 9, with flashing lights and disco music; and the *Dynasty* in the Centro Comercial del Sur, near the old Puntarenas railway station, with

soul, reggae, calypso, and even rap music. Both these have covers of about US$2 or US$3. A cheaper place is the *Salsa 54*, Calle 3, Avenida 1 & 3, with Latin music. Slightly more expensive is the *La Torre*, Calle 7, Avenida Central & 1, with a mostly gay clientele and a variety of music. In San Pedro, *Club Cocodrilo*, Calle Central opposite the Banco Anglo, is a large bar with dance floor and videos, popular with students from the nearby university and yuppies hanging on to their youth. The Cocodrilo has a reputation for serving good hamburgers.

If disco isn't your bar scene, there are several alternatives. *Charleston*, Calle 9, Avenida 2 & 4, has almost an English pub décor and plays light jazz and soft rock. Occasional live performances at weekends cost US$2 or US$3 to get in; at other times the recorded music is free (though it's also kind of dead midweek).

An American-style bar which tends to be frequented by Americans and other English-speaking foreigners is *Lucky's Piano Blanco Bar*, Avenida Central, Calle 7 & 9, which has videos of North American sports events and an occasional piano player. Others include *Nashville South*, Calle 5, Avenidas 1 & 3, which has country music and an international chef preparing chilli dogs and other bar meals and *Tiny's Tropical Bar*, Avenida 2, Calle 9, which was inhabited by middle-aged American tourists on fishing vacations the first time I stopped by but which has a dart board and attracts local ex-pat English teachers as well (second visit) – since then I've come several times to throw darts and was beaten by Randy Galati.

The *Amstel Hotel Bar*, Calle 7, Avenida 1 & 3, is a quiet place if you're fed up with all the music in other bars. Out on Avenida 2, Calle 28 is *The Shakespeare Bar*, so called because it is next to a couple of small theatres and is the place to go before or after a show. They have a dart board.

An interesting an somewhat upscale bar with delicious bocas and great mariachi music (some nights) is *México Bar* (☎ 21 8461), Avenida 13, Calle 16, next to the Barrio México church. The beers are kind of

Top: Jaguar (RL)
Bottom: Morpho blue butterfly (RL)

Top: Leaf-cutter ants at work (RT)
Bottom: White-faced monkey (RG)

pricey, but the free bocas which come with them are the best I've had. A reader recommends their margaritas – but after numerous beers & bocas, I was reluctant to try one. The bar itself is good, although the neighbourhood leading to it is a poor one; you'd be best off taking a cab.

A seven-days-a-week, 24-hour downtown bar which has been there for decades and has become something of a local landmark is *Chelle's* at Avenida Central, Calle 9. It serves simple medium-priced meals and snacks, and, of course, beer and other drinks, but its main attraction is that it's always open. You never know who may come wandering in to this harshly lit bar. Somewhat more intimate and just around the corner is *Chelle's Taberna*, Calle 9, Avenida Central & 2, which is newer but less bright. Across the street is *Besito's Bar* which is less expensive, has both Western and Costa Rican music on tape, and has several TV sets showing local sports action, especially soccer. There are many other bars in San José; this is just a selection to start with.

Most of the bars mentioned thus far charge about US$1 to US$1.50 for a beer – over US$2 is considered very expensive indeed for a beer in a bar. These bars are generally OK for women to visit. Cheaper beers, at US$0.50 to US$0.75, can be had in many bars in town, but the cheaper bars may not be suitable for women to enter alone. As you start heading west of Calle 5, towards the market area, you'll find frequent bars catering to workmen. Here you'll find cheap beer and bocas in a spit and sawdust, macho atmosphere. Cheaper bars will often advertise their beer prices on signs in the window.

Out along Calle 2 near Avenida 8 is a small red-light district with expensive strip joints. It's best avoided.

Theatre Theatres advertise in the local newspapers, including the *The Tico Times*. Although many performances are in Spanish, prices are so moderate that you'll probably enjoy yourself even if you don't understand Spanish all that well. A few performances are in English.

The most important theatre is the Teatro Nacional, which stages plays, dance, opera, symphony, Latin American music, and has similar cultural events. The season is from April to November, although less frequent performances occur during other months. Tickets start as low as US$2.

The restored 1920s Teatro Melico Salazar has a variety of performances including music and dance as well as drama. The Teatro La Máscara also has dance performances, as well as alternative theatre. The Teatro Carpa is known for alternative and outdoor theatre. The Teatro Laurence Olivier is a small theatre, coffee shop and gallery where anything from jazz to film to theatre may be performed. Nearby, the Teatro Sala Garbo offers international movies which tend towards the avant garde rather than box-office Hollywood. Teatro Chaplin is known for mime; Teatro del Angel for comedy; Teatro J J Vargas Calvo for theatre-in-the-round; Teatro Arlequin for original works; and the Teatro Eugene O'Neill for performances sponsored by the North American-Costa Rican Cultural Center. The English language Little Theatre Group (☎ 24 3643, 28 7065, 28 5774) presents two or three plays a year at the Teatro Laurence Olivier – the LTG is always on the lookout for actors, so if you plan on being around for a few months and like to act, give them a call. There are many other theatres.

Most theatres are not very large, performances are popular, and ticket prices are very reasonable. This adds up to sold-out performances, so get tickets as early as possible. Theatres rarely have performances on Mondays.

The following are some of the most important theatres:

Teatro Arlequin
    Calle 13, Avenida Central & 2 (☎ 22 0792)
Teatro Bellas Artes
    University of Costa Rica, east side of campus, San Pedro
Teatro Carpa
    Avenida 1, Calle 29 & 33 (☎ 34 2866)
Teatro Chaplin
    Avenida 12, Calle 11 & 13 (☎ 23 2919)

Teatro de la Aduana
   Calle 25, Avenida 3 & 5 (☎ 23 4563)
Teatro de la Comedia
   Avenida Central, Calle 13 & 15 (☎ 55 3255)
Teatro del Angel
   Avenida Central, Calle 13 & 15 (☎ 22 8258)
Teatro Eugene O'Neill
   Calle Los Negritos, Barrio Escalante (☎ 53 5527)
Teatro J J Vargas Calvo
   Avenida 2, Calle 3 & 5 (☎ 22 1875)
Teatro La Máscara
   Calle 13, Avenida 2 & 6 (☎ 55 4250)
Teatro Laurence Olivier
   Calle 28, Avenida 2 (☎ 23 1960, 22 1034)
Teatro Melico Salazar
   Avenida 2, Calle Central & 2
   (☎ 21 4952, 22 2653)
Teatro Nacional
   Avenida 2, Calle 3 & 5
   (☎ 21 1329, 21 4482, 21 5341)
Teatro Sala de la Calle 15
   Avenida 2, Calle 13 & 15 (☎ 22 6622, 22 6626)
Teatro Sala Garbo
   Avenida 2, Calle 28 (☎ 22 1034)

Cinemas Many cinemas show recent films from Hollywood with Spanish subtitles, and the original English sound track. Occasionally, foreign films are dubbed over in Spanish ('hablado en Español') but this is unusual. Movies are inexpensive – about US$2 per performance. Cinemas advertise in the *The Tico Times* and in other local newspapers. Some of the best cinemas are:

Bellavista
   Avenida Central, Calle 17 & 19 (☎ 21 0909)
California
   Calle 23, Avenida 1 (☎ 21 4738)
Capri 1 & 2
   Avenida Central, Calle 9 (☎ 23 0264)
Colón 1 & 2
   Paseo Colón, Calle 38 & 40 (☎ 21 4517)
Magaly
   Calle 23, Avenida Central & 1 (☎ 21 9597)
Omni
   Calle 3, Avenida Central & 1 (☎ 21 7903)
Real
   Calle 11, Avenida 6 & 8 (☎ 23 5972)
Rex
   Calle Central, Avenida 6 & 8 (☎ 21 0041)
Universal
   Paseo Colón, Calle 26 & 28 (☎ 21 5241)
Variedades
   Calle 5, Avenida Central & 1 (☎ 22 6104)

Casinos & Nightclubs Apart from the casino at Key Largo, gamblers will find casinos in several of the larger and more expensive hotels, including the Aurola, Cariari, Corobicí, Gran Hotel Costa Rica, Herradura, Irazú, Presidente, and Royal Garden. Blackjack is the most popular game, but there are others, as well as slot machines.

Some of these hotels have nightclub shows.

Sport The national sport is soccer. The Costa Rican national team qualified for the World Cup in 1990, though haven't been doing so well recently. International and national games are played in the Estadio Nacional in Parque La Sabana. The soccer season is from May to October.

La Sabana also has a variety of other sporting facilities. There are tennis courts, volleyball, basketball and baseball areas, jogging paths and an Olympic-size swimming pool, but it costs US$3 to swim there between noon and 2 pm only. Many ticos prefer the excursion to the Ojo de Agua pool (near Alajuela, frequent buses) where swimming is available all day.

The Cariari Country Club (☎ 39 2455) has the only 18 hole golf course in the country. The Costa Rica Country Club (☎ 28 9333, 28 0988) in Escazú has a nine hole course. Tennis is also available at the Cariari Country Club (☎ 39 2248) or at the Costa Rica Tennis Club (☎ 32 1266, 32 5035) on the south side of La Sabana. For working out, you can join a local gym for about US$20 a month or use the facilities in the best hotels if you happen to be staying in one. Gyms are listed under 'Gimnasios' in the telephone directory.

Things to Buy
This section deals with stores in San José. If you have the time and the inclination you can find wide selections of well-priced items in the suburb of Moravia, about eight km northeast of downtown, or by taking a day trip to the village of Sarchí, where many of Costa Rica's handicraft items are produced. (Both

villages are described in the next chapter – The Central Valley & Highlands.)

A highly recommended souvenir shop is Annemarie's Boutique (☎ 21 6063) in the Hotel Don Carlos, Calle 9, Avenida 9. This is not the usual hotel gift store with a limited selection of overpriced gift items for guests with little time to shop around; the public are welcome and both the prices and selection are very good.

Other reasonably priced stores with good selections include the government-organised crafts cooperatives such as CANAPI, Calle 11, Avenida 1; and Mercado Nacional de Artesanía (☎ 21 5012), Calle 11, Avenida 2 & 4, (there are also branches inside the Museo Nacional and in Moravia). Also reasonably priced are Arte Rica, Avenida 2, Calle Central & 2, specialising in folk art; and ANDA, Avenida Central, Calle 5 & 7, specialising in pottery and gourd crafts produced by the few local Indians. Costa Rica Expeditions Travelers Store (☎ 57 0766), Calle Central, Avenida 3, has a wide selection of crafts as well as maps and books (in English) about Costa Rica. They also sell attractive walking sticks for your next hiking expedition. Sol Maya, Avenida Central, Calle 16 & 18, sells handicrafts with a Mayan theme, mostly made from Guatemalan textiles.

La Casona, Calle Central, Avenida Central & 1, is a large complex of many stalls with a wide selection of items including imports from other Central American countries. Malety, Avenida 1, Calle 1 & 3 (☎ 21 1670) and Calle 1, Avenida Central & 2 (☎ 23 0070) specialises in leather goods, especially cases, handbags and wallets.

Some galleries carry top-quality work which is excellent but expensive (which doesn't necessarily mean overpriced). If you are looking for top quality and are prepared to pay for it, try the following selection.

La Galería (☎ 21 3436, 23 2110), Calle Central, Avenida Central & 1, is perhaps the most elegant, with good displays of pieces by renowned woodworker Barry Biesanz and other artisans.

Suraksa, Calle 5, Avenida 3, has a good

selection of gold work in pre-Columbian style and fine ceramic ware. Atmosfera (☎ 22 4322), Calle 5, Avenida 1 & 3, has paintings, wall hangings and Indian work. Magia (☎ 33 2630), Calle 5, Avenida 1 & 3, has innovative furniture made of exotic hardwoods by Jay Morrison, another well-known craftsman.

If you want to see more of the work of Barry Biesanz or Jay Morrison, call Biesanz in Escazú (☎ 28 1811, fax 28 6164) or Morrison in Santa Ana (☎ 82 6697) to arrange a viewing – by appointment only.

The Plaza de la Cultura area often doubles as an impromptu arts market, with everything from T-shirts to carvings to paintings to inexpensive jewellery. The Mercado Central, Avenida Central & 1, Calle 6 & 8, has a small selection of handicrafts (leather work, sandals, clothing, wooden toys) but is the best place to buy fresh coffee beans at a fraction of the price you'll pay at home. If you can't make it to the central market, buy the beans at any supermarket, although they are not as cheap. Also in supermarkets and liquor stores, look for Café Rica, the local liquor which looks and tastes rather like the better-known Kahlua.

Getting There & Away

San José is not only the capital and the geographical heart of Costa Rica, it is also the hub of all transport around the country.

Unfortunately, the transport system is rather bewildering to the first time visitor. Most people get around by bus, but there is no central bus terminal. Instead, there are dozens of bus stops and terminals scattered around the city all serving different destinations. There are also two airports.

Fortunately, the tourist office does pretty well in keeping up with what goes where and when, so check with them if you get stuck. The inherent friendliness of the Costa Rican people also goes a long way to easing transport difficulties – if you need directions or advice, ask.

Air SANSA and Travelair are the two domestic airlines with scheduled flights. San José

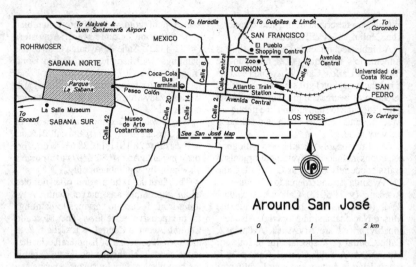

Around San José

0   1   2 km

is the hub for both of them. In addition, air taxis provide charter services to a host of airstrips all over the country.

SANSA flies between San José (Juan Santamaría Airport in Alajuela) and Golfito (one or two flights daily except Sunday, US$26), Quepos (two or three flights daily, US$15), Nosara (Monday, Wednesday, Friday, US$33), Palmar (Monday, Wednesday, Friday, US$26), Coto 47 (daily except Sunday, US$26), Tamarindo (one or two flights daily, US$33), Sámara (daily, US$33) and Barra Colorado (Tuesday, Thursday, Saturday, US$26). Return flights are later on the same day – see under respective towns for more details.

SANSA will check you in at its office downtown and provide transportation to the Juan Santamaría International Airport's domestic terminal, which is a few hundred metres to the right of the international terminal. Remember that reservations with SANSA must be prepaid to SANSA in full before they can be confirmed. You should also reconfirm in advance, preferably several times.

Travelair, the newer domestic airline, is more expensive, has a better service record,

and flies from Tobias Bolaños airport in Pavas (it's officially called an international airport because you can charter flights out of the country, but there are no scheduled international departures from this small airport). Flying with Travelair is a more relaxed procedure than flying with SANSA – they even give you a complimentary cup of coffee whilst you are waiting in their departure lounge in San José. You can buy a Travelair ticket from any travel agent or from the Travelair desk at the Tobias Bolaños airport. There are no buses to Tobias Bolaños – a taxi will be about US$3 from downtown.

Travelair flies from San José to Quepos (twice daily, US$35/60 one way/round trip), Barra Colorado (daily except Sunday, US$51/88), Golfito (daily, US$66/114), Palmar Sur (daily, US$58/100), Nosara or Samará/Carrillo (Wednesday and Sunday, US$58/100), Tamarindo (twice a day, US$66/114), Tortuguero (daily except Sunday, US$51/88), Tambor (once or twice a day, US$45/80) and Liberia (Wednesday and Sunday, US$66/114).

Airports There are two airports serving San José. These are Juan Santamaría International Airport (information ☎ 41 0744), Alajuela and Tobías Bolaños International Airport (information ☎ 32 8049, 32 2820), Pavas.

Domestic Airline Offices Apart from Costa Rica's domestic airlines (SANSA and Travelair), there are also several air taxi companies providing reasonably priced charters with small (mainly three to five passenger) aircraft to many airstrips in Costa Rica:

Aviones Taxi Aéreo SA
    Juan Santamaría Airport (☎ 41 1626, 41 2062)
Saeta
    Tobías Bolaños Airport (☎ 32 1474, 32 9514)
SANSA
    Calle 24, Paseo Colón & Avenida 1 (☎ 21 9414, 33 3258, 33 0397, fax 55 2176)
    Juan Santamaría Airport (☎ 41 8035)
Taxi Aéreo Centroamericano SA
    Tobías Bolaños Airport (☎ 32 1317, 32 1579)
Taxi Aéreo Costa Sol
    Juan Santamaría Airport (☎ 41 1444, 41 0922, fax 41 2671)
Travelair
    Tobías Bolaños Airport (☎ 32 7883, 20 3054, fax 20 0413)
Viajes Especial Aéreos SA (VEASA)
    Tobías Bolaños Airport (☎ 32 1010, 32 8043)

International Airline Offices International carriers which serve Costa Rica or have offices in San José are listed here, with their country of origin in parentheses (where it isn't obvious). Airlines serving Costa Rica directly are marked with an asterisk; they also have desks at the airport.

Aero Costa Rica*
    San Pedro (☎ 53 4753)
Aerolíneas Argentinas
    Calle 1, Avenida Central & 1 (☎ 22 1332)
Aeronica* (Nicaragua)
    Avenida 1, Calle 11 & 13 (☎ 23 7243, 55 0515)
Air France
    Avenida 1, Calle 4 & 6 (☎ 22 8811, fax 23 4970)
Alitalia (Italy)
    Calle 1, Avenida Central & 2 (☎ 22 6009, 22 6138, fax 33 7137)
American Airlines* (USA)
    Paseo Colón, Calle 26 & 28 (☎ 57 1266, 22 0786)
Avensa (Venezuela)
    Avenida Central, Calle 38 & 40 (☎ 57 1441)

Avianca (Colombia)
    (see SAM)
Aviateca* (Guatemala)
    Calle 1, Avenida 3 (☎ 33 8390, 55 4949)
British Airways
    Calle 1, Avenida 5 (☎ 21 7315)
    Calle 32, Paseo Colón & Avenida 2 (☎ 23 5648)
Continental Airlines* (USA)
    Calle 19, Avenida 2 (☎ 33 0266)
COPA* (Panama)
    Calle 1, Avenida 5 (☎ 23 7033, 21 5596)
Iberia* (Spain)
    Paseo Colón, Calle 40 (☎ 21 3311, 21 3411)
Icelandair
    Sabana Norte (☎ 22 5217)
KLM* (Holland)
    Sabana Sur (☎ 20 4111/2/3)
Korean Air
    Calle 1, Avenida Central & 1 (☎ 22 1332)
LTU* (Germany)
    Avenida 9, Calle 1 & 3 (☎ 57 2990)
Lacsa* (Costa Rica)
    Calle 1, Avenida 5 (☎ 31 0033, 21 7315)
Lan Chile
    Calle 40, Avenida 5 & 7 (☎ 57 0280)
Lloyd Aereo Boliviano
    Avenida 8, Calle 20 & 24 (☎ 55 1530, 33 6428)
Mexicana*
    Calle 38, Avenida 3 & 5 (☎ 22 1711, 33 6597, 22 7147)
SAHSA* (Honduras)
    Avenida 5, Calle 1 & 3 (☎ 21 5774, 21 5561)
SAM (Avianca)* (Colombia)
    Avenida 7, Calle 5 & 7 (☎ 33 3066)
Singapore Airlines
    Avenida 1, Calle 3 & 5 (☎ 55 3555)
TACA* (El Salvador)
    Calle 1, Avenida 1 & 3 (☎ 22 1790, 22 1744)
TWA (USA)
    Calle 1, Avenida Central & 1 (☎ 22 1332, 22 4737)
United* (USA)
    Sabana Sur (☎ 20 4844, 20 1665)
Varig* (Brazil)
    Avenida 5, Calle 3 & 5 (☎ 21 3087, 21 4004)

Bus Read the general information in the Getting Around chapter about Costa Rican bus travel before you begin taking buses around the country. This section lists the addresses and, where appropriate, phone numbers of the long-distance bus companies. Some of them have no more than a bus stop; others have a terminal.

Note that the ICT information office has up-to-date bus information. They will provide you with a computerised print-out of bus services upon request.

Try to avoid leaving San José on Friday nights and Saturday mornings when the buses are full of joséfinos off for the weekend. If you must travel then, book ahead if you can. Buses during Christmas and Easter are very crowded indeed.

The closest San José comes to having a general bus terminal is the Coca-Cola terminal, so called after a Coca-Cola bottling plant which used to exist on the site many years ago. The Coca-Cola terminal is between Calle 16 & 18, north of Avenida 1, and is one of the best known landmarks in San José.

Several companies serve a number of different towns from the Coca-Cola terminal. There are a few small signs in the terminal and it seems a little bewildering at first, but just ask someone to show you where your bus is; everyone seems to know where each bus leaves from. Several other companies have buses leaving from within three or four blocks of the Coca-Cola terminal, so this is an area to know. It is not in the best part of town, so watch for pickpockets. The area is generally safe, although late at night you might think about taking a taxi rather than walking, particularly if you are a single woman.

To/From Nicaragua & Panama There are two international bus companies with regular services to Managua (Nicaragua) and Panama City. See the Getting There & Away chapter for details of services and what to expect. TICA (☎ 21 8954), Calle 9, Avenida 2 & 4, has daily buses to Managua at 7.30 am. The trip takes 11 hours and costs US$9 from San José (it has reportedly been as high as US$17 in 1992, but was US$9 in 1993.) These buses continue to San Salvador and Guatemala City (2½ days; you sleep in hotels in Managua and San Salvador).

A cheaper but less reliable service to Managua is provided by Sirca (☎ 23 1464, 22 5541), Calle 7, Avenida 6 & 8. Their office hours are 8 am to 5 pm Monday to Friday and 8 am to 1 pm on Saturday. You have to wait on the street outside the office

for the bus to come by. Departures for Managua are on Monday, Wednesday, Friday and Sunday at 6 am (11 hours, US$8.50). They recommend that you buy tickets three days in advance.

TICA has a daily service to Panama City at 8 pm (20 hours, US$18). This company will also sell you a ticket to David, the first major town in Panama. Another company with buses to David is TRACOPA (☎ 21 4214, 23 7685), Avenida 18, Calle 4. There are daily direct buses at 7.30 am (nine hours, US$7.50).

Note that fares from Managua (or Panama City) are rarely the same as from San José because of differences in currency regulations.

To/From Southern Costa Rica TRACOPA (☎ 21 4214, 23 7685), Avenida 18, Calle 4, has five daily buses to Ciudad Neily and on to the Panamanian border at Paso Canoas. It is about seven hours to Neily, eight hours to the border. Fares are US$5.50/6.50 to Neily/Paso Canoas direct, or a little cheaper on the normal route. TRACOPA also has six daily buses to Palmar Norte, three daily buses to Golfito (eight hours, US$4.75), and a bus to San Vito (five hours direct, US$6.50; six hours normal, US$5.50). TRACOPA buses to Coto Brus, en route to San Vito, leave four times a day from Empresa Alfaro (☎ 22 2750, 23 8361), Calle 14, Avenida 3 & 5.

Buses for Puerto Jiménez in the Península de Osa leave Autotransportes Blanco at 6 am and noon from Calle 12, Avenida 9 (opposite the big Puntarenas bus terminal).

Buses to San Isidro de El General are with Transportes Musoc (☎ 23 0686, 22 2422), under the Hotel Musoc, Calle 16, Avenida 1 & 3, next to the Coca-Cola terminal. Alternatively, go with TUASUR (☎ 22 9763) which is across the street. Fares are US$3 for the three hour trip, with about 15 daily departures.

To/From Meseta Central Buses to Cartago leave several times an hour from the SACSA station (☎ 33 5350) at Calle 5, Avenida 18.

The trip takes almost an hour, depending on traffic, and costs about US$0.40. Some of these buses continue to Turrialba, but more Turrialba buses leave from the TRANS-TUSA station (☎ 22 4464) at Avenida 6, Calle 13. The two hour ride costs just over a dollar.

Microbuses for Heredia (☎ 33 8392) leave several times an hour from Calle 1, Avenida 7 & 9; the half hour trip costs about US$0.30.

Buses for Alajuela leave every few minutes from the TUASA terminal (☎ 22 5325) at Avenida 2, Calle 12. Most of these buses stop at the international airport. Some buses for Heredia also leave from across the street from here.

Buses to Grecia (one hour, US$0.40), and on seven km to Sarchí (US$0.50), leave about once an hour from the Coca-Cola terminal. It is often easier to go to Alajuela and change.

Buses for San Ramón, half way to Puntarenas, leave several times an hour from Calle 16, Avenida 1 & 3, across the street from the Hotel Musoc.

To/From the Pacific Coast Buses for Quepos and Manuel Antonio leave from the Coca-Cola terminal with Transportes Morales (☎ 23 5567). Direct buses to Manuel Antonio, with reserved seats, leave at 6 am, noon and 6 pm, and cost US$5 for the 3½ hour trip. Slower and cheaper buses to Quepos leave four times a day. Other Transportes Morales buses (☎ 32 1829) go to Jacó at 7.15 am and 3.30 pm from the Coca-Cola terminal.

Buses for Puntarenas leave every hour during the day from Calle 12, Avenida 9, with Empresarios Unidos de Puntarenas (☎ 22 0064). The two hour trip costs about US$2.40.

To/From the Península Nicoya Buses for the Península Nicoya (and its popular beaches) have to negotiate the Golfo de Nicoya, a formidable body of water. The car ferry from Puntarenas does not normally take buses. Buses either cross the Río Tempisque on the ferry, which leaves about every

hour, or take the long ___ Liberia. Thus bus tim ___ ably depending on the ___ using the ferry, whether y___ long time waiting for it.

Empresa Alfaro (☎ 22 2? ___, Avenida 3 & 5, has seven da___ ___ses to Nicoya (five hours, US$3), als_ going to Santa Cruz and Filadelfia. More interestingly, they also have daily buses for beaches at Sámara (noon) and Tamarindo (3.30 pm), as well as a bus to Quebrada Honda, Mansión and Hojancha (2.30 pm).

From Calle 12, Avenida 7 & 9 (opposite the Puntarenas terminal) is a small office with afternoon buses to Jicaral and the beaches at Bejuco and Islita (five hours, US$5.50). There is another stop for Bejuco buses from one block south of the Puntarenas terminal – check carefully to find out where the bus is leaving from.

TRALAPA (☎ 21 7202), Calle 20, Avenida 3, has daily buses to Playa Flamingo (8, 10.30 am), Junquillal (2 pm), Tamarindo (4 pm) and Santa Cruz (six daily, US$4.50).

The Pulmitan bus station (☎ 22 1650) at Calle 14, Avenida 1 & 3, has a daily bus to Playas del Coco at 10 am (US$3.50).

Buses for Playas Panamá and Hermosa leave at 3.30 pm daily from the bus stop in front of Los Rodriguez lumber store on Calle 12, Avenida 5 & 7.

These schedules are for the dry season when people go to the beach – during the wet season services may be curtailed. Beach resorts are very popular among Costa Ricans and buses tend to be booked up ahead of time. Reserve a seat if possible.

To/From North-Western Costa Rica There is no bus terminal for Monteverde, which reflects how isolated this community remains despite the enormous increase in popularity it has experienced in the past decade. Buses to Monteverde currently leave from the Tilarán terminal (☎ 22 3854), Calle 14, Avenida 9 & 11. Currently, buses leave at 6.30 am on Saturdays and 2.30 pm from Monday to Thursday for the four hour trip which costs about US$4. It is worth getting

...he day before departure (at least) ...ause the buses get booked up quickly; the ticket office is closed from 12.30 to 2 pm. Buses for Tilarán leave at 7.30 am, 12.45, 3.45 and 6.30 pm.

Buses for Cañas with Transportes La Cañera (☎ 22 3006) leave six times a day from Calle 16, Avenida 1 & 3, opposite the Coca-Cola terminal. They also have a bus for La Cruz (near the Nicaraguan border), continuing to Santa Cecilia at 2.45 pm. They also have a daily bus for Upala at 6.30 am (6 am on Saturdays). Buses for Upala also leave from Calle 12, Avenida 3 & 5, at 3 and 3.45 pm daily.

Buses to the Nicaraguan border at Peñas Blancas, with stops at the entrance to Parque Nacional de Santa Rosa and La Cruz, leave from next to the Hotel Cocorí, Calle 11, Avenida 3 & 5 (☎ 24 1968). There are three buses daily, and the cost is about US$4 for the six hour trip to the border.

Buses for Liberia (4½ hours, US$3) leave eight times a day from Pulmitan (☎ 22 1650), Calle 14, Avenida 1 & 3.

To/From Northern Costa Rica Buses to Ciudad Quesada (☎ 55 4318; two hours, US$2) via Zarcero (one hour) leave at least every hour from the Coca-Cola terminal. A few buses are express to Ciudad Quesada. (Note that Ciudad Quesada is also known as San Carlos.) From Ciudad Quesada you can take buses west to La Fortuna, the Arenal volcano, and on to Tilarán, or east towards Puerto Viejo de Sarapiquí and Río Frío). There are also buses from the Coca-Cola to Fortuna at 6.15, 8.40 and 11.30 am (☎ 32 5660).

Direct buses to Puerto Viejo de Sarapiquí (not to be confused with Puerto Viejo de Talamanca on the south-eastern Caribbean coast) leave from Avenida 11, Calle Central & 1, six times a day beginning around 6 am. Most of these buses go via Río Frío and Horquetas (for Rara Avis) and return to San José via Varablanca and Heredia; a few do the route in reverse. If going to Puerto Viejo, it makes little difference which way you go, as either way takes 3½ hours and costs about

US$3. If going to Horquetas, make sure you go via the Río Frío route or you will get stuck on the bus for 4½ hours instead of 2½. Check departures with the bus stop or the ICT – they have changed frequently in the last few years.

There are also a couple of buses for Puerto Viejo via Heredia leaving at 6 am and noon from the Coca-Cola terminal.

Buses for Los Chiles leave from Avenida 3, Calle 18 & 20.

To/From the Caribbean Coast Buses for Puerto Limón leave from Avenida 3, Calle 19 & 21, (☎ 23 7811) with at least hourly departures via Guápiles. It takes 2½ hours and costs US$3 to Limón.

For buses direct to Cahuita, Bribri and Sixaola, Autotransportes MEPE (☎ 21 0524), Avenida 11, Calle Central & 1, has three departures a day currently leaving at 6 am and 1.30 and 3.30 pm – schedules change often so check. The fare is US$5.75 to Sixaola (on the Panamanian border) and US$4.75 to Cahuita (four hours). Some MEPE buses will detour to Puerto Viejo de Talamanca en route to Sixaola.

In front of the Puntarenas station on Calle 12, Avenida 7 & 9, there is a bus stop with departures to Guápiles with a few buses continuing to Río Frío. For buses to Siquirres, go to the stop on Calle 12, Avenida 3 & 5, on the east side.

Train The railway was severely damaged in the 1991 earthquake, causing all services to be cancelled, and it is highly unlikely that the services from San José to Puerto Limón or to Puntarenas will resume. The famous and attractive route to Puerto Limón was known as the 'banana train'. Now, there is a guided banana train day tour (about US$75) which takes travellers to the lowlands by bus and then puts them on the train through some banana plantations around Guápiles, which gives them a feel for the old ride. Call Swiss Travel (☎ 31 0455) for more information.

Intertren (☎ 26 0011) has begun commuter services which link San José with Heredia. These trains leave from near the

UCR (Universidad de Costa Rica) in San Pedro at 5.45 am, noon, and 5.15 pm Monday to Friday, and go through the old Atlantic railway station in San José (Avenida 3, Calle 21 & 23) en route to the south side of Heredia, near the Universidad Nacional. There are also trains at 10 am and noon on Sundays. To get to the UCR in San Pedro, take the bus from Avenida 2, Calle 5 & 7 in San José, ask to get off at the *iglesia* (church) in San Pedro, and walk from there.

Getting Around

Downtown San José is very busy and relatively small. I always avoid taking local buses around downtown, finding it easier to walk. The narrow streets, heavy traffic and complicated one-way system often mean that it is quicker to walk than to take the bus. The same applies to driving: if you rent a car, don't drive in downtown – it's a nightmare! If you are in a hurry to get somewhere that is more than a km away, I suggest you hire a taxi.

To/From the Airport For the main international airport (Juan Santamaría) there is no airport bus as such but all buses to Alajuela will stop outside the international airport. Alajuela buses leave from Avenida 2, Calle 12 every few minutes and cost about US$0.40, irrespective of whether you go to the airport or Alajuela. (From 7 pm to midnight, buses go every 40 minutes and from midnight to 5 am, every hour.) Conventional wisdom is that these buses can't handle travellers with baggage, and that you should take a taxi. This is true. However, if you are down to your last few colones, you can still take these buses – if you have to, you could pay for an extra seat for your luggage. I wouldn't try it during rush hours, though – commuters trying to reach their jobs may not take kindly to being bumped off the bus by a backpack full of rancid clothing!

Heading into San José from the airport, you'll find the bus stop outside the international terminal, behind the car rental agencies. During the rush hour, the Alajuela

to San José bus may be full when it comes by and you may have to wait for some time.

Airport taxis are orange, and the fare to or from the airport is a set US$10 – though it has been US$10 for a few years now, and may go up.

There are no buses direct to the local airport at Tobías Bolaños. Your best bet is to take a taxi – about US$3.

Bus Local buses are very useful to get you out into the suburbs and surrounding villages, or to the airport. They have set routes and leave regularly from particular bus stops downtown. Buses run from about 5 am to 10 pm and cost from US$0.05 to US$0.30. Buses to Moravia leave from Avenida 3, Calle 3 & 5; for Escazú from Calle 16, Avenida 1 & 3; for Santa Ana from the Coca-Cola terminal; and for Pavas from Avenida 1, Calle 18 & 20. Most buses for Guadalupe leave from Avenida 3, Calle 1 & 3 (though some leave from one or two blocks away – ask).

Buses from Parque La Sabana head into town on Paseo Colón, then go over to Avenida 2 at the San Juan de Dios hospital. They then go three different ways through town before heading back to La Sabana. Buses are marked Sabana-Cementerio, Sabana-Estadio, or Cementerio-Estadio. These buses are a good bet for a cheap city tour. The Sabana-Cementerio bus has been particularly recommended. Buses east for Los Yoses and San Pedro go back and forth along Avenida 2, going over to Avenida Central at Calle 29 outbound. They start at Avenida 2, Calle 5 & 7.

If you need buses to other suburbs, enquire at the tourist office.

Taxi San José taxis are red, with the exception of airport cabs which are orange. Downtown, meters (marías) are supposed to be used but some drivers will pretend they are broken and try and charge you more – particularly if you are a tourist who doesn't speak Spanish. Driving with a broken maría is illegal and is happening less and less – but there's always a few cab drivers who will try to pull a fast one. Always make sure that the maría is working when you get in – if it isn't, you can get out and hail another taxi or negotiate a fare to avoid being grossly overcharged at your destinations.

The official 1993 rates are 80 colones (US$0.60) for the first km (which should be the total on the meter when you get in) and 35 colones for each additional km. Short rides downtown should be around US$1; longer rides around US$2. Waiting time is 300 colones per hour. San José cab drivers are the toughest in Costa Rica; on the other hand they are a lot more friendly than cab drivers in many other countries.

You can hire a taxi and driver for half a day or longer if you want to do some touring around the Meseta Central. Around US$30 to US$40 is reasonable for half a day, depending on how far you want to go. Cabs will take three or four passengers. To hire a cab, either ask your hotel to help arrange it or call one of the numbers listed below. Alternatively, talk to drivers at any cab rank. There are cab stands at the Parque Nacional, Parque Central, near the Teatro Nacional, and in front of several of the better hotels. Taxi drivers are not normally tipped in Costa Rica.

You can have a taxi pick you up if you are going to the airport or have a lot of luggage.

Car Rental There are plenty of car rental agencies if you want to drive yourself, but they are quite expensive, at least by North American standards. You should read the section on Rental and Road Safety in the Getting Around chapter before venturing onto the roads. I hired a car for part of the time whilst researching this book and had no problems – in fact, I had fun.

Car rental rates vary about 10% between companies, so shop around. There are about 40 car rental agencies in San José and new ones keep coming – look in the newspaper or the yellow pages under Alquiler de Automoviles for a comprehensive listing. The *The Tico Times* often carry ads for those companies which are having specials.

Motorbike Rental Given the narrow roads and difficult driving conditions, I cannot recommend riding a motorbike. However, if you are an experienced and careful biker, renting a motorbike is an option, but don't think about suing me if you die, 'cos I don't recommend riding motorbikes.

Rent-a-Moto (☎ 22 0055), Avenida 10, Calle 8, has 250 cc Hondas for US$35 per day including unlimited mileage, insurance and one (or two) helmets. Weekly discounts are available.

Moto-Rental (☎ 32 7850, 33 4880), Avenida 1, Calle 30 & 32, provides the same mileage/insurance/helmet deal for a 185 cc Suzuki (US$36 per day, US$210 per week) or a 200 cc Honda (US$42 per day, US$250 per week). They advertise discount prices (20% off) in the *The Tico Times* occasionally.

Heat Renta Moto (☎ 21 3789), Avenida 2, Calle 11 & 13, have also been recommended.

Renta Moto (☎ 21 3789, 21 6671, fax 21 3786), Avenida 2, Calle 11 & 13, 7th floor, has also been recommended for cheap motorbike rentals – around US$20 per day for a Honda 250 including insurance.

Bicycle Rental Mutra Tours (☎/fax 89 8191) has recently opened its 'Bike 'n Hike' shop in the Centro Comercial El Cruce shopping centre in Escazú. It offers mountain bikes for hire at US$29 per day and also organises guided and non-guided bike tours throughout the country.

Central Valley & the Highlands

The Central Valley is the popular name for the region, around San José, in the centre of Costa Rica. It is not really a valley and a more appropriate name would be the 'central plateau' or 'central tableland'. This is, in fact, the translation of the Costa Rican name for the area, Meseta Central.

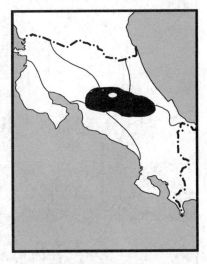

This region is both historically and geographically the heart of Costa Rica. To the north and east, the Central Valley is bounded by the mountain range known as the Cordillera Central, which contains several volcanoes including the famous Poás and Irazú.

To the south the region is bounded by the north end of the Cordillera de Talamanca and a short mountainous projection called the Fila de Bustamente. Between the Cordilleras Central and Talamanca is the beautiful Río Reventazón valley, which gives San José its historical access to the Caribbean. To the west, the plateau falls off into the Pacific lowlands.

This chapter covers the Central Valley (except San José) and, additionally, the upper Río Reventazón valley and the volcanoes of the Cordillera Central. Although not geographically part of the Central Valley, these surrounding highlands are most often visited on day trips out of San José.

About 60% of Costa Rica's population lives in the Central Valley. The region's fertile volcanic soil and pleasant climate attracted the first successful Spanish settlers. Before the arrival of the Spaniards, the region was an important agricultural zone inhabited by thousands of Indian farmers, most of whom were wiped out by diseases brought by the Europeans. The first capital city was at Cartago.

Today, four of Costa Rica's seven provinces have fingers of land within the Central Valley, and all four have their political capitals there. Thus we see an unusual situation where there are three provincial capitals within a scant 25 km of San José, which in itself is the capital of San José Province. The others are the cities of Cartago, Alajuela and Heredia, all capitals of provinces of the same name.

Despite their provincial capital status, the cities of the Central Valley do not have a well-developed hotel infrastructure. Most visitors use San José as a base for day trips to the other cities, as well as many of the other attractions of the Central Valley region. A bus ride from San José out to Central Valley towns for a day trip is as good a way as any of seeing some of rural Costa Rica – and it'll cost you next to nothing. As visitors travel throughout the area, they pass through attractive rolling agricultural countryside full of the green shiny-leaved plants bearing the berries that made Costa Rica famous – coffee.

On the way to Volcán Poás, the traveller can see huge areas of hillsides covered with what appears to be a black plastic sheet, rather like a modern environmental sculp-

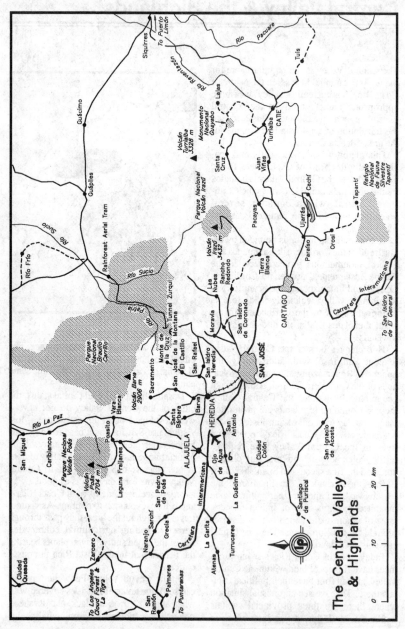

The Central Valley
& Highlands

0   10   20 km

ture. These are, in fact, *viveros* or plant nurseries. Closer inspection reveals that the black plastic is a protective mesh under which a variety of plants are grown for sale to greenhouses.

This chapter is arranged in a roughly west to east sequence around San José.

The Alajuela Area

ALAJUELA

The provincial capital of Alajuela lies about 18 km (as the crow flies) to the north-west of San José. The city is on a gently sloping hill which has an altitude of 920 metres on the south-western side of town, rising to 970 metres on the north-eastern side. As such, it is about 200 metres lower than San José and has a slightly warmer climate, thus attracting joséfinos on summer outings.

There are two cinemas, both along Avenida Central. Otherwise, there is not much entertainment, but the Parque Central is a pleasant place to relax in and the city gives a look at a more unhurried pace of Costa Rican life than the nearby capital. Several nearby villages are worth visiting also, and these are described at the end of the Alajuela section.

The city and its immediate suburbs have a population of about 50,000. The Juan Santamaría International Airport, which serves San José, is only 2.5 km south-east of Alajuela. This makes Alajuela a convenient stopping place for people wishing to catch flights.

The map shows the streets and avenues but, as with most Costa Rican towns, these are rarely used by the locals, who prefer landmark addresses.

Museo Juan Santamaría

Alajuela's main claim to fame is being the birthplace of the national hero, Juan Santamaría, after whom the nearby international airport was named.

Santamaría was the drummer boy who volunteered to torch the building, defended by filibuster William Walker, in the war of 1856. He died in this action and is now commemorated by the museum and a park in Alajuela.

The Museo Juan Santamaría (☎ 4775) is in what used to be a jail on Calle 2, Avenida 3, to the north-west of the pleasant and shady Parque Central. The museum, which contains maps, paintings and historical artefacts related to the war with Walker, is open daily from 10 am to 5 pm, except on Monday; admission is free. (The ICT in San José told me that the opening hours are 2 to 9 pm, but this wasn't the case recently. You should check.)

Two blocks south of the Parque Central is the Parque Juan Santamaría where there is a statue of the hero in action, flanked by cannons.

Festivals

The anniversary of the Battle of Rivas, 11 April, is particularly celebrated in Alajuela – home town of the battle's young hero, Juan Santamaría. There is a parade and civic events.

The Fiesta de Los Mangos is held every July, lasts over a week, and includes an arts & crafts fair, parades, and some mild revelry.

Places to Stay

There are few hotels in Alajuela. The *Hotel Rex* and *Hotel El Real* are both by the bus terminal. They are cheap and reasonably clean but not well recommended – 'much street life' as a local euphemistically told me. They would do at a pinch, however. Expect to pay about US$5 per person.

The *Hotel Alajuela* (☎ 41 1241, 41 6595; fax 41 7912; Apartado 110-4050, Alajuela), is on Calle 2, just south of the main plaza. Many of the rooms have little kitchenettes attached and the hotel is friendly, clean and well run. It has expanded recently and now has about 50 rooms but, unfortunately, it is often full. This is because of the proximity of the international airport. Rates are US$24/30 for a single/double with private hot bath. There are a few rooms with kitch-

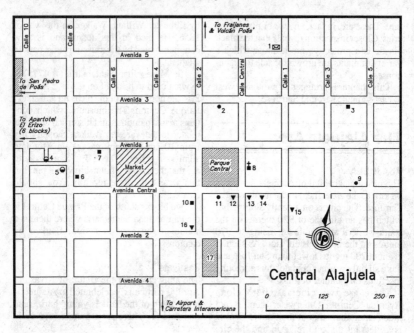

Central Alajuela

■ **PLACES TO STAY**

3 Hospedaje La Posada
6 Hotel El Real
7 Hotel Rex
10 Hotel Alajuela

▼ **PLACES TO EAT**

12 Restaurant El Cencerro
13 Mönpik Ice Cream
14 Marisquería La Sirenita
15 Kun Wa Chinese Restaurant

16 Bar Restaurant La Jarra

OTHER

1 Post Office
2 Museo Juan Santamaría
4 Bus Terminal
5 Bus Stop for San José
8 Cathedral
9 Cine Futurama
11 Cine Milan
17 Parque Juan Santamaría

---

enettes and a few cheaper rooms which lack private baths.

Another reasonably priced possibility is the *Hospedaje La Posada*, one block north and two blocks east of the Parque Central – I haven't had a chance to check this one.

The *Apartotel El Erizo* (☎/fax 41 2840; Apartado 61-4050, Alajuela) is 10 blocks west of the Parque Central and is the fanciest place in town. It has one and two bedroom apartments for US$77 and US$88. Each comes with kitchenette and TV.

About five km west of Alajuela is the *Las Orquideas Inn* (☎ 43 9346; fax 43 9740; Apartado 394, Alajuela) is an attractive Spanish-style mansion with a pool and spacious, airy rooms with wood-parquet floors. Most of these rooms have private bathrooms and cost US$50 to US$80 depending on the room. There is a restaurant and bar; call for directions.

Places to Eat

There are several recommended places near the Parque Central. The *Marisquería La Sirenita* (☎ 41 9681) has good seafood meals starting at US$3.50 and serves meat as well.

The *Kun Wa* Chinese restaurant has decent meals in the US$4 to US$6 range. The pleasant *Bar Restaurant La Jarra* is upstairs at the corner of Calle 2, Avenida 2, and has good typical food in the same price range. Some of the tables are out on little balconies with views of the Parque Juan Santamaría and statue. At the corner of the Parque Central is *Mönpik*, a favourite stand-by for ice creams and snacks.

The best and most expensive restaurant in town is on the main plaza. This is *El Cencerro* which translates into 'the cowbell' and so its speciality is, as you can guess, steaks, although they serve other food as well. Meals are in the US$6 to US$12 range.

Entertainment

At the other end of the spectrum from El Cencerro is the lively (at least on a Saturday night) *Indianapolis Taberna* on Calle 8, Avenida 1 & 3. Here, you can have a beer and a boca for US$0.90. Listen to locals singing and playing the guitar, get into a fight, make a friend for life, solve the world's problems, and drink away your money. This is one slice of tico life – but women would do best to go with a male, and speaking Spanish will help you make friends rather than get into fights.

Getting There & Away

Buses for Alajuela (US$0.40) leave San José from Avenida 2 and Calle 12 every 10 minutes between 5.30 am and 7 pm. From 7 pm till midnight, buses leave at 40 minute intervals. Late night buses are also available at less frequent intervals from Calle 2, Avenida 2. The return buses from Alajuela

leave from the stop at Calle 8, Avenida Central & 1. Behind the bus stop for San José is the Alajuela bus terminal, from where buses to other towns leave. Down on Avenida 4, Calle 2 & 4, is a microbus stop for San José.

To get to the airport, either take a San José bus and get off at the airport, or take a taxi. Taxis to the airport are available from the Parque Central at any hour of the day or night. The fare is about US$2.

OJO DE AGUA

About six km south of Alajuela are the famous Ojo de Agua springs, a favourite resort for people from both San José and Alajuela. Thousands of litres of water gush out from the spring each minute. This fills swimming pools and an artificial boating lake before being piped down to Puntarenas, for which it is a major water supply.

The recreational complex is very crowded as picnicking locals flock there at weekends – it is quieter midweek. Entrance to the complex is US$1.25 and there are places to eat, games courts and a small gym. The end of the dry season is reportedly the least impressive time to go – water levels are low, partly due to local deforestation.

Getting There & Away

Buses leave from the terminal in Alajuela. Buses also leave every hour (more frequently at weekends) from Avenida 1, Calle 18 & 20 in San José. Buses from Heredia leave from Calle 6, Avenida 6.

Drivers from San José should take the San Antonio de Belén exit off the Interamericana (in front of the Hotel Cariari) and go through San Antonio to Ojo de Agua.

THE BUTTERFLY FARM

Yes, they farm butterflies in Costa Rica and it's a fascinating process. Informative guided tours take you through tropical gardens filled with hundreds of butterflies of many species. You can see and learn about all the stages of the complex butterfly life cycle as well as find out about the importance of butterflies in nature.

Morpho butterfly

There is also a bee garden with tours discussing traditional beekeeping of stingless bees by Mayan Indians and the problems of Africanised 'killer' bees. Traditional ox cart rides are available and tropical birds abound in the gardens. Bring your camera – there are good photo opportunities.

The Butterfly Farm (☎ 48 0115) is open daily from 9 am to 5 pm. Butterfly tours last 90 minutes and run continuously from 9 am to 3.30 pm. Bee tours are available at 10.30 am, noon, 1.30 and 3.30 pm. The butterfly tour is US$11 for adults, the bee tour is US$8 (students and children receive a discount for either tour). Once your tour is over, you can stay as long as you want.

Getting There & Away

The farm is in front of El Club Campestre Los Reyes (a country club) in the village of La Guácima, 12 km south-west of Alajuela. Buses to La Guácima leave San José at 11 am and 2 pm daily, except Sunday, from a stop marked San Antonio/Ojo de Agua at Avenida 1, Calle 20 & 22. The bus returns to San José at 3.15 pm.

The Butterfly Farm also has its own bus. This collects passengers from major San José hotels at 8 and 10 am and 2 pm on Monday, Tuesday and Thursday.

There are also buses from Alajuela at 6.45,

9 and 11 am and 1 pm, leaving from 100 metres south and 100 metres west of the Supermercado Tikal (which everyone knows). Make sure your bus goes to La Guácima Abajo. The last bus returns to Alajuela at 5.45 pm.

Drivers from San José should take the San Antonio de Belén exit off the Interamericana by the Hotel Cariari and drive through San Antonio to La Guácima. There are butterfly signs as you get close. Tours are available from San José travel agencies.

LA GUÁCIMA

Apart from the Butterfly Farm, there is a motorcycle/car racetrack here, with races held on most weekends.

Near El Club Campestre Los Reyes is the *Country Inn La Guácima* (☎ 48 0179; fax 21 8245; Apartado 807-4050, Alajuela; CRBBG member). This small B&B has two rooms with private bath for US$45/60/75 for singles/doubles/triples. This includes full breakfast and transportation to/from the airport.

For information on how to get to and from the La Guácima see the previous Butterfly Farm section.

WEST TO ATENAS

West of Alajuela is a road which leads to Atenas, a small village about 25 km away. En route to Atenas you pass Zoo-Ave and La Garita. **Zoo-Ave** (☎ 43 9140) is about 10 km west of Alajuela and has a collection of tropical birds including over 60 Costa Rican species displayed in a pleasant park-like setting. There is a program to breed endangered native species and reintroduce them into the wild. There are also mammal and reptile collections.

The zoo is open daily, except Christmas, from 9 am to 5 pm; admission is US$3. If you are driving west from San José or Alajuela on the Interamericana, take the Atenas exit and continue west for 2.5 km to Zoo-Ave.

A few km beyond Zoo-Ave is **La Garita** where there is a children's amusement park called Bosque Encantado. Also in La Garita is an unusual restaurant which serves every dish you could imagine – as long as it is made from corn (maize). The restaurant, called *La Fiesta del Maíz*, is open from Thursday to Sunday.

The excursion to Ojo de Agua, the Butterfly Farm, Zoo-Ave, Bosque Encantado, and finishing at La Fiesta del Maíz is a popular weekend outing by car from San José – though roads are poorly marked and you may want to go with a tico friend. The area is famous for its *viveros* (plant nurseries), where local flora are grown and sold for use within Costa Rica.

Places to Stay

There are several small B&B places in the area. All are CRBBG members. *Ana's Place* (☎ 46 5019; Apartado 66 Atenas, Alajuela) has seven rooms, some with private bath. Rates are US$35/45 for a single/double, including breakfast. Ana's Place is near the Atenas bus station – call for directions.

Villa Tranqilidad (☎ 5460; Apartado 28-4013, Alajuela) is a modern house with a pool and garden surrounded by a coffee finca and orchard. There are four bedrooms with private bath and hot water; rates are US$35/40 for a single/double with breakfast. Airport pick-up and other meals can be arranged. The hotel is three km from the centre of Atenas – phone for directions. Spanish, English, Dutch and German are spoken.

La Piña Dorada (☎ /fax 48 7220; Apartado 523, Alajuela) is a large and comfortable house set in a spacious garden with a pool. There is a games room. Rooms are US$57 for a double with bath and hot water; a suite is US$74, including breakfast. No smoking is allowed inside the house which is almost three km south of La Garita on the road to Turrucares.

Getting There & Away

Buses go to Atenas from the San José Coca-Cola terminal several times a day, but they do not pass Zoo-Ave. To get to Zoo-Ave and La Garita take one of the buses, from Alajuela's bus terminal, to Atenas. Call

Coopetransatenas (☎ 46 5767) for bus information.

NORTH-WEST TO ZARCERO

North-west of Alajuela are the villages of Grecia (22 km), Sarchí (29 km), Naranjo (35 km) and Zarcero (52 km). They all have colourful churches, typical of the Costa Rican countryside.

All of these small towns can be reached by buses either from the Coca-Cola terminal in San José or the bus terminal in Alajuela. The drive to Zarcero is along a narrow, winding and hilly road with pretty views of the coffee fincas which cover the Central Valley hillsides.

GRECIA

Grecia is an agricultural centre (pineapples, sugar cane) and is known for its red church, something of a local landmark. There is also a small regional museum in the Casa de Cultura, which is open sporadically. Otherwise its main importance for the traveller is as a place to change buses to continue to Sarchí (although there are also direct buses there from the Coca-Cola terminal in San José).

The citizens pride themselves on the fact that Grecia was once voted the cleanest little town in Latin America!

Places to Stay

La Posada de Grecia (☎ 44 5354, 44 8660; fax 44 5321; Apartado 2-4100, Grecia, Alajuela; CRBBG member) is in an odd location – on the 3rd floor of the Tienda Raul Vega family store, by Grecia's Parque Central. There are good views of Volcán Poás and other mountains. They have three rooms with private bath for US$30 (one double bed) including continental breakfast. No smoking is allowed inside.

Another similarly priced choice is *Finca Mirador* (☎ 44 6260; Apartado 110, Grecia, Alajuela; CRBBG member). They are one km north of the Fabrica de Licores. For cheaper digs, try *Pensión Familiar* (☎ 44 5097) – I have no other details.

SARCHÍ

This small town is Costa Rica's most famous craft centre, and tour buses and locals stop here to buy crafts, particularly woodwork. It is, of course, commercial but in a charmingly understated Costa Rican way. There is no pressure to buy anything and there is the opportunity to see crafts being made.

A few decades ago, the common form of transport in the countryside was the carreta, gaily painted wooden carts drawn by oxen. Although carretas are rarely seen in use today (you'll occasionally see one in the most rural areas) they have become something of a traditional craft form and, as much as anything else, a symbol of agricultural Costa Rica.

They are used nowadays to decorate people's gardens; scaled-down versions are made for use as indoor tables, sideboards and bars, and miniature models are available for use as indoor sculptures or accent pieces. All sizes come apart and fold down for transport.

You can see them being made in several *fábricas de carretas* (cart factories) where the most interesting part of the process is watching local artisans paint the colourful mandala designs onto the carts.

The bright paintwork is also used to decorate wooden trays, plates and other souvenirs. Unpainted woodwork such as salad bowls, kitchen boards, serving dishes, jewellery boxes, letter openers, statuettes, toy cars and planes and a variety of other utilitarian knick-knacks are also sold.

These make inexpensive gifts and souvenirs and prices are slightly less than in San José.

There are also furniture factories in Sarchí. Whilst the elegantly carved headboards and bedsteads, tables and chairs, and sitting room furniture are mainly designed for local sale and use, some travellers buy one or two of the leather and wood rocking chairs – these come apart and fold down for transporting.

Whatever you do, leave a shopping trip to Sarchí until the end of your trip. Thus you won't be encumbered by presents whilst you are travelling around the country. And shop around – there are plenty of factories and stores to choose from in Sarchí.

Orientation & Information

Sarchí is divided by the Río Trojas into Sarchí Norte and Sarchí Sur and is a rather spread-out town straggling several km along the main Grecia to Naranjo road.

In Sarchí Sur is the new Plaza de la Artesanía (☎ 45 4271) – a shopping mall with about 30 souvenir stores and restaurants, as well as local musicians playing marimbas. There is an information booth with sketch maps of Sarchí. Nearby are several factories specialising in rocking chairs and other furniture – these include Los Rodriguez (☎ 45 4097), Mueblería El Familiar (☎ 45 4243), La Sarchiseña (☎ 45 4062), El Artesano (☎ 45 4304) and others. All these are on the main road.

In Sarchí Norte you'll find the main plaza with the twin-towered, typical church, a couple of hotels, and some restaurants. There are also the Banco Nacional and Banco Anglo Costarricense (☎ 45 4185). These are open from 8.30 am to 3 pm on weekdays; they cash travellers' cheques and dollars.

There are more factories and stores, including Taller Lalo Alfaro, Sarchí's oldest workshop at the far north of town, and Artesanía Sarchí (☎ 45 4267) at the south end of Sarchí Norte, specialising in typical Costa Rican clothing. Pidesa Souvenirs (☎ 45 4121), by the main plaza, specialise in hand painting all local souvenirs, including milk cans. Get a couple for that person in your life who already has everything.

Places to Stay & Eat

Few people stay here, as most visitors come on day trips. In Sarchí Norte you could try *Apartamentos Yalile* (☎ 45 4161) or *Cabinas Sarchí* (☎ 45 4425). Also in Sarchí Norte is the *Baco Steak House* (☎ 45 4121) which serves steak and seafood. *Super Mariscos* (☎ 45 4330) specialises in seafood; it is open daily except Tuesday. There are also the restaurants in the Plaza de la Artesanía in Sarchí Sur.

Getting There & Away

The quickest way to get to Sarchí is to take one of the frequent buses to Grecia from San José's Coca-Cola terminal and then connect with an Alajuela-Sarchí bus going through Grecia. If you are driving, you could choose to take the unpaved road north-east from Zarcero to Bajos del Toro and on through Colonia del Toro to the northern lowlands at Río Cuarto. The main attraction of this route is the long and beautiful waterfall north of Bajos del Toro – there are signs locally for the 'Catarata'.

Getting Around

Sarchí Taxi Service (☎ 45 4028) will shuttle you from Sarchí Norte to Sarchí Sur and drive you to any workshop you wish to visit.

SAN RAMÓN

From Sarchí, the road continues west to Naranjo where the road divides. You can continue 13 km south and west to San Ramón or 17 km north to Zarcero.

San Ramón is a pleasant small town about half way between San José and Puntarenas, just off the Carretera Interamericana joining the capital with the Pacific coast. The town is known locally as the 'city of presidents and poets' – several of them were born or lived here. Ex-president Rodrigo Carazo lives a few km to the north and owns a tourist lodge surrounded by the Los Angeles Cloud Forest. A museum in town has further information about famous native sons and daughters of San Ramón. The Saturday farmers' market is a big one – lots of locals and few tourists.

Museo de San Ramón

This museum, on the south side of the Parque Central, has interesting exhibits of local history, culture and society. It's open from 1 to 5 pm Monday to Friday. It's well worth a look – no charge.

Places to Stay

There are some cheap and basic places in town. Try *Hotel Gran* (☎ 45 6363), *Hotel El Viajero* (☎ 45 5580) or *Hotel Nuevo Jardín*.

Getting There & Away

Buses to San Ramón leave San José from in front of the Hotel Musoc on Calle 16, Avenida 1 & 3.

LOS ANGELES CLOUD FOREST

This private preserve, about 20 km north of San Ramón, is reached by the new paved road which links San Ramón with La Tigra and La Fortuna. Look for signs along the highway (which is so new that there are few landmarks) for the cloud forest and the nearby Villa Blanca Hotel – the last few km are by an unpaved but good road to the west of the paved highway.

The preserve is centred around a dairy ranch owned by ex-president Rodrigo Carazo and his wife. Some 800 hectares of primary forest have a short boardwalk trail and longer horse and foot trails leading to waterfalls and cloud forest vistas. Biologist guides are available to lead hikes and the bird-watching is good. Half-day horse rentals are US$20 and guided hikes are US$21. There are relatively few tourists in the cloud forest.

Places to Stay

The *Villa Blanca Hotel* (☎ 28 4603; fax 28 4004) has a large main lodge and restaurant with about 30 whitewashed, red-tiled, adobe cabins scattered around. The hotel is surrounded by the cloud forest described above. Rooms in the lodge are US$70 for a double whilst the rustic cabins are US$95 for a double.

The 'rustic' describes the ambiance rather than the amenities – the cabins have refrigerators, hot water, bath tubs, fireplaces and even electric kettles for hot drinks. Meals are served in the main lodge – buffet-style country cooking for US$10 a meal (US$6 breakfast). Call the hotel about day trips from San José including transportation, a guided horseback ride or hike, lunch at the hotel and snacks – all for US$70. Or ask about discounts for students and groups staying in a building with dormitory-style accommodation.

PALMARES

Driving west on the Interamericana between the turn-offs for Naranjo and San Ramón, you'll see a turn-off to Palmares, a village which is a few km south of the highway. Palmares' main claim to fame is the annual fiesta, held for 10 days in the middle of January. This country fair attracts ticos from all over the Central Valley and has events for the whole family – carnival rides, bull fights (the bull is not killed in Costa Rican fights), food and beer stands, and a variety of unusual sideshows. The 1993 fair featured robot ponies and snake caves.

There is reportedly one basic hotel.

ZARCERO

North of Naranjo, the road climbs for 17 km to Zarcero, a town at over 1700 metres at the western end of the Cordillera Central. The town is famous for its topiary garden in front of the town church. The bushes and shrubs have been cut into a variety of animal and people shapes and the effect is very pretty.

The mountainous countryside in the area is attractive and the climate cool and refreshing. The area is also well known for peach jam and homemade cheese, both of which are for sale in the town.

There are several simple restaurants around Zarcero's main square but no hotels.

Getting There & Away

Buses for Ciudad Quesada (☎ 55 4318) via Zarcero leave San José's Coca-Cola terminal every hour from 5 am to 7.20 pm. There are also buses from Alajuela. From San José to Zarcero takes two hours, from Alajuela a little less.

A day trip from San José with stops at Alajuela, Sarchí and Zarcero is certainly possible. Buses from Zarcero leave at the red bus stands at the north-west corner of the park (the church plaza with the topiary art).

Northbound buses continue over the Cordillera Central and down to Ciudad Quesada (San Carlos), 35 km away. Southbound buses go to San José every hour; some of them will drop you in Alajuela. Because Zarcero is on the busy San José to Ciudad Quesada run, buses may be full when they come through, especially at weekends.

If you are passing through Zarcero when travelling between San José and Ciudad Quesada, look out of the right-hand side for glimpses of the church and its famous topiary work.

LAGUNA FRAIJANES AREA

This small lake (☎ 46 5322 for information) is surrounded by trails, play areas and picnic sites, and is a stopping place en route to Volcán Poás. Laguna Fraijanes is 15 km north of Alajuela on Route 130 and opening hours are 9 am to 3.30 pm (except Monday).

Places to Eat

If you don't want to picnic, you'll find several recommended restaurants in the area. *Chubascos*, just north of the lake, serves typical food. *Las Fresas* (☎ 61 2397), west of the lake on the road joining Volcán Poás with San Pedro de Poás, serves steaks and pizzas. Both restaurants are good. Las Fresas is named after the many strawberry fields and blackberry patches in the area – berry drinks and shakes are a speciality of local restaurants. Further north, in the village of Poasito, there is a steak house. Several other country-style restaurants are dotted along the road to the volcano.

Getting There & Away

Coopetransasi (☎ 49 5141) has buses from three blocks west of Alajuela's Mercado Central. Weekend departures are hourly from 9 am to 5 pm; from Tuesday to Friday buses leave at 9 am and 1, 4.15 and 6.15 pm. The last bus returns at 5 pm. You can visit the lake by car en route to Volcán Poás.

PARQUE NACIONAL VOLCÁN POÁS

This 5599 hectare park lies about 37 km north of Alajuela by road and is a popular destination for both locals and visitors alike. It is one of the oldest and best known national parks in Costa Rica.

The centrepiece of the park is, of course, Volcán Poás (2704 metres) which has been active since well before records started in

1828. There have been three major periods of recorded activity, from 1888 to 1895, 1903 to 1912 and 1952 to 1954.

It appears that the volcano is entering a newly active phase and the park was briefly closed in 1989 after a minor eruption in May of that year sent volcanic ash over a km into the air.

At the present time the crater is a bubbling and steaming cauldron but doesn't pose an imminent threat – though the volcanic activity has resulted in acid rain which has damaged the coffee and berry crops of the area. You should check with either the tourist office or the SPN in San José (☎ 57 0922) for the current status of the volcano's activity and the park opening hours. Occasional closures occur depending on gaseous emissions and wind.

The mountain is composed of composite basalt. The huge crater is 1.5 km across and 300 metres deep. Geyser-type eruptions take place periodically, with peaceful interludes lasting minutes or weeks depending on the degree of activity within the volcano. Because of toxic sulphuric acid fumes, visitors are prohibited from descending into the crater, but the view down from the top is very impressive. This park is a 'must' for anyone with an interest in seeing what an active volcano looks like.

Apart from Volcán Poás itself, there is a dwarf cloud forest near the crater – the best example of this kind of habitat in the national parks system. Here you can wander around looking at the bromeliads, lichens and mosses clinging to the curiously shaped and twisted trees growing on the volcanic soil.

Birds abound, especially hummingbirds such as the fiery-throated and magnificent hummingbirds, which are high-altitude specialities of Costa Rica.

Other highland specialities to look for include the sooty robin, as well as the resplendent quetzal which has been reported here.

A nature trail leads through this cloud forest to another crater nearby (this one extinct), which forms the pretty Laguna Botos. There are other walking trails as well.

Information

There is a ranger station and small museum in the park. Current hours are from 8 am to 3 pm daily (except Monday), but these are subject to change so check in San José before you go. Entrance to the park is about US$1.50 per person. The park is very crowded on Sunday, when there are often slide shows in the museum auditorium, but it is relatively quiet midweek. The annual number of visitors is fast approaching 500,000.

The best time to go is in the dry season, especially early in the morning before the clouds roll in and obscure the view. Overnight temperatures can drop below freezing and it may be windy and cold during the day, particularly in the morning, so dress accordingly. Poás receives almost four metres of rain a year, so be prepared for it.

There are well-marked trails in the park. It is easy to walk to the active crater lookout for spectacular views; the trails through the cloud forest are somewhat steeper but still not very difficult or long.

Places to Stay & Eat

There is no overnight accommodation within the park, and camping is currently prohibited (but has been allowed in the past). Travellers who have been stuck here overnight have been able to sleep on the floor in one of the buildings of the visitor complex.

There is a cafeteria with a limited menu but bringing your own food is a good idea. There are picnicking areas and drinking water.

There are several places to stay outside the park. High up on the south-western flanks of the volcano is *La Providencia Reserva Ecológica* (☎ 31 7884, 88 0077) which is reached by taking a two km dirt road leaving from just before the national park entrance. The 572 hectare property adjoins the national park and is a working dairy ranch with about 200 hectares of primary forest and much secondary forest. There are four rustic guest cabins with kitchenette and private bathroom renting at US$63 for a double. Horseback tours with a resident biologist guide are US$25 and there are several trails. The restaurant is open to the general public and serves breakfast (US$6.50), lunch (US$11) and dinner (US$12).

About 16 km east of the volcano, near Varablanca, is the *Poás Volcano Lodge* (☎ /fax 41 9102, 55 3486; Apartado 5723-1000, San José), a dairy farm set at 1900 metres with good mountain views. Comfortable rooms are about US$40/70 for a double with shared/private bath – including breakfast. Dinner is available on request.

There is reportedly a relatively cheap place to stay about half way between the park and the village of Poasito – though I missed it when I drove by. Call ☎ 48 5213 for information.

Getting There & Away
Bus There are no public buses to Volcán Poás during the week, though there are (crowded) services on Sundays and public holidays.

On Sunday mornings in San José, a TUASA (☎ 33 7477) bus leaves from Calle 12, Avenida 2 & 4, at 8.30 am, followed by a second bus if there is passenger demand (which there usually is). Get there well before 8 am to get onto the first bus and, when you get to the volcano, make a beeline for the crater to have a chance of seeing it before the clouds roll in. The fare is US$3.50, the journey takes 90 minutes, and the return bus leaves at 2.30 pm.

Also on Sundays there is TUASA (☎ 41 1431, 41 7000) microbus leaving from Alajuela's Parque Central from opposite the Restaurant El Cencerro. It will reportedly leave as early as 8 am if it's full, so get there early. More buses will run if there are passengers. The fare is US$3.25.

Tours Many companies advertise tours which go from San José just about every day. Typically, they cost US$20 to US$70 per person and you arrive at the volcano by about 10 am or later. Some tours spend very little time at the crater, so check carefully before you fork out your hard-earned cash. The cheaper tours are large group affairs providing transportation and park entrance only and limited time at the crater. The more expensive tours include small groups, bilingual naturalist guides and lunch.

Other I would prefer to be there earlier than the bus or tour groups for the best views, so I suggest either renting a car or hiring a taxi and splitting the cost with friends. This also gets you away from the Sunday crowds. You could rent a taxi for around US$40 from San José, or US$20 from Alajuela. The ICT recommends taking one of the hourly buses from Alajuela's bus terminal to San Pedro de Poás and from there hiring a cab for about US$20 – but it seems easier to go direct from Alajuela.

If you walk, you can get local buses part of the way, but they don't run very frequently and you are still left with at least a 10 km walk (uphill all the way) from the nearest village, Poásito. There are one or two buses a day from Alajuela to Poásito and there is nowhere to stay here.

Another possibility is to take a bus from San José to Puerto Viejo de Sarapiquí via Varablanca and get off at the Poásito turn-off, about 1.5 km before Vara Blanca. From here it is three km to Poásito.

Hitchhiking is a definite possibility but there isn't much traffic – go early.

CATARATA LA PAZ
This waterfall, whose name means 'Peace Waterfall', is perhaps the most famous in Costa Rica and is about eight km north of Vara Blanca. It makes a nice side-trip after visiting Volcán Poás. The Río La Paz cascades almost 1400 metres down Poás's flanks in less than eight km, culminating in a dramatic waterfall visible from the road. A short trail leads behind the fall so that you can stand between the mountainside and the plunging water – haven't you always wanted to do that?

A local guidebook reports that 'According to experts in the subject, the drops of water are charged with negative electricity, a kind of energy that reduces the stress of modern life'.

The Heredia Area

HEREDIA

This small provincial capital lies about 11 km north of San José. Its downtown population is 30,000; if the suburbs are included there are 65,000 inhabitants.

The elevation is 1150 metres above sea level – about the same as San José. The Universidad Nacional is on the east side of town, and there is a sizeable student population which adds to the interest of the town. There is one cinema.

Things to See

The city was founded in 1706 and retains some of its colonial character – more so than the other Central Valley cities. The **Parque Central** is the best place to see the older buildings. To the east of the park is the church of **La Inmaculada Concepción**, built in 1797 and still in use. Its thick-walled squat construction is attractive in an ugly sort of way – rather like Volkswagen Beetles are attractive to many people. The solid shape has withstood the earthquakes which have damaged most of the other buildings in Costa Rica that date from this time.

To the north of the park is a **colonial fortress** simply called 'El Fortín'. The area is a national historic site. The centre of the park has a covered bandstand, where there are occasional performances. A visit to these pleasant vestiges of colonial life make a quick and easy excursion from bustling San José.

A visit to the campus of the Universidad Nacional is of interest. The marine biology department has a **Museo Zoo Marino** (☎ 37 6363, ext 2240 for opening times).

The countryside surrounding Heredia is almost completely dedicated to coffee growing. Tour companies in San José sometimes arrange visits to coffee farms (called fincas). The countryside is attractive, has several points of interest and good hotels. See the Around Heredia section for details.

Places to Stay

With San José so close, most travellers stay in the capital. There are quite a few hotels in Heredia, however, probably to cater to the student population of the nearby university. Most hotels give monthly discounts to students.

There are several cheap hotels in downtown Heredia. The basic but clean *Pensión Herediana* (☎ 37 3217) on Calle Central, Avenida 4 & 6, is family run and has an agreeable courtyard. Rooms are US$3.75 per person and there is hot water in the shared bathrooms. The friendly *Hotel Colonial* (☎ 37 5258), Avenida 4, Calle 4 & 6, is clean and family run and charges US$4.50 per person in rooms with fans. There's hot water in the communal baths. If these two are full, try the cheap and basic *Hotel El Parqueo* (☎ 38 2882), Calle 4, Avenida 6 & 8, at US$4.50 per person. It's clean enough but lacks hot water.

The *Hotel Verano* (☎ 37 1616), Calle 4, Avenida 6, has clean rooms with private hot showers for US$11/18 – it's decent value and was full on a recent visit. Also fair value is the *Casa de Huespedes* (☎ 38 3829), Avenida 8, Calle 10 & 12, which has hot water and charges US$7.25 per person in rooms with shared baths and US$9 with private bath. Another choice is the *Hotel Heredia* (☎ 37 1324), Calle 6, Avenida 3 & 5, which is clean, will change US dollars, and charges US$10/18 for singles/doubles with private bath and hot water. Meals are available.

About two km north of downtown, near the village of Barva, is *Los Jardines* (☎ 60 1904; Apartado 64-3011, Barva, Heredia; CRBBG member), a B&B in a modern house. Four bedrooms share two bathrooms with hot water. Rates are US$20/32 for singles/doubles including continental breakfast. Other meals, long-term discounts and airport pick-ups can be arranged.

On the north-west side of Heredia is *Apartotel Vargas* (☎ 37 8526; Apartado 87-1300, Heredia) which has good apartments with kitchenettes, hot-water showers, TV and laundry facilities for about US$60.

Central Heredia

A new top-end hotel is the *Hotel Valladolid* (☎ /fax 60 2912). The five storey building is about four blocks west of the university and features a sauna/jacuzzi on the top floor with good views of the surrounding area. Attractive air-conditioned rooms with kitchenette, cable TV and hot showers rent for US$85/105. A good restaurant and bar are on the premises and an adjoining complex with apartments and a pool is planned.

There are a number of middle and top-end hotels in the countryside surrounding Heredia.

Places to Eat

The *Bar/Restaurant San Antonio* at Avenida 4, Calle 6 serves decent seafood meals for about US$3 to US$4. The *Bar & Restaurant El Candil* at Calle 4, Avenida 2 & 4 is a good inexpensive restaurant serving casados for US$2.50 and other meals.

There are some student bars and cafés near the university; the *El Bulevar* and *Restaurant La Choza* have been recommended. Nearby, *Restaurant Fresas* serves meals in the US$3 to US$5 range and has an outdoor dining area. Within a block of Fresas are a couple of vegetarian restaurants which attract the

■ PLACES TO STAY		15	Mönpik Ice Cream
		24	Mönpik Ice Cream
1	Hotel Heredia		
12	Hotel Colonial		**OTHER**
16	Pensión Herediana		
18	Casa de Huespedes	2	Cruz Roja (Red Cross)
20	Hotel Verano	3	Buses to Barva
21	Hotel El Parqueo	5	Municipal Palace & Post Office
		6	El Fortín
▼ PLACES TO EAT		7	La Inmaculada Concepción
		13	Cine Isabel
4	Restaurant Fresas	14	Bus to San José
8	Restaurant La Choza	17	Bus to San José
9	El Bulevar	19	Buses to Ojo de Agua
10	Bar/Restaurant San Antonio	22	Market
11	Bar & Restaurant El Candil	23	Bus to San José de la Montaña

university crowd. *Yerba Buena* and *Natura* offer inexpensive meals (US$1.10 for a soyburger, US$2 for a full vegetarian lunch) and a variety of other products ranging from herb teas to handicrafts. Some students prefer *Pizza Hut* or *McDonald's* which are also around here.

There are clean sodas in the market for inexpensive meals. For an ice-cream or snack, there are a couple of *Mönpik* ice-cream parlours.

Getting There & Away

Bus Microbuses Rapidos Heredianos (☎ 33 8392) leave San José every few minutes from Calle 1, Avenida 7 & 9, daily from 5 am to 10 pm. Night buses leave from Avenida 2, Calle 4 & 6 every hour from midnight to 6 am.

Buses from Heredia to San José leave from Calle Central, Avenida 4 or from Avenida 4, Calle Central & 1.

The two terminals are less than a block apart. The fare for the half-hour ride is about US$0.30.

From Heredia, buses north for Barva leave from by the Cruz Roja (Red Cross) on Calle Central, Avenida 1 & 3. Buses to San José de la Montaña leave every hour from Avenida 8, Calle 2 & 4 (a recent report says that they now leave from the stop for Barva – check locally). Buses for Ojo de Agua leave from

Avenida 6, Calle 6, which is not far from the market.

Three times a day (currently at 5, 6.30 and 11.30 am – but liable to change) these buses continue past San José towards Sacramento for access to Volcán Barva in the Parque Nacional Braulio Carrillo. There is no central bus terminal; ask around for other destinations.

Train A train links Heredia with San José – the only passenger train service in the Central Valley. Intertren (☎ 26 0011) runs from San Pedro via the Atlantic train station in San José to Heredia at 5.45 am, noon and 5.15 pm, Monday to Friday. The train leaves Heredia at 6.30 am, 1 and 6 pm. There is no Saturday service. On Sunday, trains leave San Pedro at 10 am and noon, returning from Heredia at 10.45 am and 1 pm.

AROUND HEREDIA

The small town of Barva, 2.5 km north of Heredia, is a colonial town which has been declared a historic monument. It was founded in 1561 and its church and surrounding houses date from the 1700s. Although there is no particular building to see, the town as a whole has a pleasant old-world ambiance and is fun to stroll around in.

A short distance to the south-west of

Barva is the famous Café Britt Finca (☎ 60 2748) which does 'coffeetours'. These begin with a visit to the coffee finca, continue with a bilingual (Spanish-English) multimedia presentation using actors to describe the historical importance of coffee to Costa Rica. These also to show something of the production process. The presentation finishes with coffee-tasting sessions led by experienced coffee cuppers (as the tasters are called). A real eye-opening experience! Then you can buy as much coffee as you want along with coffee paraphernalia at the Café Britt gift shop.

'Coffeetours' are held at 9, 11 am and 3 pm from November to April, 10 am for the rest of the year except September when the finca is closed for maintenance. The tour costs US$12 (or US$17 if you go from San José). The Café Britt bus will pick you up from major San José hotels – call for a reservation. If you go yourself, you can't miss the signs between Heredia and Barva.

Buses from Heredia to Barva continue on to San Pedro de Barva, a further 3.5 km to the north-west. Here, there is a coffee research station – there used to be a small coffee museum as well, but it seems to have been overshadowed by the Café Britt operation. The research station is four blocks north of the San Pedro church and is open from 7 am to 3 pm, Monday to Friday. You are welcome to walk around the grounds and watch the coffee grow.

Some buses for San Pedro continue to Santa Bárbara and are marked that way. Ask at the bus stop by the Cruz Roja in Heredia.

About one km north of Barva the road forks. The right fork continues to the village of San José de la Montaña, about five km north of Barva. The village is pleasantly located at about 1550 metres on the south slopes of the Volcán Barva. The higher elevation gives a fresh nip to the air and you should bring some warm clothes, particularly if overnighting in one of the country inns north of the village.

From San José de la Montaña, three buses a day continue towards Sacramento and this is the route to the trails up Volcán Barva,

which is part of Parque Nacional Braulio Carrillo.

Three km north-east of Heredia is San Rafael de Heredia from where a road leads about eight km north to Monte de la Cruz where there is an inexpensive restaurant serving local food. From here there are great views of the mountains, the Central Valley and San José. There is a picnic spot which costs about US$0.75 to use, and there is also pleasant hiking in the area.

A couple of km before you get to Monte de la Cruz is the Club Campestre El Castillo; you can use their facilities for US$5 per day. This includes lunch, and use of their pool and exercise room. Among the attractions are an ice-skating rink and go-karts.

Some five km east of San Rafael is San Isidro de Heredia which has a couple of B&B hotels.

A new museum has opened recently in the village of Santo Domingo de Heredia, about half way between Heredia and San José. It is the Museo Joyas del Tropico Humedo (☎ 23 0343), 100 metres east of the Santo Domingo cemetery, in front of the Ministerio de Obras Públicas y Transportes school. The name of the museum means 'Jewels of the Humid Tropics' – the jewels are some 50,000 insects, spiders, centipedes and crustaceans, the lifetime collection of a North American biologist now resident in Costa Rica. Museum visits feature education and fun – there are interpretive tours and videos, and even sing-alongs! Admission, including a tour, is US$4.25 for adults and US$0.75 for children. Hours are 9 am to 5 pm daily except Monday.

Places to Stay

Santa Bárbara Just before Santa Bárbara is the *Finca Rosa Blanca* (☎ 39 9392, fax 39 9555; Apartado 41-3009 Santa Bárbara, Heredia; CRBBG member), one of the most exclusive small country hotels in Costa Rica. It has only eight suites, ranging in cost from US$131 to US$222 a double per night, including breakfast.

The most expensive room is surreal: a tower with a 360° view reached by a winding staircase made of a single tree trunk. The bathroom is painted like a tropical rainforest and has water flowing out of an artificial waterfall – not your run-of-the-mill hotel bathroom! The other rooms are also intriguing and feature murals, hand-made furniture and interesting modern architecture. There is a restaurant and bar for the guests. The owners and staff are gracious and helpful.

San José de la Montaña

A few km north of San José de la Montaña (and at a higher elevation) are several comfortable country hotels, all known for their attractive settings. Pleasant walks and bird-watching are the main activities. Although three buses a day (from Heredia to Sacramento) come close to the hotels, they will provide you with courtesy pick-up. Alternatively, get a taxi from San José de la Montaña. The hotels are small and sometimes close temporarily midweek if there is no demand. They may well be full at weekends with locals, so you should call first to make reservations, get precise directions, or arrange to be picked up.

Cabañas Las Ardillas (☎ 22 8134, 21 4294) has five cabins each with fireplace and kitchen area and accommodation for four people. There is a restaurant if you don't wish to cater for yourself. Rates per cabin are about US$48; ask about long-stay discounts.

The *Cabañas de Montaña Cypresal* (☎ 37 4466, in San José 23 1717, fax 21 6244; Apartado 7891-1000, San José) has two dozen pleasant rooms with terraces, fireplaces and private hot showers. There's a small swimming pool, jacuzzi and a restaurant. Rates are US$58/63 single/double.

The *Hotel El Pórtico* (☎ 37 6022, 38 2930, fax 38 0629, Apartado 289-3000, Heredia) is considered to be the best. It has 14 heated rooms, a restaurant, sauna and pool. Room rates are about US$55/65 single/double and it is very popular with ticos.

A steep and rather long walk or drive, about four km to the north, brings you to the friendly *Cuesta de Sanchez* (☎ 37 9851) which has double rooms for about US$20.

Monte de la Cruz

Between Club Campestre El Castillo and Monte de la Cruz you'll find a recommended small country hotel, the *Hotel Chalet Tirol* (☎ 39 7371, 39 7070, fax 39 7050; Apartado 7812-1000, San José). Accommodation is in a variety of comfortable suites set at 1800 metres in the foothills of the Cordillera Central. There is a good French restaurant and tennis courts. Pleasant trails head into the cloud forest on the grounds and beyond and horses are available for rent. Trout fishing and bird-watching are other activities. Rates range from US$92 to US$172 a double, depending on the suite. The staff will pick you up from San José or the airport; reservations are recommended. (This hotel also manages the Dundee Ranch Hotel near Carara.)

Santo Domingo de Heredia

Another good country hotel is the *Bougainvillea Santo Domingo* (☎ 40 8822, fax 40 8484; Apartado 69-2120, San José) in Santo Domingo de Heredia, about half way between Heredia and San José. There are orchards in the extensive grounds, and there is a restaurant, pool and tennis court. Shuttle buses run to San José. Rooms with balconies go for about US$69/80 single/double.

San Isidro de Heredia

This village is about eight km north-east of Heredia. About 1.5 km north of the village is *La Posada de la Montaña* (☎/fax 39 8096; Apartado 1-3017, San Isidro de Heredia; in the USA, ☎ (417) 637 2066; PO Box 308, Greenfield, MO 65661; CRBBG member), which has 12 rooms renting for US$29/35 single/double with shared bath; US$40/46 single/double with private bath and US$69 to US$133 (two to six people) for suites with kitchen, sitting room and fireplace. Breakfast is included. There are laundry facilities and meals and airport pick-up on request. The hotel is set in a pleasant garden with an orchard and flowers and has been recommended by readers.

Another place, *Finca Wa Da Da* (☎/fax 39 8284; Apartado 465-3000, Heredia, CRBBG member), has two rooms with shared bath for

US$20/35 single/double, including break-fast – other meals are provided on request. The house is in a vegetable/fruit garden and has nice views. It is a couple of km from the centre of San Isidro – call for directions.

PARQUE NACIONAL BRAULIO CARRILLO

This national park is a success story for both conservationists and developers. Until the 1970s, San José's links with the Caribbean coast at Limón were limited to the railway and a slow narrow highway. A fast, paved, modern highway was proposed as an important step in advancing Costa Rica's ability to transport goods, services and people between the capital and the Caribbean coast.

This development was certainly to Costa Rica's economic advantage, but the most feasible route lay through a low pass between volcáns Barva and Irazú to the north-west of the Central Valley. In the 1970s, this region was virgin rainforest, and conservationists were deeply concerned that the development would lead to accompanying colonisation, logging and loss of habitat.

A compromise was reached by declaring the region a national park and allowing this one single major highway to bisect it. This effectively cuts the region into two smaller preserved areas, but it is considered one national park.

The Parque Nacional Braulio Carrillo (named after Costa Rica's third chief of state) was established in 1978. The San José to Guápiles highway was completed in 1987, and 45,899 hectares have been protected from further development. The pristine areas to either side of the highway are large enough to support and protect a great and varied number of plant and animal species, and San José has its much needed modern connection with the Caribbean coast.

The way most people see the park is simply to drive through it on one of the frequent buses travelling the new highway between San José and Guápiles or Limón. The difference between this highway and other roads in the Central Valley is marked; instead of small villages and large coffee plantations, the panorama is one of rolling hillsides clothed with thick montane rainforest. About 75% of Costa Rica was rainforest in the 1940s; now less than a quarter of the country retains its natural vegetative cover, and it is through parks such as Braulio Carrillo that the biodiversity represented by the remaining rainforest is protected.

The buses travelling the new highway may stop on request, but most passengers just gaze out of the window and admire the thick vegetation covered with epiphytes (air plants) such as bromeliads and mosses. On the steepest roadside slopes there are stands of the distinctive huge-leaved *Gunnera* plants which quickly colonise steep and newly exposed parts of the montane rainforest. The large leaves can protect a person from a sudden tropical downpour – hence the plant's nickname is 'poor folks' umbrella'. A walk into the forest will give you the chance to see the incredible variety of orchids, ferns, palms and other plant life, although the lushness of the vegetation makes viewing the many species of tropical animals something of a challenge. You will certainly hear and see plenty of birds but the mammals are more elusive.

Part of the reason why there is such a huge variety of plant and animal life in Braulio Carrillo is that it encompasses a wide spread of altitudinal zones. Elevations within the park range from the top of Volcán Barva (2906 metres) to less than 50 metres in the Caribbean lowlands. Five of Holdridge's Life Zones are represented and the differences in elevation create many different habitats.

A visit to the park can consist of anything from a brief stop to see just one habitat to a difficult and adventurous trip of several days, climbing Volcán Barva and perhaps the nearby Volcán Cacho Negro (2150 metres) before descending down to the lowlands on foot. The observant naturalist may see Costa Rica's national bird, the resplendent quetzal, as well as umbrella birds, toucans, trogons, guans, eagles and a host of other avifauna.

Mammals living in the park include cats such as the jaguar, puma or ocelot; tapirs and sloths, all of which are difficult to see. More likely sightings include peccaries or one of the three species of monkeys present in the park.

Information

There are three routes to the park. One is from the new highway; the second is from the road north of San José de la Montaña towards Sacramento. On both these routes there are ranger stations from where you can get further information. The third route is north-east from San José, via San Vicente de Moravia, Paracito, San Jerónimo and Alto Palma to Bajo Hondura.

There used to be a lookout and guard station, and camping was allowed, but this last route has recently been closed because the road is in disrepair. Enquire at the national parks information office in San José for up-to-date information about the status of all these entrance routes.

Park Information Centre The park entrance on the new highway is less than 20 km north-east of San José, just past the highway toll booth. There is a sign and a ranger station and a short nature trail. Shortly afterwards, the road goes through a 600-metre-long tunnel (the Tunnel Zurqui). About 17 km beyond the tunnel, on the left-hand side, there is a parking area and sign saying 'PNBC Sector Carrillo'. From here there is a trail leading steeply down to the Río Patria, about a two hour walk away. Camping is possible there, but there are no facilities.

Near the exit from the park, where the road crosses the Río Sucio, there is an area with picnic *ramadas* (open-walled, roofed shelters) and a circular nature trail. There are various other short hikes you can take from the new road, but they are generally poorly marked.

Warning Unfortunately, there have been many reports over the last two or three years of thefts from cars parked at entrances to these nature trails, as well as armed men robbing tourists hiking on the trails.

You should check very carefully before visiting these areas – I wouldn't leave my car parked at any of these spots unless there was a park ranger on duty.

Unfortunately, the SPN don't have the money to patrol most of these places. An alternative is to go with an organised tour – but even these are prone to theft if the group is very small. I hope that this situation will improve in the near future, but meanwhile exercise extra caution.

Climbing Volcán Barva

The entrance via San José de la Montaña is the best way to go if you want to climb this volcano. From the road the track climbs to the summit of Barva, which can be climbed in about four or five hours round trip at a fairly leisurely pace. The trail goes from Paso Llano (Porrosatí) to the summit of Barva (about nine km) and returns to Sacramento if you want to make a round trip of it.

From Sacramento back to Paso Llano is about a further five km. There is a ranger station near Sacramento; check with the information office in San José to see when it may be open. Sometimes the rangers will take you up to the top; it's about four km one way.

The trail up Barva is fairly obvious and there is a sign. If you wish to continue from Barva north into the lowlands, you will find that the trails are not marked and not as obvious. It is possible, however, to follow northbound trails all the way through the park to La Selva near Puerto Viejo de Sarapiquí. A tico who has done it told me that it took him four days and is an adventure only for those people used to roughing it and able to use a map and compass.

The slopes of Barva are one of the best places in the park to see the quetzal. Near the summit there are several lakes. Camping is allowed anywhere you can pitch a tent, but no facilities are provided so you must be self sufficient.

There is plenty of water (the park receives between three and six metres of rain per year depending on locality) and there are innumerable lakes, streams, and waterfalls. This means that trails are often very muddy and that you should be prepared for rain at any time of year.

The best time to go is supposedly the 'dry' season (from December to April), but it is liable to rain then too, though less than in the other months. If going on a day trip, leave as early as possible as the mornings tend to be clear and the afternoons cloudy. The night temperatures can drop to several degrees below freezing.

Rainforest Aerial Tram

Immediately past the north-east border of Parque Nacional Braulio Carrillo, on the San José-Limón highway, you'll see this new project on the right, which should be operational by early 1994. The 1.7 km aerial tram has 20 cars, which each take five passengers and a naturalist guide.

The ride is designed to go silently through and just over the rainforest canopy and take 45 minutes each way, thus affording riders a unique view of the rainforest and unusual bird-watching opportunities.

Although there are platforms and walkways in the rainforest canopy in other countries, this is the first time (that I know of) that a canopy project on this scale has been accessible to scientists and the general public anywhere in the tropics. The cars are designed to be accessible to the disabled.

It has been my experience that groups hiking through the rainforest tend to frighten away animals, which have learnt to associate people with hunting. The aerial tram is designed to run silently and not to disturb animals. In addition, the erosion caused by hiking trails will be prevented. This looks like a good and environmentally sound tourism project – it will be interesting to monitor its success over the years.

The rainforest aerial tram is the brainchild of biologist Don Perry, one of the pioneers of canopy research (see also Rara Avis and the Books & Maps entries in the Facts for the Visitor chapter). There is a reserve (over 300 hectares) around the tram and a Centre for Canopy Exploration is planned – education and research is a major component of the project. Three km of the reserve boundary is

contiguous with the Parque Nacional Braulio Carrillo. It is also planned to open a rustic lodge by the tram, with accommodation for researchers, students and the general public.

The Rainforest Aerial Tram (☎ 25 8869) costs US$47.50 to experience. This allows two 45 minute rides (one in either direction) and a break for hiking at the end of the outbound ride. Riders should carry water and be prepared for rain – although the cars have roofs, the sides are open to the elements. There will be a restaurant, information centre and parking area at the beginning of the tram.

Call about transportation or drive yourself (just under an hour from downtown San José). The Guápiles bus will drop you off at the tram. Commercial tours will no doubt become available as soon as the project is fully operational. It is planned to run the tram continuously from dawn until dusk and also to have night tours.

Getting There & Away

Via the New Highway There are no buses going to the park. You have to either get one of the buses going through the park along the new highway and get off where you want, or go on a tour. If you take a public bus, you will have to flag one down when you want to leave. The buses are often full and don't want to stop, especially at weekends. Hitchhiking is a possibility, or you could hire a car. Note the warning in this section about visiting this area.

Via San José de la Montaña For the entrance via San José de la Montaña, three buses a day (currently at 5, 6.30 and 11.30 am) leave Heredia for Paso Llano (Porrotosí on most maps) and Sacramento. Ask the driver to set you down at the track leading to Volcán Barva. During the wet season, the bus might not make it up to Sacramento. The bus returns at 5 pm. It's about 13 km from San José de la Montaña to the park entrance.

Tours Several companies in San José offer guided day hikes to Volcán Barva, some with bilingual naturalist guides if you want help with bird-watching – they try and show people quetzals if possible. Try any of the following: Los Caminos de la Selva (☎ 55 3486), Horizontes (☎ 22 2022), or Costa Rica Expeditions (☎ 57 0766). Rates are about US$75 per person, including transportation from San José and lunch. Ask these companies about the current status of trips to Parque Nacional Braulio Carrillo along the main highway.

Robles Tours (☎ 37 2116, fax 37 1976) offers guided horse-riding in the Sacramento area, with a typical lunch in a farmhouse near the national park. The cost for a day trip including transportation from San José, breakfast and lunch is US$69.

Project Shelter International (☎ 21 9132, fax 57 2273; Apartado 3153-1000, San José) provides basic shelter with cooking facilities. Their accommodation is next to the Río Corinto, by the eastern boundaries of the national park. Mattresses are provided; bring a sleeping bag or blanket. Washing facilities are in the river, there are trails nearby and you should bring food. There is a simple soda about one km away.

Tours for two nights including breakfast are US$35 per person; transportation is by public bus (another US$1) and you are accompanied from San José by a project guide. Tours leave on Mondays.

MORAVIA

This village is named San Vicente de Moravia or San Vicente on many maps, but is known as Moravia by the local inhabitants. It lies about seven km north-east of San José and used to be the centre for the area's coffee fincas. Today, its fame is as a centre for handicrafts – especially leather, but also ceramics, jewellery and the ubiquitous wood.

The best known store (it's been there for over 70 years) is the Caballo Blanco on the corner of the spacious and attractive Parque Central. It started as a saddle shop, but now sells a good variety of leather and other goods. Other good stores nearby include La Rueda (home to an odd pair of the world's largest birds), Artesanía Bribri (which sells work made by the Bribri Indians of the Car-

ibbean slope), La Tinaja, Ceramicas Buchanan and many others.

New for the 1993 high season is the Mercado de Artesanias Las Garzas (☎ 36 0037) which is a mall-like complex with arts and crafts stores, simple restaurants serving tico food, and clean toilet facilities. The artesans' market is 100 metres south and 75 metres east of the *municipio* (town hall). Hours are 8.30 am to 6 pm daily except Sunday (9 am to 4 pm). Shoppers planning a spree should note that some stores are closed on Sunday, especially in the low season.

Places to Stay & Eat

The *Victoria Inn* (☎ 40 2320, 36 7003, fax 21 1514; Apartado 6280-1000, San José; CRBBG member) has five rooms for US$15/25 single/double with shared bath, US$20/30 with private bath and a larger room sleeping up to five for US$40. Continental breakfast is included and smoking is not allowed inside. The inn is 500 metres east and 100 metres south of the Caballo Blanco store, in front the Rincón Europeo restaurant.

El Verolis (☎ 36 0662; Apartado 597-2150, Moravia, San José; CRBBG member) has seven rooms for US$40 a double with shared bath (US$57 with private bath), including breakfast. They are 500 metres from the souvenir stores, 50 metres west and 75 metres south of La Escuela de San José.

Getting There & Away

There are frequent buses (Nos 40, 40A and 42) from Avenida 3, Calle 3 & 5 in San José to (San Vicente de) Moravia.

A taxi from downtown will cost about US$2.

CORONADO

This is the general name for several villages centred on San Isidro de Coronado, about six km east of Moravia. About one km before San Isidro de Coronado is San Antonio de Coronado, and close to this is Dulce Nombre de Coronado.

San Isidro de Coronado is at 1383 metres above sea level and is thus 200 metres higher

José. It is a popular destination ... the dry season for joséfinos looking ... escape from the city. There are some ... le restaurants but no accommodation. The village has an annual fiesta on 15 May.

Instituto Clodomiro Picado

The main reason to visit Coronado is to see the snake 'farm' at Instituto Clodomiro Picado at Dulce Nombre.

The institute is run by the University of Costa Rica and has a selection of local poisonous snakes on display. On Friday afternoon visitors can see the snakes being 'milked' for their poison which is then used to make antivenin. On other days of the week the visitor must be content with the opportunity to view the snakes, learn about the serum-making process, or buy some serum. The institute is open from 9 am to 4 pm Monday to Friday; entrance is free.

Getting There & Away

Take a bus from Avenida 3, Calle 3 & 5. From San Isidro it is one km or so back to the snake institute – ask the bus driver for directions. It is a pleasant downhill walk back to Moravia, about six km away.

LOS JUNCOS

The road east of San Isidro continues through Nubes to Los Juncos, a private cloud forest preserve on the southern edge of Parque Nacional Braulio Carrillo. The preserve, of approximately 1350 hectares, is the largest tract of privately owned virgin forest left in the Central Valley. There are excellent bird and wildlife watching opportunities here. There is also a farmhouse which once belonged to two ex-presidents of Costa Rica.

Los Juncos is owned and managed by Senderos de Iberoamérica (☎ 55 2859) which offers tours of the preserve about three times a week for US$65 per person. This includes a 6 am pick-up from San José hotels, breakfast and lunch at the farmhouse, nature hikes with a bilingual guide, and a quick souvenir stop in Moravia on the way home.

They'll also do overnight trips for US$120

per person, sleeping at the rustic farmhouse (bunk beds, shared bathrooms) and eating hearty country cooking. This seems like a good way to beat the crowds!

RANCHO REDONDO

This little community is a pleasant 16 km drive east of San José. The road climbs slowly to about 2000 metres, giving picturesque views of agricultural countryside and San José.

Places to Stay

Hacienda San Miguel (29 1094) is a beautiful country lodge with jacuzzi, sauna, pool (both the swimming and the snookering varieties!) and a relaxing recreation area with a fireplace. Room rates are US$70/82 single/double, including breakfast.

The hacienda operates horseback tours through rainforest in the 400 hectare property. Guides are bilingual naturalists and the horses are carefully selected and trained. A day tour from San José, including transportation and lunch at the hacienda, is US$55 per person.

Getting There & Away

Most people drive, but buses for Rancho Redondo (Route 47) leave San José from Avenida 5, Calle Central & 2.

The Cartago Area

CARTAGO

This is the fourth provincial capital of the Central Valley, and the most historic one. The city was founded in 1563 and was the capital of the country until 1823. Unfortunately, major earthquakes in 1841 and 1910 ruined almost all the old buildings and there is not a great deal left to see.

Cartago was built at an elevation of 1435 metres, in the valley between the Cordillera Central and Cordillera de Talamanca; Volcán Irazú looms nearby.

The city itself has a population of over 30,000 but the densely settled suburbs and

Top: Fisherman with dugout (MM)
Left: Smiles at Cuajiniquil pulpería (RR)
Right: Marcos Soto serves a cold drink at Carate pulpería (RR)

Top: Basílica, Cartago (RR)
Bottom: Volcán Arenal (RR)

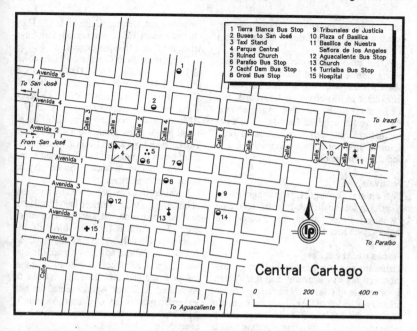

Central Cartago

Map Key:
1 Tierra Blanca Bus Stop
2 Buses to San José
3 Taxi Stand
4 Parque Central
5 Ruined Church
6 Paraíso Bus Stop
7 Cachí Dam Bus Stop
8 Orosi Bus Stop
9 Tribunales de Justicia
10 Plaza of Basilica
11 Basilica de Nuestra Señora de los Angeles
12 Aguacaliente Bus Stop
13 Church
14 Turrialba Bus Stop
15 Hospital

To San José
To Irazú
From San José
To Paraíso
To Aguacaliente

0   200   400 m

adjoining villages give the canton of Cartago a population of 110,000. The city is 22 km south-east of San José with which it is connected by a good road and frequent buses.

Things to See & Do
The most interesting sights in Cartago itself are churches.

Churches The church at Avenida 2, Calle 2, was destroyed by an earthquake in 1910. **Las Ruinas** (The Ruins) were never repaired and the solid walls of the church now house a pretty garden. Las Ruinas are a major landmark of downtown Cartago. It is a pleasant spot to sit on a park bench and watch the people of Cartago go about their business.

East of the downtown area at Avenida 2, Calle 16, **La Basílica de Nuestra Señora de los Angeles** is the most famous church of the Central Valley, if not all of Costa Rica. The Basilica was destroyed in the 1926 earthquake and rebuilt in Byzantine style.

The story goes that a statue of the virgin was discovered on the site on 2 August 1635, and miraculously reappeared on the site after being removed. A shrine was built on the spot, and today the statue, known as La Negrita, is considered a pilgrimage destination and the Virgin associated with the statue is the patron saint of Costa Rica.

La Negrita has miraculous healing powers attributed to her, and pilgrims from all over Central America come to the Basilica to worship every 2 August. There is a procession on foot from San José, 22 km away. Inside the Basilica is a chapel dedicated to La Negrita where gifts from cured pilgrims can be seen. The gifts are mainly metal (including gold) models of parts of the human body which have been miraculously healed.

Other Attractions I have recently read about a small Museo de Etnografía (☎ 51 1110), Avenida 3 & 5, Calle 3 & 5, which has pre-Columbian and colonial era exhibits and is reportedly open from 9 am to 4 pm Monday to Friday.

A few km out of the city are several interesting sights, the most famous of which is Volcán Irazú (see Parque Nacional Volcán Irazú later in this chapter). A favourite trip for locals is to the suburb of Aguacaliente, about five km south of Cartago. Here there are natural hot springs which have been dammed to form a swimming pool; it is a popular picnic spot.

Festivals

The annual 2 August pilgrimage to La Negrita at La Basílica de Nuestra Señora de los Angeles (see later in this section) is a major Costa Rican event.

Places to Stay & Eat

There are no decent hotels in Cartago and most visitors stay in nearby San José. There are a couple of cheap and basic flop houses behind what's left of the railway tracks, north of Avenida 6, Calle 3 & 5. These aren't recommended – I saw a drunk getting rolled outside of one of these hotels around sunset on a Friday night.

There are no outstanding restaurants but there are several reasonable places where you can get a meal. Just walk along the main streets of Avenida 2 and Avenida 4 downtown and take your choice. Or take a picnic lunch to one of the scenic spots in the Cartago area.

Getting There & Away

SACSA (☎ 33 5350) has buses leaving several times an hour from Calle 5, Avenida 18. Services run from about 5 am to midnight, the journey takes almost an hour depending on the traffic, and the fare is US$0.50. There are also hourly night buses.

Buses arriving in Cartago from San José come in on Avenida 2 from the west and head eastwards, stopping every few blocks, until they reach the Basilica, which is the last stop. Buses from Cartago back to San José (☎ 51 0232) leave from Avenida 4, Calle 2 & 4.

You can also take a *colectivo* (shared) taxi

from Avenida Central, Calle 11 & 13. They charge almost US$2 per person and leave when they have five passengers.

To continue from Cartago on to the town of Turrialba, take a TRANSTUSA bus (☎ 56 0073, 22 4464) from Avenida 3, Calle 8 & 10 (in front of the Tribunales de Justicia). There are buses every 30 minutes from 6 to 10.30 am and every hour from 10.30 am to 10.30 pm. It takes about 1½ hours to reach Turrialba and costs less than US$1. Some of these buses originate in San José, and come through town on Avenida 3. Space may be limited on these buses.

Local destinations are served by a variety of bus stops; if what you need isn't listed here or if the stop has moved, ask locals for directions. For Paraíso (and the turn off for Lankester Gardens), the bus leaves from Avenida 1, Calle 2 & 4. For Orosi, the bus leaves from Calle 4 near Avenida 1. The bus for the Presa de Cachí leaves from Calle 6, Avenida 1 & 2. For Aguacaliente, the bus leaves from the corner of Calle 1, Avenida 3. All of these buses are cheap and leave at least every hour.

Buses for Tierra Blanca (a village 18 km before Volcán Irazú) leave from Calle 4, Avenida 6 & 8. Buses leave Cartago at 7 and 9 am for Tierra Blanca from where you could walk or hitch to the volcano. Walkers should remember that the altitude will make the hike a breathlessly difficult one.

There is no daily bus service to Volcán Irazú. You can take a weekend bus from San José.

There is a taxi rank on the west side of the plaza and west of the ruined church. You can hire cabs to take you to any of the local destinations. A cab to Irazú costs about US$22, including a short wait at the crater.

PARQUE NACIONAL VOLCÁN IRAZÚ

The centrepiece of this national park is the highest active volcano in Costa Rica, Volcán Irazú, at 3432 metres. It is because of eruptions of this and other volcanoes that the soil of the Central Valley is so fertile. Eruptions have been recorded since 1723, when the governor of the (then) Province of Costa

Rica, Diego de la Haya Fernández, reported the event. His name is now given to one of the two main craters at the summit. The last major eruption of Irazú was a memorable one; it occurred on 19 March 1963, the day that US President Kennedy arrived on a state visit. San José, Cartago, and most of the Central Valley were covered with several cm of volcanic ash – it piled up to a depth of over half a metre in places. The agricultural lands to the north-east of the volcano were rendered temporarily uninhabitable due to the rocks and boulders hurled out of the crater. Since that explosive eruption, Volcán Irazú's activity has been limited to gently smoking fumaroles which can be observed by the curious visitor.

The national park was established in 1955 to protect 2309 hectares in a roughly circular shape around the volcano. The summit is a bare landscape of volcanic ash and craters. The Principal Crater is 1050 metres in diameter and 300 metres deep whilst the Diego de la Haya Crater is 690 metres in diameter and 100 metres deep. It contains a small lake.

There are two smaller craters, one of which also contains a lake. In addition, there is a pyroclastic (formed of fragmented rocks from volcanic activity) cone. A few low plants are slowly beginning to colonise the landscape – if it wasn't for these you might feel that you were on a different world. A few high-altitude bird species such as the volcano junco hop around. A trail about one km in length takes you from the parking lot to a lookout over the craters. A longer trail leaves from behind the bathrooms and is steeper, longer and gets you closer still to the craters. Trails are marked with a blue and white pedestrian symbol – other 'trails' which are marked by a sign saying 'Paso Restringido' (restricted or limited access) are precarious and should be avoided.

Below the summit there is a thicker cloud forest vegetation with oak and *madroño* trees covered with epiphytic plants. The lower you get, the lusher the vegetation. As you emerge from the park boundary, the land is agricultural, with much cattle and dairy farming. About five km below the summit on the left

hand side as you descend, there is the *Restaurant Linda Vista* which serves simple meals and an early breakfast. On the right-hand side about 11 km below the summit is the *Hotel Gestoria Irazú* (☎ 53 0827) where a double room with private cold shower costs about US$20; there is a poor restaurant and it is cold at night.

A little further down is a lookout over Cartago and the Central Valley; San José can be seen in the distance. The first village is called Prusia, and nearby is the Area Nacional Recreación de Ricardo Jiménez Oreamuno where there is a two km trail leading to a pretty waterfall. There are picnic sites here.

Information

There is a paved road all the way to the summit. At the summit there is a parking lot and a small information centre, open from 9 am to 4 pm. There are no permanent food services nor overnight accommodation or camping facilities. (A mobile soda wagon serves simple meals during dry season weekends.)

There is a disused observation building at the right-hand side of the end of the road (a few hundred metres past the parking lot) and you could shelter in there if desperate – broken windows, concrete floors, and garbage. A warm sleeping bag would be essential.

The entrance fee is supposed to be US$1.50 (in common with the other national parks) though half this is sometimes charged – I don't know why. During weekdays in the low season there's often no one there to collect a fee. There is no gate, so if you drive up to arrive at dawn, as I did, you won't have any problem in getting in.

From the summit, it is possible to see both the Pacific and the Caribbean, but it is rarely clear enough for this to be actually possible. The best chances for a clear view are in the very early morning during the dry season (from January to April). It tends to be cold, windy and cloudy on the summit, with temperatures ranging from -3°C to 17°C and an annual rainfall of 2160 mm. Come prepared with warm and rainproof clothes as well as food.

Getting There & Away

Buses Metrópoli (☎ 72 0651, 91 1138) operates a yellow school bus to the national park. The bus leaves San José from Avenida 2, Calle 1 & 3 at 8 am on Saturday, Sunday and holidays (and Wednesday during the high season). The bus stop is across the street in front of the *Gran Hotel Costa Rica* and the fare is US$4.50. The return bus leaves the summit parking lot promptly at 12.15 pm, allowing a little over two hours at the top.

You can also take an early morning bus from Cartago to Tierra Blanca and walk the remaining 18 or 20 km, but it is hard work at this elevation. You could also hitch, but there isn't much traffic midweek. Hiring a cab from Cartago is not too expensive if there is a group of you. I was recently quoted US$22 for the round trip with an hour's waiting time at the summit – the cab will take up to four passengers for this fare. (In 1990 I was quoted US$30 for the same trip.)

If you rent a car, you'll find the road is signed occasionally, but not at every turn. Leave Cartago from the north-east corner of the Basilica on Highway 8 which goes all the way to the summit.

At road forks, if there is no sign, look for either the more major looking road or avoid signs for highways with numbers other than 8 (you will intersect with highways 233, 230, 227, and 6 on the way up). It is not difficult to find your way.

Tours from San José will take you to Volcán Irazú for about US$20 to US$28 for a half day tour, or about US$45 to US$50 for a full day combined with visits to Lankester Gardens and the Río Orosi valley.

Finally, a company called Magic Trails (☎ 53 8146, 53 8160, fax 53 9937) has horseback tours in the Prusia area, on the south slopes of the volcano. One tour goes all the way to the summit crater by horseback and costs US$65 for the day, including lunch in an early 19th century farmhouse. Call them for more information.

LANKESTER GARDENS

This is an orchid garden run by the University of Costa Rica (☎ 51 9877). Originally a private garden run by British orchid enthusiast Charles Lankester, it is now open to the public and is frequently visited by plant lovers. The gardens are about six km east of Cartago.

To get there, catch a Paraíso bus and ask the driver to set you down at the turn off for Lankester Gardens. From the turn off it is a further one km on foot to the entrance; there is a sign.

A taxi will cost about US$2, or you can walk. Tour buses from San José often stop by the gardens either on the way to Irazú or the Río Orosi. Hours are 8 am to 3 pm daily and admission is about US$2.25. At half past the hour, free guided tours are given.

You can visit the gardens year round, but from February to April is the best time for viewing orchids in flower. With some 800 species of orchid, however, there is always something flowering year-round. This trip is recommended to all interested in plants.

RÍO OROSI VALLEY

This river valley south-east of Cartago is famous for its beautiful views, colonial buildings, hot springs, lake formed by a hydroelectric damming project, and a wildlife refuge. Most people visit the valley by taking a tour from San José or by driving their own car. It is possible to get around by public bus as well.

The first village passed is Paraíso, eight km east of Cartago. Here, you can eat at the *Bar Restaurant Continental* and other restaurants which have decent food.

Beyond Paraíso, you have the choice of going east to Ujarras and the lake formed by the Presa de Cachí (Cachí Dam) or south to Orosi.

From Cartago, buses go both to the village of Orosi and to the Presa de Cachí. The two roads are linked by a gravel road. You can drive this road in your own car, which is often used by some of the tour groups. However, if you are travelling by public bus you'll have to do one leg and then backtrack to do the other.

East of Paraíso

The Cachí bus will drop you off at **Ujarrás**, about seven km east of Paraíso. This village was damaged by the flood of 1833 and abandoned. The waters have since receded and the ruins are a popular tourist sight – the ruined 17th century church is particularly interesting to see.

A short distance above Ujarrás is a good lookout point for the artificial **Lago de Cachí**. On the north shore of the lake, about a half hour on foot east of Ujarrás, is Charrara, a government-run tourist complex with swimming pool, a reasonable restaurant, picnic areas, walking paths, and boats for hire on the lake. It is closed on Monday. The hydroelectric dam itself is at the northeastern corner of the lake.

South of Paraíso

About two km south of Paraíso is the Mirador Sanchirí tourist centre and cabins (☎/fax 73 3068). Here, there is an excellent view of the Río Orosi valley; there's also a restaurant and picnic area, and four cabins for rent (US$46 a double with private hot bath). This area gives the best views of the entire valley.

The bus continues on to the village of Orosi, about six km further south. Orosi was named after a Huetar Indian chief who lived here at the time of the conquest. The town and surrounding district has a population of about 8000 people. The main product here is coffee and a nearby finca offers tours.

Orosi, one of the few colonial towns to survive Costa Rica's frequent earthquakes, boasts an attractive church built in the first half of the 18th century – probably the oldest church still in use in Costa Rica. There is a small religious art museum (☎ 73 3051) adjacent to the church; it is open from 1 to 5 pm (but call ahead as hours change often and it is closed some days). There are hot springs and swimming pools on the east side of town.

The Orosi bus usually continues three or four km south of the village to Palomo. Near the end of the run, just after crossing a large river bridge, look on the left for the *Hotel Río Palomo* (☎ 73 3057, 73 3128, fax 73 3173; Apartado 220-7050, Cartago) which has a restaurant renowned for its fresh fish meals. The restaurant is open from 8.30 am to 5 pm daily. The motel has a swimming pool and cabins with private electric shower are US$15/25 single/double (US$6 per additional person). Some cabins have a private kitchenette.

Between Orosi and the Hotel Río Palomo there is the Orosi Coffee Adventure (☎ 73 3030, fax 73 3212; Apartado 45-7100, Paraíso, Cartago) which offers local tours. The first is at 10 am – a three hour bilingual tour of a coffee finca which includes lunch at the Hotel Río Palomo (US$21.75 per person). The second is at 2 pm and is a two hour tour without lunch for US$12.25 per person. The third is a guided horseback tour to Tapantí lasting three hours and costing US$28.

All day tours combining Tapantí on horseback, the coffee finca visit, and lunch at the Río Palomo are US$50. Call ahead for a reservation – I've heard they don't do Sunday tours (which sounds strange but call ahead.) You can also get information at the hotel.

About five km east of the Río Palomo on the road to Cachí is the Casa del Soñador (the Dreamer's House), a whimsical house designed and built by the renowned tico carver Macedonio Quesada. The house, completely built of wood and bamboo, is filled with carvings of local campesinos and religious figures. Many are life-sized, most are carved from the gnarled and twisted roots of the coffee tree, and a selection are available for sale. Entrance is free.

Most travel agencies in San José offer day tours to this area.

REFUGIO NACIONAL DE FAUNA SILVESTRE TAPANTÍ

This 5090 hectare (also reported as 4715 and 6080 hectares) wildlife refuge is in wild and wet country on the rainforested northern slopes of the Cordillera de Talamanca.

Although not a large refuge there are reportedly over 150 rivers within it, which gives an indication of the area's wetness. Waterfalls and trees abound and the wildlife is prolific, though not easy to reach because the terrain is rugged and the trails are few. Rainfall reportedly is about 2700 mm in the lower sections but supposedly reaches over 7000 mm in some of the highest parts of the reserve – maybe you should pack an umbrella. Nevertheless, Tapantí is a popular destination for dedicated bird-watchers, and the reserve opens at 6 am to accommodate them.

Quetzals are said to nest on the western slopes of the valley in which the park information centre is located. Well over 200 other bird species have been recorded, including eagles and hummingbirds, parrots and toucans, and difficult-to-see forest floor inhabitants such as tinamous and antbirds.

There are plenty of other animals: butterflies, amphibians, reptiles, and mammals. The rare jaguar, ocelot, jaguarundi, and little-known oncilla (caucel) tiger cat have been recorded here, but more usual sightings include squirrels, monkeys, raccoons and agoutis. Tapirs are occasionally seen.

Information
The refuge is open from 6 am to 4 pm. There is an information centre near the park entrance. There are a couple of trails leading from here to various attractions, including a picnic area, a swimming hole, and a viewpoint with great views of a waterfall. Fishing is allowed in season (from April to October – permit required) but the dry season (from January to April) is generally considered the best time to visit the refuge, although you should be prepared with rain gear even then. Camping may be allowed with a permit and you may be able to arrange for a ranger to show you around.

Getting There & Away
If you have your own car, you can take a gravel road (passable year round) from Orosi through Río Macho and Purisil to the refuge entrance. Most buses from Cartago to Orosi go as far as Río Palomo, from where it is a nine km walk (or hire a taxi).

There is a daily early morning bus from Cartago to Orosi going as far as Purisil, from where it is a five km walk. A taxi from Orosi costs about US$4. Some tour companies in San José do day trips with bilingual naturalist guides, including Costa Rica Expeditions (☎ 57 0766) and Horizontes (☎ 22 2022), which charge US$69 per person including lunch.

The Turrialba Area

RÍO REVENTAZÓN
From the north-east end of Laguna Cachí flows one of the more scenic and exciting rivers in Costa Rica, the Río Reventazón. (In fact, the Cachí Dam across the Río Reventazón forms the artificial lake.) The river tumbles from the lake at 1000 metres above sea level and down the eastern slopes of the mountains to the Caribbean lowlands. It is a favourite river for rafters and kayakers – some sections offer Class 3 white water, others are relatively flat and placid.

Single and multi-day river trips are offered by several agencies in San José, including: Costa Rica Expeditions (☎ 57 0766), which is the oldest and best known company; Ríos Tropicales (☎ 33 6455);

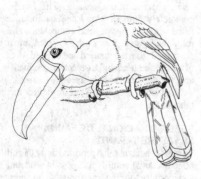

Toucan

Horizontes (☎ 222022); and Aventuras Naturales (☎ 25 3939). A day trip costs about US$69 to US$85 (depending on which section of the river you want to run) and includes everything from San José: round-trip bus transportation, a breakfast stop in a country restaurant, all river equipment and life jackets, a delicious gourmet picnic lunch on the river (I had shrimp salad as an appetiser with Costa Rica Expeditions), and several hours of guided fun on the thrilling white water. All the guides speak English.

Because of higher and more constant rainfall on the Caribbean side of the country, it is possible to run this river year round but June and July are considered the best months.

TURRIALBA

This small town is attractively perched on the Caribbean slope of the Cordillera Central at an elevation of 650 metres above sea level. It is on the banks of the Río Turrialba which flows into the Reventazón, four km to the east.

The town used to be the major stopping point on the old highway from San José to Limón but since the opening of the new highway via Guápiles, Turrialba has been bypassed by travellers to the coast and has suffered economically. Nevertheless, it is a pleasant town and makes a good base for several nearby excursions and so tourism, whilst still very low key, is becoming increasingly important.

With the surge of interest in river running during the 1980s, the town has become somewhat of a centre for kayakers and rafters. Turrialba is also an excellent base for visits to the nearby agronomical centre (CATIE) and the archaeological site at Guayabo, as well as for climbing Volcán Turrialba – all these are described later in this section.

Turrialba is a minor agricultural centre for the coffee fincas in the highlands around the town and the sugar cane and banana plantations in the lowlands to the east. The population of the town and surrounding district is about 30,000.

Places to Stay – bottom end

There are three basic and inexpensive hotels on the south side of the old railway tracks. The best of these is the *Hotel Interamericano* (☎ 56 0142) which charges US$4.50/7.25 for singles/doubles or US$7.25/11 for rooms with private bath and cold water. There is a snack bar on the premises. The nearby *Hotel Central* charges US$3 per person in rooms with shared bath. The *Hotel Chamango* is also in this price range.

The basic *Hospedaje Hotel Primavera* is OK and charges US$3 per person. The *Hotel La Roche* (☎ 56 1624) looks clean and reasonable for US$4.75/8.25 single/double. The *Pensión Chelita* (☎ 56 0214) charges US$5 per person, or US$6.50 per person in rooms with private bath.

Places to Stay – middle

The best hotel in town is the *Hotel Wagelia* (☎ 56 1596, fax 56 1566), Avenida 4, Calle 2 & 4, which charges US$24/36 single/double in rooms with private bath and hot water. Better rooms with air-conditioning and mini-refrigerator are about US$15 more. The hotel is clean and set in an attractively landscaped garden.

The restaurant on the premises is one of the best in town and has meals in the US$5 to US$10 range. The management will arrange one day Reventazón river-running excursions and other local trips.

Places to Stay – out of town

There are three small but pleasant country hotels several km east of Turrialba. About eight km away on the road to Siquirres and Limón is the *Turrialtico* (☎ 56 1111) which is known for the good tico meals served in its restaurant. There are a few rooms with private bath and hot water renting for US$20 a double (no singles) – reservations are recommended. The hotel is set on a little hill and has great views.

About 11 km away from Turrialba, also on the road to Limón, is the *Pochotel* (☎ 56 0111), which is a favourite of local river guides. The hotel is above the village of Pavones and there is a sign in the village.

There is also a tico-style restaurant here, and a tower with great views. Cabins with private bath and hot water are about US$30 a double – again, reservations are recommended.

Both of these hotels can help arrange nearby excursions or river running trips. If you call them in advance, they will pick you up in Turrialba, or you can get off the Turrialba-Siquirres bus at the appropriate spot.

About eight km south-east of Turrialba is the new and elegant *Casa Turire Hotel* (☎ 73 1111, fax 73 1075; Apartado 303-7150, Turrialba). The three-storied building boasts wide and shady verandahs and is set in well-landscaped grounds with sugar cane, coffee and macadamia nut plantations nearby. There is a swimming room, four holes of golf, and a games room. Children under 16 years are not accepted and there are no facilities for the disabled. Twelve spacious rooms with private balconies, hot water and TV are US$100/115 single/double and four suites (with king-sized beds and refrigerators) for US$150 to US$220. The most expensive suite has a jacuzzi. Meals are US$7.50, US$16 and US$18.50 for breakfast, lunch and dinner. Horse and mountain bike rental

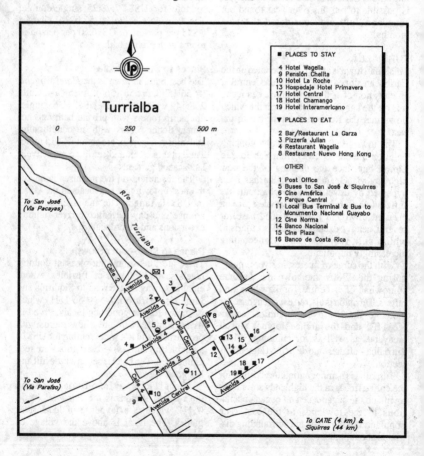

Turrialba

0   250   500 m

PLACES TO STAY

4   Hotel Wagelia
9   Pensión Chelita
10 Hotel La Roche
13 Hospedaje Hotel Primavera
17 Hotel Central
18 Hotel Chamango
19 Hotel Interamericano

PLACES TO EAT

2   Bar/Restaurant La Garza
3   Pizzería Julian
4   Restaurant Wagelia
8   Restaurant Nuevo Hong Kong

OTHER

1   Post Office
5   Buses to San José & Siquirres
6   Cine América
7   Parque Central
11 Local Bus Terminal & Bus to Monumento Nacional Guayabo
12 Cine Norma
14 Banco Nacional
15 Cine Plaza
16 Banco de Costa Rica

Río Turrialba

To San José (Via Pacayas)

To San José (Via Paraíso)

Avenida 8
Avenida 6
Avenida 4
Avenida 2
Avenida Central
Avenida 1

Calle 2
Calle Central

To CATIE (4 km) & Siquirres (44 km)

and guided walks in the rainforest and plantations are available.

Other country hotels are found near the Guayabo National Monument and at the Rancho Naturalista, described following.

Places to Eat

The hotels *Wagelia, Turrialtico, Pochotel* and *Casa Turire* all have good restaurants. The *Restaurant Kingston*, on the outskirts of town on the road to CATIE and Limón, is one of the best in Turrialba itself.

Other restaurants where you can have a decent meal for about US$2 to US$5 are *Pizzería Julian* for Italian food and *Bar/Restaurant La Garza* for a good variety of seafood, chicken and meat dishes. The *Restaurant Nuevo Hong Kong* serves slightly cheaper Chinese food.

Getting There & Away

Bus TRANSTUSA (☎ 22 4464, 56 0073) buses from San José to Turrialba leave hourly from Avenida 6, Calle 13, and take about two hours. The cost is US$1.25 direct or US$1 with stops. The route lies through Cartago and then either through Pacayas or through Paraíso and Cervantes to Turrialba. In Cervantes there is a popular country restaurant *La Posada de la Luna* which serves good local food and is especially popular at breakfast time with river-runners on their way to the Reventazón or the Pacuare. The restaurant is cluttered with bits and pieces of Costa Rican history, ranging from old guns and swords to household artefacts to archaeological pieces – an interesting place.

There are two main bus terminals in Turrialba. The Tuatusa stop on Avenida 4 near Calle 2 serves San José (you can get off at Cartago) with buses every hour. From this stop you can also go to Siquirres (connecting for Puerto Limón) with buses every two hours.

The other terminal is between Avenida Central & 2 and Calle Central & 2. This terminal has buses serving the local communities such as La Suiza and Tuís every hour, and Santa Cruz three times every afternoon. Buses to Santa Teresita (which go close to

Monumento Nacional Guayabo) leave at 10.30 am and 1.30 pm. Other local communities served include Juan Viñas, Pejibaye, Tucurrique and Pavones.

Buses to Guayabo also leave from here – the schedule is variously reported as 11 am and 5 pm on Monday and Friday; daily except Sunday; and 1 pm on Monday, 3 pm on Friday and Saturday, and 5 pm on Sunday; and other times. Probably all of these schedules have been correct in the recent past – ask locally for the current schedule.

Train Since the 1991 earthquake devastated the region, the train has not been running and, because it was already running at a loss before the earthquake, the line is unlikely to be repaired and reopened.

CATIE

This stands for the Centro Agronómico Tropical de Investigación y Enseñanza, which is known throughout Costa Rica by its acronym of CATIE (which is just as well).

The centre comprises of about 1000 hectares dedicated to tropical agricultural research and education. Agronomists from all over the world recognise CATIE as one of the tropic's most important agricultural stations.

The attractively landscaped grounds of CATIE lie just to the left of the main road to Siquirres, about four km east of Turrialba. Visitors are allowed to walk in the grounds and birders enjoy a visit to the small lake on the site where waterbirds such as the purple gallinule are a speciality. Another good birding area is the short but steep trail descending from behind the administration building to the Río Reventazón.

Those with a serious interest in tropical agriculture are encouraged to visit the facilities at CATIE. These include one of the most extensive libraries of tropical agriculture literature anywhere in the world, a teaching and research facility with student and faculty accommodation, laboratories, experimental fruit, vegetable and forest plots, greenhouses, a dairy, a herbarium, and a seed bank.

Livestock and seeds suitable for the

tropics are available for sale (although these require special permits to be exported). Research interests at CATIE include conservation of crop genetic diversity, high-yield/low impact-farming techniques for small farms, and development of agricultural strains suitable for tropical environments worldwide.

Although the grounds can be visited without prior arrangement, a tour of the complex should be arranged beforehand, either with one of the tour agencies in San José or direct with CATIE (☎ 56 6431, 56 1149). Arrangements to obtain seeds or carry out research at the centre can be made by writing to CATIE, Turrialba, Costa Rica.

MONUMENTO NACIONAL GUAYABO

Guayabo lies 20 km north-east of Turrialba and contains the largest and most important archaeological site in the country. Although interesting, it does not compare with the Mayan and Aztec archaeological sites of Honduras, Belize, Guatemala and Mexico to the north. Nevertheless, excavations have revealed a number of cobbled roads, stone aqueducts, mounds, retaining walls, and petroglyphs which can be examined by the interested visitor. Some pottery and gold artefacts have been found and are exhibited at the Museo Nacional in San José.

Archaeologists are still unclear about the pre-history and significance of the site. It seems to have been inhabited perhaps as far back as 1000 BC and reached the pinnacle of its development around 800 AD when some 10,000 people were thought to have lived in the area.

Guayabo is considered an important cultural, religious and political centre, but more precise details remain to be unearthed. The site was abandoned by 1400 AD and the Spanish conquistadors, explorers and settlers leave us with no record of having found the ruins.

The area was rediscovered in the late 19th century by Anastasio Alfaro, a local naturalist and explorer, who began some preliminary excavations and found a few pieces which are now in the Museo Nacional.

In 1968, Carlos Aguilar Piedra, an archaeologist with the University of Costa Rica, began the first systematic excavations. As the importance of the site became evident, it was obviously necessary to protect it and it became a national monument in 1973, with further protection decreed in 1980. The latest round of excavations began in 1989 and is expected to last about five years.

The monument is small, some 218 hectares, and the archaeological site itself is thought to comprise no more than 10% of the total. Most of these ruins are yet to be excavated. The remaining 90% of the monument is premontane rainforest. It is important because it protects some of the last remaining rainforest of this type in the province of Cartago, but, because of its small area, there are not many animals to be seen. Those animals which are there are interesting, however.

Particularly noteworthy among the avifauna are the oropendolas which build colonial sack-like nests in the trees of the monument. Other birds include toucans and brown jays – the latter unique among jays in that they have a small, inflatable sac in the chest which causes a popping sound to be heard at the beginning of their loud and raucous calls. Mammals include squirrels, armadillos and coatis among others.

Information

The archaeological site is being worked upon during the week and sections may be closed to visitors. Opening hours are from 8 am to 3 pm; park rangers or trained guides are available to take you around for a nominal fee. This is as much to protect the site as to give you a free tour, but it's a good deal anyway!

There is an information centre near the monument entrance where you pay the US$1.50 national parks admission fee. There is a small interpretive display and maps are available. There are trails within the monument, picnic areas, latrines and running water. Camping is allowed. You can visit the park midweek if you just want to visit the rainforest, bird-watch, picnic or camp.

Average annual rainfall is about 3500 mm and the best time to go is during the January to April dry season (when it can still rain).

Places to Stay

Apart from camping in the monument, visitors can stay in the one country hotel nearby. This is the *Albergue La Calzada* (☎ 56 0465), less than one km from the entrance to the monument. It is a small place with a few doubles at US$16 per room, shared bathrooms and electric showers. Rooms with private bathrooms are planned.

Calling ahead for reservations is recommended – the friendly and helpful owners will help you with current bus information from Turrialba and pick you up from the nearest bus stop to the hotel. Their restaurant serves good food and is open to the public.

Getting There & Away

There are buses from Turrialba to Guayabo (the community at the north entrance to the monument) on Friday, Saturday, Sunday and Monday. The schedule should be checked in Turrialba as it has changed several times.

There are also buses from Turrialba to Santa Teresita (marked as Lajas on just about every map I've seen!) which passes the turnoff to the southern entrance of the monument, a four km walk. You could try hitchhiking or hire a taxi from Turrialba (about US$15).

Tours to the monument can be arranged with travel agencies in San José, including Costa Rica Expeditions (☎ 57 0766) and Senderos de Iberoamérica (☎ 33 5760; Calle 7, Avenida 7). Tours are about US$69 including lunch in Turrialba and can be combined with visits to Irazú or Lankester Gardens.

VOLCÁN TURRIALBA

This 3329 metre high (some sources give 3339 metres) active volcano is actually part of the Irazú volcanic massif, but is more remote and difficult to get to than Irazú. The name of the volcano was coined by early Spanish settlers who named it Torre Alba or 'white tower' for the plumes of smoke pouring from its summit in early days.

The last eruption was in 1866 and today the volcano lies dormant, but it is likely that the tranquil farmlands on Turrialba's fertile soils will again be disturbed by earth shattering explosions sometime in the future.

The summit has three craters, of which the middle one is the largest. This is the only one which still shows signs of activity with fumaroles of steam and sulphur. Below the summit there is a montane rain and cloud forest, dripping with moisture and mosses, full of ferns, bromeliads, and even stands of bamboo.

To climb Turrialba, take a bus to Santa Cruz from where a 21 km track climbs to the summit. A 4WD vehicle will get you over half way; then you have to walk. It is reported that horses can be hired from the village of Pacayas (half way between Turrialba and Cartago) and there are horse trails to the summit. Guided tours involving foot or horse travel are offered in San José by Tikal Tours (☎ 23 2811) and Jungle Trails (☎ 55 3486), among others. A one day trip costs about US$70. The best time to go is the January to April dry season.

RANCHO NATURALISTA

This 50 hectare ranch is about 20 km southeast of Turrialba near the village of Tuís. The ranch has a small 10 room lodge called the *Albergue de Montaña*, which is popular with birders and naturalists. The North American owners are avid birders who have recorded over 300 species of birds within three km of the ranch. Hundreds of species of butterflies are to be found on the grounds as well. The ranch lies at 900 metres above sea level in montane rain and wet forest – there is a trail system. This is a recommended destination for people who would like some quiet days of bird-watching and nature study in a tranquil and undisturbed environment.

Costs are not cheap, but once you decide to go you'll find almost everything is included. Because the owners wish to maintain a relaxed atmosphere, they ask guests to book for a minimum of three days to enable them to enjoy and explore their surroundings at a leisurely pace. Many guests stay for a week. Accommodation is US$89 per person per day (double occupancy) in the wet season (from May to October) and US$99 during the rest of the year. Discounts for longer stays are US$500/925 per person, double occupancy for one/two weeks (from May to October) or US$605/1135 (from November to April). Single supplement is US$94 for the first three days, US$165 per week.

The prices include round trip transportation from San José, three home-cooked meals a day, maid and laundry service, guided birding trips, horse-riding, and (with stays of a week or more) a day trip to another area. About the only thing not included are bottled or canned drinks.

Rooms are comfortable, most with private bath and hot water. Three rooms share a bath if the lodge is full. Most rooms have very good or excellent views, one room lacks views and two have only fair to good views – so check which room you are reserving.

Reservations can be made with the owner, John Erb (☎/fax 39 7138; Apartado 364-1002, San José, or in the USA, Department 1425, Box 025216, Miami FL 33102-5216). He'll be happy to send you a description of each room.

RÍO PACUARE

The Río Pacuare is the next major river valley east of the Reventazón (described earlier in this chapter). It is arguably the most scenic rafting river in Costa Rica and one of the world's classic whitewater experiences. The river plunges down the Caribbean slope through a series of spectacular canyons, clothed in virgin rainforest. The Class 4 rapids are exciting and separated by calm stretches which enable you to stare at the near vertical green walls towering hundreds of metres above the river – a magnificent and unique river trip.

The Pacuare does not lend itself to one day

trips (although they are available) because it is relatively remote and inaccessible – two or even three day trips are done more often, with nights spent camping on the river banks. During the day, stops are made for swimming and exploring some of the beautiful tributaries of the main river. Some of these tributaries arrive at the Pacuare in a plunging cascade from the vertical walls of the canyon, and your raft may pass directly beneath the falls.

The usual agencies in San José do this trip. I went with Costa Rica Expeditions (☎ 57 0766) which provided excellent service; Ríos Tropicales (☎ 33 6455), Horizontes (☎ 22 0222), and Aventuras Naturales (☎ 25 3939) are other options. The river can be run year round, though June to October are considered the best months. One-day trips cost US$89, two-day trips cost about US$250 to US$300 per person, with eight passengers. Costs are more per person in smaller groups, but you can often join another group to cut costs. Combined tours with other rivers are also available.

In 1986, the Pacuare was declared a wild and scenic river and had protected status conferred upon it by the government – the first river to be so protected in Central America. Despite this, the National Electric Company began an 'exploratory feasibility study' for a hydroelectric dam scheduled for approximately the end of the century.

It is not clear whether the dam would be successful in generating electricity, but it would certainly ruin the Río Pacuare valley by flooding it, thus destroying the most beautiful tropical river valley in Costa Rica, and one of the most beautiful and unique in the world.

As of 1993, plans to build a dam continue. For more information, contact The Costa Rican Association for the Protection of Rivers (☎ 23 1925, fax 22 9936; Apartado 4600-1000, San José).

North-Western Costa Rica

Costa Rica's central highlands stretch a spectacular arm out to the Nicaraguan border. To the north-west of the Cordillera Central lie two more mountain chains, the Cordillera de Tilarán and the Cordillera de Guanacaste.

The Cordillera de Tilarán is characterised by rolling mountains which used to be covered with cloud forest. The famous cloud forest reserve at Monteverde is an important and popular destination for those wishing to see something of this tropical habitat. Separating the Cordillera de Tilarán and Cordillera de Guanacaste is Laguna de Arenal and the nearby Volcán Arenal, currently the most active volcano in Costa Rica and one of the most active volcanoes in the world. The spectacular sights and sounds of the eruptions have begun to draw visitors to the nearby town of Fortuna de San Carlos.

The Cordillera de Guanacaste is a spectacular string of dormant or gently active volcanoes, four of which are protected in the Parque Nacional Rincón de la Vieja and the Parque Nacional Guanacaste. To the west of the Cordillera de Guanacaste, shortly before reaching the Nicaraguan border, is the Península Santa Elena which contains a rare dry tropical forest habitat descending down to remote Pacific beaches. The dry forest and coastline are preserved in the beautiful and historic Parque Nacional Santa Rosa, which is well worth a visit. All in all, this is a very scenic part of Costa Rica and, apart from the Monteverde and Arenal area, one that is not much visited by foreign tourists.

This next section describes the towns, parks, reserves and mountains found along the north-western section of the Carretera Interamericana, while the second section deals with a less frequently travelled route on minor roads around the north-east side of the mountains, past the explosive Volcán Arenal and connecting eventually with the Interamericana at Cañas. If you have the time, consider taking the rougher back route. Otherwise, the well paved Interamericana

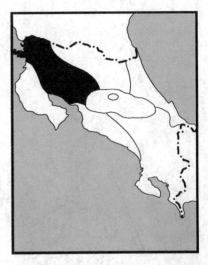

will speedily take you through this spectacular part of Costa Rica.

Interamericana Norte

Overland travellers heading from San José to Managua (Nicaragua) usually take buses along the Interamericana. This leaves San José heading west almost to Puntarenas in the Pacific lowlands and then swings north-west to the Nicaraguan border. The highway from the highlands to the lowlands is steep, winding, and often narrow. Because it is a major highway, however, it is heavily used and is plied by large trucks which come hurtling down the steep curves at seemingly breakneck speeds. Whilst the truck drivers probably know the road very well, travellers driving rented cars are advised to keep alert on this road. This advice comes from both the Costa Rican authorities and from me –

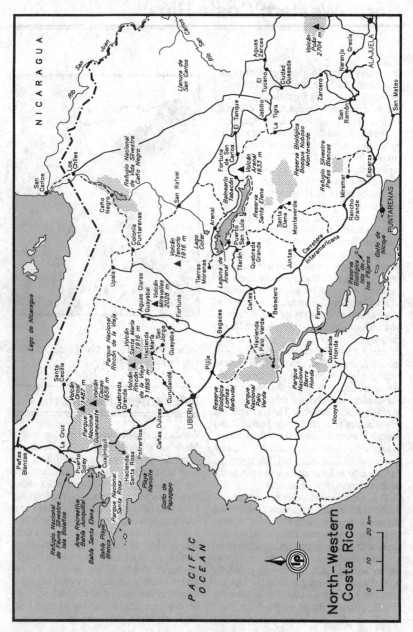

North-Western
Costa Rica

I've driven it a couple of times and found it a little nerve-racking to take a bend and be confronted by a truck trying to pass another on the narrow road.

The lowlands are reached at the village of Esparza where there is a popular roadside restaurant and fruit stalls. Tour buses and private cars often stop here for refreshments, but public buses are usually in a hurry to press on. (Esparza is linked with Puntarenas by frequent buses – see the Central Pacific Coast chapter for further information.) Five km beyond Esparza, and 15 km before Puntarenas, the Interamericana turns north-west. It continues through the small town of Cañas and the larger city of Liberia before ending up at the Nicaraguan border. Cañas and Liberia are the most important towns in the area and, although not major destinations in themselves, provide transportation and accommodation facilities. The Interamericana Norte provides the best access to the private cloud forest reserve at Monteverde and a host of national parks and reserves.

Views from the highway are spectacular, particularly at the northern end. A seat on the right-hand side of the bus as you head north will give excellent views of the magnificent volcanoes in the Cordillera de Guanacaste.

REFUGIO SILVESTRE DE PEÑAS BLANCAS

This 2400 hectare refuge is administered by the SPN. Peñas Blancas lies about six km north-east of the village of Miramar, which itself is eight km north-east of the Interamericana (see the Puntarenas section of the Central Pacific Coast chapter for details of buses to Miramar). The Miramar turn-off is at Cuatro Cruces near the rustic Miramar Restaurant. The Miramar serves tasty and inexpensive food and is a good place to stop after enduring the rigours of the descent from San José.

The road is in fairly good shape as far as Miramar, then deteriorates. You can either hike six km north-east into the refuge, or continue east on a poor road through Sabana Bonita to the tiny community of Peñas Blancas, which is within the refuge and 14

km from Miramar. An alternative approach is to head north from the Interamericana at Macacona, which is three km east of Esparza. A dirt road heads north for 20 km to Peñas Blancas – 4WD is recommended in the wet months. There are no facilities at Peñas Blancas.

The refuge clings steeply to a southern arm of the Cordillera de Tilarán. Elevations in this small area range from less than 600 metres to over 1400 metres above sea level. Variation in altitude results in different types of forest, such as tropical dry forest in the lower south-western sections, semi-deciduous dry and moist forests in middle elevations, and premontane forest in the higher northern sections. The terrain is very rugged and difficult to traverse – there are two short trails. The refuge has been created to protect the plant species in the varied habitats and also to protect an important watershed. Before the refuge's creation, however, parts of the area had been logged which is partly why it is not particularly noted for its animals.

The name Peñas Blancas means 'white cliffs' and refers to the diatomaceous deposits found in the reserve. Diatoms are unicellular algae which have a 'skeleton' made of silica. Millions of years ago, when Central America was under the sea, countless dead diatoms sank to the ocean floor and in places built up thick deposits. Diatomaceous rock is similar to a good quality chalk. The whitish deposits are found in the steep walls of some of the river canyons in the refuge.

There are no facilities at the refuge. Camping is allowed, but you must be self-sufficient and in good shape to handle the very demanding terrain. There are some hiking trails. The dry season (from January to early April) is the best time to go – I very much doubt if you'll see anyone else there. Further information can be obtained from the SPN in San José.

RESERVA BIOLÓGICA ISLA DE LOS PÁJAROS

This reserve forms part of a group of four islands (Reservas Biológicas Guayabo,

Negritos y Los Pájaros) administered by the SPN, from which permission must be obtained to visit. Isla de Los Pájaros (Bird Island) lies less than a km off the coast at Punta Morales, about 15 km north-west of Puntarenas. There are no facilities on the 3.8 hectare islet, which has a small colony of nesting seabirds. The predominant vegetation is wild guava.

With help from the national park authorities, it is possible to charter a boat to visit the island and see the birds, but camping is prohibited and normally landing is limited to researchers working on the birds. Generally speaking, biological reserves administered by the SPN were created to protect flora and fauna, and part of the protection in the more fragile areas consists of not encouraging visitors. This is a case in point.

MONTEVERDE

Monteverde is one of the more interesting places in Costa Rica and is a very popular destination for both foreign and local visitors. There are actually two Monteverdes. One is a small community founded by North American Quakers in 1951; the other is a cloud forest reserve which lies adjacent to the community.

History

The story of the founding of Monteverde is an unusual one that deserves to be retold. It begins in Alabama with four Quakers (a pacifist religious group also known as the 'Friends') being jailed in 1949 for refusing to register for the draft in the USA.

After their release from jail, a group of Quakers began to search for a place to settle where they could live peacefully. After searching for land in Canada, Mexico and Central America, they decided on Costa Rica whose lack of an army and peaceful policies matched their own philosophies. They chose the Monteverde area because of its pleasant climate and fertile land, and because it was far enough away from San José to be (at that time) relatively cheap to buy.

There were 44 original settlers (men, women and children from 11 families) who arrived in Monteverde in 1951. Many flew to San José; they loaded their belongings onto trucks and a few of the pioneering Quakers drove down from Alabama to Monteverde, a journey which took three months. If you think the roads to Monteverde are bad now, imagine what they must have been like four decades ago! The road in 1951 was an ox-cart trail and it took weeks of work to make it barely passable for larger vehicles.

The Quakers bought about 1500 hectares and began dairy farming and cheese production. Early cheese production was about 10 kg per day; today, Monteverde's modern cheese factory produces about 1000 kg of cheese daily which is sold throughout Costa Rica. The cheese factory is now in the middle of the Monteverde community and can be visited by those interested in the process.

Note that due to the Quaker influence and the high level of tourism, much of the local population speaks English and many local places are named in English as well as Spanish.

Information & Orientation

The community of Monteverde is spread out along a road running roughly north-west to south-east. At the south-east end is the biological reserve; at the north-west end, about six km from the reserve, is the village of Santa Elena. Hotels of various price levels are strung out along the road. The cheapest pensiones are found in the centre of Santa Elena.

Various businesses sell detailed maps of the area; the map in this book shows only those places which welcome the public. The best maps are published for the use of the residents of the zone – they are not readily available, to protect the privacy of the locals.

Most hotels will accept US dollars or change small sums of money. There is a bank in Santa Elena.

Santa Elena also has a small clinic (☎ 64 5076) in case of medical emergencies.

Five km north-east of Santa Elena is a new cloud forest reserve, simply called Reserva Santa Elena (see the separate entry for this reserve for details).

Responsible Tourism

Monteverde started as a Quaker community founded by peaceful people who wanted to live in a quiet and friendly environment. This has changed drastically in the last decade with the large influx of visitors. There is a limit to the number of visitors Monteverde can handle before losing its special atmosphere and there is a limit to the number of people who can visit the reserve without causing too much damage.

Quakers have traditionally been adept at peaceful resolution of problems and they are handling their new status as a tourist attraction with grace and common sense. The income from tourism is important, but preserving their own lifestyle and surroundings is equally, if not more, important to the inhabitants. Monteverde is a special but fragile place – visitors are very welcome but should remember that they are visiting a peaceful community and/or a cloud forest reserve.

Most visitors are delighted with their stay; a few complain incessantly about how muddy the trails are (you have to expect mud in a cloud forest), how boring the nightlife is (Quakers traditionally don't do much nightclubbing), or how difficult it is to see the quetzal (this is not a zoo). Monteverde is not for everybody – if clouds and Quakers, cheese and quetzals do not sound like your idea of fun, head for a resort more to your liking.

Butterfly Garden

One of the most interesting and recommended activities is visiting the Butterfly Garden (El Jardín de las Mariposas). The garden is open from 9.30 am to 4 pm daily and admission is US$5. This entitles you to a guided tour led by a naturalist (in Spanish, English or German) which begins in their information centre with an enlightening discussion of butterfly life cycles and the butterfly's importance. A variety of eggs, caterpillars, pupae and adults are examined. Then visitors are taken into the greenhouses where the butterflies are raised, and on into the screened garden, where hundreds of but-

terflies of many species are seen. The guided tour lasts about an hour, after which you are free to stay as long as you wish – there are excellent photo opportunities of the gorgeous butterflies. Keep your entrance ticket and you can visit the garden the next day if you wish.

Cheese Factory

Tours of the cheese factory (also called La Lechería or La Fábrica) can be arranged, and cheese and other dairy products can be purchased. Through a huge window behind the cheese store you can watch the workers making the cheeses. Store hours are from 7.30 to 3.30 pm daily, except Sunday when it closes at 12.30 pm. Work does not begin until 9 am (when the first tour starts).

Art Galleries

There are a number of art galleries which can be visited. They are all more than just souvenir stores for tourists. A local women's arts and crafts cooperative (CASEM) sells embroidered and hand-painted blouses and handmade clothing as well as other souvenirs. Profits benefit the local community.

The Hummingbird Gallery just outside the cloud forest reserve entrance has feeders constantly attracting several species of hummingbirds – great photo opportunities! Inside, slides and photographs by the renowned British wildlife photographer Michael Fogden are on display and for sale. There are two different daily slide shows at 9.30 am and 4.30 pm – admission is US$3.70. There is a short nature trail behind the gallery. Hours are 9 am to 5 pm daily.

Sarah Dowell's Art Gallery is in her home up a steep path through pleasant woodlands – her work is bold and distinctive and can be seen in some of the Monteverde hotels as well. There is also a small souvenir shop behind the fuel station.

El Trapiche Sugar Mill

About three km north of Santa Elena, in Cañitas, is the El Trapiche – a traditional sugar mill driven by ox power. The mill is open daily from 10 am to 7 pm and admission is US$2. Apart from sugarcane, coffee and macadamia nuts are harvested. There are daily activities: Monday – ox-driven sugarcane processing and farm tours; Tuesday and Wednesday – coffee production; Thursday and Friday – Marimba and dancing; Saturday – engine-driven sugarcane processing and product sampling. From November to February is the coffee-picking season – join in if you'd like. There is a small restaurant serving typical meals and snacks.

Hiking & Nature Trails

The Monteverde Conservation League has an office (☎ 64 5003, fax 64 5104; Apartado 10165-1000, San José) and welcomes visitors with serious questions. Office hours are 8 am to noon and 1 to 5 pm, Monday to Friday. They operate a trail called **Sendero Bajo del Tigre** (see the Monteverde map) which is open daily from 8 am to 4 pm. Parking is US$1 and the day-use fee of US$3 benefits the MCL. Children under 12 years old accompanied by adults are free. The trail is more open than in the cloud forest and hence spotting birds tends to be easier. You can join the MCL for US$25 – this entitles you to a subscription to their quarterly publication, *Tapir Tracks*.

Another small private reserve with trails is the **Reserva Sendero Tranquilo** (the Quiet Path Reserve) which limits visitation to two groups at any one time, with two to six people per group. Visitation is with a trail guide only and the average hike is three to four hours – you see no one outside your group. Information is available from the Hotel El Sapo Dorado (☎ 64 5010) or David Lowther (☎ 64 5154). The cost of the guided hike is US$12.50 per person.

A free hiking option is the track up to **Cerro Amigos** (1842 metres). This hill has good views of the surrounding rainforest and, on a clear day, of Volcán Arenal 20 km away to the north-east. The track leaves Monteverde from behind the Hotel Belmar and ascends roughly 300 metres in three km. Near the end of the track are a couple of TV/radio antennae, and so the route is easy to follow.

Horse-riding

Horseback tours are another option. There are plenty of outfitters in the area and your hotel can arrange a tour for you. One outfitter which is well recommended is Meg's Riding Stables (☎ 64 5052) which charges US$10 per hour and takes you on private trails. Other outfitters are available from about US$6 an hour and up. Apart from local tours, you can arrange all-day horse treks to view Volcán Arenal.

Festivals

A recent addition to things to do in Monteverde is their Music Festival which, the organisers hope, will continue on an annual basis. From December 1992 to March 1993, there were daily concerts (except Sunday and Wednesday) at 5 pm above the Hotel Belmar. Classical and jazz music was the mainstay of these events; call ☎ 61 2950 for information.

Places to Stay

During Christmas and Easter most hotels are booked up months ahead. During the January to April busy season, and also in July, hotels tend to be full often enough that you should telephone before arriving to ensure yourself of a place to stay. You may have to book some weeks in advance for the dates and hotel of your choice. You can write to the hotels in Santa Elena by simply addressing your letter to Santa Elena, Monteverde, Costa Rica. You can write to most of the hotels in Monteverde by addressing letters to Apartado 10165-1000, San José (unless another address is given). This is a communal box for all Monteverde mail.

Places to Stay – bottom end

Hotels The cheapest places are in Santa Elena, about five to six km from the reserve, though many people prefer to stay closer to the reserve. The hotels here are basic but adequate.

The *Hospedaje La Esperanza* (☎ 64 5068, 64 5166) has good rooms for US$4.50 per person, and has hot water in the communal showers – it looks like good value. If you can't find anyone to show you a room, ask in the store below or the house next door. Nearby, the *Pensión El Sueño* (☎ 64 5021) is a family-run place that will cook for you on request. They have basic rooms for US$3.70 per person or slightly better rooms with private bath for US$7.40 per person. There is hot water.

The *Pensión Santa Elena* (☎ 6 5051) is clean and friendly, and has electric showers in the communal bathrooms. There is a decent restaurant serving home-cooked food – breakfasts for US$3, casados for US$4.50. Lodging in small rooms costs from US$7 to US$9 per person – less when they aren't full. Luigi is the guy to talk to about horse rental and local information. Opposite, the basic *Verdulería El Tauro* has rooms at US$3 per person – there is tepid water in the communal showers. Nearby, the small, clean and friendly *Pensión Colibrí* charges US$5 per person – there is a hot electric shower in the communal bathroom. The people will cook for you on request (US$3.50 for a casado) and horse rental for US$6 an hour is available. The *Hospedaje El Banco*, behind the bank, is clean and friendly and charges about US$5 per person. The shared electric showers are warm and laundry service and meals are available on request.

The *Pensión Tucán* (☎ 64 5017) is also clean and has hot water in the shared bathrooms. The charge is US$4 to US$5.50 per person. They have a room with a private bath for US$22 for one to three people. Meals are available – the owner is a good cook. Opposite is the very basic *Pensión El Imán* which has horrible little boxes for US$3 per person – the electric showers give only cold water. You may have to go over to the Hotel Imán to get into the pensión; the hotel has a basic restaurant attached. Hotel rooms are a little better and about twice the price of the pensión.

About a half km north of Santa Elena, past the school and radio tower, is the newish and quiet *Cabinas Marlin* which has clean rooms with communal bath and hot showers for US$5 per person.

About six km north of Santa Elena, near San Gerardo Abajo, is the *El Gran Mirador* – a rustic lodge with good views of Arenal. Double rooms with private bath are US$14.70; dormitory-style rooms with shared baths are US$7.30 per person. There is a restaurant serving home-cooked meals. Guided hiking and horseback tours are available for about US$5 per person per hour – there is some primary forest and waterfalls nearby. To get to the lodge you need 4WD in the dry season or horseback in the wet months – the place is not on the beaten track. For more information, contact the Albergue Bellbird (☎ 64 5026) in Monteverde.

A couple of km south-east of Santa Elena (just under four km from the reserve) is the *Pensión Manakín* (☎ 64 5090) which charges US$5 per person in rooms with shared bathrooms. There is hot water. They have two rooms with private bath for US$20. One room sleeps two and the other sleeps three. They have good breakfasts for US$3 to US$4 and dinners for US$3 to US$5.

Camping Camping is permitted on the grounds of a few hotels – they charge about US$1.50 per person and allow you to use a shower. Hotels allowing camping include the *Pensión Flor y Mar*, the *Cabinas El Bosque*, the *Hotel Villa Verde* and the *Hotel Fonda Vela* – ask around about other places.

Places to Stay – middle
The *Albergue Arco Iris* (☎ 64 5067, fax 64 5022) is in Santa Elena. The hotel is on a small hill with views and the rooms are spacious, some with two queen-size beds and a single bed. Rates are US$30 for a double with private bath and electric showers, or US$60 with all meals. Horseback excursions can be arranged.

The *Monteverde Inn* (☎ 64 5156) is almost five km from the reserve at the end of the road leading past the Butterfly Garden. Rooms with private bath and electric showers are US$20 a double and the owners will pick you up at the bus stop if you have a reservation.

About 3.5 km from the reserve on the main road you'll find the new *Albergue Bellbird*

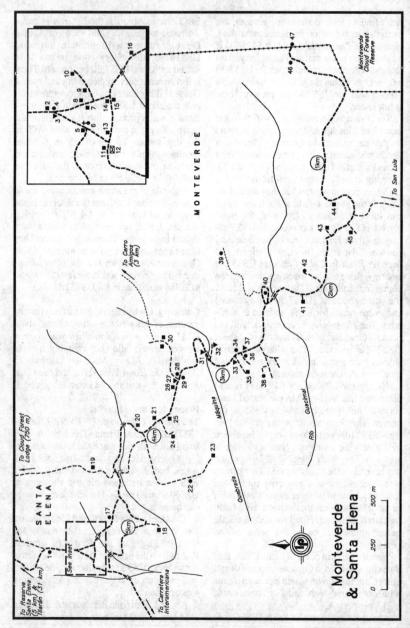

Monteverde & Santa Elena

■ PLACES TO STAY

2 Hospedaje El Banco
5 Hotel El Imán
7 Verdulería El Tauro
8 Pensión Santa Elena
9 Pensión Colibrí
10 Albergue Arco Iris (Hotel & Restaurant)
11 Hospedaje La Esperanza
13 Pensión El Sueño
14 Pensión Tucán
15 Pensión El Imán
16 Hotel Finca Valverdes
18 Monteverde Lodge
19 El Sapo Dorado
20 Hotel Heliconia
21 Hotel El Establo
23 Monteverde Inn
24 Pensión Manakín
25 Hotel de Montaña Monteverde
26 Albergue Bellbird
30 Hotel Belmar
35 Cabinas El Bosque
41 Pensión Flor Mar
43 Cabinas Mariposa
44 Hotel Villa Verde
45 Hotel Fonda Vela

▼ PLACES TO EAT

3 Soda La Central
5 Restaurant El Imán
10 Albergue Arco Iris (Restaurant & Hotel)
14 Soda Tucán
16 Restaurant Finca Valverdes
19 El Sapo Dorado
27 Soda Cerro Verde
31 Soda Manantial
32 Restaurant La Cascada
33 Restaurant El Bosque
37 Stella's Bakery

OTHER

1 School
4 Bank
6 Church
12 Post Office
17 Clinic
22 Butterfly Garden
28 Gas Station
29 Monteverde Conservation League
34 Meg's Riding Stable
36 CASEM
38 Entrance to Bajo El Tigre
39 Sarah Dowell's Art Gallery
40 La Lechería (Cheese Factory)
42 Friends' Meeting House & School
46 Hummingbird Gallery
47 Reserve Entrance & Visitor Centre

(☎ 64 5026) which has friendly owners, a restaurant, and clean, decent rooms. Introductory rates in 1993 are US$12/20 a single/double in rooms with shared hot electric bath or US$25 a double for their one room with private bath. These prices may go up when the hotel becomes better established. Complimentary coffee is served to guests.

There are a couple of relatively cheap places in Monteverde which are only 1.5 km away from the reserve. The *Cabinas Mariposa* (☎ 64 5013) is a small and friendly family-run place with just two cabins accommodating up to three people each. There is hot water. Rates are US$14.50 per person.

The *Hotel Villa Verde* (☎ 64 5025, fax 64 5115) was the closest hotel to the reserve on my recent visit. Rooms cost US$20 per person with a communal bathroom and US$30 per person for cabins with a private bath. The water was cold when I visited, though previous guests reported hot water. These rates include all three meals. The rooms are fairly basic but clean – some have a fireplace.

The *Pensión Flor Mar* (☎ 64 5009) is run by Marvin Rockwell, one of the original Quakers who was jailed for refusing to sign up for the draft and then spent three months driving down from Alabama. He and his Costa Rican wife Flory are very friendly, and their little pensión is pleasant though the rooms are simple. Rooms with shared bath are US$22 per person; with private bath, US$25 per person. This includes all three meals – they'll pack you a lunch if you ask. There are hot electric showers. Horses are available for rent. The hotel is just over two km from the reserve.

The newish *Cabinas El Bosque* (☎ 64 5129) is a couple of hundred metres behind the popular restaurant of the same name. The rooms are spacious and have private hot showers for US$20/28 single/double – good for the money. Guests get a 15% discount in the restaurant. Note that this hotel also sells bus tickets for San José.

Just outside Santa Elena is the new *Hotel Finca Valverde's* (☎/fax 64 5157) which has clean and spacious (if rather bare) rooms for US$35/44 with private bath and hot water. Most of the rooms will sleep up to four people. There is a restaurant. This hotel is a ticket agent for buses – you don't have to be a guest to buy bus tickets.

The *Hotel Heliconia* (☎/fax 64 5109) is four km away from the reserve and is another family-run hotel. Rooms with private bath are US$46 a single or double. Three meals a day cost an extra US$20 per person.

Places to Stay – top end

The *Hotel Fonda Vela* (☎/fax 64 5125; in San José ☎ 57 1413, fax 57 1416; Apartado 7-0060-1000 or Apartado 10165-1000, San José) is the closest top-end place to the reserve at just over 1.5 km away. Spacious wood-accented rooms with hot showers, some with good views, cost from US$43.50/51.50 for standard singles/doubles to US$56/69 for suites. Extra people cost from US$9 to US$14. Breakfast is US$5.50, lunch is US$8 and dinner is US$10.25 – the dining room has attractive views and the food is good. I have received several recommendations for this place. Guided horseback rides are available.

The *Hotel El Establo* (☎/fax 64 6057, in San José ☎ 25 0569; Apartado 549-2050, San Pedro, San José) is named after the stable next door. Horses are available for rent at about US$8 per hour. Rooms are fairly plain but boast some of the best mattresses in town, so at least you'll get a good night's rest. Rooms come with hot showers, carpet-

ing and access to a spacious and comfortable sitting area. Rates are US$45/55.

The *Hotel Belmar* (☎/fax 64 5201, 64 5135) is a beautiful wooden hotel on a hill, almost four km from the reserve. The road up to the hotel is steep and slippery for the last 300 metres, and cars don't always make it. But once you get there, you are rewarded with superb views of the Golfo de Nicoya when the weather is clear. Attractive rooms (most have balconies) are US$57 single/double. Breakfast is US$5, lunch or dinner is US$8, and the food is good – but the restaurant was not open to the general public recently. For US$10 you can get a ride to the reserve and be picked up again at a prearranged time.

The *Hotel de Montaña Monteverde* (☎/fax 64 5046; in San José ☎ 33 7078, fax 22 6184; Apartado 70, Plaza G Viquéz, San José) has rooms for about US$60 a double and a few suites at about US$80 a double. There is a good restaurant, and the spacious gardens are pleasant to walk around in. There is a sauna.

Both the Belmar and Montaña Monteverde will provide transport from San José on request – costs depend on the size of the group.

El Sapo Dorado (☎/fax 64 5010) was recommended for its food in the last edition of this book – now they've built a hotel and it's a nice place too. They have five large cabins, each divided into two spacious suites. Each of these has two queen-size beds, fireplace, table and chairs, balcony and private hot-water showers. There are views down to the Golfo de Nicoya, and the forest behind the hotel has trails. Their restaurant serves excellent meals, with a vegetarian main course normally being among the choices – they occasionally have live music. The restaurant is open to the public from 7 to 10 am, noon to 3 pm, and 6 to 9 pm. They also have professional massage services for US$29 per hour. Hotel rates are US$63 a double and US$12 for each extra person up to four people. Reservations are recommended.

The *Monteverde Lodge* (☎ 64 5057, fax 64 5126) is five km from the reserve and is the most upscale hotel in the Monteverde area. The rooms are larger than most, and have garden or forest views. Apart from a smoking wing, most guest rooms and the restaurant have a no-smoking policy. There is a large lobby graced by a huge fireplace and, adjoining the lobby, an indoor jacuzzi for guests to soak away the stresses of hiking steep and muddy trails.

The grounds are attractively landscaped with a variety of native plants and a short trail leads to a bluff with an observation platform. The bluff is at the height of the forest canopy – good views of the forest and a river ravine. Rooms are US$76.50/89/102.50 for singles/doubles/triples. Excellent all-you-can-eat meals are available at US$8.25 for breakfast and US$13.25 for lunch or dinner. Transport to the reserve (US$4) and San José (US$35) is available and they'll arrange guided reserve visits, horseback rides and other activities. A slide/sound show by noted area photographer and naturalist, Richard Laval, is presented most nights for US$5 (Richard contributed several of the best photos in this book).

Reservations should be made with lodge owner/operator Costa Rica Expeditions (☎ 57 0766, 22 0333, fax 57 1665) at Calle Central, Avenida 3, San José, or write to Apartado 6941-1000, San José. From the USA, mail gets there quicker if sent to CR Expeditions, Dept 235, PO Box 025216, Miami, FL 33102-5216. Complete tours with private transportation, expert bilingual naturalist guides and all the meals and accommodation are also available (for example, three days/two nights from San José, including a visit to Volcán Poás en route and a full day at the Monteverde reserve, cost US$399 per person for a group of four, US$611 per person for two).

A new top-end hotel, planned to open in late 1993, is the *Cloud Forest Lodge* (☎/fax 64 5058) being constructed about 1.5 km north-east of Santa Elena. The owners plan a forest trail through their large property and a no-smoking policy both inside the hotel and on the trails. Planned rates for the 1994 high season are about US$65 for single or double occupancy. Meals wi... US$10, US$10.50 for breakfa... dinner. Further information is av... Homestead Travel, 981 Fremont... Altos, CA 94022, USA (☎ (415) 9... ...+, fax (415) 949 1068).

Places to Eat

Many people eat in their hotels, most of which provide meals and will provide picnic lunches on request. Several hotel restaurants are open to the public, and the excellent *El Sapo Dorado* is generally well liked. There are other possibilities, however.

The *El Bosque Restaurant* is a very pleasant and popular place serving good lunches and dinners for about US$4 to US$6. It is open from noon to 9 pm daily. The restaurant is nearly three km from the reserve. Another place is the similarly priced *Soda Cerro Verde* – the food is good, but the menu has no prices and I've heard that gringos get charged more than locals. Ask before you order. There is also a soda at the reserve entrance where you can eat basic meals for under US$3. The *Soda Manantial* is another inexpensive choice in Monteverde.

The *Restaurant La Cascada* is also currently popular, especially among younger visitors and some locals who hang around for the dancing afterwards. Good dinners are served from 6 to 9 pm and main courses are in the US$4 to US$8 range. The disco/bar then takes over from 9 pm to 1 am from Thursday to Sunday.

For do-it-yourself picnic lunches, head for the nearby *Stella's Bakery* for delicious home-made bread and rolls, then go to *La Lechería* (the cheese factory) to pick up some fresh cheese. Or stop by the *Coope Santa Elena* grocery store next to CASEM.

There are cheap places to eat in Santa Elena, especially if you stick with basic plates like the casado which can be had for under US$3. Restaurants include the *Restaurant Imán* and the small *Soda Central* which puts out tasty local food. Also check out the restaurants associated with the Pensión Tucan, Pensión Santa Elena and *Albergue Arco Iris*.

Getting There & Away

Air The nearest airstrip is at Aranjuez, near the coast and just over two hours from Monteverde. Costa Rica Expeditions arrange air charters from San José to Aranjuez, continuing by car or bus to Monteverde – an expensive option.

Bus Buses to Monteverde leave San José from the Tilarán terminal (☎ 22 3854) Calle 14, Avenida 9 & 11. Currently, buses leave at 6.30 am on Saturdays and 2.30 pm from Monday to Thursday for the four to five hour trip (depending on season and road conditions). The fare is about US$4. Advance ticket purchase is recommended.

In Monteverde, most of the hotels have bus information. The hotels Finca Valverdes and El Bosque act as ticket agents for advance purchases. Buses run to San José at 6.30 am, Tuesday to Thursday, and 3 pm Friday and Sunday (sometimes also on Saturday). On Monday you could go from Santa Elena to Puntarenas and change.

In Monteverde, the last bus stop from San José is by La Lechería about 2.5 km before the reserve. Ask to be set down anywhere before there, near the hotel of your choice. Buses begin the return to San José from La Lechería.

There is also a bus from Puntarenas to Santa Elena. It leaves from the bus stop by the beach, between Calle 2 & 4, at 2.15 pm daily. The bus gets into Santa Elena about 5.30 pm and returns to Puntarenas the next day at 6 am. The bus stop in Santa Elena is by the bank.

A daily bus leaves Tilarán at noon for Santa Elena (2½ to three hours, US$2). From Santa Elena, the bus leaves for Tilarán from in front of the Hotel/Restaurant El Imán at 7 am daily.

Car Drivers will find that all the roads to Monteverde are in poor condition, and 4WD may be necessary during the rainy season. Many car rental agencies will refuse to rent you an ordinary car during the wet season if you state that you are going to Monteverde. (Ordinary cars are OK in the dry months –

but it is a slow and bumpy ride. I have heard of several instances where cars have broken down or sustained damage to the underneath – drive with care.)

There are two roads from the Interamericana to Santa Elena and Monteverde. Coming from the south, the first is at Rancho Grande, about 16 or 17 km north-west of the turn-off for Puntarenas.

All there is at Rancho Grande is the Bar Rancho Grande and a sign for 'Sardinal, Guacimal, Monteverde', both on the right (north) side of the highway. Unfortunately, the sign is so placed that you can't easily see it unless you are coming from the north, so keep your eyes peeled for the bar. The second turn-off is at the Río Lagarto bridge (just past Km 149, and roughly 15 km north-west of Rancho Grande). Here there is another not very obvious sign 'Guacimal, Santa Elena, Monteverde'. Both routes are steep, winding and scenic dirt roads with plenty of potholes and rocks to ensure that the driver, at least, is kept from admiring the scenery. (There is good bird-watching en route.)

Which road should you take? Good question. Both are about the same distance (32 or 33 km from the Interamericana to Santa Elena). The Rancho Grande road is reached more quickly from San José, and many drivers prefer it for that reason, but the Río Lagarto road seems to be favoured by bus drivers. I've been on both and can only say that both are poor but driveable. If you're driving, talk to everyone you can about current conditions and weigh up the (invariably conflicting) advice received – once you are thoroughly confused, you can begin your journey!

It is also possible to drive from Tilarán but the road is just as bad (some people say worse – a point which is debated by road-warriors having an evening drink in the hotel bars). It's driveable in an ordinary car during the dry season at least – drive carefully.

RESERVA BIOLÓGICA BOSQUE NUBOSO MONTEVERDE

When the Quaker settlers first arrived, they decided to preserve about a third of their property in order to protect the watershed above Monteverde. In 1972, with the help of organisations such as the Nature Conservancy and WWF, more land was purchased adjoining the already preserved area. This was called the Reserva Biológica Bosque Nuboso Monteverde (Monteverde Cloud Forest Biological Reserve) and became owned and operated by the Centro Científico Tropical (Tropical Science Centre) of San José. Gradually, more land was acquired and added to the reserve.

In 1986, the Monteverde Conservation League (MCL) was formed and continues to buy land to expand the reserve. In 1988, the MCL launched the International Children's Rainforest project whereby children and school groups from all over the world raised money to buy and save tropical rainforest adjacent to the reserve. This project does more than ask children to raise money for rainforest preservation – it is an educational program as well. Recent figures for the size of the Monteverde reserve is about 11,000 hectares, combined with another 7000 hectares (or more) of the Children's Rainforest.

The most striking aspect of this project is that it is a private enterprise rather than a national park administered by the government. Governments worldwide must begin to count conservation as a key issue for the continued wellbeing of their citizens, but it is interesting to see what a positive effect ordinary people can have on preserving their environment. This preservation relies partly on donations from the public.

Donations directly to the reserve can be sent to Centro Científico Tropical, Apartado 8-3870-1000, San José. Donations to the Children's Rainforest and to aid educational work and sustainable development in the local community can be sent to: Monteverde Conservation League, Apartado 10165-1000, San José.

There has been talk in recent years of combining the Monteverde reserve and Children's Rainforest along with the new Santa Elena reserve and with a large area around Volcán Arenal to create a Regional Conservation Unit (or 'megapark') covering

about 110,000 hectares. This has not happened, mainly because of the logistical, economical and social problems of involving the local landowners. Nevertheless, the region northwest of Monteverde towards Arenal is one of the wilder and more spectacular areas of the country.

Information

The information office and gift store at the entrance of the reserve is open daily from 7 am to 4 pm. For some inexplicable reason it is closed on 6 and 7 October. Entrance tickets to the reserve are bought here. Fees are US$8 per day – discounts are available for students and for weekly tickets. You may be able to buy a ticket the afternoon before, and enter the reserve at the crack of dawn – ask.

You can get information and buy trail guides, bird and mammal lists and maps here. *The Nature Trail Guide* (US$2.50) is a useful booklet in English which will enable you to hike a self-guided trail with markers. The gift shop also sells T-shirts, beautiful colour slides by Richard Laval (some of which are reproduced in this book), postcards, books, posters and a variety of other souvenirs.

Many of the walking trails are generally very muddy, and even during the dry season (from late December to early May) the cloud forest tends to be dripping. Therefore rainwear and suitable boots are recommended. (Rubber boots can be rented at the entrance for about US$1 – bring your own footwear for the best fit.) A few of the trails have recently been stabilised with concrete blocks or wooden boards and are easier to walk – it'll be interesting to see how they hold up under the pressure of thousands of visitors and torrential rainstorms. During the wet season, the unpaved trails turn into quagmires, but there are usually fewer visitors. The annual rainfall here is about three metres. (Dry season visitors who plan on staying on the main trails really don't need rubber boots – I've seen sweaty-footed hikers looking elegant in their personal pink rubber boots with barely a splash of mud on them.)

Because of the fragile environment, the reserve will only allow a maximum of 100 people in at any given time. During the busy dry season months (as well as in July) the first 100 people often arrive by early morning and then there may be a wait until late morning when the early arrivals begin departing. It is usually less crowded in the afternoons. The least busy months are May, June, September, October and November. If you are travelling in the dry season, consider going to the less crowded Santa Elena reserve, described later in this section.

It is important to remember that the cloud forest is often cloudy and the vegetation is thick. This combination cuts down on sounds as well as visibility.

I have received several letters from readers who have been disappointed with the lack of wildlife sightings in the cloud forest and they have asked me not to raise people's expectations with enthusiastic descriptions of the fauna. Personally, I find the cloud forest exhilarating and mysterious even on those cloudy and stormy days when the forest reveals few of its secrets – but I do emphasise that, for many people, the secretive wildlife is a disappointment. If your expectations are not met, I am sorry – but, please, don't blame me for that!

Guides

Although you can hike around the reserve without a guide, you'll stand a better chance of seeing a quetzal and other wildlife if you hire a guide. Half day guided hikes can be arranged at the information centre for about US$12 to US$13 per person – they leave in the early morning. For the same price, you can take a night hike into the reserve at 7.15 pm – call guide Thomas Guindon (☎ 64 5118) for information.

Most hotels will be able to arrange for a local to guide you either within the reserve or in some of the nearby surrounding areas.

The cost of a guide depends on how well known or experienced they are, but expect to start at around US$20 for half a day. The best guides will charge at least US$50 for half a day. These fees can be split up among a group, however, and so individual costs are not prohibitive. Three well known and highly recommended guides are Gary Diller (☎ 64 5045) and Richard and Meg Laval (☎ 64 5052). Meg takes people on horseriding tours; horses cost about US$10 an hour. These guides can all be contacted via the Monteverde Conservation League, Apartado 10165-1000, San José.

Because of the historical Quaker background, many locals and most guides speak English as well as Spanish.

Things to See & Do

Inside the reserve there are various marked and maintained trails. The most popular are found in a roughly triangular area ('El Triangulo') to the east of the reserve entrance – these trails are all suitable for day hikes. Longer trails stretch out east across the reserve and down the Peñas Blancas river valley (not connected with the Peñas Blancas refuge) down to lowlands north of the Cordillera Tilarán. These longer trails have shelters scattered along them every few hours – however, recent reports indicate that they are not open to the general public, though this has not always been the case. Ask at the reserve about hiking through to the northern lowlands.

The bird list includes over 400 species which have been recorded in the area, but the one that most visitors want to see is the resplendent quetzal (described in the Flora & Fauna section of the Facts About the Country chapter). The best time to see the quetzal is when it is nesting in March and April, but you could get lucky any time of year.

But there is a host of other things to observe. A walk along the Sendero Nuboso (Cloudy Trail) will take you on a two km (one way) interpretive walk through the cloud forest to the continental divide. The trail guide describes plants, weather patterns, animal tracks, insects and ecosystems which you see along the way.

Three-wattled bellbird

When I walked the Sendero Nuboso, the clouds were low over the forest and the gnarled old oak trees, festooned with vines and bromeliads, looked mysterious and slightly forbidding. Palm trees and bamboos bent menacingly over the trail and I felt as if I were walking through a Grimm fairytale – a wicked witch or grinning goblin would not be out of place.

Suddenly the cold, clammy mist was rent by the weirdest metallic BONK! followed by an eerie high-pitched whistle such as I had never heard before. I stopped dead in my tracks.

For a full minute I listened and heard nothing but the sighing of the faintest of breezes and a lone insect circling my ear. Then again, the strange BONK and whistle were repeated, louder, and high overhead. I craned my neck and searched the tree tops with my binoculars.

Finally, after several more extremely loud BONKS and whistles, I spied an odd-looking large brown bird with snow-white head and shoulders just visible on a high snag.

At first, I thought the bird was eating a lizard or small snake – through my binoculars I could clearly see the worm-like objects hanging from the bill. But then the beak gaped wide open and, instead of a seeing a reptile wriggling away, I heard another BONK and whistle. Finally, I realised that I was watching the aptly named three-wattled bellbird.

The three black, wormy looking wattles hanging from the bill were fully six cm long – about a fifth of the length of the entire bird. The metallic BONK did sound rather bell-like, but it travelled over an incredible distance. It seemed to be flooding the forest with sound, but the bird itself was probably 100 metres away or more, barely visible in the top of the cloud forest.

One animal which you used to be able to see so often that it almost became a Monteverde mascot was the golden toad. Monteverde was the only place in the world where this exotic little toad occurred. The tiny gold coloured amphibian frequently used to be seen scrambling along the muddy trails of the cloud forest, adding a bright splash to the surroundings. Unfortunately, no one has seen this once common toad since 1989, and it is a mystery what happened to it.

Recently, during a conference of herpetologists (scientists who study reptiles and amphibians) from all over the world, it was noted that the same puzzling story was occurring with other frog and toad species all over the world. Amphibians once common were now severely depleted or simply not found at all. The scientists were unable to give a reason for the sudden demise of so many amphibian species in so many different habitats.

One theory is that worldwide air quality has depreciated to the extent that amphibians, who breathe both with primitive lungs and through their perpetually moist skin, were more susceptible to air-borne toxins because of the gas exchange through their skin. Perhaps they are like the canaries miners used in the old days to warn them of toxic air in the mines. When the canary keeled over, it was time for the miners to get out!

Are our dying frogs and toads a symptom of a planet which is becoming too polluted?

Places to Stay & Eat

There is a dormitory-style refuge near the park entrance where a bunk costs a few dollars per person. These bunks are often used by researchers and may not be available to tourists – contact the reserve (☎ 64 5122) or write to the Centro Científico Tropical (☎ 22 6241; Apartado 8-3870-1000, San José) for information. I have conflicting reports about whether non-research personnel can stay here. There are kitchen facilities, or full board can be provided if arranged in advance.

Almost all visitors stay in one of the several hotels, pensións, and lodges in either the Monteverde community or in Santa Elena. The nearest hotel is just over one km from the entrance; the most distant are in the small town of Santa Elena, about five to six km from the entrance.

Getting There & Away

The entrance to the reserve is uphill from all the hotels, and there is no official public transport. The better hotels can arrange a vehicle to take you up to the reserve, or you can take your own vehicle to the small parking lot by the entrance, or walk. A taxi from Santa Elena will charge about US$5 to US$6.

There is a bus for local workers that leaves from in front of the Hotel Imán in Santa Elena at 6.30 am. It goes via the Monteverde Lodge road all the way to the reserve, picking up anybody who flags it down – the fare is under US$1. Locals tend to get charged less than gringos, but this bus service is not really designed for tourists and it's hard to get good local information about it. The service is mainly for locals who work in the hotels, reserve etc. If you happen to be at the right place at the right time, hop on the bus (and don't be obnoxious about the fare). A bus leaves the reserve mid-afternoon (recently at 3 pm) to take people back to Santa Elena.

Many visitors remark that some of the best birding is on the open road leading up to the reserve entrance, especially the final two km.

RESERVA SANTA ELENA

Also called Centro Ecológico Bosque Nuboso de Monteverde, this reserve was created in 1989 and opened to the public shortly thereafter. It provides a welcome alternative to the already over-visited Monteverde reserve. The Santa Elena Reserve is about five km north-east of the village of Santa Elena and can be reached by car or on foot (head north from Santa Elena and follow the signs). The cloud forest in the reserve is similar to Monteverde and you can see quetzals here too – I did. Within an hour or two of hiking from the entrance, you can reach lookouts where you can see Volcán Arenal exploding in the distance – I didn't. I reached the lookouts but it was too cloudy and the 20 metre visibility just didn't quite make it. Rule number 407 of cloud forest travel – it's often cloudy.

The Santa Elena Reserve is less visited than Monteverde, yet has a good (though not 'concrete blocked') trail system. I think that the Santa Elena Reserve offers a good look at the Costa Rican cloud forest, despite the cachet conferred by the Monteverde name.

The reserve has a program of cloud forest study for both local and international students. There are over eight km of trails currently open and expansion of the reserve and trail system is planned. The reserve's study and expansion programs are administered by the non-profit Cloud Forest Foundation of the Santa Elena Agricultural College, Monteverde, Puntarenas.

Information

The reserve is open daily from 7 am to 4 pm. There is an information centre at the entrance where you can see a small exhibit, obtain trail maps and information, and pay the entry fee of US$5.25 (discounts for students and locals). Rubber boots can be rented here – though I wouldn't rely on that. Bring your own for a better fit.

JUNTAS

Although marked as Juntas on all my maps, the full name is Las Juntas de Abangares. This small town on the Río Abangares used to be a major gold-mining centre in the late 19th and early 20th centuries, attracting fortune-seekers and entrepreneurs from all over the world. The gold boom is now over, but a small tourist industry is beginning in this sleepy Costa Rican town, and a museum opened in 1991. It makes an interesting side trip for travellers wishing to get away from the tourist hordes.

Named the **Ecomuseo de las Minas de Abangares**, the small museum is five km beyond Juntas and has photographs and models depicting the old mining practices of the area. It is unclear to me why a mining museum should be called an 'Ecomuseo' – it seems like everyone is trying to jump on the ecological bandwagon. In the grounds outside the museum is a picnic area and children's play area; trails above the museum lead to mine artefacts such as bits of railway. I found some good birding along these trails – it's very quiet here and the birds are rarely disturbed. Also, the area is several hundred metres above the coastal lowlands and attracts some different birds. Admission to the Ecomuseo is by contribution (100 colones suggested – about US$0.70) but there was nobody around to take it when I was there.

Places to Stay & Eat

The only place to stay is the basic *Cabinas Las Juntas* (☎ 62 0153) which has rooms with private cold showers for US$4.75/8.75 single/double. A reasonable restaurant is attached. With the new museum and tourist interest in the area, a new place to stay may open in the future.

There are several other places to eat – try the *Soda La Amistad* by the bus terminal and the *Restaurant La Familiar* on the Parque Central.

On the way out of town towards the museum, you pass the ramshackle *El Caballo Blanco* bar which is an interesting place full of mining artefacts and colourful characters. Closer to the museum is the *La Sierra Alta Super Bar* which serves cold drinks.

Getting There & Away

Bus There are buses from Cañas to Juntas at 9.30 am and 2.50 pm. There are also buses from the Puntarenas terminal in San José at 11 am and 5 pm. There are no buses to the Ecomuseo, though 4WD taxis can be hired to the Ecomuseo.

Buses leave Juntas for San José at 6 and 11 am, for Cañas at 6.30 am and 12.30 pm, and for Santa Elena at 3 pm.

Car The turn-off from the Interamericana is 26 km south of Cañas and is reasonably well signed: 'Las Juntas 6 km, Ecomuseo 11 km'. The road is paved as far as Juntas. To get to the Ecomuseo, follow the paved road for 100 metres past the Parque Central, turn left, cross a bridge and pass the Caballo Blanco on your left, then turn right; you'll see a sign for 'Ecomuseo 4 km'. The road becomes unpaved and in progressively worse shape. A couple of km past Juntas the road forks – a sign indicates a poor road, rarely used by tourists, heading left to Monteverde (30 km), and another right to the Ecomuseo (3 km). In the small community of La Sierra you can stop for a drink – you may have to park your car here and walk the last km or so. I got through to the museum in an ordinary car in the dry season – but just barely.

TEMPISQUE FERRY

About 22 km south of Cañas on the Interamericana is a turn-off to the Tempisque ferry, 25 km to the west. If you are driving to the Península de Nicoya, this will save you about 110 km of driving via Liberia. Some buses from San José to Nicoya and the Península de Nicoya beaches come this way – ask about the route in the San José bus offices. Note that bus passengers must get off, buy a passenger ticket and board the ferry on foot – don't miss the boat, because the bus won't wait.

The ferry runs every hour from 6 am to 8 pm (west-bound) and 6.30 am to 8.30 pm (east-bound). The crossing takes 20 minutes and costs US$3 per car and US$0.25 for foot passengers. The ferry holds about 10 to 20 vehicles (depending on size); you might not be able to get on at peak times, especially Sunday afternoons heading back to the mainland from the Península de Nicoya.

CAÑAS

Cañas is a small agricultural centre serving about 25,000 people in the surrounding area. It is a hot little town, 90 metres above sea level in the Guanacaste lowlands and about 180 km from San José along the Interamericana. There is not much to do in Cañas itself, but travellers use it as a base for visits to the nearby Parque Nacional Palo Verde and other reserves, the Ecomuseo and for Corobicí river trips. Cañas is also the beginning or end point for the Arenal back roads route described later in this chapter.

Places to Stay

Cañas is a cheaper place to stay than Liberia, which may be why so many long-haul truck drivers spend the night here. Get in by midafternoon for the best choice of rooms.

There are two basic but adequate hotels on the south-eastern side of the Parque Central. They are the *Hotel Guillén* (☎ 69 0070) and *Hotel Parque*. The Guillén charges US$3 per person or US$3.75 with private bath; the marginally nicer Parque charges US$3.50 per person.

The *Gran Hotel* on the north-western side of the parque charges US$3 per person, or US$9.50 for fairly basic double rooms with private bath. At the south-eastern end of town, by Avenida 2 and Calle 5, you'll find the *Cabinas Corobicí* (☎ 69 0241) which is a little more pleasant. The charge here is about US$7 per person with private bath. None of these hotels has hot showers.

The best place in downtown Cañas is the *Hotel Cañas* (☎ 69 0039; Apartado 61, Cañas, Guanacaste), Calle 2, Avenida 3. Rooms with private cold baths and fan cost US$8.50/14.50 single/double; with air-conditioning, rates are US$11/20. This hotel has a good restaurant and is very popular – the air-conditioned rooms go very fast.

The most expensive place is the *Hotel El Corral* (☎ 69 0622) which is right on the Interamericana. Clean, air-conditioned rooms with private electric showers rent for US$27/42 – overpriced, in my opinion.

You can also stay at the much better *Hacienda La Pacífica* which is five km north of Cañas (see the separate entry for the Hacienda later in this section for details). About half way between Cañas and La Pacífica is the *Capazuri Bed & Breakfast* on the northeast side of the road. This is a new operation with a friendly owner – he charges US$8 per person.

Places to Eat

The *Hotel Cañas* restaurant is good – its breakfast attracts some of the town's important people to sit around and plan the day's events. There are some decent Chinese restaurants in town. Two of the best are the *Restaurant El Primero* on the central plaza and the *Restaurant Lei Tu* just off the plaza on Avenida 1. Meals are about US$2 to US$4. There are other places nearby. Down on the Interamericana is the *Bar/Restaurant El Corral* which is run by a lady who speaks good English.

Getting There & Away

Bus Buses for Cañas leave San José six times a day from Calle 16, Avenida 1 & 3, opposite the Coca-Cola terminal. There are also TRALAPA buses from Calle 20, Avenida 3. The trip takes about 3½ hours and costs about US$2.50.

Cañas has two bus terminals. The new bus terminal and produce market is at Calle 1 and Avenida 11 – most buses leave from here. In addition, some San José buses still leave from the La Cañera terminal (not much more than a glorified bus stop) at Avenida Central and Calle 5. Perhaps by the time you read this all buses will be leaving from the new terminal.

The new terminal has daily buses to Liberia at 5.45, 7, 7.30, 9 and 11.20 am and at 3 and 5 pm. There are buses to Tilarán at 6, 9 and 10.30 am, noon, and 1.45, 3.30 and 5.30 pm. There are buses to Las Juntas de Abangares at 9.30 am and 2.50 pm; to Bebedero (near Parque Nacional Palo Verde) at 5, 9 and 11 am and 1, 3 and 5 pm; to Upala

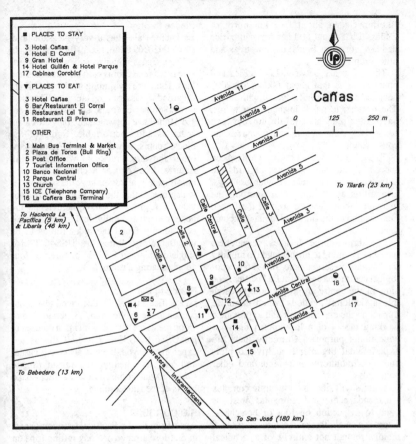

Cañas

PLACES TO STAY
3 Hotel Cañas
4 Hotel El Corral
9 Gran Hotel
14 Hotel Guillén & Hotel Parque
17 Cabinas Corobicí

PLACES TO EAT
3 Hotel Cañas
6 Bar/Restaurant El Corral
8 Restaurant Lei Tu
11 Restaurant El Primero

OTHER
1 Main Bus Terminal & Market
2 Plaza de Toros (Bull Ring)
5 Post Office
7 Tourist Information Office
10 Banco Nacional
12 Parque Central
13 Church
15 ICE (Telephone Company)
16 La Cañera Bus Terminal

To Hacienda La Pacífica (5 km) & Liberia (46 km)

To Tilarán (23 km)

To Bebedero (13 km)

To San José (180 km)

at 5.45, 9 and 11 am and at 2 and 5 pm; and to Puntarenas at 6, 6.40, 9.30 and 11 am and 12.30, 1.30 and 4.15 pm. These times are subject to change and may be curtailed in the wet season, particularly to destinations with unpaved roads. Also, not all buses originate in Cañas – many just stop here, such as the Liberia-Cañas-Puntarenas bus.

Buses for San José leave from the new terminal at 6 and 9.15 am and at 12.30 and 2.15 pm. They leave the La Cañera terminal at 4.30, 5.15, 6 and 9.15 am and 2 pm. On Sunday, the 4.30 am bus is replaced by a 5.15 pm bus.

Tours Cata Tours (☎ 69 1203) offers a variety of tours to the national parks, rivers and reserves in the nearby area, as well as to Monteverde and Volcán Arenal. Most tours leave from the Hacienda La Pacífica. Cata Tours has a San José office (☎ 21 5455, fax 21 0200; Apartado 10173-1000, San José) on Avenida 3, Calle Central & 1.

Safaris Corobicí have river rafting trips on the Río Corobicí and other local adventure tours – see below under Río Corobicí.

HACIENDA LA PACÍFICA

La Pacífica is a working hacienda just off the

Interamericana about five km north of Cañas. It has about 500 head of cattle, rice paddies, sorghum fields, cashew trees and other crops.

The difference between La Pacífica and other farms is that about 600 of its 2000 hectares have been left covered with forest. The owners, to put it in their own words, have attempted an equilibrium between rational exploitation of natural resources and conservation.

To a certain extent, this concept has been successful and many species of birds are attracted to the hacienda. Howler monkeys, armadillos and anteaters are among the mammals which can be seen in the forest. Observation of the flora and fauna is encouraged.

For almost three decades, researchers have been coming to the hacienda to monitor the habitats preserved here. In 1986 an ecological centre was created at La Pacífica. The aims of the centre are to promote research into agricultural methods which minimise impact on the environment and to provide a working model of a low-impact farm for educational purposes. Currently there are experimental organically cultivated plots and plots monitoring asparagus and other vegetables.

Visitors will find that the entire complex – hacienda, ecological centre and forest – is open to inspection on foot or horseback. There is a small library of reference books – mainly, though not entirely, of a technical nature. Bilingual naturalist guides are available for US$25 a half day (per person in groups) or US$10 per hour privately. Horses can be rented at US$25 for two hours with a guide. Bicycle rental is US$1.80 per hour or US$7.25 for eight hours. Staff can help arrange birding trips, guided visits to the national parks and float trips on the nearby Río Corobicí.

Although the hacienda is on the Pacific side of the country, it is not named after the ocean. Its name derives from Doña Pacifica Fernandéz who designed the Costa Rican flag near the turn of the century, and who was the wife of President Bernardo Soto.

Places to Stay

La Pacífica also has a very pleasant hotel (☎ 69 0050, 69 0266, fax 69 0555; Apartado 8-5700, Cañas, Guanacaste) with comfortable rooms and cabins with private baths and fans. There is a swimming pool and a highly regarded Swiss-run restaurant. The best rooms are newer (more are being built for 1994) and have hot water, and they are clean, spacious and comfortable. Some of the oldest rooms, however, are in poor shape (cold showers, cracks in walls, missing fixtures, located near a chicken coop!) – unfortunately, all rooms have the same prices which means that the worst rooms are poor value. Tour groups often stay here (taking the better rooms) and individual travellers have occasionally found the older rooms to be unsatisfactory. Rates are US$46/77 for single/double and US$95 for three or four people sharing a room.

Places to Eat

La Pacífica's tastefully decorated restaurant is open to the public from 6.30 am to 10 pm. Good meals are served, with main courses in the US$6 to US$12 range. If this is too expensive for you, there is also the pleasant and slightly cheaper restaurant *Rincón Corobicí* which is just past La Pacífica on the banks of the Río Corobicí.

RÍO COROBICÍ

Apart from the La Pacífica, tour companies in San José arrange one-day rafting trips on the Río Corobicí. Many of these use a local outfitter, Safaris Corobicí (☎/fax 69 1091, Apartado 99-5700, Cañas, Guanacaste). The emphasis is on wildlife observation rather than exciting whitewater. The river is Class I to II – in other words, pretty flat.

Safaris Corobicí have an office on the south-east side of Hacienda La Pacífica. They offer daily departures on the Corobicí – a two hour float is US$35 per person, a three hour bird-watching float covering 12 km is US$43 per person and a half day 18 km float including lunch is US$60 per person. All prices are based on a two person minimum; children under 14 accompanying

Left: Volcán Orosí from Hacienda de Los Inocentes (RR)
Right: Waterfall onto beach in Parque Nacional Corcovado (RR)
Bottom: Rafting on the Río Reventazón (RH)

Top: Poison-arrow frog (RL)
Left: Three-toed sloth (RR)
Right: Tamandua anteater (RL)

adults receive a 50% discount, and large groups can ask for a better rate, depending on group size.

Safaris Corobicí also have half day salt-water estuary trips along the Bebedero and Tempisque rivers, bordering the Parque Nacional Palo Verde, for US$50 per person (four minimum, lunch included). Animals and birds seen on some of these float trips (both Corobicí and estuary trips) include motmots, parrots, sungrebes, boat-billed and other herons, trogons, wood storks, spoon-bills, coatimundis, river otters, howler monkeys and caimans. These are good trips for nature enthusiasts – you can bring a camera and binoculars because the ride is not wild. Bring a swim suit for a refreshing river dip, and don't forget sun protection.

Apart from river floats, Safaris Corobicí have mountain-biking trips. They drive you up towards Arenal and then accompany you back on a three hour descent (longer if you want to take a lot of photographs) along paved roads with little traffic. Bikes and helmets are provided for US$43 per person.

Costa Rica Expeditions (☎ 57 0766) in San José has trips involving three hours driving, three hours rafting and three hours return driving with bilingual guides and lunch on the river. Departures are on demand and cost US$69 per person, two minimum. They can also arrange overnight tours to La Pacífica with a private vehicle and guide. Ríos Tropicales (☎ 33 6455) also offers Corobicí river trips.

BAGACES

This small town is about 22 km north-west of Cañas on the Interamericana. The main reason to stop here is to visit the national park offices or the Friends of Lomas Barbudal offices (or both).

The SPN has its headquarters here for the Area de Conservación Tempisque (ACT) which comprises the Parques Nacionales Palo Verde, Barra Honda, Marino Las Baulas, Reserva Biológica Lomas Barbudal and several small and lesser known protected areas. The ACT office (☎ 67 1062) is on the Interamericana opposite the main entry road

into the Parque Nacional Palo Verde (which is signed). The office appears to be mainly an administrative one – when I stopped by to ask a few simple questions like 'When is the best time to visit Palo Verde to see birds and other wildlife?' the staff weren't sure and suggested I talk to their biologist – who wasn't there. Oh, well. They are friendly and will try to help – you can ask them to call Palo Verde to get information direct from the rangers. Office hours are 8 am to 4 pm, Monday to Friday.

Friends of (Amigos de) Lomas Barbudal (☎ 67 1029, fax 67 1203) is a non-profit organisation begun in 1986 to protect tropical dry forest in general and Reserva Biológica Lomas Barbudal in particular. Although Lomas Barbudal is administered by the SPN, the government doesn't have enough money to conserve the area properly. 'Friends' puts a lot of work into community involvement and education, and has constructed a visitor and community centre which is staffed by locals. The organisation also works in fire management, trail construction and maintenance, land acquisitions and restoration, community development and a variety of scientific research. This is one of the most impressive grass-roots conservation organisations in Costa Rica.

You are welcome to visit their office in Bagaces – there is no street address but most Bagaceños know where it is. There's a small exhibit about the reserve and the staff will give you as much information as you can handle. They take donations too – US citizens can make tax-deductible contributions to Friends of Lomas Barbudal, 691 Colusa Ave, Berkeley, CA 94707-1517. If you want to contribute to a grass-roots conservation organisation, this is one of the best around. I made a small contribution when I stopped by – I have never before received such enthusiastic and sincere thanks as I did from the 'Friends' president, Gordon Frankie. He says every bit counts and he means it. Contributors receive the *Bee Line* bulletin which is a great combination of scientific articles written by graduate students and biology professors and poems and art work contributed by local school children. Volunteers are welcome, especially if they speak Spanish and have some background in biology.

Places to Stay

There aren't many places to stay in this small town. Try the cheap and basic *Pensión Miravalles* and the *Pensión Vargaray* – the latter with private cold water baths. *Cabinas Eduardo Vargas* has been recommended as the 'best' in town – though I didn't see them. The cheap and simple rooms have private cold showers and fans.

Getting There & Away

I didn't find a bus terminal here, but there probably is one. Most buses going to Liberia or Cañas can drop you off on the Interamericana at the entrance to town. Everything is within a few blocks of the highway.

PARQUE NACIONAL PALO VERDE

The 16,804 hectare Parque Nacional Palo Verde lies on the north-eastern banks of the mouth of Río Tempisque at the head of the Golfo de Nicoya, some 30 km west of Cañas and 30 km south of Bagaces. The national park incorporates what used to be the Refugio Nacional de Vida Silvestre Rafael Lucas Rodríguez Caballero (which is still marked on some maps).

The national park is a major bird sanctuary for resident and migrating waterfowl, as well as forest birds. A large number of different habitats is represented, ranging from swamps, marshes, mangroves and lagoons to a variety of seasonal grasslands and forests. Some 150 species of trees have been recorded in the park. A number of low limestone hills provide lookout points over the park. The dry season from December to March is very marked and much of the forest dries out. During the wet months, large portions of the area are flooded.

Palo Verde is a magnet for bird-watchers who come to see the large flocks of herons (including the country's largest nesting colony of black-crowned night-herons on Isla de Los Pájaros), storks (including the only Costa Rican nesting site of the locally endangered jabiru stork), spoonbills, egrets, ibis, grebes and ducks. Inland, birds such as scarlet macaws, great curassows, keel-billed toucans and parrots may be seen. Approximately 300 different bird species have been recorded in the park. Other possible sightings include crocodiles (reportedly up to five metres in length), iguanas, monkeys and peccaries.

Palo Verde has been combined with Parque Nacional Barra Honda and other reserves in the Península de Nicoya to form the Area de Conservación Tempisque (ACT).

Information

The recommended time for a visit is September to March because of the huge influx of migratory and endemic birds. This is one of the greatest concentrations of waterfowl and shorebirds in Central America. From December to February are the best months. September and October are very wet and access may be limited. When the dry season begins the birds tend to congregate in the remaining lakes and marshes. Trees lose their leaves and the massed flocks of birds become easier to observe. In addition, there are far fewer insects in the dry season and the roads and trails are more passable. Mammals are seen around the waterholes. Binoculars or a spotting scope are highly recommended.

The Hacienda Palo Verde research station is run by the Organization of Tropical Studies (OTS). Several trails lead from the station area into the national park and there is also an observation tower in the area.

Admission to the park is US$1.50 per day.

Places to Stay & Eat

Sometimes the research station is full of researchers or students; at other times travellers can stay here for about US$50 per day. If you wish to stay overnight at the OTS research station, make arrangements with OTS (☎ 40 9938, 40 6696, fax 40 6783); Apartado 676-2050, San Pedro, San José). Information is also available from the North American Office of OTS (☎ (919) 684 5774, fax (919) 684 5661; Box DM, Duke Station, Durham, NC 27706).

Camping is permitted near the Palo Verde ranger station, where there are toilets and shower facilities available to campers. A camping fee of US$2.25 per person is charged. If you wish to camp, let the SPN in San José or ACT in Bagaces know about it. Alternatively, try the ranger station's radiotelephone (☎ 33 4160) if you speak Spanish. For about US$8 a day you can eat meals with the park rangers if you order in advance, and you may be able to coordinate transport with a ranger going into the area. The rangers sometimes take travellers on patrol with them, often by horseback, sometimes by boat around the bird islands of the Río Tempisque. A ranger named Israel or Ismael does boat tours for about US$35 – the boat will take up to five passengers.

Getting There & Away

There are several routes into the park, but it is difficult to get there unless you have your own transportation, or hire a taxi or walk.

The most frequently used route begins in Bagaces where there is a signed turn-off from the Interamericana. From here, follow signs for the national park. At times, the road forks – if in doubt, take the fork that looks more used. If you can't decide which is the main fork, take the road that has a power line running along it. After about 28 km you reach the park entrance station, where admission fees are paid. A further eight km brings you to the limestone hill, Cerro Guayacán, from where there are good views of the park. This is where the OTS research station is found; a couple of km further are the Palo Verde park headquarters and ranger station.

The road is supposedly passable to ordinary cars all year round, but get up-to-date information if you are travelling in the rainy season. Note that the road from the Interamericana to Reserva Biológica Lomas Barbudal, which goes all the way around the reserve, eventually joins the Bagaces-Palo Verde road several km before the park entrance. Therefore both these areas can be visited without having to return to the Interamericana.

Another entrance route is to take the bus from Cañas to Bebedero. From here, a track leads into the Sector Catalina at the east end of the park. This is passable with 4WD in the dry season, or you could hike – I haven't been in this way, but it reportedly gets you to the national park in about three or four km and reaches the park headquarters about 18 to 20 km further on.

In the dry season only, it is reportedly possible to enter Palo Verde from the Península de Nicoya. Take a bus from Nicoya to Puerto Humo on the Río Tempisque. If you are driving, you can reach Puerto Humo by turning north from Quebrada Honda (six km west of the Río Tempisque ferry). I haven't taken this route either – it's reportedly drivable in the dry season and could be shorter than going all the way to Nicoya if you're coming from the east. At the tiny Puerto Humo dock, hire a boat to take you several km up the river to the national park dock. From here, a trail leads about two km to the Palo Verde ranger station and headquarters. Much of the area is flooded during the wet season.

Getting Around

Tours Safaris Corobicí has float trips along the Tempisque and Bebedero rivers which border the park (see the Río Corobicí entry for details). Horizontes (☎ 22 2022) has day tours which will pick you up from your Península de Nicoya hotel, drive you to Puerto Humo, take you on a boat ride and on-foot exploration of the park, and return. Tours include lunch and a bilingual naturalist-guide and cost US$75 per person (four person minimum). Tours are offered on Tuesday and Friday. Cata Tours (see the Cañas entry) offers float and kayak trips as well. Guanacaste Tours in Liberia also offers Río Tempisque boat tours and bird-watching. The MV *Temptress* does four and six night cruises which include Palo Verde among several other Pacific coastal parks – see Tours in the Getting Around chapter.

RESERVA BIOLÓGICA LOMAS BARBUDAL

The 2279 hectare Lomas Barbudal reserve is separated from the northern edge of Palo Verde by a narrow strip of privately owned land. About 70% of the area is deciduous forest which contains several species of endangered trees such as mahogany and rosewood as well as the co₁nmon and quite spectacular *Tabebuia ochracea* (locally called the *corteza amarilla* or yellow cortez). This tree is what biologists call a 'big bang reproducer' – all the yellow cortezes in the forest burst into bloom on the same day and, for about four days, the forest is an incredible mass of yellow-flowered trees. This usually occurs late in the dry season, about four days after an unseasonable rain shower.

During the dry season, many of the trees shed their leaves just as they do in the autumn or fall season in temperate lands. This kind of forest is known as tropical dry forest – once common in many parts of the Pacific slopes of Central America, very little of it now remains. In addition, there are riparian forests along the Río Cabuyo which flows through the reserve year-round, as well as small areas of other types of forest.

Lomas Barbudal is also locally famous for its abundance and variety of insects. There are about 250 different species of bees in this fairly small reserve – this represents about a quarter of the world's bee species. Bees here (and in nearby Palo Verde) include the Africanised 'killer' bees – if you suffer from bee allergies this is one area where you really don't want to forget your bee-sting kit. Wasps, butterflies and moths are also locally abundant.

There are plenty of birds to be seen. A check-list published by Friends of Lomas Barbudal in 1990 has 202 species, and more have been added since. Interesting species include the great curassow, a chicken-like bird that is hunted for food and is endangered. Other endangered species found locally are the king vulture, scarlet macaw and jabiru stork. Mammals which you may see include white-tailed deer, peccaries, coatimundis, and howler and white-faced monkeys. An interesting trail guide was published by the 'Friends' in 1993 under the title of *A White-faced Monkey's Guide to Lomas Barbudal*. The guide is written as if by a white-faced monkey, who gives the reader six pages of interesting details about the forest from the monkeys' perspective: 'Contrary to popular belief, we do not throw fruit or intentionally defecate on humans; however, we do have to discard our garbage *somewhere*, and if you happen to be standing beneath us, it will land on you'.

Information & Orientation

The biological reserve is administered by the SPN and is part of the ACT; information can be obtained from their office in Bagaces. The Friends of Lomas Barbudal also have an office in Bagaces and can sell you bird checklists and trail guides and give you information. (See the Bagaces entry earlier in this section for more details of both places.)

Entrance to the reserve costs US$1.50 and you can camp almost anywhere for a further US$2.25 per person (though I couldn't find anyone to take my money when I was there). The dry season is from December to April and it can get very hot then – temperatures of 38°C (100°F) are sometimes reached. During the rainy season it is a little cooler, but insects are more abundant – bring repellent.

Once at the reserve entrance, you'll find the Casa de Patrimonio which is the local (small) museum and information centre, run by the inhabitants of the nearby community of San Rafael de Bagaces. The actual reserve is on the other side of the Río Cabuyo behind the museum, but the river is not passable to vehicles so you have to wade across at this point. Alternatively, you can drive to the right towards San Ramon de Bagaces (two km) and continue around the reserve by vehicle, making short incursions at various points. It is difficult to drive into the reserve because of the river, but hikes are certainly possible. This road eventually joins up with the road between Bagaces and Palo Verde.

The Casa de Patrimonio works on a 10

days open/four days closed system, so it is a matter of luck whether they are open or not. If they are closed, go to the right for less than a km towards San Rafael de Bagaces and ask for the Familia Rosales – they have local information and can open up the Casa de Patrimonio and generally help out. You can buy trail guides, maps, T-shirts, etc here and camping is allowed in front of the Casa.

Getting There & Away
The turn-off to Lomas Barbudal from the Interamericana is at the small community of Pijije, 14 km south-east of Liberia or 12 km north-west of Bagaces. The road to the reserve is signed – it says '6 km' but it's actually just over seven km to the Casa de Patrimonio at the entrance to the reserve. The road is unpaved but open all year – some steep sections may require 4WD during and after heavy rains.

THE VOLCÁN MIRAVALLES AREA
Volcán Miravalles (2028 metres) is the highest volcano in the Cordillera de Guanacaste. It is afforded a modicum of protection by being within the Reserva Forestal Miravalles. Although the main crater is dormant, there is some geothermal activity at Las Hornillas, at about 700 metres above sea level on the south slopes of the volcano.

Volcán Miravalles is 27 km north-north-east of Bagaces and can be approached by a paved road that leads north of Bagaces through the communities of Salitral, La Ese, Guayabo, Guayabal and Aguas Claras. A parallel paved road to the east avoids La Ese and Guayabo – instead it goes through Salitral and then the community of La Fortuna before rejoining the first road before Guayabal. The road beyond Aguas Claras is an unpaved one continuing to Upala. An unpaved road joins Guayaba with La Fortuna. Near La Fortuna is the government-run Proyecto Geotérmico Miravalles – a project which is investigating the possibility of obtaining electrical power from geothermal energy. The project can be visited.

The village of Guayabal is about 30 km north of Bagaces in the saddle between Parque Nacional Rincón de la Vieja and Volcán Miravalles. Here, there is the *Parador Las Nubes* (☎ 66 1313, fax 66 2136) – they offer rustic accommodation, home-cooked meals and tours of Volcán Miravalles and other areas. A daily bus goes from Liberia to Aguas Claras.

LIBERIA
Liberia is Costa Rica's most northerly town of any importance. It is the capital of the province of Guanacaste, but the town and surrounding villages have a combined population of only about 40,000. This is an indication of how rural most of Costa Rica is once you leave the Central Valley.

The city is 140 metres above sea level and surrounded by ranches. It is a centre for the cattle industry and is also a fairly important transportation centre. Liberia is also a good base for visiting the Parques Nacionales Santa Rosa and Guanacaste, both to the north, as well as Parque Nacional Palo Verde and Reserva Biológica Lomas Barbudal to the south.

Information
There is a tourist information centre (☎ 66 1606) in a historic mid 19th century house on the corner of Avenida 6 and Calle 1. Hours are 9 am to noon and 1 to 6 pm, Tuesday to Saturday, and 9 am to 1 pm on Sunday. They have local information about hotels, bus schedules, parks information, etc and have a large-scale map for reference. It helps if you speak Spanish.

Most of the better hotels will accept US dollars, and there are also some banks.

The ICE office on Calle 6, Avenida Central & 2, has international phone and fax facilities – you can send an urgent fax overseas in a couple of minutes from here.

The town is busy during the dry season and you should make reservations for the hotel of your choice, particularly at Christmas, Easter and weekends. Conversely, the better hotels give discounts in the wet season.

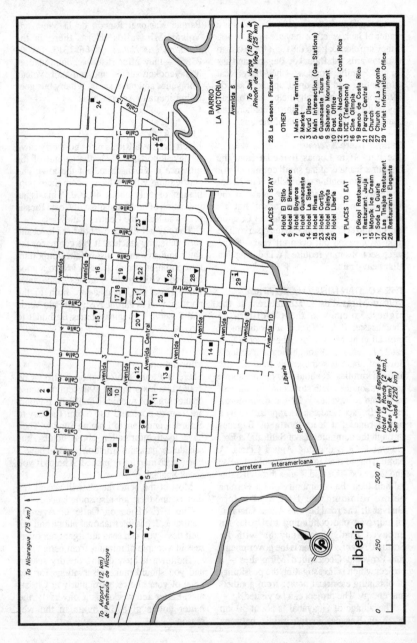

PLACES TO STAY

4 Hotel El Sitio
6 Motel El Bramadero
7 Hotel Boyeros
8 Hotel Guanacaste
14 Hotel La Siesta
18 Hotel Rivas
23 Hotel Cortijo
24 Hotel Daisyta
25 Hotel Liberia

PLACES TO EAT

3 Pókopi Restaurant
11 Restaurant Jaujá
15 Mönpik Ice Cream
17 Soda La Guaria
20 Las Tinajas Restaurant
26 Resturante Elegante
28 La Casona Pizzería

OTHER

1 Main Bus Terminal
2 Market
5 Kurd Disco
5 Main Intersection (Gas Stations)
6 Guanacaste Tours
9 Sabanero Monument
10 Post Office
12 Banco Nacional de Costa Rica
13 ICE (Telephone)
16 Cine Olimpia
19 Banco de Costa Rica
21 Parque Central
22 Church
27 Church of La Agonía
29 Tourist Information Office

Liberia

Things to See & Do

There are a number of good hotels, restaurants and bars, and the main activities are relaxing in one of them as you plan your next trip to beach or volcano.

The tourist information centre has a small museum of local ranching artefacts – cattle raising is a historically important occupation of Guanacaste province. A monument of a *sabanero* (akin to a cowboy) can be seen on the main road into town. The blocks around the tourist information centre contain several of the town's oldest houses, many dating back about 150 years.

There is a pleasant Parque Central with a modern church. Six blocks north-east of the parque along Avenida Central brings you to the oldest church in town, popularly called La Agonía (though maps show it as La Iglesia de la Ermita de la Resurrección). Strolling out there and in the surrounding blocks makes as good a walk as any in town.

There is also a cinema, the Cine Olimpía.

Places to Stay – bottom end

The *Hotel Liberia* (☎ 66 0161), just south of the parque on Calle Central, has very basic little boxes with fans for US$4.50 per person or US$11 for one or two people in rooms with private bath (cold water). The *Hotel Guanacaste* (☎ 66 2287, fax 66 0085) is affiliated with the youth hostel system and has a restaurant attached. It is on Avenida 1, a block off the Interamericana, and is popular with Costa Rican truck drivers and families and is often full. Rooms vary – some have air-conditioning and others don't; several were being remodelled in 1993. Check in early for the best rooms. Rates are about US$11/16.50/22 for single/double/triple – add US$1.50 for a fan and add US$5 for air-conditioning. IYHF members get a 10% discount. Ask the owner about bike rental and local information.

Other cheap and basic hotels include the *Hotel Cortijo* on Avenida Central, Calle 3 & 5 and the *Hotel Rivas* on the corner of the parque. Neither of these look up to much, but are probably OK – if you are on a really tight budget.

Places to Stay – middle

The *Hotel Daisyta* (☎ 66 0197, fax 66 0927) is fairly basic, but has a swimming pool and is family run and friendly. It is near the stadium on the eastern outskirts of town on Avenida 5 near Calle 13. The charge is about US$26 for a double with bath.

The *Motel El Bramadero* (☎ 66 0371), at the intersection of the Interamericana and the main road into town (Avenida Central), charges US$23/33 for singles/doubles with private bath and air-conditioning and a few cheaper rooms with fans. Rooms are plain but clean – not all of them have hot water. There is an adequate restaurant and swimming pool.

The *Hotel La Siesta* (☎ 66 0678, fax 66 2532; Apartado 15-5000, Liberia, Guanacaste) is on a quiet street – Calle 4, Avenida 4 & 6. The rates are US$25/38 for clean singles/doubles with bath (electric shower) and air-conditioning. There is a small restaurant/bar and a tiny swimming pool. This place is nothing fancy, but it does offer a quiet night's sleep and is recommended for that.

The *Hotel Boyeros* (☎ 66 0995, 66 0722, fax 66 2529; Apartado 85-1000, Liberia, Guanacaste) is also near the intersection of the Interamericana with the main road into Liberia. Rooms are US$28/39/44 for a single/double/triple with private electric shower and air-conditioning. Most rooms have small balconies or patios. There is a restaurant, adults' and kids' swimming pools, and dancing at weekends – get a room away from the music if you are looking for an early night. Otherwise, this place is a good deal.

The *Hotel La Ronda* (☎ 66 2799) is two km south of town on the Interamericana, next to the top-end Hotel Las Espuelas. It has spacious rooms with private baths and fans for US$15/20 but the empty swimming pool and unkempt appearance makes it look as if the place is about to close down; somebody needs to spruce it up a bit – it could be a nice hotel. Maybe somebody will have by the time you read this; check it out and let me know.

Places to Stay – top end

The *Hotel El Sitio* (☎ 66 1211, fax 66 2059) is on the road to Nicoya, about 300 metres west of the Interamericana. Spacious rooms with private bath (electric showers) are US$43/52 single/double with fan, or US$55/77 with air-conditioning. Because the rooms are large and well ventilated, you can get by quite well with a fan unless you demand polar temperatures in tropical rooms. The hotel is attractively decorated with original art – pre-Columbian motifs and sabanero scenes predominate and there are various Guancasteco touches. There is a decent restaurant and adults' and kids' pools.

The *Hotel Las Espuelas* (☎ 66 0144, fax 25 3987; Apartado 88-6000, Liberia, Guanacaste) is on the east side of the Interamericana, two km before you get to the main road into Liberia. It is considered the best hotel in Liberia (though the El Sitio is working hard to compete) and has pleasant grounds, a pool, restaurant and gift shop. Rooms are US$55/70 for a single/double with private bath and air-conditioning.

Many hotels (especially the more expensive ones) give substantial discounts in the low (rainy) season.

Places to Eat

The better hotels have reasonable restaurants. On the south-west side of the Parque Central, *Las Tinajas* is a good place to sit outside with a cold drink and watch the unenergetic goings on in the parque. Meals are reasonably priced. There are several Chinese restaurants (the *Restaurante Elegante* is as good as any) near the Parque Central. There are several sodas nearby too – the *Soda La Guaria* on the north-west side is cheap and popular with locals.

The *La Casona Pizzería*, Calle 1 & Avenida 4, is in a 19th century house and is a nice place with a wood-burning pizza oven, outdoor patio and small art gallery. For ice-cream, one of your best choices is *Mönpik* on Calle 2, a couple of blocks north of the parque. The *Restaurant Jauja* on Avenida Central & Calle 10 is a good general restaurant with standard meals, sandwiches,

snacks and ice cream. Perhaps the best place in town, judging by its many recommendations, is the *Pókopi Restaurant* opposite the Hotel El Sitio. They serve a variety of meals including hamburgers and sandwiches (about US$2 to US$3), fish (around US$6 or US$7) and steaks (around US$8 or US$9). Next door is the *Kurú* discotheque for you to dance off your dinner.

Getting There & Away

Air The airport is about 12 km west of town. Since early 1993 it has served as Costa Rica's second international airport – although there are no regularly scheduled international flights as yet. This may change in the near future with flights bringing sun-starved North American tourists trying to escape harsh winters by flying to Costa Rica's Pacific beach resorts.

Domestic flights are provided by Travelair (☎ 32 7883) which flies San José-Liberia-Tamarindo-San José on Wednesday and Sunday mornings, leaving San José at 9.30 am, Liberia at 10.50 am and Tamarindo at 11.25 am, returning to San José at 12.25 pm. The San José-Liberia fare is US$66 one way or US$114 for the round trip.

Bus Most visitors arrive by bus (or car). Pulmitan buses leave San José eight times a day from Calle 14, Avenida 1 & 3 (☎ 22 1650). The 4½ hour ride costs about US$3 – night buses are reportedly faster and do the trip in less than four hours.

In Liberia there is a new bus terminal on Avenida 7, a block from the Interamericana, and all buses now depart from here. Buses for San José leave at 6, 6.30 and 9 am and at 12.15 and 5 pm – more may be available as they come down from the Nicaraguan frontier. There are two companies servicing Filadelfia, Santa Cruz and Nicoya (US$1.25) with buses on the hour from 5 am to 6 pm, plus departures at 8.30 am and 7.30 and 8.30 pm. Buses for Playas del Coco leave at 5.30 and 8.15 am and 12.30, 2, 4.30 and 6.15 pm. Buses for Playa Hermosa and Playa Panamá leave at 11.30 am and 7 pm. These three are the closest beach resorts to Liberia (see the

Península de Nicoya chapter) but bus services may be curtailed in the rainy season.

Buses for La Cruz and Peñas Blancas (on the Nicaraguan border) leave at 5.30, 8.30, 9 and 11 am and noon and at 2, 6 and 8 pm – some buses stop en route from San José, but seats are usually available. These are the buses to take if you want to get dropped off at the entrance to Parque Nacional Santa Rosa. Other northbound destinations include Cuajiniquil (north side of Santa Rosa) at 3.30 pm, Santa Cecilia (passing Hacienda Los Inocentes) at 7 pm, Quebrada Grande at 3 pm, and several buses for the nearby towns of Colorado and Cañas Dulces.

Southbound buses go to Bagaces and Cañas at 5.45 am and 1.30 and 4.30 pm, to Bagaces and Aguas Claras at 1.45 pm, and to Puntarenas at 5, 8.30, 10 and 11.15 am and 3.15 pm. All these schedules are liable to change, but they give you an idea.

Taxi There is a taxi stand on the north-west corner of the Parque Central. These cabs will take you to the beaches if you can't wait for a bus. They will also take you to Parque Nacional Santa Rosa (US$15 per cab) and up the rough road to Parque Nacional Rincón de la Vieja (US$30 to US$40 per cab). Most cab drivers consider four passengers to be their limit. During the wet season, 4WD taxis are used to get to Rincón de la Vieja.

Car & Motorbike From Liberia the Interamericana heads south to Cañas (48 km) and San José (234 km). Northbound, the highway reaches the Nicaraguan border at Peñas Blancas (77 km). A paved highway to the west is the major road into the Península de Nicoya, which is famous for its good beaches, cattle ranches, terrible roads and friendly inhabitants. A poor road to the east leads to the Parque Nacional Rincón de la Vieja.

Rental cars are available – you should check their condition even more than in San José. It's probably best to rent a car in San José. In Liberia, shop around for the best deal. Sol Rent-a-Car (☎ 66 2222) and Aventura Rent-a-Car (☎ 66 2349) are in the

Motel El Bramadero. Budget and National (☎ 66 1211) are represented in the Hotel El Sitio.

Tours Guanacaste Tours (☎ 66 0306, fax 66 0307; Apartado 55-5000, Liberia, Guanacaste) is in the Motel El Bramadero and is run by a friendly English-speaking lady, Claudia Fernández de Brenes. They have a variety of day tours using air-conditioned vehicles and bilingual guides. Tours include lunch and cost from US$40 to US$90 per person, depending on the tour. There is a four person minimum – sometimes it is possible to hook up with another group. Current offerings include a Corobicí river float trip, bus and boat to Tamarindo (for turtles) and a visit to Guaitil to see Chorotega Indian ceramics, Santa Rosa & Guanacaste national parks with horse riding, Palo Verde national park and Tempisque river cruise, Rodeo Fiesta (from November to February), Volcán Arenal and Rincón de la Vieja.

PARQUE NACIONAL RINCÓN DE LA VIEJA

This 14,084 hectare national park is named after the active Volcán Rincón de la Vieja (1895 metres), which is the main attraction. There are several other peaks in the same volcanic massif, of which Volcán Santa María is the highest (1916 metres). There are numerous cones, craters and lagoons in the summit area which can be visited on horseback and foot.

Major volcanic activity occurred many times in the late 1960s, but at the moment the volcano is gently active and does not present any danger (though you should check with the SPN and local people for any change in activity before you go). There are fumaroles and boiling mud pools, steam vents and sulphurous springs to explore.

Thirty-two rivers and streams have their sources within the park, and it is therefore an important water catchment area. It was to protect this that the park was first created in 1973. Forests protect the rivers from evaporation in the dry season and from flooding in the wet season.

Elevations in the park range from less than 600 metres to 1916 metres and the changes in altitude result in the presence of four life zones. Visitors pass through a variety of different habitats as the volcanoes are ascended. Many species of trees are found in the forests. The area has the country's highest density of Costa Rica's national flower, the purple orchid *Cattleya skinneri*, locally called *guaria morada*.

Information

Because of its relative remoteness the park is not heavily visited, but several nearby lodges have recently opened just outside the park and tourism is increasing. These lodges are reached by a better road from the Interamericana. Rincón de la Vieja is the most accessible of the volcanoes in the Cordillera de Guanacaste.

Admission to the park is US$1.50 per day and camping is US$2.25 per person. The park is part of the Area de Conservación Guanacaste (ACG) which also includes the parks of Santa Rosa and Guanacaste as well as other protected areas. The ACG has its headquarters in Parque Nacional Santa Rosa (☎ 69 5598) where you can get information.

There is a park ranger station and there are trails past various volcanic features and on to the summit. The ranger station is at the Casona Santa María, a 19th century ranch house which was reputedly once owned by US president Lyndon Johnson.

Wildlife

The wildlife of the park is extremely varied. Almost 300 species of birds have been recorded here, including curassows, quetzals, bellbirds, parrots, toucans, hummingbirds, owls, woodpeckers, tanagers, motmots, doves and eagles – to name just a few.

Insects range from beautiful butterflies to annoying ticks. Be especially prepared for ticks in grassy areas such as the meadow in front of the ranger station – long trousers tucked into boots and long-sleeve shirts are some protection.

A particularly interesting insect is a high-land cicada which burrows into the ground and croaks like a frog, to the bewilderment of naturalists.

Mammals are equally varied: deer, armadillos, peccaries, skunks, squirrels, coatimundis and three species of monkeys are frequently seen. Tracks of Baird's tapir are often found around the lagoons near the summit, and you may be lucky enough to catch a glimpse of this large but elusive mammal as it crashes away like a tank through the undergrowth.

Several of the wild cat species have been recorded here, including the jaguar, puma, ocelot and margay, but you'll need a large amount of patience and good fortune to observe one of these.

Trails

There is a short nature trail through the forests around the Santa María ranger station. From the station, a trail leads three km west to sulphurous hot springs with supposed therapeutic properties. You shouldn't soak in them for more than about half an hour (some people suggest much less) without taking a dip in one of the nearby cold springs to cool off.

A further three km of hiking takes you to the boiling mud pools (Las Pailas) where you can carefully scoop out mud to make a rejuvenating (?) face pack. Be careful where you step, however, because the edges of the mudpots are sometimes weak and you could fall through and scald yourself. The Las Espuelas ranger station is near the mud pools – it's not always open but you could sleep on the porch if there are no SPN personnel to open up for you.

From the mud pools, a trail leads north. A fork to the left after about two km leads to Las Hornillas ('the kitchen stoves') which are sulphurous fumaroles about four km from the mud pools. There are waterfalls nearby. Continuing north (instead of taking the left to the fumaroles) takes you to the summit area about eight km beyond the mud pools. Below the summit is the Laguna de Jilgueros which is reportedly where you may see tapirs – or more likely their footprints if you are observant. (Note that all distances are approximate, as told to me by a park ranger. Other reports give varying distances – allow yourself plenty of time. Guides can be hired in the nearby lodges.)

Places to Stay

In the Park At the Santa María ranger station you can camp (US$2.25 per person), or a basic and inexpensive room and board can be arranged. The bunk beds are in poor shape – bring a sleeping bag.

Camping is allowed in most places within the park but you should be self-sufficient and prepared for cold and foggy weather in the highlands – a compass would be very useful. Beware of ticks in the grassy areas. The wet season is very wet, and there are plenty of mosquitoes then: dry-season camping is much better. From February to April are the best months.

Outside the Park There are two lodges near the south-west corner of the park – both are reached by the Curubundé road described in the Getting There & Away entry.

The first lodge reached is the *Hacienda Lodge Guachipelín* (☎ 41 6994, 41 6545, 41 4318, fax 42 1910; Apartado 636, Alajuela). The lodge is on the site of a 19th century ranch, parts of which are incorporated into the current building. There are plans to turn this into a museum. The hacienda has some 1200 hectares; part of this is primary forest, part is being reforested, and the rest is a working cattle ranch. Accommodation is in simple, screened rooms with electricity from 6 to 10 pm, but expansion is planned: 10 comfortable duplex cabins are to be built on a nearby ridge with volcano views. They have a simple bunkhouse (water during certain hours only) where you can stay for US$7 per person. Inside the ranch house is a dormitory with beds for US$14 per person and private rooms for US$37 a double. Showers are cold. Buffet-style meals are served for US$7 (breakfast or lunch) and US$10 (dinner).

Horses are available for US$14 a half day or US$20 a full day, and guides can also be hired to take you up into the national park. Guides charge from US$7 to US$14 per person, depending on group size, language spoken and type of tour. Mountain bike rental is planned. The lodge is still a working cattle ranch and, if you are interested, you can take advantage of this and accompany the cowboys on their chores. The lodge can provide transportation from Liberia for about US$20 round-trip per person (larger groups get discounts). The friendly English-speaking staff try to help visitors.

About five km further brings you to the *Rincón de la Vieja Mountain Lodge* (☎ 66 2369, 33 7970; fax 66 0473; Apartado 114-5000, Liberia, Guanacaste). This lodge is the closest to the park and is therefore more popular and crowded than the Hacienda Guachipelín. They are about two km from the mud pools and five km from the fumaroles described earlier. Rooms are clean and have wooden walls (which make them rather dark), and there are cold showers only. There is 24 hour electricity and the rooms are screened – insects are abundant in the wettest months and the screens help.

They have dormitory style rooms with eight bunk beds sharing a bathroom for about US$20 per person. Double rooms with private bath are US$50 and quadruple rooms (one double bed and two bunks) with private bath are about US$90. They are planning a tent camp about three km from the lodge, near the sulphurous pools to the east, where a bed will be US$17 per person and there will be shower and dining tents. Meals at the lodge are available for US$9 (breakfast) or US$12 (lunch or dinner). IYHF members can book in the Toruma Hostel in San José and receive discounts. Guides, horses and transportation from Liberia are all available – call for rates. They also have multi-day packages with tours, food and accommodation – again, call for details.

These are both relatively recent tourism developments and you can expect changes during the life of this book. Neither of these places are first class, though both are comfortable.

On a different road is the *Buenavista*

Lodge (☎/fax 69 5147; Apartado 373, Liberia, Guanacaste). This lodge is on a 1500 hectare farm and offers horseback and hiking tours into Rincón de la Vieja, bird-watching and private mud and steam pools. They have dormitory style rooms for US$15 per person and private rooms for US$50 a double.

Getting There & Away

The park is 25 km north-east of Liberia by a poor road that often requires 4WD in the rainy season but is passable in ordinary cars in the dry. To get to the Santa María ranger station, drive, walk or take a taxi (US$30 to US$40) on the road that heads north-east out of Liberia through the Barrio La Victoria suburb. After about 18 km the road passes the village of San Jorge and then continues as far as Santa María, where you can spend the night for US$2.25 if you make arrangements with the SPN in advance. There are a couple of old beds, or you can sleep on the wooden floor – bring your own sleeping bag. Mosquito nets or insect repellent are needed in the wet season. Meals can also be arranged for about US$3 each, and horses can be hired. Sometimes a ride from Liberia can be arranged when a parks service vehicle is in town.

The Parque Nacional Santa Rosa (☎ 69 5598) maintains daily radio contact with Rincón de la Vieja, or you can call the SPN radio communications office in San José (☎ 33 4160). If you want, you can simply walk the 25 km along the road – there's not much traffic and no problem if your body is up to it.

From the Santa María ranger station you can walk to the Rincón de la Vieja Mountain Lodge in about eight km, but most Mountain Lodge visitors take the following alternative route from Liberia, which also goes to the Hacienda Guachipelín.

Almost five km north of Liberia on the Interamericana there is a signed turn-off to the east onto a gravel road to the village of Curubandé, just over 10 km from the Interamericana. (Frequent public buses from Liberia to Colorado or Cañas Dulces can drop you at this turn-off, if you want to walk up. Reportedly, there are three buses a week from Liberia to Curubandé at 2.30 pm on Monday, Wednesday and Friday.)

Beyond Curubandé, the road deteriorates but is passable to ordinary cars (at least during the dry months). Blue arrows point the way to the Hacienda Lodge Guachipelín. After three km you pass through the signed entrance to the hacienda – here, there is a guarded gate (open during daylight hours) and a US$2.50 vehicle fee. This is reimbursed if you stay at the Hacienda Lodge Guachipelín, but if you continue to the Rincón de la Vieja Mountain Lodge there is no refund. (Guests going to the Mountain Lodge pass through the hacienda property; this system gives the hacienda owners their cut for allowing access to the Mountain Lodge.) The Hacienda Lodge Guachipelín is three km beyond the gate and the Mountain Lodge is five km further still.

The Buenavista Lodge is reached from the Interamericana by driving almost 12 km north from Liberia and turning right on the signed road. It is four km to Cañas Dulces (there are buses thus far from Liberia) and a further 13 km to the Buenavista Lodge.

PARQUE NACIONAL SANTA ROSA

This national park is one of the oldest (established 1971) and biggest (49,515 hectares) in Costa Rica and has one of the best developed (though still simple) camping facilities of the nation's parks.

Santa Rosa covers most of the Península Santa Elena which juts out into the Pacific at the far north-western corner of the country. The park is named after the Hacienda Santa Rosa where a historic battle was fought on 20 March 1856 between a hastily assembled amateur army of Costa Ricans and the invading forces of the North American filibuster, William Walker. In fact, it was historical and patriotic reasons which brought about the establishment of this national park in the first place. It was almost a coincidence that the park has also become extremely important to biologists.

Santa Rosa protects the largest remaining stand of tropical dry forest in Central

America, and it also protects some of the most important nesting sites of several species of sea turtles, including endangered ones. Wildlife is often seen, especially during the dry season when animals congregate around the remaining water and the trees lose their leaves. So for historians and biologists, campers and hikers, beach and wilderness lovers, this park is a great attraction.

One of the most innovative features of Parque Nacional Santa Rosa is that local people have been involved in preserving and expanding the park. Through a campaign of both education and employment, locals have learnt of the importance of conservation and have been able to put it to their own use by working as research assistants, park rangers or other staff, and also by using conservation techniques to improve their own land use on the surrounding farms and ranches. This attitude of cultural involvement has made the relationship between the national park authorities and the local people one that everybody is benefiting from. It stands as a model for the future integration of preservation and local people's interests in other parts of Costa Rica and in other countries.

The best season is the dry season, when there are fewer biting insects, the roads are more passable, and the animals tend to congregate around waterholes, making them easier to see. But this is also the 'busy' season when, particularly at weekends, the park is popular with Costa Ricans wanting to see some of their history. It is less busy midweek, but it's always fairly quiet compared to parks like Poás or Manuel Antonio. In the wet months you can observe the sea turtles nesting and often have the rest of the park virtually to yourself. The best months for sea turtles are September and October, though you are likely to see some in August, November and December as well. A recent increase in large tour groups wanting to see the turtles nesting has prompted a closure of Playa Nancite (the best-known turtle-nesting beach) to large groups, though individuals and small groups can reportedly obtain a permit to see the nesting. Visitation during turtle season is limited to 25 people per night, and you should make a reservation with the park headquarters.

Orientation

The entrance to Parque Nacional Santa Rosa is on the west side of the Interamericana, 35 km north of Liberia and 45 km south of the Nicaraguan border. From the entrance, a seven km paved road leads to the main centre of the park. Here there are administrative offices, scientist's quarters, an information centre, campground, museum and nature trail.

From this complex, a 4WD trail leads down to the coast, 12 km away. Recently, this trail was reported impassable and closed to all vehicles. Horses and walkers can use the road. About a third of the way down this trail there are two lookout points with views of the ocean. There are several beaches, with camping areas on two of them, though you need permits from the park rangers to do this and this may be prohibited during turtle nesting months. There are also other jeep, foot and horse trails which leave the main visitor complex and head out into the tropical dry forest and other habitats.

The Sector Murciélago of the park is a more recent addition which encompasses the wild northern coastline of the Península Santa Elena. There is a ranger station and camping area here. The story is that this area was once owned by Nicaraguan dictator Anastasio Somoza – after he was deposed the area became part of the national park. You can't get there from the main body of the park (except perhaps by bushwhacking). To reach the Sector Murciélago you need to return to the Interamericana and travel further north, as described in the Getting There & Away entry.

At the south-east corner of the Sector Santa Elena is the Estación Experimental Horizontes which used to be a working cattle ranch and farm, but which is now used for agricultural research projects. The area has no visitor facilities. It is best reached by a 20 km road north from the village of Guardia,

18 km east of Liberia on the Liberia-Playas de Coco highway.

The Interamericana forms the eastern border of Santa Rosa and also the western border of the new Parque Nacional Guanacaste – the two parks are contiguous.

Information

The park entrance station (just off the Interamericana) is open from 7 am to 5 pm daily. At the entrance booth you pay the US$1.50 park admission and, if you plan on camping, an extra US$2.25 per person. Maps of the park are sometimes available for sale.

It is another seven km to the park headquarters (☎ 69 5598) and campground. There are no buses so you must walk or hitch if you don't have a car. Horses are usually available for hire at the park headquarters (not expensive) and rangers may allow travellers to accompany them on their rounds of the park. Note that the park headquarters also administers the Area de Conservación Guanacaste and has information about (and maintains radio contact with) Parque Nacional Rincón de la Vieja, Parque Nacional Guanacaste and other protected areas.

La Casona

The historic La Casona (the main building of the old Hacienda Santa Rosa) houses a visitor centre and small museum. The battle of 1856 was fought around this building and the military action is described in documents, paintings, maps and diagrams. Other battles were fought in this area in 1919 and 1955. Apart from antique firearms and other weapons, the visitor can see how a typical country kitchen would have been set up in a hacienda over 100 years ago, as well as a collection of period antique furniture and tools. A display interpreting the ecological significance and wildlife of the park is also here. Some of the old rooms of La Casona are favourite bat roosts – don't be surprised if you disturb several dozen bats upon entering one of the side rooms. (And don't worry – the bats are completely harmless.)

Wildlife

Outside La Casona is a fine example of the national tree of Costa Rica, the guanacaste (Enterolobium cyclocarpum). The province is named after this very large tree species, which is found along the Pacific coastal lowlands. Nearby is a short nature trail with signs interpreting the ecological relationships between the plants, animals and weather patterns of Santa Rosa. The trail is named El Sendero Indio Desnudo after the common tree whose peeling orange-red bark can photosynthesise during the dry season when the tree's leaves are lost. The reddish bark is supposed to represent a naked Indian, though local guides suggest that 'sunburnt tourist' might be a better name. The tree is also called the gumbo limbo. Although the Indio Desnudo nature trail is a short one (a little over one km round trip) you will certainly see a variety of plants and birds and probably, if you move slowly and keep your eyes and ears open, monkeys, snakes, iguanas and other animals. Markers along the trail explain what you see – also look out for (probably pre-Columbian) petroglyphs etched into some of the rocks on the trail.

The wildlife is certainly both varied and prolific. About 260 species of birds have been recorded. A highly visible bird which is common in Santa Rosa and frequently seen and heard around the campground is the white-throated magpie jay. This raucous jay is 46 cm long and is unmistakeable with its long crest of manically curled feathers and its white under parts separated from the blue upper parts by a narrow black breast-band. The forests contain parrots and parakeets, trogons and tanagers, and as you head down to the coast you will be rewarded by sightings of a variety of coastal birds.

At dusk the flying animals you see probably won't be birds. Bats (murciélagos) are very common: about 50 or 60 different species have been identified in Santa Rosa. Other mammals you have a reasonable chance of seeing include deer, coatimundis, peccaries, armadillos, coyotes, raccoons, three kinds of monkeys and a variety of other species. There are many thousands of insect species, including about 4000 moths and butterflies. There are many reptiles – lizards, iguanas, snakes, crocodiles and four species of sea turtles.

The olive ridley sea turtle is the most numerous, and during the August to December nesting season, tens of thousands of turtles make their nests on Santa Rosa's beaches. The most popular beach is Playa Nancite where, during September and October especially, it is possible to see as many as 8000 of these 40 kg turtles on the beach at the same time! Nancite beach is strictly protected and restricted, but permission might be obtained from the SPN to see this spectacle.

After nesting has been completed, the olive ridleys range all over the tropical eastern Pacific, from the waters of Mexico to Peru. For more information, see *The Sea Turtles of Santa Rosa National Park* by Stephen E Cornelius (National Parks Foundation, Costa Rica, 1986). This beautifully illustrated 80 page paperback is written in English and is available in Costa Rica. Recently, it was out of print, but may be reprinted again or available in reference collections.

The variety of wildlife reflects the variety of different habitats protected within the boundaries of the park. Apart from being the largest remaining stand of tropical dry forest in Central America, habitats include savannah woodland, oak forest, deciduous forest, evergreen forest, riparian forest, mangrove swamps and coastal woodlands.

Surfing

Playa Naranjo, the next major beach south of Playa Nancite, is near the southern end of the national park's coastline. The surfing here is reportedly good, especially near the Witch Rock area. A group of surfers wrote to me about camping and surfing here for several days in 1993. They had a great time but had to pack everything – surfboards, tents, food and drinking water, though there was brackish water available for washing off after a day in the waves. The hike in takes several hours.

Research

Santa Rosa is a mecca for scientists, particularly tropical ecologists. Near the park headquarters there is simple accommodation for researchers and students, many of whom spend a great deal of time both studying the ecology of the area and devising better means to protect the remaining tropical forests of Costa Rica.

Tropical ecologist Dr Daniel H Janzen has spent much of his research time in Santa Rosa, and has been a prime mover in the conservation of not just this national park, but also in the creation of the conservation area or 'megaparks' system which will make protection of all the national parks more effective. He has been very vocal about how the needs of local people must be addressed in order for conservation to become truly effective on a long-term basis. Most recently, Janzen has been involved in the INBio project to catalogue as many species as possible and to screen them for potential pharmaceutical value.

Janzen has also done much solid research on the tropics and is noted for a plethora of scientific papers. The titles of these range from the whimsical ('How to be a fig' in *Annual Review of Ecology & Systematics* vol 10, 1979) to the matter-of-fact ('Why fruits rot, seeds mold, and meat spoils' in *American Naturalist* vol 111, 1977) to the downright bewildering ('Allelopathy by myrmecophytes: the ant *Azteca* as an allelopathic agent of *Cecropia*' in *Ecology* vol 50, 1969). But perhaps Janzen's strangest claim to fame, among students of ecology at least, is his experiment on tropical seeds where he studied how seed germination was effected by the seeds being eaten and passed through the digestive systems of a variety of animals. Facing a lack of suitable animal volunteers, Janzen systematically ate the seeds himself, then recovered the seeds and tried to germinate them. Tropical ecology can be a messy business!

Places to Stay & Eat

There is a campground at the park headquarters. Facilities are not fancy but do include drinking water, picnic benches, flushing toilets and cold-water showers. Large fig trees provide shade. The campsites on the coast (when open) also have drinking water and latrines, but no showers. If you make arrangements with the ranger station (☎ 69 5598) in advance, you can eat meals at the park headquarters for about US$11 per day. Otherwise, bring your own food – there is none for sale in the park. Camping fees are US$2.25 per person.

Getting There & Away

To get to the main park entrance by public transport, take any bus between Liberia and the Nicaraguan border and ask the driver to set you down at the park entrance. The ranger on duty has a timetable of passing buses for when you are ready to leave. There are about seven buses a day heading to the border or to Liberia and San José. If you are driving, watch for the km posts on the side of the road – the park entrance is about 300 metres south of Km 270.

To get to the northern Sector Murciélago of the park, go 10 km further north along the Interamericana, then turn left to the village of Cuajiniquil, eight km away by paved road. There are passport controls both at the turn-off and in Cuajiniquil itself, so don't have your passport buried. Buses go here once or twice a day from La Cruz, but it's probably easier to hitch or walk the eight km if you don't have a car. At Cuajiniquil there is a basic soda/pulpería but no accommodation. (The paved road continues beyond Cuajiniquil and dead-ends at a marine port, four km away – this isn't the way to the Murciélago sector, but goes towards Area Recreativa Bahía Junquillal.) Park rangers told me it was about eight km beyond Cuaijiniquil to the Murciélago ranger station by poor road – 4WD is advised in the wet season, though you might make it in a high-clearance ordinary vehicle if you drive carefully. At the Murciélago ranger station you can camp and, if you advise the SPN or Santa Rosa headquarters in advance, eat meals. The dirt road continues beyond the ranger station for about 10 or 12 more km,

reaching the remote bays and beaches of Bahía Santa Elena and Bahía Playa Blanca. This road may be impassable in the wet season.

AREA RECREATIVA BAHÍA JUNQUILLAL

This 505 hectare recreation area is part of the Area de Conservación Guanacaste, administered from the park headquarters at Santa Rosa. The quiet bay and protected beach provide gentle swimming, boating and snorkelling opportunities and there is some tropical dry forest and mangrove swamps. Short trails take the visitor to a lookout for marine birding and to the mangroves. Pelicans and frigatebirds are seen, and turtles nest here in the appropriate seasons. Volcán Orosí can be seen off in the distance.

Information

There is a ranger station which is in radio contact with Santa Rosa (☎ 69 5598). Entrance to the recreation area is US$1.50 and camping is allowed for US$2.25 per person. During the dry season especially, water is at a premium and is turned on for only one hour a day (5 to 6 pm when I was there). There are pit latrines, and the area is very quiet.

Getting There & Away

From Cuajiniquil (see under Santa Rosa) continue for two km along the paved road and then turn right onto a signed dirt road (the sign may say Playa Cuajiniquil, but it's the correct turn). Four km along the dirt road (passable to ordinary cars) brings you to the entrance to Bahía Junquillal. From here, a poorer 700 metre dirt road leads to the beach, ranger station and camping area.

PARQUE NACIONAL GUANACASTE

This newest part of the ACG was created on 25 July 1989, Guanacaste Day. The park is adjacent to Parque Nacional Santa Rosa, being separated from that park by the Interamericana, and is only about five km north-west of Parque Nacional Rincón de la Vieja.

The approximately 36,000 hectares of Parque Nacional Guanacaste is much more than a continuation of the dry tropical forest and other lowland habitats found in Santa Rosa. In its lower western reaches it is an extension of Santa Rosa's habitats, but the terrain soon begins to climb towards two volcanoes, Volcán Orosí (1487 metres) and Volcán Cacao (1659 metres). Thus it enables animals to range from the coast to the highlands, just as many of them have always done.

Scientists have come to realise that many animal species need a variety of different habitats at different times of year, or at different stages of their life cycles, and if habitats are preserved singly the animals within may not survive well. If a series of adjoining habitats is preserved, however, the survival of many species can be improved. This is one of the main reasons for the formation of the 'megaparks' such as the ACG.

Not all the preserved areas are natural forest. Indeed, large portions of the ACG are ranchlands. But researchers have found that if the pasture is carefully managed (and much of this management involves just letting nature take its course) the natural forest will reinstate itself in its old territory. Thus crucial habitats are not just preserved, but in some cases they are also able to expand.

Research Stations

Research is an important aspect of Guanacaste and there are no less than three biological stations within the borders. They are all in good areas for wildlife observation or hiking.

Maritza Biological Station This is the newest station and has a modern laboratory. To get there, turn east off the Interamericana opposite the turn-off for Cuajiniquil (see Parque Nacional Santa Rosa). The station is about 17 km east of the highway along a dirt road that may require a 4WD vehicle, especially in the wet season. The main problem with driving the road is entering it from the Interamericana – there is a very steep kerb –

but once you've negotiated that, the going gets better.

From the station at 600 metres above sea level there are trails to the summits of Volcán Orosí and Volcán Cacao (about five to six hours). There is also a trail to a site where Indian petroglyphs have been found, about an hour away.

Cacao Biological Station This station is high on the slopes of Volcán Cacao at an elevation of about 1060 metres above sea level. The station is reached from the south side of the park. At Potrerillos, about nine km south of the Santa Rosa park entrance on the Interamericana, head east for about seven km on a paved road to the small community of Quebrada Grande (marked as Garcia Flamenco on many maps). A daily bus leaves Liberia at 3 pm for Quebrada Grande. From the village square, a 4WD road heads left (north) towards the station, about 10 km away. You can reach about half way in a vehicle, them either walk or, if you have called ahead, be met by horses to take you to the station. From the station there are trails to the summit of Volcán Cacao and to the Maritza Biological Station.

Pitilla Biological Station This station is a surprise – it lies on the north-east side of Volcán Orosí in forest more like that found in the Caribbean slope than on the Pacific, although the Pacific is only 30 km to the west whilst the Caribbean is 180 km to the east. The station is on the eastern side of the continental divide, so the rivers flow into the Caribbean and the climate and vegetation are influenced by the Caribbean.

To get to the station, turn east off the Interamericana about 12 km north of the Cuajiniquil turn-off, or three km before reaching the small town of La Cruz. Follow the paved eastbound road for about 28 km to the community of Santa Cecilia. From there, ask about the poor dirt road heading 10 or 12 km south to the station – you'll probably need 4WD. (Don't continue on the unpaved road heading further east – that goes over 50 km further to the small town of Upala.)

Places to Stay & Eat

In the Park Since the creation of the new national park, the biological research stations have become available for tourist accommodation. Maritza or Cacao are where you are most likely to be allowed to stay – Pitilla is the province of research biologists or students. The stations are all quite rustic, with dormitory-style accommodation for 30 to 40 people and shared cold-water bathrooms. A bed and three meals costs about US$20 a day. Permission to camp near the stations can also be obtained; the fee is about US$2.25 per night. Horses are often available for hire. You should make arrangements to stay in the stations with the SPN in San José or (better) at the Santa Rosa headquarters. Park personnel in Santa Rosa may be able to arrange transport from the park headquarters to the biological stations for about US$10 to US$20, depending on where you go.

Outside the Park There are two lodges within a few km of the park boundaries, one on the south side and one on the north. Either of these can be used as a base to explore the national park.

The *Santa Clara Lodge* (☎ 26 4921, fax 66 0475; Apartado 17-5000, Quebrada Grande, Liberia, Guanacaste) is on the south side of the park. This is a small, rustic, friendly, family-run lodge in a working dairy farm on the banks of the Río Los Ahogados (the River of the Drowned) – I forgot to ask about the reason for this not-very-reassuring name. A cold-water mineral spring near the lodge is channelled into a dip pool – the locals claim the water is good for the skin. Rooms are clean but very small and simple. Electricity is available from 6 to 10 pm; otherwise, candles are provided. Showers are cold.

The four rooms inside the lodge share a bathroom. The rates during the high season are US$24/41/54 for a single/double/triple, which seems pricey for a shared cold shower! (Low-season rates are US$19/34/46 including breakfast.) A cabin with private cold bath is US$59 for up to three people.

Meals are US$5 for breakfast and US$6.25 for lunch and dinner. This is filling campesino-style cooking, and you can eat with the family if you want.

The lodge is about seven km due south of Parque Nacional Guanacaste and nine km west of Parque Nacional Rincón de la Vieja. Horseback tours are available around the ranch, to a local bauxite mine and, at weekends, to an ostrich farm (unique in Costa Rica as of this writing) which is on the western outskirts of the nearby village of Quebrada Grande. Tours cost from US$20 to US$40. They also advertise bird-watching, though they seem to be more into cattle, mining and ostrich raising than anything else. Ask them about visiting the national parks. The lodge is reached by heading four km south of Quebrada Grande on a dirt road (see under Cacao Biological Station for details about reaching Quebrada Grande).

The *Hacienda Los Inocentes* (☎ 66 9190); in Heredia (☎ 39 5484, fax 37 8282; Apartado 1370-3000, Heredia) is a working cattle ranch on the north side of Parque Nacional Guanacaste. This ranch appears to be more interested in wildlife and conservation than the Santa Clara Lodge. The hacienda building itself is a very attractive century-old wooden house converted into a comfortable, though not luxurious, country lodge owned and operated by the Viquez family, who have been here for generations. About a third of the 1000 hectare ranch is for cattle raising; the rest is mainly secondary forest with some primary forest suitable for bird and animal watching. During my most recent visit there were howler monkeys seen frequently on foot trails by the nearby Río Sábalo, as well as a variety of parrots in the forest and king vultures overhead. Guests can also watch the ranch workers and attend the daily 3 pm milking sessions.

Trips into Parque Nacional Guanacaste can be arranged, and Volcán Orosí, looming high on the horizon about seven km to the south, can be climbed. Naturally, horses are available (by this stage in the chapter, you probably realise that horses are an important way of getting around rural Costa Rica). The lodge building has about a dozen spacious wooden bedrooms upstairs – each room has its private bathroom with electric shower on the ground floor, so though you never have to share a bathroom, you do have to walk downstairs to reach it. The upper floor is surrounded by a beautiful shaded wooden verandah with hammocks and volcano views. Accommodation is US$29 per person and meals are US$6 for breakfast, US$12.50 for lunch or dinner – the food is good. You can wander around at will, but guided tours are extra. Horse rental is US$10 a half day.

Reach the hacienda by driving 15 km east of the Interamericana on the paved road to Santa Cecilia. It is just over half a km from the entrance gate to the lodge itself. Buses from San José to Santa Cecilia pass the lodge entrance about 7.30 pm and buses from Santa Cecilia returning to San José pass the lodge around 5.15 am. More frequent buses join La Cruz with Santa Cecila and can drop you at the hacienda entrance. Taxis from La Cruz charge about US$10 for the 20 km ride.

Getting There & Away

See the descriptions of the three biological research stations and two nearby lodges for details on how to get to the park. Also see under Parque Nacional Santa Rosa which adjoins the park.

REFUGIO NACIONAL DE FAUNA SILVESTRE ISLA BOLAÑOS

This 25 hectare island is a national wildlife refuge because brown pelicans, magnificent frigatebirds, American oystercatchers and other seabirds nest here. There are about 500 pelicans in a nesting colony on the north end of the island and some 1000 frigatebirds nesting on the southern cliffs. The island is about 80 metres high at its highest point. The refuge is part of the ACG administered in Parque Nacional Santa Rosa (see above for details).

The island is in Bahía Salinas on the Nicaragua-Costa Rica border. The nearest point on the mainland is Punta Zacate, 1.5 km away, but there is no road here. The nearest habitation is at Puerto Soley, about six km

south-west of La Cruz by road. From Puerto Soley you can hire a boat to take you the four km across the bay to the refuge.

There are no facilities on the island, and you should contact the Santa Rosa headquarters for permission if you need to land on the island. No permit is necessary for bird-watching from a boat.

LA CRUZ

This is the first/last settlement of any size before reaching the Nicaraguan border at Peñas Blancas, 20 km further north on the Interamericana. It's a small town, and everything is within two or three blocks of the Parque Central with its bright blue concrete benches. The town is on a small hill overlooking the Bahía Salinas in the distance – there is a good lookout point.

Places to Stay & Eat

The *Cabinas Maryfel* (☎ 66 9096) opposite the bus station is cheap and clean. The nearby *Pensión La Tica* is more basic. A couple of blocks before you reach the Parque Central are *Cabinas Santa Rita* (☎ 66 9062) which has clean rooms with private cold showers for US$14.50 a double – this place is the best choice, popular and often full, especially in the dry season. Another choice is the *Hotel El Faro* on the road between the gas station on the Interamericana and the town – cheap and basic but reasonably clean.

The *Restaurante Dariri*, a couple of blocks before the parque, is a small, friendly *tipico* place open from 7 am to 9 pm. Gallo pinto with egg is about US$1.25, a casado is US$2.25, and fruit salads, pizzas and seafood are also available. Just past the parque is the hole-in-the-wall *Soda Santa Marta* which serves cheap local breakfasts and meals. The *Restaurante Ehecatl* (locally called *el mirador* or 'the lookout point') is on the bluff overlooking Bahía Salinas – good views and decent lunches and dinners.

Getting There & Away

Bus Buses connect La Cruz with San José, Liberia and the Nicaraguan border. Buses come through on the way to San José five times a day, to Liberia five times a day and to the border nine times a day.

In La Cruz, the bus station is next to a pulpería (☎ 66 9108) which sells tickets and has bus schedules. Many of the southbound buses begin at the border and locals complain that it's sometimes difficult to get on by the time the bus comes through La Cruz. If this is the case, you could try back-tracking 20 km to the border and catch a bus there – though many of the buses to the border originate in Liberia or San José and may also be full as they come through La Cruz. Catch-22.

Local buses leave La Cruz for Santa Cecilia (passing Hacienda Los Inocentes) at 5 and 10.30 am and at 1.30, 7 and 7.30 pm – in Santa Cecilia there is a basic pensión and connections with buses on to Upala in the northern lowlands. Call the Santa Cecilia public telephone (☎ 66 9105) for further information. There are also local buses from La Cruz to Puerto Soley at 5 am and 1 pm and to Cuajiniquil at 12.30 pm.

Taxi A taxi to the border charges about US$6.

PUERTO SOLEY

A six km dirt road (normally passable to ordinary cars) leads down from the lookout point in La Cruz to the small fishing community of Puerto Soley on the coast. Here there is a very basic bar and restaurant where you can ask about renting a boat to visit the Isla Bolaños refuge. Expect to pay about US$20 per hour for a boat which will hold eight or 10 passengers.

One map shows an archaeological site named 'Las Pilas' in the area – I haven't been there but you could ask around if you're interested.

Places to Stay On Bahía Salinas, about 1.5 km past Puerto Soley, is the *Las Salinas Trailer Park y Cabinas* (in San José ☎ 33 6912, 28 2447, 28 0690; Apartado 449-1007, San José). They have cabins with private showers for about US$25, a restaurant, a camping and picnic area, beach access and clean public showers. Boats can be rented

here to visit Isla Bolaños and other places; horse rental is also available.

PEÑAS BLANCAS

This is the border with Nicaragua – it is a border post, not a town. There is nowhere to stay.

See the Getting There & Away chapter for full details of crossing the border here in either direction.

The Arenal Route

The route described here goes from San José in a north-westerly direction through Ciudad Quesada, Fortuna, Arenal and Tilarán, connecting with the Interamericana at Cañas. From Cañas you could head north towards Liberia and Nicaragua, or turn south along the Interamericana and thus make a loop trip back to San José. The recent increase in popularity of Fortuna as a base for visiting the active Volcán Arenal has led to a rise in tourism to the area and you will find adequate bus connections if you are not in too much of a hurry. Drivers can do the complete circuit on paved roads, with the exception of a 10 km stretch on the north shores of the Laguna de Arenal. It is also possible to connect with Monteverde, although the roads are not in such good shape, and with the northern lowlands of Costa Rica.

CIUDAD QUESADA

The name of this small city is often abbreviated to Quesada. To make things even more complicated, the locals know it as San Carlos and local buses often have San Carlos as the destination. Quesada lies at 650 metres above sea level on the north-western slopes of the Cordillera Central, overlooking the plains of Llanura San Carlos stretching off to Nicaragua. The population including outlying suburbs is about 30,000.

Roads north and east of the city take the traveller into the Northern Lowlands. Roads to the north-west lead to Fortuna and the spectacular Volcán Arenal, and over the mountains to the Interamericana.

Quesada is not an important tourist destination but does make a convenient place to spend the night if you like to travel slowly and see some of Costa Rica's smaller towns. Its importance is as a centre for the agriculture on the northern slopes of the Cordillera Central and in the Llanura San Carlos – the Feria del Ganado or cattle fair which is held every April is the biggest in the country. This is accompanied by a horse parade – if you're interested in horses, check out the saddlemakers in town. *Talabarterías* or saddle-shops are found near the town centre – they make and sell some of the most intricately crafted leather saddles in Costa Rica.

The focal point of Quesada is the large Parque Central with shade trees and benches. Almost everything of importance is either on this square or within a few blocks of it. Shoppers could check the cooperative crafts store on the north side.

Emergency medical attention is available from the Hospital de San Carlos (☎ 46 1176).

Places to Stay – bottom end

The cheapest place is the *Hotel Terminal* (☎ 46 2158) which is in the bus terminal, half a block from the plaza. This hotel is very basic and noisy and not particularly recommended.

Budget travellers should stroll along the first two blocks of Calle 2, north of the Parque Central. There is a street produce market along here and also several bottom-end hotels, including the following.

The *Hotel Cristal* (☎ 46 0541) has basic but OK rooms for US$3.30/6 a single/double or US$5/8.50 with private bath. Opposite is the similarly priced *Hotel Ugalde* (☎ 46 0260). On the next block, the *Hotel Axel Alberto* (☎ 46 1423) is the same price too and looks cleanest. The *Hotel Los Helechos* is nearby. None of these have hot water.

The *Hotel El Retiro* (☎ 46 0463, 46 1900) is on the Parque Central and charges about US$7/12 for singles/doubles. Rooms are basic but clean and have private baths with electric showers. There is a parking lot. The family-run *Hotel del Valle* (☎ 46 0718) is 200 metres north and 50 metres west off the Parque Central and charges US$7.25/12 for rooms with private electric showers.

Places to Stay – middle

The *Hotel La Central* (☎ 46 0301, 46 0766, fax 46 0391) is also on the Parque Central. Most rooms have private bath, some with hot water, for around US$12 per person. There is a restaurant.

The *Hotel Conquistador* (☎ 46 0546) is 500 metres south of the parque on Calle Central and is the most comfortable place close to the centre. Clean rooms with private hot showers are about US$10.50/18.50 for singles/doubles.

On the outskirts of town is the *Balneario San Carlos* (☎ 46 0747) which has cabins with private baths renting for about US$16 a double. There is a swimming pool and restaurant. Five km north of town, on the road to Fortuna, is the *Hotel La Mirada* (☎ 46 2222) which has good views of the Llanura San Carlos. Rooms with private hot baths are about US$25 a double, and there is a restaurant.

Places to Stay – top end

The *El Tucano Hotel & Country Club* (☎ 46 1822, fax 46 1692; Apartado 114-1017, San José) is eight km north-east of Quesada on the left hand side of the road leading to Aguas Zarcas – look for the large white gate. Facilities include a recommended restaurant, swimming pool and sauna, a casino, and various sports facilities ranging from tennis courts to miniature golf. Nearby thermal springs are tapped into three small hot pools where you can soak away your ills. The thermal waters are said to have medicinal and therapeutic properties. Horse, boat and vehicle excursions can be arranged to anywhere in the region. The whole complex is well-run and popular, and has expanded from about three dozen rooms to over 90 in the last few years.

Rooms are about US$63/76/89/100 for one to four people and there are a few more expensive suites. Day visitors using the pools and facilities are charged almost US$4. (Outside the hotel is a public park and recreation area named Aguas Termales de la Marina – popularly known as El Tucanito by the locals – through which flows the same hot river used in the hot springs. You can bathe directly in the hot springs for well under US$1.) Both the hotel and hot springs can be reached from Quesada by taxi or by a variety of buses to Puerto Viejo, Pital, Venecia, Río Frío etc.

Also worth mentioning is the top-end Tilajari Resort Hotel, 18 km north of Quesada in Muelle San Carlos – see the Northern Lowlands chapter for full details.

Places to Eat

Apart from the hotel restaurants, there are several places to eat within a couple of blocks of the main plaza. One of the better ones is the *Tonjibe* on the plaza itself, though several others look just as good.

Getting There & Away

Buses to Quesada leave San José from the Coca-Cola terminal about every hour during the day. The journey costs US$1.50 and is an attractive ride over the western flanks of the Cordillera Central, reaching 1850 metres at Laguna, just beyond Zarcero. Then begins the long and pretty descent to Quesada at 650 metres. The bus makes many stops and takes three hours unless you get a directo all the way to Quesada (two hours).

The bus terminal in Quesada is half a block from the Parque Central. Buses return to San José about every hour during the day. Buses to Fortuna take two hours and leave at 6, 9.30 and 10.30 am and at 1, 3.30 and 6 pm. Buses to Tilarán take about four or five hours and leave at 6.30 am and 3 pm.

Eastbound buses leave for Río Frío (via Venecia, Puerto Viejo de Sarapiquí and other intermediate communities) at 6 and 10 am, and at 3 pm. Buses for Puerto Viejo leave at 5 am and 5.30 pm and there are other buses for small local villages to the east. Buses north to Los Chiles leave nine times a day and north-west to San Rafael de Guatuso five

times a day. Ask at the bus terminal for other local destinations.

FORTUNA

Officially called La Fortuna de San Carlos, this small town (population about 5000) is the nearest to the spectacular Volcán Arenal. Fortuna is about 250 metres above sea level and has excellent views of the 1633 metre volcano only six km away to the west. The volcano has attracted many travellers and Fortuna's tourist industry has expanded greatly in recent years – there were about four hotels in 1990 but over a dozen in 1993. Various other attractions are found in the area – a lovely waterfall, hot springs, a lake and tours to caves and the nearby Caño Negro wildlife refuge (described in the Northern Lowlands chapter).

Information

There is a tourist information office on the main street on the south side of the church and soccer field, though it was closed when I stopped by. Most of the hotels will be more than happy to provide tourist information.

There is a bank which changes money, but faster service can often be obtained in some of the local hotels and restaurants for almost the same rates as in the bank. One traveller reports that the Restaurant El Jardín will accept US dollars and travellers' cheques.

Emergency medical attention is available from Clinica de la Fortuna (☎ 47 9142).

Local Tours

A number of tour operators have sprung up in the last few years. Many operate out of hotels. Prices and quality of tours can vary substantially, so shop around and try and talk to someone who has just been on a tour to see what's good. Two freelance guides who hang out in front of the El Jardín restaurant are Ronald Bermudez and Hugo Murillo – they speak English and have been recommended for their budget prices. Bermudez is also found at the Cabinas Via Fortuna. There are other decent guides.

The most popular tour is, of course, a visit to Volcán Arenal. You can go by day or night.

If the weather is clear, red hot lava rolling down the slopes and being ejected from the crater can be seen at night. Many tours include a soak in the Tabacón hot springs. (Both Arenal and Tabacón are described in detail further in this chapter.) Night tours leave at 7 pm every day and cost from US$6 to US$8 per person – shop around. Discounts are sometimes available if you buy the tour through the hotel you are staying at. Tours are also available to Fortuna falls by horseback (half day, US$15 per person), Caño Negro (US$25 and up for a full day), the caves at Venado, fishing on Laguna de Arenal, and other local places on request.

One interesting tour is a hike from Fortuna to Santa Elena and Monteverde – this costs about US$120 but can be split between a group of up to eight people. It takes a long day for the guided hike – you return the next day by bus to get your gear or, if you carry everything with you, you can stay on in Santa Elena for as long as you like.

La Catarata de La Fortuna

A visit to this long and narrow waterfall is one of the area's most popular excursions, after the obligatory visits to the Arenal volcano and lake. It is easy to visit the falls from town – you don't need a guide unless you want one.

From the south side of the church there is a signed road (the sign claims it is 5.5 km to the falls). After a few paved blocks, the road becomes dirt and makes several twists and turns but each one of these is marked (watch carefully for signs which are not always very obvious). It is a pleasant walk through agricultural countryside. (I drove there once in the dry season in a rented car, but recent reports indicate that you really need 4WD or, better still, walk or ride a horse.) Early risers will find good birding along this road.

At the overlook to the falls you must park on the road. (There was a small parking area there once – it may be replaced.) From here there's a good view of the long ribbon-like falls cascading down the far side of a very steep forested canyon. There's plenty of water, even in the dry season. An extremely

steep trail descends down to the base of the falls, but it might be too slippery and muddy in the wet season to be usable, even with hiking boots.

Places to Stay – bottom end

Fortuna is becoming popular not just with foreign travellers but also with ticos interested in seeing the famous exploding volcano. During weekends, especially in holiday periods, the cheaper hotels can be full, so try and arrive early or make a reservation if possible. Prices tend to be a little higher during holiday weekends and lower when the town isn't full. More hotels will probably be opening in the next couple of years.

The *Hotel Central* (☎ 47 9004, fax 47 9045; Apartado 003, La Fortuna, San Carlos, Costa Rica) is a popular budget travellers' choice. There is a tour desk here for the volcano and other places. Basic but clean small rooms are US$4.50 per person with shared bath – the two bathrooms have electric showers but only one warms the water. Nevertheless, I recommend this hotel because of the following experience.

When I arrived at 6 pm on a busy weekend the hotel was full except for one room which was reserved by someone who was coming in on the last bus at 7.30 pm. I asked the landlady to let me have the room if, after the bus came in, there was a 'no show'. She agreed. At 7.30, I was back at the hotel and waiting to see what would happen. By 8 pm it was clear that the person with the reservation had not arrived on the last bus (which stops within two blocks of the hotel) and so she agreed to release the room to me. Less than a minute later, another couple walked in looking for a room. The landlady told them that she was full.

I was impressed by the fact that she held the reservation until the last bus had discharged all its passengers; I was even more impressed by the fact that she gave me the room (even though I had not yet finished registering) when she could have given it to a couple and charged the higher double rate. The moral of this story for budget travellers is that if you make a reservation, this hotel (at least) will hold your reservation even when it's full – but if you do miss the last bus, make sure you call if you still want the room.

With the increase in tourism, a number of small, family-run places have cropped up

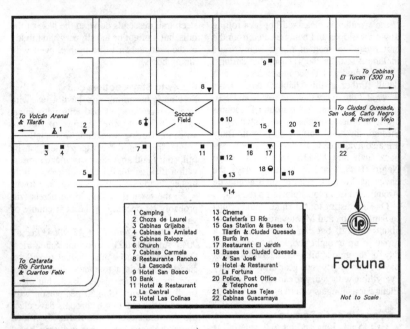

1 Camping
2 Choza de Laurel
3 Cabinas Grijalba
4 Cabinas La Amistad
5 Cabinas Rolopz
6 Church
7 Cabinas Carmela
8 Restaurante Rancho
   La Cascada
9 Hotel San Bosco
10 Bank
11 Hotel & Restaurant
   La Central
12 Hotel Las Colinas
13 Cinema
14 Cafetería El Río
15 Gas Station & Buses to
   Tilarán & Ciudad Quesada
16 Burío Inn
17 Restaurant El Jardín
18 Buses to Ciudad Quesada
   & San José
19 Hotel & Restaurant
   La Fortuna
20 Police, Post Office
   & Telephone
21 Cabinas Las Tejas
22 Cabinas Guacamaya

Fortuna

Not to Scale

recently, each with just a few simple rooms with private bath and electric showers. They charge about US$7 per person and include the following: the *Cabinas Grijalba* (☎ 47 9129), the *Cabinas Carmela* (☎ 47 9010; Apartado 265-4400, San Carlos) and *Cabinas La Amistad* (☎ 47 9035). These places will help arrange local tours and are a good way to help locals cash in on the tourism boom.

Cuartos Felix, about three km out of town towards the Catarata Río Fortuna, is another inexpensive place – quiet and friendly. Although I didn't check it out, you might try the *Cabinas El Tucan* east of town which opened in 1993.

The *Cabinas Las Tejas* (☎ 47 9077) charges about US$6 per person – shared electric showers. The rooms are clean and vary from doubles to dormitory style. They rent bicycles, have a liquor store, and provide local tour information. The *Cabinas Vía Fortuna* (☎ 47 9139), also called the Vía

Fortuna Guest House, is 500 metres east of town along the main road. They charge about US$5.50 per person, are clean, and have shared bathrooms. Reportedly, they'll allow you to camp and use their facilities.

The *Hotel La Fortuna* (☎ 47 9197) is expanding. They have a few rooms with shared cold showers for US$3 per person, but most of their rooms have private electric showers and cost US$15 a double or US$22 a triple. There is a restaurant and a tour desk. *Cabinas Rolopz* (☎ 47 8058) has clean rooms with private electric showers for US$14.50/17 for singles/doubles. The new *Cabinas Guacamaya* (☎ 47 9087) is about US$20 for a double.

Camping You can camp at the west end of town across the street from Cabinas Grijalba or ask around for another campsite on the outskirts near the town cemetery. Both places have cold showers and toilets available. Fees are about US$1.50 per person.

Places to Stay – middle

The pleasant *Burío Inn* (☎/fax 47 9076; in San José ☎ 28 0267, 28 6623; Apartado 1234-1250, Escazú, San José) advertises B&B for US$20 per person but when I was there recently they told me it was US$12 per person. It depends on the season and how full they are. IYHF members receive discounts – the Toruma in San José can make reservations for US$10 per person. The hotel is popular, especially with European visitors, and has small, clean rooms with private electric showers. They arrange tours to the volcano as well as fishing trips on the lake with well-known local guide, Peter Gorinsky

The *Hotel Las Colinas* (☎ 47 9107) is also clean and good. Their rooms are US$13/24 and the owners are friendly and helpful with arranging tours.

The *Hotel San Bosco* (☎ 47 9050, fax 47 9178) has fans and hot private showers in all the rooms. Older rooms are US$12/21/25 for singles/doubles/triples and newer, airier and more spacious rooms are US$25/35/42 – note that there are very few single rooms available. Tours are arranged here.

In the village of El Tanque de La Fortuna which is seven km east of Fortuna, is the *Hotel Rancho Corcovado* (☎/fax 47 9090; Apartado 25, El Tanque de La Fortuna, San Carlos) which has a swimming pool and restaurant, and arranges local tours and horse rental. Double rooms are US$46. They are planning on building some suites and a private airstrip for charter planes.

Places to Eat

The place where everyone seems to eat is the central and popular *Restaurant El Jardín*. If you're on a budget, you can get a casado for about US$2.50; other meals are somewhat pricier but good. Beers are just under US$1. This is the place to eat, drink and meet people. Quieter places include the attractive, thatch-roofed *Restaurante Rancho La Cascada* on the corner of the soccer field. This is popular with tour groups and the food is good, though slightly pricier than at the El Jardín. If economising, try the pasta napolitana for under US$3.

Budget travellers will find the usual local dishes at reasonable prices in the following places. The *Restaurant La Fortuna* (in the hotel of the same name) features a few vegetarian as well as meat dishes. The restaurant in the *Hotel Central* is also reasonable and popular. The *Cafetería El Río* serves good, inexpensive food in a simple setting. There are a few other cheap places.

At the west end of town, *Choza de Laurel* features a serve-yourself tico buffet – get there early for the best choices. Later on, the food dries out. Just under two km west of town on the road to the volcano is the recomended *La Vaca Muca* – an attractive tico-style country restaurant with good food. Meals are in the US$4 to US$8 range.

Getting There & Away

Bus Direct buses from San José to Fortuna leave the Coca-Cola terminal at 6.15. 8.40 and 11.30 am. Alternatively, take one of the frequent buses to Ciudad Quesada and connect there with an afternoon bus. There are also buses from Tilarán.

In Fortuna, there are two bus stops. The one in front of the gas station is for buses to Tilarán; the one across from the Hotel La Fortuna is for San José buses. Buses for Ciudad Quesada leave from both bus stops. Direct buses for San José (US$2.50, four hours) leave at 1.20 and 2.45 pm. Buses for Ciudad Quesada leave at 5, 6, 7 and 10 am. Reportedly, the 7 am bus is a slow local one and the 10 am bus connects in Ciudad Quesada with a San José bus.

In addition, there are buses *de paso* which come through Fortuna from somewhere else en route to Ciudad Quesada – these are at about 10 am and 3.30 pm. Buses for Tilarán leave at 8 am and 4 pm – these come from Ciudad Quesada, but there are usually seats available. There is a 5 am bus to San Ramón (where you can connect with buses to Puntarenas on the Pacific coast). There is a 6 pm bus for El Tanque de La Fortuna and on to Guatuso. For other northern destinations, go to Ciudad Quesada and change buses.

Car & Motorbike Drivers should know about the new route to San José which was opened in 1993. Most drivers come via Zarcero and Ciudad Quesada; the new road roughly parallels the old one about 10 km to the west. It begins in San Ramón (see the Central Valley & Highlands chapter) and heads north to La Tigra. It is paved between San Ramón and La Tigra and is a narrow winding road which, because it is so new, is still largely unsettled. It gives tantalising looks at rain and cloud forest and mountain views. Unfortunately, the road is so narrow and winding that there is almost nowhere to pull over to take a photograph or change a flat tyre. Drive defensively.

About one km south of La Tigra there is a small sign for 'Bosque Eterno de los Niños – 5 km'. This road peters out in the Children's Rainforest, from where you could try and hike into the Cordillera de Tilarán and Monteverde (though I haven't done this). In La Tigra you could stay at the cheap Cabañas Los Ríos. Shortly north of La Tigra, the paving stops. You can either take a rough road nine km east to Jabillo where you can pick up the paved Ciudad Quesada-Fortuna road (which is what I did in a car), or you could try continuing due north to Fortuna, about 15 km away – I have no idea if this section is passable to an ordinary car.

WEST OF FORTUNA

The following places can be visited by taking the bus to Tilarán, or driving or walking.

About six or seven km from Fortuna **Jungla & Senderos Los Lagos**. Trails and a dirt road climb steeply to two lakes in the foothills of the volcano, about three km away from the entrance. You may be able to drive up. Rowboats can be hired. Day use costs US$0.80, overnight use (camping) is US$1.50, bathrooms are available and there is reportedly good bird-watching as well as volcano watching.

Three km along the main road beyond the entrance of Los Lagos is the Restaurant Los Lagos, which is operated by the same people and serves good fish dinners. You could camp here too, and trails lead up to the lakes.

Two km further, or 12 km from Fortuna, you reach the **Balneario Tabacón** which is a bathing resort built around the Tabacón hot springs. This is a good spot from which to view Volcán Arenal, and many tours to the volcano include a visit and a soak in the natural hot pools. There is a tourist complex with a jacuzzi, water slide and a variety of cold and hot swimming and soaking pools – a bar and restaurant is attached. The area is open from 10 am to 10 pm daily and there is a US$10 admission fee. You don't have to pay admission if you just want to visit the bar and restaurant from where you can watch either the bathers bathing or Arenal exploding, depending on where you sit. The views are good, especially on a clear night when your dinner is enhanced with periodic volcanic fireworks to liven up what could be called a hot date. Meals here are good but not cheap – US$6 to US$12. The owners are friendly and will tell you of big plans to open cabins, etc – they've been telling everyone this for some years now, and there is still no sign of accommodation. Maybe next year...

Across the street is another facility with minimal development; you can bathe in the same thermal springs for US$2. Take your choice. Locals say there are places where you can bathe for free – ask around.

VOLCÁN ARENAL

The best night-time views of the volcano are to be had from the west side of the volcano looking east at the red lava flows. The degree of activity varies from week to week; sometimes it can be a spectacular display of flowing red hot lava and incandescent rocks flying through the air. At other times the volcano subsides to a gentle glow. It is possible to camp on the west side of the volcano, and there is a volcano observatory where you can stay overnight.

The volcano was dormant until 1968 when huge explosions triggered lava flows which killed several dozen people living in the area. Despite this massive eruption, the volcano retained its almost perfect conical shape and with its continuing activity Arenal is everyone's image of a typical volcano. Occasionally, the activity quietens down for a few weeks, but generally Arenal has been producing huge ash columns, massive explosions and glowing red lava flows almost daily since 1968. I visited the volcano first in 1981 and several times since then, most recently in 1993 – every time it was exploding several times a day.

Every once in a while, perhaps lulled into a sense of false security by a temporary pause in the activity, someone tries to climb up to the crater and peer within. This is very dangerous – climbers have been killed or maimed by explosions. The problem is not so much getting killed (that's a risk the foolhardy insist is their own decision) but rather risking the lives of Costa Rican rescuers. (I must admit that I was young and impetuous enough to climb the volcano in 1981 and came close to terminating my climbing career just below the summit. I strongly discourage anyone from attempting the climb.)

Some maps and books discuss the Area de Conservación Arenal, which includes the volcano, Monteverde and all the area in between – in other words, most of the Cordillera de Tilarán. This area is rugged and varied and the biodiversity is high. It contains roughly half of the species of land-dwelling vertebrates (birds, mammals, reptiles and amphibians) known from Costa Rica. So far, this entire area is not officially protected, but there are plans to incorporate parts of it into the national park system (the Monteverde area is already privately protected).

Arenal Volcano Observatory

This private observatory was established in 1987 on a macadamia nut farm on the south side of Volcán Arenal. Vulcanologists from all over the world have come to study the active volcano, and recently researchers from the Smithsonian Institution in Washington DC were here on an expedition. A seismograph operates around the clock.

There is a small lodge which can be used as a base to explore the nearby countryside. Trips can be made to see recent lava flows from the volcano or to climb Arenal's dormant partner, Volcán Chato, which is 1100 metres high and only three km southeast of Volcán Arenal. There is a lake in Chato's summit crater, and canoes and paddles are provided for those who can't resist the chance to take a boat out on a volcano.

Local guides (with limited English) are available from the lodge for US$5 per person to climb Volcán Chato or visit lava flows. (There are trails up Chato and a guide is not essential.) You can wander around the macadamia nut farm or through the primary forest which makes up about half of the 347 hectare site. Guided walks are US$5 per person and horse rental is US$5 per hour. There is good birding as well as good volcano views. Fishing trips are US$25 per hour per person (two-person minimum). Motorboats, fuel, tackle, lunch and fishing guide are provided. Full day Caño Negro tours are US$45 per person (four minimum).

The observatory, lodge and tour services are run by Costa Rica Sun Tours (☎ 55 2112, fax 55 3529; Apartado 1195-1250, Escazú) at Avenida 7, Calle 3 & 5, San José. The company is run by the English-speaking Aspinall family who have many years of experience in environmental tourism in Costa Rica and do a good job.

Because the lodge is small, reservations are essential. Most of the rooms have bunk beds sleeping up to six people; all rooms have private baths with hot water. There is a restaurant and a small vulcanology exhibit. You can call the lodge (☎ 69 5033) but reservations are best made with Costa Rica Sun Tours. Rates are US$46/57/69 for single/double/triple and meals are US$6/8.50/10 for breakfast/lunch/dinner. (Children get discounts: 10 to 14 year olds pay 75%, four to nine year olds pay 50%, unders fours are free.) You can also arrange tours which include transportation from San José, guides and combinations with Monteverde if desired – call Costa Rica Sun Tours for details.

Camping

You can camp for free on the west side of the

volcano. There are no facilities – you need to bring everything. The camping area is a few km before the Arenal Observatory Lodge – see the Getting There & Away entry for directions. This is also the area through which all the tours come, so if you want some privacy, head away from the main parking area. Note that there are some 'Peligro' signs: *peligro* means danger – all visitors and campers should stay below these signs. Developed camping with basic facilities is available at Jungla & Senderos Los Lagos (see the West of Fortuna entry).

Getting There & Away

Transport from San José to the Arenal Observatory Lodge is approximately US$120 one way, but the vehicle takes up to six passengers and the cost is split between the passengers. If you want to make your own way there, you normally need a 4WD vehicle as there are two rivers to ford, though you may get by in a regular car in the dry months. Otherwise, take a bus to Fortuna and hire a 4WD taxi to the lodge (about US$10). The hearty could take a Quesada (or Fortuna) to Tilarán bus and then walk to the entrance.

The entrance to the observatory is marked by a sign reading 'El Parqueo', about four km beyond Balneario Tabacón on the Fortuna to Tilarán road. Turn left off the main road and follow a dirt road for about three km to a fork where there is a large orange sign with Volcán Arenal information. The right fork goes down to Laguna de Arenal, about two km away; the hard left fork peters out in the lower slopes of Volcán Arenal (this is where the tours go and where you can camp – it's about two km to the very end of the road); and the road bending slightly to the left follows electrical pylons for about 3.5 km to the Río Agua Caliente. Here, on the left, there is a very simple shelter of logs and earth that looks like it would withstand a major explosion.

The observatory and the Volcán Arenal are separated by the Agua Caliente river valley which acts as a protection against lava flows. On the other side of the river there is a sign indicating 'Macadamia' to the left and

'Tilarán' to the right. (This is an alternative road to Tilarán, rarely used and passable only with 4WD and plenty of time and perseverance.) Follow signs for 'Macadamia' to the observatory, about three or four km further. A second stream, the Danta, is crossed on the way. The observatory entrance is through a gate just past the second river, up the hill and the first left.

ARENAL

This small village, sometimes called Nuevo Arenal, replaced the earlier Arenal which was flooded by the lake formed in 1973. It is the only town of any size between Fortuna and Tilarán, and also the only town on Laguna de Arenal.

Arenal village itself has little to offer beyond a fuel station, a couple of simple places to stay and a bus stop near the parque. Local tour guide Ramón Swartzentruber has an office opposite the bus stop – he speaks English. The Arenal botanical gardens, about seven km south-east of Arenal, are open from 9 am to 4 pm daily except in October when they are closed. Admission is US$3.50. They reportedly have many orchids in their collection and the gardens are apparently well laid out, with good lake views. For more information call ☎ 669 5266 ext 273.

Places to Stay

Opposite the bus stop is a small hotel and restaurant with the somewhat mystifying name of *La Cage des Tigres* (☎ 69 5266, ext 112). They have three rooms with private bath for US$15 a double and serve good fish dinners for around US$6. There are also reports of a *Hotel Restaurant Lajas* and *Cabinas Rodriguez* but I have no details.

Roughly 1.5 km east of Arenal is the *La Casona del Lago* (☎ 31 4266) which is affiliated with the Costa Rican youth hostel system, with headquarters at the Toruma Hostel (☎ 24 4085) in San José. There are four rooms each with bunk beds for four people. Reservations and information can be obtained at the Toruma, though I have received a report that a reservation was lost. Make sure all reservations are confirmed in writing. Overnight rates for IYHF members are US$15 including breakfast; non-members pay US$25. Lunches and dinners are US$5 and US$6. Local tours to either the Venado caves (see the Northern Lowlands chapter) or Volcán Arenal and Tabacón are US$65 for one to four people – get a group together.

Two km north-west of Arenal is *Chalet Nicholas* (☎/fax 69 5387; Apartado 72-5710, Tilarán, Guanacaste). This is a small but comfortable B&B place charging US$40 a double. Along the 28 km of road joining Arenal with Tilarán, a few other B&B places are beginning to advertise – keep your eyes open for signs and check them out if you wish.

A few km off the main road between Fortuna and Arenal is the *Arenal Lodge* (☎ 46 1881 for the lodge; for information (☎ 28 2588, fax 28 2798; Apartado 1139-1250, Escazú), an exclusive small country hotel with pleasant grounds and great views of the volcano. Horse riding and birding are possibilities, but the lodge's main function is to provide fishing excursions on Laguna de Arenal accompanied by expert fishing guides. Inside the hotel there is a library and billiards room to while away the evenings. The rates for comfortable rooms are US$55/69/80 for singles/doubles/triples; suites cost US$80/92/103. Fishing packages are about US$150 per day, everything included.

Two or three km west of Arenal is a sign for the *Ecoadventure Lodge Coter* (☎ 21 4209, fax 21 0794; Apartado 6398-1000, San José) which is operated by Tikal Tours of San José. A four km unpaved but OK road leads to the lodge, which is near Lago Coter. The emphasis is on natural history and adventure – amenities include telescopes for volcano watching, naturalist guides for bird-watching, bicycles, surfboards, canoes and horses. There are trails and board walks through the nearby cloud forest, and bird-watching is promising – the lodge brochure claims over 350 species of birds have been recorded in the area. A variety of nearby excursions are available. There is a fireplace and relaxation area – billiards, TV and a small library. Food is buffet-style and plentiful; bathrooms (with hot water) are shared. Rooms are clean, simple but comfortable. Most visitors come on complete packages that include tours and activities led by naturalist guides and all meals and lodging. Prices range from US$269 for two nights and three days to US$726 for seven nights and eight days per person (double occupancy). Contact the lodge about shorter stays or individual activities.

About 10 km west of Arenal is the small *Mirador Los Lagos* (☎ 69 5484). I haven't checked this one out, but it reportedly provides good lake views, comfortable cabins with private bath, tasty meals and all the local tours. Rates are about US$45 a double.

Getting There & Away

Bus Buses to Quesada via Fortuna leave at 8 am and 1.30 pm. There are several buses daily to Tilarán (many begin in Ciudad Quesada). There is also an afternoon bus for San Rafael de Guatuso – the bus is simply marked 'Guatuso' and goes to several other small villages in the northern lowlands.

Car & Motorbike It is about 39 km from Fortuna and 28 km from Tilarán. Most of the road is narrow and winding, and there is an unpaved section of about eight km on the east side which may cause delays in the wet season, although ordinary cars usually get through.

TILARÁN

This is a small, quiet market town 550 metres above sea level near the northern end of the Cordillera de Tilarán; Laguna de Arenal is the principal attraction, some five km to the north-east of the town. Cattle farming is important in the area and there is a rodeo and fiesta (Días Cívicas) during the last weekend in April. This is very popular and hotels are often full at that time. There is another fiesta on 13 June.

The pleasant climate, rural atmosphere, annual rodeo and proximity of Laguna de Arenal have brought about the development of a small tourist industry. Fishing, boating, windsurfing and horse riding can be arranged at several places in the area.

The local tourist information office publishes a leaflet proclaiming Tilarán as 'the city of broad streets, fertile rains, and healthful winds, in which friendship and progress is cultivated'. I have no quibbles with that.

Places to Stay – bottom end

The *Hotel Central* (☎ 69 5363) is near the south-east corner of the town church, 50 metres from the parque and 350 metres south of the principal entrance road into town. Basic but clean rooms are US$3.75 per person; cabins with private bath are US$10 single or double.

The friendly and recommended *Cabinas Mary* (☎ 69 5479) on the south side of the parque is good, clean and pleasant, and has a reasonably priced restaurant attached. Rooms with private bathroom and electric showers are US$6/11 single/double. Rooms with communal bath are US$4.50 per person.

Cabinas Lago Lindo is a block from the Parque Central and offers eight clean rooms for about US$6 per person – it is new and may expand.

The basic *Hotel Grecia*, on the west side of the plaza, charges about US$5 per person or US$11 for a room with private bath (single or double).

Places to Stay – middle

The best place in town (when I visited, at least) is *The Spot Hotel* (☎ 69 5711, fax 69 5579). The Spot is supposed to be a partial translation of Tilarán – 'spot of many waters' in the Guatuso language. I don't know any Guatuso speakers who could confirm that – maybe it's just a nice story. The hotel charges US$32/42. A restaurant is attached.

The friendly and recommended *Cabinas El Sueño* (☎ 69 5347) is less than a block away from either the Parque Central or the bus terminal. It looks very clean and has a restaurant. Rooms with private bath and warm water are US$15/25 single/double. One reader, however, complained that rooms

lacked fans and mosquitos prevented sleep – mosquitos are not often a problem and few hotels have fans in Tilarán. During the rainy season you might try asking at the desk for a fan if mosquitos are bothering you.

The *Cabinas Naralit* (☎ 69 5393) is behind The Spot. Pleasant rooms with private baths and hot water, some with TV, rent for about US$21/26 for singles/doubles. There is a restaurant and bar attached.

Places to Eat

The best place to eat in town, if you insist on nothing less, is the somewhat pricey *Catala* restaurant in The Spot Hotel. The restaurant under the *Cabinas Mary* is fairly inexpensive and well recommended. The *El Parque* restaurant under the Cabinas Sueño is midway between the other two in price and is OK.

Getting There & Away

Bus Autotransportes Tilarán buses from San José cost about US$2.50 and take four hours. They leave four times a day from Calle 14, Avenida 9 & 11. Buses from Puntarenas leave at 11.30 am and 4.30 pm. Buses from Ciudad Quesada via Fortuna leave at 6.30 am and 3 pm. There are seven buses a day from Cañas.

Buses from Tilarán leave from the bus terminal, half a block from the parque central as you head away from the cathedral. Buses to San José leave daily at 7 and 7.45 am and 2 and 4.50 pm, but the Sunday afternoon departure is usually sold out by Saturday. Buses between Tilarán and San José go via Cañas and the Interamericana, not via the Quesada-Fortuna-Arenal route. Buses to Arenal leave at 10 am and 4 pm.

Buses to Ciudad Quesada leave at 7 am and 12.30 pm; to Puntarenas at 6 am and 1 pm; and to Santa Elena (near Monteverde) at noon. Buses for Cañas (where the Interamericana is joined) leave five times a day. There is a daily noon bus for San Rafael de Guatuso. Buses for a variety of small local towns also leave from this terminal.

Car & Motorbike Tilarán is 24 km by paved road from the Interamericana at Cañas. The route to Santa Elena and Monteverde is unpaved and rough, though ordinary cars can get through with care.

LAGUNA DE ARENAL

This artificial body of water was formed by a dam built in 1973 at what is now the eastern end of the lake, flooding small towns such as Arenal and Tronador. Laguna de Arenal now supplies water for Guanacaste and hydro-electricity. The dam can be seen from the Fortuna-Tilarán road. There are also many good views over the lake from the road, and sometimes the volcano can be seen smoking quietly near the eastern shores. This is Costa Rica's largest lake. Winds are often strong and steady, especially at the western end during the dry season, and the lake is recommended for sailing and windsurfing. See the Tilarán entry for more windsurfing information.

Rainbow bass (locally called *guapote*) weighing up to four kg are reported by anglers, who consider this to be a premier fishing spot. Boats and guides can be hired for fishing expeditions – ask at any of the major hotels in the area.

Although Tilarán is becoming known as a windsurfing centre, the lake Laguna de Arenal is actually about five or six km away by a hilly road. The lake has a year-round water temperature of 18 to 21°C with one metre high swells and winds averaging 20 knots in the dry season, a little less in the wet. May and June then September and October are the least windy months, December to February are the most windy. Maximum winds often go over 30 knots and windless days are a rarity. These consistently high winds attract experienced windsurfers – complete beginners may have a hard time learning under these conditions.

Places to Stay

The *Cabinas Puerto San Luis* (☎ 69 5750, fax 69 5387) is on the shores of Laguna de Arenal. Rooms all have private electric shower, refrigerators and TV and rent for US$27/48 including breakfast. Seven windsurfing boards can be rented for US$25 per person and lessons can be arranged. The owner told me that the lake in front of the hotel is a little less windy than other areas and so is suitable for people with less experience. The hotel also has boats for rent and can take you on fishing or sightseeing trips.

The *Hotel Tilawa Viento Surf* (☎ 69 5050, fax 69 5766; Apartado 92, Tilarán, Guanacaste) is a full-service windsurfing resort which opened for the 1993 dry season. They have by far the best selection of sailboards to rent in the area. Call them for full details of their rental fleet – they have dozens of rigged and ready boards of different makes, sizes and types suitable for a variety of experience and performance levels.

The hotel also offers a swimming pool, tennis court, horse and mountain bike rental, day tours, a restaurant and bar. For dedicated windsurfers, they offer a package for about US$600 per person (based on double occupancy) which includes seven nights accommodation with continental breakfast, a complete week of windsurfing including fully rigged board, and use of the pool and tennis facilities. They'll pick you up in San José if you reserve a week's package. Call them about shorter visits. And what if the winds fail? They claim that it's windy on 360 plus days a year and guarantee that you'll get a shorty board (2.65 metres – 8½ feet – or smaller) up and planing or they'll refund your money. They recommend that you bring a shorty wet suit and helmet if you wish – they provide the rest.

Getting There & Away

Puerto San Luis can be reached from Tilarán on the Tronadora bus which leaves Tilarán at 11.30 am and 4 pm. (Tronadora is a village a couple of km beyond Puerto San Luis).

Local buses from Tilarán to Nuevo Arenal (10 am and 4 pm) and Tierras Morenas (11.30 am and 4 pm) pass by the Tilawa resort, which is about nine km from Tilarán. Taxis are available to both places.

The Northern Lowlands

The traveller heading north from San José, over the volcanic ridges of the Cordillera Central, soon arrives in the flat tropical lowlands stretching from just 40 km north of the capital to the Nicaraguan border and beyond. The northern halves of the provinces of Alajuela and Heredia both contain large tropical plains, called *llanuras*. It is the northern slopes of the central mountains and the two llanuras beyond which are described in this chapter.

The original vegetation of much of the northern lowlands is mixed tropical forest, becoming increasingly evergreen as one heads east to the Caribbean. The climate is generally wet and hot. The dry season is more pronounced in the western part of the northern lowlands, near the slopes of the Cordillera de Guanacaste, but as one moves east towards the Caribbean the dry season tends to be shorter and not entirely dry. Much of the original vegetation has been destroyed and replaced by pasture for raising cattle, which is the main industry of most of the northern lowlands.

In much of the more remote areas near the Nicaraguan border, especially in the Llanura de los Guatusos and the Llanura de San Carlos, the pastureland floods extensively during the wet season, creating vast swamps and lakes. One such area has been protected in the Refugio Nacional de Vida Silvestre Caño Negro – one of the more remote of Costa Rica's national refuges and parks. Other swamp areas have been changed to rice cultivation.

The northern lowlands generally have a very low population density, with no large towns, few small towns, rough roads, poor public transport and relatively little in the way of tourist facilities. A major exception to this is in the north-eastern lowlands around the small town of Puerto Viejo de Sarapiquí, which is well served by public buses. Here there are a number of hotels, and nearby there are several tourist lodges and a

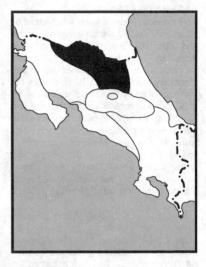

biological station. The Puerto Viejo area is the destination of most visitors wanting to see some of the northern lowlands.

The Caño Negro area has recently seen an increase in visitation. Visitors travelling between Puerto Viejo and the popular Volcán Arenal (see the North-Western Costa Rica chapter) are starting to discover this area, which now has several hotels, the wildlife refuge with excellent bird-watching, and a number of small towns which have not yet been much visited by gringos.

The Caño Negro Area

From Muelle San Carlos, two paved roads head out across the northern lowlands. These are the road north-west to San Rafael and Upala, and the road north to Los Chiles. The Caño Negro area is between these two roads.

Volcán Arenal (RR)

Left: Hiking, Reserva Biológica Bosque Nuboso Monteverde (RR)
Right: Donald Perry's Automated Web for Canopy Exploration (AWCE), Rara Avis (AB)
Bottom: Tractor transportation to Rara Avis (AB)

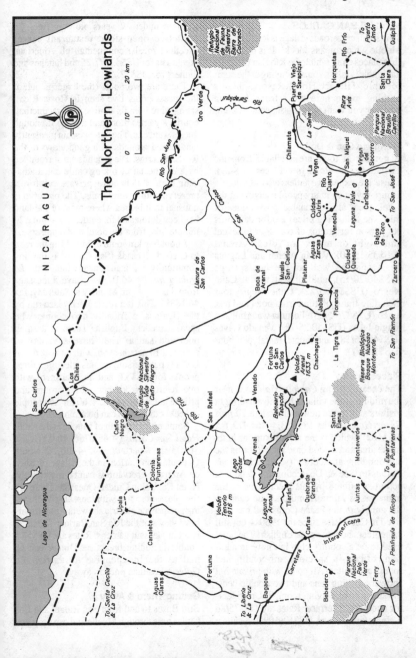

MUELLE SAN CARLOS

This small crossroads village is locally called Muelle which means 'dock'. It is one of the first places from which the Río San Carlos is navigable. Unless you are staying at the comfortable Tilajari Hotel Resort, there's nothing to do here apart from deciding whether you want to go north, south, east or west.

Things to See & Do

A number of tours are available from the Tilajari Resort Hotel (see Places to Stay). These are expensive unless you can join a group – with so many people staying at the hotel, there are reasonable possibilities of this. The following prices are for day tours per person for groups of two, four to seven, and eight or more: to Volcán Arenal (US$35/15/10), Volcán Arenal and Laguna de Arenal as well as the hot springs (US$40/20/15), guided boat trip at Caño Negro (US$57/35/22), Caño Negro tour including transportation from hotel and box lunch (US$87/45/25), Fortuna waterfall and jungle lakes (US$40/25/18), Venado Caves (US$40/25/18) and horse rental per hour (US$10/8/7).

Places to Stay

The cheap-looking *Cabinas Violetas* is near the middle of the village, but most overnight visitors stay at the new and modern *Tilajari Resort Hotel* (☎ /fax 46 1083, ☎ 46 0979, fax 46 1462), which is the most luxurious hotel in the area and a good base for exploring the surrounding attractions (see the previous Things to See & Do section for details of activities offered by this hotel). One of the managers is Jaime Hamilton, who came to the area with the Peace Corps and has now lived in Costa Rica since the 1960s – but still remembers how to speak English! The hotel used to be a country club but now, in addition, offers 48 spacious, air-conditioned rooms and suites. All come with private hot showers, ceiling fans and two double beds; the suites have a living room, TV, refrigerator and private terrace. Rates are US$75/86 a single/double and US$109 for the suites;

children under 12 years old stay free. An attractive open-sided restaurant serves excellent meals: continental/full American breakfasts for US$4.25/7.25 and lunches and dinners for US$12.

There are two pools (the larger is one of the nicest pools I've seen in Costa Rica), sauna, three tennis courts, two racquetball courts, a games room and a disco if enough guests want one. The hotel is set in pleasantly landscaped grounds with good views of the Río San Carlos. The grounds are surrounded by a 240 hectare working cattle ranch adjacent to a 400 hectare private rainforest preserve with several trails. The preserve is unusual in this area where most of the land has been deforested for cattle. It is about a 20 minute hike from the hotel to the preserve.

About five km south of Muelle on the road to Ciudad Quesada (San Carlos) is the tiny community of Platanar, near which is the *La Quinta Inn* (☎ 46 0731 – leave a message from 8 am to 4 pm, Monday to Saturday; fax 46 1631). This is a rustic B&B place run by the Ugaldes, a friendly tico couple who speak excellent English. There is a small pool and sauna. They have a variety of rooms; a 10 person cabin with bunk beds for US$11 per person; rooms sleeping three people for US$33; and an apartment with two bedrooms, kitchen, sitting room and private hot shower for US$60 for five people – weekly discounts can be arranged.

Some nine km north of Muelle is the small *Hotel San Carlos* (☎ 46 0766, 46 0301, fax 46 0391; Apartado 345-4400, Ciudada Quesada, San Carlos) in the village of Boca de Arenal. Reservations can be made at the Hotel Central in Ciudad Quesada. There are five pleasant rooms with fans, air-conditioning and private electric showers – two rooms have views of the Río San Carlos. The hotel is set in pleasant gardens. Rates are US$58 a double including breakfast. Dinner can be had at the inexpensive *Restaurant La Galería* less than one km away.

Getting There & Away

Bus Buses to and from San Rafael and Los Chiles pass through Muelle and can drop you off. (See the entries for those towns for details.)

Car & Motorbike Drivers will find paved roads north to Los Chiles (74 km), east to Aguas Zarcas (22 km) and Puerto Viejo (55 km), south to Ciudada Quesada (21 km) and on to San José (124 km), west to Fortuna (28 km) and Volcán Arenal, and north-west to San Rafael (58 km). This is certainly a cross-roads town.

SAN RAFAEL (DE GUATUSO) AREA

Although marked on most maps as San Rafael, this small community is locally known as Guatuso. About 6000 people inhabit the town and the surrounding district. San Rafael is on the Río Frío, 19 km north-east of the village of Arenal by poor dirt road or 40 km north-west of Fortuna (de San Carlos) by paved road. This latter road gives good views of Volcán Arenal to the south.

About 10 km before San Rafael, a dirt road heads south for about 10 km to Venado (which means 'deer') where there are basic cabinas and a public telephone (☎ 46 1954).

Things to See & Do

Four km south of Venado are caves which can be explored – an entry fee of about US$3 is charged, and you should be prepared with several sources of light and clothes which you don't mind getting wet and dirty. There are local guides in Venado or you can take a tour from any of the larger hotels in the Caño Negro and Fortuna area. There is an afternoon bus from Ciudad Quesada.

Just before reaching San Rafael the road passes through the Reserva Indígena Guatuso, although there is nothing that obviously demarcates the reserve.

Places to Stay & Eat

There are a few cheap and basic places to stay – the 'best' of them appears to be *Hotel Las Brisas* (☎ 46 2087). Other possibilities are the *Cabinas El Gordo* (☎ 46 2017), *Hotel La Macha* and *Hotel Almendras*.

There are a handful of inexpensive eateries; I had a good casado for less than US$2

at the *Restaurant El Turista* whilst I listened to the manager trying to sell me some real estate! Did I look like a tourist?

About 20 km west of San Rafael is the *Hotel de Montaña Magil* (☎ 33 5991, 21 2825, fax 33 6837). This small lodge (about a dozen rooms) is on the low eastern slopes of Volcán Tenorio and is hard to reach on a dirt road but the owner says that ordinary cars can make it even in the wet season. Alternately, ask the lodge to arrange transport for you – buses leave San José at 8.30 am on Wednesday and Saturday, returning late the following afternoon and arriving in San José about 10 pm. This alternative costs US$225 per person, including round trip transportation, guided tours en route to the hotel, all meals, a welcome cocktail and overnight accommodation – recommended.

Good rooms are about US$120 a double including meals, and there are tours and horse-riding (half day horseback tours cost US$15) available. Local attractions include the caves at Venado, Volcán Arenal, a crocodile farm, a private rainforest preserve and Caño Negro.

Getting There & Away

Buses leave about every two hours for either Tilarán or Ciudad Quesada (some continue to San José). Cuidad Quesada is the most frequent destination.

A good unpaved road leads 40 km north-west to Upala – this is normally driveable with an ordinary car all year round.

From San Rafael you can hire a boat in the wet season to take you up the Río Frío to the Refugio Nacional de Vida Silvestre Caño Negro.

UPALA

This small town is nine km south of the Nicaraguan border, in the far north-eastern corner of the northern lowlands. About 10,000 people live in Upala and the surrounding district. Dirt roads lead up to and across the border, but these are not official entry points into either Costa Rica or Nicaragua. There is a passport check by the bridge at the south end of town (coming from

San Rafael) and another near Canalete (coming from the Interamericana).

Upala is the centre for the cattle and rice industries of the area. A few remaining Guatuso Indians live in the region. It has become increasingly important in recent years – a paved secondary road from the Carretera Interamericana was opened in the 1980s and so there are good bus connections with San José. Few travellers go to Upala, however, and those that do are mostly heading to or from Caño Negro. The trip to Upala and its surroundings is an interesting off-the-beaten-track experience.

Places to Stay & Eat

Although few travellers come through, Upala is visited by relatively large numbers of ticos, especially businesspeople midweek, when the hotels may well be full. Call ahead and get there early in the week for the best choice of rooms.

A popular place is the *Cabinas & Restaurante Buenavista* (☎ 47 0063). The pleasant, open-sided restaurant is in a breezy location overlooking the river just to the right after you cross the bridge entering the town from the south. The cabins are 200 metres away into town and offer clean rooms with fans, private cold showers and parking for just US$3.50 per person – a good deal if you can get in because it's often full, especially midweek.

Another choice is the *Hotel Restaurante Upala* (☎ 47 0169) which has basic rooms with private cold showers for US$4.50/6.75 single/double. They are a couple of blocks from the bus station. Other OK cheapies include the *Hotel Rosita* and *Cabinas Maleku*. The *Cabinas del Norte* (☎ 47 0061) is right next to the bus station and market, so they are apt to be noisy. *Hospedaje Rodriguez* looks like the most basic of the lot.

Getting There & Away

There are buses from San José at 6.30 am and at 3 and 3.45 pm. There is a 3.30 pm bus from Ciudad Quesada. There are buses at 5.45, 9 and 11 am and at 2 and 5 pm from Cañas.

From the Upala bus station there are buses to San José (US$4, five to six hours) at 5 and 9 am and 2 and 3.30 pm, (though only the 5 am and 2 pm departures were running recently). There is a 9 am bus to Ciudad Quesada, buses to Cañas at 6, 9 and 11 am and 1 and 4.30 pm, and buses to a variety of small local destinations, including Santa Cecilia, once or twice a day.

If you are driving to Upala, have their documents accessible for passport controls near Upala.

REFUGIO NACIONAL DE VIDA SILVESTRE CAÑO NEGRO

This 9969 hectare refuge is of interest especially to bird-watchers, who come to see a variety of waterfowl such as anhingas, roseate spoonbills, storks, ducks, herons and the largest Costa Rican colony of the olivaceous cormorant. The refuge is the only place in Costa Rica where the Nicaraguan grackle regularly nests. In addition, pumas, jaguars and tapirs have been recorded here more than in many of the other refuges. It certainly is in a remote and little populated area which is conducive to these rare large mammals. Many smaller mammals have also been reported.

The Río Frío flows through the refuge. During the wet season the river breaks its banks and forms an 800 hectare lake which is best visited by boat for bird-watching. During the dry months of January to April the lake shrinks, and by April has virtually completely disappeared – until the rains in May begin. During the dry season there are some foot and horse trails, but by boat is the only way to go for the rest of the year. From January to March is the best time for seeing large flocks of birds, though smaller flocks can be seen year-round.

Orientation & Information

In the tiny community of Caño Negro you'll find a ranger station where you can stay. They can be reached on channel 38 on the SPN radiotelephone (☎ 33 4160) – around 8 to 9 am is a good time, the rangers told me. Park entrance is US$1.50, camping is

US$2.25, or you can stay in the rangers' house for US$7.50 if it's arranged in advance. There are cold showers, and meals can be arranged. Fewer people come midweek.

The Caño Negro public phone (☎ 46 1301, 46 1303) allows you to leave messages (in Spanish) to arrange for local boatmen. Boats can be hired for about US$11 per hour (including driver) to take you on fishing and birding trips. Fishing is not allowed from April to June, but during the rest of the rainy season you can catch a variety of fish if you have a licence. Two local guides which have been recommended are Elgar Ulate and Vicente Mesa (though I have met neither.) Horse rental can also be arranged. There are no hotels in Caño Negro, but *El Machón* will cook meals for you.

Things to See & Do

Several hotels in this area arrange tours to Caño Negro (see the Muelle San Carlos and Fortuna entries). In San José, Horizontes (☎ 22 2022) operates three day/two night tours for US$310/560 single/double, visiting Volcán Arenal on the first day and Caño Negro on the second day, staying overnight both nights at the Tilajari Resort Hotel. Meals and bilingual naturalist guides are also included in the cost. Cheaper tours are advertised in *The Tico Times* and at travel agents.

Getting There & Away

The reserve can be reached by road from Upala or by boat from Los Chiles.

From Upala Take the road south-east towards San Rafael. After 11 km, at the community of Colonia Puntarenas, there is a signed turn-off for Caño Negro. It is 26 km away by very rough road, though the first half (as far as Angeles) has been worked on recently. I just barely got through in my little rented car in the dry season (I hope the car rental companies aren't reading this!) but you'll probably need 4WD in the wet. I've read reports of a daily bus between Upala and Caño Negro, but it wasn't running when I was there. Pick-up trucks drive along this road a couple of times a day and will pick up people.

From Los Chiles Access from Los Chiles is easier – you just take a boat along the Río Frío. These are day trips, described under Los Chiles, following. There are no ranger stations and camping facilities on this side, though during the rainy season you could hire a boat to take you across the lake to the community and ranger station at Caño Negro.

To get from Los Chiles to Caño Negro by land, the Río Frío must first be crossed. There is no bridge, so you need to get a boatman to ferry you across; then you could walk or hire horses along the track to Caño Negro. Apparently, the road is passable to 4WD – except that you need to figure out a way across the river first. I've read reports that a bus goes from Los Chiles to Caño Negro – but unless it's an amphibian bus it'll have problems.

LOS CHILES

Los Chiles is about 70 km north of Muelle by paved road or 25 km north-east of Caño Negro by horse trail. The small town is on the Río Frío, three km before the Nicaraguan border. About 8000 people inhabit the Los Chiles district. Although the town is midway between the Pacific and Caribbean coasts, the elevation is only 43 metres above sea level – not for nothing is this region called the northern lowlands.

Los Chiles was originally built to service river traffic on the nearby Río San Juan, the south bank of which forms the Nicaragua-Costa Rica border for much of the river's length. A landing strip connected Los Chiles with the rest of the country. Since the construction of a road there are no scheduled services, although aerotaxis can be hired from San José.

Crossing the Border

In the 1980s, Los Chiles was on an important supply route for the Contras, which explains why the authorities are still touchy about the border crossing here. In fact, until Violeta

Chamorro became Nicaraguan president in 1990, this crossing was closed except to ticos and Nicaraguan *nicas*. Recently, though, this crossing was reported open to all travellers with proper documents.

The *migración* office in the centre of town (ask anyone for directions) is open from 8 am to 4 pm, Monday to Friday. If you are really set on leaving Costa Rica for Nicaragua this way, check with the immigration office in San José before departing. (See the Getting There & Away entry for more details.)

Si a Paz

An interesting side effect of the Contra-Sandinista hostilities was that many of the local inhabitants living on or near the Río San Juan left for a safer area. Because fighting in the area was relatively low key compared to, for example, Vietnam, where defoliants and herbicides destroyed much of the countryside, most of the rainforest in the Río San Juan area has been protected from colonisation and preserved. Whilst forests were being cut for pasture in northern Costa Rica, the San Juan area remained free of farmers.

Since the cessation of hostilities in 1990, the colonists are slowly drifting back. This slow drift will soon become a wave as word gets out that the area is both safe again and untouched. Regular discoveries of unexploded mines in the area are stemming the tide of settlement temporarily.

Meanwhile, environmentally aware Costa Rican authorities are working with their Nicaraguan counterparts in an attempt to establish an international park – a national park which spans the border. The proposed name of the park is Si a Paz (literally, 'yes to peace'). It is hoped that it will stretch from the Caño Negro refuge north to Lago de Nicaragua and east through a large tract of primary rainforest in south-eastern Nicaragua and along the San Juan to the Caribbean coast, joining up there with the existing Barra del Colorado refuge. This park is part of the proposed Paseo Pantera – an innovative new project to preserve biological

diversity and enhance wildlife management throughout the Caribbean side of Central America. Paseo Pantera is the brainchild of the Carr brothers, sons of Archie Carr Junior who founded the Caribbean Conservation Corporation and is considered the father of turtle conservation in Central America. For more information, contact the CCC (see the National Parks entry in the Facts about the Country chapter).

Boat Tours

From the main highway you have to drive west through town to reach the Río Frío. At the boat dock you can hire a boatman to take you up the Río Frío during the dry season and all the way into Lago Caño Negro during the rainy season. Boat rental is about US$45 to US$80, depending on the size and type of boat (a canopied boat is usually more expensive; it protects you somewhat from direct sun and rain, but cuts down a little on your field of view). Boat tours last about five hours; if there is a small group of you, this is a good way to go. Individual budget travellers will save money by hooking up with the tours offered in Fortuna. These tours are recommended if you enjoy watching wildlife – there are plenty of monkeys, caymans, sloths, turtles, lizards, butterflies, toucans, parrots and other birds to be seen. Wildlife sightings are comparable to the more frequently visited Tortuguero.

Places to Stay & Eat

The 'best' hotel is probably the *Hotel Carolina* (☎ 47 1151, 47 1116) which is a block west of the police post on the main road at the entrance of town (or about four blocks from the Parque Central – it is not a large town). Basic rooms with fans and private cold shower go for US$5.50/10.50 single/double and cheaper rooms with shared bath are available. Nearby, close to the police post, is the *Soda Sonia* which is one of the better places to eat tico food in.

A block to the west of the Parque Central is the *Hotel Río Frío* (☎ 47 1127) which has cheaper rooms with shared bath. Another cheap and basic choice is the *Hotel Central* on the north-east corner of the parque. The *Restaurant El Parque* serves pretty good tico food, and the *Los Pinos*, a couple of blocks east of the parque, serves ice creams, juices and snacks and is locally popular.

Getting There & Away
Bus Nine buses a day run between Ciudad Quesada (San Carlos) and Los Chiles. There are also less frequent services to and from San José.

Car & Motorbike A paved road connects Los Chiles with Muelle, 70 km to the south. A dirt road goes north three km to the border, from where only a rough trail continues into Nicaragua.

Boat Most border crossers take a boat along the Río Frío to San Carlos, 14 km north of the border. San Carlos is at the point where the Río Frío and Río San Juan empty into Lago de Nicaragua; it has a few very basic pensiones. Passenger boats leave at 8 am and charge just under US$4 per passenger. Boats leave San Carlos about every two days to cross the lake to the important Nicaraguan town of Granada.

San José to Puerto Viejo

Puerto Viejo de Sarapiquí can be approached from San José either from the west or the east, so a round trip can be done without backtracking. The western route, via Heredia, Varablanca, Catarata La Paz, La Virgen and Chilamate is paved and hence preferred in the rainy season. The eastern route via the new highway through Parque Nacional Braulio Carrillo and the turn-off (about 13 km before Guápiles) to Horquetas and Puerto Viejo is almost paved and may be completely so by the time you get there.

WESTERN ROUTE
San José to San Miguel
The western road is a spectacular one which is a favourite of tour companies. The road leaves San José via Heredia and Barva and continues over a pass in the Cordillera Central between Volcán Poás to the west and Volcán Barva to the east. The steep and winding mountain road climbs to over 2000 metres just before the tiny community of Varablanca.

A couple of km past the highest point, there is a turn-off to Poasito and Volcán Poás. Then begins a dizzying descent with beautiful views. People on tours or with their own vehicles can stop for photographs or for high and middle elevation bird-watching. Travellers on public buses must be content with window gazing.

About eight km north of Varablanca, the Río La Paz is crossed by a bridge on a hairpin bend. On the left side of the bridge is an excellent view of the spectacular Catarata La Paz (described in the Central Valley & Highlands chapter). Several other waterfalls may be seen, particularly on the right-hand side (heading north) in the La Paz river valley, which soon joins with the Sarapiquí river valley.

About six or seven km beyond Catarata La Paz there is a turn-off to the right on a dirt road leading to **Colonia Virgen del Socorro**, a small community several km away across the river. This road (which may require 4WD) is famous among birders, who will often spend several hours looking for unusual species along the quiet road, with forest, a river, clearings and elevational changes contributing to species diversity in this one spot.

On one of my birding trips to this area, a friend who had been birding in Costa Rica for over a decade saw his first solitary eagle, a large and uncommon bird which likes remote forested mountainous terrain and is therefore difficult to see. This was a big find. My observations were less unusual but more colourful. I saw the sunbittern (a water bird with a striking sunburst pattern on its spread wings) and the psychedelically coloured redheaded barbet, which has a thick greenish-yellow bill, bright red head and eyes, orange breast, black face with little bristles surrounding the beak, green back, yellow belly streaked with green, olive legs and a bluish-white stripe on the neck. The area is certainly a birder's delight.

Costa Rica Expeditions (☎ 57 0766) organises birding day trips to the area for US$69 per person, two people minimum.

Barely a km north of the turn-off for Virgen del Socorro, just past the community of Cariblanco (which has one of the only gas stations on this road), is a turn-off to the left which leads along a poor dirt road to the attractive **Laguna Hule**. The nine-km road is just passable to ordinary cars in the dry season, but 4WD is advised in the wet. The lagoon is the remnant of a volcanic crater and is set amidst luxuriant rainforest – though away from the lake, most of the forest has gone. The lake is reputedly good for fishing.

About seven km north of the Virgen del Socorro turn-off, the road forks at the community of San Miguel. The west-bound fork goes to Ciudada Quesada, about 35 km away by paved road, whilst the north fork heads for Puerto Viejo to the north-east.

West of San Miguel

The west-bound road hugs the northern limits of the Cordillera Central and there are occasional views of the northern lowlands. About 14 km west of San Miguel along this road is the village of Venecia where there is a basic pensión. Halfway between San Miguel and Venecia is the hamlet of Río Cuarto from which an unpaved road heads south-east past the beautiful waterfall near Bajos del Toro and on to Zarcero (see the Central Valley & Highlands chapter).

A few km north of Venecia is the pre-Columbian archaeological site of **Ciudad Cutris** which can be reached by 4WD vehicle or on foot. The site has not been properly excavated, has no tourist facilities, and is on private land. Enquire locally about permission to see the site.

About eight km west of Venecia is the small town of **Aguas Zarcas** which is the

main settlement between the Puerto Viejo and Caño Negro areas. There are a few cheap and basic but clean places to stay, including *Hotel La Violeta* (☎ 47 4015) which charges US$3/5.25 with shared bath or US$7.25 for a double with a private cold shower (these go fast). *Cabinas Adriana* has rooms with communal bathrooms for US$3 per person.

San Miguel to Puerto Viejo

The road north from San Miguel drops for 12 km to the village of **La Virgen** (not Colonia Virgen del Socorro mentioned previously) which is truly in the northern lowlands. The now flat road goes through mainly agricultural country a further 13 km to **Chilamate** and on six more km to Puerto Viejo. Lodges along this route include Rancho Leona near La Virgen, and Islas del Río and Selva Verde, both near Chilamate. These lodges are described below as are several others in the Puerto Viejo area.

Río Sarapiquí Trips Parts of the Sarapiquí are good for river-running from May to November. The put-in point is usually around La Virgen del Socorro, from which Class II and III rapids are encountered. Alternatively, you can put in at Chilamate, from which it is a more gentle float with mainly Class I and maybe a few Class II rapids. Check to ensure you are signing up for the level you want. Tours run most days with one company or another and cost about US$70 per person. Costa Rica Expeditions (☎ 57 0766), Horizontes (☎ 22 2022) and Ríos Tropicales (☎ 33 6455) all run day trips which involve 3½ hours driving from San José, four hours on the river and 3½ hours back to San José. Lunch and bilingual river guides are provided.

Another option is a kayak tour operated by Rancho Leona in La Virgen (see the Rancho Leona entry later in this section).

EASTERN ROUTE

After visiting the interesting Puerto Viejo area, you can return to San José via the eastern road. (You can also arrive in Puerto

Viejo by the eastern road, reversing this route. Buses go in both directions.)

About four km south-east of Puerto Viejo the road passes the entrance to La Selva Biological Station (described later in this chapter). About 15 km further is the village of **Horquetas**, from where it is 15 km to the rainforest preservation project and lodge at Rara Avis (also described later in this chapter).

From Horquetas the straight, paved road continues about 17 km through banana plantations to the main San José-Puerto Limón highway near the tiny village of Santa Clara. Turn east for Guápiles and the Caribbean; turn west for San José. This route to San José takes you through the middle of the Parque Nacional Braulio Carrillo.

About two km south of Horquetas, an unpaved road goes east for nine km to the village of **Río Frío**, which is an important banana centre. This used to be on the main road between Santa Clara and Horquetas, and some buses still go through here, even though it is about nine km further and the road is not paved. Río Frío has an airstrip. Flights can be chartered to and from here – it is the nearest point to Tortuguero which can be conveniently reached by road. There is a basic hotel here, the *Pensión Ana*, a couple of simple restaurants and a bus stop. Buses between San José and Puerto Viejo often stop here for a meal break. You can catch buses several times a day from here to Puerto Viejo, San José or Guápiles.

Bananas

Everywhere you look in this region you'll see banana plants. Bunches of bananas are often covered with large blue plastic sacks whilst the fruit is still on the tree. The plastic keeps the plants warm (like in a miniature greenhouse) and also concentrates ethylene gas which is produced by ripening fruit.

Strange-looking little tractor trains pull wagons loaded with fruit to processing centres. In some plantations, bunches of bananas are hung on wire contraptions which are pushed by workers into the processing area. The bananas are washed and sprayed to

prevent molding and then shipped off in crates and boxes to the coast and the world.

Recent reports have criticised the banana companies for a multitude of ills over the decades. The rainforests have been replaced by plantations, blue plastic bags litter and clog the streams and rivers, and the insecticide and fungicide sprays used have caused health problems, including sterility, in thousands of workers. These problems have been largely ignored, mainly because the plantations gave workers mimimum housing and a livelihood, and bananas have been, along with coffee, the main source of foreign income for Costa Rica. Slowly, however, the health and environmental problems are being addressed – though the damage already done cannot be easily reversed, some attempt is now being made to minimise further pollution, degradation and sickness.

PUERTO VIEJO DE SARAPIQUÍ

The locals simply refer to the town as Puerto Viejo, but its full name distinguishes it from another popular destination – Puerto Viejo de Talamanca on the Caribbean coast.

The town is at the confluence of the Río Puerto Viejo and the Río Sarapiquí. About 5500 people live in the Puerto Viejo district, which, despite its ramshackle appearance, has an interesting history. It used to be an important port on the trade route to the Caribbean before the days of roads and railways. Boats plied down the Sarapiquí as far as the Nicaraguan border and then turned east on the Río San Juan to the sea. With the advent of roads and railways, Puerto Viejo lost its importance as a river port, although adventurous travellers can still sail down the Sarapiquí in motorised dugout canoes.

Today, the region is known for its nearby undisturbed premontane tropical wet forest which extends out from the northern arm of Parque Nacional Braulio Carrillo. A biological research station and several forest lodges nearby have made this undisturbed habitat accessible to scientists and travellers.

A few km south-east of Puerto Viejo is a women's herb cooperative called MUSA. It is a small farm which produces herbs for medicinal, culinary, cosmetic and incense purposes. Products are for sale and visits are encouraged.

There is no dry season in this area, but late January to early May is the less wet season. A weather station at La Selva, just outside Puerto Viejo, records about 170 mm of rain in February (the driest month) and close to 500 mm in December, the wettest month. The drier season means fewer insects and less muddy trails, but it's never really dry.

Places to Stay & Eat

Although most foreign visitors stay in one of the more expensive lodges in the Puerto Viejo area, budget travellers will find a few cheap and basic hotels in Puerto Viejo itself. Most are along the one main street, so you won't have any difficulty in finding them. The problem is that the best cheap rooms are often full with local workers who use them on a long-term basis, and so choice of rooms may be limited.

The *Cabinas Restaurant Monteverde* (☎ 76 6236) charges US$6.60/9.60 for fairly basic singles/doubles with private cold-water shower and fan. The restaurant here is popular and reasonable. The *Restaurant Cabinas La Paz* (☎ 76 6257) has some basic and rather poor older rooms with private bath for US$5/9 and some better newer rooms for US$7.25/11. Another basic cheapie is *Hotel Santa Martha* for about US$3 per person – rooms all share baths and the place looks pretty run-down, though the people are OK. If all these are full, budget travellers could try *Soda Cabinas Yacaré* in the small village of Guaria, almost three km west of Puerto Viejo on the main road. There are several inexpensive restaurants, bars and sodas.

A new middle-range place in Puerto Viejo is the *Hotel El Bambú* (☎ 76 6005, fax 76 6132), or in San José (☎ 25 8860; Apartado 1518-2100, Guadalupe). This new building is right next to the Cabinas Monteverde and has nine rooms, two apartments with kitchenette and living room, a bar, restaurant and tour services – though these were not yet fully operational when I stopped by in 1993. Introductory prices for comfortable new

rooms with fans, TV and hot water were US$45/70/90/100 for one to four people, including breakfast. Children under 12 years old stay free if they are with their parents. The dining room offers breakfast (US$4.50) lunch and dinner (US$8). The hotel will arrange transportation from San José for US$20 per person, one way (a minimum of four people).

Getting There & Away

Bus Buses from San José leave six times a day (from 7 am to 4 pm) from a marked bus stop on Avenida 11, Calle Central & 1. Departure times and routes have changed frequently recently so check for up-to-date information. Most go via Río Frío and Horquetas; one express bus at 10 am avoids Río Frío and is faster. One bus at 7 am goes via the western route, the others go via the eastern route. Either way, the fare is US$3 and the trip takes about 3½ hours (about two hours on the express). Check with the San José tourist office for the latest schedule, or go to the bus stop and hang around until a bus comes by. The drivers know the schedules. There are also a couple of buses a day from the Coca-Cola terminal.

From Ciudad Quesada (San Carlos), there are buses at 5, 6 and 10 am and at 3 and 5.30 pm – these hours are also subject to frequent change.

Buses return from Puerto Viejo to San José seven times a day between 4 am and 4.30 pm. The bus stop is on the main street – ask anyone. A nearby stop has buses for Ciudad Quesada five times a day.

Taxi There is a taxi sign on the main street of Puerto Viejo. There aren't many taxis, but if you wait by the stand one will eventually cruise by. (Conveniently, the bar behind the taxi stand has a serving window to the street, so you can have a beer while you're waiting.) Taxis will take you to the nearby lodges and biological station for US$2 to US$5.

Boat The port is small and not busy. There are a few motorised dugouts available for hire. A daily boat leaves at 11 am for Oro

Verde and Río San Juan – the fare is US$2. There is nowhere to stay except at Oro Verde (though you could ask around for accommodation).

Local lodges can arrange transportation almost anywhere. One boatman who has been well recommended is William Rojas (☎ 76 6260; leave a message in Spanish). He will take you anywhere, including down the Sarapiquí and San Juan to the Caribbean and south to Tortuguero for about US$250 – the boat can take a group of about eight or 10 people. He'll also take you to other places.

Sailing down the Sarapiquí is full of surprises. If the water is low, dozens of crocodiles are seen sunning on the banks. If the water is high, river turtles climb out of the river to sun themselves on logs. In trees on the banks, you may see monkeys, iguanas, or maybe a snake draped over a branch. Birds are everywhere.

I was lucky enough to see a sleeping sloth which looked just like a greenish-brown blob on a branch because of the algae which grows in the fur of this lethargic mammal. When my boatman suddenly cut the engine, I turned around to see what was the matter. He grinned and yelled, in his none-too-good English, 'Slow! Slow!'. It was obvious that we were going slow, and it took me a while to realise that he was trying to say 'Sloth!' How he managed to make out the blob on a branch as a sloth is one of the mysteries of travelling with a sharp-eyed campesino.

It was not until the dugout had gently nosed into the bank beneath the tree, and the sloth raised a languid head to see what was going on, that I finally realised what we were stopping for.

We continued on down to the confluence of the Sarapiquí with the San Juan, where we stopped to visit an old Miskito Indian fisherman named Leandro. He claimed to be 80 years old, but his wizened looking frame had the vitality of a man half his age. From the bulging woven grass bag in the bottom of his fragile dugout, Leandro sold us fresh river lobster to accompany that evening's supper.

The official border between Nicaragua and Costa Rica is the south bank of the San Juan, not the middle of the river, so you are technically travelling in Nicaragua when on the San Juan. This river system is a historically important gateway from the Caribbean into the heart of Central America. Today, it remains off the beaten tourist track and is a worthwhile trip to see a combination of rainforest and ranching, wildlife and recent war zones, deforested areas and protected areas. It's not an easy or comfortable trip – but it's a good one.

Around Puerto Viejo

LODGES WEST OF PUERTO VIEJO
Selva Verde

Selva Verde is in Chilamate, about seven km west of Puerto Viejo. It is a private finca which has been turned into a tourist facility. Well over half of its approximately 200 hectares is forested; the rest contains the lodge buildings in attractively landscaped grounds.

The main lodge (called the River Lodge) has 45 double rooms in a series of modules surrounding a large conference hall. This facility is often used by Elderhostel groups, and slide shows, lectures and discussions on a variety of topics are presented on nights when Elderhostel groups are there and at irregular intervals at other times. The dining area is in a large thatched building linked to the bedrooms by a long covered walkway. Meals are served buffet-style at set times. There is a small reference library for guests.

Rooms are rustic but comfortable, with private hot showers and large communal verandahs with hammocks and forest views. Rates are US$80/130 single/double including meals. There are also some new bungalows sleeping up to four people which are cheaper per person if occupied by three or four people, as well as a few rooms with communal baths which are a little cheaper.

The lodge is owned and operated by Holbrook Travel of the USA. Because of the travel agency connection, the lodges are popular with tour groups from the USA and other countries. Reservations can be made in San José (☎ 20 2121, fax 32 3321) or in the USA with Holbrook Travel (☎ (904) 373 7118, fax (904) 371 3710; 3540 NW 13th St, Gainesville, FL 32609, USA).

Things to See & Do There are several km of walking trails through the grounds and into the forest (premontane tropical wet forest); trail maps are available or you can hire a bilingual guide from the lodge. There are plenty of birds and butterflies, and observant visitors may see mammals, frogs and reptiles.

On a recent visit I saw a pair of nesting sunbitterns on the banks of the Río Sarapiquí. Stiles & Skutch write, in their authoritative *A Guide to the Birds of Costa Rica* that '[the sunbittern's] nest has rarely been found, and the best available account of its breeding is that of a pair that nested in the gardens of the Zoological Society of London more than a century ago.' Seeing a pair of sunbitterns on a nest in the wild is not a bad way to start a day of birding.

There is also a garden of medicinal plants as well as a butterfly garden, planted with flowers, shrubs and trees designed to attract a variety of butterfly species. Guests at the lodge can visit for free, others pay a few dollars admission.

Bilingual guides charge US$24 for a four hour hike or US$36 for a six hour hike on the trails. This is for up to three hikers – larger groups pay a little more. Various boat tours on the Río Sarapiquí are also available. You can rent a small boat or canoe with a guide for four or five hours for US$45 per person. You can rent a large canopied boat seating up to 25 passengers for about US$13 per person for large groups, for a three hour trip with a driver but no bilingual guide. Mountain bikes can be rented for US$25 a half day and horse rental can also be arranged.

Getting There & Away Buses en route to Puerto Viejo will drop you off at the entrance – all the drivers know where it is. Buses from Ciudad Quesada pass by the front of the lodge five times a day and from San José six times a day. Taxis from Puerto Viejo to the lodge cost about US$3 or US$4. If you make arrangements with Selva Verde, they will provide transport from San José for US$70 one way – the vehicle will take one to four passengers. Larger groups pay US$85 (five to seven), US$120 (eight to 12), US$150 (13 to 20 passengers).

Islas del Río
A km or two west of Selva Verde, at the community of Bajos de Chilamate, is the Islas del Río lodge which re-opened in 1992 under new tico ownership. There are about three km of trails which can be visited on foot or horseback – some trails may involve some stream crossings. The lodge is called Islas del Río because tributaries of the Sarapiquí have divided the grounds into small islands. Longer foot or horseback tours beyond the lodge area into the rainforest are also available.

There are about 33 rooms, of which half have private baths with electric hot showers (or, in some cases, bathtubs). The other rooms have shared bathrooms (one between two rooms) or communal bathrooms (one between several rooms). A large open dining room serves good tico fare. Some rooms will sleep up to six people. Rates with private bathroom are US$42/68 single/double and on up to US$108 for six people; with shared bathroom, US$37/58 to US$96; with communal bathroom, US$30/44 to US$78. Meals are US$3 for breakfast and US$6 for lunch or dinner.

Members of the Costa Rican or International Youth Hostel Federation receive discounts – recently, hostellers who bought entire packages (accommodation plus three meals) were charged between 20% and 33% less, depending on the size of the group. Check with the Hostel Toruma (☎/fax 24 4085) in San José about details.

Reservations can be made at Islas del Río (☎ 71 68 98), in San José (☎ 33 0366, fax 33 9671). See the Selva Verde entry for transport details.

Rancho Leona
This rustic lodge is 19 km west of Puerto Viejo in the village of **La Virgen**. Kayaking trips are the main focus: most guests take a trip of one or more days on the Sarapiquí, though you are welcome to hang out at the lodge, swim in the nearby river or hike to riversides and waterfalls. Guides are available, and all the people who work there speak English. Accommodation at the lodge is in bunks, and there is a laid-back family atmosphere. Solar-heated showers, a restaurant

and bar, and a games/reading area are all available.

Most guests come on the one day/two night trip which gives you two nights at the lodge with a day of kayaking. The price is US$75 per person and includes kayak and equipment, river guide, transportation to put-in and take-out points, and a picnic lunch. They also offer multi-day trips to Caño Negro (five days) and other places on request. The one day trip is designed for all levels; a brief introductory lesson is provided for those with no experience. Experienced kayakers can arrange for adventurous trips on rivers with Class III and IV rapids.

Reservations can be made at Rancho Leona, La Virgen de Sarapiquí, Costa Rica (☎ 71 6312 at the lodge or, if you can't get through, call ☎ 39 9410).

Buses from San José and Ciudad Quesada can drop you in front of the lodge on their way to Puerto Viejo. All the drivers know Rancho Leona in La Virgen. Buses from Puerto Viejo to San José or Ciudad Quesada can drop you there too; the 6 and 7.30 pm buses from Puerto Viejo have been ending their runs in La Virgen recently.

LODGES NORTH OF PUERTO VIEJO
El Gavilán

El Gavilán is a private 180 hectare preserve about four km north-east of Puerto Viejo. The lodge used to be a cattle hacienda and is surrounded by attractive gardens with large trees – great for bird-watching. There is also a variety of tropical fruit harvested for meals. Horses are available for hire and guides will take you into the rainforest, which is over a km from the lodge. Or you can wander around at will. There is an outdoor jacuzzi for relaxation.

A variety of boat trips are available, ranging from short jaunts down the Río Sarapiquí for a couple of hours to multi-day trips down the Sarapiquí to the San Juan and then on to the coast and down to Barra del Colorado or Tortuguero.

The lodge has 14 simple but good-sized rooms, each with an electric hot shower and fan. Rates are US$47/70 single/double

including breakfast. Tico-style lunches or dinners are available for US$10. Note that their restaurant will serve no alcohol – bring your own if you wish. Guided hiking or horseback tours are US$17 per person; Sarapiquí river rides are US$23 per person; day tours to the Río San Juan are US$65.

To get here, take any Puerto Viejo bus and then a taxi for about US$2 or US$3. Boatmen from the Puerto Viejo dock (if you can find one readily available) will take you for about the same price. El Gavilán will arrange transportation from San José for US$20 per person one way or US$25 round trip. They also offer day trips from San José, including a ride on the Río Sarapiquí and lunch, for US$70 per person. Overnight packages, including transportation from San José, accommodation, meals and tours, start at US$380 a double for two days and one night and go to US$760 a double for five days and four nights.

Reservations can be made in San José (☎ 34 9507, fax 53 6556; Apartado 445-2010, San José). There is no phone at the lodge.

The prices given for accommodation at El Gavilán are the officially advertised prices if you just show up and there's space, you can often get a discount.

Oro Verde

Oro Verde is a larger private preserve on the Sarapiquí near the Nicaraguan border, two to three hours by motorised dugout from El Gavilán. The owner, Wolf Bissinger, says that preserving the tropical forests near Oro Verde is a prime concern. When he bought Oro Verde, it came with about 500 hectares of land. Adjoining property has been added, and now Oro Verde contains about 2500 hectares, of which 80% is forested. Work is going on to expand the boundaries of the Oro Verde preserve to include more of the remaining stands of rainforest at the northern end of the Sarapiquí.

The very rustic lodge is set in a clearing surrounded by rainforest. The dining building with its huge cone-shaped thatched roof is only three km from the Nicaraguan border.

Although some of the land between Puerto Viejo and Oro Verde remains forested, the majority of the banks of the Sarapiquí have been turned to cattle pasture, with the river being the main highway for the ranchers.

Many of the people working at Oro Verde are local campesinos who speak little or no English. Sometimes there is a bilingual nature guide available, at other times tours are offered with campesinos who have been raised in the countryside. They are often the best spotters of interesting animals, birds and plants. In addition, the policy of hiring locals to work on private preserves is a sensible one – if you tell a parent with children to feed that they can't chop down particular tracts of forest, it is important to offer viable economic alternatives.

Accommodation at Oro Verde is spartan – which is an attraction or an inconvenience, depending on your point of view. There are eight cabins with private (cold) bath and five with shared bath. High season rates are US$35/58/76/93 for one to four people – for some strange reason, rooms with private and shared bathrooms cost the same. Meals are US$6 for breakfast and US$10 for lunch or dinner.

Discounts for students and large groups are available – a large dormitory-style building has 15 bunk beds. A group staying in the dormitory pays as little as US$15 per person. Basic food is provided and you can cook for yourself. There is a propane stove – but make sure that propane is available. There is no electricity

Three day/two night package tours leave San José on Fridays and Sundays. Packages cost US$195 per person and include bus and boat from San José to the lodge, all meals, a guided boat tour, and accommodation.

Reservations can be made in San José at the Oro Verde office (☎ 33 6613, fax 23 7479; Apartado 7043-1000, San José). Their street address is Avenida 2, Calle 17 & 19. This office also runs the Playa Chiquita Lodge on the Caribbean. There is no telephone at the lodge itself.

Getting There & Away If you are not on a tour and have not arranged transportation, take the 11 am passenger boat from Puerto Viejo – all the boatmen know the Oro Verde Lodge and can drop you there for about US$2 or US$3.

LA SELVA

La Selva (not to be confused with Selva Verde in Chilamate) is a biological station, not a lodge, though you can stay here if you have an advance reservation. The biological station is the real thing – teeming with research scientists and graduate students using the well-equipped laboratories, experimental plots, herbarium, and library to investigate the ecological processes of the rainforest.

La Selva is run by the Organization for Tropical Studies (OTS) which is a consortium founded in 1963 with the purpose of providing leadership in education, research and the wise use of tropical natural resources. Member organisations from the USA, Puerto Rico and Costa Rica include 46 universities and two museums.

Many well-known tropical ecologists have received training at La Selva. Twice a year OTS offers an eight week course open mainly to graduate students of ecology. The students visit several of the other OTS sites, but La Selva is the biggest and most frequently used one. Course work is gruelling, with classes, discussions, seminars and field work running from dawn till dusk and beyond every day. Various other courses and field trips are also offered. There are many long-term and ongoing experiments under way at La Selva, and many researchers come here year after year.

Information

The area protected by La Selva is about 1500 hectares of premontane wet tropical rainforest. About 90% of the land has not been disturbed. It is bordered to the south by the 44,000 hectares of the Parque Nacional Braulio Carrillo, thus affording a large enough area to enable a great diversity of species to live here. Over 400 species of birds have been recorded at La Selva, as well as over 100 species of mammals, and thousands of plants and insects.

You can visit La Selva all year round, but with almost 200 mm of rain falling in each of February and March (the driest months) you should be prepared with rainwear or an umbrella.

Insect repellent, a water bottle, clothes which you don't mind being covered in mud, and footwear suitable for muddy trails are also essential. The total annual rainfall is 4100 mm, and temperatures average 24°C but are often higher. The elevation is about 35 metres at the research station and goes up to about 150 metres by the time Braulio Carrillo is reached.

There is a small exhibit room and a gift shop selling books, maps, posters and T-shirts.

Walking Trails

Bird-watching in particular is excellent because of the very well developed trail system at La Selva. A few of the trails have a boardwalk to enable relatively easy access even during the wet season (though watch your footing – those wet boards can get very slick).

Most of the trails are simply dirt tracks which ramble off into the rainforest, but they are marked with posts every 50 metres so that you don't lose your way. The posts are labelled with the distance you have walked. In all, there are 25 maintained trails ranging from 200 metre long boardwalks to difficult, steep and often muddy trails five km long. The total length of trails is about 50 km. Hikes can combine a variety of different trails so that you can do a round trip loop lasting from one hour to a full day. The most popular trails are maintained regularly and well – others are infrequently maintained and may involve making detours around fallen trees and through thick vegetation or having to wade through streams or swamps.

The trail guide *Walking La Selva* by R Whittall & B Farnsworth (1989) is available from the OTS. Other booklets about La Selva are also available, including *A Biologist's Handbook* by D B & D A Clark, codirectors

of the station. The handbook describes two nature trails in fascinating detail. Local guides are sometimes available to take you around.

Warning The well-developed trail system tends to lull some visitors into a sense of false security. This is a wilderness area, and you must watch where you step. There are plenty of poisonous snakes. Also watch where you put your hands and where you sit. Many of the plants have very sharp thorns or stingers. Worse still, the large black ant *Paraponera clavata*, which can reach up to three cm in length, is quite common and delivers a vicious bite.

Places to Stay & Eat

You can come on a day trip or stay overnight. There are simple but comfortable bungalows with four bunks per room, and a limited number of singles and doubles. Bathrooms are communal, but there are plenty of them. There is a dining room serving meals, although researchers and students always have priority. If there is room available, tour groups (especially birding ones) and individual travellers can use the facilities, but reservations must be made in advance. There is usually space available if reservations are made a few weeks in advance, though during the popular dry season, the place may be fully booked for two or three months ahead.

The rates are US$84 per person per day for tourists; researchers stay for half price and students (working or studying at La Selva) even less. This is, after all, a research station. Prices include three meals a day, and a maximum of 65 people can stay at La Selva. Beer is available if ordered in advance; other alcohol is not available. Laundry machines are available in the afternoons only.

If you don't want to stay here overnight, day visits can also be arranged – though the number of visitors is limited and day visits, too, are booked weeks or even months ahead in the dry season. Day visits cost US$17 per person and include use of the trails and lunch. Lunch is supposedly available from noon to 1 pm, though I and other day visitors have found that lunch is served at noon and if you aren't there on time, there are pretty slim pickings by 12.15.

Reservations should be made with OTS (☎ 40 9938, 40 6696, fax 40 6783), Apartado 676-2050, San Pedro, San José. Information is also available from the North American Office of OTS (☎ (919) 684 5774, fax (919) 684 5661) Box DM, Duke Station, Durham, NC 27706. La Selva has phones and an address to contact the research station and facilities, not to make reservations (☎ 71 6897, fax 71 6481), Apartado 53-3069, Puerto Viejo de Sarapiquí.

Just outside La Selva is the *Sarapiquí Ecolodge* (☎ 35 9280, 53 2533, fax 53 8645). This is on an 80 hectare dairy ranch run by the Murillo family. Rustic accommodation in bunks in the family ranch house is available for US$45 per person, including country-style meals. The nearby Río Puerto Viejo (a tributary of the Sarapiquí) provides swimming and boating. Horses can be rented and boat tours are available.

Getting There & Away

The public bus to Puerto Viejo via the Río Frío and Horquetas route can drop you off at the entrance to La Selva, about three km before Puerto Viejo. From the entrance it is almost a two km walk to the research station. Taxis from Puerto Viejo will take you there for about US$3.

OTS runs buses from San José to La Selva and back on Monday, Wednesday and Friday. The fare is US$10 and reservations should be made when you arrange your visit. Researchers and students have priority.

OTS also runs a van service into Puerto Viejo and back several times a day (except Sunday, when there is only one trip).

RARA AVIS

Rara Avis is a remote private preserve of 1335 hectares of tropical rainforest between 600 and 700 metres in elevation on the northeastern slopes of the Cordillera Central. The land borders the eastern edge of the Parque Nacional Braulio Carrillo. The rainforest

preserve was founded by Amos Bien, an American who came to Costa Rica as a biology student in 1977. As has happened to many biologists who have worked in the tropics, he became fascinated by the incredible complexity of the rainforest ecosystems. But instead of becoming a research biologist bent on discovering more about the rainforest, Amos decided that he wanted to help preserve it. The result is the Rara Avis preserve, in my mind the most interesting tropical rainforest preservation project in Costa Rica.

The logic behind Rara Avis is simple. Tropical rainforests are being destroyed all over the world for one reason only – money. Biologists and conservationists, meteorologists and environmentalists can all provide pressing reasons why the world's rainforests must be protected, but unless economic reality is addressed, destruction of the rainforest will continue. Rara Avis was created with the goal of demonstrating that an intact and preserved rainforest could be just as profitable, if not more so, than one that is logged and turned into cattle pasture, which has been the fate of much of Costa Rica's tropical rainforests.

Certainly, international aid and a national parks scheme go part of the way towards preserving rainforests. But much deforestation occurs in many small operations run by private individuals. It is these individuals for whom Rara Avis is setting an example of what can be done to both preserve and profit from rainforest.

The most obvious solution is ecotourism, and Rara Avis has two lodges, one fairly simple and moderately priced, the other more comfortable and more expensive. But campesinos trying to make a living in the rainforest are rarely going to have the resources to build and run tourist lodges. Rara Avis is unique in Costa Rica in that it is developing other methods of non-destructive profit from the forest, which is a major reason why I believe it is the most interesting and worthwhile private preserve in Costa Rica.

One method is by ecologically sound production and harvesting of forest products on a sustained yield basis. This is already a viable option in some parts of the Amazon – for example, rubber tapping and brazil nut harvesting both work best in an intact forest rather than in plantations where these plants have been shown to be susceptible to epidemics. Recently, biologists at Rara Avis have rediscovered the dappled understorey palm, *Geonoma epetiolata*, which had been considered extinct in Costa Rica for about half a century. It is an attractive palm that grows only in deep shade, with potential as an ornamental house plant. Harvesting just the seeds for growing the plant in nurseries could provide a significant income. It may also be possible to cultivate this plant commercially in the rainforest understorey.

Tree and orchid seedlings are another potential source of income. Orchids from the wild were formerly obtained by cutting down the tree on which they were growing. Work is now going on to try and cultivate orchids domestically from seeds – until now a difficult task. Seeds are collected from the rainforest canopy using methods such as the AWCE (see following). Tree seedlings grown in and collected from the rainforest are useful in maintaining genetic diversity in reforestation projects.

Some philodendron species produce aerial roots which are harvested and treated by local artisans to provide wicker. This product can then be woven into baskets, furniture, mats and other utilitarian items. A local craftsman, Federico Vargas, has been actively producing wicker furniture from philodendron roots for some years and recently has appeared on CNN television and was featured in a documentary made by Cultural Survival. The philodendron is a rainforest plant, and workers at Rara Avis are studying the ecology of the plant to determine what a sustainable harvest size would be, and whether it would be an economically practical crop.

Another profitable enterprise is butterfly farming. At Rara Avis, Isidro Chacón, curator of entomology at the Museo Nacional in San José, is working on sustainable butterfly farming in a project funded by the Worldwide Fund For Nature.

The project is to raise certain species of moths and butterflies for sale to European tropical hothouses. It is difficult to raise butterflies economically in Europe. They are important in the hothouses both as an attraction in themselves and as natural pollinators. Another purpose of the project is to learn more about these insects and provide education.

Straightforward biological research is also a goal at Rara Avis – but with an innovative twist. It is here that biologist Donald Perry built his Automated Web for Canopy Exploration (AWCE). This is a radio controlled ski-lift type machine which is able to travel up, down and along about four hectares of forest canopy. Recent studies have shown that the rainforest canopy is the new frontier of natural history. Until recently, researchers had to be content with examining the canopy through binoculars, trying to peer through the rare gaps in the rainforest. Little did they know that many thousands of new species remained to be discovered in the rainforest canopy. Some species of birds which had been recorded only a handful of times were found to be abundant in the canopy. Many epiphytic plants, mosses, beetles, ants and other insects, frogs, reptiles, fungi, parasites and a host of other creatures spend their entire life cycles in the rainforest tree tops, and were unknown to scientists until exploration of the canopy began recently.

The story of the AWCE can be read in Donald Perry's book *Life Above the Jungle Floor* (1986, Simon & Schuster). Much of the preliminary research for the project was done at the La Selva Biological Station. The final product was built at Rara Avis, and interested visitors can see and sometimes even ride on the machine. This depends on whether it is being used for research, and whether there is a qualified operator available. If you can go on the AWCE, be prepared to sign a lengthy legal waiver in case of any accident. This is, after all, a new and experimental set up, but visitors insist on riding it. It cost me US$25 for a ride, and gave me a completely new perspective of the rainforest.

Although Don Perry still visits and works at Rara Avis part of the time, much of his time is spent developing the new Rainforest Aerial Tram project (see the Central Valley & Highlands chapter for details).

You can also take hikes along the trail system at Rara Avis, either alone or accompanied by biologists who work as guides. The bird-watching is excellent, with a list of about 340 species, and growing. Birds seen here but not very often elsewhere include the blue-and-gold tanager, the black-and-yellow tanager, and the snowcap hummingbird (all of which I saw near the lodge) as well as many others.

Very common mammals include whiteface, spider and howler monkeys, coatimundis, banded anteaters and paca. Peccaries, jaguars, tapirs and sloths are also present in reasonable numbers, but are harder to see.

Insects are, of course, abundant, and the plants and trees are as varied as anywhere in the tropics – there are over 500 species of trees known on the property, which is more than the tree species in all of Europe. There are reference books available at the lodge.

Rara Avis can be visited all year round. The dry season is from January to December inside the lodge. Outside, it rains over 5000 mm every year and there are no dry months, although from February to April is slightly less wet. This is definitely rainforest.

A short trail from the lodge leads to La Catarata – a 55 metre high waterfall which cuts an impressive swath through the rainforest. With care, it is possible to take a gloriously refreshing swim at the base of the falls.

You should be aware, however, that flash floods have been known to surge through the La Catarata area and, very sadly, three young Canadians were drowned in such a flood in 1992.

Since then, an alarm system has been installed which goes off when a sudden rise in water levels upstream is detected – ask for local advice before swimming.

Places to Stay & Eat

El Plastico is at the edge of the preserve, 12 km from Horquetas by very bad road through farmland. (Horquetas itself is about 18 km south of Puerto Viejo and 10 km west of Río Frío.) It is a ramshackle building built in 1964 by prisoners from a now defunct jungle penal colony. The prisoners were given pieces of plastic to sleep under – hence the name. The building was abandoned in 1965 and renovated for Rara Avis in 1986. It is available mainly for use by biologists, students and groups. Accommodation is quite basic – 40 bunk beds in about seven rooms. There are communal showers with hot water on demand, and an open-air dining area with simple but plentiful and tasty food. Accommodation is US$45 per person per day, including meals.

Owner Amos Bien is emphatically interested in educating visitors to the rainforest and has an attractive system of discounts for various groups. Working biologists and students groups on courses receive a discount. Costa Rican citizens and residents receive a 30% discount. Members of the IYHF who book at the Toruma Hostel in San José are charged US$35 per day. People staying over five days also receive discounts.

A further three km of equally bad (if not worse) road through rainforest brings you to the *Waterfall Lodge*, named after the fall nearby. This is a rustic but comfortable and attractive jungle lodge. Rooms have private showers and hot water, and have balconies overlooking the rainforest. Even when it's pouring outside, you can watch birds from your private balcony. Because access is time-consuming and difficult, a two day minimum stay is recommended. Prices include meals, guided walks and transport from Horquetas. There is no electricity but kerosene lanterns are provided. The open-air dining room serves good and plentiful meals. The rates are US$85 per person per day in single rooms, US$75 per person in doubles and US$65 per person in triples or quads. Children under 16 years sharing rooms with their parents are half price. Anybody wanting an in-depth immersion into the rainforest can stay here for five days or more at a 20% discount for the fifth and subsequent days.

You can also buy shares in the Rara Avis SA corporation. These cost US$1800 for a block of three shares. They enable the project to expand and work on rainforest preservation research, and entitle shareholders to two free nights (for two people) at the lodge each year. Eventually, it is planned to pay dividends to the stockholders.

Reservations are more or less essential. Contact Amos Bien (☎/fax 53 0844), Apartado 8105-1000, San José.

Getting There & Away

First get a bus to Horquetas – you are given a schedule when you make your reservation. Here you will be met and transported to Rara Avis. This latter transportation is another major reason why I love Rara Avis. The road is so bad that a 4WD won't make it for most of the year. The road climbs from Horquetas at 75 metres to the lodge at 710 metres above

sea level. En route, two rivers must be forded (there are foot bridges). So what does 'transportation' mean?

A tractor is used to pull a wagon with padded bench seats. The 15 km trip takes three to five hours, and the ride is not a smooth one. Occasionally, the tractor breaks down or the mud is simply too deep (too thick? too sticky? too runny? too disgusting for words?) for the tractor to get through. In which case you walk the rest of the way.

Horses are available if you want to ride or to transport luggage. Take heart – the tractor nearly always gets about nine km of the way up, often makes it to El Plastico (the 12 km mark) and sometimes might even make it to the lodge. The way to look at it is that getting there is a good introduction to what the rainforest is like – and all just part of the adventure. Many people have suggested to Amos that he fix the road – but I like it just fine the way it is. It makes arriving at Rara Avis just that little bit more special.

The Caribbean Lowlands

The Caribbean and Pacific coasts of Costa Rica are very different. The Pacific coast is indented and irregular, while the Caribbean is a smooth sweep of beaches, mangroves and coastal swamp forest. The tidal variation on this smooth coastline is very small. The Pacific has a dry season; the Caribbean is wet all year round (though from February to March and September to October are less rainy). About half of the Caribbean coastline is protected by two national parks and two national wildlife refuges, while less than 10% of the Pacific is so protected. The most luxurious beach resorts have been developed on the Pacific; the Caribbean coast is visited not simply for a relaxing beach experience but also for wildlife and culture.

The entire Caribbean coast is part of Limón Province, which covers 18% of Costa Rica but has only 7.5% of the population, making it the second most sparsely populated province in the country (after Guanacaste). One third of the province's 240,000 inhabitants are Blacks, mainly of Jamaican descent. Most of them live on or near the coast and many still speak delightfully archaic English. They add a cultural diversity missing in the rest of Costa Rica. Also, in the southern part of the province, several thousand indigenous Bribri and Cabecar people survive.

Partly because of the low population of the region, and partly because, until the 1949 constitution, Blacks were legally discriminated against, the Caribbean lowlands have been much slower to be developed than the Pacific. There are fewer roads and more areas which can be reached only by boat or light aircraft. Limón province has less than 10% of the country's hotel rooms, while the Pacific coastal provinces of Guanacaste and Puntarenas have a combined total of about 40%. Traditionally, Costa Ricans from the populous Central Valley have vacationed on the Pacific, and even today the Caribbean is not a primary destination for most nationals.

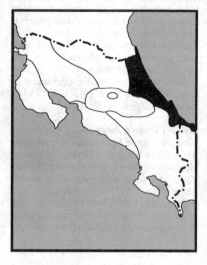

This is slowly beginning to change with the opening, in 1987, of the San José-Guápiles-Puerto Limón highway which cuts driving time to the coast in half, but traditions die hard.

Foreign travellers, on the other hand, are more attracted to the Caribbean, partly for the romance associated with the word 'Caribbean' and partly for the cultural diversity found there. The main road from San José to the Caribbean ends at the provincial capital at Puerto Limón. From here there is just a single road heading south along the coast to the Panamanian border. Northbound travellers must rely on boats to take them up the coastal waterway, locally known as *los canales*, through wilderness areas, past remote fishing villages, and on to Nicaragua. Limited access has helped maintain a sense of traditional values in the inhabitants, which makes a Caribbean visit certainly more interesting, if not as luxurious, as a trip to the Pacific beaches.

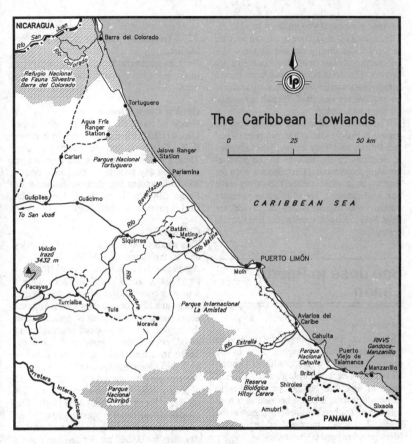

The Caribbean Lowlands

NICARAGUA
Río San Juan
Barra del Colorado
Río Colorado
Refugio Nacional de Fauna Silvestre Barra del Colorado
Tortuguero
Agua Fría Ranger Station
Cariari
Parque Nacional Tortuguero
Jalova Ranger Station
Parismina
Guápiles
Guácimo
To San José
Río Reventazón
CARIBBEAN SEA
Batán
Matina
Siquirres
Río Matina
Río Pacuare
Volcán Irazú 3432 m
PUERTO LIMÓN
Moín
Pacayas
Turrialba
Tuis
Parque Internacional La Amistad
Aviarios del Caribe
Moravia
Cahuita
RNVS Gandoca-Manzanillo
Río Estrella
Parque Nacional Cahuita
Puerto Viejo de Talamanca
Manzanillo
Carretera Interamericana
Parque Nacional Chirripó
Reserva Biológica Hitoy Cerere
Shiroles
Bribri
Bratsi
Amubri
Sixaola
PANAMA

0   25   50 km

There are exceptions, of course. Tortuguero and Barra del Colorado both have 1st class lodges in wilderness areas and the hotel quality is improving in the south. But most of the Caribbean coast has a gentle, laid-back, unhurried feel to it. If a small coastal village with simple accommodation is more to your liking than elaborate tourist developments, I think you'll find what you are looking for right here.

The devastating earthquake that struck Costa Rica on 22 April 1991 had its epicentre south of Puerto Limón, which was the city most seriously affected by the disaster.

Roads were closed (at least 17 bridges were impassable), the railway was destroyed, thousands of buildings suffered damage and parts of the coastline rose by more than a metre, in some cases exposing coral reefs.

At the time of writing, both roads from San José to Puerto Limón (the old and slow road through Turrialba and the new highway through Guápiles) have been repaired but still show signs of earthquake damage. Once they get to the flatlands on the way to Puerto Limón, highway motorists tend to speed – beware of very severe dips in the road every few km. Some of these dips could certainly damage your car if you hit them at 80 km/h. The highway is also prone to closure because of mud slides during the wet season – closures normally last from a few hours to a day or two. The southbound road from Puerto Limón has suffered severe cracking and potholes – average speeds of 20 km/h are normal for long stretches.

The famous 'jungle train' railway from the capital to Puerto Limón has also been closed indefinitely and there are no plans to reopen it. Sections of the railway in the banana-growing areas around Guápiles are open for 'banana train' tours (see the Train entry in the San José chapter). The only trains currently running with regular passenger services are from Puerto Limón south to the Río Estrella valley.

San José to Puerto Limón

GUÁPILES

This town is the transport centre for the Río Frío banana-growing region. It is in the northern foothills of the Cordillera Central, 62 km north-east of San José, and is the first town of any size on the San José-Puerto Limón highway. It could be used as a base for visiting the banana-growing region to the north, if you are interested in seeing that. Most people speed on through.

Places to Stay & Eat

None of the hotels in town are very good. Perhaps the best is the *Keng Wa* (☎ 71 6235), near the old railway station, or the nearby *Hotel Hugo Sanchez* (☎ 71 6197). Rooms with private bath are about US$10 a double. There are a few cheaper hotels.

A few km before Guápiles is the new *Casa Río Blanco* which is a small B&B operated by North Americans. I haven't been there but the owners tell me that they have accommodation for up to six people and all rooms have private hot showers. No smoking is allowed and meals can be prepared on request. Local

tours are available – write to Apartado 241-7210, Guápiles-Pocosí for rates and information.

There are several inexpensive places to eat in Guápiles but no particularly noteworthy ones.

Getting There & Away

Buses to San José (US$1.20) or Puerto Limón (US$1) leave about every hour. Buses to Río Frío leave three or four times a day. There are also buses to Cariari, from where one bus a day goes to Puerto Lindo on the Río Colorado in the Refugio Nacional de Fauna Silvestre Barra del Colorado. The road is paved as far as Cariari.

GUÁCIMO

This small town is 12 km east of Guápiles and is the home of EARTH (Escuela de Agricultura de la Región Tropical Húmeda) (☎ 55 2000, fax 55 2726). This school has a four-year college-level program designed to teach students from all over Latin America about sustainable methods of agriculture in the tropics. There is a banana plantation and a 400 hectare forest reserve on the grounds. There are nature trails, and horse rental is available. Overnight visits can be arranged – the campus accommodates visitors in 32 double rooms with fans and private hot showers. Rates are about US$27/40. The campus dining room is open to guests.

Costa Rica Expeditions in San José has day tours for US$69 per person (four people minimum) accompanied by bilingual naturalist guides and including lunch; they can also arrange overnight accommodation.

Another site of interest is Costa Flores (☎ 76 5047, in San José ☎ 20 1311, fax 20 1316; Apartado 4769, San José) north of Guácimo on signed roads. This is a 120 hectare tropical flower farm – they say they are the largest in the world. Six hundred varieties of tropical plants from 30 countries are grown here for export. Visitors and shoppers are welcome – call for information.

The 24 hour gas station on the main highway at the entrance to Guácimo is a popular stopping place for truckers and tico families – the food is inexpensive and quite good. Aficionados of truck-stop menus may want to give the tico version a try.

SIQUIRRES

This town, 25 km east of Guácimo, used to be an important railway junction until the closure of the railway in 1991. It remains significant as the road junction of the old San José-Turrialba-Puerto Limón route with the new highway to the coast. The old route is slower but very scenic, for those with a little more time on their hands. Siquirres is the last town of any size before Puerto Limón, about 58 km further east.

Places to Stay & Eat

There are a number of cheap and basic hotels, all near the old railway station which is two blocks from the bus station. There are several restaurants. The best is just off the highway, a km or two south-east of Siquirres at a small tourist complex near the Río Pacuare.

Getting There & Away

Buses leave about every hour to Guápiles (US$0.55), San José (US$1.45) and Puerto Limón (US$0.60).

PUERTO LIMÓN

This port is the capital of the province of Limón and many ticos refer to the city as, simply, Limón. The mainly Black population of Limón and the surrounding district is about 70,000, thus almost a third of the province's inhabitants live in and around the provincial capital.

Limón is quite lively and busy, as ports tend to be, and sometimes you may hear some coastal music. Generally, though, Limón is not considered a tourist town, although there are good quality hotels and a beach resort at Playa Bonita, four km north of the town centre. Most people just spend a night en route to somewhere else, though you may be the type of traveller who finds tropical ports to be interesting and want to spend a few days getting to know this one.

Orientation

The streets are very poorly marked. Most streets have no signs, though I found one with two different street signs on it. Apart from this, the streets and avenues go up one number at a time (Calle 1, Calle 2, etc) as opposed to going up in twos, as they do in San José and most other towns. Locals get around by city landmarks. Some of the major ones are the market, Radio Casino and the town hall *(municipalidad)* on Parque Vargas. If you ask where Calle 5 and Avenida 2 is, most people will have no idea. (It's 500 metres west of the municipalidad, or 100 metres west of the south-west corner of the market.)

Avenida 2 is considered one of the main streets – Parque Vargas, the municipalidad, the market, a couple of banks, the museum and the San José bus terminal are all on or just off this street.

Limón is on the rocky Punta Piuta; the point shelters the main port at Moín, about six or seven km west of Limón.

Information

Tourist Office Though there is no tourist office, Helennik Souvenirs Shop (☎ 58 2086) is helpful with local information. It is on Calle 3, Avenida 4 & 5. Medical attention in the Caribbean area is available from the Hospital Tony Facio (☎ 58 2222) in Limón.

Money The Banco de Costa Rica and other banks will change money; street money-changers hang out around the market. Change as much money here as you'll need for your trips on the coast, as exchange facilities are not great along the coast (though the better lodges and hotels accept cash US dollars or even travellers' cheques).

Immigration For those few arriving at Limón by sea, there is a Migración office on the north side of Parque Vargas. Visa extensions are normally given in San José, just 2½ hours away by bus.

Post & Telecommunications CORTEL, the post and telegram office, is at Calle 5,

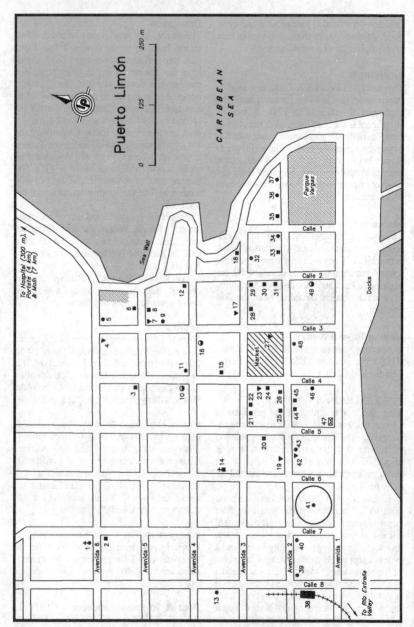

■ PLACES TO STAY

2	Hotel Puerto
3	Hotel Ng
6	Hotel Lincoln
8	Nuevo Hotel Internacional
12	Hotel Venus
15	Nuevo Hotel Oriental
18	Park Hotel
20	Pensión El Sauce
21	Pensión Los Angeles
22	Hotel El Caño
24	Hotel Los Angeles
25	Hotel Linda Vista
26	Hotel Fung
28	Hotel Acon
29	Cariari Hotel
30	Hotel Palace
31	Hotel Río
33	Hotel Las Palmeras
35	Hotel Caribe
44	Hotel Miami
45	Hotel King

▼ PLACES TO EAT

4	Restaurant Sien Kong
7	Restaurant International
17	Mönpik
19	Soda Restaurant Yans
23	Restaurant Chong Kong
27	Restaurant Doña Toda
35	American Bar
42	Palacio Encantador Restaurant
48	Mares Soda Bar/Restaurant

OTHER

1	Church
5	Gas Station
9	Helennik Souvenirs Shop
10	Bus to Moín
11	Radio Casino
13	Police
14	Cathedral
16	Bus to Cahuita, Puerto Viejo & Sixaola
32	Fire Station (Bomberos)
34	Banco de Costa Rica
36	Town Hall (Municipalidad)
37	Migracíon
38	Railway Station
39	Bar Estadio
40	Gas Station
41	Baseball Stadium
43	ICE Telephones
46	Museo Etnohistorico de Limón
47	Post Office
48	Banco Nacional de Costa Rica
49	Buses to San José

Avenida 1. ICE, the telephone and fax office, is on Avenida 2, Calle 5 & 6.

Warning People have been mugged in Limón, so stick to the main well-lit streets at night. Also watch for pickpockets during the day. These are fairly normal precautions in many port cities – Limón is not especially dangerous.

Things to See
The main attraction is **Parque Vargas** in the south-eastern corner of town by the waterfront. The park has tall attractive palms and other tropical trees, flowers, birds and sloths hanging out (literally) in the trees. It's not easy to see the sloths, but they are there. Passers-by will help you spot one.

From the park it's a pleasant walk north along the **sea wall** with views of the rocky headland upon which the city is built.

There are no beaches in Limón but at **Playa Bonita**, four km north-west of town, there is a sandy beach which is OK for bathing. There are places to eat and picnic areas, and the backdrop of tropical vegetation is attractive.

On his fourth and last trans-Atlantic voyage, Columbus landed at **Isla Uvita**, which can be seen about a km east of Limón. It is possible to hire boats to visit Isla Uvita, and the better hotels can organise tours there. Tours to Tortuguero, Cahuita and other destinations of interest can also be arranged from all the better hotels (as well as in San José).

Another focal point of the town is the colourful **public market** which has a variety of cheap places to eat and plenty of bustling activity.

The **Museo Etnohistórico de Limón** (☎ 58 2130 or 58 3903) has a small exhibit about the the landing of Columbus, displays of local indigenous and of Afro-Caribbean cultural artefacts, and details of the building of the railway from San José to the coast in the 1880s and Puerto Limón's subsequent growth as a seaport. Museum hours are erratic, but it is usually open from Tuesday to Friday, and sometimes on Saturday.

Festivals
Columbus Day (12 October, locally known as El Día de la Raza) is celebrated with more than the usual enthusiasm because of Columbus's historic landing on Isla Uvita. Tens of thousands of visitors, mainly ticos, stream into town for street parades and dancing, music, singing, drinking and general carrying on which goes on for four or five days. Hotels are booked well in advance of this event. The locals call this their annual Carnaval, although in other parts of Latin America, Carnaval is celebrated in the days leading up to Lent.

Places to Stay
Since the opening of the new highway in 1987, hotels all along the Caribbean have been in much greater demand. This is particularly true of weekends during the San José holiday seasons (Christmas, Easter, January, February) and during the Columbus Day celebrations on and around 12 October. You should call in advance if possible during those periods.

Some hotels reportedly operate on two price structures – one for locals and a higher one for visitors. There's not much you can do except go to another hotel if you don't like the price.

Places to Stay – bottom end
The cheapest hotels have little to recommend them except price. Prostitutes and their clients reportedly use some of these hotels but, whilst not salubrious, these places don't seem particularly dangerous either – though single women should use their best judgement. They basically are places to crash for a night.

The impecunious might try the basic *Pensión Los Angeles*, which is just US$3 per

person but has few singles, or the similarly priced *Pensión El Sauce* – neither are particularly good. The *Hotel Río* seems to be popular with local workers and looks OK and reasonably clean for US$3.60 per person – there are very few single rooms available.

The *Cariari Hotel* (☎ 58 1395) has small, basic rooms with no fans for US$3.60 per person and has single rooms – it's as good as any. It supposedly has a 2nd-floor balcony for street watching, but I didn't go up there. The *Hotel Venus* is similarly priced and reasonably clean and the *Nuevo Hotel Oriental* (☎ 58 0117) is US$7.20 a double and OK. The basic *Hotel El Caño* (☎ 58 0894) is adequate for US$4.80 per person.

The *Hotel Ng* (☎ 58 2134) is filled with workers during the week but less busy at weekends. It seems clean and honest for US$5.50/9.50 single/double or US$7/11 with private cold shower. The *Hotel Fung* (☎ 58 3309) is also OK and charges US$5.75/10.25 with communal bath or US$11.50 for a double with private cold shower. Some rooms have fans. A good basic choice in this price range is the *Hotel King* (☎ 58 1033) which is well run and cheerful. They charge US$5.20 per person in rooms with communal bath and have doubles with private cold shower for US$13.25. Most rooms have fans. Another reasonable choice for about US$5 or US$6 per person is the pleasant *Hotel Linda Vista* (☎ 58 3359).

The *Hotel Palace* (☎ 58 0419) charges US$6.25/11 for basic rooms with communal baths. It's in an interesting-looking old building around a courtyard with flowers.

Other hotels in this price range include the *Hotel Las Palmeras* with private baths but no singles – reportedly prostitutes use it; the poor *Hotel Lincoln* which is run-down and overpriced and the *Hotel Los Angeles* (☎ 58 2068) which charge US$11 for a double with fan and US$14 with air-conditioning, but they won't show you the room before you register. The *Hotel Caribe* has rooms with private bath for US$7.30 per person, but is over a bar and looks overpriced and has been described as a 'party hotel'.

The *Park Hotel* (☎ 58 3476) has rooms

with private cold shower and fans starting at US$9.50/13, but these are noisy and nothing special. Nicer rooms are US$12/16. The best rooms have sea views and electric showers but are often full – they are in the middle category. Rates are US$15/19. There is a simple but adequate restaurant. This old hotel used to be the best in town, but...

Places to Stay – middle

The clean *Hotel Miami* (☎ 58 0490, fax 58 1978; Apartado 266, Puerto Limón) charges US$11.25/17 for single/double rooms with private cold shower and fan; air-conditioned rooms are US$13.50/20.50. There is a cafeteria. The newer *Hotel Puerto* (☎ 58 1095) has clean, quiet rooms with private electric showers for about US$10 per person. It has a few rooms with one double bed which costs US$15 per couple.

The *Nuevo Hotel Internacional* (☎ 58 0662; Apartado 288, Puerto Limón) opened in 1993 and has good, clean rooms with private bath and electric showers. Rates are US$12.50/17 with fans and US$26 a double with air-conditioning. It competes with the traditionally top downtown *Hotel Acon* (☎ 58 1010, fax 58 2924; Apartado 528, Puerto Limón) which charges US$22/29 for large but rather bare singles/doubles with private electric showers and air-conditioning. It has a restaurant and dancing at weekends.

There are also some good hotels on the coast just north-west of Limón. If you are driving you can reach them by taking the Moín turn off to the left, about six km before reaching Limón from San José; this avoids downtown Limón altogether. If you do go this way, three km after turning off the main highway, just before Moín docks, take a right for Portete and Playa Bonita, and follow the coast road east past the coastal hotels, eventually reaching Limón itself. If you are not driving take the Moín bus, although it is often very crowded; a taxi would be a better way to go.

About four km out of Limón, or 2.5 km from the Moín dock, is *Cabinas Cocori* (☎ 58 2930, Apartado 1093, Puerto Limón)

which is on the small beach at Playa Bonita. The owner has the delightful name of Maria de McGuinness. They have cabins with fan, kitchenette and refrigerator. Rates are US$45 for up to five people, though they told me that I could have one to myself for US$20 because they weren't full. They are planning to add a swimming pool and air-conditioned rooms in 1994 and expect to charge about US$35/40 for singles/doubles.

Places to Stay – top end

Across the street from the Cabinas Cocori (see above for directions) is the *Hotel Matama* (☎ 58 1123, 58 4200, fax 58 4499; Apartado 686, Puerto Limón). It is about 300 or 400 metres to the small beach at Playa Bonita. They have a swimming pool, bar and restaurant. Their air-conditioned rooms are in a variety of bungalows and cabins – they have eight double rooms, four rooms sleeping four and four rooms sleeping six. The buildings are set in hilly gardens with jungle vegetation; inside some of the bathrooms there are miniature jungle gardens which I rather liked. It made a nice change from the thousands of hotel bathrooms it's been my good fortune to gaze at. The showers are electric but seem to work quite well.

The *Hotel Maribu Caribe* (☎ 58 4010, 58 4543, fax 58 3541; Apartado 623, Puerto Limón, or, in San José, ☎ 53 1838, fax 34 0193; Apartado 1306-2050, San José) is just over a km east of the Matama, or about three km north-west of Puerto Limón. It is on a small hill which catches ocean breezes and has a good view. There are two pools and a restaurant and bar. Accommodation is in attractive, private, air-conditioned, thatched bungalows and costs US$80/91 for singles/doubles. This place also has electric showers, but they seem to do the trick. Both these top-end hotels will arrange tours.

Places to Eat

There are many snack bars and sodas around the market – one of the best is *Restaurant Doña Toda* where snacks and simple meals cost around US$2. There are several cheap bar/restaurants near the market, especially

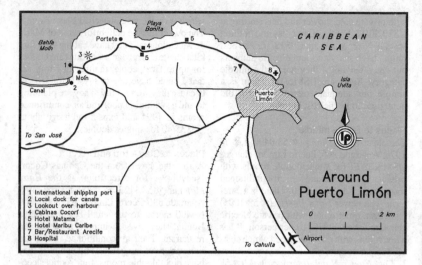

```
1 International shipping port
2 Local dock for canals
3 Lookout over harbour
4 Cabinas Cocorí
5 Hotel Matama
6 Hotel Maribu Caribe
7 Bar/Restaurant Arecife
8 Hospital
```

Around
Puerto Limón

across the street on the west side. One of these is the *Restaurant Chong Kong* with Chinese meals for about US$3 to US$5. Rather more upmarket, popular and clean is the *Mares Soda Bar/Restaurant* on the south side of the market. It serves a variety of snacks and meals for US$3 to US$7. For desserts there's always *Mönpik* for good ice creams.

Chinese food is often the best bet for inexpensive eating. The best Chinese restaurant is the *Sien Kong*, with meals from US$5 to US$10. Two clean places a couple of blocks west of the market are the *Palacio Encantador* and the *Soda Restaurant Yans* – the latter with a small menu but very popular among locals.

The better hotels have decent restaurants open to the public. These include the *Park, Miami, Acon, Nuevo Internacional, Matama* and *Maribu Caribe* in roughly ascending order of price. Another good choice is the *Bar/Restaurant Arecife* (☎ 58 4030) which is about 500 metres north-west of town on the road to Portete. It serves good seafood. A few hundred metres further is *Springfields* which used to specialise in Jamaican food – I don't know if it's still open so ask locally.

The *American Bar* by Parque Vargas has slightly pricey but filling meals and is a popular hang-out for a variety of coastal characters – sailors, ladies of the night, entrepreneurs, boozers, losers and the casually curious. There are plenty of other drinking joints.

Getting There & Away

Limón is the transportation hub of the Caribbean coast.

Air The airstrip is about four km south of town, near the coast. Since the opening of the new road in 1987, regular flights are no longer available, although charters from San José can be arranged. Travelair planned scheduled flights to Limón, but there wasn't enough interest.

Bus Buses from San José to Limón leave about every hour from near the Atlantic railroad station in the capital. Buses return to San José with two companies, the offices of which are side by side on Calle 2, a block east of the market. Buses with one or the other of the companies leave every hour on the hour, from 5 am to 8 pm. The fare is US$3 for the 2½ to three hour ride. From the same bus terminal there are buses to Siquirres and Guápiles many times a day.

Buses heading south leave from a block north of the market. Currently, buses from Limón to Sixaola leave at 5 and 10 am, and 1 and 4 pm. The buses stop at Cahuita (US$0.80), Puerto Viejo (US$1.20), Bribri (US$1.40) and Sixaola (US$2, three hours). The buses are crowded, so try to get a ticket in advance and show up early to get a seat. Advance tickets are sold next to the soda by the *parada* (bus stop).

Buses also leave from here to Penshurst and Pandora (Valle de La Estrella) several times a day. From Pandora you can go to the Reserva Biológica Hitoy Cerere.

Train The 'jungle train' railway from San José was destroyed in the 1991 earthquake and there are no plans to reopen this route.

There are trains to the Río Estrella valley, south of Puerto Limón en route to Cahuita. This used to be a freight train which was disrupted by the 1991 earthquake; the line reopened in April 1993, carrying both passengers and cargo. Departures from Puerto Limón are at 4 am and 3 pm, Monday to Friday. The train goes through many villages, ending up at the Banana Fincas on the Río Ley, a tributary of the Río Estrella. The journey takes about 1½ hours and costs US$1.50 to the end of the line. Return trains leave at 5.50 am and 4.50 pm.

Car & Motorbike If you are driving, fill up in Limón because there are no gas stations in Cahuita or Puerto Viejo. There is one in Pandora in the Valle de La Estrella. If you plan on doing a lot of driving, consider bringing a spare can of fuel.

Boat Limón is the country's major Caribbean port, and cruise ships occasionally dock here for a short visit. Boats to Tortuguero and further north leave from Moín, about seven km north-west of Limón.

Getting Around

Taxi A taxi to Cahuita costs about US$20. If

you do this trip at night, make sure you have a hotel reservation in Cahuita. Taxis to the good hotels around Portete charge about US$3.

MOÍN

This port is about seven km west of Puerto Limón. The main reason to come here is to take a boat up the canals to Parque Nacional Tortuguero and on to Refugio Nacional de Fauna Silvestre Barra del Colorado.

The canals are so called because they are not all natural. There used to be a series of natural waterways north of Limón as far as Barra del Colorado, but they were not fully connected. In 1974, canals were completed to link the entire system, thus avoiding having to go out to sea when travelling north from Moín. This inland waterway is a much safer way to go than travelling up the coast offshore.

After the 1991 earthquake, travel up the canals was severely disrupted. For a while there was little boat traffic to Tortuguero. Then the riverside village of Matina, on the Río Matina half way between Puerto Limón and Siquirres, began providing access to the canals. Other villages were also used as departure points. In 1993, boats left from both Moín and other areas. Sometimes the canals are blocked north of Moín by water hyacinths or log jams, in which case Matina or other ports are used until the blockage is cleared. If you are on a booked tour, you'll go the way they take you (funny how that is!) but if you are completely independent, you'll probably go via Moín because it has easier bus connections.

Places to Stay & Eat

There is nowhere decent to stay in Moín (stay in Limón). There are a couple of simple restaurants near the dock area.

Getting There & Away

Bus Buses to Moín leave from Limón several times an hour, starting at 6 am. The bus stop is opposite Radio Casino, at Calle 4, Avenida 4.

Boat The majority of travellers get to the national parks on organised tours with prearranged boat or plane transport. These tours are usually good but not very cheap, although you can pay for just the travel portion and then stay in cheaper accommodation in Tortuguero.

It is possible to arrange transportation independently of an organised tour, especially if you speak Spanish. The harbour authority, JAPDEVA, no longer has public boats to Tortuguero – their boat *Gran Delta* is out of commission.

The thing to do is go down to Moín dock early and start asking around. The boat dock for Tortuguero is about 300 metres to the left of the main port, through a guarded gate. There are passenger and cargo boats leaving most days, but it takes a little bit of asking around about schedules and availability. Some boats are officially cargo only, though you might persuade the captain to allow you aboard. The trip to Tortuguero can take from 2½ hours to all day, depending on the type of boat.

Most travellers end up taking a private boat; when I was there, boatmen offered a private day trip for two people including box lunch for US$150. Others offered the round trip for US$50 per person with a three person minimum and said that you could arrange beforehand to return on a different day. Others offered a one-way passage for US$35 if they had room. Bargaining ability may be helpful in getting slightly lower prices, especially if there is a group of you, but don't expect great price reductions. There are often boatmen hanging around the dock area in the early morning and boats normally leave between 7 am and 8 am. The trips take about five hours to Tortuguero (allowing for photography and wildlife viewing). After lunch and a brief time in Tortuguero, the return trip is done in 2½ hours. There is a locked and guarded parking area for those driving a car (but don't leave valuables in the car).

Other Routes A combination of asking around, hitchhiking, luck, bus, boat, patience and time may get you to Tortuguero (and beyond to Barra del Colorado). Budget traveller Ursula Hoelzli from Canada described an unconventional trip she and a friend made in early 1993.

There were no public boats from Moín so they hitched/bussed to Matina, where they found a very basic hotel for US$5 a double. Boats available here were as expensive as in Moín, so they took a morning bus to Batán and from there another bus to San Rafael (locally called Freeman, after the local banana plantation) near the mouth of the Río Pacuare. Locals told them a boat would be by at 2 pm; finally, at 5.30 pm a cargo boat passed by and gave them a ride to Parismina (described later).

They spent the following morning at the Parismina dock, got a ride in the early afternoon to Tortuguero on a passing tourist boat (US$7.25 per person), and camped at Tortuguero for a few days. They encountered a man from Barra del Colorado (also described later) who gave them a ride to his village, where they stayed with a family. They caught a daily 4.50 am boat to Puerto Lindo, 30 minutes away on the Río Colorado, from where a 6 am bus took them to Cariari, taking two hours. (Boat and bus from Barra del Colorado to Cariari was US$6.60 per person).

From Cariari there are buses to Guápiles and on to San José. Try calling the Soda La Parada (☎ 76 7120) in Cariari for bus times.

The North Caribbean

PARISMINA

This small village is at the mouth of the Río Parismina, about 50 km north-west of Limón, just over half way between Limón and Tortuguero village and a few km south of the southern border of Parque Nacional Tortuguero.

Parismina boasts two of the best fishing lodges on the Costa Rican Caribbean. Record-breaking Atlantic tarpon and snook are the fish to go for. Offshore reef fishing is also good. Traditionally, from January to mid-May is the tarpon season and from September to November is the season for big snook – however, all the locals will tell you that you can get into good fishing any month of the year, because these fish don't migrate.

Note that while most of the lodges

described here and elsewhere in the book will provide tackle, inveterate anglers will probably prefer to bring their own. Lures and other essentials are sold by the lodges but, because of import duties, are more expensive than at home. Lures are not included in the packages. The lodges will be happy to advise you about all aspects of fishing equipment if you make a reservation with them.

Places to Stay

The *Parismina Tarpon Rancho* (☎ 35 7766; prefers to take reservations in the USA (☎ 1 (800) 531 7232, (210) 377 0451, ☎ /fax (210) 377 0454; PO Box 290190, San Antonio, TX 78280, USA) and provides everything you need for deep-sea fishing for US$2190 a double for three days of fishing to US$2095/3390 a single/double for seven days of fishing. Rates include transport from San José, boats and gear in Parismina, accommodation, meals and a night in San Jose's Aurola Holiday Inn at either end of your stay. The owners also run Golfito Sailfish Rancho and will arrange fishing packages with three days on one coast and four on the other.

The *Río Parismina Lodge* (☎ 22 6633) prefers you to make reservations in the USA, (☎ 1 (800) 338 5688, (210) 824 4442, fax (210) 829 3770; PO Box 460009, San Antonio, TX 78246-0009, USA). It is a new fishing lodge that also provides local nature tours on request. The lodge has a swimming pool, jacuzzi and nature trails on its 20 hectare property. They provide absolutely everything (except tips for fishing guides and lodge staff) in their all-inclusive fishing packages, which include a night in a 1st class San José hotel at either end of your lodge stay. Rates vary from US$1500/2800 a single/double for three days of fishing to US$2500/4200 a single/double for seven days of fishing. Extra days of fishing are US$250 per person.

If you just want budget accommodation, there are a couple of cheap and pretty basic cabinas charging about US$15 a double; one is the *Parismina Lodge* (☎ 76 8636) – I haven't been there.

Getting There & Away

You pass here on the canal boats to Tortuguero, but some visitors fly in to the local airstrip (charter flights only).

PARQUE NACIONAL TORTUGUERO

This 18,946 hectare coastal park is the most important breeding ground for the green sea turtle in all of the Caribbean. There are eight species of marine turtles in the world; six nest in Costa Rica and four in Tortuguero. The many turtles give the national park its name. The Tortuguero nesting population of the green turtle, *Chelonia mydas*, has been continuously monitored since 1955, and is the best studied. Comparatively little is known about other marine turtles.

Parque Nacional Tortuguero is under extreme pressure. With only a handful of personnel to work in the three ranger stations, the protected area is being encroached upon by loggers, banana and oil palm plantations, ranches and colonists. Arriving by air is frightening. If you fly in, you'll see nothing but plantations and cattle ranches until you reach the Caribbean. At the last possible moment, there is a narrow swath of coastal land which looks relatively undisturbed. Visitors arriving by boat are treated to rainforest views along the canal banks – but a few minutes walk into the forest will reveal that the forest views are cosmetic in many cases. The western parts of the national park are being eroded and it is difficult to stop this effectively. Nevertheless, locals are becoming increasingly aware of the problems of forest loss, you can still see more wildlife here than in many parts of Central America, and I encourage you to discuss conservation issues with local boatmen, tour operators and whomever else you come across on your journey.

Information

Humid is the driest word I can think of to describe Parque Nacional Tortuguero. With rainfall of 5000 to 6000 mm throughout the park, it is one of the wettest areas in the country. Rainwear is a must all year round: an umbrella is a good idea. There is no dry

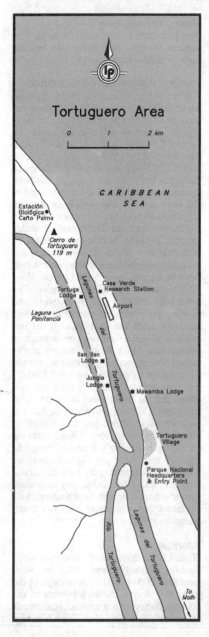

Tortuguero Area

0   1   2 km

CARIBBEAN
SEA

Estación
Biológica
Caño Palma

Cerro de
Tortuguero
119 m

Tortuga
Lodge

Casa Verde
Research Station

Laguna
Penitencia

Airport

Ilan Ilan
Lodge

Jungle
Lodge

Mawamba Lodge

Tortuguero
Village

Parque Nacional
Headquarters
& Entry Point

Río
Tortuguero

Lagunas del Tortuguero

To
Moín

season, although it does rain less in February and March and again in September. The average temperature is 26°C but it is often hotter during the middle of the day. Bring insect repellent – you'll use it.

There are three ranger stations. The Jalova ranger station is on the canal at the south entrance of the national park. Here, there is a short nature trail. The Agua Fría ranger station is near the western edge of the park, on the slopes of the Lomas de Sierpe (334 metres) which are the highest hills on the North Caribbean coast. Agua Fría reportedly can be reached from Cariari by poor unpaved roads through the villages of Maquilla (Maravilla on some maps) and La Fortuna (which is not marked on any map I've read). From La Fortuna there is a trail to the ranger station, several km away. This is a trip for the intrepid.

Most vistors go to the Tortuguero ranger station which is at the north end of the park along the canal. This is the park headquarters. (The village of Tortuguero is a few minutes walk away, just beyond the park boundary.) At the park headquarters there is a small exhibit room and information is available. The entrance fee to the park is US$1.50 per day – most visitors pay the fee at the headquarters. The ranger station can be reached by SPN radio/telephone (☎ 33 4160) – it helps if you speak Spanish.

From the headquarters there is a one km long nature trail, which is maintained, and some other trails in poor condition. You can walk along the beach north for five km (officially outside the park) or south for 30 km. Park rangers will take you on guided walks to see the turtles laying – they leave at 8 pm during the season and cost US$5. Other guided hikes and boat trips can also be arranged through the park headquarters.

Although the beaches are extensive, they are not suitable for swimming. The surf is very rough, the currents strong, and, if that's not enough to faze you, sharks regularly patrol the waters.

Turtle Watching

Travellers are allowed to visit the nesting

Top: Boathouse, Tortuguero (RR)
Bottom: Banana plantation (RR)

Top: Cabinas Black Sands (Bri-bri thatched roof), Puerto Viejo de Talamanca (RR)
Left: Parque Nacional Cahuita (RR)
Right: Puerto Viejo de Talamanca (RR)

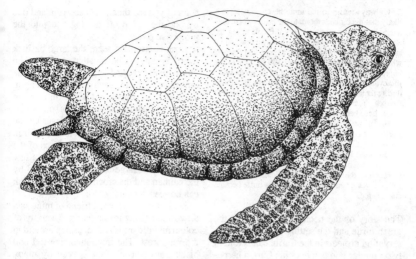

beaches and watch the turtles lay their eggs or observe the eggs hatching. However, camera flashes and flashlights may disturb the laying or attract predators to the hatchlings, so you should check with park rangers or researchers working at the Casa Verde centre for instructions. Often, researchers or park personnel will accompany visitors to the best viewing areas and explain what is going on.

If you are unable to visit during the green turtle breeding season, you can see leatherback turtles from February to July, with a peak in April and May. Hawksbill turtles nest from July to October and loggerhead turtles are also sometimes seen. Stragglers have been observed during every month of the year. Only the green turtle nests in large numbers; the other species tend to arrive singly.

Since the active protection of the nesting beach in Tortuguero, the green turtle population has recovered to some extent. In other areas, turtles are still harvested, but limits and quotas have been set.

Green Turtles Scientists write that anywhere from several hundred to over 3000 female green turtles come to the Tortuguero nesting beach during any given season. The season is from July to early October, with the highest numbers nesting in late August.

Mating occurs at the beginning of the breeding season, but the fertilised eggs which result from the mating are not laid until the female returns in subsequent seasons. During a season, an individual female may come ashore as many as seven times to lay eggs, though two or three times is more likely. During the two weeks between layings, the females spend their time in the water close to shore.

About 100 eggs are laid during any one session; these are deposited in a depression in the sand which the female makes with her flippers, and are then covered over for protection.

The incubation period is about two months, after which the hatchlings scramble out of the nest and head for the sea, usually under the cover of darkness. About half of the hatchlings make it to the water; many are preyed upon by birds, coatimundis, dogs and other animals. Once they make it to the sea, they are eaten by fish and other predators, so it is estimated that less than 1% of eggs eventually become breeding adults.

Females do not lay in successive years, but return every three years on average. During the intervening years, they migrate hundreds of km to feeding grounds elsewhere, often to the Miskito coast of Nicaragua. Tens of thousands of breeding females have been tagged at Tortuguero, and they have never been recovered in other breeding grounds, showing that they always return to the same beach to nest. It is likely that the females return to the beach where they hatched, but it has proved very difficult to tag the newborn hatchlings (which weigh only a few grams) and subsequently recover them as breeding females which weigh from 60 kg to over 200 kg. One of the biggest gaps in the understanding of the green turtle life cycle is knowing what happens to the hatchlings during their first year of life after they disappear into the sea. Year old youngsters weighing about 500 grams have been recovered.

Green turtle meat has long been eaten on the Caribbean coast. In addition, the eggs are (erroneously) considered to have aphrodisiac properties, the shell is used for ornaments and jewellery, and even the skin has a market. In the early and middle parts of this century, the huge nesting colonies of green turtles were harvested so thoroughly that the turtle became endangered.

The story of the decline and return of the green turtle and the setting up of turtle conservation projects in the Caribbean is told in two popular books by Archie Carr, a herpetologist who has done much work on turtles and played an important role in getting Tortuguero protected. The books are *The Windward Road*, A A Knopf, New York, 1956, reprinted 1979, Florida State University Press, Gainesville, Florida; and *So Excellent a Fishe*, 1967, Natural History Press, New York.

Other Wildlife

Turtles are certainly the most famous attraction at Tortuguero, but they are by no means the only one. The national park offers great wildlife viewing and bird-watching opportunities, both from the few trails within the park and on guided or paddle-yourself boat trips. All three of the local species of monkeys (howler, spider and white-faced capuchin) are often seen. Sloths, anteaters and kinkajous are also fairly frequently sighted. Manatees are protected but not often seen. Peccaries, tapirs and various members of the cat family have also been recorded, but you have to be really lucky to see them.

The reptiles and amphibians are also of great interest. Apart from the sea turtles, there are seven species of freshwater turtles. Look for them lined up on a log by the river bank, sunning themselves. It seems that as

soon as you see them, they see you, and one by one they plop off the log and into the protective river.

Lizards are often seen; the large basilisk lizard is among the most interesting. The impressively crested males look like little dinosaurs and can reach a metre in length. They have large rear feet with skin flaps on each toe enabling them to run on water, giving them their nickname of Jesus Christ lizard. Younger, smaller individuals can run as far as 20 metres across the surface of the water, but larger adults manage only a few metres. These large lizards are upstaged by the caiman and the crocodile, both of which can be seen here.

Snakes are also seen; a friend of mine saw a two metre long fer-de-lance. A variety of colourful little frogs and toads hop around in the rainforest. The thumbnail-size red and black poison-arrow frog is seen by many observant visitors, and the not so little marine toad is also common. This toad can reach 20 cm in length and weigh over a kg. About 60 species of amphibians have been recorded in the park.

Birds There are over 300 species of birds recorded in the Tortuguero area. These include oceanic species such as the magnificent frigatebird and royal tern; shore birds such as plovers and sandpipers; river birds such as kingfishers, jacanas and anhingas; and inland forest species such as hummingbirds and manakins.

Many migrant birds from North America pass through on their way south for the North American winter or north for the North American summer.

The variety of habitats contributes to the diversity of birds. On just one boat ride near Tortuguero I saw six species of herons, including the chestnut-bellied heron which *A Guide to the Birds of Costa Rica* describes as an uncommon to rare resident in humid lowland forests of the Caribbean slopes.

Tours

Mitur Tours Mitur (☎ 55 2031, 55 2262, fax 55 1946; Apartado 910-1150, San José), on

Paseo Colón, Calle 20 & 22, runs three day/two night tours to Parque Nacional Tortuguero, staying at the Ilan Ilan lodge, across the river from Tortuguero village. On the first day they drive you from San José to Moín (or another dock), where you board one of their boats, *Colorado Prince* or *Tortuguero Prince*, for a five to six hour journey through the canals to Tortuguero. The journey itself is part of the adventure – the boat slows down for photographs, and a bilingual guide identifies what you see. On the second day, guided walking and boat tours of the area are provided. A night visit to the beach is added during the turtle nesting season. You return by boat and bus on the third day. The cost is US$198 per person, double occupancy, and includes transport by bus and boat, guides, tours, accommodation in rooms with private bathrooms, meals in the lodge, and picnic lunches on the boat. Single occupancy is US$30 extra. There are usually three departures a week; on Tuesday returning Thursday, on Friday returning Sunday, and on Sunday returning Tuesday. If there is room available they will take extra passengers for US$30 one way to or from Tortuguero (you provide your own accommodation). Extra nights can also be arranged.

Cotur Tours Similar tours at similar prices are provided by Cotur (☎ 33 0155, 33 6579, fax 33 0778; Apartado 1818-1002, San José), Calle 36, Paseo Colón and Avenida 1 (50 metres north of the Toyota dealership). They use the boats *Miss Caribe* and *Miss América*, and stay in the Jungle Lodge, which also has rooms with private bath.

Mawamba Lodge A third choice is the Mawamba Lodge (see the Places to Stay section) which runs similar tour packages at slightly higher prices.

Tortuga Lodge This lodge, described in the Places to Stay section, is famous for both its wildlife tours to the park and beaches, and as a fishing lodge. The head guide and general manager, Eduardo Brown Silva, holds a world fishing record for cubera snapper, and other fishing records for Costa Rica. Tarpon season is from January to June, with 40 kg fish being routinely caught, and fish twice that size having been landed. From July to December is snook season. These average one to five kg, but fish of 24 kg have been caught here. January to May and August to October are the best months. Fishing for other fish is possible: shark, snapper, ray, grouper and jewfish are all caught.

Boat rental for natural history tours (with motor and guide) costs US$35 per hour and takes up to five people.

Night tours of the canals, with a superpowerful searchlight to seek out crocodiles, sleeping animals and night animals on the prowl, cost US$27.50 per person (two person minimum) and last about three hours. Boat rental for fishing (with motor, guide and tackle) costs US$40 per hour (two persons per boat). Speedboats from Moín to the lodge cost US$50 per person (three minimum, five maximum, 2½ hours). Slower boats taking four hours cost US$350 for up to 12 passengers. The confirmed air fare from San José to Tortuguero in single engined aircraft with five seats is US$95 per person, but if there is empty seat at the last minute, you can have it for US$45.

Reservations can be made with Costa Rica Expeditions in San José at Calle Central & Avenida 3. From outside Costa Rica, write to Department 235, PO Box 025216, Miami, FL 33102-5216, USA.

Places to Stay

Apart from camping, there is nowhere to stay in the park itself. Just outside the north boundary of the park in the village of Tortuguero (see following) you can find basic, inexpensive accommodation, food, boats and guides. North of the village there are a few comfortable and more expensive jungle lodges between one and four km away.

Camping You can camp outside the park headquarters for US$2.25 per person – just make sure your tent is waterproof. Drinking water and pit latrines are provided. The daily admission fee is an extra US$1.50 per person.

Lodges The newer *Mawamba Lodge* (☎ 23 2421, 33 1206, fax 22 4932; Apartado 6618-1000, San José), Avenida 10, Calle 24, is a nice lodge on the Tortuguero village side of the canal, which means you can walk to the village about one km away and can also go down to the beach. (From the other lodges, you need to take a boat across the canal to the village, if you want to go there.)

Costa Rica Expeditions (☎ 57 0766, fax 57 1665) runs the *Tortuga Lodge*, without a doubt the most comfortable and elegant place to stay in the Tortuguero area. The lodge is on 20 hectares of private grounds, just across from Archie Carr's famous Casa Verde turtle research station. The buildings are in attractively landscaped gardens with a large variety of ornamental tropical trees, palms, shrubs, orchids and other flowers. These attract many birds, so you can birdwatch from the lodge itself.

Beyond the gardens the tropical rainforest begins, and a troop of howler monkeys is usually heard within a few minutes walk of the lodge. The rooms are spacious and screened, and have private baths and fans. The food is plentiful and very well prepared. A radiotelephone is available to make connections with anywhere in the world. The staff and guides are good and speak English.

You can get to the lodge by boat, or by flying in to the Tortuguero airport nearby. Costa Rica Tours will make all arrangements for the type of tour you want. Current high-season prices are US$65.50/77.50/91.75 for one, two or three people in standard rooms, or US$93.50/113/130 in deluxe rooms. Large and delicious 'all-you-can-eat' meals are served and cost US$8.25 for breakfast, US$13.25 for lunch or dinner. See the preceding Tours section for information on the tours run by this lodge.

The *Ilan Ilan Lodge* and *Jungle Lodge* are mentioned in the preceding Tours section.

Getting There & Away

Most visitors either arrive by boat along the canals on day trips, or continue through the park to either the village of Tortuguero, or to one of the nearby lodges.

There is an airport four km north of the park – see under Tortuguero for details.

Day trips to Tortuguero are offered from some of the Limón hotels, but these do not give enough time at the park. They are better than nothing if you are pressed for time. Day tours are also offered from San José but, if you allow for four or five hours of total driving time, this makes for a long and tiring day and again gives inadequate time in the park. Best are overnight trips with early morning or evening visits to the park along the canals.

TORTUGUERO

The inhabitants of this sleepy little village make most of their living from turtles and the national park. They work in the hotels and tour lodges or as park rangers or researchers, or guides and boatmen; and a few do a little farming and fishing. Generally speaking, a good balance has been struck between the interests of the local people, visitors and the turtles. This is mainly because access is limited to boats and planes – if there were a road here it would undoubtedly be a different story.

Instead of harvesting the turtles, the people exploit them and the accompanying park in non-destructive yet economically satisfactory ways. In the centre of the village is an informative kiosk explaining the natural history, cultural history, geography and climate of the region. The community appears to take some pride in 'its' turtles and national park.

Green Turtle Research Station

This is locally known as 'Casa Verde' (Green House), probably because of its (at one time) greenish paint job rather than because of the green turtles. Green turtle research has been carried out from here since 1954. The station is next to the airstrip, about four km north of Tortuguero.

Canoeing

Several places in Tortuguero just north of the entrance to the park have a sign announcing boats for hire. You can paddle yourself in a dugout canoe for about US$1.25 to US$1.50 per hour, or go with a guide for about US$2.50 to US$3 per person per hour. Some of the local guides are Damma, Bananero and Jim.

In the village centre is a pulpería where you can ask about other guides or boat rentals. The La Culebra ('The Snake') Centro Social next to the pulpería is another place to ask. Although it is cheaper to paddle your own canoe, it is well worth hiring a guide, at least for a few hours, because you get to see so much more.

Guides can also be hired from the nearby lodges. These guides use motorboats and are substantially more expensive – their tours cover more ground, and they normally switch the motor off and paddle for a while.

Hiking

Apart from visiting the waterways of the park and the beaches, a climb can be made of 119 metre high Cerro de Tortuguero, about six km north-east of the village. You need to hire a boat and guide to get there. Cerro Tortuguero is the highest point right on the coast anywhere north of Limón – it actually lies just within the southern border of Refugio Nacional de Fauna Silvestre Barra del Colorado. There are views of the forest, canals, sea and birds.

Places to Stay & Eat

Tortuguero Village Tortuguero has several cheap places. The friendly and family-run *Hospedaje Mariscal* has small rooms with shared bath and fans for US$10.50 a double. The owner of the clean *Cabinas Sabina* charges about the same in her breezier upstairs rooms; downstairs rooms are US$4.50 per person. Food is available here. If these are full, ask around; you may be able to stay in someone's house. Another choice is the similarly priced *Cabinas Tatané* which is a five minute boat ride away – ask at the pulpería to get in contact with the owner.

Restaurants charge about US$3 to US$4 per meal, and it is fairly basic food. Some travellers report that slightly cheaper and better meals are available by asking around and eating in private houses. One of the cheapest places seems to be the *Soda La Liliana* which serves basic casados for US$3.

A recommended cook is *Miss Juni* who cooks for the national park rangers and will cook for travellers with a day's notice. She charges US$2.50 for breakfast and US$4.75 for dinner. She is planning on building cabinas.

Las Brisas del Mar is a local bar with cheap beers and cabins alongside – the cabins looked closed down on my last visit. Other local places are opening up with the increase of tourism.

Casa Verde At the *Casa Verde* there are basic dormitory rooms which accommodate 18 people, and camping outside is possible; a rain roof is being built to provide shelter for campers. There are communal kitchen and bathroom facilities, and electricity. The station accommodates researchers and student groups, but is not designed for tourists. Permission to stay and more information is available from the Caribbean Conservation Corporation (☎/fax 25 7516), Apartado 246-2050, San Pedro, San José; or from the CCC (☎ (904) 373 6441, fax (904) 375 2449), PO Box 2866, Gainesville, FL 32602, USA.

COTERC The acronym stands for Canadian Organization for Tropical Education and Rainforest Conservation – a non-profit organisation. They operate the Estación Biológica Caño Palma in the Caño Palma area just north of Cerro Tortuguero and about seven km north of Tortuguero village. Although the biological station is actually within the southern boundary of Refugio Nacional de Fauna Silvestre Barra del Colorado, access is easiest from Tortuguero.

The station is a research and education facility but will accommodate naturalist guests when space is available. The buildings are 200 metres from the Caribbean, but separated from it by a river. Rivers, streams and lagoons can be explored and there is a trail system into the rainforest. Visitors stay in a simple dormitory with a capacity of 13 people – bunks and bedding are provided. There are outdoor showers and bathrooms. There is also a covered hammock area with four hammocks, a study area, kitchen and dining area. Rates in 1993 were US$35 per person per day including three meals and use of trails accompanied by local guides (this will probably be subject to a US$5 to US$10 increase in 1994/95). Guided boat excursions are US$25 per half day.

The station can be reached by hiring a boat from Tortuguero. If you make prior arrangements, the staff will pick you up either in Tortuguero airport or village for US$10.

For further information and reservations, contact Marilyn Cole, COTERC (☎ (416) 683 2116, fax (416) 392 4979), PO Box 335, Pickering, Ontario L1V 2R6, Canada. Drop-in visitors can usually find space.

Lodges See Places to Stay in the Parque Nacional Tortuguero entry for details of the lodges near Tortuguero. The two lodges across the river from Tortuguero are used by the tour companies, but you could probably stay in one of them for about US$30 if they have room.

About a km north of Tortuguero, the *Mawamba Lodge* caters mainly to pre-arranged groups but would rent you a room if they are not full – about US$30/45 single/double. The luxurious *Tortuga Lodge* about four km north of the village on the other side of the canal is another possibility.

Getting There & Away

Air The small airport is four km north of Tortuguero by the Casa Verde, across the canal from the Tortuguero Lodge. Travelair (☎ 32 7883, 20 3054, fax 20 0413) has flights from San José at 6 am daily except Sunday. The return flight leaves at 7 am. Fares are US$51 one way or US$88 round trip. Travelair has an office next to the souvenir shop in Tortuguero village. Planes can also be chartered in to this airport.

Boat See the Moín section or Tours above for details of boats.

REFUGIO NACIONAL DE FAUNA SILVESTRE BARRA DEL COLORADO

At 92,000 hectares, Barra del Colorado is the biggest national wildlife refuge in Costa Rica. It is virtually an extension of Tortuguero National Park and the two are combined to form a Regional Conservation Unit.

There are several differences between Tortuguero and Barra del Colorado: Barra (a common name for the area) is not as famous for its marine turtles (although they are found in the reserve); it is more remote; and it is more difficult to visit cheaply.

Despite being a national wildlife refuge, people come here for the sportfishing rather than for natural history tours. But there are also similarities: Barra receives as much rainfall as Tortuguero, and has much of the same variety of wildlife, also best seen from a boat.

The northern border of the refuge is the Río San Juan (the Nicaraguan border). The area was politically sensitive during the 1980s, which contributed somewhat to the isolation of the reserve. Since the relaxing of Sandinista-Contra hostilities in 1990, it has become easier to journey north along the Río Sarapiquí and east along the San Juan to the reserve. This would be an interesting trip.

The western part of the refuge is less known, but that doesn't mean no-one goes there. Infrared satellite photography is showing large amounts of unauthorised logging and road construction at the western boundary of the refuge. Undoubtedly, illegal logging activity is going on within Barra del Colorado, but there are not enough reserve wardens to be able to police the area properly. The western part of the refuge is now accessible to vehicles and there is a daily bus (road and weather conditions allowing) to Puerto Lindo on the Río Colorado in the heart of the reserve. This road brings in loggers, ranchers, farmers and colonists and does not bode well for the western part of Barra del Colorado, but the eastern sections are very swampy and not conducive to easy logging, so that area, at least, may change less.

Surprisingly, there are over 2000 inhabitants in the area, and they want the rough road to Puerto Lindo to be improved and are petitioning the government to make the road all-weather.

Places to Stay

Most visitors stay in the village of Barra del Colorado, though there is also the possibility of staying at a field station at Caño Palma, which is the south end of the refuge. It is much closer to the Tortuguero airport and village than it is to the village of Barra del Colorado (see the Tortuguero section).

In the village of Barra del Colorado, the cheapest hotel is next to the airport at *Cabinas Tarponland* (☎ 71 6917). Rooms are about US$30 a double and the owner both knows the area well and is very helpful in arranging local trips and transportation.

If the Tarponland is too expensive for you, you are allowed to camp in the refuge, but there are no facilities. You may be able to find somewhere inexpensive to stay with a family in Barra del Colorado village if you ask around.

The rest of the lodges detailed here operate expensive all-inclusive sportfishing charters. ('All-inclusive' does not include tips to fishing guides and lodge staff.) Tarpon from January to May and snook in September and October are the fish of choice – but there is decent fishing all year round.

The *Isla de Pesca* (☎ 71 6776; in San José ☎ 23 4560, fax 55 2533, Calle 24, Paseo de Colón) offers both fishing charters and 'tropical river safaris'. Their river safaris fly into Barra del Colorado from San José, visit Tortuguero, stay overnight in Isla de Pesca, and return to San José via the Río San Juan and Río Sarapiquí, and bus from Puerto Viejo de Sarapiquí. The two day/one night tour costs US$290 per person (two minimum) and is a comfortable and efficient way of seeing this part of Costa Rica. Fishing packages range from three days to a week at a cost comparable to other lodges.

Another good fishing lodge is *Casa Mar* (☎ 41 2820; in the USA ☎ 1 (800) 327 2880, (305) 664 8833 or (305) 664 4615, fax (305) 664 3692), PO Box 787, Islamorada, FL 33036). It's a small lodge set in a pleasant garden. All-you-can-eat home-cooked meals are included in the rates. They prefer to book seven day, Saturday to Saturday, fishing charters, though you can stay for as few as three days if you wish, preferably either arriving or departing on a Saturday. They have two seasons: from January to mid-May and September to October. Their seven day charters are US$2495/3990 a single/double, including round-trip air travel from San José, all fishing, accommodation, meals and an open bar. They will make San José hotel reservations (at additional cost) upon request.

The longest established and best known lodge on the Caribbean coast is the excellent *Río Colorado Lodge* (☎ 32 8610, 32 4063, fax 31 5987; Apartado 5094-1000, San José; in the USA ☎ 1 (800) 243 9777, fax (813) 933 3280). They have an office in the Hotel Corobicí in San José. The attractive tropical-style lodge buildings are built on stilts near the mouth of the Río Colorado. Rooms have fans and electric showers, and are breezy and pleasant. The food has been recommended and is all-you-can-eat family style. For relaxation after a day of fishing there is a happy hour with free rum drinks, a lounging area with a pool table and other games, and a video room with satellite TV. Most guests are anglers but non-fishing visitors can stay here for US$75 a day including meals. The lodge is open all year round and offers boat, bilingual guide, all meals and accomodation for US$378/676 per day single/double. Transportation to the lodge is extra, a fishing licence costs US$30 and you should bring your own tackle (they have some loaner equipment) and provide transportation to the lodge.

The lodge will also arrange complete packages, including licence, flights from and to San José, a hotel night in San José at either end of your trip, airport transfers and services described above for three full days fishing for US$1520/2620 a single/double or five full days fishing for US$2285/3990. They locally advertise $uper $ummer $aver $pecials from 15 June to 15 August – three full days of fishing, a fishing licence, three nights at the lodge, all meals, and air travel from San José for US$675 per person (or US$460 for two days). They'll take you fishing in Nicaragua on request (an extra US$25 per day) and could arrange transportation from or to San José via the Río Sarapiquí and Río San Juan if you wanted them to.

Getting There & Away

Air Many visitors arrive by air from San José. You can charter a light plane or take a regularly scheduled flight. SANSA flies on Tuesday, Thursday and Saturday at 6 am, returning at 6.50 am; the fare is US$26 each way. Travelair flies daily except Sunday at 6 am, returning at 7 am; the fare is US$51 one way or US$88 round trip. (Note that these airlines depart from different airports in San José.)

Bus There is a daily 6 am bus leaving from the small riverside community of Puerto Lindo, about half an hour by motorboat up the Río Colorado. The bus goes to the town of Cariari (two hours) from where there are buses to Guápiles. The road is sometimes closed after heavy rains, but provides the cheapest link with San José for local inhabitants. I don't know what time the Cariari to Puerto Lindo bus leaves. Try calling the Soda La Parada (☎ 76 7120) for bus information.

Boat A few of the boats from Moín to Tortuguero continue to Barra, but there is no regular service. Boats can be hired in Tortuguero to take you up to Barra for about US$50; they'll take three to five passengers. If you don't have a group and have time on your hands, you could probably do it cheaper by asking the locals and going with them.

Boats are available between Barra and Puerto Lindo to meet the bus to Cariari. The boat leaves at 4.50 am.

Occasional and irregular passenger boats go from Barra to Puerto Viejo de Sarapiquí via the Río San Juan and Río Sarapiqui, or boats can be hired to do this trip anytime.

Crossing to Nicaragua

Day trips along the Río San Juan and some offshore fishing trips enter Nicaraguan territory but no special visa is required (though your passport should be carried for checkpoints along the San Juan). The Nicaraguan village at the mouth of the Río San Juan is San Juan del Norte – there are no hotels here though accommodation can be found with local families. San Juan del Norte is linked with the rest of Nicaragua by irregular passenger boats sailing up the San Juan to San Carlos on Lago de Nicaragua. However, this is not normally used as an entry point into Nicaragua – ask locally about the possibilities.

The South Caribbean

A road (still badly potholed and broken up since the 1991 earthquake) leads south-east of Puerto Limón, approximately paralleling the Caribbean coast, until Sixaola on the Panamanian border is reached. The road provides access by car and bus to most of the southern Caribbean coast and this area is more visited than the coast north of Puerto Limón.

AVIARIOS DEL CARIBE

This small wildlife sanctuary and B&B (fax 58 4459 – they check the fax about twice a week; Apartado 569-7300, Limón) is 31 km south of Limón, or about one km north from where the coastal highway crosses the Río Estrella. The sanctuary is an 88 hectare island in the delta of the Río Estrella, and the owners (Luis and Judy Arroyo) have recorded 255 species of birds here – and are still counting. After the 1991 earthquake the coast rose about a metre in this area, the buildings were destroyed and the island became partly attached to the mainland. It remains protected nevertheless, and a variety of local nature-oriented excursions are offered. The most popular is the US$25 kayak tour which lasts about three hours. A guide paddles you quietly through the Estrella delta, getting close to a variety of birds and animals. Sloths, monkeys, caiman and river otters are seen – in fact, there is an orphaned sloth, named Buttercup, on the grounds. Buttercup's mother was killed by a car and the owners have raised the youngster, who was about five weeks old when they found it. They also have all sorts of interesting other animals, as well as an ant house and a poison-arrow frog hatchery!

The small B&B is an attractive place to stay. Art by Mindy Lighthipe graces the walls – her paintings of butterflies are stunning. A balcony provides a view of the garden and forest, and there is a library and a games room. Rooms are spacious with fans, comfortable beds, restful décor and well-designed bathrooms with hot water. Rates, including breakfast, are about US$46/70 single/double. Dinners are available on request.

Any bus to Cahuita will drop you off at the entrance.

VALLE DEL RÍO ESTRELLA

The Estrella river valley is a long-established cacao-growing region. There are plantations of several other types of tropical fruit as well. This is the only place in the Caribbean lowlands where trains still run regularly. (See the Limón entry for details of timetables.) You can also reach here by road by turning right (west) on the signed road just south of the bridge over the Río Estrella. This is the route to Hitoy Cerere.

RESERVA BIOLÓGICA HITOY CERERE

This 9154 hectare reserve is 60 km south of Limón by road, but only half that distance as the vulture glides. Although not far from civilisation, it is one of the most rugged and rarely visited reserves in the country. There is a ranger station but otherwise there are no facilities – no campsites, nature trails or information booths. The reserve lies between about 150 and 1000 metres in elevation on rugged terrain on the south side of the Río Estrella valley.

Although few people come here, that is no reason for ignoring it. The reserve sounds like a fascinating place and, being so rarely visited, offers a great wilderness experience in an area which has been little explored. It has been called the wettest reserve in the parks system – expect almost four metres of rain each year in these dense evergreen forests.

Hiking is permitted but the steep and slippery terrain and dense vegetation make it a possibility only for the most fit and determined hikers. Heavy rainfall and broken terrain combine to produce many beautiful streams, rivers and waterfalls. Hiking along a stream bed is one way of getting through the dense vegetation. Reportedly, there is one more-or-less maintained trail leading south of the ranger station for several km. There are many different plants, birds, mammals and other animals – many of which have not yet been recorded because of the remoteness of the site.

Information

Visitors should call the Servicio de Parques Nacionales in San José to make sure that somebody will be at the ranger station when they arrive. Sleeping at the ranger station for a small fee is a possibility if arranged in advance.

Getting There & Away

Take a bus or train to Valle la Estrella from Limón. From the end of the bus line it is about a further 10 or 15 km to the reserve along a dirt road. There are 4WD taxis available to drive you there for US$10 or so. The drivers are reliable, and will come back to pick you up at a prearranged time. From Cahuita (about 30 km away) 4WD taxis will take you to the reserve for about US$30.

CAHUITA

This is a small village about 43 km south-east of Limón by road. It is known for the attractive beaches nearby, many of which are in the Parque Nacional Cahuita which adjoins the village to the south.

Until the 1970s, Cahuita was quite isolated from the rest of Costa Rica. A ride in an old bus on a dirt road, a river crossing by wobbly canoe, and a train ride were required to get to Limón – this journey could take half a day. Now the paved road which links Cahuita to Limón has cut the journey to a 45 minute drive under good conditions (though road conditions after the 1991 earthquake made this journey twice as long at the time of writing). The 1987 opening of the new road from Limón to San José means that Cahuita is now three to four hours from the capital by car. Despite this, the area retains much of its remote, provincial and unhurried flavour. Most Costa Ricans still use the Pacific coast for their beach vacations, and there are few luxury hotel developments on the Caribbean. Those hotels which do exist tend to be in high demand at weekends and school holidays (from mid-December to February, Easter), particularly during the highland dry season (from January to May), so travel midweek if you can. If you have to arrive on a Friday or Saturday, make a reservation or get there very early in the day.

The approximately 3500 inhabitants of the Cahuita district are predominantly Black and many speak a Creole form of English. This can be confusing at first, because some phrases do not mean the same as other speakers of English are used to. For example 'All right!' means 'Hello!' and 'Okay!' means 'Goodbye!'.

The people are of Jamaican descent and colonised the Costa Rican coast in the middle of the 19th century. They used to subsist mainly by small-scale farming and fishing, but tourism is becoming an increasingly important part of the economy. The influx of tourist cash helps improve the standards of living but at a cultural cost. Traditional ways of life slowly become eroded and, inevitably, the local people have some difficulties in adjusting to the new, and sometimes demanding or obnoxious, tourist population. Nevertheless, much of the Creole culture remains for those who look for it, particularly in cooking, music and knowledge of medicinal plants.

Cahuita is expanding as a tourist destination, with more hotels being built and other facilities being developed. But the main street is still made of sand – more suited to horses and clunky wheeled bicycles than the cars and 4WDs which tourists drive amidst clouds of choking dust. One local lady told me that the tourists' vehicles were the biggest problem that tourism has caused; she couldn't even hang her laundry out to dry in front of her house because of the dust. This is an example of the clash between 20th century tourism and a 19th century way of life – travellers are urged to enjoy their visit but to try not to impose their own values upon the areas they are visiting.

Information

Tourist Office Tourist information is available from places listed in the following Tours & Rentals section.

Money It's best to bring what you think you'll need. However, Cahuita Tours will change travellers' cheques if they have enough colones, and the better hotels will help you out as well.

Telephone Cahuita has only one telephone number: ☎ 58 1515. To call a hotel, call the Cahuita number and ask for the place you want or the extension if you know it. To make outbound calls, go to the public phone office at the Soda Uvita near the parque or to Cahuita Tours.

Warnings Many travellers enjoy their visit to the area – others find that the coastal way of life is not for them.

One couple told me that they felt uncomfortable in Cahuita because they met a few young men in a bar who accused them of being racist for not buying them drinks. The couple had also been offered drugs (which they had refused) when walking along the beach. Their hotel room had cockroaches and they'd had to wait an hour in a local restaurant before they were served. They felt as if they were unwelcome outsiders and did not enjoy their stay.

It is true that there are some people living on the coast who try to take advantage of tourists, but this is not generally a major problem. Most travellers find that the relaxed pace, the mainly friendly people, the lack of a highly developed tourist infrastructure, the cultural diversity, and the attractive environment all contribute to an enjoyable visit. But travellers should beware of rip-offs. Keep your hotel room locked and the windows closed. There have been several reports of theft from rooms, including the 'fishing' technique which involves slicing open the netting over a window and using a long, hooked stick to fish out whatever valuables are 'caught'. Never leave gear unattended on beaches when swimming, don't walk the beaches alone at night, and be prudent if entering some of the local bars.

Not many of the locals are into smoking ganga or snorting coke – but those who are will probably be found hanging around the few bars in town. They don't reflect the population as a whole, who are not particularly happy with young travellers coming on a search for drugs and a permanent high. Beware of drug sellers who may be in cahoots with the police.

I have heard complaints from solo women travellers who feel that some of the local men are too demanding in their romantic advances. Female travellers may feel that travelling with a friend is safer than travelling alone. Some women do travel alone and do have a good time, but not everyone is adept at avoiding unpleasant situations.

'Safe sex' is rarely practised here, but casual sex is a temptation. AIDS and other sexually transmitted diseases are certainly here. If you can't resist anyone who gently lays their hand on yours and enticingly whispers, 'Black and White; White and Black', you should bring your own condoms. Better still, talk to the locals about AIDS – it's in Costa Rica but few ticos know much about it.

Please note that, despite the casual atmosphere both here and in other coastal areas, nude bathing is definitely not accepted. Also, wearing skimpy bathing clothes in the villages is frowned upon. Wearing at least a T-shirt and shorts is expected and appreciated.

And a final point. Both locals and readers report that a few of the European owners of some of the Cahuita accommodation are insensitive – indeed racist – in their attitudes to the local Black population. Obviously, this is not a blanket statement for all lodges operated by Europeans and applies to only a handful of places, but be aware of this problem and, if you sense it happening, take your business elsewhere.

Beaches

There are three nearby beaches within walking distance. At the north-west end of Cahuita there is a long black-sand beach with good swimming. Some people think that the black-sand beach has better swimming than the white-sand beach at the eastern end of town. This latter beach is in the national park, and a trail in the jungle behind the beach leads you to a third beach about six km away. These last two beaches are separated by a rocky headland with a coral reef offshore that is suitable for snorkelling. This is more fully described in the section on Parque Nacional Cahuita.

Tours & Rentals

There are currently three places which rent equipment and arrange tours; Moray's (☎ ext 216), Cahuita Tours and Rentals (☎ ext 232) and Lunazul Viajes (☎ ext 243). Other places may open by the time you get there. You should shop around for the best deals – the following prices are approximate. These places rent mask, snorkel and fins (US$5 per day), bicycles (US$5 to US$10 per day), surfboards (US$10 per day) and binoculars (US$4.50 per day).

Boat trips to the reef in a glass-bottomed boat, with snorkelling opportunities, are US$15 per person for three or four hours. Drinks are provided. Day trips to Tortuguero are about US$60 to US$70. Guided horseback and hiking trips into the local national park areas are available, as are a variety of

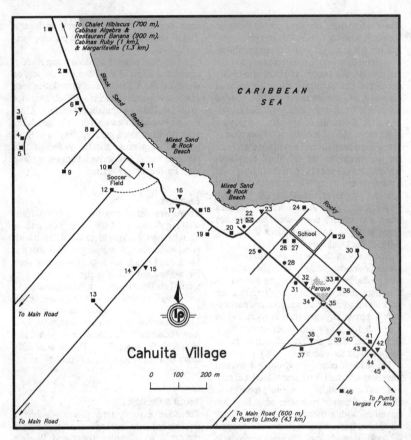

To Chalet Hibiscus (700 m),
Cabinas Algebra &
Restaurant Banana (900 m),
Cabinas Ruby (1 km),
& Margaritaville (1.3 km)

CARIBBEAN
SEA

Black Sand Beach

Mixed Sand
& Rock
Beach

Mixed Sand
& Rock
Beach

Rocky shore

Soccer
Field

School

Parque

To Main Road

Cahuita Village

0   100   200 m

To Main Road

To Punta
Vargas (7 km)

To Main Road (600 m)
& Puerto Limón (43 km)

taxi services and visits to places like Hitoy Cerere and the Bribri indigenous reserves.

Often, the best prices are available directly from the guides. The Asociación Talamanqueño de Ecoturismo y Conservación (ATEC), based in Puerto Viejo de Talamanca (which see for more information), has local guides who will take you on half to full day hiking tours through old cacao plantations and into the rainforest around Cahuita – the emphasis in these tours is the Afro-Caribbean lifestyle plus natural history. They also have visits to Parque Nacional Cahuita and bird-watching walks. Some local guides which have been recommended are Carlos Mairena and Jose McCloud (☎ ext 288) and Walter Cunningham (☎ ext 229) who specialises in birding. They charge about US$15 per person for a three hour tour, but will give students and groups a discount.

Places to Stay
Reservations are recommended for Friday and Saturday in the dry season. Remember that all Cahuita has only one telephone number: ☎ 58 1515. Just the extensions are given following.

■ PLACES TO STAY

1 Bungalow Malú
2 Hotel Jaguar
3 Cabinas Topo
4 Cabinas Iguana
5 Cabinas Jardín Tropical
6 Cabinas Brigitte
8 Cabinas Black Beach
9 Jardín Rocalla
10 Atlántida Lodge
12 Cabins Colibrí Paradise
13 Cabinas Margarita
18 Cabinas Bello Horizonte
19 Cabinas Tito
20 Moray's
24 Cabinas Surfside
26 Cabinas Smith
27 Cabinas Surfside (Main site)
29 Cabinas Brisas del Mar
30 Cabinas Jenny
33 Cabinas Safari
36 Cabinas Palmer
37 Cabinas Correoso
40 Cabinas Vaz
41 Hotel Cahuita
43 Cabinas Sol y Mar
46 Cabinas Rhode Island

▼ PLACES TO EAT

7 La Ancla Restaurant & Reggae Bar
11 Restaurant Brisas del Mar
14 Cafeteria Vishnu
15 Pizzería El Cactus
16 Las Rocas
17 Pastry Shop
23 Miss Edith's
27 Restaurant Surfside
32 Pizzería Revolución
34 Salon Vaz
38 Restaurant El Tipíco
39 Restaurant Defi
40 Restaurant Vaz
42 Restaurant Cahuita National Park
43 Soda Sol y Mar
44 Restaurant Vista del Mar

OTHER

20 Moray's
21 Police
22 Post Office & Telegrams
25 Cahuita Tours & Rentals
28 Hannias Bar
31 Soda Uvita & Public Phone
35 Bus Stop
36 Lunazul Viajes
45 Kelly Creek Station (Parque Nacional Cahuita Entrance)

Places to Stay – bottom end

Budget travellers will find that the cheapest hotels in Cahuita are not as cheap as some parts of Costa Rica. Single travellers, in particular, will have a hard time in finding cheap rooms because many are rented by the room for two, three or four people. Prices have as much as doubled since the last edition – so don't be surprised if they continue to rise. Most hotels have cold water only unless I specify otherwise.

There are no real campsites in town, though you can put up your tent behind the Cafeteria Vishnu if you want. Facilities are very basic and the charge is about US$1.50 per person.

In a good location near the beach, one of the least expensive places is *Cabinas Bello Horizonte* (☎ ext 206) which has five basic but clean rooms with communal bathrooms

for US$5.50 per person and three cabins with private shower for US$25. The *Cabinas Brigitte* has a few basic rooms for US$7.25/9 single/double and rents horses too – among the cheapest horseback rates in town. Ask about bicycle rentals as well. *Moray's* (☎ ext 216) has some very basic rooms for US$9 a double. A reader writes that *Erica's Cabinas* (near Cabinas Margarita) has two clean rooms each with two beds for US$7.25 per room – the shower is outside. (I didn't see this place when I was there, so it's not on the map.)

Cabinas Correoso (☎ ext 214) offers clean and good accommodation for US$12.50/15 a double/triple with bath and fan. *Cabinas Surfside* (☎ ext 246) has modern, plain, concrete-block rooms, but they are clean, and have a fan and a private bath. Rates are US$12 for a double and there is a restaurant on the premises. I've had reports that they've recently begun charging each guest US$3.30 extra and providing breakfast. They have a couple of better cabins a block away, right near the rocky shoreline, for US$17. *Cabinas Vaz* (☎ ext 218) has clean concrete-block rooms with bath and fan for US$14.50/18.50 single/double (some sleep up to five people) – though the loud music from the restaurant downstairs can be heard in the rooms above it. The *Cabinas Rhode Island* (☎ ext 264) has some very clean small rooms for US$15.50 a double and some good larger rooms for US$18.50/22 a double/triple with bath and fan.

If you want to stay away from town, try *Cabinas Algebra* (☎ 58 2623 – leave a message) which is over 2.5 km north-west of town on the black beach road. They have simple but adequate cabins with shower and fan for about US$20 and a decent restaurant is attached. About 100 metres further out is the similarly priced *Cabinas Ruby*.

Places to Stay – middle

The clean *Cabinas Smith* is run by a friendly woman and has good rooms with electric showers and fans for US$22/26 a double/triple. *Cabinas Black Beach* (☎ ext 251) has some pleasant rooms with balcony and private bath for US$21 a double or about US$30 for four (there is a double bed and a bunk bed). *Cabinas Margarita* (☎ ext 205) has clean rooms with cold water for US$21 and with hot water for US$26. *Cabinas Brisas del Mar* (☎ ext 267) charges US$22 for clean double rooms with cold showers. The *Cabinas Sol y Mar* (☎ ext 237) has decent rooms with fan and shower for US$22. *Cabinas Jenny* (☎ ext 256) also charges US$22 for the cheapest rooms; US$27 gets you a upstairs room with sea views and private bath.

The *Hotel Cahuita* (☎ ext 201) is one of the few places in this price range that has single rooms – they charge US$12.50 per person which is OK for a single but over-priced for a double. The rooms have fans and private bath, but the ground floor units are

rather dank. Opposite is a hotel which has been under construction since at least 1990 – who knows when it might open. The *Cabinas Palmer* (☎ ext 243) is owned by friendly locals who operate a tour agency and beach store (selling stuff like sunscreen and camera film – not beaches). The plain but clean rooms have cold showers and rent for US$20/25 single/double – some larger rooms have kitchenettes. Across the street, the same people own the *Cabinas Safari* (☎ ext 243) with a few newer, nicer rooms for US$30 – still cold water though.

Jardín Rocalla has just one nice cabina for US$25. *Bungalow Malú* has a few pleasant rooms with electric showers for US$30. *Cabinas Jardín Tropical* has two nice cabins with refrigerator for US$30. *Cabinas Iguana* has a couple of nice rooms with shared showers for US$14.50 a double (usually full of long-stay guests) and a couple of even nicer cabins with refrigerator and hot plate, sleeping two to four people for US$25 to US$40. *Cabinas Topo* has one nice cabin with hot showers for US$40. None of these places has a phone, and all are small, quiet and out of the way.

Cabinas Tito (☎ ext 286) has pleasant rooms with cold showers and fans, some with kitchenette, for US$22/30/40 for single/double/triple. If you really want to get away from the Cahuita scene, the *Chalet Hibiscus* (fax 58 1543) are set in attractive beach-side gardens with many flowering bushes and plants. They are almost 2.5 km north-west of the main bus stop in 'downtown' Cahuita, if you're looking for peace and quiet. Pleasant, rustic-looking wooden rooms with private cold shower, table fans, and mosquito screens are US$35 a double. Closer to town, the *Cabinas Colibrí Paradise* (☎ ext 263) is also attractive, in a quiet location behind the soccer field. It's easy enough to walk there on a footpath from the beachside road, but if you have a car you need to drive in from the main Puerto Limón-Sixaola road. The handful of cabins come with fans, kitchenette, refrigerator, and electric showers and rent for US$35.

The *Atlántida Lodge* (☎ ext 213) is a nice place with about 30 thatched-roof rooms set in pleasant gardens. Rooms with fans and hot showers go for US$40/46/52 for single/double/triple including full breakfast. The owners and staff are friendly and helpful. The lodge is about a km north-west of the bus stop – if you have a reservation they'll pick you up. They also have a private bus from San José several times a week – call for times. The fare is US$30 direct to the lodge.

The *Hotel Jaguar* (☎ ext 238; in San José 26 3775, fax 26 4693; Apartado 7046-1000, San José) is opposite the black-sand beach and just under two km from downtown: two minutes to an ocean dip and 22 minutes walk to downtown. The hotel is set in extensive grounds – the forest at the back has trails, and sloths and other animals have been reported frequently. The helpful Canadian/tica owners, the Vigneaults, are usually in evidence. The modern buildings house some of the most spacious rooms in Cahuita. Although they lack fans, they are built in such a way that cross-breezes and natural ventilation keep the rooms airy and comfortable – an interesting design which saves on electricity. All rooms come with private bathroom; about half of them have hot showers. Rates are US$30/55 single/double and are good value when you consider that they include breakfast and dinner. Breakfasts are good and varied, but the dinners are among the best along the entire coast. Paul Vigneault is often found in the kitchen working on his latest favourite new dish. The menu changes every night. Recent repasts have included corvina steamed in banana leaves in herbs, chicken in papaya sauce, steak in peanut sauce, and breadfruit french-fries. Call it Nouvelle Cahuita style – it's good.

Places to Eat

An eatery that has attracted the attention of travellers over the years is *Miss Edith's*. Guide books rhapsodised about Miss Edith 'cooking up a storm' of Caribbean food – and she has been so successful that the restaurant is no longer a little local place on the front porch of someone's home, but is a popular and often crowded tourist hang-out. The food is still good, however – the varied meals on the tourist menu are around US$6 to US$9. Locals and savvy budget travellers can get a decent casado for about US$3. Alcohol wasn't served on my last visit. (As the local people get older, they traditionally earn a place of respect in the community. This is reflected by their form of address; they are called Miss or Mister, followed by their first name – hence, Miss Edith. You wouldn't refer to a young person in this way.)

Several places have opened over the last few years and are currently very popular. One of those most in vogue is *Restaurant Defi* which plays Caribbean music (occasionally live) and has sand (as opposed to sawdust) on its wood floors. They serve anything from creole cooking to Italian food (rasta pasta?) and are open from early breakfast till late. Service is laid back.

There are two well-recommended restaurants on a side-road north-west of downtown. The reasonably priced *Cafeteria Vishnu* is a good choice for vegetarian eaters – choices include home-made granola, milkshakes and multigrain bread (though hamburgers are also served). They are open only for breakfast and lunch. Across the street, the *Pizzería El Cactus* serves a US$5 pizza that will feed most very hungry people and will do for two if you're not starving – they are open just for dinner. Closer to downtown, the *Pizzería Revolución* is also quite popular – one reader describes it as 'new age rasta' (you figure that out!) They serve local and vegetarian food as well.

Out along the road towards the black-sand beach are *Las Rocas* and *Restaurant Las Brisas del Mar* – a couple of popular beachfront restaurants. They're good places for a meal or a beer and a snack whilst being cooled by ocean breezes – but the beachfront location means slightly higher prices. Near to Las Rocas is the *Pastry Shop* which bakes delicious bread, cakes and pies. The *La Ancla Restaurant and Reggae Bar* (locally known as 'Samwell's') is another choice – a limited menu but a popular place for a beer with the rastas. For people staying in the places north-west of town, the *Restaurant Banana* by the Cabinas Algebra sells good local food. About 500 metres further north is the Canadian-run *Margaritaville* which advertises home-cooked dinners daily from 6 pm.

Back in the heart of town, the *Restaurant Cahuita National Park* is by the entrance to the national park and is a little pricey, but popular because of its location. They serve breakfast, lunch and dinner. The food is quite good and the place tends to be frequented by tourists who eat and drink at the outside tables – the locals drink inside. The newer *Restaurant Vista Del Mar* across the street is also open all day long and serves seafood. Near the Vista del Mar there is a little snack hut which is open erratically, selling delicious home-made empanadas and other snacks until they're gone. Local ladies sometimes set up shop and sell home-made stews and snacks direct from the cooking pot – a popular location is in front of the Salon Vaz at night when the disco is going.

Nearby are the *Soda Sol y Mar*, for breakfasts and other meals, and the *Restaurant Vaz*, for meals and drinks. Both are attached to the cabinas of the same names – the Vaz is recommended for good gallo pinto for breakfast and shrimp for dinner. The nearby *Restaurant El Típico* has a variety of pricey but good local food – budget travellers should order the usual casado for US$3. The *Salon Vaz* is more of a bar than a restaurant but serves local food during the day. A hotel with a decent restaurant is the *Surfside* with meals around US$5 or US$6. Some of the best dinners are at the previously mentioned *Hotel Jaguar* – you should make a reservation if you aren't staying there.

Entertainment

This can be summed up in one word: bars. The 'safest' bet is any one of the restaurants mentioned above. *Defi's* and *Las Rocas* are among the most popular. *Hannias Bar* is a nice local bar tended by Lloyd, who is a real gentleman. He runs a tight ship and doesn't allow troublemakers in there. For a little bit of local colour, the *Salon Vaz* is open all day and into the night and is known for its cracking loud games of dominoes. At night, the back room pounds to the sounds of a Caribbean disco which is usually crowded and is the most happening place in town – though be prepared for people bumming free drinks or offering ganga, coke or free love.

Getting There & Away

Buses from San José to Sixaola stop at Cahuita. There are three daily departures with Autotransportes MEPE (☎ 21 0524) leaving from Avenida 11, Calle Central & 1. The fare is US$5.75 for the four hour ride. Buses return to San José from the crossroads in the middle of Cahuita at 6.30 and 9.30 am, and also 4 pm. These buses leave from Sixaola and, given the current pot-holed road conditions, are often 20 or 30 minutes late by the time they pass through Cahuita. Schedules are liable to change so ask locally about these times, and the following ones.

Buses to Limón (US$0.80) leave from the same intersection at 6.30 and 10 am, and 12.30, 1.30 and 4.30 pm.

Buses to Puerto Vargas, Puerto Viejo, Bribri and Sixaola (US$0.80) leave from here at 5.50 and 11 am, and 2 and 5 pm. Buses to Puerto Viejo and Manzanillo leave at 7 am and 3 pm.

PARQUE NACIONAL CAHUITA

This small park of 1067 hectares is one of the more frequently visited national parks in Costa Rica. The reasons are simple: easy access and nearby hotels combined with attractive beaches, a coral reef and a coastal rainforest with many easily observed tropical species. They all combine to make this a popular park. Fortunately, Cahuita is still relatively little visited compared to Manuel Antonio on the Pacific coast.

The park is most often entered from the east end of Cahuita village, through the Kelly Creek entrance station and booth (but see the Getting There & Away section for other suggestions). Almost immediately, the visitor sees a two km long white-sand beach stretching along a gently curving bay to the east.

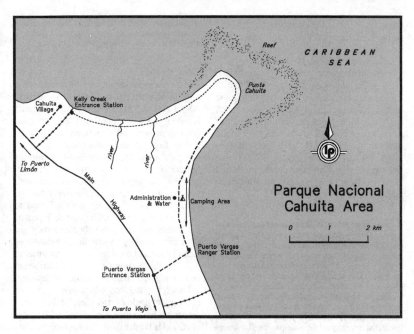

About the first 500 metres of beach have warning signs about unsafe swimming, but beyond that, waves are gentle and swimming is safe. (But take a friend – it is unwise to leave clothing unattended when you swim.)

A rocky headland known as Punta Cahuita (Cahuita Point) separates this beach from the next one, Playa Vargas. At the end of Playa Vargas there is the Puerto Vargas ranger station, which is about seven km from Kelly Creek. The two stations are linked by a trail that goes through the coastal jungle behind the beaches and Punta Cahuita. At times, the trail follows the beach; at other times hikers are 100 metres or so away from the sand. A river must be waded near the end of the first beach – the water can be thigh deep at high tide. Various animals and birds are frequently seen, including coatimundis and raccoons, ibises and kingfishers. From the Puerto Vargas ranger station, a one km road takes you out to the main coastal highway where there is another park entrance station.

Information

The park entrance stations are open daily from 8 am to 4 pm and the entry charge is US$1.50. No-one stops you from entering the park on foot before or after these hours. However, if you are driving to the Puerto Vargas area (where you can camp), you'll find a locked gate will prevent entry to vehicles out of hours.

There is not much shade on the beaches so remember to use sunscreen to avoid painful sunburn in the tropical sun. Don't forget your sensitive untanned feet after you take your shoes off on the beach. Also, carry drinking water and insect repellent.

Howler Monkeys

I have a special memory of the trail behind the beaches. I was hiking along it early one morning when I began to notice a distant moaning sound. It seemed as if the wind in the trees was becoming more forceful and I wondered whether a tropical storm was brewing. I decided to continue, and as I did so the noise became louder and eerier. This was definitely unlike any wind I had heard – it sounded more like a baby in pain.

I am not normally afraid of sounds, but the cries began sounding so eerie that I had to reason with myself that there was nothing to be apprehensive about. Finally, after much hesitant walking and frequent examinations of the forest through my binoculars, I found the culprit – a male howler monkey, the first I had ever seen. At the time, I knew only that their name related to their vocalisations and I had no idea how weird and unsettling these could be.

Only males howl, and to do so they are equipped with a specialised hyoid bone in the throat. Air is passed through this hollow and much enlarged bone, producing the strange and resonant call which can carry up to a km. The hyoid bone contributes to the typically thick necked appearance of the monkeys, which are often seen (or heard) in Parque Nacional Cahuita.

The call itself advertises the presence of a troop of monkeys in the area. This means that they can eat their favourite diet of succulent young leaves without being challenged by neighbouring troops. Thus troops

remain spaced apart, foraging efficiently and relying on safe howling rather than dangerous fighting to retain their claim to a particular patch of forest.

Coral Reefs

The monkeys and other forest life are not the only wildlife attractions of this national park. About 200 to 500 metres off Punta Cahuita is the largest living coral reef in Costa Rica (though very small compared to the huge Barrier Reef off Belize, for example). Corals are tiny, colonial, filter-feeding animals (cnidarians, or, more commonly, coelenterates) which deposit a calcium carbonate skeleton as a substrate for the living colony. These skeletons build up over millenia to form the corals we see. The outside layers of the corals are alive, but, because they are filter feeders, they rely on the circulation of clean water and nutrients over their surface.

Since the opening up of the Caribbean coastal regions in the last couple of decades, a lot of logging has taken place, and the consequent lack of trees on mountainous slopes has led to increased erosion. The loosened soil is washed into gullies, then streams and rivers, and eventually the sea. By the time the coral reef comes into the picture, the eroded soils are no more than minute mud particles – just the right size to clog up the filter-feeding cnidarians. The clogged animals die, and the living reef along with them.

After deforestation, the next step is often plantations of bananas or other fruit. These are sprayed with pesticides which, in turn, are washed out to sea and can cause damage to filter-feeding animals which need to pass relatively large quantities of water through their filtering apparatus in order to extract the nutrients they need.

The 1991 earthquake also had a damaging effect on the reef. The shoreline was raised by over a metre, exposing and killing parts of the coral. Nevertheless, some of the reef has survived and remains the most important in Costa Rica.

It is important to note that the coral reef is not just a bunch of colourful rocks. It is a living habitat, just as a stream, lake, forest,

Howler Monkey

or swamp is a living habitat. Coral reefs provide both a solid surface for animals such as sponges and anemones to grow on and a shelter for a vast community of fish and other organisms – octopi, crabs, algae, bryozoans and a host of others. Some 35 species of coral have been identified in this reef, along with 140 species of molluscs (snails, chitons, shellfish and octopuses), 44 species of crustaceans (lobsters, crabs, shrimps, barnacles and a variety of fleas, lice and others), 128 species of seaweeds and 123 species of fish. Many of these seemingly insignificant species are important links in various food chains. Thus logging can have much greater, and unforeseen, negative effects than simply getting rid of the rainforest.

On a more mundane level, the drier months in the highlands (from February to April), when less run-off occurs in the rivers and less silting occurs in the sea, are considered the best months for snorkelling and seeing the reef. Conditions are often cloudy at other times.

Camping

Camping is permitted at Playa Vargas, about one km from the Puerto Vargas ranger station. There are outdoor showers and pit latrines at the administration centre near the middle of the camping area. There is drinking water, and some sites have picnic tables. The area is rarely crowded, in fact it is often almost empty and most people opt to camp close to the administration centre for greater security – it is safe enough if you don't leave your gear unattended. Easter week and weekends tend to be more crowded, but the campsite is rarely completely full. The daily camping fee is US$2.25 per person. With a vehicle it's possible to drive as far as the campsite via the Puerto Vargas ranger station.

Getting There & Away

It's very easy to just walk in from downtown Cahuita through the Kelly Creek entrance station. However, if you want to do the day hike all the way along the coastal part of the park, I suggest you take a Cahuita to Sixaola

or Puerto Viejo bus around 6 am and ask to be put down at the Puerto Vargas park entrance road. A one km walk takes you to the coast, and then you can walk the further seven km back to Cahuita.

PUERTO VIEJO DE TALAMANCA

This small village is locally known as Puerto Viejo – I give its full name to avoid confusion with Puerto Viejo de Sarapiquí. In some ways, Puerto Viejo is a more tranquil and lower key version of Cahuita. There is more influence of the local Bribri indigenous culture and there is much less development. Also, Puerto Viejo has the best surfing on this coast, if not the whole country.

The village is 18 km south-east of Cahuita by road, but it can also be reached from Cahuita by walking along the beach at low tide – don't get cut off by the tides: get local advice about this. (One couple reported that they were robbed doing this hike.) The inhabitants traditionally lived by small-time agriculture and fishing, although catering to tourists is now becoming a minor industry. The mixture of Black and indigenous culture is very interesting: you can buy Bribri handicrafts and listen to reggae or calypso music; take horse rides into local indigenous reserves or go fishing with the locals; go surfing and swimming; or hang out with the old-timers and talk. There's plenty to do, but everything is very relaxed. Take your time and you'll discover a beautiful way of life – rush through and you'll end up with a feeling of frustration.

Poor surfing conditions in September and October mean that these are the quietest months of the year. It rains year round, but there are often periods of a few dry days during the less wet months of February to early May, and September to October. But don't rely on it – it can rain every day for a week during those months as well!

Information

Tourism Information The acronym ATEC stands for Asociación Talamanqueña de Ecoturismo y Conservación, which has its headquarters in Puerto Viejo. Their office is open from noon to 6 pm daily. This is the place to come for tourist information if you are interested in the local culture and environment. ATEC is a non-profit grassroots organisation which began in the 1980s to promote local tourism in a way that supports and enhances local people and communities whilst providing a meaningful and enjoyable experience for the traveller wishing to learn something about the region.

ATEC is also commited to environmentally sensitive tourism and conservation. The organisation's current president, Mauricio Salazar, is a Bribri local who knows the area exceptionally well.

ATEC can provide you with information ranging from the problems caused by banana plantations, to homestays with local people, to how to arrange a visit to a nearby indigenous reservation. ATEC is not a tour agency, but will arrange tours to local areas with local people and, as such, are recommended. Tours include emphases on natural history, bird-watching, indigenous and Afro-Caribbean culture, environmental issues, and snorkelling and fishing. (There are over 350 birds recorded in the area; one group reported 120 species sighted on a two day trip.) ATEC trains local guides to provide you with as much information as possible and they do a good job – if all your questions aren't satisfactorily answered, follow up at the ATEC office. Most tours involve hiking – ask about levels of endurance necessary. Fairly easy to difficult tours are available.

Tour prices aren't dirt cheap, but are fair value. The idea is to charge less than the big tour companies, but more than guides might make working for the big tour companies. This avoids the middle person and gives more profits to local guides, whilst saving the traveller some money.

A percentage of fees goes to ATEC educational programs and to local indigenous reservations etc. Tour prices range from about US$12.50 per person for half day trips, early morning birding hikes and night walks. All-day trips are about US$25, and a variety of overnight trips is available, the price depending on your food and lodging needs.

Group sizes are limited to six for outdoor activities.

ATEC can arrange talks and slide shows about a variety of local issues for around US$45 per group. They can arrange meals in local homes for around US$4 per person, depending on the meal required.

There is no telephone at the Puerto Viejo office – just show up to arrange tours, obtain information, or buy one of their books. If you wish to make advance reservations or require information in advance, you can leave a message (☎ 58 3844) and ask ATEC to return your call collect at a specified time – you may not always be able to get through. You can also send a fax to ANAI (fax 53 7524 in San José) though it takes a few days to get messages from there. Mail (which takes one to two months) can be addressed to Mauricio Salazar, President, ATEC, Puerto Viejo de Talamanca, Limón, Costa Rica.

Money Almost nobody accepts credit cards and the nearest bank is in Bribri (see following) so try and bring as many colones as you'll need. Some of the local stores will change cash US dollars and maybe travellers' cheques if they have enough colones on hand.

Telephone There are only two public telephones in Puerto Viejo. The Hotel Maritza (☎ 58 3844) and the Pulpería Manuel León (☎ 58 0854) allow the public to use their phones. If you need to call someone in Puerto Viejo, call one of these numbers and ask them to tell your party to call you back, otherwise you have no way of knowing if they received your message. This system works, but is not completely reliable. It should be limited to important calls. A handful of hotels have their own phone.

Books Some of the older Black inhabitants of the area told their life stories to Paula Palmer, who collected this wealth of oral history, culture and social anthropology in two books which are sometimes available in San José or Puerto Viejo. They are well worth reading: *What Happen: A Folk*

History of Costa Rica's Talamanca Coast (Ecodesarrollos, San José, 1977) and *Wa'apin Man* (Editorial Costa Rica, 1986). (Both books may have been reprinted more recently by other publishers.)

('What happen' or 'Wa'apin man' are common forms of greeting among Costa Rican coastal Blacks. North American travellers will have no difficulty in relating this to the 'What's happening' of Afro-Americans; travellers from other areas may find this greeting somewhat mystifying. 'All right' is probably as good a response as any.)

Taking Care of Sibö's Gifts – An Environmental Treatise from Costa Rica's KéköLdi Indigenous Reserve by Paula Palmer, Juanita Sánchez and Gloria Mayorga, was recently available in English at the ATEC office. ATEC also produces a booklet titled *Welcome to Coastal Talamanca*, crammed full of useful information.

Warning For years, Puerto Viejo has had the reputation of being a peaceful and safe place. This was shattered in April/May 1993 when a gang of muggers began robbing tourists at machete point. Locals reported about two dozen attacks (fortunately, no injuries) with the targets being people walking alone in unlit areas after dark. Police presence has been beefed up in the area and things should return to normal soon – but ask locally about the advisability of walking unlit streets alone.

Insects There seem to be plenty of them – if you intend staying in the cheapest hotels, bring insect repellent or mosquito coils if you are very sensitive to bugs.

Indigenous Reserves

There are several reserves in the Caribbean slopes of the Cordillera de Talamanca as well as the Reserva Indigena Cocles/KéköLdi which comes down to the coast just east of Puerto Viejo. Together with the nearby national parks and wildlife reserves they are part of the Amistad-Talamanca Regional Conservation Unit or 'megapark'. They protect the land against commercial develop-

ment in a variety of ways. Hunting is prohibited except for Indians hunting for food. Entrance to the reserves is limited to those visitors who receive the necessary permits from the Reserve Associations – these are difficult to obtain for the Talamanca reserves. Mauricio Salazar can guide you on day tours to the small KéköLdi reserve (twice a week, US$24.50 per person including lunch, two minimum, six maximum, 10% of tour cost goes directly to the reserve).

The Talamanca-Cabécar Reserve is the most remote and difficult to visit. The Cabécar indigenous group is the most traditional and the least tolerant of visits from Westerners. The Bribri people are more acculturated. Access to the reserves is generally on foot or horseback.

Surfing

The people at the Hotel Puerto Viejo are local surfing experts and many surfers stay here. The waves are best from December to early March, and there is another mini-season for surfing in June and July. From late March to April, and in September and October, the sea is at its calmest. Surfers tell me that the most exciting surfing is on the famous La Salsa Brava outside the reef in front of Stanford's Restaurant. If you lose it, you're liable to smash yourself and your board on the reef, so this is for experienced surfers. If this doesn't appeal to you, Playa Cocles, about two km east of town, has good and less damaging breaks. Ask about other places.

Horse-Riding & Cycling

Several places rent bicycles – the Soda Irma, Soda Tamara, Bela Soda and behind the Hotel Puerto Viejo. Ask around about others. Talk to ATEC about horse rentals.

Places to Stay

There are a number of places to stay, but most of them are small. They tend to be full during weekends in the surfing season, and during Christmas and Easter. You should arrive early, and preferably midweek, if you have no reservations. Reservations can be made by writing to the place you choose, Puerto

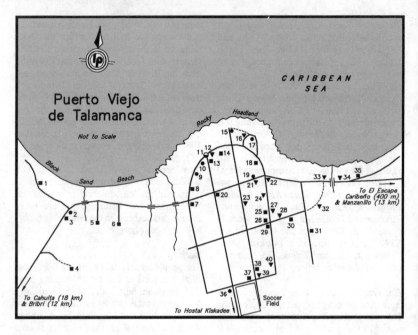

Puerto Viejo de Talamanca

	PLACES TO STAY	16	Jhonny's Place
1	Cabinas Black Sands	21	Soda Tamara
3	Cabinas Las Brisas	22	Restaurant El Parquecito
4	Cabinas Chimuri	23	Café Pizzería Coral
5	Cabinas Playa Negra	24	Caramba Restaurant
6	El Pizote Lodge	25	Restaurant MexiTico
7	Pensión Agaricia	27	Miss Dolly (bakery, medicinal plants)
8	Hotel Ritz	28	Bela Soda
13	Cabinas Diti	32	Soda Irma
14	Hotel Maritza	33	Stanford's Restaurant Caribe
18	Cabinas Manuel	34	Restaurant Bambu
20	Cabinas Grant	39	Garden Restaurant
25	Hotel Puerto Viejo	40	Miss Sam (bakery & soda)
26	Cabinas Stanford		
29	Cabinas Tamara		OTHER
30	Cabinas Casa Verde		
31	Cabinas Spence	2	Pulpería Violeta
35	Cabinas Salsa Brava	9	La Taberna de Popo
37	Hotel Pura Vida	10	Abastecedor Central (shop)
38	Cabinas Jacaranda	11	Bus Stop
		15	Pulpería Manuel León (public phone)
▼	PLACES TO EAT	17	Police & Post Office
		19	ATEC
12	Soda Priscilla	33	Stanford's Disco
		36	School

Viejo de Talamanca, Limón – allow two months. Alternatively, try calling one of the public phone numbers and leaving a message for the hotel to call you back. Many of the cheaper hotels don't like to take reservations – Catch-22.

Few of Puerto Viejo's hotels have hot showers. Note that there are many more places to stay strung out on the road from Puerto Viejo to Manzanillo, described in the next section.

Places to Stay – bottom end

In some of the cheaper hotels, the cold-water showers may only work intermittently, but bucket baths are usually available in this case. The majority of hotels will provide either mosquito netting or fans (a breeze fanning the bed will keep mosquitoes away). Check the facilities before getting a room.

Most of the rates below are for one night in the high season. For long stays, or during the low season, discounts can often be arranged.

Note that, apart from the places listed below, local people may hang out a 'Rooms for Rent' sign and provide inexpensive accommodation. ATEC will recommend local families to stay with if you wish.

A good shoestring-budget place is the friendly *Hostal Kiskadee* which is a six or seven minute walk south-east of the soccer field. The path is steep and could be slippery after rain, so carry a flashlight if arriving after dark. Simple dormitory-style accommodation is provided for US$3.75 per person and an extra US$0.75 gets you kitchen privileges.

The *Hotel Puerto Viejo* has 20 double rooms and is the biggest place in town. It is popular with surfers and budget travellers. The bare, basic but clean upstairs rooms are US$5.20 per person; a few downstairs rooms are not as good and are a little cheaper. Also popular with surfers is the basic *Cabinas Manuel* (☎ 58 0854) which has a poor water supply. Rooms with private bath are about US$10, but there are four beds and you can reportedly sleep four people in there for the same price as one (I couldn't find three vol-

unteers to try this with me). Another cheapie is the *Hotel Ritz* which charges only US$6 for a double room with private bath – it's reasonably clean.

Cabinas Jacaranda has quite pleasant rooms and provides fans and mosquito nets – not bad for US$10.50/12 single/double (good value at the double rate). It also has a few doubles with private bath for US$15.

Cabinas Las Brisas (over a km west of town) is locally known as 'Mister O'Conner's' after the owner. He has four basic but decent rooms for US$7.25 per person. Still further west is *Cabinas Black Sands* – an attractive thatched cabin in the local Bribri style, set in a pleasant garden near the beach. There are three basic rooms each with two beds and mosquito nets, and communal kitchen and bathroom facilities. This is a nice place to stay for peace and quiet near the beach – though restaurants are not very close. Rates are US$11/14 single/double and you get a discount if you book all three rooms (six beds). They are very popular and often booked up in the high season.

Several places charge US$14.50 for a room, irrespective of whether one or two people use it (triple occupancy may be possible). These include *Cabinas Diti* which is decent and has private baths – ask at Taberna de Popo for information.

Cabinas Stanford is also OK and has private baths and fans – ask at Stanfords restaurant for information. *Cabinas Salsa Brava* has basic rooms with private baths and good views of the Salsa Brava section of the shoreline.

The *Hotel Pura Vida* charges US$13/17 single/double in rooms with fans and sinks – shared baths are down the hall. The place is attractive and clean. *Cabinas Casa Verde* has pleasant cabins with occasionally warm water in the communal bathroom – rates are US$12.50/18.50 for singles/doubles.

Cabinas Spence has decent rooms with private bath for US$15.50 single or double occupancy. The *Hotel Maritza* (☎ 58 3844) charges US$18.50 for a double in nice cabins with fan, private bath and electric shower. It also has a few very cheap and basic rooms with shared bath over its attached restaurant.

Places to Stay – middle

Cabinas Grant (☎ 58 2845) has decent rooms with private bath and fan for US$21, single or double. The owners are helpful with local advice and are planning on building a restaurant. *Cabinas Tamara* has rooms ranging from small doubles for US$18.50, to doubles with refrigerator and kitchenette for US$22 and a larger room with refrigerator and kitchenette for US$31. All have private baths and fans and are quite good.

The clean *Pensión Agaricia* is run by a tico artist and his Belgian wife and has a pleasant and quiet atmosphere. Rooms with fans and shared bath are US$20/25 – I've read nothing but recommendations for this place, which reflects the owners and atmosphere rather than the rooms themselves which are completely acceptable but not out of the ordinary. One of the rooms has a good sea view – but I shouldn't be telling you this because it'll be taken when you get there. Oh, well...

Another place out of town that is well worth seeking out is *Cabinas Chimuri* run by ATEC president, Mauricio Salazar (and his European wife, Colocha), who knows as much about the Bribri culture as anyone in Puerto Viejo.

There are a few small, simple attractively thatched A-frame cabins in the Bribri style on stilts renting for US$17/22 single/double and one quadruple cabin going for a few dollars more. There are communal kitchen and simple bathroom facilities. The cabins are set in a 20 hectare private preserve with trails and good bird-watching possibilities. This is the place to go for trips to the local indigenous reserves and to learn more about ATEC and the Talamanca region.

The *Cabinas Playa Negra* (☎ 56 1132, 56 6396) is on a quiet road just west of town. The telephone numbers are in Turrialba, not in Puerto Viejo, but reservations can be made. They have several family-style houses with two or three rooms, kitchen, bathroom

(cold water) and TV which rent for US$37 and sleep up to six.

About half a km east of town is *Escape Caribeño* (☎ 58 3844, Apartado 704-7300, Limón) which has pleasant bungalows with fans, private bath, refrigerator and porch for US$29/34 single/double. Kitchen privileges are available.

Places to Stay – top end

About a km west of town on a quiet back road is the relatively comfortable *El Pizote Lodge* (☎ 58 1938; in San José, ☎/fax 29 1428; Apartado 230-2200, Coronado). This is the fanciest hotel in Puerto Viejo. The rooms are large and clean, but don't have private baths. That is not a real problem, however, as there are four shared bathrooms for eight rooms. There are also pleasant wooden bungalows with private baths which are more expensive. The lodge is set in a pleasant garden, there are bicycles, horses and snorkelling gear for rent to clients, and boat and snorkelling tours are planned. Good meals are available in the rather pricey restaurant (US$8 breakfast, US$16 dinner). Rooms are US$31/46/60/70 and bungalows are US$62/75/90/102 for one to four occupants.

Places to Eat

Several small locally owned places serve meals and snacks typical of the region – ask at ATEC for recommendations if you'd like to eat with a family or small local place. ATEC president, Mauricio Salazar, mentions the following possibilities for reasonably priced local eateries and food. The bakery and soda at *Miss Sam* and *Soda Irma* are run by ladies who are long-term residents. Doña Juanita cooks out of her house near the 'Rooms for Rent' sign shortly before the Cabinas Las Brisas as you enter Puerto Viejo. Doña Guillerma does the same a couple of hundred metres away – ask locally for directions.

Miss Dolly sells only baked goods – no meals – and her wide knowledge of local medicinal plants and herbs is interesting. She will take interested visitors on plant walks. *Bela Soda* has cheap but good breakfasts.

The *Restaurant Bambu* is inexpensive and good value if you avoid the tourist menu – a casado is US$2.25 and a beer is US$0.75. The place is a popular bar in the evenings. *Jhonny's Place* keeps sharp-eyed readers busy writing letters to me about the misspelling – I just write what the sign says! Meals here are Chinese-style and filling, prices are low and quality is acceptable – recommended for those bringing large appetites and small bank accounts.

The *Café Pizzería Coral* has breakfast daily, except Monday, from 7 am to noon. They serve a variety of healthful items such as yoghurt and granola, home-made whole wheat bread, and, of course, the tico speciality – gallo pinto. Eggs and pancakes are also served. In the evenings, they bake great home-made pizzas – all kinds of tasty varieties. Prices are moderate. Also good for breakfasts and snacks throughout the day is the friendly *Soda Tamara* – they have coconut bread and cakes and casados in the evening. *Soda Priscilla* has also been recommended for cheap food.

Stanford's Restaurant Caribe is good for seafood which ranges from US$3 to US$8 depending on how exotic a meal you order. They have a lively disco at weekends. *Restaurant El Parquecito* is quite good and has meals ranging from a US$3 casado to a US$4.50 fish fillet or pork chop, to shrimp and lobster dishes for a reasonable US$7.25. The *Restaurant MexiTico* in the Hotel Puerto Viejo serves Mexican-style snacks and meals at reasonable prices. The *Caramba Restaurant* serves French food and wine – I haven't tried it but a reader tells me it's good. There is also a restaurant at the *Hotel Maritza*.

The very best place in town at time of writing is the warmly recommended *Garden Restaurant*. They serve Caribbean, Asian and vegetarian food. Try the Jerk Chicken (a Jamaican dish), chicken curry or well-prepared red snapper. Desserts are also good. Vegetarian main courses begin at about US$5.50; others start at US$6.50 and go up from there – red snapper is US$8 for example. Service and preparation are a step

or three above what you might expect in such a small, out-of-the-way town. They are closed on Wednesday.

Entertainment
La Taberna de Popo is a good and popular bar which plays both Caribbean and rock music and has live entertainment on occasion. Stanford's Disco is a dancing place at weekends. The Restaurant Bambu has a popular bar.

Getting There & Away
From San José, Autotransportes MEPE (☎ 21 0524) has three buses a day leaving from Avenida 11, Calle Central & 1. Two of these will drop you off at the intersection almost six km from Puerto Viejo but the 3.30 pm bus will go into town – check with the bus company to confirm this. If you don't want to walk the last five km, call the Hotel Maritza or Pulpería Manuel León to arrange for a taxi pick-up.

Alternatively, go to Puerto Limón, where buses leave from a block north of the market at 5 and 10 am, and 1 and 4 pm. It takes about 1½ hours and costs US$0.90 to Puerto Viejo. Buses continue to Bribri and Sixaola from the bus stop marked on the map.

Buses leave Puerto Viejo at 6 am and 1 and 4 pm for Cahuita and Limón; there is no 1 pm bus on Sunday. A 7 am bus goes directly from Puerto Viejo to San José. The fare is US$5.75.

There are also buses from Limón to Manzanillo, passing through Puerto Viejo around 7.30 am and 4 pm. Manzanillo to Limón buses pass through at about 9.15 am and 5.15 pm.

EAST OF PUERTO VIEJO
A 13 km dirt road heads east from Puerto Viejo along the coast, past sandy beaches and rocky points, through the small communities of Punta Uva and Manzanillo, through sections of the Reserva Indigena Cocles/KéköLdi and ending up in the Refugio Nacional de Vida Silvestre Gandoca-Manzanillo. The locals mainly use horses and bicycles along this narrow and sandy road,

though vehicles get through. Drive slowly and carefully – not only are there horses and bicycles, but there are slick little one-lane bridges offering the unwary driver an intimate visit to the creek below.

This road more or less follows the shoreline, and a variety of places to stay and eat can be found strung along the road. Most have opened in the last few years – this area is experiencing a minor boom in tourism. The local people realise that the tourist industry is a double-edged sword and are trying to control its development to ensure that Talamanqueños benefit fairly. They are hampered by a bureaucratic jungle within which such apparently straightforward things as the borders of the KéköLdi reservation and the Gandoca-Manzanillo refuge are poorly defined. Some of these problems are addressed briefly below; interested Spanish-speaking visitors should try and read the novel *La Loca de Gandoca* (see Books in the Facts for the Visitor chapter for a brief review).

Places to Stay & Eat

These are listed here in the order that they are passed as you leave Puerto Viejo.

Playa Cocles Two km east of town, Playa Cocles has very good surfing. Surfers stay at the *Cabinas & Soda Garibaldi* which charges US$12 for fairly basic rooms with private bath and sea views. Just before Garibaldi is the more expensive *Surf Point* and there are also several houses renting rooms. *Kapalapa* is a pub with music and videos and has a few bottom-end rooms to rent.

Playa Chiquita There are several places at Playa Chiquita, a small beach about four km east of Puerto Viejo. First is the *Picasso Hotel* which looks OK and then *Tío Lou's Resorts* (☎ 26 3131) which are slightly more upscale cabins – I didn't have time to check them when I came through. The most luxurious place on this beach is *Villas del Caribe* (☎ 33 2200, fax 21 2801) which has nice beach-front apartments with sea views, hot showers and fans, and can sleep up to five

people; sample rates are US$115/126 double/triple. They give discounts to drop-in guests if they are not full.

These apartments are owned by Canadian environmentalist Maurice Strong, organiser of the 1992 'Earth Summit' in Río de Janeiro. In 1992, reports emerged in *The Tico Times* that part of the hotel had been built illegally within the limits of the KéköLdi indigenous reservation and the Gandoca-Manzanillo national wildlife refuge. Strong asserted that, according to Minister of Natural Resources, Hérnan Bravo, the hotel land was not in the reservation/refuge. Later, it was discovered that a mistake had been made, not least of which was that the land had been surveyed as part of the wildlife refuge but, in fact, should have been included in the indigenous reservation. Meanwhile, the KéköLdi association is studying the problem and is not taking action until studies have been finished. It should be noted that several of the small places mentioned here (including, but not limited to, the Picasso, the Dasa and the Maracú) apparently have also been in violation of reservation or refuge boundaries – but their impact has been minimal.

Just beyond the Villas del Caribe, *Cabinas Dasa* has a two-bed room with shared bath for US$14/18 single/double, and a four-bed room with private bath for US$20 to US$35 depending on the number of people. They also have a cabin with private bath and kitchenette for up to six people. This costs about US$50 per night, but a two day minimum stay is preferred. Reservations can be made in San José (☎ 53 3431, 20 4089 or 36 2631). Close by, *Maracú* has two simple cabins with a stove and two beds each, and there is a shared bathroom. Rates are about US$7 per person. Reservations can be made (☎ 25 6215).

About 400 metres further (five km from Puerto Viejo) is the entrance, on the right, to *Hotel Punta Cocles* (☎ 34 0306, fax 34 0014; Apartado 2692, San José) which has several dozen comfortable rooms, some with air-conditioning, some with kitchenettes, and all with private electric showers and private patios. There is a swimming pool, restaurant, bar and local trails into the forest. Guides and rental items (snorkels, surfboards, binoculars, horses and bicycles) are available. Rooms are US$63/75/86 for one to three guests; larger rooms with kitchenettes are more.

A further 400 metres brings you to the *Miraflores Lodge* (☎ 33 5127, fax 33 5390; Apartado 7271-1000, San José; CRBBG member). This small B&B lodge is 500 metres from the beach and offers about eight rooms in an attractive private home. Rooms with bath and electric shower are US$46/57 single/double; rooms with shared bath are a few dollars cheaper. Some of the large rooms can sleep several people, but children are not permitted and smoking is outside only. Full breakfast is included. The place is small and popular, so reservations are recommended. The owner will arrange local tours with an emphasis on natural history and culture.

There are half a dozen small restaurants within a few hundred metres, as well as houses advertising 'Rooms for Rent'. The *Restaurant Las Palmitas* offers meals, simple cabins, and a camping area. *Elena Brown's Soda & Restaurant* is a nice litle local place to eat. Others are *Pinguin Soda* and *Soda Acuarius* – the latter bakes homemade bread, has a couple of basic rooms for rent and also has a rustic house to rent for about US$300 per month.

Almost six km from Puerto Viejo is the attractively thatched *Playa Chiquita Lodge* (☎ 33 6613, fax 23 7479; Apartado 7043-1000, San José) which is owned by Wolf Bissinger who also operates Oro Verde on the Río Sarapiquí (see The Northern Lowlands chapter). Playa Chiquita Lodge is 200 metres from the beach – you can't see the ocean from the lodge because Wolf wanted to leave the intervening forest standing. Instead, a short but scenic jungle hike leads to the beach. Rooms are spacious and have fans and private bath – a few have electric showers. There is a good restaurant on the premises, open to the public. Breakfasts are US$6, lunches and dinners are US$10. Local guided tours by boat or van can be arranged. High season room-rates are US$35/58/76/92

for one to four people – take off about 20% for low season.

Punta Uva Seven km east of Puerto Viejo is the Punta Uva area which has several places to stay and eat. A sign advertises 'Caminata Guiada al Bosque' (guided forest hikes) and there is a trail going up into the forest along the Quebrada Ernesto. Ask at the house near the sign for guides and horses if you want. Just beyond, on the right, is the *Soda & Restaurant Naturales* set up on a hillside in the forest with good sea views – a nice place. They serve good local seafood and drinks and have a small crafts and T-shirt store. They used to be closed on Wednesday, but recently they were closed on Thursday instead.

Just beyond is *Selvin's Cabins* with several basic rooms for about US$10 a double and a cabin with private bath for four people at US$26. There is a decent restaurant and bar which is closed on Monday. Two hundred metres further along is the reasonably cheap and popular *Walaba Cabinas* (☎ 25 8023) with both basic rooms and dormitories – they were full when I passed by so they can't be too bad. Another km (now about eight km from Puerto Viejo) brings you the *El Duende Feliz* Italian restaurant which has a couple of house rentals nearby.

Just beyond Punta Uva, about nine km east of Puerto Viejo, is *Las Palmas Beach Resort* (☎ 55 3939, fax 55 3737; Apartado 6942-1000, San José). This 60-room resort (more rooms are planned) offers comfortable rooms with ocean views, private hot showers and air-conditioning for about US$70 a double. There is a pool, lighted tennis court, bar and restaurant, horse and bike rental, and swimming, snorkelling and scuba diving. They provide daily round-trip transportation from San José for US$30. Unfortunately, this resort has been built within the boundaries of the Gandoca-Manzanillo national wildlife refuge and has violated a number of environmental and legal laws. This has caused the Ministry of Natural Resources to order the hotel to be torn down, a decision which has been revoked by the Supreme Court. Meanwhile, the owner, Jan Kalina, born in Czechoslovakia but a Canadian resident, was ordered deported because he was in Costa Rica on an expired tourist visa. In a long, drawn-out legal battle, one thing remains clear: whereas local conservation organisations reported the many infringements early on, government bureaucracy, ineptitude and confusion has led to a chaotic situation not only with this development, but with the tourism boom on the entire coast.

The next few km are within the wildlife refuge and are presently devoid of tourist developments, although the village of Manzanillo has basic facilities within the refuge.

Getting There & Away
See the Manzanillo entry.

MANZANILLO
The village school of Manzanillo is 12.5 km from Puerto Viejo (Manzanillo village already existed when the Gandoca-Manzanillo refuge was established in 1985). The schoolmaster, Don German, is a fountain of local information.

The road continues for about one more km and then peters out. From the end of the road, footpaths continue around the coast through Gandoca-Manzanillo.

Places to Stay & Eat
Near the bus stop in Manzanillo, there is the basic *Cabinas Maxi* charging about US$7.25 per room. There is a restaurant, bar and even a disco here at weekends. Several local ladies will prepare traditional Caribbean meals in their homes for travellers – ask around.

A walk of 10 minutes or so towards Puerto Viejo will bring you to the *Pulpería Mas por Menos* where you can buy basic food and other supplies and where a public phone was recently installed.

Almonds and Corals Lodge Tent Camp (☎ 72 2024, fax 72 2220) is opening a tent camp in the Manzanillo area at the end of 1993. They plan on 20 tents for two people, four tents for four people; each tent on a raised wooden platform and containing single beds, fan, light, table and hammock. A central lodge will provide family-style dining, and there will be showers and toilet facilities. Guided hikes, snorkelling, bicycle rent, bird-watching and horseback riding will be offered. Rates will be US$29/40 single/double and US$11.50 for each extra person. Meals will be US$6 for breakfast and US$10 for lunch and dinner.

Getting There & Away
Buses leave Limón for Manzanillo at 6 am and 2.30 pm, passing through Cahuita, Puerto Viejo and arriving in Manzanillo about 2½ hours later. The fare is US$1.90. Return buses leave Manzanillo at 8.30 am and 4.30 pm.

REFUGIO NACIONAL DE VIDA SILVESTRE GANDOCA-MANZANILLO
This refuge lies on the coast around Manzanillo and continues south-east as far as the Panamanian border. It encompasses 5013 hectares of land plus 4436 hectares of sea. This is the only place in the country apart from Cahuita where there is a living coral reef. It lies about 200 metres off-shore and snorkelling is one of the refuge's attractions.

The land section has several different habitats, not least of which is farmland. The little village of Manzanillo is actually in the reserve. There is an area of rainforest and there are also some of the most beautiful beaches on the Caribbean, unspoilt and separated by rocky headlands. Coconut palms form an attractive tropical backdrop. There is a coastal trail leading 5.5 km from Manzanillo to Punta Mona. South of this trail is an unusual 400 hectare swamp containing holillo palms and sajo trees. One map shows a trail that leaves from just west of Manzanillo and skirts the southern edges of this swamp and continues to the small community of Gandoca, roughly eight or 10 km away. Experienced hikers could follow the Punta Mona trail, but a guide may be necessary for the trail to Gandoca. Ask locally.

Beyond Punta Mono is the only red mangrove swamp in Caribbean Costa Rica, protecting a natural oyster bank. In the nearby Río Gandoca estuary there is a spawning ground for the Atlantic tarpon, and cayman and manatees are reported. The endangered Baird's tapir is also found in this wet and densely vegetated terrain.

Marine turtles have nested on the beaches at the south-east end of the refuge. The first few months of the year are the best times to see this. Local conservation efforts are underway to protect these nesting grounds – an increase in human population in the area has led to inceased taking of turtle eggs to the point where not enough are left to allow the species to continue. The people taking turtle eggs may be doing it out of economic necessity, but destroying this resource will not solve anyone's problems. Currently, there is a grassroots organisation which is working with locals to protect the sea turtles – they definitely need volunteers if you are interested in sea turtle conservation. Long hours, no pay, hot and humid conditions, and a chance to help sea turtle conservation and see a remote part of Costa Rica – if this appeals to you, write for information to ANAI, 1176 Bryson City Rd, Franklin, NC 28734, USA; in San José, (☎ 24 6090, 24 3570, fax 57 7524). If you can't volunteer, contributions are welcome – they are tax-deductible in the USA for US taxpayers.

The variety of vegetation and the remote location attract many tropical birds. The very rare harpy eagle has been recorded here, and other birds to look for include the red-lored parrot, the red-capped manakin and the chestnut-mandibled toucan among hundreds of others. The birding is considered to be very good. I saw a flock of several hundred small parakeets come screaming overhead at dusk – quite a sight and quite a sound!

Information

Ask for Florentino Grenald who lives in Manzanillo and acts as the reserve's administrator. He has a local bird list and can recommend guides. A local boatman, Willie Burton, will take you boating and snorkelling from Manzanillo. His house is the last one on the road through Manzanillo before you reach the trails for Punta Mona. If you have a car, you can leave it by his house

while you go hiking. Horses and guides can also be hired locally. ATEC in Puerto Viejo has a variety of tours into the refuge, including day and overnight trips by foot, horse or boat.

Places to Stay

Camping is permitted, but there are no organised facilities. Reportedly, camping on the beach is best – fewer insects and more breezes. At Punta Mona, a local farmer named Emilio will let you camp near his house and will provide meals if arranged in advance (contact ATEC). Most visitors take day hikes and stay in the Puerto Viejo area.

Getting There & Away

See the Manzanillo entry.

BRIBRI

This small village is passed en route from Cahuita to Sixaola. It is the end of the paved (and badly pot-holed) coastal road; from Bribri a 34 km gravel road takes the traveller to the Panamanian border.

Bribri is the centre for the local indigenous communities in the Talamanca mountains, although there is not much to see here.

The Ministry of Health operates a clinic in Bribri which serves both Puerto Viejo and the surrounding Indian communities. There is a Banco Nacional de Costa Rica here, also serving Puerto Viejo (about 12 km away). There are several phones (☎ 58 0092, 58 2981, 58 2983, 58 3353, 58 0150).

Places to Stay

There are a couple of basic places to stay and restaurants in Bribri. *Cabinas Piculino* has been recommended, though I haven't checked them out. Buses sometimes stop for a meal or snack at the *Restaurant King-Giung* which has reasonable Chinese and tico food.

Getting There & Away

Bribri is a regular stop for all buses to and from Sixaola. Buses leave from Bribri via the communities of Chase and Bratsi (public ☎ 71 2125) to the village of Shiroles (public

☎ 76 2064), 17 km away. From here, horse and foot traffic continues on into the indigenous reserves. One village that can be reached is Amubri (☎ 76 2215), which reportedly has a mission with a place to stay.

SIXAOLA

This is the end of the road as far as the Costa Rican Caribbean is concerned. Sixaola is the border town with Panama, but few foreign travellers cross the border here – most overlanders go via Paso Canoas on the Carretera Interamericana.

Sixaola is an unattractive little town, with nothing to recommend it except the border crossing itself, which is fairly relaxed. Most of the town is strung out along the main street. The public phone is ☎ 76 2152. Remember that Panama's time is one hour ahead of Costa Rica's.

For full details of crossing the border at this point, see the Getting There & Away chapter.

Places to Stay & Eat

There are two *Restaurants Central*, one of which has an extremely basic pensión attached. There are a couple of other places: ask around. Accommodation is generally unappealing, though OK for the unfastidious looking for something different. It's best to get here as early as possible if going to or coming from Panama. There is better accommodation on the Panamanian side.

The best restaurant in Sixaola is the *El Siquerreno*, but it's not always open. There are several other places to eat – when I went through at about 10 o'clock one morning, every restaurant had a bunch of argumentative drunks in it. Maybe it was the day after payday for workers on the local cacao fincas.

Getting There & Away

Direct buses from San José leave three times a day from Avenida 11, Calle Central & 1. If you take the first bus you should be in Sixaola by late morning. Buses return to San José (six hours, US$5.75) at 5 and 8 am, and 2.30 pm. There are also three buses a day to and from Limón.

Taxis with 4WD are available to visit local villages. You can reach Gandoca (in the Refugio Nacional de Vida Silvestre Gandoca-Manzanillo) from here.

Southern Costa Rica

The southbound Carretera Interamericana leaves San José to the east and skirts Cartago before truly heading south. The highway begins to climb steadily, reaching its highest point at over 3300 metres near the sombrely named 3491 metre peak of Cerro de la Muerte (Death Mountain).

This area is about 100 km by road south of San José and is often shrouded in mists. The next 30 km stretch is a particularly dangerous section of highway.

From the high point, the road drops steeply to San Isidro de El General at 702 metres.

San Isidro is the first important town south of Cartago, and is the main entry point for the nearby Parque Nacional Chirripó which contains the highest mountains in Costa Rica.

From San Isidro, the Carretera Interamericana continues south-east through mainly agricultural lowlands to the Panamanian border, a little over 200 km away.

There are no more big towns, but there are several smaller ones which are of interest to those visitors wanting to see some of Costa Rica which is not on the normal 'gringo trail'. From these towns roads lead out to some of the more remote protected areas in the country.

These include the magnificent wilderness of Parque Nacional Corcovado in the Península de Osa, the rarely visited and difficult to get to Parque Internacional La Amistad, and the Wilson Botanical Gardens, to name but a few.

From highlands to tropical lowlands, there is a variety of beautiful wilderness parks and preserves – and not many tourists. Slow down and take some time to check it out if you can.

Note that little, yellow-topped, numbered posts are located along the Carretera Interamericana. These are km markers which are found south of San José and are referred to in the text.

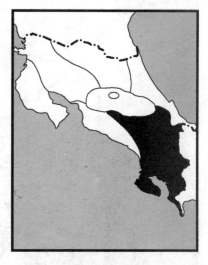

San José to Palmar

LA RUTA DE LOS SANTOS

The route of the saints is so-called for the villages it passes through – Santa María de Dota, San Marcos de Tarrazú, San Pablo de León Cortés, San Cristóbal Sur and several others named after saints. The towns in themselves are not especially exciting but the drive takes you through typical hilly farm country – coffee, cattle and clouds. Narrow, steep roads twist through splendid scenery – green and inviting or dark and forbidding, depending on the weather.

Places to Stay

Several of the towns have inexpensive country hotels, though most visitors tend to just drive through on a day trip. Try one of the following: *Hotel Santa María* (☎ 74 1193) in Santa María de Dota; *Hotel Marilú*

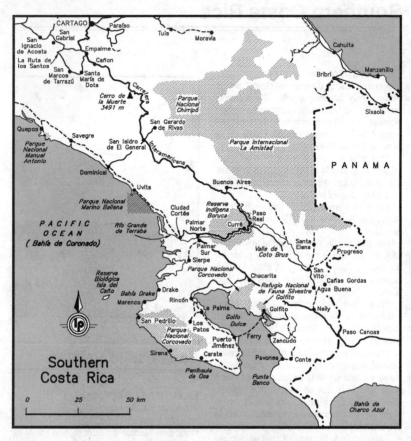

Southern
Costa Rica

PACIFIC
OCEAN
(Bahía de Coronado)

0   25   50 km

PANAMA

(☎ 77 6110), *Hotel Zacatecas* (☎ 77 6073), *Hotel Continental* (☎ 77 6225) and *Hotel Tarrazú* in San Marcos de Tarrazú.

Getting There & Away

Most visitors drive south on the Carretera Interamericana to Empalme, a small gas station/soda stop about 25 km south of Cartago. Shortly beyond there a paved road turns west to Santa María de Dota, about 10 km away, San Marcos (a further seven km) and San Pablo (a further four km). From there a choice of paved roads takes you back to the Interamericana via San Cristóbal or winding north through San Gabriel and other villages to San José. A regular car can travel on these roads, but maps and road signs are poor – ask locals for directions.

There are bus services. Autotransportes Los Santos (☎ 27 3597) leaves from Calle 21 Avenida 16 bis in San José for Santa María de Dota several times a day.

GENESIS II

At about 2360 metres above sea level, this private nature reserve is possibly the highest in the country. Situated in the Cordillera de Talamanaca, the reserve covers 45 hectares,

Top: Hiking, Parque Nacional Corcovado (RR)
Middle: Golfo Dulce getaway (MM)
Bottom: Tortuguero Canal (RG)

Top: Parque Nacional Chirripó, highest in Costa Rica (RR)
Left: Climbing in Parque Nacional Chirripó (RR)
Right: La Paz waterfall (RR)

almost all of which is virgin cloud forest (or, technically, tropical montane rainforest). This consists of evergreen and oak forest with epiphytic bromeliads, ferns, orchids, lichens, mosses and other plants covering every available surface. This is the place to stay to look for highland species of birds, plants and butterflies. Some of the more spectacular birds include the resplendent quetzal, collared trogon and emerald toucanet – about 200 birds are predicted for this highland region and identifying and classifying all the birds present in the reserve is an ongoing project.

There are about 20 km of trails within the reserve. The 'dry' season is from January to May but it can rain any time, so rain gear is essential. Mornings are usually clear – even during the rainy season. Average annual rainfall is 2300 mm. The altitude makes the weather cold – bring warm clothes.

Places to Stay

Accommodation is not fancy. There are six simple guest bedrooms (double bed or two singles) in the main house and two separate cabins sleeping up to four people. All guests share the two hot-water showers and toilets in the main house. Electricity is available. Tasty family-style meals are served using fresh garden and local produce.

The English-speaking owners suggest a minimum stay of three days and recommend a week. Rates for three days are US$380/460 for single/double and US$200 for each additional person. Weekly rates are US$700/890 plus US$370 for each additional person. Longer stays are discounted. Rates include accommodation, meals, guide services and transfer from San José. Write to Steve & Paula Friedman, Apartado 10303-1000, San José, or fax 51 0070, Apartado 655-7050, Cartago. A San José contact is Eric or Lee Warrington (☎ 25 0271).

Getting There & Away

The turn-off for Genesis II is at the Cañon church, just south of Km 58 on the Interamericana. Turn east and follow the rough road four km to the refuge. I couldn't get through in my ordinary car – either use 4WD or arrange for the owners to pick you up in San José (or at the Cañon church if you are travelling by bus).

ALBERGUE DE MONTAÑA TAPANTÍ

This small highland hotel (☎ 32 0436, 33 0133, fax 33 0778; Apartado 1237-1000, Pavas) is the most comfortable place to stay on the Interamericana between San José and San Isidro de El General. There is a garden and some remnants of high-altitude cloud forest – a good spot for some roadside birding. The hotel is north of Km 62 on the Interamericana.

Rooms are brightly decorated and have sitting areas or terraces or both. The private bathrooms have hot water, and room heaters are available. Rates are US$58 a double and US$90 a quadruple. They have a good restaurant with meals for US$5 to US$7 – it's open to the public.

CABINAS CHACÓN

Cabinas Chacón (☎ 71 1732 – often busy) is a small family-run hotel where the highland birding is excellent. Quetzals have been reported here regularly every April and May (the breeding season) but are often seen during the rest of the year. In fact, many people feel this is one of the best places in the country to see quetzals. The trout fishing in the Río Savegre is also very good. The seasons are from May and June for fly fishing, and from December to March for lure fishing.

The hotel is on the Chacón farm which was literally carved out of the wilderness by Don Ephraim Chacón in 1957 – an interesting story in its own right. The elevation here is about 2000 metres. The farm is now part apple orchard, part dairy ranch and part virgin forest. There are several trails; one km, eight km and longer. The owners are enthusiastic about their birds and usually know where the quetzals are hanging out.

Telephoned reservations are needed to stay at the Cabinas Chacón. There are hot showers, and rooms cost about US$36 per person, including home-cooked meals. The restaurant is popular with ticos at weekends.

Note that Cabinas Chacón is also known as Albergue Río Savegre and Finca Zacatales – it's all one and the same.

Getting There & Away
The cabinas are in the tiny community of San Gerardo de Dota, which is nine km west of the Interamericana at Km 80. Buses to San Isidro de El General can drop you off at 'La Entrada a San Gerardo' from where the Chacóns will pick you up for US$12 if you have a reservation. Or walk – it's downhill.

You can drive down there, but the road is very steep, though passable to an ordinary car in good condition.

CERRO DE LA MUERTE
The mountain overlooking the highest point on the Carretera Interamericana got its name before the road was built – but the steep, fog-shrouded highway in the area is known as one of the most dangerous for accidents in Costa Rica. Take care if driving. During the rainy season, landslides may partially or completely block the road. I drove over the pass one dark and misty night with visibility of about three car lengths, speeding along at about 15 km/h – frightening!

This area is the northernmost extent of the *páramo* habitat – a highland shrub and tussock grass habitat more common in the Andes of Colombia, Ecuador and Peru than in Costa Rica. Nevertheless, here it is – and you can drive through it. Birders look for highland bird species here, such as the sooty robin, volcano junco and two species of silky flycatchers.

Tours
Costa Rica Expeditions (☎ 57 0766) has one-day guided birding trips to Cerro de la Muerte for US$69 per person, minimum of four people.

Horizontes (☎ 22 2022) has three day two night-guided excursions to the area, overnighting at the Albergue de Montaña Tapantí. Rates are US$305 per person, double occupancy, including meals.

Places to Stay
About five km beyond the highest point is the *Hotel Georgina* where buses often stop for a meal and toilet break. Rooms are about US$5 per person, simple meals are served, and there is good high-altitude birding nearby.

SAN ISIDRO DE EL GENERAL
Some 136 km from San José, San Isidro is the most important town on the southern Interamericana. The town and its surrounding district have a population of about 40,000.

The Río General valley is important for agriculture, as you can see when descending from the bleak páramos of Cerro de la Muerte through the increasingly lush farming country of the valley. San Isidro is the commercial centre of the coffee fincas, cattle ranches and plant nurseries which dot the mountain slopes. In addition, the town is an important transport hub.

It is a bustling, pleasant and fairly modern town. There is a small museum, but otherwise there really is not much to see or do here, though its position as a gateway to other places makes it of interest to the traveller. San José to the north and Panama to the south-east are the most obvious important destinations, of course, but in addition a road to the north-east leads to the village of San Gerardo de Rivas, where the ranger station for Parque Nacional Chirripó is found. Another road to the south-west leads to the Pacific coast and beaches at Dominical, which allows a round trip to be made from San José to Dominical and Parque Nacional Manuel Antonio without retracing your route. Other minor roads lead into quiet farming country. River-running trips on the nearby Río General and Río Chirripó can be arranged in San José, with overnight stops in San Isidro.

Information
You can change money in the bank on the Parque Central, as well as at another bank a block away. The post and telegram office is a block south of the park.

The regional park service office for the Reserva de la Biosfera La Amistad (which includes the Parque Nacional Chirripó) (☎ fax 71 1115) is on the Interamericana at the north end of San Isidro. Hours are 8 am to noon and 1 to 4 pm, Monday to Friday.

Things to See & Do

Museo Regional del Sur This small regional museum at Calle 2 & Avenida 1 has a small display of items of local cultural, social, historical and archaeological interest. Hours are 8 am to noon and 1 to 4.30 pm,

Monday to Friday – definitely subject to change.

In the same complex is a cultural centre with a theatre, art gallery and lecture hall.

River Running Costa Rica Expeditions (☎ 57 0766) has three and four-day river running trips on the Río Chirripó from mid-June to mid-December. This is a mainly Class IV river.

Trips include round-trip transportation from San José, all boating gear including life vests, tents for camping by the side of the river, expert bilingual river guides and all

San Isidro de El General

0   250   500 m

■ PLACES TO STAY

4 Hotel Amaneli
5 Hotel Balboa
8 Hotel Iguazu
10 Hotel Lala
11 Hotel El Jardín
12 Hotel Astoria
20 Hotel Chirripó
25 Pensión Eiffel

▼ PLACES TO EAT

9 Restaurant El Tenedor
11 Restaurant El Jardín
14 Restaurant Hong Kong
20 Café & Restaurant Chirripó

OTHER

1 Reserva de la Biosfera La Amistad office
2 Gas Station
3 Musoc & TUASUR Buses to San José
6 Banco Nacional de Costa Rica
7 Museo Regional del Sur & Centro Cultural
13 Banco Anglo Costarricense
15 Texaco Gas Station & Buses to Puerto Jiménez
16 Parque Central
17 Cathedral
18 TRACOPA Bus Terminal
19 Banco de Costa Rica
21 Post Office & Telegrams
22 Mercado Municipal
23 New Bus Terminal
24 Buses to Dominical, Uvita & Quepos

To San José (136 km)

Carretera Interamericana

Avenida 5

Avenida 3

Avenida 1

Avenida Central

Avenida 2

Avenida 4

Avenida 6

To Dominical (34 km)

Río San Isidro

To Hotel del Sur (6 km) & Panama (220 km approx)

meals. Costs depend on the number of people. Sample rates for a four day trip are US$436 per person with eight passengers, and substantially more per person with fewer participants. It is sometimes possible to join other groups if there are not eight of you.

Running the Río General is also possible, although none of the major river running outfitters are currently offering it. Ask around if you have a group and want to go – something can be arranged.

Festivals The annual fair is held during the first week in February (occasionally beginning at the end of January) and features agricultural, horticultural and industrial shows and competitions.

San Isidro is the patron saint of farmers, who bring their stock into town to be blessed on the saint's feast day – 15 May.

Places to Stay – bottom end

The *Hotel El Jardín* has been recommended by budget travellers for clean, basic rooms and a cheap restaurant. Rooms are US$3.30 per person. The cheapest place in town is the *Hotel Lala* (☎ 71 0291) which charges US$2.20 per person in basic rooms, or US$5.50 (one or two people) for a room with a double bed and private cold-water shower. It's not bad for the price. The *Hotel Balboa* can also be tried. The *Hotel Astoria* (☎ 71 0914) has very basic box-like rooms for US$2.75 per person, or slightly better boxes for US$3.25 to US$4 per person with private cold shower.

The *Hotel Chirripó* (☎ 71 0529) is modern and good value for US$4.75/8.50 single/double or US$7/11.50 in rooms with private electric shower. It has a decent restaurant.

The *Pensión Eiffel* (☎ 71 0230) is a cheap hotel near the new bus terminal – it will probably begin getting more business as the bus companies begin moving there.

Places to Stay – middle

The *Hotel Iguazu* (☎ 71 2571) is good, clean and secure. Rooms with private electric showers are US$8.25/12 single/double. Also

good is the *Hotel Amaneli* (☎ 71 0352) which charges US$7 per person in rooms with private electric shower and fans.

The *Hotel El Tecal* (☎ 71 0664, 71 0431) is six km south-east of town on the right of the Interamericana. It has small but clean rooms with hot showers for US$9/13.

The best hotel is about seven km southeast of town, on the left side of the Interamericana. This is the *Hotel del Sur* (☎ 71 0233, fax 71 0527; Apartado 4-8000, San Isidro de El General, Pérez Zelédon) with a swimming pool, tennis court and a pleasant restaurant and bar. Rooms with private bath, hot water, air-conditioning, telephone and TV available on request are US$20/26.50 single/double. Cabins with fan, refrigerator and hot water, sleeping up to five people, are US$35.

Places to Eat

There are many inexpensive sodas downtown and in the market/bus terminal area – this is the place for travellers watching their colones.

The *Restaurant El Jardín* in the hotel of the same name is cheap and good. The *Hotel Chirripó Cafe* opens at 6 am for breakfast – it is inexpensive and popular. The *Hotel Chirripó Restaurant* has pleasant plaza views and is good value – a casado is US$2.50. The *Panadería El Tío Marcos* on the same block has good pastries and other baked goods. The *Restaurant El Tenedor* next to the Hotel Iguazu has a balcony overlooking a busy street and serves meals from US$1 (hamburgers) to US$5; pizzas are a speciality. The *Restaurant Hong Kong* on the park has been recommended for, predictably, Chinese food. The *Café del Teatro* in the Museo Regional/Centro Cultural complex has also been recommended for snacks and coffees.

About 2.5 km from the town centre on the road to Dominical is *Non Plus Ultra Bar/Restaurant* – it has been recommended for steaks, though I haven't tried it.

Getting There & Away

Buses leave San José from Calle 16, Avenida

1 & 3 (near the Musoc Hotel) about 15 times a day for San Isidro. The fare is about US$3 and the ride takes three hours.

The new bus terminal/market complex in San Isidro was due to open in 1993. Buses still leave from a variety of terminals and bus stops scattered throughout town (see map), but these services will slowly gravitate to the new terminal – you should enquire locally.

Buses to San José with Musoc (☎ 71 0414) or TUASUR (☎ 71 0419) leave from Calle 2 and the Interamericana 15 times a day from about 5 am to 4.30 pm.

Buses for San Gerardo de Rivas (for Parque Nacional Chirripó) leave at 5 am and 2 pm and take two hours. The morning bus leaves from the Parque Central and the afternoon bus leaves from the south side of the new bus terminal.

Buses leave for the coast at Quepos via Dominical at 7 am and 1.30 pm, and for Uvita via Dominical at 3 pm. Departures are from Calle 1, Avenida 4 & 6 – there is a little store here which sells tickets but it's not well marked.

TRACOPA (☎ 71 0468) at Calle 3 and the Interamericana has buses southbound. The ticket office is open from 7 am to 12.30 pm and 1.30 to 4 pm from Monday to Saturday – at other times buy tickets on the bus. Buses for Buenos Aires, Palmar Norte and Neily leave at 4.45, 7.30 am and 12.30 and 3 pm. Buses to Buenos Aires, Paso Real, San Vito (3½ hours, US$2.75), Sabalito and Agua Buena leave at 5.30 am and 2 pm. TRACOPA buses from San José pass through San Isidro at approximately the following times for the following destinations – tickets are sold on a space-available basis: to Canoas at 8.30 am and 3.45, 7.30 and 9 pm; to Golfito at 10 am and 6 pm; to Ciudad Cortés (near Palmar Norte) at 11.30 am and 5.30 pm; to Coto 47 (near Neily) at 1.30 pm; to San Vito and Agua Buena at 9 and 11.30 am and 2.45 and 5.30 pm; to Davíd, Panama, at 10 am and 3 pm.

Buses to Puerto Jiménez leave from the fruit stand by the Texaco station on the Interamericana. According to the ICT, departures are at 5.30 am and noon, but locals told me that was the time the buses left San José and that they came through San Isidro at about 8 am and 2.30 pm and that tickets are sold on a space-available basis – so check carefully for the current situation. The five to six hour ride costs about US$4.

You can hire a 4WD taxi to San Gerardo de Rivas for US$16. A taxi to the Hotel del Sur is about US$3.

Getting Around
City buses leave from the north-west side of the Parque Central.

SAN GERARDO DE RIVAS
This small village, about 20 km north-east of San Isidro, is the entry point to Parque Nacional Chirripó (described following). The elevation here is about 1350 metres, the climate is pleasant, and there are hiking and bird-watching opportunities both around the village and in the above park.

Information
The Chirripó ranger station is about one km below the village on the road from San Isidro.

Places to Stay
Just below the ranger station is the simple and basic *Cabinas La Marín* with a couple of rooms for US$3 per person. As you head up to the village from the ranger station you pass several more simple hotels. The *Cabinas & Soda El Descanso* owned by the friendly and helpful Francisco Elizondo family is a good choice. They charge US$3 per person in small but clean rooms. There is an electric shower and decent meals are available on request.

Further up is the new *Cabinas Elimar* which has simple but spacious rooms with private electric shower. Each room has one double and one single bed and rents for US$14.50. They have a restaurant which opens on request.

About one km above the ranger station, in the centre of San Gerardo, is the *Soda & Cabinas Chirripó* which has clean, small rooms for US$2 per person. An electric shower is available. Next door is the village pulpería (☎ 71 0433, ext 106) which is the only phone in town. If you speak Spanish, you can call the pulpería and leave a message for one of the hotels – either they'll call you back or you can tell them when you'll call again and they can stand by.

About 1.5 km below the ranger station, in the community of Canaán, is the *Chirripó Lodge* which has basic rooms with four beds for about US$3 per person. You can leave a message with the Canaán pulpería (☎ 71 0433, ext 101). The lodge rents hiking gear: a sleeping bag for US$9, a stove for US$5.

Getting There & Away

Buses leave San Isidro at 5 am and 2 pm and take almost two hours to get to San Gerardo de Rivas (there is another San Gerardo – ask for the full name). The final stop is outside a cantina just beyond the ranger station – you have to continue on foot to the places to stay in San Gerardo. Return buses leave from the cantina at 7 am and 4 pm.

If driving, head south of San Isidro on the Interamericana, crossing the Río San Isidro at the south end of town. About half a km further, cross the Río Jilguero and look for a steep turn up to the left, about 300 metres beyond the Jilguero. (There is a 'Pollo Brasilia' sign opposite the turn-off, but the road itself is not signed until you've been on it for a few hundred metres!) The ranger station is about 18 km up this road, which is steep and gravelled but passable to ordinary cars.

PARQUE NACIONAL CHIRRIPÓ

This is Costa Rica's main mountain park and, at 50,150 hectares, the nation's largest national park. There are three peaks of over 3800 metres, including Cerro Chirripó itself which, at 3819 metres, is the highest mountain in the country. In fact, of all the Central American countries, only Guatemala has higher mountains. Most of the park lies at over 2000 metres above sea level, and there are hiking trails and two simple mountain huts for people wishing to spend a few days

hiking at high altitude. I remember when I first visited Chirripó, in 1981, I had spent almost a year travelling around tropical Central America and was delighted to find a park where I could get away from the heat for a while!

The park entrance at San Gerardo is at 1350 metres, and so the elevation gain to the top of Chirripó is about 2.5 km straight up! That is a lot of climbing.

Fortunately, there is an easy-to-follow trail all the way to the top, and no technical climbing is required. Almost all visitors use this trail to get up to the top, though alternatives are discussed below. Walking at the lower elevations is also rewarding, with excellent views and good bird-watching.

The climb is a fascinating one because it goes through constantly changing scenery, vegetation and wildlife as you ascend. After passing through the pasturelands outside the park, the trail leads through tropical lower montane and then montane rainforests. These are essentially evergreen forests with heavy epiphytic growths in the trees, and thick fern and bamboo understoreys. Emerging above the main canopy (25 to 30 metres) are oak trees reaching 40 or even 50 metres in height.

These highland forests are home to such birds as the flame-throated warbler and buffy tufted-cheek, to name but two. Blue and green frogs and lime-coloured caterpillars thickly covered with stinging hairs make their way across the trail and Baird's tapir lurks in the thick vegetation – though you are much more likely to see squirrels than tapirs. Eventually, the trail climbs out of the rainforests and into the bare and windswept páramo of the mountain tops.

The Chirripó massif is part of the Cordillera de Talamanca which continues to the north-west and south-east.

The national park's eastern boundary coincides with the western boundary of the huge and largely inaccessible Parque Internacional de La Amistad, and thus most of the Talamancan mountains are protected. Chirripó and La Amistad parks, together with some biological reserves and several large Indian reservations, make up the Reserva de La Biosfera La Amistad.

Orientation & Information

The dry season (from late December to April) is the most popular time to go. During weekends, and especially at Easter, the park is relatively crowded with Costa Rican hiking groups. The mountain refuge may well be full – and camping is not allowed at the summit to protect the delicate páramo ecosystem. February and March are the driest months, though it may still rain sometimes.

During the wet season, you are likely to have the park to yourself. I have spent almost two weeks backpacking in the park during the wet season and found that it rarely rained before 1 pm – and I didn't see anybody. A great wilderness experience. But it is as well to remember that as much as 7000 mm of annual rainfall has been recorded in some areas of the park.

The ranger station in San Gerardo is a good place to ask about weather conditions and get an idea of how many people are in the park. Officially, you need to make a reservation with the park service to stay in the huts near the summit. When I asked about making a reservation at the park's service office in San José, I was told that there was a six week waiting list! Other travellers give similar reports. In reality, there are a lot of no-shows. You should just go to San Gerardo and ask the ranger for a permit – it helps if you speak Spanish. When I was there in March 1993, the ranger told me there were 13 people at one hut, which has a maximum capacity of 40. So much for a six week waiting list. Occasionally, travellers may find that the huts are, indeed, full – but if you can wait a day or two, space will become available. The week before Easter and the Easter weekend are usually reserved well ahead, but there are rarely problems at other times.

You can contact the ranger station directly by the Servicio de Parques Nacionales radio-telephone (☎ 33 4160) but you need to speak Spanish. You can also try to contact them from the regional office in San Isidro. Ranger station hours are from 5 am to 5 pm daily.

At the ranger station pay the approximately US$1.50 daily park entrance fee plus US$3 per night in the huts. Drivers can leave vehicles near the ranger station and excess luggage can be locked up for US$0.75. Maps available at the station are very sketchy. Good topographical maps from the IGN are available from San José (though huts and trails are not marked). Chirripó lies on the corner of four 1:50,000 scale maps, so you need maps 3444 II San Isidro and 3544 III Durika to cover the area from ranger station to the summit of Chirripó itself, and maps 3544 IV Fila Norte and 3444 I Cuerici to cover other peaks in the summit massif. (Topographical maps are nice to have but not essential.)

Mule hire can be arranged with the locals – ask in the hotels or ranger station. You can ride a mule or just have one to carry your gear. The locals will not normally rent the animals without a local guide to come with you. Expect to pay about US$25 per day for a guide and a pack animal.

Climbing Chirripó

From the ranger station it is a 16 km climb to the Chirripó summit area. Allow seven to 16 hours to reach the huts, depending on how fit and motivated you are. Anybody can show you the beginning of the trail, which is signposted at approximately two km intervals and easy to follow once you are on it.

There used to be three huts spaced out along the last hour of the trail. There are two currently in use, and they are very close to one another. They are equipped with a sleeping platform and wood stove. However, there is very little dead and down wood available in the páramo and burning it is unjustified. Rangers will sometimes bring supplies of wood up from the forest by mule, but you should carry a camping stove. It can freeze at night so have warm clothes and a good sleeping bag. There is a cave (sleeps about six people) about half way along the trail if you don't want to go from ranger station to huts in one day. There is also an open-sided insect-ridden hut about half way up which can provide shelter. Carry water along the trail, particularly during the dry season when there is only one place to get water before the huts.

From the huts it is a further four km or so to the summit – allow at least two hours if you are fit. A minimum of two days is needed to climb from the ranger station to the summit and back again. Three days would be better. If you don't return to San Gerardo by 4 pm, you'll miss the last bus out.

Almost every visitor to the park climbs the main trail to Chirripó and returns the same way. Other nearby mountains can also be climbed, up fairly obvious trails leading from the huts. These include Cerro Ventisqueros, at 3812 metres just seven metres lower than Chirripó and the second highest peak in the country, and several other peaks over 3700 metres. Some maps show a couple of rarely used, non-maintained wilderness trails leading north and south out of the park, but these are extremely difficult to find and are not recommended.

An alternative, rarely used route to Chirripó is to head north of the ranger station to the community of Herradura, three km away. Here, guides can be hired to take you up a new trail entering the mountains from the west side. An overnight camp is necessary below Cerro Urán – the rangers will permit you to camp on this rarely used route. Ask locally about other, rarely used, routes through the forest up to the mountain.

Apparently, there are a couple of places to stay beyond Herradura. One is called *Ojo del Agua* and is three km beyond Heradura, and the other is *Pensión Quetzal Dorado*, three hours hike beyond Herradura. Both offer beds, horses and bird-watching opportunities – ask locally.

BUENOS AIRES

This small village is 64 km south-east of San Isidro and three km north of the Carretera Interamericana. The village is in the centre of an important pineapple-producing region. You could stop here as an entry point for the rarely visited Parque Internacional de La Amistad and several Indian reserves to the north and Reserva Indígena Boruca to the south. A road east of Buenos Aires goes through remote country and Indian reserves eventually joining with the San Vito road at Jabillo. You won't see other tourists.

Places to Stay

There are a couple of cheap and basic places to stay in Buenos Aires.

A new 'back to the earth' project has recently opened its doors to tourism. The private *Reserva Biológica Durika* is about 20 km north of Buenos Aires on the flanks of Cerro Durika in the Cordillera de Talamanca. A couple of dozen people live here in a more or less independent and sustainable manner – classes are offered in yoga, vegetarian cooking, meditation etc. Community members are committed to local conservation. Visitors are welcome – there are several rustic cabins with showers and bathroom at the Finca Anael on the reserve. Birding and hiking are the main activities – there is a resident birding guide. Rates are US$40 to US$55 per cabin and include vegetarian meals and transportation from Buenos Aires. (This is about an hour in a 4WD vehicle followed by an hour on foot or horseback.) I've never been there, but it sounds like a good place for really getting away from it all in the mountains. Reservations are taken in English (☎ 40 2320, fax 23 0341), in Spanish (☎ 78 0028, fax 78 0003) or write to Apartado 9, Buenos Aires, Puntarenas Zona Sur, Costa Rica.

Getting There & Away

There are buses from San Isidro, or you can take any southbound bus on the Carretera Interamericana and ask to be put down at the turn-off for Buenos Aires.

PASO REAL

This is the point where the Interamericana reaches the intersection of the Río General with the Río Terraba. The Interamericana turns west towards Palmar Norte. Travellers wishing to continue east to San Vito cross the

Río Terraba on a small car ferry which runs 24 hours and costs US$1.30 for car and driver. Signage on the Interamericana is poor: if heading southbound, there is a small sign for Paso Real; if heading northbound there is a sign for San Vito.

RESERVA INDÍGENA BORUCA

This reserve is centred around the village of Boruca, about 20 km south of Buenos Aires. It is one of the few Indian reserves where visitors are not unwelcome, perhaps because Boruca is only some eight km west of the Carretera Interamericana.

The Borucas are known for their carvings, both of balsa wood masks and decorated gourds. The women use pre-Columbian back-strap looms to weave cotton cloth and belts. These can sometimes be bought from the locals. Generally, the people live a simple agricultural life in the surrounding hills.

If you are simply driving through the area on the Carretera Interamericana, you can stop at the community of Curré, a few km south-west of Paso Real. There is a small crafts co-operative store here, and it sells Boruca work.

Festivals

New Year's Eve and 8 February are important fiesta times. New Year's Eve is celebrated in Boruca with the three day Fiesta de los Diablitos (little devils). Men in devil costumes represent the Indians in their fight against the Spanish conquerors. The Spaniards, represented by a man in a bull costume, lose the battle. A similar fiesta is held in Curré in February – a recent report gives 8 February as the date, but check locally.

Places to Stay

There is no hotel as such, but accommodation can be arranged with a local family in Boruca by asking at the village pulpería. This is for culturally sensitive travellers who can respect and appreciate the local lifestyle.

Getting There & Away

Ask a bus driver to drop you off at the Entrada de Boruca, which is about two km south of Curré on the Carretera Interamericana. From there it is an eight km hike. A school bus from Buenos Aires leaves on school days (from March to early December) at 1.30 pm and takes about two hours to Boruca via a different route.

PALMAR NORTE & PALMAR SUR

These two places are basically the same town on different sides of the Río Terraba, which the Interamericana has been following for the last 40 km (if you are southbound). Palmar is about 125 km south of San Isidro and 95 km north-west of the Panamanian border.

The town is the centre of the banana-growing region of the Valle de Diquis, and is also a transportation hub. You might find yourself staying here en route to the Sierpe, Bahía Drake and the Corcovado region.

The area is also of interest to archaeologists because of the discovery of almost perfect stone spheres up to 1½ metres in diameter. These were made by pre-Columbian Indians, and similar spheres have been found on Isla del Caño (now a Biological Reserve) – but exactly who made them and how remains a mystery. Ask in town if you want to see the spheres *(esferas de piedra)* – they are found in a variety of places including backyards and in banana plantations.

Palmar Norte has hotels, buses and a gas station, and Palmar Sur has the airport. The Banco Anglo Costarricense is on the Interamericana in Palmar Norte.

Places to Stay & Eat

There are two hotels on the Interamericana and two more in the town centre, scant blocks from the highway (it's not a big town). On the Interamericana near the north end of town is the *Cabinas Tico Aleman* (☎ 75 6232) which has clean rooms with private bath and fan for US$7 per person. Nearby, next to the Chevron station, the *Cabinas & Restaurant Wah Lok* has rooms with fan and shower for US$10.50 a double.

In town, the *Hotel Xenia* (☎ 75 6129) is 150 metres east of the TRACOPA bus terminal. It's supposedly the cheapest place, but when I was passing through there was nobody at the reception desk. I took a quick peek – it looks OK. *Cabinas Amarillas* (☎ 75 6251) is 300 metres east of TRACOPA, by the soccer field. They have clean, secure rooms with private bath and fan for US$10/15.

There are several inexpensive restaurants, of which the *Chan Yeng* opposite the Supermercado Terraba has been recommended.

Getting There & Away
Air There are flights from San José with SANSA on Monday, Wednesday and Friday at 9.30 am arriving 10.05 am (US$26), continuing on to Coto 47. Return flights to San José are at 10.20 am via Coto 47 reaching San José at 11.45 am.

Travelair has flights leaving San José at 8.10 am daily via Golfito, arriving in Palmar Sur at 9.50 am. Direct return flights are at 10.05 am. The fare is US$66 one way and US$114 for the round trip.

The airport is in Palmar Sur. Taxis usually meet incoming flights and charge US$2 to Palmar Norte or US$12.50 to Sierpe. The Palmar Norte to Sierpe bus passes through Palmar Sur – you can board it on a space-available basis.

Bus TRACOPA has buses to San José at 5.25, 7.30, 8.15 and 10 am and 1, 2.30 and 4.45 pm from Monday to Saturday. On Sunday buses leave at 7.30 and 8.15 am and 12.15, 1, and 3 pm. Buses for San Isidro leave daily at 6.30 and 9.30 am and 2.30 and 4 pm. Southbound buses sell tickets on a space-available basis only.

Buses go 14 km to Sierpe (US$0.50) from in front of the Supermercado Terraba about five times a day between 6 am and 5.30 pm. Taxis charge about US$12.50 to Sierpe.

Car & Motorbike A paved road from Palmar Norte goes seven km west to Ciudad Cortés, from where a rough 20 km road goes northwest along the Pacific coast through Coronado as far as Tortuga Abajo. Beyond that a poor track suitable for 4WDs continues

32 km via Uvita to the coastal village of Dominical. This road is currently being worked on and should be passable to ordinary cars by the time you read this.

Palmar to Corcovado

SIERPE
This small village is on the Río Sierpe, about 30 km from the Pacific Ocean. Boats to Bahía Drake can be hired here and most of the lodges in Bahía Drake will arrange boat pick-up in Sierpe for their guests.

Places to Stay & Eat
Hotel Margarita has basic but very clean small rooms for US$2.25 per person. The hotel is on the corner of a grassy square about three blocks from the dock – there is no sign but the Bazar Jennifer clothing store is right next to it.

A block from the dock is the new *Hotel Pargo* (☎ 75 6485) which has good rooms with fans and private hot shower for US$16.50/20 and with air-conditioning for an extra US$5. It has a decent soda attached.

The *Cabinas Estero Azul* (☎ 33 2578, 21 7681, fax 22 0297) is a new outfit about two km before you get to Sierpe. They have cabins sleeping up to three with fans, private bath and refrigerator for US$40. They also offer sportfishing and natural history boat tours for about US$250 per day – the boats will take up to four people. However, the place was empty when I stopped by – they don't seem to have much business.

I've also heard there is an Italian-run lodge across the river – but I couldn't find it.

The most popular restaurant is the *Las Vegas Bar/Restaurant* right next to the boat dock. The *Restaurant Piccoli* serves Italian food.

Places to Stay – Río Sierpe
Just over half way between Sierpe and the ocean is the *Río Sierpe Lodge* (☎ 20 2121, 20 1712, fax 32 3321; Apartado 818-1200, Pavas). This small, rustic but comfortable

and well-run lodge offers nature and birding tours, diving and sportfishing for its guests. There are eight rooms each with private solar-heated bath. The rooms are usually double occupancy but are spacious enough to sleep five people – student discounts are available. The food is good and varied and there is a recreation area with a large library of paperback books. There are several trails around the lodge suitable for bird-watching. The staff are helpful and friendly.

Room rates include meals, taxes, soft drinks and road/river transfer from Palmar to the lodge. Independent travellers are charged US$78/130 single/double. Optional full day excursions (two person minimum) include Parque Nacional Corcovado or Isla Caño (US$55 per person), tidal basin angling (US$80) and Pacific Ocean angling (US$160). Half day trips to Isla Violines (good birding) are US$25 and mangrove excursions (more birds) are US$35. These can be combined into excursion packages for naturalists or anglers – these go from three days/two nights to six days/five nights and internal flights are included. There are substantial discounts for naturalist or student groups of eight or more – call the lodge for details.

They also do two day overnight camping treks into the rainforest and through remote villages for US$65 per person or US$125 on horseback. They have dive packages available which include boats, all gear and a PADI or NAUI certified divemaster – you just need your swim wear, mask and a diver certification card. Prices (including lodging, meals, and flights/transfers from San José) range from US$395 per person for three days/two nights to US$820 for six days/five nights with a six person minimum – add about 50% if there are just two of you. There are US$20/day discounts if you bring your own BC and regulator.

Getting There & Away

Road Buses between Sierpe and Palmar Norte leave five times a day between 5.30 am and 3 pm. A taxi charges about US$12.50.

Boat If you have not pre-arranged a boat pick-up with a Bahía Drake or Río Sierpe lodge, ask around at the dock next to the Las Vegas Bar. The going rate is about US$15 per person to Bahía Drake – if there is a group. The Hotel Pargo is planning on buying a boat and providing local transportation and tour services in 1994.

The trip out to Bahía Drake is a scenic and interesting one: first along the river through rainforest, then through the estuary with mangroves, and on through the tidal waves, currents and surf of the river mouth into the ocean. Keep your eyes open for monkeys, sloths, herons, macaws, parrots, kingfishers, ibises and spoonbills along the river and dolphins, boobies, frigatebirds and pelicans along the coast. The river mouth has a reputation for being dangerous – and it is in a small dugout. But the larger boats with strong engines used by the lodges don't have any problems – though it's pretty exciting riding the swells and avoiding the splashes.

BAHÍA DRAKE

Bahía Drake (pronounced 'dra-cay' by locals) is both 16th century history and natural history. Sir Francis Drake himself supposedly visited the bay in March of 1579, during his global circumnavigation in the *Golden Hind*. The bay is only a few km north of Parque Nacional Corcovado, which can be visited from here. Reserva Biológica Isla del Caño can also be visited from Bahía Drake.

Agujitas is a small village on the bay, with a pulpería, a public phone and a school. You can visit Agujitas and pick up a cola or beer, watch the local kids coming home from the school, and chat with the locals. Most people who visit tend to stay in their lodges, but the locals enjoy talking with travellers, so stop by.

Places to Stay

Most visitors stay in one of the lodges on or near Bahía Drake. Travellers on a low budget can stay in one of the cheaper hotels near Agujitas.

The *Bahía Drake Wilderness Camp*

(☎ fax 71 2436) is run by an American, Herb Michaud, and is the longest established of the Bahía Drake lodges. The camp is on a low headland, so you can explore the tide pools or swim in the ocean (although the swimming is rocky and depends on the tide). It has enthusiastic naturalist guides who can take you to see and experience all the local habitats. Snorkelling gear and fibreglass canoes can be borrowed and horses, diving gear and fishing gear are available for rent. You can canoe up the Río Agujitas at high tide to explore the forest and look for birds and monkeys.

The wilderness camp hires friendly local people to work in the lodge, and their kids are often running around which makes the place far from impersonal. Although the place is called a 'wilderness camp', the accommodation ranges from tents to comfortable cabins. The rooms have fans and private solar-heated showers, and several have patios with ocean views. A generator provides electricity from 4 pm to 4 am. Radiotelephone provides links with the outside world. Tasty and ample home-cooked meals are provided in the screened dining room, just a few metres away from the Pacific Ocean. There is a nice bar.

Accommodation prices include three meals a day: 19 rooms with private shower cost US$84/132 single/double; four large walk-in tents with electricity and beds are US$64/92 – access to bathrooms is nearby. Corcovado and Isla del Caño tours are about US$40 per person. Offshore fishing boats including food, bait and fishing gear can take up to three anglers for about US$250.

Packages for four days/three nights, including day tours to Corcovado and Isla del Caño, bilingual guides, air/bus/boat transfers from San José, snorkelling gear, and all meals are US$492/888. Four day/three night packages including two days fishing are US$650/1270. Dive packages are available on request.

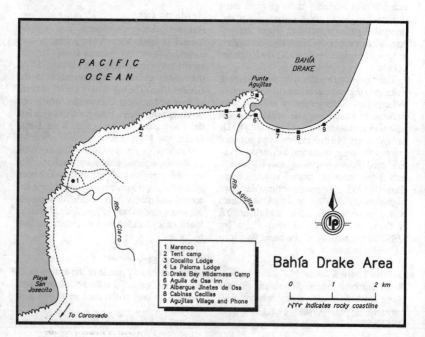

PACIFIC OCEAN

BAHÍA DRAKE

Punta Agujitas

Río Agujitas

Río Claro

Playa San Josecito

To Corcovado

1 Marenco
2 Tent camp
3 Cocalito Lodge
4 La Paloma Lodge
5 Drake Bay Wilderness Camp
6 Aguila de Osa Inn
7 Albergue Jinetes de Osa
8 Cabinas Cecillas
9 Agujitas Village and Phone

Bahía Drake Area

0   1   2 km

∿∿∿ Indicates rocky coastline

A five minute walk up a hill behind Bahía Drake brings you to *La Paloma Lodge* (☎ fax 39 0954, radiotelephone at lodge 39 2801; Apartado 97-4005, San Antonio de Belén, Heredia, Costa Rica). Its hilltop location gives splendid ocean and forest views and catches whatever sea breezes may waft by. There are plenty of birds around – scarlet-rumped tanagers and common tody flycatchers were nesting right next to the dining room when I visited. English-speaking guides with biology degrees are on hand to help guests identify what they see. Snorkelling gear can be borrowed and nature tours, fishing, horseback and canoeing are available. Corcovado tours are US$55 per person, Isla del Caño tours are US$65 per person – group rates on request. Sportfishing boats are available for US$350 per day.

All the buildings are elevated on stilts to take maximum advantage of breeze and views. There is a row of five cabins, each with a private bathroom and a private balcony with hammock and a good view. Rates are US$80/126 single/double including meals and boat pick-up from Sierpe. Three spacious thatched-roof bungalows, surrounded by forest and with a wrap-around balcony, can sleep up to eight people on two levels – great for families. Each bungalow has a private bathroom. Rates are from US$160/190 for double/triple. Electric power is available at night. Excellent meals are served in a beautiful dining room/club house with a high thatched roof.

Because of its smaller size, the lodge owners try and give personalised service to their guests. Package and group rates are available on request.

A path leads west of La Paloma, down the hill, to Playa Cocalito – a small beach about five minutes away. Most of the shoreline in the area is rocky and this little beach is the best bet for an ocean swim – though not at high tide. Right behind the beach is the *Cocalito Lodge* (☎ 75 6150, fax 75 6291; in Canada, ☎ (519) 782 4592; Apartado 63, Palmar Norte). This is a small, laid-back and very friendly lodge owned by Canadians. There are seven rooms sleeping from two to six people. Three rooms have their own bathroom downstairs, the other four have private in-room bathrooms. Lighting is by candle, except for a tiny hydroelectric system which provides power for the kitchen. Their professional chef prepares excellent seafood, grilled, barbecued and spiced with fresh herbs from their garden. Walk-ins are welcome at their restaurant – candle-lit dinners are about US$11 each. There is a small paperback library and pleasant bar.

Local guides are used for excursions to all the usual destinations – tours start at US$30 a day for hikes up to waterfalls, and US$50 for Corcovado, Isla del Caño, and mangrove tours. They can also set you up with horses and local guides for overnight jungle trips for US$100 per person.

Room rates are a modest US$30 per person, or US$50 including meals. You can camp here for US$7 if you are backpacking through – this gives use of showers, bathrooms and restaurant. They will also organise complete packages with air transport from San José and bus/boat to the lodge.

On the east side of the Río Agujitas is the *Aguila de Osa Inn* (☎ 32 7722; Apartado 10486-1000, San José; PO Box 025312 £250, Miami, FL 33102-5312). There are seven cabins with private bath, fans and nice views for US$98/160 single/double with all three meals. They offer all the usual local tours, fishing charters and scuba packages ranging from US$1200 for two people for three nights and two days of diving to US$2660 for two people for seven nights and six days of diving. Two tanks, weights, divemaster and boat are provided for divers.

Continuing east along the shores of Bahía Drake brings you to *Albergue Jinetes de Osa* about five minutes away. Isabela in San José (☎ 53 6909) can make reservations for the albergue, which is a small four-bedroom lodge owned by a friendly local couple. Each room has a double and single bed – the bathroom is shared. There is electricity from 6 to 9 pm. They charge US$30/60/75 for single/double/triple including three meals. A small boat is available on request for tours to Corcovado and Isla del Caño – prices are the cheapest in the area, but don't expect a fast boat with bilingual naturalist guides. Horse rental is available for US$20 for half a day.

A few hundred metres further east is *Cabinas Cecilia*, also on the beach. The Agujitas pulpería (☎ 71 2336) can pass on a message. There are two double rooms for US$25 per person including three meals. Two more rooms, each with bunk beds for six people, are US$20 per person, including meals. The bathroom is shared. They can also arrange cheap tours.

Getting There & Away

Most people arrive by boat from Sierpe after either flying to Palmar Sur or travelling by road. If you have a lodge reservation, this will be arranged for you. There is an airstrip near Bahía Drake which can be reached by chartered flights from San José – this is an expensive option which can be arranged by the lodges. It is only a couple of hours faster than taking the scheduled SANSA or Travelair flights and continuing by taxi and boat.

A road links Agujitas with Rancho Quemado – a tiny community to the east – but this road is in terrible shape and accessible only to 4WD in the dry season. But it explains the few trucks and 4WDs seen in the village. You can also reach Rancho Quemado on foot or by horseback; Pedro Garro at the Albergue Jinetes de Osa can give you information, rent horses, and tell you of a friend who will give you a place to stay. From Rancho Quemado there is a daily bus to Rincón, on the road to Puerto Jiménez. There is talk of a road linking Agujitas with Sierpe – this probably won't be built for some years yet.

Backpackers occasionally hike in from Parque Nacional Corcovado. From San Pedrillo at the north end of the park, beach trails lead to Bahía Drake. It takes two to three hours to hike from San Pedrillo to Marenco (see following), and a further one to two hours to hike from Marenco to Bahía Drake. (If you have a reservation at one of the lodges, they can arrange to pick you up or drop you off in San Pedrillo.) Ask around at the lodges in the Bahía Drake area for a

boat on to Sierpe. If you want to hike into Corcovado from Bahía Drake, it can be done fairly easily along the coast in about four to five hours. Dropping tides are always the best for coastal walks – high tides may cut you off or delay you. Ask locally.

Note that there is a tent camp between Bahía Drake and Marenco. There are 10 large tents, a dining room, several bathrooms and showers. The charge is US$45 per person including three meals. The tent camp is used mainly by anglers who are deep-sea fishing in the area. For more information, call Expediciones Tropicales (☎ 33 9135, 33 3892; fax 23 6728; Apartado 659-1150, La Uruca).

MARENCO

Marenco is about three or four km southwest of Bahía Drake and five km north of Corcovado – it is the closest place to stay on the north side of the national park if you want comfortable accommodation. It used to be a biological station but is now a private Costa Rican-run tropical forest reserve set up to protect part of the rainforest. As such, the reserve plays an important role as a buffer zone around Parque Nacional Corcovado. Ecologists know that the conservation of a protected area is much enhanced if the region beyond the park boundary is carefully managed. This is the case with Marenco. Not only is the habitat conserved, but employment is provided for local people who work as boatmen, guides and hotel staff.

The 500 hectare reserve is set on a bluff overlooking the Pacific and is a good place for trips to Corcovado, Isla del Caño, or simply into the forest surrounding the station. There are four km of trails around Marenco and many of the plant, bird and other animal species seen in Corcovado can be found in the Marenco area. A favourite hike is to the Río Claro which literally cascades through the reserve. There are beautiful swimming holes to reward you at the end of a sweaty hike. Bilingual naturalist guides are on hand to take visitors on excursions to rainforest, beach or islands. In addition, self-guiding nature trail booklets are available to those wishing to explore alone. Horses are available for rent.

I recently received a report that some tourists are overcharged (US$170 per night), that the food is poor, the drinking water improperly treated, the beds are uncomfortable, and that the natural history guides are poorly trained. For US$170 per night it's not a good deal – though it may be just be worth the US$80 that drop-ins pay.

I've also read positive reports about the place – which is certainly well situated. Perhaps the writers of the complaint just hit it at a bad time – which can happen anywhere. I found the people there polite when I visited though I've never taken a tour with them.

Tours

Most people come on a package deal which includes transport and local tours. A minimum of two nights is required. The most complete package is for five days and four nights, including chartered flights from San José and return, a day boat trip to Isla del Caño, guided day hikes to Corcovado and Río Claro rainforest, and all accommodation, food, transfers and taxes. This package costs US$690 per person in bungalows, US$640 in cabins. Cheaper packages with fewer options are available. Student and group discounts are available. For information and reservations contact Marenco Tropical Forest Reserve (☎ 21 1594, 33 9101, fax 55 1340; Apartado 4025-1000, San José).

Places to Stay & Eat

Accommodation is in rustic cabins and bungalows which are elevated enough to catch the breeze. Each room has a private bathroom and a verandah overlooking the Pacific Ocean. There are four bunks in each room, but double occupancy is the rule except for student or discounted groups. A generator runs for a few hours in the evening. Meals are served family style in the dining room, and a small library of reference books is available.

There are eight small cabins and 17 more spacious bungalows, but the reserve may well be full during the 'dry' busy months of December to April when advance reservations are needed. During the rest of the year, you can often get in by making a reservation just a day or two in advance. The wettest months are September and October, when the lodge may well be almost empty. Overnight stays for drop-ins are US$85 per person including meals, but tours are extra.

Getting There & Away

Marenco will make all arrangements for its guests. Most guests enter via Palmar or Bahía Drake airports and then boat in, though other routes can be arranged. Note that there is no dock at Marenco. Arriving guests transfer from launches to small boats which are anchored off-shore – you will almost certainly get your feet wet.

RESERVA BIOLÓGICA ISLA DEL CAÑO

This 300 hectare island is roughly 20 km west of Bahía Drake. The reserve is of interest to snorkellers, divers, biologists and archaeologists. About 5800 hectares of ocean are designated as part of the reserve.

Snorkellers will find incredibly warm water (about body temperature!) and a good variety of marine life ranging from fish to sea cucumbers. Scuba diving trips are arranged by the Bahía Drake/Río Sierpe lodges – there are coral reefs and underwater rock formations as well as an abundance of sea life. A tropical beach with an attractive rainforest backdrop provides sunbathing opportunities, and a trail leads inland, through an evergreen rainforest, to a ridge at about 110 metres above sea level.

Near the top, look for some of the rock spheres which were made by pre-Columbian Indian people. Although these spheres have been found in several places in southern Costa Rica, archaeologists are still puzzling over their functions. Trees include milk trees (which exude a drinkable white latex), rubber trees, figs and a variety of other tropical species. Birds include coastal and oceanic species as well as rainforest inhabitants, but wildlife is not as varied or prolific as on the mainland.

Places to Stay

Camping is allowed, but you need permission from the Servicio de Parques Nacionales first. There are no facilities. The reserve is administered by the Parque Nacional Corcovado and there is a ranger station by the landing beach.

Getting There & Away

Most visitors arrive with a tour. These can be arranged with any of the lodges north or south of Corcovado.

PARQUE NACIONAL CORCOVADO

This national park has great biological diversity and has long attracted the attention of tropical ecologists who wish to study the intricate workings of the rainforest. The 41,788 hectare park covers the south-western corner of the Península de Osa and protects at least eight distinct types of habitat. This assemblage is considered both unique and the best remaining Pacific coastal rainforest in Central America. In addition, the park has recently acquired a further 12,751 hectares on the north-western side of the Golfo Dulce.

Because of its remoteness this rainforest remained undisturbed until the 1960s when logging began in the area. The park was established in 1975, but a few years later a small gold rush in the area led to several hundred miners moving into the park. Their activities began silting up rivers, disturbing wildlife and destroying forest. In 1986 the miners were forcibly evicted from the park and now there is an uneasy truce between the park authorities and the miners who are working the lands neighbouring the park. On my last visit, in 1993, I found sites with evidence of miners still working within the park.

Whilst it is important to preserve the biodiversity and unique environment found in the park, it is understandable that local people also want to improve their lives. The mining operations within the park were mainly of the gold panning variety, rather than large-scale dredging operations, and the miners were often poor people trying to

make a living. The Costa Rican authorities, ever mindful of the concepts of peaceful conflict resolution, are trying to work with both conservationists and miners to work out a compromise which allows the people to work without endangering the rainforest protected in the park. It will be interesting to see whether these conflicts will be resolved.

Information

There are five ranger stations. Four of them are at the edges of the park, and the fifth one, the park headquarters at Sirena, is in the middle of the park. There are trails linking these stations, and you can camp at all of them. Camping costs US$2.25 per person per night. In addition, you must pay the daily park fee of US$1.50. If you make arrangements a week or more in advance, the rangers can provide basic meals for about US$10 per day. Camping facilities consist of tent space, water and latrines.

Sirena, the park headquarters, provides the only shelter in the park. You still need a sleeping bag and insect netting (or use your tent) – you will have a breezy attic area with a roof over your head. There is also a bunkhouse for which you should make reservations in advance. There is also an airstrip at Sirena.

Reservations for meals at any ranger station or to sleep in the Sirena bunkhouse can be made through the Servicio de Parques Nacionales office in San José, by radiotelephone (☎ 33 4160) direct with the ranger station, or through the park's office in Puerto Jiménez (☎ 78 5036, fax 78 5011). Allow a few days for arrangements to be made. Self sufficient backpackers can just show up and pay their daily fees as they go.

Because Corcovado has the best trail system of any rainforest park, it attracts a fair number of backpackers – sometimes as many as two dozen people may be camped at Sirena during the dry season, though there are fewer people at the other stations. I have heard complaints from a few budget travellers that the combined daily park and camping fee (US$3.75 per person per day) is too expensive. It is worth noting, in this context, that the national parks are inadequately funded and that park fees help to keep the parks open. Many countries which rely on tourism as a mainstay of their economy, for example Kenya, Nepal and Ecuador, have much higher national park fees. The fee to enter the Galápagos Islands of Ecuador is currently US$80 per visitor. If you want to see the rainforest today and have it around for your children and grandchildren to see a few decades from now, then the modest entrance fee is not too much to pay.

Wildlife

The wildlife within the park is varied and prolific. Corcovado is home to Costa Rica's largest population of the beautiful scarlet macaw. Many of the other important or endangered rainforest species are protected here: tapirs, five cat species, crocodiles, peccaries, giant anteaters, sloths and monkeys. The rare harpy eagle, which is almost extinct in Costa Rica, may still breed in remote parts of Corcovado. Almost 400 species of birds have been seen here, as well as about 140 mammals and over 500 species of trees.

One day I was hiking a trail south of Sirena with some friends when we stopped to look at one of the more common rainforest mammals, an agouti. With binoculars, we were all getting excellent looks at this reddish-brown rodent, which looks like an oversized rabbit with a squirrel-like face and an almost non-existent tail. Suddenly, I saw a slight movement in the bushes behind the agouti and, through binoculars, I found myself staring face to face at a small ocelot. I almost jumped out of my jungle boots in excitement – a jungle cat in the wild! It took a long steady look at me and then melted into the undergrowth. No one else in my group had seen it.

That same afternoon, apart from the agouti and ocelot, I saw all four species of Costa Rican monkeys, a white-nosed coati, and a goodly number of tropical birds including trogons, scarlet macaws, a nesting common black hawk, a spectacled owl and many others. The secret to seeing so much wildlife on one hike is to go in a small group, to hike on a trail that has few visitors, to keep your eyes peeled and, above all, to have a reasonable amount of good luck. Good luck to you, too!

Harpy eagle

Walking Trails

One of the most exciting aspects of Corcovado for visitors is that there are long-distance trails through the park, leading to several ranger stations. Unlike many of Costa Rica's other lowland rainforest parks, backpackers can hike through Corcovado. The trails are primitive, and the hiking is hot, humid and insect ridden, but it can be done. For the traveller wanting to spend a few days hiking through a lowland tropical rainforest, Corcovado is the best choice in Costa Rica.

It is safest to go in a small group. One reader claims that he hiked through the park alone and suffered several misadventures.

First, he was treed by a herd of 50 to 100 white-lipped peccaries which milled around underneath his tree clicking their teeth in a menacing fashion. Then he was robbed by a gang of youths who apparently were Panamanian poachers capturing scarlet macaws and endangered squirrel monkeys for illegal sale to zoos, collectors and pet shops. Having lost, among other things, his insect repellent, his trip ended uncomfortably with hundreds of itchy bug bites.

If, after reading his story, you still want to go, you'll have an easier time of it in the dry season (from January to April) rather than slogging around in calf-deep mud during the wet season. There are fewer bugs in the dry season, too.

You can hike in from the north, south, or east side of the park (see Península de Osa & Golfo Dulce map) and exit a different way, thus not having to retrace your steps. From the north, walk in along the coast from Marenco and arrive at the San Pedrillo ranger station less than an hour after entering the park. From San Pedrillo it is an eight to 10 hour hike to Sirena – check the tide tables or ask at the station. Most of the first few hours are through coastal rainforest, then the trail follows the beach. En route you'll pass the beautiful waterfall plunging onto the wild beach of Playa Llorona. A few hundred metres south of the waterfall, a small trail leads inland to a cascading river and a refreshing swimming hole. The Río Llorona must be forded and, at the Playa Corcovado two or three hours later, the Río Corcovado must also be crossed. About a km before reaching Sirena you must ford the Río Sirena which can be chest deep in the rainy season and is the largest river on the hike. The entire distance from San Pedrillo to Sirena is about 23 km. The northern trail is the least frequently used one.

From the south, take air or land transportation to Carate from where it is a one to two hour hike to the park station at La Leona. From there it is six to seven hours hike to Sirena, but check that the tides are low – it is a beach hike with several rocky headlands to cross and high tides can cut you off. If you look carefully, you can usually find trails going inland around the headlands. Often, these inland trails give the best chances to see mammals – though jaguars have been seen loping along the beach. Keep your eyes open for paw prints. The entire distance from Carate to Sirena is about 16 km.

From the east, take a bus to La Palma from where it is three or four hours along a rough road to Los Patos ranger station. The road is passable to 4WD vehicles and you may be able to hitch a ride – but don't count on it. From Los Patos, the trail undulates steeply through hilly forest for two or three hours before flattening out near the swampy Laguna Corcovado. It is about 20 km from Los Patos to Sirena – allow six to eight hours.

Note that I give fairly conservative times – fit hikers with light packs can probably move faster.

Getting There & Away

One of the Bahía Drake lodges can give you a boat ride to San Pedrillo or Llorona in the north; otherwise walk.

From Puerto Jiménez it is about 40 or 45 km around the southern end of the Península de Osa as far as Carate, where there is an airstrip, pulpería and the comfortable Corcovado Lodge tent camp – see the following entry. A truck or 4WD leaves Puerto Jiménez at 7 am on Monday, Wednesday, Thursday and Saturday for US$4 per person. At other times you can hire the vehicle for US$40. The return from Carate is around 10 am.

Several buses a day go from Puerto Jiménez to La Palma where there are a few pulperías. At La Palma, you can catch buses southbound back to Puerto Jiménez or northbound to the Interamericana and San Isidro or San José.

You can also arrange to fly into either Sirena or Carate with chartered aircraft from San José, Golfito or Puerto Jiménez. The Servicio de Parques Nacional sometimes has planes going in – ask about it. They may take passengers if space is available.

CORCOVADO LODGE TENT CAMP

This comfortable tent camp is just 500 metres from the southern border of Parque Nacional Corcovado, and 1.5 km west of Carate along the beach. Owned and operated by Costa Rica Expeditions, it makes an excellent base from which to explore Corcovado as well as being a restful place to stay for those who have hiked through the national park.

A sandy beach fronts the camp. A steep trail leads to the rainforest 100 metres away where a 160 hectare private preserve is available for hiking and wildlife observation. Currently, the lodge is low impact, with 20 tents, two bath houses (with eight individual showers, toilets and wash basins), a dining room and a bar/lounge area. A small genera-

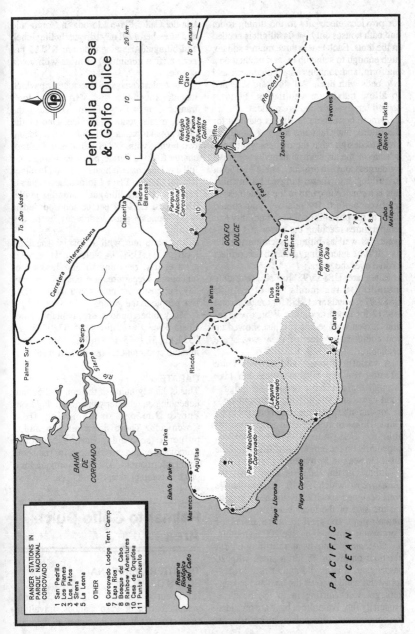

Península de Osa & Golfo Dulce

RANGER STATIONS IN
PARQUE NACIONAL
CORCOVADO
1 San Pedrillo
2 Los Planes
3 Los Patos
4 Sirena
5 La Leona

OTHER
6 Corcovado Lodge Tent Camp
7 Lapa Rios
8 Bosque del Cabo
9 Rainbow Adventures
10 Casa de Orquídea
11 Punta Encanto

tor provides electricity to the dining room and bath houses only – a flashlight is needed in the tents. Each tent is three metres square, high enough to stand up in, and pitched on a platform, and contains a canopied deck and two beds with linen. All sides are screened to allow maximum ventilation. Food is served family-style and is excellent.

A more permanent facility is planned for the future, but plans are moving slowly in order to design what the owners want to be a 'state of the art environmentally sensitive wilderness tourism project'. There's no point in rushing into these things... Meanwhile, this is a chance to camp in the wilderness in relative comfort. By relative, you should think of the possibility of high humidity and temperatures reaching the upper 30s Centigrade, as well as biting insects during the day. It'll be interesting to watch this project evolve over the years.

Rates are US$55/93 for single/double including three meals – tent only is US$23/29. Meals are US$8 for breakfast and US$12 for lunch or dinner. Whilst reservations are encouraged, if you just showed up you could eat or sleep if there was space available.

A variety of tours and activities are offered. You can take the three km hike through the rainforest behind the lodge – good views and lots of birds and monkeys – or you can hike along the beach into the park. Guided hikes to more remote areas are available for US$14 to US$36 per person, depending on the length and difficulty of the hike. Horses can be rented.

Unique to the lodge is their boat, the *Guacamaya*, which is a 10 metre inflatable craft designed specifically to safely negotiate the surf of the local beaches, enabling passengers to visit remote parts of Corcovado. Powered by two 200 hp motors, the *Guacamaya* moves at a thrilling 64 km per hour empty or 48 km/h laden with 20 passengers. It is a wild and exciting ride – spray and wind fly over the boat and passengers get wet. Surfing in to the beach is especially fun. Waterproof bags are provided for cameras and binoculars during trips to Isla del Caño, Playa Llorona in Corcovado and elsewhere. All day trips including lunch and bilingual captain/guide are US$55 per person (five minimum) or more with fewer people.

Most guests arrive on a package trip which includes round-trip flights from San José, transfers, luggage transfer from Carate to the lodge, meals, tours and guide. One of the most popular packages is for three days and two nights, with SANSA flights to Golfito, charter flight to Carate, preserve hiking tour, full day *Guacamaya* boat excursion to either Isla del Caño or Playa Llorona, seven meals and services of a bilingual naturalist guide. These cost US$414 per person and depart every Monday, plus Wednesday in the dry season.

The same tour with a Spanish-speaking local guide is US$295. Note that day three is a travel day, returning to San José about lunchtime. Departures are possible on any day, but cost more unless you have four or five people in the group.

Many other options are available from Costa Rica Expeditions (☎ 57 0766, 22 0333, fax 57 1665) in San José. The lodge is in radio communication with San José.

CARATE

This is the beginning of the end of the road, depending on whether you are arriving from Puerto Jiménez or departing from Corcovado. There is an airstrip and a pulpería (see under Parque Nacional Corcovado and Puerto Jiménez for transportation information). Ask at the pulpería for a place to camp or sleep.

Palmar to Golfo Dulce Area

THE INTERAMERICANA SOUTH OF PALMAR

It is about 95 km from Palmar to the Panamanian border at Paso Canoas, travelling south-east on the Interamericana all the way.

About 40 km south of Palmar, at Chacarita, a turn-off to the west leads to Puerto Jiménez (76 km) and Parque Nacional Corcovado. About 65 km south of Palmar, at Río Claro, a turn-off to the south-west leads to Golfito (26 km) which is the largest town south of San Isidro. The small town of Neily (on the Interamericana) is reached some 80 km south of Palmar, and a further 17 km brings you to the border.

GOLFITO

Golfito is named after a tiny gulf that emerges into the much larger Golfo Dulce, a large Pacific Ocean gulf just west of Panama. It is the most important port in the far southern part of Costa Rica, although its maritime importance has declined greatly in recent years. From 1938 to 1985 Golfito was the centre of a major banana growing region, and for many years was the headquarters of the United Fruit Company. But a combination of declining foreign markets, rising Costa Rican export taxes, worker unrest, and banana diseases led to the closing of the United complex in 1985. Some of the plantations have since been turned to African palm-oil production, but this didn't alleviate the high unemployment and economic loss caused by United's departure.

In the late 1980s a small tourism industry began in the area and has blossomed in the last couple of years. The town is pleasantly situated and visitors often stop by for a day or two en route to somewhere else. There are good surfing and swimming beaches nearby (though none in Golfito itself – Playa Cacao, across the little gulf, is the closest). The town is surrounded by the steep hills of the Refugio Nacional de Fauna Silvestre Golfito which creates a splendid rainforest backdrop and has good bird-watching opportunities. There are a couple of good fishing/boating marinas. Boats and light planes cross the Golfo Dulce to the Península de Osa, where the Parque Nacional Corcovado is found. There is a growing number and good variety of hotels and there are a few jungle lodges nearby.

In an attempt to boost the economy of the region, Costa Rica has built a new duty-free facility in the northern part of Golfito. 'Duty free' is a misnomer, because items for sale here are still heavily taxed and do not offer significant savings for foreign tourists. Nevertheless, the taxes here are substantially lower than elsewhere in Costa Rica, and this attracts ticos from all over the country into visiting Golfito on shopping sprees for microwave ovens and TV sets. In order to do so, however, they must spend at least 24 hours in Golfito, which tends to put hotel rooms at a premium at weekends.

Golfito is still, superficially, two towns strung out along a coastal road with a backdrop of steep thickly forested hills. The southern part of town is where you find most of the bars and businesses – this sector feels pleasantly decrepit in the way tropical seaports tend to be, but without the usual hustle and danger. In fact, Warner Brothers chose this site to film their new movie *Chico Mendes* – the true story of a Brazilian rubber-tapper's efforts to preserve the rainforest – and you can see the movie set, complete with plaza and fake church and other buildings, near the Golfito gas station.

The northern part of town was the old United headquarters, and retains a languid, tropical air with its large, well-ventilated homes with verandahs and attractively land-scaped surroundings. Several of these houses now offer inexpensive accommodation. The airport and duty-free zone is at this end.

The port is a well-protected one and a few foreign yachts on oceanic or coastal cruises are usually found anchored here.

Information

Arriving yachties will find the port captain (☎ fax 75 0487) and immigration authorities opposite the Muelle Bananero (old Banana Company Dock). Hours are 7 to 11 am and 12.30 to 4 pm, Monday to Friday. There have been several complaints reported locally and in the press of an overly officious cop, nick-named 'Rambo', who boards boats, conducts searches improperly, and attempts

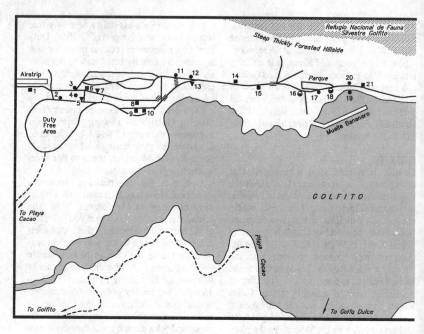

	PLACES TO STAY
1	Hotel Sierra
6	Hotel Costa Sur
8	Casa Blanca
9	Hospedaje Familiar
10	El Manglar
14	Cabinas Wilson & Soda/Cabinas Santa Marta
15	Cabinas Princesa de Golfo
21	Hotel del Cerro
22	Pensión Minerva
24	Hotel/Restaurant Uno
26	Hotel Golfito
29	Hotel Costa Rica Surf
30	Cabinas Mazuren
34	Hotel Delfina

▼	PLACES TO EAT
5	Bar Restaurant Cazuelita
7	Jardín Cervecero
13	Soda Miriam
23	Bar Restaurant Samoa
24	Hotel/Restaurant Uno

27	Pequeño Restaurant
28	El Jardín Restaurant
29	El Balcon Restaurant
32	La Eurakita Restaurant

	OTHER
2	Aero Costa Sol
3	Airport Terminal
4	Travelair
11	Refugio Nacional de Fauna Silvestre Golfito administration
12	School
16	Club Latino & Bus Stop to Neily
17	Banco Nacional de Costa Rica
18	TRACOPA Bus Terminal
19	Taxi boats
20	ICE Building
25	Muellecito
26	Banco de Costa Rica & Gas Station
30	Laundry
31	Post Office
33	Marea Baja Discotheque
35	Eagle's Roost Marina

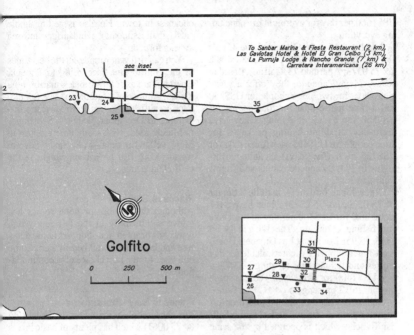

To Sanbar Marina & Fiesta Restaurant (2 km),
Las Gaviotas Hotel & Hotel El Gran Ceibo (3 km),
La Purruja Lodge & Rancho Grande (7 km) &
Carretera Interamericana (26 km)

Golfito

0   250   500 m

Plaza

to intimidate visitors and extort bribes. Carry documentation at all times.

Many of the places around Golfito lack telephones and communicate with one another by VHF radio. If you need to reach someone by VHF from Golfito, ask at the following places in Golfito for the use of their VHF: El Balcon Restaurant, Las Gaviotas Hotel, Sanbar Marina, Eagle's Roost Marina and others. Laundry service is available next to the Cabinas Mazuren in the south part of town. Emergency medical attention can be obtained at the Hospital de Golfito (☎ 75 0011).

Sportfishing & Boating

The Sanbar Marina accommodates foreign yachts and is also the home of Phoenix Charters (☎ 70 0735; in the USA, ☎ 1 (800) 733 4742, fax 504 837 1544; 3850 N Causeway Blvd, 2nd Floor, Metairie, LA 70002, USA). This is a first-class operation with trips ranging from two to five days of fishing.

Anglers sleep on a 19 metre mothership complete with air-conditioned state rooms with private bath. A bar and restaurant serve gourmet meals. Smaller boats zoom out to the best sites – no time is wasted leaving hotels and motoring out to the fishing grounds.

Rates range from US$355 per person per day (six people, five days) to US$900 per person per day (two people, three days) including flights from San José and overnight in first class hotels at either end of the trip. Cheaper charters without San José hotels and in different boats are available. Diving and sightseeing trips can also be arranged.

Eagle's Roost Marina (☎ 75 0838; in the USA, ☎ (714) 632 5285) has a floating dock marina with full services accommodating foreign yachts for US$30 a day or US$10 per foot per month. They have a 16 metre sportfishing boat sleeping four anglers which charters for US$1250 per day, or

US$1660 per day for overnight trips, including everything.

Another option is Captain Steve Lino's Golfito Sportfishing (☎ 75 0353, 88 5083, fax 75 0373; Apartado 73, Golfito). Based in nearby Playa Zancudo, they offer a seven metre boat for two/three people for US$350 and a nine metre boat for four people for US$550 for a day of fishing. They have multi-day offshore fishing packages for three people for US$495 each (three days) or US$725 each (five days) including overnights in Playa Zancudo cabins and flights from San José.

Other local outfitters include Leomar (☎ 75 0230, fax 75 0373) which have a 6.7 metre boat for US$450 per day and can take you fishing or diving. The *Venecia* (☎ 33 9355, 33 9567 or ask at Las Gaviotas Hotel) is a 13 metre trawler yacht available for day cruises and fishing trips (costing US$800 a day, US$1400 for two days). There is space for four to 12 passengers.

Golfito is also the pick-up and drop-off point for deep sea fishing at the Golfito Sailfish Rancho which is operated by the same people who run Parismina Tarpon Rancho on the north Caribbean coast. Information on both these luxury sport-fishing lodges is available from PO Box 290190, San Antonio, Texas 78280, USA (☎ 1 (800) 531 7232 or (210) 377 0451, fax (210) 377 0454 in the USA; 35 7766 in Costa Rica).

Rates vary from US$2790/3885 for double/triple occupancy for three days of fishing to US$3600/4790/6285 for single/double/triple occupancy for seven days of fishing – and they guarantee hooking a sailfish or marlin on any trip. Rates include a night in San José at either end of the trip and everything in between. They also offer split weeks with three days on one coast and four days on the other.

If these prices are simply out of your reach, ask around for Banana Joe who can be reached on the VHF radio or found at the Eagle's Roost Marina. He offers water taxi services, and has a nine metre launch which can be used for fishing, snorkelling or sightseeing trips. His 'no frills' services are the cheapest in town. He also is getting hobie cats (small sailboats), windsurfers and sea kayaks for rent.

You can fish year round, but the best times in the Golfito area (according to Phoenix Charters) are as follows: black marlin, blue marlin, grouper – December to May; dorado, Pacific sailfish – November to May; snook – October to December; wahoo – September to March; roosterfish – any time but best in May; yellowfin tuna – any time. Several world record fish have been caught in the Golfo Dulce area.

Places to Stay

Although the number of hotel rooms has grown significantly in the last few years, weekends bring in tico shoppers at the duty-free and hotels may well be full then. Come midweek for the best choice of accommodation.

Places to Stay – bottom end

The cheapest place in town is the *Hotel Uno* (☎ 75 0061) which has plenty of basic boxes without fans for US$1.75 per person. Most rooms lack a window. A better budget choice is the small but friendly *Cabinas Mazuren* (☎ 75 0058; Apartado 82, Golfito) which has two rooms with shared bath for US$3 per person and three rooms with private bath and fan for US$3.75 per person. The *Hotel Delfina* (☎ 75 0043) has basic rooms without fans, and many without windows, for US$3.75 per person. They also have better rooms with private baths and fan for US$14.50 single or double.

Another choice is the *Hotel Golfito* (☎ 75 0047) which has rooms with private bath and fan for US$9, either single or double occupancy. The *Hotel Costa Rica Surf* (☎ 75 0034; Apartado 7, Golfito) has rooms with fan and shared bath for US$5.75/7.25. Rooms with fan and private bath go for US$11/16. Many of the rooms either lack windows or have skylights. There are a few air-conditioned rooms with hot showers – but these are usually booked up. The hotel is popular with North Americans and hosts

American Legion meetings on the first Tuesday of the month.

In the quieter north end there are several families which take guests. The friendly *Hospedaje Familiar* (☎ 75 0217) is also known as 'El Vivero' because the owner, Robert Beatham, grows and sells ornamental plants. They charge US$4.40 per person in airy rooms with fans and shared baths. Across the street, the family-run *Casa Blanca* (☎ 75 0124) has rooms with fans and private bath for US$8.75 single or double. The nearby *El Manglar* (☎ 75 0510) and the *Cabinas Wilson* (☎ 75 0795) are similarly priced.

There are several other houses in the area around the parque, about one km south of the north end. These include the *Casa de Huespedes Felicia* (☎ 75 0539), the *Cabinas Marlin* (☎ 75 0191), the *Soda/Cabinas Santa Marta* (☎ 75 0508) and others – ask around. They charge in the range of US$2 to US$4.50 per person. The *Cabinas Princesa de Golfo* (☎ 75 0422) has rooms with fan and private bath for US$11/13 single/double.

If you're stuck, try the run-down-looking *Pensión Minerva* for cheap digs. I couldn't raise the owner when I stopped by. Also look at the *Hotel del Cerro* (see following) which has cheap 'backpacker rates'.

Places to Stay – middle

The friendly *Hotel del Cerro* (☎ 75 0006, fax 75 0551), owned by longtime local resident Luis Wachong, is near the north end of town and has great views of the bay and a pleasant, reasonably priced restaurant. They have a large variety of clean rooms, ranging from dormitories with shared bath (there are plenty of bathrooms) for US$5 per person ('backpacker rates') to rooms with fans and private bath (US$10/15 single/double) to air-conditioned rooms with phones and hot water for US$25 a double.

Right in the north end is the recently refurbished *Hotel Costa Sur* (☎ 75 0871, fax 75 0832) which has spotless rooms with fans and electric showers for US$24 (single or double) and with air-conditioning, one

double and two single beds for US$46. A nice restaurant and bar are on the premises.

The Swiss-run *La Purruja Lodge* (fax only 75 0373; Apartado 83, Golfito) is seven km south of town on the main road into Golfito. It has nice cabins with fans and private bath for about US$15 a double. Meals, transportation into Golfito and tours of the Península de Osa are available.

At the entrance of Golfito, about three or four km south of town, is *Hotel El Gran Ceibo* (☎ 75 0403) which has pleasant rooms with fans and private bath for US$17 a double and a few air-conditioned cabins for US$29. The local Golfito bus terminates outside.

Almost opposite, right on the coast, is the well-known and recommended *Las Gaviotas Hotel* (☎ 75 0062, fax 75 0544; Apartado 12-8201, Golfito). It is set in a tropical garden, and has an excellent restaurant with good prices, a café, a bar, two pools and a boat dock from which you can watch the *gaviotas* (gulls). The 18 spacious rooms with air-conditioning or fans and hot water are US$38 a double, and three larger cabins with kitchenettes overlooking the ocean cost US$47.

Places to Stay – top end

Golfito's luxury hotel is the *Hotel Sierra* (☎ 75 0666, fax 75 0087; Apartado 37, Golfito; or ☎ 33 9693, fax 33 9715, Apartado 5304-1000, San José). Located between the airstrip and the duty-free zone, the hotel offers two restaurants, rooms service, bar, two pools and local tours. There are 72 large air-conditioned rooms with fans, telephone, TV and hot water for US$60/72 a single/double.

Places to Eat

Budget travellers will find several restaurants where meals start at US$2 to US$3. *Restaurant Uno* (☎ 75 0061) has been around for decades and serves decent Chinese food and fish dinners. Luis Brenes *Pequeño Restaurant* (☎ 75 0220) is very popular with local ticos and gringos and a good place for swapping information and meeting people. Luis lived in Los Angeles for years, but likes Golfito much better and is an amiable and helpful host. A recent arrival on the scene is the *El Jardín Restaurant* (☎ 75 0235) which has a chalkboard menu of specials and a friendly, 'Ask for what you want and well try to cook it' attitude. They have a paperback book exchange. The *Soda Muellecito* is popular for early breakfasts by the Muellecito (little dock).

The US-run *El Balcon* above the Hotel Costa Rica Surf has a variety of meals ranging from US$2 to US$7. Breakfast is also served. It has VHF radio communication with many of the local lodges etc and the bar is a popular gathering/information centre. There is a dart board, paperback book exchange and a pleasant view of the gulf. The nearby *La Eurekita* is a breezy open-air restaurant selling good fruit juices and slightly pricey but good tico dishes.

Heading north takes you past the *Bar Restaurant Samoa* in a large thatched building which you can't miss. Continental cuisine (with a French and Italian emphasis) is offered with meals around US$5. In the north zone, *Bar Restaurant Cazuelita* (☎ 75 0921) has been recommended for Chinese meals. Nearby, the *Jardín Cervecero* (☎ 75 0126) in a typical two storey house in the Alamedas *barrio*, claims to have the coldest beer in town and serves good seafood and steaks in a family environment. It opens around 8 am. Also in the northern zone, the *Soda Miriam* and a couple of other cheap sodas are popular with workers and students at the nearby school.

Heading south of town, the floating *Sanbar Fiesta Restaurant* (☎ 75 0874) is part of the Sanbar Marina – the gangplank entrance to the restaurant can be an easy few steps or a steep climb, depending on the tide. Once aboard, you'll find friendly staff and an innovative menu of excellent food at competitive prices – most plates are around US$7 or US$8 and are delicious. There is a bar and a TV beaming in the US CNN network by satellite.

The *Las Gaviotas Hotel* restaurant is open from 6 am to 10 pm and serves an excellent variety of food at good prices – it is locally popular. A little further out of town is *Río de Janeiro Restaurant* which is known for big portions and good variety – from US$2 cheeseburgers to US$12 jumbo shrimp plates. Seven km south of town, the rustic, thatched-roof *Rancho Grande* serves country-style tico food cooked over a wood stove. Prices are very reasonable – it's worth the trip out here. Hours are 7 am to 10 pm.

Entertainment

Apart from the popular bars already mentioned, there is the *Marea Baja Discotheque* (☎ 75 0139) with dancing, especially at weekends.

Things to Buy

Assuming you're not in town to load up at the duty-free, you might want to check out the Surfari Souvenir Shop which has a good selection of local T-shirts and crafts, as well as Guatemalan textiles and Panamanian *molas*.

Getting There & Away

Air SANSA (in Golfito ☎ 75 0303; in San José 33 3258, 33 0397) flies from San José daily, except Sunday, at 6 am returning to San José at 7 am. There is a second flight on Wednesday, Thursday and Friday leaving San José at 1 pm, returning at 2 pm. The flight takes 45 minutes and the fare is US$25.50. Flights are often fully booked but it's worth getting on the waiting list and showing up at the airport because there are frequent 'no-shows'.

Travelair (in Golfito ☎ 75 0210; in San José 32 7883, 20 3054) flies from San José every day at 8.10 am. The flight takes one hour and costs US$66 one way, US$114 round trip. The return flight to San José leaves at 9.30 am, makes a quick stop in Palmar Sur, and arrives in San José at 10.55 am.

Local airlines Aeronaves (in Golfito ☎ 75 0278, 75 0631; in San José 32 1413) and Aero Costa Sol (in Golfito ☎ 75 0607, fax 75 0035; in San José ☎ 41 1444, 41 0922) have three to five passenger light aircraft which can be chartered to San José, Palmar Sur, Puerto Jiménez, Corcovado and anywhere you want to fly in the southern zone. You have to charter the whole plane and fill it up with three to five passengers. A three seat (270 kg maximum) charter to San José is about US$370, to Sirena about US$140, and to Puerto Jiménez US$50. There are daily scheduled passenger flights to Puerto Jiménez for US$11 at 6 am and 1 pm (if there is enough demand). The flight takes seven minutes and luggage is limited to 10 kg maximum.

The airport is almost four km north of the town centre.

Bus TRACOPA (☎ in Golfito 75 0365, in San José 21 4214) has daily buses at 7, 11 am and 3 pm from San José to Golfito (eight hours). The buses leave from Avenida 18, Calle 4. Return buses from Golfito leave at 5 am and 1 pm daily. Fares are US$4.75 to San José and US$3.50 to San Isidro. TRACOPA's office hours in Golfito are 6 to 11.30 am and 1.30 to 4 pm from Monday to Saturday, and 7 to 11 am on Sunday and holidays.

Buses for Ciudad Neily leave every hour from the bus stop outside the Club Latino at the north end of town. They will pick up passengers in town as they pass through for the one hour trip to Neily. Buses for the surfing area of Pavones and for the beach at Playa Zancudo leave from the Muellecito. Departures depend on the weather, the condition of the road and the condition of the bus – ask locally. Services may be interrupted during the rainy season – it's a poor road. During the dry season, the bus leaves at 2 pm for Pavones (three hours) and at 1.30 pm for Zancudo (three hours) with a transfer at the Río Conte. In the wet season, you'll probably have to take a boat.

Boat There are two main boat docks for passenger services (apart from the various marinas). The Muellecito is the main dock in the southern part of town. Taxi boats leave from the dock opposite the ICE building near the north end of Golfito.

The daily passenger ferry (☎ 78 5017) to Puerto Jiménez was suspended in 1991 and 1992 but was running again in 1993, so check locally for the current situation. At the time of writing, the ferry left at 11.30 am from the Muellecito. It takes 1½ hours and costs US$2.50.

A guy called Miguel (nicknamed 'Macarela') takes people from the Muellecito to Playa Zancudo at 1 pm on Monday, Wednesday and Friday (perhaps more often if there are enough passengers – but don't rely on this). He charges about US$2 per person. Banana Joe goes to Zancudo for about US$22 per boatload and other destinations on request.

Taxi boats (☎ 75 0712, 75 0357) leave from the dock opposite the ICE and can take eight or more passengers. They have services to Playa Zancudo for US$22 to US$51, depending on the size and speed of the boat and who you talk to. Other destinations (Pavones, Puerto Jiménez, Punta Encanto, Rainbow Adventures, Casa Orquideas and others) can also be reached for US$35 to US$65.

Getting Around
Bus City buses go up and down the main road of Golfito for about US$0.15 per ride.

Taxi Colectivo taxis go up and down the main road from the airport down to Las Gaviotas. Just flag them down if they have a seat. The set fare is US$0.75.

A private taxi from downtown to the airport costs about US$2.

PLAYA CACAO
This beach is opposite Golfito and offers the closest clean swimming to town.

Places to Stay & Eat
The best known place is the *Shipwreck Hotel & Bar* run by shipwreck survivor, Captain Tom, and his wife, Rocio. The Captain has been a local character for about four decades and has many stories to tell. The 'hotel' is

three double cabins in a beached boat – cold showers are available in the Captain's house nearby. Rates are US$10 per cabin. The bar speciality is jungleburgers – and a wide variety of drinks and beer. Make sure you read and sign the Shipwreck guest book. Captain Tom will let you camp nearby and rents tents if you want.

Nearby are the newer *Las Palmas* (☎ 75 0457, fax 75 0373; Apartado 98, Golfito) which offer six spacious cabins with high thatched roofs and tiled floors for US$30 a double. Each cabin has a private bath, and lighting is by candle. Meals are sometimes available.

Siete Mares restaurant is open from 7 am to 9 pm for inexpensive breakfasts, lunches and dinners. They specialise in local dishes and seafood.

Getting There & Away

The five to 10 minute boat ride costs US$0.75 per person (three minimum). You can also get there by walking or driving along a dirt road west and then south from the airport – about 10 km total from downtown Golfito. (This road is motorable most of the time.)

REFUGIO NACIONAL DE FAUNA SILVESTRE GOLFITO

This small (1309 hectare) refuge was originally created to protect the Golfito watershed. It encompasses most of the steep hills surrounding the town, and whilst the refuge has succeeded in keeping Golfito's water clean and flowing, it has also had the side effect of conserving a number of rare and interesting plant species. These include a species of *Caryodaphnopsis*, which is an Asian genus otherwise unknown in Central America, and *Zamia*, which are cycads. Cycads are called 'living fossils' and are among the most primitive plants. They were abundant before the time of the dinosaurs but relatively few species are now extant. *Zamia* are known for the huge, cone-like inflorescences that emerge from the centre of the plant, which looks rather like a dwarf palm.

Other species of interest include many heliconias, orchids, tree ferns and tropical trees including copal, the kapok tree, the butternut tree and the cow tree, so called for the copious quantities of drinkable white latex which it produces.

The vegetation attracts a variety of birds such as scarlet macaws, and a variety of parrots, toucans, tanagers, trogons and hummingbirds. Peccaries, pacas, raccoons, coatimundis and monkeys are among the mammals which have been sighted here.

Information

The refuge administration is in the old banana company building near the north end of town. Camping is permitted in the refuge, but there are no facilities – most people stay in Golfito.

Rainfall is very high, with October, the wettest month, receiving over 700 mm. From January to mid-April is normally dry.

Getting There & Away

About two km south of the centre of Golfito, a gravel road heads inland, past a soccer field, and up to some radio towers (Las Torres), seven km away and 486 metres above sea level. This is a good access road to the refuge (most of the road actually goes through the middle of the preserve). You could take a taxi up first thing in the morning and hike down, birding as you go. There are a few trails leading from the road down to the town, but there is so little traffic on the road itself that you'll probably see more from the cleared road than the overgrown trails.

Another possibility is to continue on the road heading north-west from the Hotel Sierra, past the end of the airstrip. The pavement soon ends and a dirt road continues about three km to a sign for Senderos Naturales (nature trails). Here, two somewhat overgrown trails plus the abandoned road provide good birding, with crested guan, slaty-tailed trogon, rufous-tailed jacamar and orange-billed sparrow among the species reported by birders.

There is also a very steep hiking trail which leaves from almost opposite the Bar

Restaurant Samoa. A somewhat strenuous hike (allow about two hours) will bring you out on the road to the radio towers, described previously. The trail is in fairly good shape, but easier to find in Golfito than at the top. Once you reach the radio tower road, return the way you came or, for a less knee-straining descent, head down along the road.

NORTH ALONG THE GOLFO DULCE

Taxi boats can take you out of Golfito and up along the north-east coast of the Golfo Dulce, past remote beaches and headlands interspersed with several jungle lodges. The backdrop to the coastline is mainly virgin rainforest; indeed, the Parque Nacional Corcovado has recently acquired an extension along this coast.

Punta Encanto

About 10 km west of Golfito as the crow flies, or about 25 minutes by taxi boat, brings you to the Punta Encanto Lodge (☎ 75 0171; Apartado 157, Golfito) which opened in late 1992. The rustic lodge has nine comfortable rooms with private bath and excellent family-style meals. The 7.5 hectare property has nature trails and waterfalls (a guided two hour walk is US$6 per person), and swimming, snorkelling and canoeing are other activities. Boats are available for fishing (US$35 per hour) and local tours.

Lodge rates are US$120 a double, including three meals. If you stay for three days, they'll pick you up from Golfito – otherwise, hire a taxi boat (US$50 per boat load).

Casa de Orquídea

This private botanical garden is a veritable Eden. Surrounded by primary rainforest, the garden has been lovingly collected and tended by Ron and Trudy MacAllister who have homesteaded in this remote region since the 1970s. They first planted fruit trees simply to survive and soon became interested in plants. Self-taught botanists, they have amassed a wonderful collection of tropical fruit trees, bromeliads, cycads, palms, heliconias, ornamental plants and over 100

varieties of orchids, after which their garden is named.

The gardens are open from 7 to 10 am from Sunday to Thursday (the early hours avoid the wilting heat of the midday sun). Guided tours last from two to three hours and cost US$5 per person. The tours are fascinating and fun – touching, smelling, feeling and tasting is encouraged. I chewed on the pulp surrounding a 'magic seed' whose effect was to make lemons taste sweet instead of sour. I also saw bats hanging out in a 'tent' made from a huge leaf, looked for insects trapped in bromeliad pools, photographed torch ginger in glorious flower, smelt vanilla, and learnt about orchids life cycles. The MacAllisters host natural history courses for students – they encourage interested schools to write to them at Apartado 69, Golfito, or leave a message with Bob Hara (☎ 75 0353) in Playa Zancudo.

Casa de Orquídea is between Punta Encanto and Rainbow Adventures lodges on the Golfo Dulce coast. It is accessible only by boat, and transport and tours can be arranged with these lodges, as well as Banana Joe and Sanbar Marina in Golfito and Zancudo Boat Tours.

There is one rustic cabin available for rental periods of a week or more. The screened two room cabin can sleep up to four, has a private bath, refrigerator and kitchenette, and runs on 12 V electricity. Linens and kitchenware are furnished, but you need to bring your own food. Fruit can be picked if it's in season. Rates are US$150 a week or US$500 a month, including round trip transportation from Golfito.

Rainbow Adventures

This private 400 hectare preserve is bordered by the new Parque Nacional Corcovado extension at the far north-east corner of Golfo Dulce. It is reached by a scenic 45 minute boat ride from Golfito to Playa Cativo beach – one of the attractions of the trip is 'shooting the rock' where the boat hurtles through a narrow gap between a rocky islet and the coast. At the preserve, you can walk, swim or snorkel along the 1.5 km long Playa Cativo or wander into the nearby forest. I saw howler monkeys and olingos (carnivorous mammals in the raccoon family) just a few metres away from the lodge.

The heart of Rainbow Adventures is a unique three-storey lodge built on Playa Cativo. The all-wood, wide-balconied, rustic appearance of the lodge belies the elegance within – handmade furniture, silk rugs, turn-of-the-century antiques and fresh flowers make this a special place in the wilderness. The 1st level is the dining room, lounge and relaxation area and the remaining two levels are guest rooms. These are not for the average tourist who may seek four walls and a bed. Instead, half walls (enough to ensure privacy) allow guests beautiful and unimpeded views of the rainforest, the beach and the gulf. Each bed is equipped with a fine-meshed mosquito net which can be raised or lowered as desired. It's almost like camping in the jungle, but with all comforts including private bath, comfortable beds and balconies.

The three rooms on the 2nd level cost US$130/160 single/double and the 3rd floor 'penthouse' room is US$135/165. There are also two attractive and spacious wooden cabins, each with a large bedroom, a private bathroom, and a spacious verandah – one had a pair of variable finches nesting immediately outside when I visited. The bedroom can be partitioned off into two mini-bedrooms suitable for parents with children, though tight for adult couples. Rates are US$150/180 single/double plus US$40 for extra people. All prices include meals (buffet style – vegetarian, dairy free etc available on request), soft drinks, snacks, beer with meals, transportation from and to Golfito airport, a tour of nearby jungle and use of snorkelling gear (although it's always best to bring your own to ensure the best fit).

Boats are available for US$35 per hour per boat (up to four passengers) for fishing or boat tours. Guided jungle tours are US$4 per hour per person. Information and reservations are available in the USA from Michael Medill (☎ (503) 690 7750, fax (503) 690 7735; 5875 NW Kaiser Rd, Portland, OR 97229); in Costa Rica (☎\fax 75 0220; Apartado 63, Golfito). Note that the telephone is in Golfito and has staff standing by only from 8 to 9 am on Monday and Friday – there is no phone at the lodge.

Cabinas Caña Blanca

A couple of km north of Playa Cativo brings you to a small beach with two well-designed and comfortable cabins. Each comes with private bath, refrigerator, kitchenette and spacious verandah. Guests bring and cook their own food and have access to rainforest trails and a beach – this is for people who want to do their own thing in a remote area. Rates are US$70 a double and include transportation from Golfito if you stay for three nights. The owners, Veronica and David Corella, live nearby and offer boat and fishing excursions for US$35 an hour.

For information and reservations, write to Apartado 34, Golfito, or leave a message with Bob Hara (fax 75 0373) at Playa Zancudo.

PLAYA ZANCUDO

This beach, on the south side of the mouth of the Río Coto Colorado, about 15 km south of Golfito, is a popular destination for locals, who claim that this long black-sand beach has the best swimming in the area. The surf is gentle. The beach is busy during the dry season but is quiet at other times.

There are mangroves in the area around the river mouth which may offer bird-watching possibilities. Steve Lino's Golfito Sportfishing operates out of Playa Zancudo (see Sportfishing under Golfito). Zancudo means 'mosquito' – although there aren't too many insects, it's still worth bringing insect repellent.

Places to Stay & Eat

There are few single rooms. I've received complaints about single travellers being charged the triple rate in rooms with three beds. On a busy weekend, there's not much you can do about this, but at quieter times you should get a single rate.

Many hotels are known locally by the name of their owner – both official and local names are given here. Most hotels have a restaurant attached. New places are opening at frequent intervals. *Restaurant & Cabinas Tranquillo* (also known as Reiner's Place after owners Reiner and Maria Kraemer) is a decent budget place popular with European budget travellers. Basic rooms are US$7.25 per person and newer cabins are opening in 1993. They have a simple and inexpensive restaurant – one traveller reports that Maria is the best cook in town. Reiner also operates the new *Las Vistas* cabins which are good value at US$7.25 per person – but you have to walk almost an hour south along the beach to reach them. Write to Apartado 152, Golfito for more information.

One of the cheapest places is *Cabinas Suzy* which has basic rooms with shared bath for US$6 per person and some slightly more expensive rooms with private bath. They serve decent casados for US$2.50. *El Coquito* has basic rather stuffy cabins with private bath for US$7.25 per person and a restaurant serving good inexpensive meals. Friendly and popular *Cabinas Petier* (☎ 77 3027, also known as Froylan's Place) has simple rooms with fans and private bath for US$7.25 – a restaurant is attached. *Río Mar* (☎ 75 0350, also known as Franklin's Place) has four cabins with fans, private bath and three beds for US$7.50 per person – though Franklin's wife seems reluctant to charge the per person rate to single travellers. They also have a six bed cabin with private bath, fans and kitchen for US$45.

The *Rancho Zancudo* (☎ 73 3027) had no sign in front recently but has reasonably comfortable rooms with fans and private bath for US$20 per room. *Los Almendros* (☎ 75 0515, also known as Roy Ventura's Place) is one of the oldest places to stay at Zancudo and has a faithful local clientele. Pleasant rooms with private bath and fans rent for US$20/30 single/double. There is a restaurant with good food and a priceless menu – if you want to know how much they are going to charge, ask before you eat. They have 6.7 metre boats available for all day

fishing trips – US$250 for one or two anglers.

Cabinas Sol y Mar (☎ 75 0353, fax 75 0373; Apartado 87, Golfito) is a quiet, friendly well-run place about 20 minutes down the beach to the south. The owners, Bob and Mónica Hara, are a good source of information on the area and speak Spanish, English and German. They have four nice cabins with private bath and fans for US$20/25. Next door is their restaurant which serves good food for reasonable prices in a relaxed atmosphere. Horse rental is available for US$7.25 an hour. They can also arrange fishing and boating excursions.

Near the Sol y Mar is *Zancudo Boat Tours* (better known as Susan & Andrew's, also known as Cabinas Los Cocos). They were primarily a boat taxi/tour service but have recently opened two cabins with private bath, refrigerator, kitchenette and deck. Rates are US$30 a day, US$200 a week, US$600 a month. Phone them through Sol y Mar or write to Apartado 88, Golfito.

Estero Mar (☎ 75 0056), also known as Mauricio's, serves decent tico food at reasonable prices, and is a popular bar. It has the Zancudo public telephone and may rent sleeping space if all else fails.

Getting There & Away

Boat or bus from Golfito is the usual way to get here. Miguel Macarela has boat service back to Golfito at 6 am on Monday, Wednesday and Friday – about US$2 per person. The bus, when it runs, leaves *El Coquito* at 5 am and takes about three hours, with a transfer at the Río Conte.

Zancudo Boat Tours charges US$7.25 per person to Golfito and US$11 per person to Pavones or Puerto Jiménez (three passengers minimum). For tours elsewhere, they charge US$15/20/25 per hour for two/three/four passengers. Contact them through Cabinas Sol y Mar.

PAVONES

About 10 km south of Zancudo is the Bahía de Pavón, which is supposed to have some of the best surfing on the Pacific side of

Central America. The area is known locally as Pavones.

The best season is from April to October when the waves are at their biggest and the long left can reportedly give a three minute ride. An apocryphal story has it that the wave passes so close to the Esquina del Mar Cantina that you could toss beers to surfers as they come by on their boards. (Camera, anyone?) This is definitely not the beach to bring your small children to for a gentle paddle. The best season coincides with the rainy months, which makes transport there more difficult.

There is no phone in Pavones. I'm told that Winfred Zigman, a German ham radio operator living in Pavones, provides weather information for surfers and sailors and is a way of making outside contact in an emergency.

Places to Stay & Eat

Pensión Maurem has very basic rooms for US$3 per person. The popular *Esquina del Mar Cantina* has breezy upstairs rooms for US$7.25 a double and US$14.50 a triple. You get lulled to sleep by the sounds of the surfing sea – and the bar below. The bar owner has some other cabins nearby – described as hot and airless. Some new cabins are being built behind the pulpería. Ask around for other cheap places to stay.

About 10 minutes walk away is *Cabinas Mira Olas*, Apartado 32, Golfito. They have two simple but pleasant cabins with private baths and solar-heated showers and electricity. One rents for US$10/15 single/double or US$90 a double per week; the other has a kitchenette and rents for US$15/18. Mail reservations are accepted – send a US$20 money order made out to Paul Romano to guarantee the first night and allow at least six weeks. You could also use Coopersamic radiotelephone (☎ 75 0120) and ask for Mira Olas, or call on VHF channel 74.

I've recently heard that the *Impact Surf Lodge*, run by a helpful guy named Ted McGrath, provides decent rooms and all meals.

Camping on the beach is a possibility, but

watch your stuff. Thefts from tents have been reported so don't leave your campsite unattended.

Getting There & Away

The daily bus leaves for Golfito at 5 am from the soccer field. It returns from Golfito at 2 pm. The road has recently been graded so this service may improve. A 4WD taxi will charge about US$30 to US$40 from Golfito.

Walter Jiménez is a local boatman who can take you to Zancudo, Golfito and elsewhere.

TISKITA JUNGLE LODGE

This is a private biological reserve and experimental fruit farm on 160 hectares of land at Punta Banco, about 30 km due south of Golfito and 10 km from the Panamanian border. About 100 hectares are virgin rainforest. Tiskita also has a coastline with tide pools and beaches suitable for swimming.

The lodge is run by Peter Aspinall, who was born in Costa Rica. His passion is homesteading and he has an orchard with over 100 varieties of tropical fruits from all over the world. He plans to ship the most suitable of these fruits to San José and abroad. Meanwhile, guests are able to sample dozens of exotic fruits and fruit drinks during their visit to the lodge.

There are trails in the surrounding rainforest, which contains waterfalls and rivers suitable for swimming in. The tide pools have a variety of marine life such as chitons, nudibranchs, bristle and feather worms, starfish, sea urchins, anemones, tunicates, crabs and many shells. Ask for booklets describing the rainforest trail, the tide pools and the land crabs, and for a butterfly list.

Bird-watchers will find the combination of rainforest, fruit farm and coastline produces a long list of birds. The fruit farm is particularly attractive to frugivorous (fruit-eating) birds such as parrots and toucans, which can be more easily observed in the orchard than the rainforest. Nature trails into the forest help the birder see the more reticent species, and a local checklist is

Top: Lodge at Rainbow Adventures, Parque Nacional Corcovado (MM)
Left: Muellecito, Golfito (RR)
Right: Isla del Caño from Marenco (RR)

Top: Snack stop at Soda La Balsa, by Paso Real ferry crossing (RR)
Left: Cashew with developing fruit (MM)
Right: Delicious anona (custard fruit) (MM)

available. This includes such exotic-sounding names as yellow-billed cotingas, fiery-billed aracaris, green honeycreepers, and lattice-tailed trogons – to name a few. Monkeys, sloths, agoutis, coatimundis and other mammals are often seen. Of course, insects and plants abound.

Accommodation is in nine rustic cabins with private bath and Pacific Ocean views. The private baths are on the outside of the cabins, allowing rainforest views as you shower. A splendid way to start the day. Electricity is provided by solar and hydroelectric power – you should bring a flashlight. There is a lodge with a small library and informal relaxation area and a dining room serving home cooked food.

Reservations are essential, because the lodge is sometimes full with birding groups and the like. Make reservations with Costa Rica Sun Tours (operated by the Aspinalls), (☎ 33 6890, 55 3418, fax 55 4410; Apartado 1195-1250, Escazú, Costa Rica). The lodge is closed from 15 September to 31 October due to heavy rains and for maintenance.

Daily rates are US$63/74/85.50 for single/double/triple. Breakfasts are US$7.25, lunches and dinners are US$11. Children aged between three and 10 years pay 50% of the adult charge, between 10 and 14 years pay 75%.

Many people come on a package tour which includes accommodation, meals, aircraft flights from San José to Tiskita, airport transfers, and two guided walks by local naturalists. These packages cost US$880 for two people for three days/three nights or US$1240 for two for seven days/seven nights. Packages including 4WD travel from Golfito to Tiskita or flying visits to Corcovado are available on request. Boogie boards, snorkelling gear and horse rental (US$25) are also available.

Getting There & Away

It is possible to drive to the lodge with a 4WD vehicle, but most people opt to fly to the nearby airstrip. Getting there yourself is rather difficult but can be done by public transport or your own vehicle in the dry season. Ask the Aspinalls for directions.

PUERTO JIMÉNEZ

This small town can be reached from the Interamericana along 44 km of paved road from Chacarita to the small town of Rincón, followed by 32 km of gravel road to Puerto Jiménez. It is also almost 20 km away from Golfito by sea, across the Golfo Dulce. With a population of some 4000, Puerto Jiménez is the only town of any size on the Península de Osa.

Until the 1960s, the Península de Osa was one of the most remote parts of Costa Rica, with exuberant rainforests and a great variety of plants and animals. Then logging began, and later gold was discovered, creating a minor gold rush and increased settlement. In the face of this, the Parque Nacional Corcovado was created in 1975. Around the park, logging and gold mining go on, but within the park a valuable and unique group of rainforest habitats are preserved.

The gold rush and logging industry, along with the accompanying colonisation, has made Puerto Jiménez a fairly important little town and, because access is now relatively straightforward, there is a burgeoning tourist industry. Ticos come to Puerto Jiménez partly for its slightly frontier atmosphere and partly for the pleasant beaches nearby. Foreigners tend to come because this is the entry town to the famous Parque Nacional Corcovado which has an administration/information office here. It is a pleasant and friendly town and still remote enough that you can see parrots and macaws flying around. I saw four scarlet macaws flying over the south end of town on my most recent trip.

Information

Corcovado information office (☎ 78 5036) is open from 8 am to noon, and 1 to 4 pm daily. They have up-to-date information on how to get to the park. Next door, the Banco Nacional de Costa Rica buys dollars and gold.

The Restaurant Carolina is an informal but useful information centre and can arrange

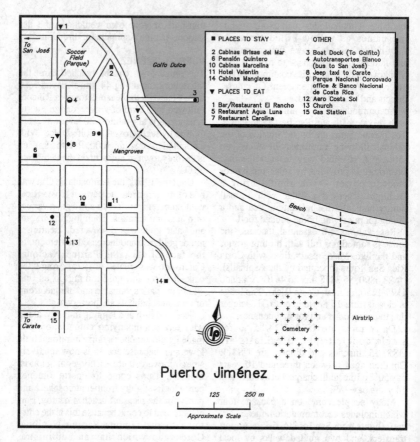

■ PLACES TO STAY		OTHER
2 Cabinas Brisas del Mar		3 Boat Dock (To Golfito)
6 Pensión Quintero		4 Autotransportes Blanco
10 Cabinas Marcelina		(bus to San José)
11 Hotel Valentin		8 Jeep taxi to Carate
14 Cabinas Manglares		9 Parque Nacional Corcovado
		office & Banco Nacional
▼ PLACES TO EAT		de Costa Rica
1 Bar/Restaurant El Rancho		12 Aero Costa Sol
5 Restaurant Agua Luna		13 Church
7 Restaurant Carolina		15 Gas Station

Puerto Jiménez

```
0        125        250 m
Approximate Scale
```

local transportation and accommodation. A store near the restaurant will change dollars. Emergency medical treatment can be obtained at the Clínica CCSS, Puerto Jiménez (☎ 70 5029, 7 5061).

Places to Stay & Eat

During Easter week, all the hotels are full. During weekends in the dry season, most hotels are also full. Call ahead to make reservations, or arrive midweek.

The cheapest place in town is the *Hotel Valentin* which has tiny airless rooms and no fans, but is at least clean. Rooms are US$2.25 per person. The *Pensión Quintero* (☎ 78 5087) has slightly bigger rooms, is also clean, but still has no fans. Shared bathroom facilities are very basic, and the rates are US$3.75 per person.

The friendly *Cabinas Marcelina* (☎ 78 5007) offers clean rooms with fans and private bath for US$6/10.50 single/double. *Cabinas Brisas del Mar* (☎ 78 5012) has clean rooms with private shower for US$14.50 – the few singles are usually full with long-term guests. (This place is up for sale – so prices may change.) The best place is *Cabinas Manglares* (☎ 78 5002, fax 78

5121; Apartado 55-8203, Puerto Jiménez) which is away from the town centre and has a pleasant restaurant attached; the food is good. Spacious rooms with fans and private bath (which used to be US$8.25 in the last edition of this book) are now US$25/30 – I guess they'll charge whatever the market will bear. They also run local tours.

About 600 metres west of the soccer field, on the main road into town, is *El Bambu* where you can camp for about US$1.50 per person.

In town, the *Restaurant Carolina* is a good place to eat. Near the boat dock the *Restaurant Agua Luna* has seafood and a sea view. Nearby, the *Bar/Restaurant El Rancho* serves meals and has a happy hour.

Getting There & Away

Air Aero Costa Sol (☎ 78 5017) has a daily flight to Golfito at 6 am, and another at 1 pm if there is passenger demand. The fare is US$11 for the seven minute flight. They also have SANSA information for connecting with Golfito to San José flights. Office hours are from 6 am to 7 pm in the busy dry season.

Three seater aircraft can be chartered into Corcovado for about US$167; five seaters cost US$185. A five seater charter to San José is about US$400. Ask at Aero Costa Sol or Restaurant Carolina for details.

Bus A new company, Autotransportes Blanco, has two buses a day via San Isidro (US$4) to San José (nine hours, US$6.50) at 5 and 11 am. The bus stop is half a block south of the soccer field – you should buy tickets in advance, especially for the 5 am departure. Ticket office hours are from 7 am to 6.30 pm. In San José, buses leave at 6 am and noon from Calle 12, Avenida 9.

There are also two buses a day at 5.30 am and 2 pm for Neily (four hours, US$2.50). The San José and Neily buses will take you the 23 km to La Palma, which is the eastern exit/entry point for the Parque Nacional Corcovado. A few buses a day go the 14 km to Dos Brazos, where there are gold mines.

Buses may run to Golfito if the ferry is not running. Ask around for other destinations.

Truck To go south of Puerto Jiménez to Carate, at the southern end of Corcovado, take a truck. They leave from near the Restaurant Carolina on Monday, Wednesday, Thursday and Saturday at 7 am. There may be more departures in the dry season; one departure may be cancelled in the wet. The fare is US$4 per person. At other times you can hire a truck or 4WD taxi for about US$40 or US$50. Ask for Cyrilo Espinosa.

Boat The passenger ferry to Golfito (☎ 78 5017) leaves daily at 6 am, takes 1½ hours and costs US$2.50. This ferry was cancelled in 1991/92 but was running again in 1993, so check locally to confirm.

Tours Corcovado Tours, based in the Cabinas Manglares (see Places to Stay), has local tours. Day trips to Corcovado are US$35 per person (four minimum) and they also offer day hikes, visits to local gold mines, horse-riding on the beach, and boat trips.

SOUTH OF PUERTO JIMÉNEZ

It is about 40 to 45 km by dirt road around the tip of the Península Osa to the Parque Nacional Corcovado. The US Army Corps of Engineers was working on the road in 1993. This project is somewhat controversial. On the one hand, the better road improves communications and opens up the region to colonisation – on the other hand, a relatively unspoiled part of Costa Rica may be devastated if uncontrolled logging, mining, ranching and other development occurs without a well-thought-out and properly implemented plan. The unique and outstanding Parque Nacional Corcovado is especially threatened by development in the area.

Whatever the pros and cons of the road building project, new bridges and graded surfaces have made the road passable to any vehicle for the first 10 km and work is proceeding fast. I just barely made it to Lapa Rios, 19 km from Puerto Jiménez, in my rented 2WD car in the 1993 dry season but the road may be all-weather by 1994.

Beyond Lapa Rios, high clearance or 4WD are required – ask locally.

Lapa Rios
This is an upscale wilderness resort situated in a 400 hectare private nature reserve in the southern Península de Osa. The preserve is 80% virgin forest and much of the remainder is scheduled for reforestation. The wilderness resort is a million dollar plus project which opened in 1993 with a commitment to conserve and protect the surrounding forest.

The main activities are hiking the extensive trail system and nature observation. Most of the trails are steep and not recommended for people with walking limitations, though there is a three km road on the property which gives easy access to the rainforest.

A medium difficulty trail system near the lodge gives scenic looks at a waterfall and huge strangler fig as well as good birding. Longer, more difficult trails require guides (US$15 to US$25 depending on length) and include a hike to the border of the Corcovado park, a wild and difficult trek to a 30 metre waterfall and others. An overnight camping trip with guide, dinner, platform tent in the rainforest and a night walk (by flashlight) is available for US$50.

A beach about one km from the lodge offers tide pools, surfing, swimming and snorkelling opportunities. Boogie boards, snorkelling gear (US$10/15 for half/full day) and surf boards (US$15/25) can be rented. Horse rental is from US$25 per half day (two people minimum) or try your hand at gold panning with a guide (US$25). Full-day boating excursions to Corcovado and Isla Caño or fishing trips can be arranged (about US$500 per day, five or six people).

The lodge has a pool, restaurant, bar, reading room and good views. Fourteen bungalows, each with solar-heated showers, electricity, two queen-size beds, large screened view windows and ample deck, rent for US$143/229/292/389 for one to four people, including three meals and transfer from Puerto Jiménez.

Make reservations in Puerto Jiménez (☎/fax 78 5130; Apartado 100, Puerto Jiménez). Lapa Rios can be reached by Spanish-speaking radiotelephone (☎ 75 0210) from 8 am to 5 pm Monday to Friday, and 8 to 11.30 am on Saturday. Information in Puerto Jiménez is available at the Aero Costa Sol office.

Bosque del Cabo
South of Lapa Rios, the road continues through the Cabo Matapalo area, the southernmost cape on the peninsula. There are stands of virgin forest interspersed with cattle ranches and great ocean views.

Bosque del Cabo is a wilderness lodge set in about 140 hectares, half of it virgin forest. There are four thatched-roof bungalows with ocean views (whales pass by from December to March), comfortable beds and solar showers. There is electricity in the main lodge where food is served.

Bird-watching in the area is excellent and hikes can be taken through the forest, to the ocean, to nearby rivers and to a waterfall. Large flocks of scarlet macaws are commonly seen.

Horse-riding (US$15 per person), tide pool exploration and swimming are all options. Day trips to Corcovado are about US$100 per person (two people) or less for groups.

Rates are US$75/110 for singles/doubles, including three meals. Reservations can be made with the owners, Philip and Barbara Spier, who pick up faxes in Puerto Jiménez (fax 78 5073) or write to Apartado 2907-1000, San José. Get there by taking a taxi from Puerto Jiménez, or the scheduled truck to Carate will drop you off.

House for Rent
Near the tip of the peninsula there is an exclusive private home available for US$150 per day (four people) or US$200 (six people). Kitchen facilities are available and there are wildlife watching opportunities. For more information, fax 78 5045.

The Far South-East

NEILY

This town, 17 km north-west of the Panamanian border by road, is nicknamed Villa by the locals. It is also sometimes referred to as Ciudad Neily. It is the main centre for the banana and African oil-palm plantations in the Coto Colorado valley to the south of town. At just 50 metres above sea level, it is a hot and humid place, but otherwise pleasant and friendly.

A road goes 31 km north to the attractive little town of San Vito at a cooler 1000 metres.

Neily's main importance to the traveller is as a transport hub for southern Costa Rica, with roads and buses to Panama, San Vito and Golfito, as well as to a host of small local agricultural settlements.

Information

There are a number of banks where you can change money. Operator-assisted telephone calls can be made from the public booths in the Cabinas El Rancho hotel. There is a hospital about two km south of town on the Interamericana.

Places to Stay

There are a number of hotels, all fairly cheap. The cheapest is the basic but friendly *Pensión Elvira* (☎ 75 3057) which charges about US$2.50 per person or US$3 with a fan and shared cold showers. Other cheap and basic places are the *Pensión Bulufer* (☎ 75 3216), *Hotel Las Vegas* (☎ 75 3205), *Pensión Familiar, Hotel El Viajero, Hotel Nohelia* and *Hotel Villa*.

The *Cabinas El Rancho* (☎ 75 3201, 75 3104, 75 3008, 75 3060) is locally popular and reasonable value at US$4.50 per person in simple rooms with private bath and fans. The *Hotel Musuco* (☎ 75 3048) offers small basic rooms for US$4 per person or US$5.50 with bath and fan. *Cabinas Andrea* (☎ 75 3784) has decent rooms with bath and fans for US$6 per person. Other clean possibilities are the *Cabinas Fontana* and *Cabinas Heyleen*.

Places to Eat

The *Cabinas El Rancho* has a reasonable restaurant attached. The best place in town is the *Restaurant La Moderna* which has a variety of meals ranging from hamburgers and pizza to chicken and fish. Meals are in the US$2 to US$5 range. *La Esquina Dulce* serves ice cream, pizza and snacks and has a couple of outside tables.

The *Bar Europa* is run by a friendly Belgian woman, Lillian, and is a good place for a drink in the evening. Lillian prepares good European-style food if you give her a couple of days notice.

Getting There & Away

Air SANSA has flights from San José to Coto 47 at 9.30 am on Tuesday, Thursday and Saturday. The 45 minute flight costs US$26 and returns from Coto 47 to San José at 10.30 am.

On Monday, Wednesday and Friday, the flight leaves San José at 9.30 am, stops at Palmar Sur, and arrives at Coto 47 at 10.45 am, returning direct to San José at 11 am.

Coto 47 is about seven km south-west of Neily, and is the closest airport to Panama. Some of the local buses pass near the airport.

Bus TRACOPA buses from San José leave five times a day from Avenida 18, Calle 4. Most of these buses continue on to the Panamanian border at Paso Canoas after stopping at Neily.

In Neily, the bus terminal is at the northeast end of town next to the market. Buses for San José (eight hours, US$5.50) leave at 4.30, 6, 8.30 and 11.30 am and 3.30 pm. Buses for San Isidro leave at 7 and 10 am and 1 and 3 pm. Buses leave for the frontier at Paso Canoas 19 times a day between 6 am and 6 pm. Buses for Golfito (1½ hours, US$0.55) leave 13 times a day between 6 am and 7.30 pm. Buses for San Vito (2½ hours, US$1.50) leave at 6 am and 1 pm via Agua Buena, and 11 am and 3 pm via Cañas Gordas. Buses for Puerto Jiménez leave at 7

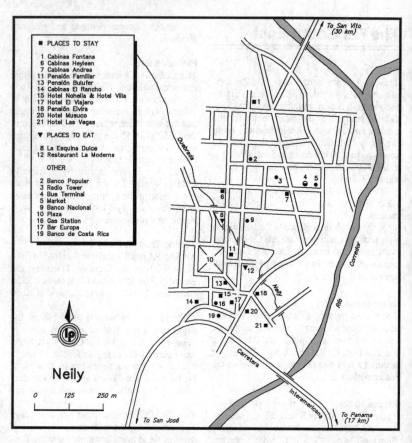

PLACES TO STAY

1 Cabinas Fontana
6 Cabinas Heyleen
7 Cabinas Andrea
11 Pensión Familiar
13 Pensión Bulufer
14 Cabinas El Rancho
15 Hotel Nohella & Hotel Villa
17 Hotel El Viajero
18 Pensión Elvira
20 Hotel Musuco
21 Hotel Las Vegas

PLACES TO EAT

8 La Esquina Dulce
12 Restaurant La Moderna

OTHER

2 Banco Popular
3 Radio Tower
4 Bus Terminal
5 Market
9 Banco Nacional
10 Plaza
16 Gas Station
17 Bar Europa
19 Banco de Costa Rica

To San Vito (30 km)

Quebrada

Corredor

Río

Neily

Neily

Carretera

Interamericana

To San José

To Panama (17 km)

0   125   250 m

am and 2 pm and take five to six hours. Buses for Cortés (near Palmar) leave at 9 am, noon and 2.30 and 4.15 pm.

Many local communities are served, including the Fincas 40, Pueblo Nuevo, Piñuelas and Zancudo – these services may depend on how much it has been raining.

Taxi Taxis with 4WD are available to take you almost anywhere. From Neily to Paso Canoas costs about US$6; to Coto 47 the fare is about US$2.50. Taxis between Coto 47 and Paso Canoas will cost you about US$8.

SAN VITO

With a population of about 10,000, this pleasant town at 980 metres above sea level offers a respite from the heat of the nearby lowlands. The drive up from Neily is a very scenic one, with superb views of the lowlands dropping away as the bus climbs the steep and winding road up the coastal mountain range (called Fila Cruces). Drivers should note that the road is steep and unpaved for 19 km to Agua Buena – it's passable to ordinary cars but with care. After Agua Buena the road is paved to San Vito.

Some buses from Neily go via Cañas

Gordas, which is on the Panamanian border but is not an official crossing point – although you can see Panama. There is reportedly a pensión here.

The bus continues through Sabalito (which has a gas station and basic hotel) before reaching San Vito. Other buses go more directly via Agua Buena, passing the Wilson Botanical Gardens about six km before reaching San Vito.

You can also get to San Vito from San José via the Valle de Coto Brus – this route is also scenic and involves crossing the upper Río Terraba by ferry, soon after leaving the Carretera Interamericana. (A bridge is planned, but the ferry is more fun.) This road is paved all the way.

San Vito was founded by Italian immigrants in the early 1950s, and today you can still hear Italian spoken in the streets.

The most exciting thing to do in San Vito itself is to eat Italian food in one of the Italian restaurants. San Vito is also a good base for visits to the Wilson Botanical Gardens and to the Parque Internacional La Amistad.

Places to Stay

The *Hotel Tropical* is friendly and secure. Basic rooms are US$2.50 per person, but a disco downstairs may keep you awake at weekends and buses getting gas at the station across the street may wake you up in the morning. The *Hotel Colono* is another cheap and basic choice.

For US$5 per person, you can stay at the *Cabinas Las Mirlas* (☎ 77 3054) which is clean, quiet and pleasant with private electric showers. Windows open onto an orchard. Go down the drive about 150 metres to the house on the right to ask about these cabins.

The *Hotel Collina* charges US$4.50/7.25 for single/double rooms with private cold shower. The attached bar is locally popular. The *Hotel Pittier* (☎ 77 3006) is about the same price but you need to call the owner to open it up. The *Cabinas Las Huacas* (☎ 77

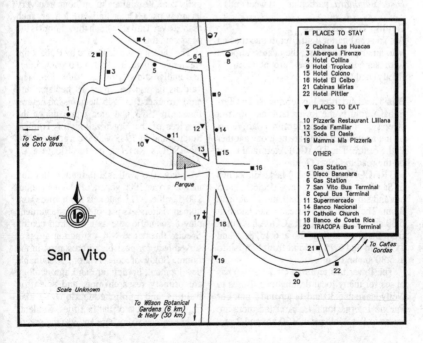

PLACES TO STAY

- 2 Cabinas Las Huacas
- 3 Albergue Firenze
- 4 Hotel Collina
- 9 Hotel Tropical
- 15 Hotel Colono
- 16 Hotel El Ceibo
- 21 Cabinas Mirlas
- 22 Hotel Pittier

PLACES TO EAT

- 10 Pizzería Restaurant Liliana
- 12 Soda Familiar
- 13 Soda El Oasis
- 19 Mamma Mia Pizzería

OTHER

- 1 Gas Station
- 5 Disco Bananara
- 6 Gas Station
- 7 San Vito Bus Terminal
- 8 Cepul Bus Terminal
- 11 Supermercado
- 14 Banco Nacional
- 17 Catholic Church
- 18 Banco de Costa Rica
- 20 TRACOPA Bus Terminal

To San José via Coto Brus

Parque

San Vito

Scale Unknown

To Wilson Botanical Gardens (6 km) & Nelly (30 km)

To Cañas Gordas

3115, 77 3517) has decent new rooms which are fair value for US$6.25/11 with private electric showers. The *Albergue Firenze* (☎ 77 3206) has OK rooms with private electric shower in this price range.

The *Hotel El Ceibo* (☎ 77 3025) is the best in town. It has older rooms with cold showers for US$6.75/11.75 and newer, nicer rooms with electric showers for US$10/18.25.

Places to Eat
The *Hotel El Ceibo* has a reasonable restaurant. Italian restaurants include the *Pizzería Restaurant Lilliana* which has pizza, Italian and local food for US$3 to US$4, and the slightly fancier *Mamma Mia Pizzería*, which is another good choice.

The *Soda El Oasis* has cheap meals and served me a memorably excellent cup of the local Coto Brus coffee – thick, chocolaty and very strong. Perhaps I just got lucky. Nearby, the *Soda Familiar* has cheap meals and is locally popular. After dinner, check out the *Disco Bananara*, particularly at weekends.

Getting There & Away
Air You can charter light aircraft into the San Vito airstrip. Otherwise, the nearest airports with scheduled services are at Coto 47 (Neily) and Golfito.

Bus There are three bus terminals. The Terminal Cepul is the lower terminal down a steep side street and the Terminal San Vito is on the main street. Both are near one another in the centre. The TRACOPA terminal is out on the road to Cañas Gordas.

TRACOPA (☎ 77 3410) has a direct bus to San José (about six hours, US$6.50) at 5 am and slower buses at 7.30 and 10 am and 3 pm. They also have buses to San Isidro at 6.30 am and 1.30 pm. TRACOPA has buses from San José to San Vito at 6.15, 8.15 and 11.30 am and 2.15 pm and from San Isidro at 5.30 am and 2 pm.

The lower bus terminal (☎ 77 3010) has buses for many local destinations. Buses to Neily leave at 5.30 and 11 am and 2 pm. For Parque Internacional La Amistad there are buses to Las Mellizas at 9.30 am and 2 pm,

to Las Tablas at 10.30 am and 3 pm, and to Cotón at 3 pm. Other nearby destinations served include Río Sereno on the Panamanian border, Los Reyes, Cotón and Los Planos.

The main street terminal has buses to Neily at 7 am, Paso Real at 4 pm, Las Mellizas at 5 pm, Santa Elena at 10 am and 4 pm (this bus goes near La Amistad) and Las Tablas at 11.30 am, connecting with a bus to Colorado on the edge of La Amistad.

WILSON BOTANICAL GARDEN
This garden, six km south of San Vito, is very well laid out and many of the plants are labelled. Wandering around the grounds is fun, and the labels turn the walk into a learning adventure. There are many trails, each named for the plants found alongside. They include the Heliconia Loop Trail, Bromeliad Walk, Tree Fern Hill Trail, Orchid Walk, Fern Gully, and Bamboo Walk. Most of these trails take 30 minutes to an hour at a very leisurely pace. Other trails are longer, such as the River Trail for which three hours is the suggested time.

The garden was established by Robert and Catherine Wilson in 1963 and became internationally known for its collection. The gardens themselves cover 10 hectares and are surrounded by 145 hectares of natural forest. In 1973, the area came under the auspices of the Organization for Tropical Studies and in 1983 was incorporated into UNESCO's Reserva de La Biosfera La Amistad.

Today, the well-maintained collection includes over 1000 genera of plants in about 200 families. This attracts both birds and human visitors. As part of OTS, the gardens play a scientific role as a research centre. Species threatened with extinction are preserved here for possible reforestation in the future. Study of conservation, sustainable development, horticulture and agroecology are primary research aims and scientific training and public education are also important aspects of the facilities. Students and researchers stay here and use the greenhouse and laboratory facilities. Members of the public can also be accommodated.

The dry season is from January to March, when it is easier to get around the gardens. Nevertheless, the vegetation in the wet months is exuberant with many epiphytic bromeliads, ferns and orchids being sustained by the moisture in the air. Annual rainfall is about 4000 mm and average high temperatures are about 26°C.

Information

The gardens are open daily from 7.30 am to 4 pm. Foreign travellers are charged US$2/4 to get in for a half/full day whilst ticos are charged US$0.30 in an attempt to foster interest in plant conservation among locals. A trail map is provided. The money goes to maintaining the gardens and research facilities.

Places to Stay & Eat

Overnight guests can be accommodated if reservations are made in advance with OTS (☎ 40 6696; fax 40 6783; Apartado 676-2050, San Pedro, San José). The dry months (especially February) and July and August are popular with visiting research and student groups, who have priority. Make reservations as far in advance as possible for these months.

Accommodation is available for 32 people in a number of rooms with shared bathrooms and hot water. Meals and laundry facilities are provided for overnight guests. Rates are about US$50 per person per night, including meals. Lunch only can be arranged for US$11. Meals are a tasty affair, shared with interesting scientists, graduate students and other researchers working here. You can call the gardens direct (☎ fax 77 3278) if you are already in San Vito – they may be able to accommodate or feed you if there is space available, although reservations are requested. Also call the gardens direct to arrange guided tours.

Otherwise, stay in San Vito.

Getting There & Away

Buses between San Vito and Neily (and other

destinations) pass the entrance to the gardens several times a day. Ask at the bus terminal about the right bus, because some buses to Neily take a different route. A taxi from San Vito to the gardens costs US$2 to US$3. It is a six km walk from San Vito, mainly uphill, to the gardens (and downhill back). A sign near the centre of town claims '4 km' but it's six. Trust me.

PARQUE INTERNACIONAL LA AMISTAD

This huge park is by far the largest single protected area in Costa Rica. It is known as an international park because it continues across the border into Panama, where it is managed separately.

Combined with Chirripó and several indigenous reservations and biological reserves, La Amistad forms the Amistad-Talamanca Regional Conservation Unit. Because of its remoteness and size, the RCU protects a great variety of tropical habitats ranging from rainforest to páramo and so has attracted the attention of biologists, ecologists and conservationists worldwide. In 1982, the area was declared the Reserva de La Biosfera La Amistad by UNESCO, and in 1983 was designated a World Heritage site. Approximately 250,000 hectares are a strictly protected core area which will remain untouched. A further 340,000 hectares are buffer zones with controlled management and development. These are joined by some 440,000 hectares on the Panamanian side.

Conservation International and other agencies are working with the Costa Rican authorities to implement a suitable management plan. This plan must preserve the wildlife and habitat, and develop resources, such as hydroelectricity, without disturbing the ecosystem or the traditional way of life of the Indian groups dwelling within the reserve.

Reserva de La Biosfera La Amistad has the nation's largest populations of Baird's tapirs, as well as giant anteaters, all six species of neotropical cats – jaguar, puma (or mountain lion), margay, ocelot, tiger cat (or oncilla) and jaguarundi – and many other more common mammals. Over 500 bird species have been sighted (more than half of the total in Costa Rica) and 49 of these species exist only within the biosphere reserve. In addition, 115 species of fish and 215 species of reptiles and amphibians have been listed and more are being added regularly. There are innumerable insect species. Nine of the nation's 12 Holdridge Life Zones are represented in the reserve.

The backbone of the reserve is the Cordillera de Talamanca, which, apart from having the peaks of the Chirripó massif, also has many mountains over 3000 metres in elevation. The thickly forested northern Caribbean slopes and southern Pacific slopes of the Talamancas are also protected in the park, but it is only on the Pacific side that ranger stations are found. These are on access roads that are outside the actual park boundaries.

Within the park itself, development is almost non-existent, which means backpackers are pretty much left to their own resources. Hiking through steep, thick and wet rainforest is both difficult and lacking in the instant gratification of seeing, say, grizzly bears and North American bison in Yellowstone National Park, or lions and leopards in Kenya's national parks. It is because of the lack of human interference that the shy tropical mammals of Costa Rica are present in relative abundance at La Amistad – but expect to work hard for a glimpse of them. Bird-watching, on the other hand, will usually be more successful.

Information

Obtaining information from the Servicio de Parques Nacionales in San José is difficult – this is such a remote area that nobody knows much about it.

Park headquarters is at Progreso, near the Zona Protectora Las Tablas. From Progreso, a nine km trail heads uphill into the Las Tablas area where you can camp and bird-watch. This is the best 'developed' area.

There is also a station at La Escuadra, almost 20 km north of Santa Elena, and in the Colorado area.

Places to Stay

A family in the Las Tablas area provides food and accommodation on their ranch – ask around.

La Amistad Lodge is a new operation in the Las Tablas zone. They have 10 double rooms sharing four baths with hot and cold showers. Family-style meals are served and electricity is available a few hours a day (bring a flashlight). There is no telephone at the lodge. Rates are US$65 per person including meals and guide service. There are plans to build more cabins in 1994. For reservations and information contact Giselle Sibaja at Tropical Rainbow Tours (☎ 33 8228).

Getting There & Away

From San Vito, buses for Las Mellizas and Las Tablas pass near Progreso. A bus also goes to Santa Elena for access to La Escuadra and Colorado ranger stations.

Taxis with 4WD can usually be hired from the nearest towns to get you to the park stations, but be prepared to do a bit of asking around before finding someone who knows the way. You could also try exploring the area in a rented 4WD. This is a trip only for those adventurers with plenty of time.

Costa Rica Expeditions in San José will arrange a four day/three night excursion to the Las Tablas zone, staying at the Las Tablas lodge, for US$425 per person (minimum four people).

PASO CANOAS

This small town is on the Interamericana at the Panamanian border, and is therefore the main land port of entry between Costa Rica and Panama. It is a popular destination for ticos who come here on shopping trips to buy goods more cheaply than in San José. Therefore hotels are often full with bargain hunters during weekends and holidays, at which time you should go on to Neily, 17 km away. Most of the shops and hotels are on the Costa Rican side.

See the Getting There & Away chapter for full details of the border crossing to or from Panama.

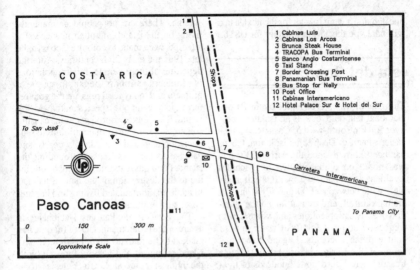

Paso Canoas

1 Cabinas Luis
2 Cabinas Los Arcos
3 Brunca Steak House
4 TRACOPA Bus Terminal
5 Banco Anglo Costarricense
6 Taxi Stand
7 Border Crossing Post
8 Panamanian Bus Terminal
9 Bus Stop for Nelly
10 Post Office
11 Cabinas Interamericano
12 Hotel Palace Sur & Hotel del Sur

Information

Paso Canoas has a gas station. Money-changers hang out around the border, and give better rates than banks for exchanging cash US dollars to colones. You can also convert excess colones to dollars, but this exchange is not as good. Try to get rid of as much Costa Rican currency as possible before crossing into Panama. Colones are accepted on the border, but are difficult to get rid of further into Panama. Other currencies are harder to deal with. Travellers cheques can be negotiated with persistence, but are not as readily accepted as cash. There are banks but they are only open in the mornings from Monday to Friday. The Panamanian currency is the balboa, which is on par with and interchangeable with cash US dollars.

Places to Stay & Eat

The *Hotel del Sur* and the *Hotel Palace Sur* next door are the cheapest places to stay – around US$3 per person.

The *Cabinas Interamericano* has clean rooms with private bath and fan for about US$4.75 per person.

Cabinas Los Arcos charges about US$8.75 for a double with private bath and fan. Next door is the *Cabinas Luis* in the same price range.

There are a number of cheap sodas where you can eat. One of the better restaurants is in the *Cabinas Interamericano*. Also try the *Brunca Steak House* which is popular with international truck drivers.

Getting There & Away

Air The nearest airport to the border is at Coto 47, near Neily (see the Neily section). The SANSA agent is at the Cabinas Interamericano.

Bus Buses from the TRACOPA terminal in San José leave several times a day, but make reservations if you're travelling on Friday night because the bus is usually full of weekend shoppers. The same applies to buses leaving Paso Canoas on Sundays. Direct buses leave Paso Canoas for San José at 4 and 9 am and 1 pm – the fare is US$6.50 for the seven hour trip. Slightly slower buses leave at 7.30 am and 3 pm (US$5.20).

Buses for Neily leave about every hour during daylight hours, from less than 100 metres away from the border. If you just miss one and don't want to wait for the next, a taxi will take you the 17 km to Neily for US$6.

Isla del Coco

This island, which is occupied by the Parque Nacional Isla del Coco, is an isolated one – over 500 km south-west of Costa Rica, in the eastern Pacific. Despite its isolation, Cocos has been known since the early 1500s and was noted on a map drawn by Nicholas Dechiens as far back as 1541. It is extremely wet, with between 6000 and 7000 mm of annual rainfall, and thus attracted the attention of early sailors, pirates and whalers, who frequently stopped for fresh water and, of course, fresh coconuts. Legend has it that some of the early visitors buried a huge treasure here but, despite hundreds of treasure-hunting expeditions, it has never been found. The heavy rainfall has enabled the island to support thick rainforest which soon covers all signs of digging.

Because of its isolation, Isla del Coco has evolved a unique ecosystem, which is why it is protected by national park status. Over 70 species of animals (mainly insects) and 70 species of plants are reportedly endemic (occurring nowhere else in the world) and more remain to be discovered. Bird-watchers come to the island to see the colonies of seabirds, many of which nest on Cocos. These include two species of frigatebirds, three species of boobies, four species of gulls and six species of storm petrels among the 76 birds listed for the park. Three of the birds are endemic: the Cocos Island cuckoo, Cocos Island finch, and Cocos Island flycatcher. (The Cocos Island finch is part of the group of endemic finches studied in the Galápagos Islands by Darwin – although the Cocos species was not discovered until almost 60 years after Darwin's visit to the Galápagos.)

There are two endemic lizard species. The marine life is also varied, with sea turtles, coral reefs and tropical fish in abundance. Snorkelling and diving are possible and plea-surable. There are no people permanently living on the island, although unsuccessful attempts were made to colonise Cocos in the late 19th and early 20th centuries. After the departure of these people, feral populations of domestic animals began to create a problem and today feral pigs are the greatest threat to the unique species native to the island. The pigs uproot vegetation, causing soil erosion which in turn contributes to sedimentation around the island's coasts and damage to the coral reefs surrounding the island. Feral rats, cats and goats also contribute to the destruction of the natural habitat. In addition, unregulated fishing and hunting poses further threats.

The Servicio de Parques Nacionales is aware of the problem, but lack of funding has made it difficult to do anything about it. The island is rugged and heavily forested, with the highest point at Cerro Yglesias (634 metres). As a practical matter, how can you remove a large population of feral pigs from a thickly vegetated and hilly island which is 12 km long and five km wide?

Information

There is a park station and permission is needed from the parks service to visit it. There are some trails, but camping is not allowed. The few visitors who come stay on their boat.

Tours

Okeanos Aggressor (☎ 1 (800) 348 2628, (504) 385 2416, fax (504) 384 0817; PO Drawer K, Morgan City, LA 70381, USA) has 10 day dive charters leaving from Puntarenas about 12 times a year. They have space for 21 passengers. Rates are US$2595 per person from San José including everything except alcohol, crew tips and US$25 for park fees. Compressed air is provided for divers and the charter includes seven days of diving with four dives per day. Diving equipment can be rented and the trip is recommended for experienced divers.

Tropical Sceneries (☎ 24 2555, fax 33 9524; Apartado 2047-1000, San José) also arranges diving trips to the island.

Central Pacific Coast

Costa Rica's major Pacific coastal town is Puntarenas, about 110 km west of San José by paved highway. This has traditionally been the town for highlanders to descend to when they wanted to spend a few days by the ocean, but there are now many other popular vacation spots on the Pacific coast south of Puntarenas.

These include swimming and surfing beach resorts, sportfishing towns, well-developed and almost undeveloped beaches, a biological reserve, a national marine park and the famous coastal national park at Manuel Antonio.

Generally speaking, the Pacific coast is better developed for tourism than the Caribbean, and if you are looking for some luxury, it is easy to find here. On the other hand, you can also find deserted beaches, wildlife and small coastal villages.

There are marked wet and dry seasons along the Pacific coast. The rains begin in April, and from May to November you can expect a lot of precipitation. This eases in December and the dry season continues for the next four months.

The dry months coincide with Costa Rican school vacations in January and February, and the biggest holiday of the year at Easter. So the dry season is the high season – wherever you travel on the Pacific coast, expect a lot of visitors and make sure you have hotel reservations at weekends.

During Easter week, most beach hotels are booked weeks or months in advance. If you travel during the low (wet) season, you'll see fewer visitors and have little difficulty in booking into hotels.

Low season discounts (ranging from 10% to 40% or even 50%) are worth asking about. (The prices given throughout this chapter are the high season rates.)

Average temperatures on the coast, year round, are about 22°C minimum and about 32°C maximum. The dry season is generally a little hotter than the wet.

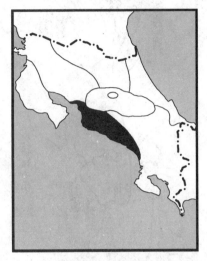

PUNTARENAS

This city of 95,000 inhabitants is the capital of the province of Puntarenas, which stretches along the Pacific coast from the Golfo de Nicoya to the Panamanian border.

During the 19th century, in the days before easy access to the Caribbean coast, Puntarenas was Costa Rica's major port.

Goods such as coffee were hauled by ox cart from the highlands down the Pacific slope to Puntarenas, from where they were shipped around the Horn to Europe. A long trip!

After the railway to Puerto Limón was built, Puntarenas became less significant but still remained the most important port on the Pacific side of the country. This changed in 1981 when a new port was opened at Caldera, about 18 km south-east of Puntarenas by road. This new facility has become the major Pacific port.

Despite the loss of shipping, Puntarenas remains a bustling town during the dry

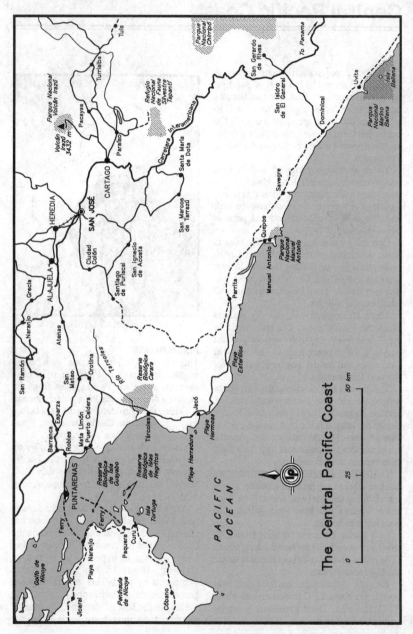

The Central Pacific Coast

season, when tourists arrive. During the wet months, however, the city is much quieter.

There are plenty of sandy beaches, but unfortunately they are too polluted for swimming (although the local kids do so). You can walk along the beach, or the aptly named Paseo de los Turistas beach road stretching along the southern coast of town, but if you want to swim, stick to your hotel pool.

Although the town is popular with Costa Rican holiday makers, foreigners tend to look for a destination where they can swim. There are plenty of possibilities in the towns and beaches south of Puntarenas, and many people go there and avoid Puntarenas completely.

The locals have a reputation for friendliness. Hang out on the beach front with the tico tourists, and check out the busy comings and goings during the season. Walk by the church – perhaps the most attractive building in Puntarenas. Some people even like to come during the wet season when it is quiet and fresh with daily rain showers. It certainly is the closest coastal town to San José for a quick getaway – although there are plenty of better beaches elsewhere.

Orientation

The geographical setting of the town is an intriguing one. Puntarenas literally means a 'sandy point' or sand spit. The city is on the end of a sandy peninsula that is almost eight km long but only 600 metres wide at its widest point (downtown) and less than 100 metres wide in many other parts. The city has 60 Calles from west to east but has only five Avenidas running north to south at its widest point. Driving into town with the waters of the Pacific lapping up on either side of the road is a memorable experience. Make sure you leave or arrive in daylight hours to see this.

With such a long, narrow street configuration, you are never more than a few minutes walk away from the coast.

Information

There are several banks along the two blocks of Avenida 3 between Calle Central & 3.

Puntarenas does not have the normal parque central or town square. Be careful of thieves and pickpockets, especially along the beach.

Emergency medical attention is available from the Hospital Monseñor Sanabria (☎ 63 0033), eight km east of town.

Beaches

There are also good beaches and resorts in the Península de Nicoya on the other side of the Golfo de Nicoya, and passenger and car ferries leave Puntarenas for the peninsula daily. So if you're heading for Nicoya, you can spend a night or two in Puntarenas en route.

Festivals

Apart from the usual tico holidays, Puntarenas celebrates the Fiesta del Virgen del Mar on the Saturday closest to 16 July. There is the usual parade, except that the gaily decorated floats really do float – fishing boats and elegant yachts are beautifully bedecked with lights, flags and all manner of fanciful embellishments as they sail around the harbour. There is also a carnival, boat races, and plenty of food, drink and dancing.

Places to Stay – bottom end

One of the cheapest hotels is the basic and rather noisy *Hotel Río* (☎ 61 0331) on Calle Central, Avenida 3, just next to the old Paquera boat dock. The dock/market area is a little rough but the management is friendly. Rooms with fans and communal bathrooms are US$3.75/5.80 for singles/doubles and rooms with private shower are US$6.50/ 11.60. On the east side of the market is the *Pacífico* (not to be confused with the El Oasis del Pacífico), a flophouse inhabited by drunks and prostitutes – not recommended unless you are desperate.

For US$3.75 per person, stay in the basic but friendly *Pensión Cabezas* (☎ 61 1045) on Avenida 1, Calle 2 & 4. The rooms are small but clean and have fans – this is one of the best choices in this price range. Other basic hotels charging US$3.75 per person include the following. The *Pensión Chinchilla* (☎ 61 0638) on Calle 1, Avenida

Central & 2, is clean and secure, as is the *Pensión Montemar* (☎ 61 2771) on Avenida 3, Calle 1 & 3. The *Pensión Juanita* (☎ 61 0096), in an interesting-looking house on Avenida Central, Calle Central & 1, has boxy little rooms and charges an extra US$1.50 for a portable fan. There is also the *Pensión El Nido* (☎ 61 2471), Avenida 1, Calle 4 & 6, which has fans, and the *Pensión Gutierrez* around the corner which looks the most basic of the lot.

The *Hotel Ayi Con* (☎ 61 0164, 61 1477) on Calle 2, Avenida 1 & 3, has rather basic but clean rooms – this is locally considered the 'best' budget hotel. Rates are US$4.50 per person in rooms with fans, US$6 per person in rooms with fans and private cold shower, and US$7.25 per person with shower and air-conditioning.

The Youth Hostel Association in San José (☎/fax 24 4085) can make reservations (strongly suggested) for members at the *Cabinas San Isidro* (☎ 21 1225, 63 0031; fax 21 6822) for US$9 per person. San Isidro is a Puntarenas suburb about eight km east of downtown Puntarenas, and there are buses to and from town. The cabinas are near a beach, and there are cooking facilities, a restaurant, and a swimming pool. Ask the bus to drop you off at the Monseñor Sanabria Hospital bus stop, from where it's about a 300 metre walk. Rates are more expensive for non-IYHF members.

Places to Stay – middle

The *Gran Hotel Imperial* (☎ 61 0579) is a large old wooden hotel on Paseo de los Turistas and Calle Central, near the bus stations. The place has atmosphere. The rickety upstairs rooms have balconies, some with ocean views, but bathrooms are shared. Rates are US$9 per person. Darker downstairs rooms have private bathrooms and fans and rent for US$10.50 per person.

The family-run *Cabinas Central* (☎ 61 1484), on Calle 7, Paseo de los Turistas & Avenida 2, is clean, safe and friendly. The rooms are small but have private baths and fans for US$11/18. (Note that Calle 5 is mistakenly signed Calle 7 at the Paseo de los

Turistas end – this can lead to confusion in finding the hotel.)

The *Hotel Cayuga* (☎ 61 0344), on Calle 4, Avenida Central & 1, gets mixed reports. My room with private bath had no hot water but did have a very efficient air-conditioning system, which was a relief in the hot temperatures. The rooms are uninspiring but clean and the restaurant attached to the hotel is quite good, although not very cheap. There is a locked parking lot behind the hotel. Rates are US$11/16 for a single/double – not a bad deal. They also have a nicer suite with TV and refrigerator for US$30 a double. Reservations can be made at Apartado 306-5400, Puntarenas, Costa Rica.

The *Cabinas El Jorón* (☎ 61 0467) on Avenida 4 bis, Calle 25, has both small, rather dark rooms and roomier cabins. The rooms have private baths, air-conditioning and a refrigerator (locally called a 'refri'), and cost US$18 for a double; the more spacious cabins are a little more expensive.

The *Hotel Las Hamacas* (☎ 61 0398, 61 1799), on the Paseo de los Turistas, Calle 5 & 7, is popular with younger ticos. There is a pool, restaurant, disco and bar, so it can get a bit noisy if your room is close to the revelries. Simple rooms with private cold bath and fan are US$11.50/20, or a few dollars more for air-conditioning.

The *Gran Hotel Chorotega* (☎ 61 0998) at Avenida 3, Calle 1, has had a recent facelift and price increase. Clean rooms with a private bath and fan are US$24 for a double; rooms with communal baths are US$16 a double.

The French-owned *El Oasis del Pacífico* (☎ 61 0209), on Paseo de los Turistas, Calle 3 & 5, has a heavily chlorinated pool, disco, restaurant, bar and parking, and seems popular with tico families on vacation. Simple rooms with private shower and fan rent from US$26 a double to US$63 for five people.

The *Hotel La Punta* (☎ 61 0696), on Avenida 1 and Calle 35 at the far western point of town near the car ferry terminal, is a well-run, clean little hotel which is popular with older North Americans. English is

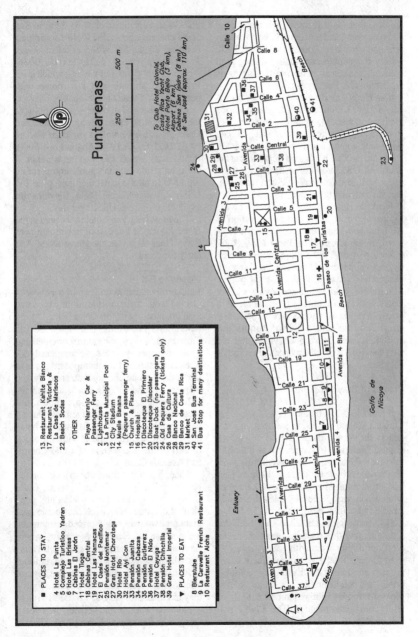

Puntarenas

0   250   500 m

To Club Hotel Colonial,
Costa Rica Yacht Club,
Hotel Porto Bello (3 km),
Airport (6 km),
Cabinas San Isidro (8 km)
& San José (approx. 110 km)

Estuary

Golfo de
Nicoya

Beach

■ PLACES TO STAY

4 Hotel La Punta
5 Complejo Turístico Yadran
6 Hotel Las Brisas
7 Cabinas El Jorón
11 Hotel Tioga
18 Cabinas Central
19 Hotel Las Hamacas
21 El Oasis del Pacífico
25 Pensión Montemar
27 Gran Hotel Chorotega
30 Hotel Río
32 Hotel Ayí Con
33 Pensión Juanita
34 Pensión Cabezas
35 Pensión Gutiérrez
36 Pensión El Nido
37 Hotel Cayuga
38 Pensión Chinchilla
39 Gran Hotel Imperial

▼ PLACES TO EAT

8 Bierstube
9 La Caravelle French Restaurant
10 Restaurant Aloha

13 Restaurant Kahite Blanco
17 Restaurant Victoria &
   La Casa de Mariscos
22 Beach Sodas

OTHER

1 Playa Naranjo Car &
   Passenger Ferry
2 Lighthouse
3 La Punta Municipal Pool
4 City Stadium
14 Muelle Banana
   (Paquera passenger ferry)
15 Church & Plaza
16 Hospital
17 Discoteque El Primero
20 Discoteque DiscoMar
23 Boat Dock (no passengers)
24 Old Paquera Ferry (tickets only)
26 Casa de Cultura
28 Banco Nacional
29 Banco de Costa Rica
31 Market
40 San José Bus Terminal
41 Bus Stop for many destinations

spoken, there is a pleasant bar, small pool and restaurant, and the rooms have hot water, fans and a balcony. Rooms are US$26/33.50 – only the double rate applies during high season weekends. The mail address is Apartado 228, Puntarenas.

The *Hotel Las Brisas* (☎ 61 4040; Apartado 83-5400, Puntarenas) on Paseo de los Turistas, Calle 31, near the west end of Puntarenas, is a quiet, clean and pleasant hotel with a good restaurant and small pool. Rates are US$22/30 for a single/double at the back and US$34/44 at the front with a sea view. All rooms have air-conditioning, private bath and hot water.

Near the north end of Calle 74 in the suburb of Cocal, at the narrowest portion of the peninsula some three km east of downtown, is the *Costa Rica Yacht Club* (☎ 61 0784; Apartado 2530-1000, San José) which caters to members of both local and foreign yacht clubs as well as the general public. Rooms are spartan but spotless, with hot water and air-conditioning, and there is a pool. Standard rooms are US$15/19 single/double and superior rooms are US$22/31, which are good value, but it's very hard to get in – the place is often full of yachties.

Places to Stay – top end

The *Hotel Tioga* (☎ 61 0271, fax 61 0127; Apartado 96-5400, Puntarenas), Paseo de los Turistas, Calle 17 & 19, was opened in 1959 and is the 'grand dame' of the downtown hotels. There are 46 rooms, but as it's often full, call ahead. All rooms have air-conditioning and private bath, most with hot water. The more expensive rooms have balconies with a sea view; cheaper ones are inside around the pool. Rates range from US$29 to US$43 for a single, and US$37 to US$57 for a double, and this includes breakfast in the 4th floor dining room with ocean view.

In Cocal suburb, next to the Yacht Club, are two good hotels with mooring facilities, pools, air-conditioning, hot water, clean, pleasant rooms and restaurants, both of which are recommended. The *Club Hotel Colonial* (☎ 61 1833, fax 61 2969; Apartado

368-5400, Puntarenas or ☎ 55 3232 in San José) charges about US$30/48 for singles/doubles. To the left is the excellent *Hotel Porto Bello* (☎ 61 1322, fax 61 0036; Apartado 108-5400, Puntarenas) which is set in pleasant grounds and has rooms with patios for US$46/60 single/double.

At the other end of town near the point of the sand spit at Paseo de los Turistas and Calle 35, is the *Complejo Turistico Yadran* (☎ 61 2662, fax 61 1944; Apartado 14-5000, Puntarenas) which has two restaurants, a children's and adults' pool, comfortable rooms with all the usual facilities, plus TV, US$64/80; suites are US$94. Bicycles are available for hire at US$12 per day.

The most luxurious hotel in the area is the *Hotel Fiesta*, 11 km east of downtown near Playa Doña Ana (see the Playa Doña Ana entry for details).

Places to Eat

Eating in Puntarenas (at least in the cheaper places) tends to be a little more expensive than in other parts of Costa Rica. Many restaurants are along the Paseo de los Turistas and so tend to be tourist oriented and a little more pricey – but not outrageously so. The cheapest food for the impecunious is in the sodas around the market area, by the Paquera boat dock. This area is also inhabited by sailors, drunks and prostitutes, but seems raffish rather than dangerous – during the day at least. There are also several inexpensive Chinese restaurants within a block or two of the intersection of Calle Central and Avenida Central.

There is a row of fairly cheap sodas on the beach by the Paseo de los Turistas, Calle Central and 3. They serve snacks and non-alcoholic drinks. Three blocks to the east there are two reasonably priced restaurants, the popular *La Casa de Mariscos*, where English is spoken, and the *Restaurant Victoria*, which serves Chinese food and seafood.

Just west of the Hotel Tioga are several international restaurants to choose from – they have meals in the US$5 to US$10 range – more for shrimp and lobster, less for a snack. The *Restaurant Aloha* (☎ 61 0773) is one of the better ones in town. Half a block further is the *La Caravelle* French restaurant which is popular and often crowded; it is closed on Monday. Just beyond is a German style bar and restaurant, the *Bierstube* (☎ 61 0330). Apart from beer, it has a variety of snacks and light meals.

On the north side of town, at Avenida 1 and Calle 19, is the *Restaurant Kahite Blanco* (☎ 61 2093) which is a rambling restaurant popular with the locals. It serves good seafood in the US$3 to US$7 range. They have music and dancing at weekends.

Most of the better hotels have decent restaurants. Ones which have been particularly recommended are at the hotels *Porto Bello, Colonial* and *Las Brisas*.

Entertainment
During the day, laze around the municipal pool at the very point of Puntarenas – nice ocean views through the fence. There are adult and kids pools and entrance is US$0.90 or US$0.55 for kids aged under 11 years. Pool hours are 9 am to 4.40 pm, Tuesday to Sunday.

Look for plays and concerts being presented at the Casa de Cultura during the high season (from December to Easter).

There are several dancing spots. On Paseo de los Turistas near Calle 7 are the *Discoteque DiscoMar* and the *Discoteque El Primero*. Several of the hotels, including the *Yadran* and *Hamacas*, may have dancing some nights.

Getting There & Away
Air There are no regularly scheduled flights here, but you can charter a plane to the Chacarita airstrip, six or seven km east of downtown Puntarenas.

Bus The drive from San José takes less than two hours and costs about US$2.40. Buses leave frequently from Calle 12, Avenida 9 – there may be a wait during holiday weekends. From Puntarenas, buses for San José leave frequently from the terminal on Calle 2, just north of the Paseo de los Turistas.

Across the Paseo from the San José bus terminal is a covered bus stop right by the ocean, from where buses leave to many nearby destinations. There are 12 buses daily to Miramar (near the Refugio Silvestre de Peñas Blancas) and buses inland to Esparza every hour or so. Buses to Liberia leave at 5.30, 7 and 9.30 am and 3 and 5.20 pm. Other buses include the 11.30 am and 4.30 pm departures for Tilarán, a bus to Guácimal at 1 pm, and a bus for Santa Elena (near Monteverde) at 2.15 pm. Buses to Quepos (which could drop you at Jacó) leave at 5 and 11.30 am and 2.30 pm. (The 11.30 am bus may be canelled in the wet season.) Buses serving the communities on the coast north of Puntarenas include a 1 pm bus to Pitahaya, a 12.15 pm bus to Chomes, and buses to Costa de Pajaro at 10.45 am and 1.15 and 4.30 pm.

Buses for the port of Caldera (also going past Playa Doña Ana and Mata Limón) leave from the market about every hour and head out of town along Avenida Central.

Train The train station is at the eastern end of downtown, but passenger services to San José were discontinued in 1991.

Boat There are two ferry terminals. The Conatramar terminal (☎ 61 1069, fax 61 2197) at the north-west end of town has a car/passenger ferry which does the 1½ hour trip to Playa Naranjo, on the Península Nicoya west of Puntarenas. There are departures at 4, 7 and 10.30 am and 1.30 and 4 pm daily during the high season – some crossings may be cancelled during the low season. The fare is US$1.10 for adults, half fare for children, US$8.10 for car plus driver, and US$2.50 for bicycles and motorbikes. There is rarely any problem with getting a passenger ticket, but cars may be turned away, so try to get in line a couple of hours early. (Note that if you want to continue from Playa Naranjo without a car, the only buses meeting the ferry go to Nicoya.)

The Paquera ferry (☎ 61 3034, 61 2830) departs from the Muelle Banana at the north end of Calle 9, behind the Banana Bar. (The old terminal at the dock behind the market sells tickets only.) The ferry is for foot and bike passengers only. There are daily departures at 6.15 am and 3 pm for the village of Paquera, a 1½ hour ride away to the southwest across the Golfo de Nicoya. During the high season, an 11 am departure is added. The fare is US$1.50 for adults, US$1.20 for motorbikes and US$0.90 for bicycles and children aged under 11. En route, the ferry passes near the Reserva Biológica de Isla Guayabo, which is known for its seabird colonies. Buses heading further south into the Península Nicoya meet the ferries in Paquera.

You can charter boats to the above destinations, and others throughout the Golfo de Nicoya. Small boats holding up to six passengers are available from Taximar (☎ 61 1143, 61 0331) for US$20 to US$40 per hour, depending on the size and type of boat.

Taxi Bus lines can be very long during dry season weekends. A taxi back to San José costs about US$80. You can also get taxis to take you south to other beach destinations.

Getting Around

Buses marked 'Ferry' run up Avenida Central and go to the Contranamar (Playa Naranjo) terminal, 1.5 km from downtown. The taxi fare from the San José bus terminal to the ferry terminal is about US$2.

Several boat tour companies can take you to visit local beaches and islands described in the following entries. Calypso Tours (☎ 61 0585) is by the Yacht Club and is the longest established and best known operator. Others include Bay Island Cruises (☎ 31 2898, 39 4958), Fantasy Yacht Cruises (☎ 55 0791) and Blue Seas (☎ 33 7274). Fred Wagner at Casa Alberta (☎/fax 63 0107) in Roble (10 km east of town) offers fishing trips for US$195 per day and cheaper local sightseeing cruises.

ISLA TORTUGA

This is actually two uninhabited islands off the coast of the Península Nicoya near Paquera. There are beautiful beaches for snorkelling and swimming.

The islands can be reached by daily boat tours from Puntarenas. Tours from San José cost US$70 per person and include continental breakfast in San José, a private bus to Puntarenas, boat trip to the islands, delicious picnic lunch and cocktails on the beach, time for swimming, snorkelling and sunbathing, and transport back to San José. The fare from Puntarenas is marginally cheaper. The two island biological reserves of Guayabo and Negritos, famous for their seabird colonies, are passed en route.

Although this trip is not cheap, the yacht *Calypso* (in San José ☎ 33 3617, fax 33 0401; in Puntarenas ☎ 61 0585) has built up a reputation for excellence in food and service for this trip and has many repeat customers. Reservations can be made at Apartado 6941-1000, San José. *Calypso* has been operating since the mid-1970s (I have received complaints that it's getting a little crowded compared with earlier years) and there are now other companies which also do the trip. These include Bay Island Cruises (☎ 31 2898, 39 4958) and Fantasy Yacht Cruises (☎ 55 0791). Better hotels in Puntarenas and San José, and travel agents in San José, can book this cruise for you.

RESERVAS BIOLÓGICAS DE ISLAS GUAYABO & NEGRITOS

These islands in the Golfo de Nicoya are well known seabird sanctuaries, and for the protection of the birds, no land visitors are allowed except researchers with permission from the Servicio de Parques Nacional. The reserves can be visited by boat however, and you can observe many of the seabirds from the boats. The Paqueras ferry is the cheapest way to get fairly close, and the Isla Tortuga trips and chartered boats are another way to go.

Isla Guayabo is a 6.8 hectare cliff-bound rocky islet about eight km south-west of Puntarenas, and two km south-east of Isla San Lucas. There is very little vegetation. Costa Rica's largest nesting colony of brown pelicans (200 to 300 birds) is found here, and the peregrine falcon overwinters on the island. Both Guayabo and Negritos have magnificent frigatebird and brown booby colonies.

The Islas Negritos are two islands 16 km south of Puntarenas, with a combined size of 80 hectares. Although they are only a few hundred metres from the Península de Nicoya, both these biological reserves are more frequently visited by boat from Puntarenas, though you may be able to find someone from Paquera to take you out in a boat. Islas Negritos are covered with more vegetation than Guayabo, and frangipani, gumbo limbo and spiny cedar have been reported as the dominant trees.

OTHER ISLANDS

The Golfo de Nicoya has dozens of other islands, some of which can be visited and others which are privately owned. The **Isla Muertos** (locally called Isla Gitana) is 13 km south-west of Puntarenas and only a few hundred metres away from Bahía Gigante on the Península de Nicoya. There is a small lodge (✆ 61 2994) here with cabins for about US$60 a double including meals. This is a private place with attractive beaches where you can get away from it all. Call for information, reservations and to arrange pick-up from Puntarenas or Paquera. The **Isla Jesuita**, a few km to the south, also has a lodge.

Isla San Lucas, five km west of Puntarenas, used to be a prison and visitors were allowed. The prison was closed in 1992 and now no visits are allowed, although there has been sporadic talk of turning it into a resort.

ESPARZA

This small town is about 20 km inland from Puntarenas, and the two are linked by hourly buses. It is a clean and pleasant town, with a few inexpensive hotels which can provide an alternative to Puntarenas. These include the *Pensión Cordoba* and *Pensión Fanny* (✆ 63 5158) which charge about US$3 or US$4 per person, and the more expensive *Hotel Castanuelas* (✆ 63 5105) which has rooms with private baths and fans for US$11 a

double, and with air-conditioning for US$14.50 a double.

PLAYA DOÑA ANA

This is the first clean beach south of Puntarenas, and is about 13 km away from downtown. There are actually two beaches a few hundred metres from one another: Boca Barranca and Doña Ana. Surfing is reportedly good at both beaches. The Doña Ana beach has been developed for tourism – there is a sign on the Costanera Sur (coastal highway) south of Puntarenas but it's not easy to see. The *Soda Doña Ana* is by the turn-off. At the beach entrance there is a parking lot (US$0.75). Daily use fee for the beach is US$0.75 for adults, half that for children. There are snack bars, picnic ramadas and changing areas.

Places to Stay

On the east of the Costanera Sur, 0.5 km north of Playa Doña Ana, is the *Hotel Río Mar* (✆ 63 0158) which has rooms with private bath and fan for US$14/19. There is a restaurant and bar.

The *Casa Canadiense* (✆ 63 0287; Apartado 125, El Roble, Puntarenas; CRBBG member) has four cabins with fans, hot water, kitchenette and ocean views for US$40/52 single/double. There is a pool. Children are not allowed.

On the west side of the Costanera Sur, 1.3 km north of Doña Ana, is the biggest resort hotel in the area. The *Hotel Fiesta* (✆ 63 0808, 63 0185, fax 63 1516, Apartado 171-5400, Puntarenas) has 191 standard rooms, 34 luxury rooms with ocean view, 18 time-shared condos with kitchenette, 12 junior suites, four master suites and a presidential suite. There are several restaurants and bars, pools, tennis courts, volleyball, casino, gym, disco, bicycle and car rental, full tourist agency, and so on. There is a beach outside and you can walk to Doña Ana. Although tours to local national parks, volcanoes and reserves are available, most guests treat the place as a destination in itself. A standard room with two queen-size beds is US$107, deluxe rooms are US$137 for single/double occupancy.

Getting There & Away

You can get to this area from Puntarenas on buses heading for Caldera. Hotel Fiesta guests can take a daily bus from San José at 2 pm, returning from the hotel at 9.30 am. The fare is US$15.

MATA LIMÓN

This is an old beach resort which has long been popular with locals from Puntarenas as well as highlanders. It is near the new port of Caldera, and buses from Puntarenas to Caldera will get you to Mata Limón. The turn-off is 5.5 km south of Playa Doña Ana.

The resort is around a mangrove lagoon which is good for bird-watching (especially at low tide) though not very good for swimming. The village is divided into two by a river, with the lagoon and most facilities on the south side.

Places to Stay & Eat

Try the *Hotel Viña del Mar* or the *Cabinas Cecilia*. There are several restaurants, of which the *Costa del Sol* has been recommended.

DUNDEE RANCH HOTEL

Just over nine km south of the Mata Limón turn-off on the Costanera is the exit for this hotel, two km off the highway. It is only 60 km from the San José international airport via Orotina and Atenas. The hotel is a working ranch in the dry Pacific slopes and has comfortable air-conditioned rooms, a pool, restaurant and bar, and tours are available to the surrounding sights of interest. You can see wildlife on the premises. I haven't stayed here, but have received good reports. Rates are US$87 for single/double occupancy, including breakfast. Make reservations at Dundee Ranch Hotel (☎ 46 8776, fax 39 7050) Apartado 7812-1000, San José.

HACIENDA SANTA MARTA

This working ranch in a renovated hacienda has recently opened to the public under the auspices of the folks who run the Rosa Blanca Country Inn near Heredia. Visitors can hike, ride horses, watch birds or relax by the pool. There are six cabins renting for about US$70 a double. Further information is available at (☎ 53 6514, fax 34 0958; Apartado 463-1000, San José).

RESERVA BIOLÓGICA CARARA

This 4700 hectare reserve is at the mouth of the Río Tarcoles, about 50 km south-east of Puntarenas by road or about 90 km west of San José via the Orotina highway. The reserve is surrounded by pasture and agricultural land, and forms an oasis for wildlife from a large surrounding area. It is the northernmost tropical wet forest on the Pacific coast, in the transition zone to the tropical dry forests further north, and five of Holdridge's Life Zones occur within the park. Therefore Carara has both an abundance and variety of wildlife. There are also archaeological remains which you can see with a guide – but they are not very exciting ruins.

If driving from Puntarenas or San José, pull over to the left immediately after crossing the Río Tarcoles bridge. Carefully scan the river, particularly the muddy banks, and you will often be rewarded with a view of basking crocodiles. Binoculars help a great deal. A variety of water birds may also be seen – herons, spoonbills, storks and anhingas. Some 0.6 km further south on the left-hand side is a locked gate leading to the Laguna Meandrica trail. A further 2.4 km brings you to the Carara administration building/ranger station which is open from 8 am to 4 pm. There are bathrooms, picnic tables and a short nature trail. You can get information here and pay the US$1.50 fee to enter the reserve. I found the ranger here to be knowledgeable and helpful.

Visitors are advised that cars parked at the Laguna Meandrica trail have been broken into. Recently, there have been guards on duty from 8 am to 4 pm in the high season – but this doesn't help for a crack-of-dawn bird walk. Early risers are advised to park their cars in the much safer parking lot at the Carara ranger station and walk north along the Costanera Sur for 2.4 km. Go in a group and don't carry unnecessary valuables.

A variety of forest birds inhabit the reserve, but can be difficult to see without an experienced guide. The most exciting bird for many visitors is the brilliantly patterned scarlet macaw which is seen here, especially in June and July. Other birds to watch for include guans, trogons, toucans, motmots and many other forest species. Monkeys, squirrels, sloths and agoutis are among the more common mammals present.

The dry season from December to April is the easiest time to go – though the animals are still there in the wet months! Rainfall is almost 3000 mm annually, which is less than the rainforests further south. It is fairly hot, with average temperatures of 25°C to 28°C – but it is cooler within the rainforest. Make sure you have insect repellent. An umbrella is important in the wet season, and occasionally needed in the dry months.

Tours

If you are not experienced at watching for wildlife in the rainforest, you will have difficulty in seeing very much. Going on a tour with a guide is expensive, but worthwhile if you want to see a reasonable number of different species. Geotur (☎ 34 1867), Costa Rica Expeditions (☎ 57 0766) and other companies have day tours to Carara from San José for US$69 per person. It takes about 2½ hours to drive down from San José.

Places to Stay

Camping is not allowed and there is nowhere to stay in the reserve, so most people come on day trips. There is talk of opening a camping area inside the park in 1994. The nearest hotels are at Tárcoles, two or three km south of the reserve, or at Jacó, 22 km south.

Getting There & Away

There are no buses to Carara, but you can get off any bus bound for Jacó, Quepos or Manuel Antonio. This may be a bit problem-atical at weekends when buses are full, so go midweek if you are relying on a bus ride.

Many of the remoter parts of the Pacific coast are best visited by car.

TÁRCOLES

Two km south of the Carara ranger station is the Tarcoles turn-off to the right (west) and the Hotel Villa Lapas turn-off to the left. Turn right for a km, then right at the T-junction to the village, with cabins and a beach, and continue past the village for two or three km to reach the mudflats of the Río Tarcoles – this is a good area to explore for birders looking for shorebirds, particularly at low tide.

Places to Stay

In the village there are several cabins including the *Hotel Carara* (☎ 61 0455) which has fairly basic rooms with showers ranging from US$23 to US$38 a double depending on whether you want fans, views or air-conditioning. The *Cabinas Villa del Mar* (☎ 61 2478) has simple cabins with kitchen, fan and shower, and sleeps up to nine people for US$30 or US$22 a double.

Half a km inland from the Tárcoles turn-off is the new *Hotel Villa Lapas* (☎ 88 1677; Apartado 476-4005, Cuidada Cariari, San José, ☎/fax 39 4104). The hotel has a small pool and pleasant gardens surrounded by hillside and forest. A horse/foot trail leads to a waterfall about an hour away. The 30 rooms are plain but clean, spacious and airy; they have fans and private hot showers. There is a restaurant/bar.

The *Tarcol Lodge* (☎/fax 39 7138; Apartado 364-1002, San José, Costa Rica; in the USA, Dept 1425, Box 025216, Miami, FL 33102-5216), on the south bank of the Río Tárcoles, a few hundred metres from the beach, is a new lodge opened in mid 1993. It is run by the same folks who have the Rancho Naturalista near Turrialba and the focus will be similar – birding and nature tours, comfortable lodging and good food.

The lodge is reached by driving 3.7 km to the right from the T-junction before the village of Tarcoles. It is surrounded by the river on three sides at high tide, but at low tide the exposed mud and sandflats may have thousands of shorebirds searching for food – bring binoculars. The lodge is small – five bedrooms sharing two bathrooms – but will probably expand. Rates are US$85 per person or US$520 per person per week from November to April; rates are US$75/420 for the rest of the year, including transportation from San José (with a three day minimum stay), guided tours, meals and lodging. Bottled drinks are extra and people arranging their own transportation get a small discount. Guided tours are led by naturalist guides and visit two different trails in Carara or are boat tours on the estuary at high tide, either at night or during the day. All four tours are provided for visitors who stay a week. Weeks can also be split between the Tarcol Lodge and Rancho Naturalista.

Just over three km south of the Tárcoles turn-off is the *Chalets Paradise* which offers double rooms for US$30 – OK but nothing special. There is a pool. A few km further south are the luxurious *Hotel Punta Leona* and *Hotel Villa Caletas* described under Jacó.

PLAYA HERRADURA

The Herradura turn-off is on the Costanera Sur 3.5 km north of the turn-off to Jacó. The good gravel road leads three km west to Playa Herradura – a quiet, sheltered, palm-fringed, black-sand beach.

Places to Stay

Development is minimal. At the point where the road reaches the beach is a campsite with bathrooms available. The cost is US$2.20 per person.

Nearby is the *Cabinas Herradura* (☎ 45 5775, 64 3181) which charges US$30 for cabins which sleep six people, but may charge more during dry season weekends. There is also the similarly priced *Cabinas del Río* (☎ 64 3029) about half a km before you reach the beach. There is a simple restaurant on the beach.

JACÓ

Jacó is the first developed beach town on the Pacific coast as you head south. Its proximity to San José makes it popular and crowded by Costa Rican standards, though it will seem relatively quiet to many visitors who may be used to shoulder-to-shoulder sunbathing on their own crowded beaches. Jacó has something of a reputation as a 'party beach' – especially during the dry season – but it is pretty sedate compared to some of the North American party beaches like Daytona Beach in Florida. Nevertheless, it is popular with young people and vacation package visitors (especially from Canada). Swimming is possible, though you should be careful of rip currents and avoid the areas nearest the estuaries, which are polluted.

The turn-off from the Costanera Sur for Jacó is just 3.5 km beyond Herradura, so you have the choice of beaches. Jacó Beach is about two km off the Costanera. The beach itself is about three km long, and hotels and restaurants line the road running behind it. Development has been fast in Jacó – perhaps too fast. The word in Costa Rica is that Jacó suffers from sewage problems: the septic tanks used by the majority of hotels are inadequate to handle the large volume of sewage. There are many quieter and less crowded places elsewhere. Despite this, Jacó continues to grow and draw tourists.

Jacó is also something of a surfers' hangout, although Playa Jacó itself does not offer the best surfing. To get better surfing, head out to Tivives and Boca Barranca on the way back to Puntarenas, or to Hermosa, Esterillos and Bejuco south of town. Playa Hermosa has the most consistent surf. You need either a rental car or a taxi to get to most of these places easily.

Information

The Clínica CCSS de Jacó (☎ 64 3228) provides emergency medical care. Several banks change money. The ICE office has international telephone and fax. There is a laundry service next door.

There is a *supermercado* and a number of stores where you can buy your own food and several souvenir shops where you can spend the money you saved by buying your own food.

Several places advertise bike rentals. These usually cost about US$1.50 an hour or US$7.25 a day.

Fishing boat charters are available from the Hotel Cocal for a half day (US$160 for one or two people) or full day (US$150 per person, three to five people) and to Isla Tortuga (US$70 per person, six to 10 people).

The Nucleo de Turistas Bribri provides beach access for day visitors for US$0.75 per person. This gives use of locked storage facilities, showers, bathrooms and parking.

The Unicornio Ranch rents horses and provides tours. The main tour company is Fantasy Tours. Both are on the main road.

Places to Stay

Reservations are strongly recommended during the December to April dry season, and definitely required during Easter week and most weekends. There are plenty of places to stay – but travellers on a shoestring budget will not find many good deals, especially if looking for single rooms. Camping is an option.

Low-season discounts are available in most hotels, as are surfers' discounts – the latter probably because surfers tend to stay for days or even weeks. If you plan on a lengthy stay (surfer or not) ask for a discount. The rates given here – are full high-season rates, but discounts could be as high as 40% to 50% if you're staying for several nights in the low season.

Playa Jacó is a growing resort – you can expect more hotels to open in the future.

Places to Stay – bottom end

At the south end of town, the *Cabinas Calypso* (☎ 64 3208) charges US$14.50 for a very basic double room with shared bath. The *Cabinas Andrea* (☎ 64 3089) has two double and one quad room sharing a bath for US$14.50 a double. Fans are available. The nearby *Cabinas Las Brisas* (☎ 64 3074) has very beat-up old rooms with bath and fan for

US$11 a double, or US$22 a double for larger and newer rooms. This hotel is for sale – so who knows what it will end up as.

Closer to the centre, the *Cabinas Bohío* (☎ 64 3017) has basic old cabins for US$18 which will sleep three or four people (as well as nicer, newer, pricier cabins). The *Cabinas Cindy* on the same street is also cheap. The *Cabinas Supertica* (☎ 21 8136) has four basic old cabins with kitchen, refrigerator, bath and fan. The cabins will sleep up to six people for US$36 but double occupancy is a steep US$25. The *Cabinas Emily* (☎ 64 3328) and the *Cabinas García* (☎ 64 3191) both have reasonable rooms with bath and fan for about US$22 a double; the Emily has some cheaper rooms with shared bath which are popular with shoestringers. Also in this price range is the basic but friendly *Cabinas El Recreo* (☎ 64 3012).

Up at the north end of town, try the *Cabinas Antonio* (☎ 64 3043) which has clean rooms with bath and fan for US$18 a double – one of the better deals for under twenty bucks. Across the street, the *Hotel Mariott* charges US$22 for a basic room with bath but no fan – three people can sleep in the room. The nearby *Cabinas Garabito* is another bottom-end option.

Camping *Camping El Hicaco* (☎ 64 3004) in the centre charges US$1.80 per person and is friendly. They have picnic tables, bathrooms and a lock-up for your gear. The campsites are sandy rather than grassy, which, a camper told me, cut down on the problems of chiggers. For US$1.50 per person, there are also *Camping El Estero*, *Camping Madrigal* (☎ 64 3230), *Camping Garabito* and the lot outside the *Mariott Hotel* – all these are grassier.

Places to Stay – middle

Los Ranchos (☎/fax 64 3070; Apartado 22, Playa Jacó) is very popular with English-speaking visitors and has many repeat clients. There is a pool, pleasant garden, small paperback library and friendly staff offering local tour and surfing information. Rooms are quiet and have fans, refrigerator,

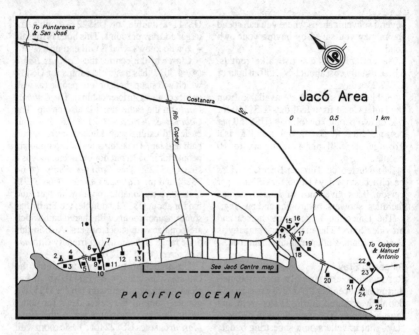

kitchenette and private bath with warm water. Rates are good value at US$34 for three people in the smaller upstairs rooms. The larger downstairs rooms go for US$46 for three or four people and there are bungalows sleeping up to six for US$11.40 per person (four people mimimum). Surfers get a 20% discount, and cheaper single and double occupancy can be arranged if space is available.

The *Cabinas Alice* (☎ 64 3061) has fairly simple but clean rooms with private bath and fan for US$19/29 single/double. Their restaurant has been recommended. The *Cabinas Marea Alta* (☎ 64 3317) has fairly basic cabins with either one double and two single beds or one double, one single and a kitchenette. The cabins rent for US$33 at weekends and US$25 midweek. The *Chalet Santa Ana* (☎ 64 3233) is in a quiet area at the far south end of town. The rooms are OK and rent for US$25 a double with bath (hot water) and fan or US$36 with a kitchenette.

Some rooms sleep up to five. The nearby *Cabinas El Naranjal* (☎ 64 3006) has a good restaurant and spacious, clean but bare rooms with hot showers and fans for US$25 or US$33 a double, depending on the size of the room. Quads are US$40. Also nearby, the *Cabinas Catalina* (☎ 64 3194) has a pool and rooms with kitchenette and ocean views for about the same price.

The *Cabinas Bohío* (☎ 64 3017) has, apart from its bottom-end rooms, some newer cabins with two double beds, bathroom, kitchenette, refrigerator and fan for US$42 (two to four people). There is a decent restaurant on the premises. The *Apartamentos El Mar* (☎ 64 3165) has clean good-sized apartments with hot water, kitchenette and fan for US$62 for five people – a good deal. It has a few doubles for US$37 and there is a small pool. The *Zabamar Resort* (☎/fax 64 3174) has one of the cleanest pools in Jacó and a small, reasonably priced breakfast/snack bar. Clean, pleasant rooms are

■ PLACES TO STAY

2	Camping El Estero
3	Cabinas Playa del Sol
4	Cabinas Gaby
5	Apartamentos Pochote Grande
7	Cabinas Antonio
8	Cabinas Las Palmas & Cabinas Garabito
10	Hotel El Jardín
11	Hotel Mariott
12	Hotel Jacó Beach
15	Cabinas El Naranjal
18	Hotel Jacó Fiesta
19	Chalet Santa Ana
20	Cabinas Catalina
21	Hotel Marparaíso
24	Camping Madrigal
25	Hotel Club del Mar

▼ PLACES TO EAT

6	Los Faroles
7	La Fragata
9	El Verano, Doña Cecilia, Casita del Maíz & other restaurants
10	Restaurant El Jardín
13	Restaurant Gran Palenque
16	Soda Perla del Mar
17	Soda Estrella del David
23	Restaurant El Bosque

OTHER

1	Disco Upe
14	Palacio Municipal
22	Gas Station

US$35 a double with fan, or US$50 with air-conditioning.

At the far north end of town, the *Cabinas Gaby* (☎ 64 3080, fax 41 5922; Apartado 20-4050, Alajuela) has pleasant rooms with kitchenettes, hot water and a choice of fans or air-conditioning. There is a small pool and a shady garden. Rooms are US$36 a double. Across the street, the *Cabinas Playa del Sol* (☎ 64 3016) has clean rooms with kitchenette, bath and fans for US$36 a double or US$48 for five people.

Also at the north end, the Belgian-owned *Hotel El Jardín* (☎ 64 3050) is known for its decent French restaurant. Rooms are simple but clean and have hot water; rates are US$30 to US$37 a double, depending on the room. There is a pool. Nearby, the *Cabinas Las Palmas* (☎ 64 3005) has a variety of rooms set in pleasant gardens. Rooms with bathroom, fan and kitchenette are about US$40 a double, and without kitchenette are about US$25. The bathrooms have electric showers.

Other acceptable possibilities for double rooms under US$40 include the *Cabinas La Sirena* (☎ 64 3193), *Hotel Lido* (☎ 64 3171) and the *Cabinas Mar de Plata* (☎ 64 3580). The *Apartotel Sole d'Oro* (☎ 64 3172) has clean, modern, spacious rooms with kitchen-

ette, hot water and fan. They sleep up to four people and are usually full with French-Canadian tour groups during the high season but charge US$55 if you can get in. During the low months of May and June and from August to November they charge US$30 midweek and US$35 at weekends.

About four km south of the Restaurant El Bosque on the Costanera there are a couple of mid-range hotels offering both good access to Playa Hermosa and discounts to surfers. These are *Cabinas Vista Hermosa* (☎ 64 3422) and *Cabinas Las Olas*.

Places to Stay – top end

The *Apartotel Gaviotas* (☎ 64 3092, fax 64 3054) has 12 spacious and modern apartments with a kitchenette, refrigerator, sitting area, fans and hot water. There is a fine pool, a bar and a TV room. It's a few hundred metres walk to the beach – if you can put up with that then you'll find this to be one of the best deals in town for the money. A double is US$44 and a unit sleeping four to six people rents for US$58. About 100 metres further inland is the *Cabinas Paraíso del Sol* (☎ 64 3250, fax 64 3137; Apartado 92-4023, Jacó, Puntarenas). They have nice rooms with fans or air-conditioning, kitchenettes and hot water. There is a small pool and a bar.

Rates are US$50 in a room sleeping up to four – also a reasonable deal.

The German-owned *Hotel Cocal* (☎ 64 3067, fax 64 3082; Apartado 54, Playa de Jacó) is good value for US$30/44 for singles/doubles. The pleasant rooms have hot water and fans – add US$5 for air-conditioning. There is a nice pool, good restaurant with ocean views and a bar. The *Villas Miramar* (☎ 64 3003) is also a good place with large rooms, kitchenettes, refrigerator, hot water, fans and a pool. It is set in a pleasant and quiet garden with picnic/barbecue areas. Rates are US$42/52/62 for two/four/six people. Other good places with similar facilities include *Apartamentos Pochote Grande* (☎ 64 3236; Apartado 43, Jacó) which is US$65 for a unit sleeping three people, and *Apartotel Flamboyant* (☎ 64 3146; Apartado 018, Jacó) which is US$50 a double.

The *Hotel Jacó Beach* (in Jacó, ☎ 64 3064, 64 3032, fax 64 3246; in San José, ☎ 20 1441; in the USA, ☎ 1 (800) 272 6654; Apartado 962-1000, San José) is by far the biggest hotel in Jacó, with over 100 rooms. It is connected with the Hotel Irazú in San José, and many Canadian charter groups stay here. This is a full beach resort, with bicycle, surfboard, kayak, boat and car rentals. There is a restaurant, disco, swimming pools and sunbathing areas. Rooms are air-conditioned and have hot water. Rates are US$58/74 for a single/double and US$100 for a suite. The other big resort hotel in town is the *Hotel Jacó Fiesta* (☎ 64 3147, fax 64 3148; Apartado 38, Jacó) which is slightly lower key and has air-conditioned rooms (with kitchenettes) sleeping one to four people for US$73. The *Hotel Club del Mar* (☎ 64 3194; Apartado 107-4023, Jacó) has air-conditioned rooms on the beach ranging from US$55 to US$95 for a double, depending on the room. Some rooms have kitchens, balconies and sitting areas. There is a pool, restaurant and pleasant gardens, and the

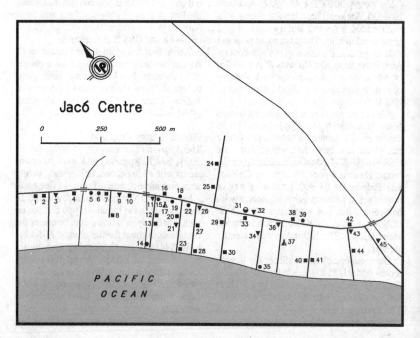

owners speak Spanish, Swahili and a spot of English.

Other places in this price range include the *Tangerí Chalets* (☎ 64 3001, 42 0977; Apartado 622-4050, Alajuela) with spacious chalets with three bedrooms and kitchen. They prefer long-term guests. There is also the *Hotel Marparaíso* (☎ 64 3025; Apartado 24, Jacó) and the *Jacó La Costa Condominiums* (☎ 64 3465, 64 3466).

The *Hotel Copacabana* (☎ /fax 64 3131, Apartado 150, Jacó) is a new, Canadian-run hotel near the beach. The owners will help to arrange car rentals or tours to nearby national parks etc. There is a pool, restaurant and bar with satellite TV. Rooms with fans and hot showers are US$44/57 single/double and air-conditioned suites with kitchenette are US$103 for up to four people.

North of Jacó there are two top-end hotels. The *Hotel Villa Caletas* (☎ 88 2402, 22 2059, fax 22 2059; Apartado 12358-1000, San Jóse) is eight km north of the Jacó turn off the Costanera. A one km dirt road leads to the beautiful hotel decorated with art and antiques. There are great views, a pool (US$7 for non-guests) overlooking the views, and a fine restaurant. It is about one km down a steep trail to the beach. Air-conditioned rooms have private balconies and range from US$97 to US$125. À la carte meals are US$7.40 for breakfast and US$19.50 for lunch or dinner, including taxes.

The *Hotel Punta Leona* (☎ 61 1414; in San José (☎ 31 3131, fax 32 0791; Apartado 8592-1000, San José) is 11 km north of the Jacó turn-off from the Costanera. A guard station lets guests onto the four km dirt road to this exclusive resort with access to remoter beaches. Rooms are US$50/75 single/double; apartments range from US$100 to

■ PLACES TO STAY	▼ PLACES TO EAT
1 Jacó La Costa Condominiums	3 Pura Vida
2 Cabinas García	9 Killer Munchies Pizzería
4 Cabinas Emily	11 La Ostra
7 Cabinas La Sirena	21 Susie Q's
8 Hotel Lido	23 Restaurant El Bohío
10 Tangerí Chalets	26 Restaurant Flamboyant
12 Cabinas Mar de Plata	32 Pizzería Guilloly & Soda Nena
13 Los Ranchos	34 Restaurante Piccola
16 Cabinas Supertica	36 Pancho Villas
17 Camping Garabito	43 Restaurant Sen Ly
20 Cabinas Cindy	45 Soda Helen
23 Cabinas Bohío	
24 Cabinas Paraíso del Sol	
25 Apartotel Gaviotas	OTHER
27 Villas Miramar	
28 Apartotel Flamboyant	5 Unicornio Ranch
29 Zabamar Resort	6 Nucleo de Turistas Bribri
30 Hotel Cocal	14 Disco Papagayo
33 Cabinas El Recreo	15 Banco de Costa Rica
37 Camping El Hicaco	18 ADA Car Rental
38 Cabinas Andrea	19 Fantasy Tours
40 Cabinas Las Brisas	22 Laundry; ICE phone & fax
41 Cabinas Alice	31 Bus Stop & Supermercado
42 Cabinas Marea Alta & Cabinas Calypso	33 Banco Nacional
	35 Discoteca La Central
44 Apartotel Sole d'Oro & Apartamentos El Mar	39 Red Cross

US$160, have kitchenettes, and will sleep four people.

South of Jacó is the *Terraza del Pacífico* (☎ 64 3222, 64 3444, 64 3424; Apartado 168, Jacó). This elegant new hotel is just over three km south of the Restaurant El Bosque on the Costanera. Spacious rooms have air-conditioning, TV and hot water and the hotel has children's and adults' pools, a bar, and restaurant. Rates are US$74/86 for singles/doubles.

Places to Eat

Shoestring travellers will find that the set menus at the sodas and restaurants used by the locals are the best deals for budget meals. At the north end, the *Restaurant El Verano* has fried chicken for US$2, the *Restaurant Doña Cecilia* has casados for US$2.50 and the *Restaurant Casita del Maíz* charges US$3 for a casado. Other cheap eats are the *Picnic Inn* opposite the Disco La Central (for fried chicken) and *Soda Nenas* for good casados. Also try the *Soda Helen* which is open from 7 am to 10 pm during the high season, and the sodas *Estrella del David* and *Perla del Mar* at the south end.

Italian food lovers will find the *Pizzería Guilloly* (which also shows surfing videos) is inexpensive but adequate – small individual pizzas are US$3 to US$6 depending on the toppings. *Killer Munchies Pizzería* is twice that price but serves 'gourmet' pizza and is very popular with tourists. Italian food is also served at *Pura Vida* and *Restaurante Piccola*.

Pancho Villas advertises Mexican food but is disappointing – their international food is much better. Meals average US$7. *Restaurant Sen Ly* serves satisfactory Chinese food. *Susie Q's* is open from 6 to 9 pm for pretty decent ribs, steak and barbecue dinners in the US$4 to US$8 range. The *Restaurant El Jardín* serves French food and is slightly pricey but good. The *Restaurant Gran Palenque* serves excellent Spanish food for around US$6 or a paella for about US$12 and has been well recommended. It is closed on Tuesdays.

Several restaurants serve interna-

tional/tico food. The *Restaurant El Bohío* is quite good and has a sea view. It is open for breakfast and serves dinners in the US$3 to US$7 range (except for shrimp or lobster at US$18). The *Restaurant Flamboyant, Los Faroles, La Fragata* and *La Ostra* are all currently popular and reasonable – take your pick. Out on the Costanera, the *Restaurant El Bosque* has been recommended for breakfast – though I never did make it out there.

The best hotels have decent restaurants.

Entertainment

The *Disco La Central* is the hip place for foreign travellers and is in the middle of town. The *Disco Papagayo* is also central and tends to attract a more local crowd. *Disco Upe* at the north end of town is quieter and is a nice late-night place. The *Hotel Jacó Beach* also has a disco.

Getting There & Away

Bus There are direct buses from the Coca-Cola terminal in San José, leaving at 7.15 am and 3.30 pm daily. The journey takes about three hours and costs about US$3. Buses between either San José or Puntarenas and Quepos could drop you off at the entrance to Jacó. Buses tend to be full at weekends – get to the terminal as early as possible.

Buses leave from Jacó for San José at 5 am and 3 pm daily. An 11 am bus may be added in the high season. Departures for Puntarenas are at 6.45 am, noon and 5 pm; and for Quepos at 6.30 am and 4 pm – but it's best to enquire locally, especially for Puntarenas and Quepos departures. The bus stop is just north of the supermercado in Jacó and there is another stop near the crossroads at the north end of town. You can phone for bus information in Jacó (☎ 64 3135, 64 3074). Most hotels know the current time-table.

If you are staying at the Hotel Jacó Beach you can take advantage of their daily shuttle bus to and from the Hotel Irazú in San José. American Limo Bus (☎ 22 8134, fax 21 4590) leaves San José at 9 am and returns from Jacó at 2 pm daily. Their air-conditioned buses have a snack bar, TV and a bathroom. Fares are US$15 or US$25 round-trip.

Taxi Taxi 30-30 (☎ 64 3030) will get you anywhere – for a price.

Car Car rental agencies in Jacó include ADA (☎ 64 3207), Budget (☎ 64 3112) and Elegante (☎ 64 3224).

Getting Around

Bus The Jacó shuttle bus goes from the Hotel Jacó Beach at the north end and stops outside Fantasy Tours, Apartotel Sole d'Oro, Hotel Club del Mar and Terraza del Pacífico Hotel (south of Jacó) and at other points on demand. Departures from the Hotel Jacó are at 9 and 10.30 am and 2, 3.30, 5 and 7 pm. Departures from Terraza del Pacífico are at 9.10 and 11.10 am and 2.45, 4.10, 5.40 and 7.30 pm. The fare is about US$0.75 to Terraza del Pacífico and half that to Jacó. There are no buses on Sunday and Monday mornings.

Other Transport You can get a taxi or rent a car to get around; for details, see the preceding Getting There & Away section.

JACÓ TO QUEPOS

The paved Costanera continues south-east from Jacó to Quepos, 65 km away. The road parallels the Pacific coastline, but only comes down to it a few times. The route has a few good beaches (some with good surf) which are rather off the beaten track and most easily visited by car, though you could get off buses to Quepos or Manuel Antonio and walk down to the beach.

The first beach is **Playa Hermosa** about five km south of Jacó. This beach stretches for about 10 km and is for expert surfers – there is an annual contest here in August.

Esterillos Oeste and Esterillos Este are about 22 km and 30 km respectively south-east of Jacó. Between the two, the Esterillo Beach stretches for several deserted km. At Esterillos Este is the recommended and good *Hotel El Delfín* (☎ 71 1640; Apartado 37, Parrita, Puntarenas). Rooms with private bath (hot water) and balcony with sea views are in the top-end price range. There is a restaurant and pool. There is also cheaper accommodation in Esterillos.

Infrequently visited beaches beyond Esterillos include Playa Bejuco and Playa Palma, both reached by short side roads from the Costanera. **Parrita**, a bustling little banana town on the river of the same name and 40 km from Jacó, has a couple of basic hotels. The coastal road is now inland and continues so until Quepos. The last section is unpaved but is passable in all weathers with normal cars. There are plans to pave this section soon. African oil-palm plantations stretch for several km before Quepos is reached.

QUEPOS

This town gets its name from the Quepoa Indian tribe, a subgroup of the Borucas, who inhabited the area at the time of the conquest. The Quepoa people declined because of diseases brought by the Europeans, internecine warfare with other Indian groups, and being sold as slaves. By the end of the 19th century there were no pure-blooded Quepoa left, and the area began to be colonised by farmers from the highlands.

Quepos first came to prominence as a banana-exporting port. Its importance has declined appreciably in recent decades because of disease which has severely reduced banana crops. African oil-palm has replaced bananas as the major local crop but, as it is processed into oils used in cosmetics, machine oils and lard, the finished product is much less bulky than bananas.

Consequently Quepos has not been able to recover as a major shipping port. Instead, it has become important as a sportfishing centre and also as the nearest town to the Parque Nacional Manuel Antonio, which is only seven km away and one of the most visited national parks in Costa Rica. There are regularly scheduled flights and buses from San José, and the tourist industry has enabled Quepos to find a new economic niche for itself.

Information

The La Buena Nota store (☎ 77 0345) at the entrance to town sells beach supplies and acts as an information centre for tourists. A second store is planned for the Manuel Antonio beach area just beyond the El Karahé Hotel.

The Banco Nacional de Costa Rica changes US dollars, and is extremely air-conditioned – a cool wait. There are several other banks too. The post office is on the north side of the soccer field at the east end of town.

The Super Mas grocery store is one of the best bets for picnic supplies etc. There are laundry services on the south side of the soccer field and around the corner from the Soda Isabel.

The Hospital Dr Max Teran V (☎ 77 0020) provides emergency medical care for the Quepos/Manuel Antonio area. It is on the Costanera Sur.

The annual Fiesta del Mar (Sea Festival) takes place near the end of January with processions, street dancing and general revelry.

Note that the beaches are not recommended for swimming because of pollution.

Sportfishing

Sportfishing is big in the Quepos area. Offshore fishing is best from December to April and sailfish are the big thing to go for, though marlin, dorado, wahoo, amberjack and yellowfin tuna are also caught. You can fish inshore year-round; mackerel, jack and roosterfish are the main attractions. Places chartering out sportfishing boats may take you out sightseeing, snorkelling or diving if they don't have any anglers.

Sportfishing information and charters are available from Quepos Sportfishing Information Centre (☎/fax 77 0106; Apartado 122-6350, Quepos), a couple of hundred metres north of the bridge at the north-west end of Quepos. They have a seven-metre boat carrying up to five anglers for US$650 a day or US$400 a half day, and a 10-metre boat for US$275/175 for full/half day. All tackle, bait, bilingual guide and food is included. Another recommended company is Costa Rica Dreams (☎ 39 3387, fax 39 3383; Apartado 79-4005, Belén, Heredia) which has nine-metre boats holding four anglers for US$595 per day and eight-metre boats for US$395/275 for full/half day charters.

Treasure Hunt Tours (☎ 77 0345; Apartado 187-6350, Quepos) offers a boat for three people for US$300/180 for full/half days of fishing, diving or touring. Ask at the Buena Nota store.

If you are not in a group, go anyway. You can often join up with a small group to fill up a boat.

Places to Stay

Quepos has benefited from the current tourist boom and general overcrowding at Manuel Antonio, and the number of hotels here has more than doubled since the last edition of this book. Hotels tend to be full during weekends in the dry season. They are cheaper here than on the way to and at Manuel Antonio. You can get wet season discounts.

Places to Stay – bottom end

The *Hotel Majestic* has basic boxes for US$3.75 per person – the cheapest in town. The *Hotel Luna* (☎ 77 0012) is equally basic for US$4.40 per person. The *Hospedaje La Macha* (☎ 77 0216) is basic but clean and the rooms have fans – it's OK for US$5.50/10 single/double. Other basic cheapies are the *Hospedaje Araya* at US$5.50 per person and the *Hotel Linda Vista* at US$7.25/8.75.

The *Cabinas Kali* has simple rooms with fans and private baths for US$7.25/11 – it was recently popular with German-speaking travellers. The *Cabinas Doña Alicia* (☎ 77 0419) has clean rooms with private bath and two double beds for US$14.50 for up to four people – good value if you want to share. They also have singles and doubles for US$11.

The *Hotel Ipakarahi* (☎ 77 0392) has pleasant, clean rooms with private bath and fan, not to mention a writing desk and chair, for US$14.50 – one of the nicer places for two people. Also good value is the *Cabinas*

Top: Crab, Parque Nacional Corcovado (RR)
Bottom: Golden toads mating (RL)

Top: Playa Cativo at Rainbow Adventures, Parque Nacional Corcovado (MM)
Bottom: Truck drivers take a beach break, Península de Nicoya (RR)

Mary (☎ 77 0128) which charges US$7.25 per person in clean rooms with private bath. There are only three rooms, of which two are air-conditioned – good luck in getting in. The *Cabinas El Cisne* (☎ 77 0522) is also good value at the same price. Others which have acceptable rooms with private bath for US$7.25 per person include the *Hotel El Parque* (☎ 77 0063), the *Hotel Ramus* (☎ 77 0245) and the *Hotel Mar y Luna* (☎ 77 0394) – this last also has rooms with shared baths for US$5.50 per person. The *Cabinas Villa Verano* (☎ 77 0236) has good clean rooms with private bath for US$11/14.50 single/double, as does the *Cabinas Horcones* (☎ 77 0090) north of town for US$9 per person.

Places to Stay – middle

The *Hotel Ceciliano* (☎ 77 0192) charges US$22 for a clean double room with private bath and US$14.50 with communal bath. The *Hotel Quepos* (☎ 77 0274, Apartado 79, Quepos) above the SANSA office is similar and charges US$11/14.50 with shared bath and US$14.50 per person with private bath – they'll give discounts for stays of over two nights. Both hotels are popular. The *Cabinas Helen* (☎ 77 0504) has decent rooms with private bath for US$14.50/22. The French-run *Hotel Voilá Voilá* (☎ 77 0124) has clean rooms with tepid private showers and is good value for US$20 per room. The *Apartotel Los Corales* (☎ 77 0006) is also good value for a room with kitchenette, refrigerator and bathroom for US$25.50. All these places have fans.

A good choice for various budgets is the *Hotel Malinche* (☎ 77 0093). It has older rooms for US$14.50/17 with private cold shower and fans. Newer and nicer rooms, with private hot shower and fan, are US$14.50 per person or US$25 per person if you want air-conditioning. *Villas Cruz* (☎ 77 0271) has nice rooms with private bath, fan and refrigerator for US$27.50 – the upstairs rooms are slightly nicer. It also has a two-bedroom villa with TV and nice views for US$60.

The *Hotel Paraíso* (☎ 77 0082) charges US$31/41 for rooms with kitchenette, refrig-

erator, air-conditioning and private cold showers. Larger units with hot showers are US$52. Rates include breakfast. The *Hotel Viña del Mar* (☎ 77 0070) has new rooms with hot showers and air-conditioning for US$25/45.

Places to Stay – top end

The *Villas Morsol Inn* (☎ 77 0307, Apartado 256, Quepos) has new, nice, air-conditioned rooms with a refrigerator and hot shower for US$45/57. Similar prices are charged at the *Hotel Sirena* (☎ 77 0528, fax 77 0171) with modern air-conditioned rooms, private hot showers, a pool and a restaurant.

The best hotel in Quepos is the *Hotel Kamuk* (☎ 77 0379, fax 77 0258; Apartado 18-6350, Quepos). All rooms have air-conditioning, hot water and phone and there is a bar, restaurant, coffee shop and casino (but no pool). Standard rooms are US$57 for one or two people. Better rooms, with balcony and ocean view, are US$79 for two or three people and there are larger rooms with balconies for US$96 (up to three people) or US$113 for four people.

Places to Eat

The *Soda El Kiosko* at the south end of town has a menu in English and tries to attract foreign tourists – they have simple but good food, though it's not particularly cheap. Cheap snacks are available at the *Soda Nahomi* at the east end of town on the way out to Manuel Antonio beach.

In the centre of town there are several reasonable places, of which the *Restaurant Ana* is one of the cheapest for set casados – about US$2.20. The *Bar Restaurant La Central* is also inexpensive and the *Soda Isabel* is a little less cheap but still good value. There are several inexpensive eateries around the market and bus station, including the *Quepoa* on the south side, a no-name place at the south-east corner and the *Soda La Coquita* in the market. Just east of the market is *Pizza Gabriel* with good individual pizzas for US$3 to US$5.

The *Gran Escape Bar* is popular with sportfishing visitors and other tourists and is

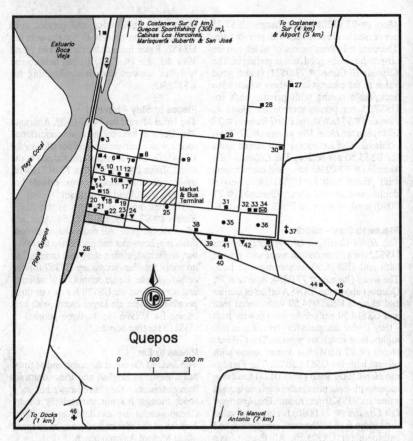

To Costanera Sur (2 km),
Quepos Sportfishing (300 m),
Cabinas Los Horcones,
Marisquería Jiuberth & San José

To Costanera
Sur (4 km)
& Airport (5 km)

Estuario
Boca
Vieja

Playa Cocal

Playa Quepos

Market
& Bus
Terminal

Quepos

0   100   200 m

To Docks
(1 km)

To Manuel
Antonio (7 km)

one of the more lively bars. They also serve very good food, though appreciably more expensive than the sodas – a fish dinner with a beer came to about US$9. They are closed on Tuesday. *George's American Bar & Grill* is popular and crowded for breakfast, lunch and dinner. An example of their prices is the fried fish dinner for US$5.50. The *Marisquería Jiuberth* is similarly priced and is a good seafood place.

Entertainment

The *Arco Iris Riverboat Bar* (☎ 77 0449) has dancing at weekends, and serves food as

well. Across the street, the *Mirador Bahía Azul* has sea views and is a popular place for a beer, as is the *Gran Escape Bar*. The *Hotel Kamuk* has a casino.

Getting There & Away

Air SANSA (☎ 77 0161) has flights from San José at 8 am daily. During the dry season it also has afternoon flights at noon on Sunday, 3 pm daily except Sunday, and 4 pm on Monday, Friday and Saturday. The flight takes 20 minutes, costs US$15, and returns for San José 20 minutes after arriving in Quepos. These times are subject to change –

so check again. Make reservations and pay for your ticket well in advance to ensure a confirmed reservation. Reconfirm your flight as often as you can. Flights are often full, with a waiting list.

Travelair (☎ 32 7883, 20 3054) has daily flights in smaller aircraft at 8.10 am. The flight takes 30 minutes, costs US$35 (US$60 round trip) and returns to San José at 9 am.

It is also possible to charter light planes to Quepos. Nahomi Travel will help with airline reservations. They'll also arrange airport transfers for US$2.25 from anywhere in the Quepos-Manuel Antonio area. The airport is five km away from Quepos. There is an airport tax of US$2.25 per passenger.

Bus Buses leave San José several times a day from the Coca-Cola terminal. Direct express buses leave for Manuel Antonio (3½ hours) at 6 am, noon and 6 pm and there are regular

services to Quepos (five hours) leaving at 7 and 10 am and at 2 and 4 pm. You can also get here from Puntarenas, San Isidro and Dominical.

The ticket office in the Quepos bus terminal is open from 7 to 11 am and 1 to 5 pm daily except Sunday, when it closes at 2 pm. There are regular services to San José at 5 and 8 am and 2 and 4 pm daily (US$3). Direct buses leave three or four times a day (US$5) from Manuel Antonio and pick up passengers in Quepos before continuing directly to San José. In the high season, bus tickets to San José are bought days in advance – buy a ticket as early as you can.

Buses to Puntarenas (3½ hours, US$2.75) via Jacó (two hours, US$1.50) leave at 4.30 am and 3 pm. There are seven daily buses to Parrita. Bus leave for San Isidro (via Dominical) at 5 am and 1.30 pm. Buses go to Hatillo (near Dominical) at 9.30 am and 4 pm and to various local communities in the agricultural country surrounding Quepos.

Buses for Manuel Antonio leave 13 times a day between 5.40 am and 9.30 pm during the high season, returning from Manuel Antonio as soon as they arrive. There may be more buses at weekends and fewer in the dry season. The 20 minute trip costs about US$0.30.

Taxi Quepos Taxi (☎ 77 0277) will take you to Manuel Antonio for about US$3.

Getting Around
Elegante Rent-a-Car (☎ 77 0115) has an office in Quepos – I suggest you arrange car rentals in advance in San José to pick up cars here, as they are in short supply.

Pico Motor Scooter Rental (☎ 77 0125) costs US$25 per day.

QUEPOS TO MANUEL ANTONIO
From the port of Quepos, the road swings inland for seven km before reaching the beaches of Manuel Antonio village and the national park. The road goes over a series of hills with picturesque views of the ocean. Along this road, every hilltop view has been commandeered by a hotel which lists 'ocean views' as a major attraction. Certainly, these views are often magnificent. Most people staying in these pricey hotels expect, and get, good services. These hotels are generally so pleasant and comfortable that spending the whole day there is an attractive alternative to visiting the national park.

The Manuel Antonio area has been discovered and it is no longer the beautiful unspoilt gem that it was as recently as a decade ago. The prolification of hotels in an area where the sewerage system is primitive at best has led to serious threats of pollution to the once pristine beaches. The famous national park is being overwhelmed by visitors. Hotel prices average much higher here than in the rest of the country. This is perhaps the most publicised stretch of coast in Costa Rica.

Note that the road is steep, winding and very narrow. There are almost no places to pull over in the event of an emergency. Drive and walk with extreme care.

Places to Stay
The first hotel on the road to Manuel Antonio after leaving Quepos is middle priced; almost all the rest are all top end – at least price-wise. The hotels are listed here in the order that they are passed as you travel from Quepos to Manuel Antonio. The rates quoted include tax for the high and dry season (from December to April). Substantial discounts (40% is not unusual) are available in the wet season. Reservations are a must for weekends and sometimes midweek in the dry months.

Many of these hotels (even the most expensive ones) will not accept credit cards or personal cheques, so you need cash or travellers' cheques. Ask about this when calling for reservations. Most of the places are small and intimate – many have less than a dozen rooms.

The Manuel Antonio area is experiencing a tourist boom, and many of these hotels were built or opened in the late 1980s and early 1990s. More are expected to open.

Places to Stay – middle
Cabinas Pedro Miguel (☎ 77 0035) is up the hill out of Quepos, about one km out of town on the right. It has fairly basic rooms at US$21 for a double with bath, or cabins with kitchenettes for US$29 to US$37 which will sleep three or four people. The place is family run and friendly, and they'll cook for you. They are nearly always full, so must be doing something right. The only other mid-priced hotel before reaching Manuel Antonio is the *La Colina* (☎ 77 0231) which offers B&B-style accommodation for about US$45 a double.

Places to Stay – top end
The *Hotel Plinio* (☎ 77 0055; fax 77 0558; Apartado 71-6350, Quepos) has recently been remodelled and has rooms with fans for about US$51 and air-conditioned suites for about US$85 a double. There is hot water, the rooms are attractive and there are plenty

of nooks for hammocks and relaxing. Breakfast is included and both the restaurant and the hotel is recommended. Just beyond is the *El Miradór del Pacífico* (☎/fax 77 0119; Apartado 164-6350, Quepos) which has air-conditioned rooms with fans and private hot showers – the rooms lead to a verandah with attractive views. Rates range from US$52 to $82 a double, depending on the room. *Mimo's Hotel* (☎/fax 77 0054) is new and has spacious rooms with air-conditioning or fans, hot water and a pool. Rates are US$65 to US$90 for doubles, including breakfast.

Hotel Bahías (☎ 77 0350, fax 77 0279; Apartado 186-6350, Quepos) used to be just a restaurant (and a good one) but is now also a hotel. Pleasant air-conditioned rooms with hot water are US$91 a double, or US$114 with a jacuzzi. The oddly named *Suia Bya Ba* (☎ 77 0597, fax 77 0279) is French-owned and offers double rooms with fans and hot water for about US$60.

The *Hotel Las Charrúas* (☎/fax 77 0409; Apartado 38-6350, Quepos) is named after a Uruguayan Indian tribe and features a Uruguayan steak house and balconied rooms with fans and hot water for US$75 a double. The Canadian-run *Hotel Lirio* (☎ 77 0403; Apartado 123-6350, Quepos) has spacious rooms with hot water and fans and there is a small pool. Rates are US$80 a double. *Villa Las Amapolas* is similarly priced and has a jacuzzi.

The Norwegian-owned *Hotel Villa Oso* (☎/fax 77 0233; Apartado 128-6350, Quepos) has great views and rooms featuring kitchenette, refrigerator, hot water, fans and furnished balconies for US$57 to US$80 a double (add US$12 for a third person) and an apartment with full kitchen for US$98 a double or US$132 for quad. The owner is somewhat of a character – I like this place.

With about 30 rooms, the *Hotel Divisimar* (☎ 77 0371, fax 77 0525; Apartado 82-6350, Quepos) is one of the bigger hotels. Horseback, sea kayak and fishing tours are available. There is a pool and restaurant set in a pleasant garden. Air-conditioned rooms with plenty of hot water are US$82 a double and suites are US$110. The hotel is popular with affluent ticos as well as foreign tourists. Across the street is the newly refurbished *Hotel Casablanca* (☎/fax 77 0253; Apartado 194-6350, Quepos) which has spacious rooms with fans and hot water for US$70 a double and suites for US$170. There is a very small pool, a nice garden and a good view.

Down the side road behind the Casablanca are two of the region's most exclusive hotels. The internationally acclaimed *Hotel La Mariposa* (☎ 77 0355, 77 0456, fax 77 0050; Apartado 4-6350, Quepos) has 10 luxurious private villas, each with splendid views. Murals, flowers, hammocks and balconies are for the enjoyment of the guests and there is a pool and excellent restaurant. Children under 15 years are not allowed. As the hotel says, 'Only those who know how to do absolutely nothing, and do it well, can understand this paradise.' (Staff will, however, arrange all the usual activities on request.) Rates (with taxes and gratuities and including continental breakfast and dinner) are US$145 for one person, US$75 for each additional person. The restaurant is open to the public with a day's notice. Reservations, with first and last night deposits, are essential: in the USA (☎ 1 (800) 223 6510) and in Canada (☎ 1 (800) 268 0424). Credit cards and personal cheques are not accepted.

About one km down a very steep gravel road brings you to *Makanda by the Sea* (☎/fax 77 0442; Apartado 29-6350, Quepos) which vies with the Mariposa for peaceful luxury and attentive, helpful staff. There are six studios in a rainforest setting with good chances of seeing monkeys during your stay. A pool with a superb view is planned for 1994. Studio 1 (the largest) has a vista which took my breath away – the entire wall is open to the rainforest and the ocean. The unit has a full kitchen, dining area, king-sized bed, balcony, Japanese garden and large bathroom with hot shower. This rents for US$195 a double.

Three smaller studios below can all be interconnected to create personalised accommodation. Each has a king-sized bed, kitchenette and bathroom. Two have a balcony and small Japanese garden and rent for US$143 a double; the third has a terrace and is US$103 a double. There are also two large individual studios similar to Studio 1, but with two bedrooms, for US$195 a double and US$17 for additional guests. Children under 15 years are not allowed and prepaid reservations are required (credit cards accepted).

The *El Dorado Mojado* (☎ 77 0368; in San José (☎ 33 3892, 33 9135, fax 23 6728; Apartado 238-6350, Quepos) has pleasant and spacious rooms with air-conditioning and kitchenette for US$75 a double and villas with full kitchens for US$125 – these will sleep up to four people, though the fourth bed is a foldaway in the kitchen area. A pool is planned for 1994.

In the same area is the *Hotel Byblos* (☎ 77 0411, 72 0217, fax 77 0009; Apartado 112-6350, Quepos). Spacious and comfortable bungalows and cabins are set in the rainforest – there are distant ocean views from the restaurant. Rooms have either air-conditioning or fans, hot water, refrigerator, TV and can accommodate up to four people. There is a pool, jacuzzi and a French restaurant with a good reputation. This place tries to compete with La Mariposa and the Makanda – their restaurant is certainly excellent but I have received complaints about their service. I found the desk staff had a snotty attitude when I stopped by – perhaps this will improve. Rates are US$232 for a double including breakfast and dinner; US$60 per extra person.

The *Villas Nicolas* (☎/fax 77 0538; Apartado 26-6350, Quepos) has a variety of comfortable rooms, suites and villas. All have hot water, fans and a small or large balcony. There is a pool. The cheapest rooms start at US$70 a double and lack ocean views. Bigger rooms with hammocks and views are US$85; with kitchen US$98 to US$124; suites with two bedrooms, two bathrooms, two balconies with hammocks and a kitchen are from US$157 to US$175 for four persons. *Hotel & Villas Mogotes* (☎/fax 77 0582; Apartado 120-6350, Quepos) has great views, a pool and restau-

rant. Music buffs delight in recounting that this was the summer home of North American singer Jim Croce (1942-73) – this coast must have been incredibly peaceful in those days. Some rooms have fans but most have been or are being converted to air-conditioning. Most have good views – the cheapest don't. Double rooms start at US$90 and larger villas with kitchenettes go for up to US$180.

The *El Colibrí* (☎ 77 0432, fax 77 0279; Apartado 94-6350, Quepos) is set back on a side road. Colibrí means 'hummingbird', and there are certainly plenty of these in the pleasant gardens in which the 10 cabins are set. There is a pool. The cabins have hot water, a kitchenette with refrigerator, and fans. Rates are US$57/68.50/80 for a single/double/triple, and pre-teen children are not allowed – the place is tranquil. *La Quinta* (☎ 77 0434; Apartado 76-6350, Quepos) have five spacious cabins set in pleasant and quiet gardens. Cabins have balconies, views, fans, and some have kitchenettes. There is a small pool. Rates are US$70 for a double, or US$95 for a cabin sleeping up to four with kitchenette.

The *Costa Verde* (☎ 77 0584, fax 77 0560) is the sister hotel of the San José Costa Verde (Apartado 89, Escazú, San José for both hotels); in the USA (☎ 1 (800) 231 RICA). They have a variety of apartments and condominiums, 28 in all, most with kitchenettes and balconies. Rates are US$74 to US$90 a double and there are a few larger villas sleeping up to six people for about US$120.

The *Hotel Arboleda* (☎ 77 0092, ☎/fax 77 0414; Apartado 55-6350, Quepos) is the biggest hotel in the area. There are some three dozen stone cabins, some near the beach and others scattered down a forested hillside. The hotel has a pool and restaurant. Some cabins have fans, other have air-conditioning, while a few lack hot water. The rates are about US$63/74 single/double (with fans) or US$86/97 (air-conditioned).

On the final hill before reaching Manuel Antonio is the *Hotel Karahé* (☎ 77 0170, ☎/fax 77 0152; Apartado 100-6350, Quepos). You could easily walk to the national park from here in about 20 leisurely minutes. There is a pool, spa, restaurant and three levels of rooms. The oldest cabins have superb views and are reached by climbing an interminable flight of steep stairs – a 'ski lift' is planned. These rustic wooden cabins sleep up to three, have hot water, fans and refrigerators, and rent for US$75/80/103 single/double/triple. Lower, more modern spacious rooms with air-conditioning and ocean views rent for US$86/92/115 and air-conditioned junior suites by the ocean are US$108/115/143. All rates include breakfast.

A couple of minutes walk beyond the Karahé the beach level is reached and there is more accommodation along here and in Manuel Antonio village (all of it cheaper) described following.

Places to Stay – houses

For people who want to stay for at least a week or more, it is possible to rent a house and cater for yourself. The owner of La Buena Nota (☎ 77 0345) has two houses near the Hotel Mariposa and knows about others. The Biesanz family (☎ 49 1507) has quiet houses nearby. Howard and Carolyn (☎ 77 0331) have three houses. Ask around about others.

These houses are generally comfortable and fully equipped, and you can expect to pay between US$350 and US$650 a week.

Places to Eat

Many of the hotels mentioned above have good restaurants open to the public – the *La Mariposa, Byblos, Plinio, Bahías* and *Arboleda* hotels have all been recommended. The Plinio serves excellent Italian and German food, Byblos specialises in French, Arboleda is a Uruguayan steak house, and La Mariposa and Bahías are international. All are pricey by Costa Rican standards – the Plinio and Bahías are the least expensive and the most popular. Bahías began life as a bar/restaurant before becoming a hotel. If you are not staying in these places, you should make reservations (a day in advance in some cases).

Another good place is the *Restaurant Barba Roja* (☎ 77 0331), opposite the Hotel Divisimar. The name means 'red beard', and the place has well-prepared North American food (hamburgers, sandwiches, Mexican, steak and seafood) and there is a great view. Fish dinners are around US$8, hamburgers start at US$3 and their 'margarita sunsets' are good whilst the sun goes down. There is both inside and outside dining. Breakfast, lunch and dinner is served from Tuesday to Sunday – good value and recommended.

Other noteworthy places along the road are *La Arcada* which serves good Italian dinners, the French *La Brise*, by the entrance of the La Quinta hotel, and the *Iguanazul Restaurant & Bar* which has excellent piña daiquiris and good views.

Getting There & Away

Many visitors get here by private or rented car, which enables them to drive the few km to Manuel Antonio. Drive carefully on this narrow, steep and winding road. Others rely on the Quepos taxi service, the Quepos-Manuel Antonio bus service, walk or hitchhike down to the park.

MANUEL ANTONIO

The small village at the entrance to the national park has a number of less expensive hotels and restaurants and is popular with younger international travellers. The same advice regarding hotel reservations during the high season applies here – the village is packed during Easter week, and few rooms are available at weekends. The same comments about poorly regulated development and subsequent pollution and litter also apply – the government periodically tries to control development but this has not been very effective. In an effort to protect the nation's coasts, a law was passed in the late 1970s making all of Costa Rica's beaches national and public property and closed to any kind of construction within 50 metres of the high tide mark. It remains unclear what to do with those hotels and restaurants which violate the law but were built before the law was passed.

There is a good beach (Playa Espadilla) but swimmers are warned to beware of rip currents. The town is generally safe, but swimmers should never leave belongings unattended on the beach here, or on the national park beaches. Make sure your hotel room is securely locked when you are out, even briefly.

Tours & Rentals
Ríos Tropicales (☎/fax 77 0574; in San José ☎/fax 55 4354) is in the Iguana Tours office next to the Villas Nicolas. They rent snorkelling, surfing and sea-kayaking gear. They offer river-running trips down the Río Naranjo from June to November (if the water is high enough) as well as sea-kayaking and snorkelling tours. A full day is about US$55, depending on the tour.

There are stables (☎ 77 0355) opposite the Cabinas Piscis. The horses are well looked after. Rent a horse for US$30 for two hours – get cheaper rates for longer rides and groups.

Places to Stay – bottom end
The cheapest place is *Costa Linda* (☎ 77 0304; Apartado 62-6350, Quepos) affiliated with the Ticalinda budget travellers' hotel in San José. It is behind the Pargo Rojo restaurant, is reasonably clean and charges US$5.50 per person in basic stuffy rooms with shared cold showers. A bigger cabin sleeping up to six is US$36 with a private bath. Other basic cheapies are the *Cabinas Grano de Oro* (☎ 77 0578), which doesn't like to take phone reservations and the *Cabinas Anep* (☎ 77 0565) which has some rooms with private (cold) bath. Both charge US$7.25/11.

The *Cabinas Irarosa* has simple but clean rooms with fan and private cold bath for US$14.50/20. The *Cabinas Manuel Antonio* (☎ 77 0212) has basic rooms with private cold shower – the main attraction is that they are right on the beach. Rooms are US$25 to US$30 and will sleep up to four – they are usually full of young international travellers and are a fun place to stay. A few small rooms at the back are US$6 per person. The *Hotel*

Manuel Antonio opposite is open or closed, depending on who you talk to – they had US$22 doubles with private bath recently. People camp next to the hotel for US$1.50 per person – watch your possessions at ALL times.

Places to Stay – middle
The *Cabinas Ramírez* (☎ 77 0510) has rather dank rooms with private cold bath and fans for US$25 a double or US$30 a triple. During the high season it may be difficult to get cheaper single or double rates. The nearby disco may preclude sleep. For the same price, the *Cabinas Piscis* (☎ 77 0046; Apartado 219-6350, Quepos) is better – the cabins are close to the beach and has an inexpensive restaurant.

The *Hotel Vela Bar* (☎ 77 0413; Apartado 13-6350, Quepos) has large pleasant rooms for US$25/35 for a single/double with private bath; larger rooms with a kitchenette are US$65. The owners are pleasant and run a popular restaurant. The *Hotel Del Mar* (☎ 77 0543; Apartado 77-6350, Quepos) has simple but clean, spacious rooms with fans and private cold showers for US$35/40.

The *Cabinas Los Almendros* (☎ 77 0225; Apartado 68-6350, Quepos) has large, quiet and pleasant rooms for US$40 a double with cold water and fans and for US$64 with hot water and air-conditioning. A decent restaurant is attached. The *Cabinas Espadilla* (☎ 77 0416; Apartado 195-6350, Quepos) has helpful owners and spacious clean rooms with private cold bath and fan. Rooms with kitchenette and sleeping up to four cost US$50; some cheaper rooms without kitchenette are also available.

Places to Stay – top end
The *Cabinas Espadilla* (see above) has a new annexe across the street that has larger air-conditioned rooms with hot water and sleeping up to four for US$75 at high-season weekends (less midweek). The new *Hotel Villabosque* (☎ 77 0401) has nice rooms with fans, balconies and hot water for US$70 a double or US$80 with air-conditioning.

Places to Eat

The *Vela Bar* is the best and priciest restaurant in Manuel Antonio. They serve a variety of meals, including a few vegetarian plates, for from US$6 to US$12. The restaurants at the *Hotel Villabosque* and the *Cabinas Los Almendros* are also good and slightly cheaper. The restaurant at the *Hotel Manuel Antonio* is cheaper still and popular.

The *Restaurant Mar y Sombra* (☎ 77 0003) is also popular and serves seafood. It has casados and chicken and pasta plates for about US$3 and fish dinners for twice that. There are good sunset views. The *Restaurant y Soda Marlin* is often crowded and has meals for around US$3 to US$5. They serve breakfasts. There are a number of other cheap sodas and roadside stands in the beach area – *Restaurant Las Olas* and *Pearl's Soda* have been recommended.

The *Discoteque Amor y Mar* (☎ 77 0510) serves fairly cheap meals, if you can stand the invasively loud disco music. As you might expect, there is dancing here some nights. The *Bar del Mar* (☎ 77 0543) is a quiet place for a drink or snack, and rents surfboards and snorkels.

Getting There & Away

Direct buses from San José leave the Coca-Cola terminal at 6 am, noon and 6 pm daily during the dry season; one of these departures may not run in the wet. Return buses leave from near the Restaurant Las Olas at 6 am, noon and 5 pm daily, plus 3 pm on Sundays. They will pick you up from in front of your hotel if you are on the road to flag them down, or from the Quepos bus terminal. Note that direct buses to San José cost about US$1 less from Quepos. Buy tickets in advance if possible, particularly at weekends when they sell out days ahead. Try calling ☎ 77 0263 for bus reservations in Manuel Antonio.

Buses for destinations other than San José leave from Quepos. Buses from Manuel Antonio to Quepos leave about 13 times a day from 6 am to 9.50 pm – more often in dry season weekends and less often on the wet season.

All flights to Manuel Antonio go to Quepos.

PARQUE NACIONAL MANUEL ANTONIO

At 683 hectares, Manuel Antonio is by far the smallest park in the national parks system, but it is also one of the most popular ones. This is because of its beautiful forest-backed tropical beaches, dramatic rocky headlands with ocean and island views, prolific wildlife, and maintained trail network.

Fortunately, Manuel Antonio was declared a national park back in 1972, thus preserving it from hotel development. The many hotels in the area north of the park, however, have made this gem of a park the focus of much visitation. Clearly, large numbers of people in such a small area will tend to detract from the experience of visiting the park. Idyllic and romantic beaches have to be shared with others, wildlife is either driven away or, worse still, taught to scavenge for tourist handouts, and there are inevitable litter and traffic problems.

Several steps have been taken to minimise pressure on the park. Camping is no longer allowed. Apart from an information centre and lavatory facilities, there are no buildings inside the park – no souvenir stands, restaurants, snack bars, gift shops or picnic shelters. Vehicular traffic is prohibited within the park (and arriving on foot is a minor adventure in itself). Still, the heavy pressure of visitors has led to serious discussions of closing the park on certain days of the week or limiting the number of visitors entering the park at any one time. Rules like these may have come into effect by the time you read this.

If you want to avoid the crowds, go early in the morning, midweek during the rainy season.

Information

There is a visitor information centre just before Playa Manuel Antonio. Drinking water is available at the information centre and there are toilets nearby. The park is officially open from 7 am to 4 pm, and guards come round in the evening to make sure that

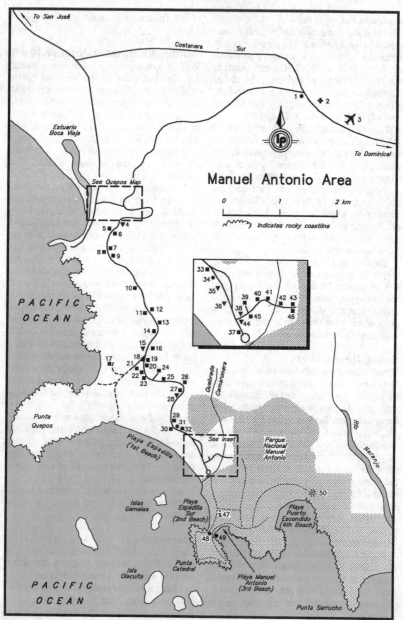

To San José

Costanera   Sur

To Dominical

Estuario
Boca Vieja

See Quepos Map

Manuel Antonio Area

0   1   2 km

indicates rocky coastline

PACIFIC
OCEAN

33
34
35
36
39 40 41
38   42 43
45   46
37 44

Quebrada Camaronera

Punta
Quepos

Playa Espadilla
(1st Beach)

See inset

Parque
Nacional
Manuel
Antonio

Río Naranjo

Islas
Gemelas

Playa
Espadilla
Sur
(2nd Beach)

147

48 49

Punta
Catedral

Playa Manuel
Antonio
(3rd Beach)

Playa
Puerto
Escondido
(4th Beach)

50

Isla
Olacuita

PACIFIC
OCEAN

Punta Serrucho

nobody is camping. It used to be possible to camp, but heavy user pressure has caused the closure of the campsite and visitors have to stay outside the park.

The beaches are often numbered – most people call Playa Espadilla (outside the park) first beach, Playa Espadilla Sur is second beach, Playa Manuel Antonio is third beach, Playa Puerto Escondido is fourth beach, and Playita is fifth beach. Some people begin counting at Espadilla Sur, which is the first beach actually in the park, and so it can be a bit confusing trying to figure out which beach people may be talking about.

The average daily temperature is 27°C and the average annual rainfall is 3800 mm. The dry season is not entirely dry, merely less wet, and so you should be prepared for rain then too (although it can also be dry for days on end). Make sure you carry plenty of drinking water and sun protection when visiting the park. Insect repellent is also an excellent idea.

Entrance into the park is US$1.50 per day.

Walking Trails

Visitors must leave their vehicles at the south end of the road in Manuel Antonio village. (Sometimes, there aren't enough parking spaces.) The Quebrada Camaronera estuary divides the southern end of the village from the park and there is no bridge, so the estuary must be waded to gain access. The water may be ankle deep at low tide and thigh deep at high tide (spring tides in the rainy season have been known to be chest high), so prepare yourself to get at least a little wet.

Once across the estuary, follow an obvious

trail through forest to an isthmus separating Espadilla Sur and Manuel Antonio beaches. This isthmus is called a *tombolo* and was formed by the accumulation of sedimentary material between the mainland and the peninsula beyond, which was once an island. If you walk along Playa Espadilla Sur, you will find a small mangrove area. The isthmus widens out into a rocky peninsula, with forest in the centre. A trail leads around the peninsula to Punta Catedral from where there are good views of the Pacific Ocean and various rocky islets which are bird reserves and form part of the national park. Brown boobies and pelicans are among the seabirds which nest on these islands.

You can continue around the peninsula to Playa Manuel Antonio, or you can avoid the peninsula altogether and hike across the isthmus to this beach. At the western end of the beach, during low tide, you can see a semicircle of rocks which archaeologists believe were placed there by pre-Columbian Indians, and which functioned as a turtle trap. The beach itself is an attractive one of white sand, and is popular for bathing. It is protected and safer than the Espadilla beaches.

Beyond Playa Manuel Antonio, the trail divides. The lower trail is steep and slippery during the wet months, and leads to the quiet and aptly named Playa Puerto Escondido ('hidden port beach'). This beach can be more or less completely covered by high tides, so don't get cut off. The upper trail climbs up to a bluff overlooking Puerto Escondido and Punta Serrucho beyond – a nice view. I have a map showing a trail continuing from here to the Playita, but it seems that it is now closed; check with park rangers.

Monkeys abound in the park, and it is difficult to spend a day walking around without seeing some. White-faced monkeys are the most common, but the rarer squirrel monkeys are also present and howler monkeys may be seen. Sloths, agoutis, peccaries, armadillos, coatimundis and raccoons are also seen quite regularly. Over 350 species of birds are reported for the park, and

a variety of lizards, snakes, iguanas and other animals may be observed. All of the trails within the park are good for animal watching – ask the rangers where the most interesting recent sightings have occurred. There is a small coral reef off Manuel Antonio beach, but the water is rather cloudy and the visibility limited. Despite this, snorkellers can see a variety of fish as well as marine creatures like crabs and corals, sponges and sea snails, and many others.

Immediately inland from the beaches is an evergreen littoral forest. This contains many different species of trees, bushes and other plants. A common one to watch out for is the manzanillo (little apple) tree, *Hippomane mancinella*; this tree has fruits that look like little crab apples and which are poisonous. The sap exuded by the bark and leaves is also toxic, and causes the skin to itch and burn, so give the manzanillo a wide berth. There are warning signs prominently displayed by examples of this tree near the park entrance.

THE ROAD TO DOMINICAL & SAN ISIDRO

It is not possible to continue further south along the coast from Manuel Antonio. You have to backtrack to Quepos, and from there head four km inland to the Costanera Sur. It is 44 km from Quepos to the next village of any size, Dominical. The road is gravel and easily passable in the dry season, but requires some care to negotiate with an ordinary car in the wet. Residents of this area have long complained to the government that the Costanera Sur should be paved and, in June 1993, organised a massive protest by blockading Quepos and effectively shutting down that town plus Manuel Antonio. Many travellers were stranded. The government is promising to pave and improve this road soon – maybe it'll be paved by the time you get there, though don't bank your last colón on it.

The drive is through km after km of African oil-palm plantations, with identical-looking settlements along the way. These are minor centres for the palm-oil extracting process. Each settlement has a grassy village square, institutional-looking housing, a store, church, bar and, somewhat strangely, an Alcoholics Anonymous chapter. Playas Savegre and Matapalo may be worth a look if you are a beach lover; there are no noteworthy facilities at these.

About a km before reaching the Río Barú is the private nature reserve at Hacienda Barú, described following. A bridge crosses the Río Barú and immediately beyond is the village of Dominical on the south-east side of the river mouth. From the west side of the bridge, a steep but paved road climbs 34 km inland to San Isidro de El General. Thus, if you can negotiate the somewhat rough Quepos to Dominical road, a round trip from San José to Quepos, Dominical, San Isidro and back to San José is quite possible and, indeed, makes a good excursion.

HACIENDA BARÚ

This private nature reserve covers only about 330 hectares but manages to pack a large number of species into its small size. This is because its location on the steep coastal hills encompasses a variety of habitats including three km of beach, 16 hectares of mangroves, one km of the Río Barú, pasture and plantations, and lowland and hilly rainforest up to 320 metres above sea level. About 80 hectares are undisturbed primary rainforest, 50 hectares are rainforest that was selectively logged almost two decades ago and then left, and 25 hectares are secondary forest growing on abandoned pastures. In addition, the reserve contains several pre-Columbian village sites and cemetery sites (including a tomb which was not found by grave robbers) as well as several petroglyphs. The Museo Nacional is beginning to study the area.

The Hacienda Barú bird list is well over 300 species and growing; the mammal list is 56 species (including 23 bats); the amphibian and reptile list is 35 species and there are many frogs, toads and snakes which are yet to be identified; and the plant list is far from complete with over 100 trees and 75 orchid species. An impressive list!

The owners, Jack and Diane Ewing, have lived and raised their family here since 1970.

They are a delightful couple with a fund of stories to tell and information to dispense. When they first arrived, transportation was mostly by horseback – now the road goes by and tourism is increasing. Nevertheless, Barú still has a remote feel to it and communication is by radio. The Ewings are working hard at preserving the area and are active in encouraging and helping their neighbours to do likewise – they want to be ready to handle properly the inevitable growth in tourism which has already begun.

Information

Obtain information and make reservations for tours or accommodation with Selva Mar (☎/fax 71 1903; attention Jack or Diane Ewing, Apartado 215-8000, San Isidro de El General). Selva Mar is in daily radio contact with Hacienda Barú – 24 hours advance notice is appreciated.

The Ewings's El Ceibo gas station, which Diane proudly claims has the cleanest gas station toilets (I made an unannounced stop there just to verify this phenomenon) in Costa Rica, is 1.7 km north of the hacienda. A variety of groceries, fishing gear, tide tables and other useful sundries is available – this is one of the few gas stations in the country which sell more than just gas.

Tours

Tours available at Hacienda Barú include a 2½ hour lowland birding walk (US$12.50); a rainforest hike including lunch (US$25); an all day hike from mangroves to hilly rainforest with a visit to the pre-Columbian cemetery, including lunch and snack (US$30); and an overnight stay in the rainforest with meals and comfortable camping (US$60). These prices are for one person and are cheaper per person in groups. A maximum of eight people are allowed in the rainforest so that you don't meet other hikers. Horseback rides (US$15 for two hours, US$3 per extra hour) are also available. These prices include native guides. Jim Zook, a very knowledgeable English-speaking naturalist and ornithologist, will accompany any tour for an additional US$50 per day.

Places to Stay

There is a simple three-bedroom cabin and five more are due to open in late 1993. The cabins are a few hundred metres beyond the gas station and each will have a kitchen, refrigerator, electric shower, sitting room and insect screens. High-season rates are US$35 to US$70 for two to six people. Alternatively, stay in nearby Dominical or in one of several local places south of the village. The Ewings are in radio contact with many of these and will help you make reservations if you leave a message with Selva Mar.

Getting There & Away

The Quepos-Dominical-San Isidro bus stops outside the hacienda entrance. The San Isidro-Dominical-Uvita bus will drop you at the Río Barú bridge, just over a km from the hacienda.

DOMINICAL

This quiet coastal village is 1.2 km south of Hacienda Barú. The Dominical beach is a long one and has a reputation for strong rip currents, so exercise extra caution. Despite this, a good number of surfers hang out here and the area has a growing reputation as a place to get off the beaten track. A small ecotourism industry is developing and local operators, led by the owners of the Hacienda Barú, are banding together in an effort to promote the area without spoiling it. Apart from surfing, attractions include rainforest hiking and camping, wildlife observation, horse-riding, fishing and visits to the nearby Parque Nacional Marino Ballena.

Information

There are public phones outside the Soda Laura and Cabinas Coco. Selva Mar (☎/fax 71 1903) will pass on radio messages for some local businesses if you leave a message (see the Hacienda Barú section).

Fishing

Steve Wofford of Reel 'n Release has been recommended for deep-sea fishing trips. He charges US$425 for four people for a full day – everything included. He'll also help with snorkelling or diving charters. Contact him through Selva Mar.

Places to Stay – bottom end

Even the cheap places are not very cheap – free camping on the beach is an option. The least expensive accommodation is at the basic but clean *Cabinas Coco* (☎ 71 2555). It is on the main street and charges US$7.25/11 for singles/doubles. Others on the main street include the following.

The best value is at *Albergue Willdale* (also called Cabinas Willy) with clean, spacious rooms with private electric showers and fans for US$18/22/26 for singles/doubles/triples. Reserve rooms through Selva Mar. *La Residencia* charges US$22 for clean, if small, double rooms with private electric shower and fans. *Jungle Jim's* (☎ 71 2095) is similarly priced for clean rooms with a communal shower, but the accompanying 'sports bar' and live music may preclude an early night. They also rent houses by the week. This place is up for sale, so it may have changed names by the time you read this.

Cabinas Nayarit (☎ 71 1878) is closer to the beach and charges US$22 for rather grim rooms with private bath and fan; up to three people can sleep in a room. They also have cheaper rooms without bath. About one km south of town is the *Cabinas Roca Verde* which charges US$18 for simple cabins with private bath – they'll sleep up to three people and are OK.

Places to Stay – middle

For more upscale accommodation, try the newer *Hotel Río Lindo* by the Restaurant Maui at the entrance to Dominical. They have ocean and river views and clean, attractive, spacious rooms with hot showers go for US$40 a double. Unfortunately, I've received comments that the walls are thin and you can hear your neighbours – this is a common problem in many hotels.

Just beyond the entrance into Dominical a

sign points under the bridge to *Cabinas Río Mar* (☎ 71 2333, fax 71 2455 in San Isidro) – it's supposedly 400 metres but was closer to 800 on my odometer. They have small clean cabins with kitchenettes, private hot showers and fans for US$40 a double or larger cabins with kitchen, refrigerator, private hot-water bathroom and two or more bedrooms for about US$92. They also have a few standard rooms with bath for US$23/29 for singles/doubles.

Places to Stay – south of Dominical

There are several interesting places to stay south of town. Contact them via the Selva Mar radio (☎/fax 71 1903) or from the Hacienda Barú or Albergue Willdale.

Just over two km south of the Cabinas Roca Verde in Dominical, along the gravel road to Uvita, a sign points to a road to the left for *Cabinas Bellavista*. Owned by longtime resident Woody Dyer, this remote lodge is in a revamped farmhouse 500 metres above sea level. A balcony gives superb ocean views and there is rainforest and a waterfall nearby. Accommodation is rustic but clean; there is no hot water. Six rooms in the main building are US$20/30/40 for one to three people; bathrooms are communal. Meals are available for US$10 per day. A guesthouse for up to eight people and including kitchen facilities is planned for mid-1993; it will have a private bathroom and a kitchen. Rainforest/waterfall hiking tours with lunch and local guide are US$35 per person, and horse rental is available.

This place is so remote because it is difficult to get to. You need 4WD to get up their road, which is locally called the *Escaleras* (Staircase). If you don't have 4WD, they'll pick you up in Dominical for US$10.

Also on the Escaleras road is the *Finca Brian y Milena*, Apartado 2-8000, San Isidro de El General, Costa Rica. This is a small, isolated working farm surrounded by rainforest. They have a cabin sleeping up to five (with portable cots); this has a bathroom. Rates are US$25 a single and US$15 per additional person. There is also the aptly named Birdhouse Cabin which shares the

bathroom with the main house; rates are US$15/25 for single/double. Country-style meals are US$10 per day and a hot tub is available. If you don't have 4WD, you can either hike (1½ hours) or ride a horse (US$7.50 per hour) to get to their place. They arrange rainforest/waterfall tours of one to five days (with optional camping or visits with campesino families). A one day trip is US$30 for one person and US$10 for each additional person up to six; a five night trip is US$190 for one person and US$60 for each additional. Prices include food and native guides.

Also on the Escaleras road is *Villa Cabeza de Mono* run by the folks at the Albergue Willdale in Dominical. This mountain villa with superb views, small swimming pool, kitchen and room for up to six people can be rented by the day or week. Bring food and cook for yourself or hire a cook. You need 4WD to get there.

Cabinas Punta Dominical (☎ 25 5328 in San José, fax 53 4750 in San Isidro), Apartado 196-8000, San Isidro de El General, is 3.5 km south of Dominical. Built high on a rocky headland named, appropriately enough, Punta Dominical, the cabins are isolated and attractive, yet retain a modicum of comfort. Four pleasant cabins with fans, private baths with electric showers, and a porch to hang a hammock, rent for US$45 for a double and US$75 for six people. Reservations are recommended, especially at weekends, and should be prepaid in San José for confirmation. The cabins overlook a rocky beach; there is a sandy beach nearby and boat trips can be arranged. The restaurant on the premises is widely regarded as the best in the area.

Seven km south of Dominical is *Cabañas Escondidas* (Apartado 364, San Isidro de El General, or leave a message with Selva Mar; CRBBG member). The cabins are set in very attractive gardens surrounded by 20 hectares of rainforest and are a tranquil alternative to other accommodation. The women running the place offer classes in tai chi and chi kung, give therapeutic massage, and provide gourmet vegetarian meals, as well as arrange the usual guided rainforest hikes, snorkelling trips and horseback rides. You can walk to the beach in about 10 minutes. Three cabins with ocean views and private baths are US$45 for a double plus US$11 for additional people – this includes breakfast. Other meals are US$8 with advance notice. There are also two private 'ranchos' which are simple sleeping platforms with thatched roofs and great views; it's almost like sleeping out in the forest. Bathrooms are in the main house. These rent for US$26 for two people. A couple more cabins are planned for 1994, one with kitchen facilities.

Places to Eat

There are several inexpensive sodas in Dominical, of which the best are the *Soda Laura* and *Soda Nanyoa*. They open by about 6.30 am for breakfast and serve casados for about US$2. The pleasant tico-owned *Restaurant Maui* is more upscale and has decent meals ranging from US$2 to US$7. The US-owned *Jungle Jim's* is pricey by local standards but the food is nothing special. They call themselves a 'sports bar' and have a satellite dish to capture all the latest North American baseball. Rock and reggae, surfers and sportfishers, beer and 'babes' complete the picture.

Head down to the previously mentioned *Cabinas Punta Dominical* for the best meals in the area. Their excellent restaurant is open from 8 am to 8 pm daily. Sample prices are US$3.50 for a casado, US$4.50 for fried fish and US$14 for a shrimp or lobster dinner.

Getting There & Away

Buses leave Quepos at 5 am and 1.30 pm, passing through Dominical about two hours later and continuing about 1½ hours to San Isidro. A bus leaves Uvita at 6.30 am, passing through Dominical around 8 am and continuing to San Isidro. Buses leave San Isidro at 7 am and 1.30 pm for Quepos and at 3 pm for Uvita, passing through Dominical about 1½ hours later. The bus stop in Dominical is by the pulpería next to the Soda Laura.

UVITA

This village is 17 km south of Dominical and is the end of the road as far as the central Pacific coast is concerned. This is the entry point for the new Parque Nacional Marino Ballena.

A local family, the Duartes, offer trail rides from Rancho La Merced on the coast up to 600 metres above sea level, returning through the rainforest on foot and stopping at their finca for a campesino-style lunch. They have homesteaded the area for over three decades and continue to live without roads or electricity. They operate a *trapiche* or sugar mill in the traditional way – by oxen power. The trapiche is visited on the tour which costs US$35 for one person, US$30 for additional people and includes lunch and a local guide. Add US$25 for an English or French-speaking guide. These tours give you a look at traditional Costa Rican life and give the Duartes an income which encourages them to preserve the rainforest on their land. Contact them through Selva Mar radio (☎/fax 71 1903).

Places to Stay

Cabinas Los Laureles has three cabins with bathrooms. The smallest, with a double bed, is US$22; the largest, with two double beds, is US$29. They can arrange horseback tours. You'll find the cabins a few hundred metres to the left of the El Coco Tico *abastecedor* (general store), 17 km south of Dominical. There is a sign. Nearby the previously mentioned *Rancho La Merced* is planning on opening a cabin soon. Both places can be contacted through Selva Mar.

Getting There & Away

A bus leaves San Isidro for Uvita at 3 pm daily, returning at 6.30 am. Ask locally for the bus stop.

The gravel road from Dominical is passable to cars all year.

Beyond Uvita, a poor dirt road follows the coast as far as Tortuga Abajo, 16 km away. This stretch was suitable only for 4WD when I was there, but construction of new bridges and road improvements undertaken during

1993 may make the road passable year-round to all cars – ask locally. There are several remote beaches along here. Beyond Tortuga Abajo, the road improves and continues 20 km to Ciudad Cortés and seven more km to Palmar Norte. There are plans to eventually pave this road and connect the central Pacific coast with southern Costa Rica, but it looks like it will be close to the end of the century before this project may be completed. Meanwhile – this is an adventure for drivers of 4WD vehicles, or backpackers who want to walk it. Let me know how it goes!

PARQUE NACIONAL MARINO BALLENA

This national marine park was created in 1990 to protect coral and rock reefs in 4500 hectares of ocean around Isla Ballena, south of Uvita. The island has nesting colonies of magnificent frigatebirds, blue-footed boobies and other seabirds, as well as many green iguanas and basilisk lizards. Humpback whales migrate through the area and may be sighted from December to March. The Spanish word for whale is *ballena* – this gives the name to the vaguely whale-shaped island as well as the park. Both common and bottle-nosed dolphins are found here all year round and there is a good variety of other marine life.

From Punta Uvita heading south-east, the park includes 13 km of sandy and rocky beaches, mangrove swamps, river mouths and rocky headlands. By Costa Rican law, the first 50 metres of coast above the high tide mark are protected from development and are accessible to everyone – not just here but throughout the country. The sandy beaches are the nesting sites of olive ridley and hawksbill turtles during the rainy months of May to November, with peak laying occurring in September and October. All five kinds of Costa Rica's mangroves

occur within the park: red, tea, black, white and (rarest) the buttonwood mangroves.

Information

The ranger station is in the community of Bahía, the seaside extension of Uvita. The rangers told me that you can hire boats from Bahía to Isla Ballena for about US$15 to US$20 per hour; landing on the island and snorkelling is permitted. From the ranger station you can walk out onto Punta Uvita and snorkel. This is best on a dropping/low tide (especially when the tides are not extreme). High and extreme tides make the water turbid. The park entrance fee is US$1.50.

Places to Stay

Because the park is so new, there were no official campsites when I visited in 1993. Therefore camping along the beaches was free. A campsite with pit toilets and water is planned near the ranger station – this will cost the usual fee which is currently US$2.20 per person per night.

See under Uvita and Dominical for other accommodation.

Getting There & Away

Locals tell me that the daily Uvita-San Isidro bus begins and ends in Bahía – ask locally for the bus stop.

If you are driving south from Dominical, you'll pass the 'Parque Nacional Marino Ballena' sign almost 17 km south of the Cabinas Roca Verde in Dominical. Past the sign is the abastecedor where you turn right. When the road forks, turn left and cross a river (high clearance needed in the wet months), reaching the coast 2.5 km from the abastecedor. Here, there is a public phone and basic stores and a soda. The ranger station is a few hundred metres to the right.

Several Dominical area hotels arrange transportation and boat trips to the park.

Península de Nicoya

This peninsula juts south from the north-western corner of Costa Rica and, at over 100 km in length, is by far the largest in the country. Despite its size, it has few paved roads and most people get around on gravel or dirt roads. Some of Costa Rica's major beach resorts are here, often remote and difficult to get to, and offering beaches and sun rather than villages, culture or wildlife. Most visitors come for the beaches and if all you want to do is swim, sunbathe and relax, then you'll probably enjoy a few days on part of the beautiful shoreline of the peninsula. Otherwise, you could become bored very quickly. An adventurous traveller, however, may still discover remote beaches and villages where a friendly conversation with a smiling local could be more memorable than a hammock on the beach.

There are several small wildlife reserves and a national park found in the peninsula that are worth visiting if you are in the area. In 1940 about half of the peninsula was covered with rainforest; this had been mostly cut down by the 1960s. Much of the peninsula has been turned over to cattle raising, which, along with tourism, is the main industry.

The main highway through the peninsula begins at Liberia and follows the centre of the peninsula through the small towns of Filadelfia and Santa Cruz to Nicoya, which is the largest town in the area. (Nevertheless, it is a small town.) From Nicoya, the main road heads east to the Río Tempisque ferry or south-east to Playa Naranjo from where the ferry to Puntarenas leaves several times a day. These roads are good, and, for the most part, paved. Many drivers arrive from the main part of Costa Rica by taking the car ferry from Puntarenas to Playa Naranjo or the car ferry across the Río Tempisque. In this chapter, however, I describe the peninsula from north to south.

From this main central highway, side roads branch out to a long series of beaches

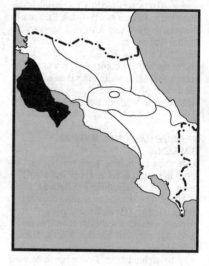

stretching along the Pacific coastline of the peninsula. Many of these roads are gravel or dirt and may be in poor condition. Once you get to the beach area of your choice, you are usually stuck there and cannot continue north or south along the coast for any long distance because there is no paved coastal road. If you have a 4WD vehicle, it is possible to follow the coast (more or less) on the poor dirt roads. In an ordinary car or if you are travelling by bus to the next set of beaches, you often need to backtrack to the main central highway and then come back again on another road. Some beaches have a hotel but no village, and bus service may be nonexistent. If there is a small village, the bus service is often limited to one per day. Many visitors come by car rather than relying on the bus services, though there is no problem with using buses if you have plenty of time and patience. Note that bus services may be curtailed during the wet season, when few ticos go to the beach.

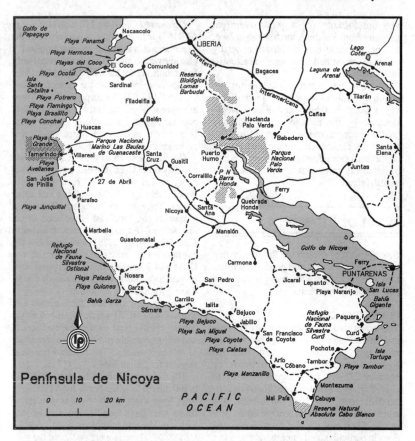

Península de Nicoya

The beaches at Tamarindo, Nosara, Sámara and Tambor have regularly scheduled flights from San José with SANSA or Travelair. This avoids the difficulties of road travel but limits your visit to just one beach. Some people rent a car (4WD is useful in the dry season and recommended in the wet – many car hire companies won't allow you to rent an ordinary car to go to the Península de Nicoya in the wet season) but this is an expensive option if you are going to park your car by the beach for a few days. If you decide to hire a car, be prepared for a frustrating lack of road signs and gas stations.

Fill up whenever you can and ask frequently for directions.

Budget travellers using public buses should allow plenty of time to get around. Hitchhiking is a definite possibility – given the paucity of public transport, the locals hitchhike around the peninsula more than in other parts of Costa Rica. If you want to cook for yourself, bring food from inland. Stores are few and far between on the coast, and the selection is limited and expensive.

What this all means is that most of the Península de Nicoya beaches are more suitable for a leisurely visit of several days. If you are looking for a quick overnight getaway from San José, the beaches at Jacó, Manuel Antonio or Cahuita are generally easier to get to and have more of a tourist infrastructure.

As with beach areas throughout the country, you should have reservations during dry season weekends and Easter week. Because of the remote nature of many beaches, reservations are a good idea at any time. Prices in this chapter are the high and dry season prices (from December to Easter). Substantial rainy season discounts are usually given.

West of Liberia

Beaches west of Liberia are linked with that town by a paved road and good bus service. Consequently, they are amongst the most popular on the peninsula.

PLAYAS DEL COCO

This beach area is only 35 km west of Liberia and (of the Península de Nicoya beaches) the most easily accessible by road from San José. It is attractively set between two rocky headlands. There are a number of hotels to choose from, a small village, good bus connections from San José and Liberia, and more nightlife than most beaches on the peninsula. Thus is a popular resort for young ticos in particular, and foreign travellers to a lesser extent. However, the beach has a reputation for strong rip currents and is somewhat shabby and littered because of the high visitor use and the nearby fishing harbour.

Places to Stay & Eat

Camping is possible if you don't mind the ambiance of the construction site and chickens scratching around the palm trees. Follow signs to the campsite which is about 150 metres from the beach. The place seems secure and there are several bathrooms and showers available. The rates are US$1.50 per person per night.

Cabinas El Coco (☎ 67 0110, 67 0276, fax 67 0167) is to the right as you arrive at the beach and is one of the cheaper hotels. It's also known as Casino Playa del Coco. Fairly basic rooms at the back are US$11.75/15 for singles/doubles and at the beachfront are US$14.50/17.50, all with private bath. There are dozens of rooms and the place is fairly popular though not anything special. There is a decent mid-priced restaurant on the premises and a disco next door.

Cabinas Luna Tica (☎ 67 0127; Apartado 67, Playas del Coco, Guanacaste) has rather stuffy rooms with private bath, fan and a double bed for US$20 as well as some larger rooms. They are on the beach. There is a restaurant and breakfast is included in the low season. Across the street, the *Anexo Luna Tica* (☎ 67 0279) is cheaper but the rooms seem breezier and better for US$11/14.50 single/double. All rooms have private bath and fan; a few have air-conditioning for a few more dollars.

Other cheapies include the *Cabinas Las Brisas* (☎ 67 0155) which is just before the parque central next to the Pronto Pizzería and has reasonable rooms. An unsigned set of cabins is nearby. The *Pronto Pizzería* is popular for Italian food.

The *Cabinas Chale* (☎ 67 0036, 67 0303) is 100 metres from the beach and a 600 metre walk from town, to the right as you arrive (there are signs). Good rooms with private bath, fan and refrigerator are good value for US$18/24. There is a big pool, and the staff is friendly.

The *Hotel Palmas del Coco* (☎ 67 0367, fax 67 0117; Apartado 188-5019, Playas del Coco, Guanacaste) is on the left side of the plaza as you enter town. Clean spacious rooms with fans, private bath and hot water are US$25 single or double. There is a good restaurant on the premises.

The *Cabinas Costa Alegre* (☎ 67 0218) is almost five km before you reach the beach on the road from Liberia. It has cabins with kitchenette, fan and private bath, which sleep up to five people for US$50. There is a pool and restaurant.

The best hotel is the *Flor de Itabo* (☎ 67

0011; Apartado 32, Playa del Coco, Guanacaste) which is almost a km from the beach, on the right hand side as you arrive. There is a good restaurant and both children's and adults' pools. The spacious air-conditioned rooms have hot water. The rates are US$65/72 for a single/double room, and cabins with kitchenettes and refrigerator start from US$80. The cabins have one double and two single beds each. The owners are friendly and will help arrange fishing and diving excursions, and there are horses for rent.

Getting There & Away

Pulmitan (☎ 22 1650) has a bus leaving San José from Calle 14, Avenida 1 & 3 daily at 10 am (US$3.50). The return leaves Playa del Coco at 9.15 am daily. Arata buses (☎ 66 0138) from Liberia leave at 5.30 and 8.15 am and 12.30, 2, 4.30 and 6.15 pm during the dry season (less frequently in the wet). They return from Playas del Coco about one hour later. A taxi from Liberia costs US$12 to US$15.

PLAYA HERMOSA

This gently curving and relatively safe beach is about seven km north of Coco, and it is quieter, cleaner and less crowded. The main 'action' is at the north end where there is a small resort.

Aqua Sport (☎ 67 0450, 67 0158), near the middle of the beach, rents bicycles, kayaks, surfboards, snorkelling gear etc. They can also arrange boat excursions for anglers, divers and sightseers. They have a grocery store and public telephone, and will change cash dollars and travellers cheques.

Places to Stay & Eat

The previously mentioned *Aqua Sport* has a good seafood restaurant with international dishes – it has received several recommendations.

Cabinas Playa Hermosa (☎ 67 0136) is a quiet and pleasant hotel near the south end of the beach. Clean rooms with fans, private baths and electric showers are US$20/30 for a single/double. There is an Italian restaurant on the premises. Nearby, there are some cheaper ocean-front restaurants serving fresh fish. Cheaper cabins are available in this vicinity.

The *Hotel Condovac La Costa* (☎ 67 0267, 67 0283, fax 67 0211; in San José ☎ 21 2264, 21 8949; Apartado 55-1001, Plaza Víquez, San José) at the north end is a condominium complex with about 100 units renting for US$115 a double. Each has a kitchenette, hot water and air-conditioning. There are tennis courts, a pool, discotheque, restaurant and bar on the grounds, and diving, snorkelling, fishing, kayaking, boating and horse-riding can be arranged.

Near Condovac is the smaller but similarly priced *Hotel Los Corales* (☎ 67 0255, fax 55 4978) which offers air-conditioned cabins sleeping up to eight people. Each cabin has a kitchen and hot shower; there is a pool and jacuzzi, but it is a couple of minutes walk away from the beach.

The new Canadian-owned *Hotel El Velero* (☎/fax 67 0310; Apartado 49-5019, Playa Hermosa, Guanacastre) has good rooms with private bath and air-conditioning for about US$76 a double. It has a pool and restaurant and offers sailing courses for snorkelling, scuba diving or just enjoying the sunset.

Getting There & Away

Empresa Esquivel (☎ 66 1249) buses leave Liberia at 11.30 am and 7 pm, passing Playa Hermosa on their way to Playa Panamá. Buses return from Playa Panamá at 5 am and 4 pm. An express bus leaves San José from Calle 12, Avenida 5 & 7 at 3.30 pm and takes five hours to reach Playa Panamá. It returns from Playa Panamá at 5 am. A taxi from Liberia is about US$12 to US$15, and a taxi from Coco is about US$4.

PLAYA PANAMÁ

This protected dark-sand beach is one of the best swimming beaches in the area. It is about three km north of Playa Hermosa, and is the end of the road. There is a basic store and a bar. It is possible to camp on the beach at *Jardín del Mar* (☎ 31 7629); they have showers and rent tents for US$5, or bring your own for less. One reader reports seeing sloths around the campground.

The government-run Papagayo Project has slated the area for hotel development and there will probably be cabins and hotels there soon.

See Playa Hermosa for how to get there.

NACASCOLO

This is a pre-Columbian Indian ruin north of Playa Panamá. There isn't a great deal to see, but you can get here by boat across the Bahía Culebra from Playa Panamá. Ask around for someone to take you over. It is possible to camp at Nacascolo, but there are no facilities or drinking water.

PLAYA OCOTAL

This attractive but small beach is three km south of Coco by unpaved road. It offers good swimming and snorkelling, and scuba diving is available. The nearby Isla Santa Catalina is a recommended diving spot – there are others. Accommodation here is good but not cheap. The south end of the beach is recommended for snorkelling.

Places to Stay

The *Hotel El Ocotal* (☎ 67 0012, 67 0230) is on a cliff with great views. Rooms are US$86/101 single/double with hot water, air-conditioning and refrigerator. There is a pool, restaurant, tennis court and boating facilities. Dive packages cost about US$500 per person, double occupancy, for four days, including two days of boat diving with two tanks each, overnight accommodation and breakfast. Equipment and transportation from San José is included. You can rent all the gear, get instruction and do day dives if you don't want to go on a package. Sportfishing is available for about US$250 a day.

The *Hotel Bahía Pez Vela* (☎ 67 0129, 21 1586; Apartado 7758-1000, San José) is a comfortable and attractively located sportfishing resort which offers complete individualised three day fishing packages for about US$4000 (these are supposedly some of the best fishing packages in the country, though I just didn't happen to have four

grand to check it out). Attractive air-conditioned rooms with private bath and hot water (without fishing) are about US$70 a double. There is a restaurant and good snorkelling nearby.

Vista Ocotal (☎ 67 0429) has air-conditioned villas sleeping up to five people. Each villa has a kitchen and private bath; there is a pool and bar, and boat excursions are available. Rates are start at US$73 a double or US$80 for five people.

Between Playas del Coco and Playa Ocotal is the newish *Hotel Villa Casa Blanca* (☎ 67 0448; CRBBG member), a few minutes walk from the beach. This is a small B&B hotel with about 10 pleasant rooms, each with private bath and fan, renting for US$52/58 (including breakfast). There is a pool.

Santa Cruz & Surrounds

To visit beaches further south than Ocotal, you have to return to the main peninsula highway at Comunidad. Then head south for 12 km through the little town of Filadelfia, the community of Belén (18 km) and the small town of Santa Cruz (35 km south of Comunidad).

From Belén, a paved road heads west 25 km to the small community of Huacas, from where shorter unpaved roads radiate to a number of popular beach areas. From Santa Cruz, a 16 km paved road heads west to the tiny community of 27 de Abril, from where unpaved roads also radiate to a number of beaches. It is possible to drive from 27 de Abril to Huacas, thus making all the beaches described in this section accessible from Santa Cruz.

Filadelfia and the beaches near Huacas are described first, then Santa Cruz and the beaches reached via 27 de Abril.

FILADELFIA

Filadelfia is about 32 km from Liberia. The population of Filadelfia and the surrounding district is 6600.

Places to Stay

There is an inexpensive hotel here, the *Cabinas Amelia* (☎ 69 8087) which is three blocks from the parque central.

Getting There & Away

The bus terminal, half a block from the parque central, has several buses a day to San José and hourly buses passing through en route to Nicoya or Liberia.

PLAYA BRASILITO

The road from Huacas hits the ocean at the village of Brasilito, which has a few small stores and restaurants and the cheapest accommodation in the area. There is a beach, but the other beaches nearby are better.

Places to Stay & Eat

About half a km before reaching Brasilito is the *Cabinas Conchal* (☎ 67 4257), with clean, spacious rooms with fans and private bath for US$22/29 single/double. They can arrange bicycle and horse rentals as well as boating and fishing excursions. Nearby is the new *Cabinas El Caracol* which looks about the same price range.

On the plaza in Brasilito, ask about the *Cabinas Olga* (☎ 67 4013 – no sign) which has basic rooms with private bath and fan for US$11. It is away from the beach side of the plaza. On the beach side is the *Hotel Brasilito* (☎ 67 4237) which has simple rooms with private bath and fan for US$30/40. There is a restaurant attached. There are a couple of other simple places to eat. The *Iguana Verde Bar* is popular with divers and other travellers.

About half a km north of Brasilito and set back from the beach somewhat is *Villas Pacifica* (☎ 67 4137) which has air-conditioned condo units with kitchens and satellite TV for about US$100 and up. The premises have a pool, restaurant, bar, ocean views and can arrange fishing etc.

Camping is possible – ask around.

Getting There & Away

See under Playa Flamingo for details.

PLAYA CONCHAL

About two km south of Brasilito, Playa Conchal is so-called for the huge numbers of shells *(conchas)* which are piled up on the beach.

Places to Stay

The new *Condor Club Hotel* (☎ 67 4050, fax 67 4044; in San José ☎ 31 7326, fax 20 0670) has functional rooms with air-conditioning, fans, TV, private hot bath and king-size bed for US$86. There is a restaurant, bar, pool and disco, all with good views.

A reader writes that a farmer near the beach rents cabins and allows camping and use of showers for a small fee.

Getting There & Away

See under Playa Flamingo for details.

PLAYA FLAMINGO

Three or four km north of Brasilito, the road comes to Flamingo, a beautiful white-sand beach. It has been developed for sportfishing and boating and is one of the better known beaches in Costa Rica. Many maps mark the beach with its original name, Playa Blanca, but it is now known as Playa Flamingo after the famous Flamingo Beach Hotel. (There are no flamingoes in Costa Rica.)

There is no village here, so if you are looking for life beyond the hotels, forget it unless you want to walk a couple of km to Brasilito. But if you want comfortable hotels, a pretty beach and boating facilities – and have enough money to pay for them – this is a popular destination.

Places to Stay & Eat

There are no cheap places here. At the far end of the road, the famous *Flamingo Beach Hotel* (☎ 67 4010, fax 67 4060; reservations ☎ 39 1584, fax 39 0257; Apartado 692-4050, Alajuela) has everything you might want for a beach resort vacation. There are three swimming pools, restaurants and bars, casino, snorkelling, boating, diving and fishing facilities. Car rental is also available. Rates are around US$110/120 for a single/double and suites with kitchenettes are more expensive.

Some other luxurious accommodation have opened in recent years. *Hotel Flamingo Marina Resort* (☎ 67 4141, fax 21 8093) offers a variety of rooms (US$109) and suites (US$183). There is a pool, jacuzzi, restaurant and the nearby marina. Other possibilities are the *Hotel Villas Pacifica* (☎ 67 4137/8/9) and the *Villas Flamingo* (☎ 67 4196, 67 4258). A house reservation agency (☎ 67 4007, 67 4009) will reserve a house or condo for extended stays near the beach.

Apart from the hotel restaurants, there is the relatively inexpensive restaurant, *Marie's*, with a variety of snacks and meals.

Getting There & Away
Air The Flamingo Beach Hotel has a private airstrip and plane charters are possible. Alternatively, you can fly to Tamarindo which is the nearest airstrip with scheduled flights. It is about 20 km from Tamarindo and, if you have hotel reservations, you can arrange to be picked up.

Bus Empresa El Folklorico (☎ 68 0545) in Santa Cruz has buses for Playas Conchal, Brasilito, Flamingo and Potrero daily at 4 and 10.30 am and also 2 pm. Buses return at about 6 and 8 am and at 2 and 5 pm – ask about the nearest stop. TRALAPA (☎ 21 7202) has several daily buses from Calle 20, Avenida 3 in San José to Santa Cruz and direct buses from San José to Flamingo at 8 am (express) and 10.30 am (regular). Buses return to San José (five to six hours, US$3.50) at 7 am and 2 pm. Tourist agencies in San José can make reservations for luxury air-conditioned beach buses which will take you there in comfort for about US$20.

Car The road is paved as far as Brasilito. Beyond that it is passable to ordinary cars in the dry season. The worst stretch is the final two or three km to the Flamingo Beach Hotel – if you are driving in the wet season, call ahead to see if you'll need 4WD.

PLAYA POTRERO
This beach is six or seven km north of Brasilito, separated from Flamingo by a rocky headland. There is a small community at Potrero, and this is the end of the bus line.

Isla Santa Catalina is a rocky islet 10 km due west of Playa Pan de Azúcar. It is one of the few places in Costa Rica where the bridled tern is known to nest, from late March to September. Bird-watchers could hire a boat from any of the nearby resorts to go and see this bird in season.

Places to Stay
There are hotels on Playa Potrero a couple of km before reaching the tiny village of Potrero. The *Hotel Bahía Flamingo* (☎ 67 4014, fax 67 4183) has cabins with kitchenettes, fans and hot water for about US$70 a double, and cheaper rooms without kitchenettes. There is a pool and a reasonably priced restaurant. Snorkelling, fishing and boating gear are available for rent, as are bicycles. They had a PADI dive sign outside when I passed through – call them about dive trips.

Cabinas Cristina (☎/fax 67 4006) is about 700 metres away from the sea – if you can handle that, then you'll find these cabins good value for the area. There is a small pool, the management is friendly, and local tours and boat rentals can be arranged. Cabins with kitchenette, refrigerator, fans and private bath are US$22/29 for singles/doubles and US$48.50 for five people. There is an inexpensive restaurant nearby.

A few hundred metres before reaching these hotels you'll find a camping area on the beach.

Getting There & Away
See under Playa Flamingo for details.

PLAYA PAN DE AZÚCAR
This small white-sand beach is two or three km north of Potrero and is the last beach reachable by road. The waters are protected by rocky headlands at either end of the beach and offer good snorkelling.

Places to Stay

The *Hotel Sugar Beach* (☎ 67 4242) is a small hotel attractively located above the Playa Pan de Azúcar. Good air-conditioned rooms with private bath and hot water are about US$85 for a double. The restaurant is good and has a great view. There is some forest in the area and you can watch monkeys and birds from near the hotel. Boat charters are available for fishing, diving and snorkelling. Horse rental is also available.

Getting There & Away

The nearest bus goes to Playa Potrero, from where you'll have to walk about four or five km. Or drive.

PLAYA TAMARINDO

Instead of turning north from Huacas to Brasilito and Flamingo, you can head south on to Tamarindo. The first eight km of the road south of Huacas are paved as far as Villareal and the last five km are unpaved but in good shape. The village of Tamarindo is spread along the last 1.5 km. Both commercial fishing and tourism are of economic importance here.

The beach is large and attractive. Both surfing and windsurfing are good, and there is a wildlife refuge and marine national park nearby. Parts of the beach have rip currents or have barely submerged rocks, so make local enquiries before swimming. This beach has better access by public transport than most of the beaches in the area and is a little more developed. But the beach is large enough that you can still find stretches for yourself.

Tamarindo is definitely popular with surfers. There are good waves at the river estuary north of town and at Playa Grande across the estuary. There is some surfing right off Playa Tamarindo, but the rocks make for limited space. Playa Langosta, a couple of km south of Tamarindo, is a favourite and uninhabited surfing beach. About six or seven km further south is Playa Avellanes, described later in this section.

Tours & Rentals

Papagayo Excursions (☎/fax 68 0859) near the entrance of town arranges excursions such as boat tours, scuba diving, snorkelling, sportfishing, horse rentals and visits to turtle nesting areas on Playa Grande and in the new Parque Nacional Marino Las Baulas. In the centre of town near the Hotel El Milagro is a place called Tamarindo Boutique which rents surfboards, kayaks, snorkels, bikes and other beach gear. The friendly Iguana Surf Shop has reasonably priced kayak and surfboard rentals and meets other beach needs.

Places to Stay & Eat

These will be described in the order they are passed as you enter town on the dirt road. The distance between the first and last place is about 1.5 km. First on the left is the *Hotel Pozo Azul* (☎ 67 4280; in Santa Cruz, ☎ 68 0147), which is several minutes walk from the beach. Whilst the hotel is rather spartan looking, the rooms all have private bath with a choice of fans or air-conditioning. Most rooms have a kitchenette and refrigerator, and there is a pool. Rates are US$21/27 for singles/doubles with fan and US$34 with air-conditioning.

Shortly beyond is the *Pueblo Dorado Hotel* (☎/fax 22 5741; Apartado 1711-1002, San José) which is very clean and has a pre-Columbian motif throughout. There is a small pool and restaurant. Sportfishing and touring can be arranged. Pleasantly bright air-conditioned rooms with electric showers are US$50/60 single/double. Almost opposite the hotel is the well-liked *Johan's Bakery* which opens around 6 am for sales of fresh pastries, croissants etc. They also make pizzas and stay open till about 8 pm.

A couple of hundred metres beyond is the *Hotel/Restaurante El Milagro* (☎ 41 5102, fax 41 8494; Apartado 145-5150, Santa Cruz, Guanacaste). This used to be just a restaurant but a new hotel, under European management, has been added. The staff speaks some Spanish, English, Dutch, French and German. (I can personally attest that at least the first three languages are spoken well, but why can't they speak

Polish? Niesprawiedliwie!) They have a pool, a recommended restaurant and a bar, and attract young adults. Local tours of all kinds are arranged. Nice rooms with fan and private electric shower are US$40/46 single/double, including breakfast. Air-conditioned rooms are planned for 1994 – they cost about US$57.

About half a km up a hill to the left brings you to the new, elegant and luxurious *El Jardín del Edén* (☎ 67 4111, in San Jóse ☎/fax 20 2096, 24 9763; Apartado 1013-1000, San Jóse). This friendly Italian-French run hotel has beautiful and spacious rooms, each with a private patio (nice views) and sitting area. All rooms have fans, a refrigerator and private bath with hot water. Most are air-conditioned, and two apartments have a kitchenette. There is a big pool, jacuzzi, bar and restaurant. All the usual local tours can be arranged. Most rooms are large and rent for US$103/126 a single/double. A few smaller rooms rent for US$86/97. Some of the the large rooms will sleep up to four people; extra adults pay US$17; extra children under 12 years pay US$11.50; kids under five years are free. The apartments are US$149. These prices include continental breakfast. The restaurant specialises in French and Italian dishes.

Back down on the main road through town, you'll see the *Coconut* – a pricey but popular French restaurant with a romantic atmosphere and good food. Shortly beyond are two of the cheapest places to stay in town. On the right, *Hotel Dolly* has long been popular with backpackers and budget travellers. Unfortunately, Dolly isn't doing so well these days and her restaurant is closed. The basic old rooms seem to have been closed down too. Nevertheless, newer double rooms with fans and private bath are quickly snapped up at US$22. Opposite, *Cabinas Marielos* (☎ 41 4843) provides similar accommodation and prices. It's hard to get single rates during the high season.

A few hundred metres beyond is the large *Hotel Tamarindo Diriá* (☎ 68 0652, 68 0474; in San José ☎ 33 0530, fax 55 3355) which is popular with German-speaking tourists (though Spanish and English is spoken). They have a pool, restaurant, bar and make all tour arrangements. Air-conditioned rooms with cable TV and hot-water bathrooms are US$84/90 single/double. One reader tells me that, during the wet season, the management brings mosquito repellent around to the diners at its outdoor restaurant! (There is indoor seating as well.)

Another 300 metres brings you to the end of the road. Here, you'll find another old and reasonably priced favourite – the *Cabinas Zullymar* (☎ 26 4732). The main problem for budget travellers is that there are no single rates (at least during the high season), but the place is popular. Basic rooms with private bath and fan are US$22/27 for doubles/triples; better rooms with refrigerator are US$25/31 for doubles/triples; the best rooms are air-conditioned and have a refrigerator and electric warm shower for US$42/48 for doubles/triples. Opposite, they have a good and reasonably priced restaurant. There are several other restaurants clustered around here, most in the lower-middle price range.

Just beyond the end of the road is the *Tamarindo Resort Club* (☎ 68 0883) which has many air-conditioned cabins with kitchenettes for about US$80. A recent report tells me it's closed, so check first.

Another recent budget recommendation is *Cabinas Rosa Mer* which is in front of some rental and souvenir shops and is reportedly the cheapest place in town.

Getting There & Away

Air The Tamarindo airstrip is about four km away from the village: a hotel bus usually is on hand to pick up arriving passengers. The Hotel Milagro is the SANSA agent and the Hotel Pueblo Dorado is the Travelair agent.

SANSA has flights from San José to Tamarindo on Monday, Wednesday and Friday at 8.45 am, arriving at 9.20 am and leaving for San José at 9.35 am. There are also flights on the same days at 6 am, arriving at Tamarindo at 6.35 am, continuing to Nosara and then Sámara before returning to San José. On Tuesday, Thursday, Saturday and Sunday, flights leave San José at 9 am for Tamarindo, continuing to Sámara before returning to San José. Flights may be less frequent in the wet season. The fare to/from San José is US$33; the fare from Tamarindo to either Nosara or Sámara is US$22.

Travelair has flights from San José to Tamarindo daily except Wednesday and Sunday at 9.30 am, arriving at 10.30 am. On Wednesday and Sunday, the 9.30 am flights go via Liberia and arrive at Tamarindo at 11.05 am. There are also daily flights from San José to Tamarindo at 3 pm, arriving at 4 pm. Return flights to San José leave Tamarindo 20 minutes after arriving. Fares are US$66 one way, US$114 round trip.

Road TRALAPA (☎ 21 7202) buses leave from Calle 20, Avenida 3 in San José at 4 pm daily for Tamarindo (about six hours). Their 6.45 am bus from Tamarindo takes people to Santa Cruz to change for a bus to San José. Empresa Alfaro (☎ 22 2750, 23 8229) at Calle 14, Avenida 3 & 5, San José also has a daily bus at 3.30 pm. Their bus returns from Tamarindo direct to San José at 5.45 am. A bus leaves Santa Cruz at 6.45 am and 8.30 pm daily for Tamarindo.

A taxi from Santa Cruz should cost about US$12 to US$15. Allow twice that from Liberia.

If you are driving, the better road is from Belén to Huacas and south. It is also possible to drive from Santa Cruz 17 km to 27 de Abril on a paved road and then north-west on a dirt road for 19 km to Tamarindo, but this route is rougher, though still passable to ordinary cars.

PARQUE NACIONAL MARINO LAS BAULAS DE GUANACASTE

Formerly a national wildlife refuge, this national marine park was created in 1991 and covers about 500 hectares on the north side of the Río Matapalo estuary, just north of Tamarindo village. In addition, 22,000 hectares of ocean are also protected. Most of the land portion is mangrove swamp containing all six of the mangrove species found in Costa Rica – two species of black mangrove as well as tea, white, red and buttonwood.

This creates a great habitat for caimans and crocodiles as well as numerous bird species, including the beautiful roseate spoonbill.

But the main attraction and *raison d'être* of the park is undoubtedly Playa Grande, which is an important nesting site for the leatherback turtle *(baula* in Spanish). These turtles are the largest in the world, and adults average an incredible 360 kg each; though specimens in excess of 500 kg are not particularly rare. The nesting season is from October to March (especially from November to January), and more than 100 reptiles may be seen laying their eggs on Playa Grande during the course of a night.

Playa Grande is also a favoured surfing beach. So far, surfers and turtles have co-existed within the national park with few problems. The park was created more to control unregulated tourism and to protect the nests from poaching.

Until recently, tourists arrived by the boat-load and harassed the animals by using flash photography, touching the animals and generally acting like yahoos. Now turtle-watchers pay a US$1.50 entry fee to the park and must watch the activities from specified viewing areas.

Other things to look for when visiting this reserve are howler monkeys, raccoons, coatis, otters and a goodly variety of crabs.

Places to Stay

Most people stay in Tamarindo, just south of the park. At the north end of Playa Grande (at the north end of the park) there are a couple of small hotels.

Hotel Las Tortugas (☎/fax 68 0765; Apartado 164, Santa Cruz, Guanacaste) has air-conditioned rooms with private bath starting at US$80. There is a pool, jacuzzi and restaurant and tours to the national park and elsewhere can be arranged.

The hotel is right on the beach. A few hundred metres back from the beach is the *Cabinas Playa Grande* (☎ 37 2552), which has rooms with private bath and fans, some with kitchenette, starting from about US$26 a double. There is a restaurant.

Getting There & Away
Land There are no buses to Playa Grande. You can drive to Huacas and then take the dirt road through Matapalo to Playa Grande. This is a dirt road which may be hard to negotiate in a regular car during the wet months of May to November. If you are staying at the Cabinas Playa Grande, ask them to pick you up from the Matapalo turn-off (where the bus from San José can drop you off). Local hotels will organise turtle-watching tours in season. Tours are also offered by Guanacaste Tours (☎ 66 0306, fax 66 0307) in Liberia and CATA Tours; in San José (☎ 21 5455, fax 21 0200; in Cañas, ☎/fax 69 1203).

Boat Boat tours are available from agencies in Tamarindo or through your hotel.

PLAYA AVELLANES
This popular surfing beach has both left and right breaks. It is about seven km due south of Tamarindo, but closer to 10 km if you walk in along the beaches. Otherwise you have to drive inland to Villareal and then south towards San José Pinilla on a good dirt road, then towards the beach on a poorer road which requires 4WD in the rainy season – and maybe during the dry months too. Alternatively, from 27 de Abril take the road to Playa Junquillal and, four km before reaching Junquillal, turn north at Paraíso and head for Playa Avellanes. This route also requires 4WD and maybe a river crossing in the wet season.

Places to Stay
The attractive *Lagartillo Beach Hotel* (☎ 57 1420) has rooms with private bath and fan for US$40/50 single/double. There is a pool and restaurant and there is forest around the grounds. There are also a few cheap cabinas and camping areas.

PLAYA JUNQUILLAL
This is a wide and wild beach, with high surf, strong rip currents and few people. The beach is two km long and has tide pools and

pleasant walking. The local people go surf fishing here.

Junquillal is about midway between Las Baulas de Guanacaste and Ostional. Sea turtles nest here, but in smaller numbers than at the refuges. There is no village as such, but there are several places to stay. Because of the length of the beach and the lack of a village, the beach is uncrowded.

Places to Stay & Eat
As you arrive, the first place you pass is the entrance to the North American-run *Hotel Iguanazul* (☎/fax 68 0783; Apartado 130-5150, Santa Cruz, Guanacaste). It's about a km from the entrance to the hotel itself, which is elegant and secluded but friendly and fun. Airy and attractive rooms with fans and private hot showers are US$55/70 single/double. There is a pool, good restaurant and good view of the beach. Snorkelling gear (US$5 a half day) and horse rental (US$10 an hour) are available and sportfishing, diving and local tours can be arranged.

About one km beyond the Iguanazul entrance there are two cheaper places near the beach. The cheapest is the *Hotel Playa Junquillal* which charges US$11 per person in basic rooms with private showers. These are often full in the dry season – you can try calling the Paraíso pulpería (☎ 68 0446) and leave a message. There is a restaurant/bar. You could camp here (US$4 per night for use of bathrooms) – or you could probably camp almost anywhere along the beach if you had your own food and water. Almost opposite is the French-run *Hibiscus Hotel* (☎ 41 2282, Apartado 163-5150, Santa Cruz, Guanacaste) which has pleasant rooms with fans and private electric shower for US$40/46 single/double.

About half a km beyond the Hibiscus, the *Hotel Villa Serena* (☎ 68 0737; Apartado 17, Santa Cruz, Guanacaste) is a small, elegant and intimate hotel for lovers and nature lovers. Children are not encouraged. The owners are always in residence to ensure everything is satisfactory. There is a small pool, sauna, tennis court, and horses for rent. Spacious rooms with fans, private hot-water bathrooms and patios facing the beach rent for US$80/120 including three good continental style meals. They are usually full during the dry season, so make reservations.

The *Hotel Antumalal* (☎ 68 0506; Apartado 49, Santa Cruz, Guanacaste) is almost a km beyond and is the end of the road. There are two dozen attractive cabins with private bath and fans, some with air-conditioning. There is a pool, discotheque and tennis court, and wild monkeys reportedly visit the grounds. Rates are about US$70/90 single/double.

Apart from the hotels, there is nowhere to eat unless you return four km to the village of Paraíso where there are a few simple local restaurants, sodas and bars.

Getting There & Away
Bus TRALAPA (☎ 21 7202, 68 0392) Calle 20, Avenida 3 in San José has a daily bus to Junquillal at 2 pm taking about six hours. The return bus leaves Junquillal at 5 am. There is also a daily TRALAPA bus from Santa Cruz at 6.30 pm, returning at 4.45 am. The bus may go only as far as Paraíso, which is four km by foot or taxi from the beach.

There is a luxury bus service to Playa Junquillal from the Gran Hotel in San José, with pick-ups at all major hotels. The bus leaves San José at 6 am on Tuesday, Thursday and Saturday and leaves Junquillal at 2 pm on Wednesday, Friday and Sunday. The fare is US$30 or US$50 round trip, including snacks. Make reservations with Exotur (☎ 27 5169, ☎ /fax 27 2180).

Car & Motorbike If you are driving, it is about 16 km by paved road from Santa Cruz to 27 de Abril, and a further 17 km by unpaved road via Paraíso to Junquillal.

From Junquillal you can head south by taking a turn-off about three km east of Paraíso. This road is marked 'Reserva Ostional' and I'm told is passable in ordinary cars, at least during the dry season. Most people visiting the beaches south of Junquillal reach them from Nicoya. Expect to have to ford some rivers (especially if it has been raining), and carry spare every-

thing. There are no gas stations on this coastal dirt road, and it carries little traffic.

SANTA CRUZ
This small town is on the main peninsula highway 25 km south of Filadelfia, 57 km south of Liberia and 23 km north of Nicoya. A paved road leads 16 km west to 27 de Abril from where dirt roads continue to Playa Tamarindo, Playa Junquillal and other beaches. Santa Cruz makes a possible overnight stop when visiting the peninsula – it gives the visitor a chance to experience Costa Rican life in a small country town.

About three city blocks in the centre of town were burnt to the ground in a devastating fire in 1993. A major town landmark is the Plaza de Los Mangos, a large grassy square named after the four mango trees growing on the north side. Many town addresses are given from that plaza.

There is an annual rodeo and fiesta during the second week in January. There is a small tourist office (☎ 60 0748) 100 metres north of the Plaza de Los Mangos. The population of Santa Cruz and the surrounding district is over 15,000.

Places to Stay & Eat
The *Pensión Isabel* (☎ 68 0173) is on the south-west corner of the Plaza de Los Mangos and has basic but OK rooms for about US$4.50 per person. Cheap and basic wooden boxes are available at the *Pensión Pampera*, 100 metres west and 150 metres south of the Plaza de Los Mangos. Another cheapie is the *Hospedaje Amadita*, 250 metres north of the same Plaza. Also try the family-run *Hospedaje y Restaurante Avellanas* (☎ 68 0808) which is 150 metres north of the Banco Anglo Costarricense. They charge about US$8 for a double with bath. A block away is the cheaper *Posada Tu Casa* with basic but clean rooms and friendly people.

The new *Cabinas La Estancia* (☎ 68 0476, fax 68 0348) is 100 metres west and 50 metres south of the Plaza de Los Mangos. Clean rooms with fans, TV and private bath rent for US$20/26 single/double. On the northern outskirts of town, near the intersection with the main peninsula highway and about 500 metres north of the Plaza de Los Mangos, is the best hotel in town – the *Hotel Diria* (☎ 68 0080; Apartado 58, Santa Cruz, Guanacaste). It has a pool and restaurant, and air-conditioned rooms with private bath cost US$24/41 for a single/double. Occasionally, the hotel may host entertainment at weekends – live marimba music or recorded dance music are possibilities. (Marimbas are wooden xylophone-like instruments of African origin, although some musicologists claim that the Central American version is of Guatemalan Indian origin.)

Check out *La Fabrica de Tortillas*, on a side street 700 metres south of the Plaza de Los Mangos. It's a huge corrugated metal barn which looks like a factory. Inside are plain wooden tables and you eat whatever is available – always homemade typical food cooked right in front of you in the woodstove kitchen. It's interesting, and the food is tasty and inexpensive. Hours are from 5 am to 6.30 pm.

Getting There & Away

There are two bus terminals and some other bus stops. Check your departure points carefully. Transportes La Pampa (☎ 68 0111) buses leave from the terminal on the north side of the Plaza de Los Mangos to Nicoya 14 times a day from 6 am to 9 pm and to Liberia 13 times a day from 5.30 am to 7.30 pm.

The main terminal is 400 metres east of the centre. TRALAPA (☎ 21 7202, 68 0392) has buses leaving Calle 20, Avenida 3 in San José six times a day for Santa Cruz (five to six hours, US$4.50). Buses to San José leave Santa Cruz at 3, 4.30, 6.30, 8.30 and 11.30 am and at 1.30 and 2 pm. Expect one or two buses fewer in the wet season. Alfaro buses between San José and Nicoya also go through Santa Cruz. Buses to Puntarenas leave at 6.20 am and 3.20 pm. Various local villages are also served, including Guaitil about six times a day.

Empresa El Folklórico (☎ 68 0545) has beach buses leaving from the main terminal

and from a bus stop 100 metres south and 50 metres west of the Plaza de Los Mangos. They have buses for Playas Conchal, Brasilito, Flamingo and Potrero at 4 and 10.30 am and 2 and 6.30 pm during the dry season – fewer in the wet. Some TRALAPA beach buses also go via Santa Cruz. A bus leaves for Junquillal at 6.30 am and Tamarindo at 6.45 am and 8.30 pm.

GUAITIL

An interesting excursion from Santa Cruz is the 12 km drive by paved road to the small pottery-making community of Guaitil. Get there by taking the main highway towards Nicoya and then taking the signed Guaitil road to the left, about 1.5 km out of Santa Cruz. This road is lined by trees and is very attractive in April when all the trees are in bloom. The road used to be the main highway to Nicoya and passes the small town of Santa Bárbara before reaching Guaitil where you can see people making pots outside their houses.

The attractive pots are made from local clays and using natural colours in the pre-Columbian Chorotega Indian style. They come in a variety of shapes and sizes – many of the huge pots seen decorating houses and hotels in Guanacaste come from here. Ceramics are for sale outside the potters' houses in Guaitil and also in San Vicente, two km beyond Guaitil by unpaved road. Approximately 100 families are engaged in this industry.

Tours to Guaitil are arranged by Guanacaste Tours in Liberia. There are local buses from Santa Cruz. If you are driving, you can continue on the unpaved road through to Nicoya.

The Nicoya Area

To visit any of the beaches south of Junquillal, many people return to the main peninsula highway and go through Nicoya, 23 km south of Santa Cruz. Dirt roads to the south-west reach the attractive beaches at

Playas Nosara, Garza, Sámara and Carrillo and the wildlife refuge at Ostional. There are airstrips with scheduled flights at Nosara and Sámara/Carrillo. Paved roads east of Nicoya pass the national park at Barra Honda en route to the Tempisque car ferry to the main part of Costa Rica. Paved and unpaved roads to the south-east lead to Playa Naranjo and the Puntarenas car ferry. Travellers using public buses will find it difficult to continue further south to the popular beach at Montezuma and other areas – you'll need to return to Puntarenas and take the passenger ferry back to Paquera.

NICOYA

Nicoya is the most important town on the peninsula and has a population of about 25,000 (including the surrounding district). The town is named after the Chorotega Indian chief Nicoya who welcomed Spanish conquistador Gil González Dávila in 1523. The Indians presented the Spaniard with rich gifts, which is part of the reason why the country became known as Costa Rica. The Chorotegas were the dominant Indian group in the area at the time of the conquest, and many of the local inhabitants can claim to be at least partly of Indian decent.

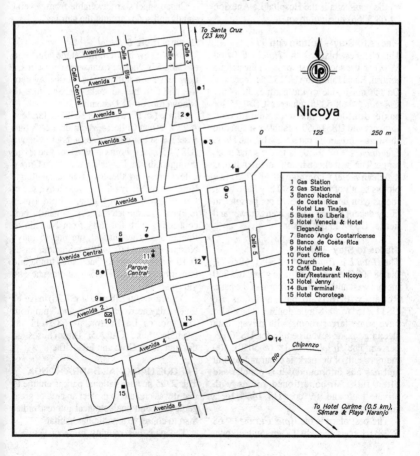

Nicoya

0   125   250 m

1 Gas Station
2 Gas Station
3 Banco Nacional
   de Costa Rica
4 Hotel Las Tinajas
5 Buses to Liberia
6 Hotel Venecia & Hotel
   Elegancia
7 Banco Anglo Costarricense
8 Banco de Costa Rica
9 Hotel Alí
10 Post Office
11 Church
12 Café Daniela &
   Bar/Restaurant Nicoya
13 Hotel Jenny
14 Bus Terminal
15 Hotel Chorotega

To Santa Cruz
(23 km)

Avenida 9
Calle 1 Bis
Calle 1
Calle 3
Calle Central
Avenida 7
Avenida 5
Avenida 3
Avenida 1
Avenida Central
Calle 5
Parque Central
Avenida 4
Avenida 6
Chipanzo
Río
To Hotel Curime (0.5 km),
Sámara & Playa Naranjo

A major landmark is the shining white colonial church of San Blas, dating back to the mid-1600s. The church is slowly undergoing restoration but can be visited. There is a small collection of local pre-Columbian and colonial artifacts. Look for it on the north-east corner of the attractive Parque Central, which is an inviting spot to rest and people watch.

Nicoya is now the commercial centre of the cattle industry as well as the political capital and transportation hub of the peninsula. US dollars can be exchanged at one of the several banks in town. The main hospital on the peninsula is the Hospital La Anexión (☎ 68 5066) north of town.

Places to Stay – bottom end

The cheapest place is the *Hotel Ali* (☎ 68 5148) on the south-west corner of the parque central. Basic rooms are US$3.25 per person. On the north side of the parque, the *Hotel Venecia* (☎ 68 5325) charges US$7.25 for basic double rooms with shared cold showers and US$14.50 a double with private showers – no single rates. Nearby, the *Hotel Elegancia* (☎ 68 5159) is in the same price range. The best cheap hotel, but often full, is the clean *Hotel Chorotega* (☎ 68 5245) two blocks south of the parque. They have basic rooms with fans for US$3.75 per person and fairly decent rooms with private shower and fan for US$7.25 per person.

Places to Stay – middle

The *Hotel Las Tinajas* (☎ 68 5081, 68 5777, fax 68 5096) is clean and quite good. It is 200 metres west and 100 metres north of the park. Rooms with private bath and fans are US$11/15 for a single/double. They also have some larger rooms with private bath sleeping six or seven people for US$6 per person. The *Hotel Jenny* (☎ 68 5050), 100 metres south of the park, is clean and helpful and has bus information. It is popular and often full. Air-conditioned rooms with private bath and TV cost US$14/21 for a single/double.

The best place is the *Hotel Curime* (☎ 68 5238) which is about half a km south of town on the road to Playa Sámara. There is a pool and restaurant, and rooms have air-conditioning, TV, a refrigerator and private electric showers. The rates are US$25 per person.

Places to Eat

There are three or four Chinese restaurants in the town centre and they are considered the best places to eat. *Café Daniela*, a block east of the park, serves breakfasts, burgers, pizzas, and snacks and is popular. Next door, the Chinese-run *Bar/Restaurant Nicoya* is good for standard meals.

Cheap snacks are available from several stands and sodas around the parque.

Getting There & Away

There is a new bus terminal at the south end of Calle 5 in Nicoya from where most buses now leave. An antique bus on display here was the first bus to make the San José to Nicoya run, on 11 December 1958.

Alfaro (in Nicoya ☎ 68 5032, in San José ☎ 22 2750) at Calle 14, Avenida 3 & 5, San José, has six or eight buses a day to Nicoya (US$4.50, six hours). Most of these go through Liberia, Filadelfia and Santa Cruz – a few cross on the Río Tempisque ferry. Buses from Nicoya to San José leave seven times a day between 4 am and 4 pm. Buses to Playa Naranjo leave at 5.15 am and 1 pm, connecting with the ferry from Naranjo to Puntarenas. There is a 1 pm bus to Playa Nosara, a 3 pm bus to Playa Sámara, buses at 10 am and 3 pm to Quebrada Honda and one or two a day to a variety of other nearby villages.

Departures for Liberia (US$1.25) leave 17 times a day between 4.30 am and 7 pm from Transportes La Pampa (☎ 68 0111) at Avenida 1 and Calle 5. These buses go through Santa Cruz and Filadelfia.

PARQUE NACIONAL BARRA HONDA

This 2295 hectare national park is unique in that it was created to protect an area of great geological and speleological interest rather than to conserve a particular habitat.

The park lies roughly midway between

Nicoya and the mouth of the Río Tempisque in a limestone area that has been uplifted into coastal hills over 500 metres in height. A combination of rainfall and erosion has created a series of deep caves, some in excess of 200 metres in depth. There are reportedly 42 caves, but only 19 of them have been explored, and so Barra Honda is of special interest to speleologists looking for something new.

The caves come complete with stalagmites, stalactites and a host of beautiful and (to the non-speleologist) lesser known formations with intriguing names such as fried eggs, organs, soda straws, popcorn, curtains, columns, pearls, flowers and shark's teeth. Cave creatures, including bats, sightless salamanders, fish in the streams running through the caves, and a variety of invertebrates, live in the underground system. Pre-Columbian human skeletons have also been discovered, although who these people were or how they got into the caves remains a mystery.

A few of the caves have access for the general public. The 55 metre deep Terciopelo Cave is one of the most beautiful and frequently visited. Visitors may require permits from the Servicio de Parques Nacionales to enter some of the other caves. These include: Santa Ana, the deepest, at 249 metres; the Trampa ('trap'), which has a vertical 52 metre drop; the Nicoya, where human remains were found; and the Pozo Hediondo ('stink-pot'), which has a large bat colony.

Above the ground, the Barra Honda hills have trails and are covered with the deciduous vegetation of a tropical dry forest. The top of Cerro Barra Honda boasts a lookout with a good view of the area. There are waterfalls in the rainy reason and animals year-round. Howler and white-faced monkeys, armadillos and coatimundis are seen. Amazonian skunk (also called the striped hog-nosed skunk) *Conepatus semistriatus* are supposedly frequently sighted.

Information

The dry season is considered to be the best time for caving because entering the caves is dangerous and discouraged during the rainy months. However, you can come any time to climb the hills, admire the views and observe the wildlife. If you come in the dry season, however, be sure to carry several litres of water and let someone know where you are going. Two German hikers died at Barra Honda in 1993; they planned a short hike of about 90 minutes and didn't want to hire a local guide. They got lost, had no water and died of dehydration.

There is a ranger station in the south-west corner of the park where basic sketch maps and information may be obtained. Park entry is US$1.50 per day. About 350 metres beyond the station there is an area with latrines and water where camping is permitted for US$2.20 per day. Trails from the ranger station lead to the top of Cerro Barra Honda – allow about a half day for the round trip.

The park is part of the Área de Conservación Tempisque (☎ 67 1062), with administrative headquarters in Bagaces. You should obtain permits from them if you wish to explore the cave system. If you want to hire a guide, contact Las Delicias.

Proyecto Las Delicias

This locally run project provides a basic tourist infrastructure as well as work for local people. Just outside the park entrance they have food, accommodation, guide services and information. This is an excellent way to involve the local population in conserving the area – it is a new project and it will be interesting to see how it evolves.

Three small cabins with a shower and six beds are available for US$11 per person. Camping is US$2.20 per person. A simple restaurant serves typical local meals. A guide service is available for hiking the trails within the park and also for descending into the most popular caves. A descent costs about US$50 for a group of up to eights cavers. This covers the costs of guide and equipment – ladders and ropes are used and you should be reasonably fit. To reserve accommodation or guide service, call the park-side community of Santa Ana (☎ 68 5580). Guides are also available from Barra Honda (☎ 68 5406), El Flor and Corralillo (☎ 68 5455). Only Spanish is spoken.

Getting There & Away

Getting to the park is somewhat confusing, because a map shows two ways to enter the park. Barra Honda is shaped like an inverted U; at the east end is the village of Quebrada Honda, with a dirt road leading north from it into the park. Past reports indicate that there was an administration centre here, but it is now closed and this is no longer the best way to enter the park.

The west arm of the inverted U is the way to the ranger station. If you are driving from the Tempisque ferry, you will see a sign on the right hand side for 'Barra Honda' about 16 km after leaving the ferry and 1.5 km before you reach the main peninsula highway between Nicoya and Carmona. If you are driving from the peninsula highway, take the turn-off for the Tempisque ferry and look for the Barra Honda road to your left after 1.5 km – there is no sign if you are coming this way. From the turn-off, the road goes four km to the small community of Nacaome, from where a signed dirt road goes a further six km into the park. The community of Santa Ana is passed en route. This road has some steep and rough stretches, and you may require 4WD in the rainy season.

No buses go to the park, but you can get a bus from Nicoya to Nacaome (the bus may be signed Barra Honda) and walk the last six km. There is also a daily bus from Nicoya to the village of Santa Ana, which is two or three km from the ranger station. A bus also goes from Nicoya to Corralillo, about four km from the park entrance.

RÍO TEMPISQUE FERRY

The car and passenger ferry crossing is 17.5 km from the main peninsula road. See the description of the Río Tempisque ferry in the North-western Costa Rica chapter for more details.

PLAYA NOSARA

This attractive white-sand beach is backed by a pocket of luxuriant vegetation which attracts birds and wildlife. The area has not been logged, partly because of the nearby wildlife refuge and partly because of real estate development – an unlikely sounding combination.

There are many houses and condominiums, some of which are lived in year-round, and others which can be rented by the week or month. The permanent occupants are mainly foreign (especially North American) retirees. The expatriate community is interested in protecting some of the forest, which makes Nosara an attractive area to live in, and you can see parrots and toucans, armadillos and monkeys just a few metres away from the beach.

The small beaches of Playa Pelada and Playa Guiones, a couple of km south of Playa Nosara, are both attractive and worth visiting. Playa Guiones has corals and the best snorkelling opportunities, Playa Pelada has a simple restaurant near which you can camp, and Playa Nosara has surf.

Note that the village and airport of Nosara are five km inland from the beach. Basic food supplies and gas are available in the village. Thus the Nosara area (three beaches, airport and village) is very spread out and lacks a real 'centre'. This makes it hard to get around if you don't know the place – ask for local help and directions.

Places to Stay & Eat

Budget travellers will want to either camp on the beach or stay in the village, inland. In the village are the basic but adequate *Cabinas Chorotega* (☎ 68 0836) which charges US$7.25 per person in rooms with fans. *Cabinas Agnel* has clean rooms with fans and private bath for US$8.75 per person. *Betty's Restaurant* on the soccer field serves Mexican food and *La Lechuza* on the outskirts of the village is locally popular. There are other sodas and restaurants.

A few minutes walk from Playa Pelada is the reasonably priced and recommended *Rancho Suizo Lodge* (Apartado 14, Bocas de

Nosara, Guanacaste 5233). Run by René and Ruth, a friendly Swiss couple, the lodge provides pleasant bungalows with private bath and fan for US$29/40 single/double. There is a small pool and restaurant (make advance reservations for dinner) and horse rental and local tours (eg turtle watching in season for US$20) can be arranged on request. The contact in San José is Saragundi Tours (☎ 55 0011, fax 55 2155).

The Italian/Swiss-run *Estancia Nosara* (☎/fax 68 0378; Apartado 37, Nosara, Guanacaste) is about 1.5 km away from the beach at the south end of the Nosara area. Despite this, it is a attractive place to stay with a nice pool, tennis, restaurant and bar surrounded by plenty of trees. Bicycles are rented for US$7 per day and horse rentals and tours are available on request. Rooms with refrigerator, kitchenette, private electric showers and fans are US$40/47 single/double.

A recommended place to stay is the well-run *Hotel Playa Nosara* (☎ 68 0495; Apartado 4, Nosara, Guanacaste). It is attractively located on a hill top between Playas Pelada and Guiones and has beautiful beach views from the balconied rooms. There is a pool and restaurant. The North American owners speak six languages and will help with organising local tours. Rooms have private baths with hot water and fans, and cost about US$57/75 for a single/double.

The *Condominio Los Flores* (☎ 68 0696) is perched on a hill overlooking the beach and rents two-bedroom apartments with kitchens and hot water. Expect to pay about US$500 per week. If you are interested in long-term (minimum one week) rental of a house, try calling ☎ 68 0747. Houses start at about US$250 per week.

The *Gilded Iguana Bar & Restaurant* (☎ 68 0749) has been recommended for its famous Black Panther cocktail and good sandwiches and snacks – but I couldn't find it when I passed through town. OK, so I'm stupid (or they've closed). They have apartments with kitchenettes for rent.

Down on Playa Pelada, grab a casado for just US$3 at *Olga's Bar & Restaurant* or get a fish dinner for about US$5 to US$6. Another restaurant which has been recommended is *Casi Paraíso*.

A new hotel at the south end of the beaches has locals up in arms because the construction has been insensitive to their efforts to conserve the area. Locals say that forest has been replaced by large open areas with non-native plants, wildlife has been driven away, and roads have been torn up but not repaired.

Getting There & Away

Air SANSA (☎ 21 9414) has flights from San José to Nosara on Monday, Wednesday and Friday. Flights leave at 6 am, stop at Tamarindo, arrive at Nosara at 7.05 am, continue to Sámara and get back to San José at 8.25 am. The fare is US$33 from San José and US$22 from Tamarindo. Make reservations well in advance during the dry season, and reconfirm frequently.

Travelair (☎ 68 0836 in Nosara, 32 7883 in San José) has flights from San José direct to Nosara at 10 am on Wednesday and Sunday, arriving at 10.55 am and stopping in Sámara en route back to San José. The fare is US$58 one way, US$100 round trip.

Road The 35 km dirt road from Nosara to Nicoya (via Guastomatal) is a poor one – locals told me it was passable only to 4WD vehicles and there are no signs. Most people take the longer road past Playa Garza and Playa Sámara to Nicoya – this is about 60 km and is not in great shape either. It has many sudden dips and washboarded areas and there may be rivers to ford in the wet season – but this is the way the bus comes, and there are signs. You may have some difficulty in getting through in an ordinary car during the rainy season. It is also possible to continue north, past Ostional, to Paraíso and Junquillal, though you may need 4WD in the rainy season.

There is a daily bus from Nicoya at 1 pm. Buses return to Nicoya at 6 am. The journey lasts 2½ to five hours depending on road conditions.

REFUGIO NACIONAL DE FAUNA SILVESTRE OSTIONAL

This coastal refuge includes the beaches of Playa Nosara, Playa Ostional, the mouth of the Río Nosara, and the beach-side village of Ostional.

The reserve is a narrow strip about eight km long but only a few hundred metres wide. The protected land area is 162 hectares; 587 hectares of adjoining sea are also protected.

The main attraction and reason for creation of the refuge is the annual nesting of the olive ridley sea turtle on Playa Ostional. This beach and the Playa Nancite in Parque Nacional Santa Rosa are the most important nesting grounds for the olive ridley in Costa Rica (see Parque Nacional Santa Rosa for more information). The nesting season lasts from July to November, and August to October are peak months.

The turtles tend to arrive in large groups of hundreds or even thousands of individuals – these mass arrivals, or *arribadas*, occur every three or four weeks and last for about a week, usually on the dark nights preceding a new moon.

However, you can see turtles in lesser numbers almost any night you go during the nesting season. Villagers will guide you to the best places.

Coastal residents used to harvest both eggs and turtles indiscriminately and this made the creation of a protected area essential for the continued wellbeing of the turtles. An imaginative conservation plan has allowed the inhabitants of Ostional to continue to harvest the eggs from early layings. Most turtles return to the beach several times to lay new clutches, and earlier eggs may be trampled or damaged by later layings. Thus it seems reasonable to allow the locals to harvest the first batches and sell them – they are popular snacks in bars throughout the country.

The leatherback and Pacific green turtle also nest here in smaller numbers. Apart from the turtles, there are iguanas, crabs, howler monkeys, coatimundis and many birds to be seen. Some of the best bird-watching is at the south-east end of the refuge, near the mouth of the Río Nosara, where there is a small mangrove swamp.

The rocky Punta India at the north-west end of the refuge has many tide pools abounding with marine creatures such as sea anemones, sea urchins, starfish, shellfish and fish-fish. Along the beach are thousands of almost transparent ghost crabs, bright red Sally Lightfoot crabs and a variety of lizard. The vegetation behind the beach is sparse, and consists mainly of deciduous trees such as frangipani and stands of cacti.

The rainy season is from May to December and the annual rainfall is about 2000 mm. The best time to see the turtles is the rainy season, so be prepared. Average daytime temperatures are 28°C. There is a Universidad de Costa Rica research station and the villagers of Ostional are helpful with information and will guide you to the best areas. Ostional has a small pulpería where you can get basic food supplies. Beware of very strong currents off the beach – it is not suitable for swimming.

Places to Stay

Camping is permitted, but there are no camping facilities. The *Hospedaje Guacamaya* next to the Ostional pulpería (☎ 68 0467 and ask for Melvin Chavarría) has a five basic box-like rooms for rent at US$3 per person – bring mosquito coils. They are usually full during the best turtle-nesting nights.

Getting There & Away

The refuge begins at Playa Nosara, and Ostional village is about eight km north-west of Nosara village. This unpaved road is passable, but some minor rivers need to be forded in the wet season, so 4WD or at least high clearance may be needed. From the road joining Nosara beach and village, turn north just before the Supermercado La Paloma. After 0.4 km take the right fork and continue another 0.4 km across the Río Nosara over a new bridge. After the bridge there is a T-junction; take the right fork and continue another 1.2 km to a T-junction where you take the left fork. From here continue on the main road north to Ostional about 5.5 km away. Reports indicate that the road from Santa Cruz to just before Paraíso and south along the coast to Ostional is better – but I haven't taken it.

During the dry months, there is a daily bus from Santa Cruz at noon – this may or may not run during the wet season, depending on road conditions. Many of the better hotels in the region offer tours to Ostional during egg-laying periods. Tours are also offered by Guanacaste Tours (☎ 66 0306, fax 66 0307) in Liberia and CATA Tours (in San José (☎ 21 5455, fax 21 0200; in Cañas ☎/fax 69 1203).

BAHÍA GARZA

This small bay is about 10 km south of Nosara along a dirt road. A beach is picturesquely set in a rocky cove with an island at the mouth of the bay.

Places to Stay

There is one good hotel, the *Villagio Guaria Morada* (☎ 68 0784, 33 2476, fax 22 4073; Apartado 860-1007, Centro Colón, San José). There are 30 pleasant cottages, each with private bath, renting for US$130 a double including breakfast and dinner. There is a good restaurant, pool and disco, and horse-riding, fishing and snorkelling can be arranged.

PLAYA SÁMARA

This beach is 16 km south-east of Bahía Garza and about 35 km south-west of Nicoya. Sámara has a beautiful, gentle, white-sand beach which has been called one of the safest and prettiest in Costa Rica. It has gained much popularity in recent years. Former president Oscar Arias has a vacation house near here, as do many other ticos. It is also a favourite beach for tourists, and has an improving bus and air service.

The village has a general store, a disco-theque and a couple of basic hotels, restaurants and bars. The Pulpería Mileth has a public phone and bus information. Things are a little spread out – ask for directions. Local inhabitants (other than retirees) do a little farming and fishing.

Places to Stay & Eat

You can camp near the *Soda Yuré* for about US$1.50 per person or at *Coco's* for about US$2.25 per person. *Soda Yure's* offers cheap typical food – casados are US$2.50 and other plates are about US$4, but no beer is served. Ask around for other places to camp.

A popular cheap and basic place to stay is the *Hotel Playa Sámara* (☎ 68 0724) which charges about US$6 per person. There is a cheap but reasonable soda attached, and a disco next door. *Cabinas & Comedor Arenas* (☎ 68 0445) is better and has rooms with private bath and fan for US$29 a double – they'll give you the room for US$14.50 a single if there is space. Other cheap and basic places to try is the *Cabinas Sámara* (☎ 68 0222) which has rooms with private baths, and the cheaper *Cabinas Magaly* which has rooms with shared bath.

The French-Canadian-run *Albergue Casa del Mar* is next to the Super Sámara grocery store and charges US$20/30 for singles/doubles in spacious, very clean and pleasant rooms with fans. The bathrooms are separate. Continental breakfast is included. Opposite, a house advertises rooms for rent.

Next to the Cabinas Arenas is the *Hotel Sámara Beach* (☎ 68 0445, in San José 33 9398) which has rooms with private bath and fans for US$55 a double and with air-conditioning for US$65. They have a small pool. Nearby is *Colocho's* – a restaurant which advertises international food.

The German-run *Hotel Marbella* (☎ 33 9980) is set inland somewhat and offers clean rooms with private hot shower and fans for US$42/46 single/double. The hotel has received several recommendations. There is a pool, restaurant and bar, and tours and horse rental can be arranged.

The best hotel is at the south end of the beach, a little over a km from the village. This is the *Hotel Las Brisas del Pacífico* (☎ 68 0876, in San José 33 9840; Apartado 129-6100, San José). There is a pool, jacuzzi and a good restaurant with a German chef known for his delicious desserts as well as tasty meals. The hotel has a gift shop and horses, boats, surfboards and diving gear are available for rent. Comfortable and spacious rooms, all with private hot showers, are US$60 a double with fan, larger bungalows are US$85 a double and air-conditioned suites are US$110 a double. A third person can be added for US$17, but single rates are difficult to get during the dry season.

Getting There & Away
Air The SANSA agent is at the Hotel Las Brisas del Pacífico and the Travelair agent is at the Hotel Sámara Beach. The airport is between Playa Sámara and Playa Carrillo and serves both communities. Sometimes the airport is referred to as Carrillo.

SANSA has flights on Monday, Wednesday and Friday leaving San José at 6 am and stopping at Tamarindo and Nosara before arriving at Sámara at 7.35 am. The return flight to San José direct leaves at 7.50 am and takes 35 minutes. On Tuesday, Thursday, Saturday and Sunday, SANSA's flight leaves San José at 9 am, stops at Tamarindo and arrives at Sámara at 10.05 am, leaving at 10.20 am for San José. The fare from San José is US$33; the fare from Tamarindo is US$22.

Travelair has flights on Wednesday and Sunday at 10 am, stopping at Nosara before arriving at Sámara at 11.10 am. The return flight to San José direct leaves at 11.40 am and takes 50 minutes. The fare from San José is US$58 one way or US$100 round trip.

Road Empresa Alfaro (☎ 22 2750 in San José) has a daily bus to Sámara at noon taking six hours. The bus returns to San José at 4 am (it may leave at 1 pm on Sunday – check locally). Tickets and bus stop are at Pulpería Mileth. Buses from Nicoya leave at 8 am and 3 pm, take about two hours and cost US$1.25. The return is at 6 am and 4 pm. On weekends buses leave only at 4 pm and during the wet season there is only one bus a day, and it takes longer. The buses from Nicoya continue on to Playa Carrillo.

See under Nosara for a description of the road between Nicoya and Sámara.MARA

PLAYA CARRILLO
This beach is three or four km south-east of Sámara, and is a smaller, quieter version of it. On a recent dry-season visit, I saw only four or five people on the beach here. The two beaches are separated by the narrow Punta Indio and thus the beaches are almost, but not quite, contiguous.

Places to Stay
There are a few cheap places, including basic rooms offered by the *Bar El Mago* and the cabins rented by the *artesanía* store near the huge strangler fig tree by the beach. These rent for about US$11 per person.

The most famous place is the Japanese-run *Guanamar* (same management as the Hotel Herradura in San José (☎ 39 0033, fax 38 2388) which is attractively located at the south end of the beach on a cliff with good views and ocean breezes. There is a pool and restaurant. Rooms with ocean view, private bath and fans are US$140 for a double; without ocean views, US$115. There is a private airstrip into which you can charter planes. Horses, mountain bikes and snorkelling gear are all available for about US$7 per hour – discounts for half and full-day rentals. Boogie boards are US$4 per hour and sea kayaks are US$10 per hour. Water skiing is also available. Sportfishing, however, is the big and most expensive attraction.

Getting There & Away
See under Playa Sámara.

The Southern Peninsula

SOUTH-WEST COAST
It is possible to continue south-east beyond Playa Carrillo, more or less paralleling the coast, to reach the southern tip of the peninsula. There are various small communities and deserted beaches along this stretch of coast, but accommodation and public transport is minimal. Thus this area is very much separated from Nicoya, although it is close to it.

Places to Stay & Eat

Playa San Miguel has an unnamed beach hotel where very basic cabins rent for US$3.75 per person. A bar/restaurant is attached.

In San Francisco de Coyote, a small village four km inland from Playa Coyote, there are a couple of sodas and pulperías. The friendly folk at *Soda Familiar* offer clean beds for US$3.75 per person and horse rental for US$10. The family-run *Rancho Loma Clara* is similarly priced. Both places prepare simple country meals. The *Centro Social Los Amigos* offers beer and pool. (The telephone number for San Francisco de Coyote is ☎ 67 1236 – leave a message.)

About 300 metres from Playa Coyote is the *Bar/Cabinas Veranera* which offers cheap accommodation.

You could camp in several places if you had a car and were self sufficient.

Getting There & Away

Bus The bus company at Calle 12, Avenida 7 & 9, opposite the Puntarenas bus terminal in San José, has a daily bus which crosses the Golfo de Nicoya on the Puntarenas ferry and continues through the villages of Jicaral, San Francisco de Coyote and on to Bejuco. The bus leaves San José at 3 pm, passing San Francisco de Coyote at 10 pm and arriving at Bejuco at 11 pm. The return bus leaves Bejuco at 4 am and passes through San Francisco de Coyote at 5 am.

There don't seem to be buses from Nicoya, and I was unable to discover any other bus services further south along this coast.

Car & Motorbike It is about 70 km by very rough road from Playa Carrillo to the town of Cóbano – allow about four hours for the trip if you have a 4WD vehicle and encounter no delays. Several rivers have to be forded, including the Río Ora about five km east of Carrillo. This river can be impassable at high tide, even to 4WDs, so check the tides and water levels.

An easier route, if you are driving, is to head inland from Playa Carrillo, through the communities of San Pedro, Soledad (also known as Cangrejal) and Bejuco and down to the coast at either Islita (to the north-west) or Jabilla (to the south-east). This loop takes about 18 km and is very steep in places – I got through in a regular car in the dry season, but you'll probably need 4WD in the wet.

Adventurous drivers with 4WD (or maybe a regular car in the dry season) could continue on past Playa Coyote, Playa Caletas, Playa Arío and Playa Manzanillo (camp at any of these places if you are self-sufficient) before heading inland via Río Negro to Cóbano, Montezuma and Cabo Blanco. These last three places are usually reached by the road which connects with the Puntarenas to Playa Naranjo ferry and follows the south-eastern part of the peninsula; they are described in the next section.

SOUTH-EAST CORNER

From Nicoya, buses go south-east to the car ferry terminal of Playa Naranjo, about a 72 km drive. To travel beyond Playa Naranjo you need your own transportation – all buses either end at the car ferry or cross over to Puntarenas. If you want to go further south and don't have your own car, cross the Golfo de Nicoya on the car ferry to Puntarenas and then recross the gulf on the Puntarenas-Paquera passenger ferry. Buses go from Paquera further south.

Two villages of note on the Nicoya-Playa Naranjo run are Jicaral and Lepanto. Buses from San José go through Jicaral once a day on their way to the south-west peninsula (see above). There are a couple of cheap and basic places to stay here, including the *Hospedaje El Malinche* (☎ 64 0083), *Pensión San Martín* (☎ 64 0169) and the better *Hotel Guamale* (☎ 64 0073) behind the church. There are 4WD taxis available to take you anywhere you want to go.

Near Lepanto there are salt pans visible from the road. This is a good place to stop and look for waders – I saw roseate spoonbills here, among others.

PLAYA NARANJO

This village is the terminal for the Puntarenas

car ferry. The beach is not very exciting. Most ferry passengers continue on to Nicoya by bus or drive further south into the Península de Nicoya. Several hotels offer lodging for those waiting for a ferry.

Places to Stay

The *Hotel El Paso* (☎ 61 2610; Apartado 232-2120, San José) has clean rooms with fans for US$16.50/21 single/double, with private bath for US$25/29 single/double, and with air-conditioning and TV for US$41 a double. An air-conditioned cabin with refrigerator, TV and private bath rents for US$66 for six people. There is a good restaurant serving fresh seafood and a pool.

The *Hotel Oasis del Pacífico* (☎/fax 61 1555; Apartado 200-5400, Puntarenas) has adult's and children's pools, pleasant grounds, and horses and boats for rent. Sportfishing is available. The restaurant is good and not too expensive. Rooms with fans and private bath have hammocks in their patios and rent for US$44/58 for a single/double. Day use of pools, hammocks and showers is US$3. The hotel's brochure claims that 'your room is free any day the sun don't shine'.

Getting There & Away

All transport is geared to the arrival and departure of the ferry. The hotels pick up ferry passengers if they know you are coming – although you could walk as it's not far.

Buses meet the ferry and take passengers to Nicoya, three to four hours away. There are no other public transport options except for 4WD taxis, which can take you to Paquera for about US$25.

The ferry (☎ 61 1069 for information) leaves daily at 5.15 and 8.30 am, noon, and 3 and 6 pm. (Some crossings may be cancelled in the rainy season.) Fares for car and driver are US$8.10, US$1.10 for adults, US$0.60 for children and US$2.50 for bicycles and motorbikes. Note that on most buses using the ferry, passengers have to get off the bus to buy a separate ticket – don't dally in the nearby sodas, as the bus may leave without you!

BAHÍA GIGANTE

This bay is about nine km south-east of Playa Naranjo.

Places to Stay

The good *Hotel Bahía Gigante* (☎ 61 2442) has pleasant views of the bay, and large forested grounds where you can hike and bird-watch. Monkeys and other mammals can be seen. Tours to a nearby waterfall or boat trips to the nearby islands can be arranged, and fishing and horse-riding is available. There is a restaurant and pool. Spacious rooms with fans and private baths are US$35/40 single/double; there are also some more expensive condo apartments. They'll pick you up at Playa Naranjo.

PAQUERA

It is about 25 km by road from Playa Naranjo to the village of Paquera which is four km from the Paquera ferry terminal. Most travellers pass straight through on their way to or from Montezuma – perhaps that is a good reason to stop here for a night and meet some locals for a change. There is a Banco de Costa Rica.

Places to Stay

There are a couple of cheap hotels in the village. The *Cabinas Ginana* (☎ 61 1444, ext 119) is considered the best with rooms with private showers and fans renting for about US$11 a double. There are also the *Cabinas Rosita* (☎ 61 1444 ext 206) and some family hospedajes.

Down by the ferry dock, a sign points the way to *Fred's Folly* (☎ 88 2014), three km away along the coast on a driveable unpaved road. They have cabins for US$39 and offer meals, fishing trips and excursions to Isla Tortuga.

Getting There & Away

Boat The passenger ferries operate to Puntarenas at 8 am and 5 pm daily, plus 12.30 pm in the high season. Ferries leave

Puntarenas for Paquera at 6.15 and 11 am (high season), and 3 pm. The fare is US$1.50 for adults, US$1.20 for motorbikes and US$0.90 for bicycles and children. Crossing time is about 90 minutes.

Road A very crowded truck takes passengers into Paquera village. Most travellers take the bus from the ferry terminal to Montezuma (two hours, US$2.50). The bus can be crowded; try to get off the ferry early to get a seat. During the wet season this bus may only go as far as Cóbano, six km short of Montezuma, and you may have to continue by 4WD. A 4WD taxi to Montezuma costs about US$29; taxis usually meet the ferry.

Parts of the road from Paquera to Montezuma have been paved, though much remains unpaved. Work is slowly progressing on paving this road, which will undoubtedly change this part of Costa Rica.

There are no southbound buses. A 4WD taxi to Playa Naranjo is about US$25.

REFUGIO NACIONAL DE VIDA SILVESTRE CURÚ

This small 84 hectare refuge is at the eastern end of the Península de Nicoya, about five km south of Paquera village. Despite its small size, a great variety of habitats exists here. There are deciduous and semideciduous forests with large forest trees, mangrove swamps with five different mangrove species, sand beaches fringed by palm trees, and rocky headlands. The forested areas are the haunts of deer, monkeys, agoutis and pacas, and three species of cat have been recorded. Iguanas, crabs, lobsters, chitons, shellfish, sea turtles and other marine creatures are found on the beaches and in the tide pools. The snorkelling and swimming is good. Birders have recorded 115 species of birds, but there are probably more. For such a small place, it has a lot of wildlife.

An intriguing feature of this national wildlife refuge is that it is privately owned. The owners, Señora Julieta Schutz and children (☎ 61 2392, 26 4333), can provide tours, rustic accommodation, and home-cooked meals if arranged in advance. The Schutzs

consider Curú to be a living laboratory for researchers and students (who have priority for the rooms) but travellers are sometimes accommodated. Most of the better hotels in the area will arrange day tours to Curú. The reserve is not signed and is down a dirt road (as is everything in this area). Call in advance if you want to visit to get directions, and make sure the gate is open.

PLAYAS POCHOTE & TAMBOR

These two long beaches are protected by the Bahía Ballena (Whale Bay), the largest bay on the southern peninsula coastline. The beaches begin 14 km south of Paquera at the tiny community of Pochote in the north, and stretch for about eight km to the village of Tambor – they are divided by the narrow and wadable estuary of the Río Pánica. The calm beaches are safe for swimming, and whales are sometimes sighted in the bay.

Places to Stay & Eat

At Playa Pochote, stay at the quiet and friendly *Zorba's Place* (☎ 61 3233 for messages). Yes, the owners are Greek/Costa Rican. They have simple but clean rooms on the beach at US$18 a double or US$29 a double with private bath. There are fans, breakfast is included, and there is a restaurant with meals for about US$5. There's not much else in the immediate vicinity – the owner told me that Erich von Daniken has stayed here for weeks whilst writing his books.

Right in the middle of the Bahía Ballena shoreline is the *Hotel Playa Tambor* (☎ 61 2039; fax 61 2069) which, with over 400 guest rooms, is by far the largest hotel in the country. It is also the most controversial in the history of tourism in Costa Rica. The Spanish owners, Grupo Barceló, were sued in 1992 for a long series of environmental violations during construction. These include illegally filling in a swamp, taking massive amounts of sand off beaches and gravel from rivers (causing serious erosion), improperly treating sewage, and harassing passers-by on the beach. (By law, the first 50 metres of all Costa Rican beaches are public property and available to everyone.) Hundreds of hotel staff live in housing with far worse sewage and water facilities than the hotel. Some workers have complained of inadequate health care and safety rules – two employees have died in accidents in questionable circumstances.

The Costa Rican Supreme Court ordered the project halted in April 1992 and, in September 1992, the Minister of Tourism ordered Grupo Barceló to stop building within the 50 metre zone. Necessary permits for the project had not all been obtained. Despite these restraining orders and alleged violations, the project proceeded as planned and opened in November 1992. This led to criticism of the government for their perceived inability to enforce the law and has also has led to boycotts of the hotel by tourism operators who feel that the highly touted 'environmentally sensitive ecotourism' image of Costa Rica is being destroyed. Some European groups are even calling for a boycott of all tourism in Costa Rica until the environmental and social impact of the hotel has been studied and the problems addressed. Grupo Barceló is planning eight such hotels in Costa Rica.

If you'd like to stay here, rooms are about US$217/251 a single/double including all meals and services. Tennis, a theatre, shops, pool activities etc are available.

At the south end of the bay, in the village of Tambor, is the *Hotel Dos Lagartos* (☎ 61 1122, ext 236). It is clean and friendly, and has beach views and a restaurant. A few rooms with private bath and fan are US$23 a double; most rooms have shared bathrooms and cost US$8.50/12.50 for singles/doubles. Tours can be arranged to nearby areas.

Nearby are several places to eat of which *Cristinas Restaurant* is considered the best. You can get supplies at *Pulpería de Los Gitanos*; next door is *Los Gitanos Bar/Restaurant*. There are also some beach-front sodas. About one km south is the *Bahía Ballena Yacht Club* which has a good restaurant and bar open to the public from 10 am to 10 pm, Tuesday to Sunday. They also provide mooring facilities, boat rentals,

water taxi services and scuba diving. There is a camping site half way between Tambor and the yacht club.

The *Hotel Tango Mar* (☎ 61 2798, fax 55 2697; in San José ☎ 23 1864; Apartado 3877-1000, San José; CRBBG member) is three km south of Tambor village. This is an attractive and secluded beach-front resort with a pool, golf course, tennis court and restaurant. The club is built on 50 hectares of property and has some primary forest left. Tours are available, and you can rent 4WDs, horses, and boating, fishing and diving gear. Spacious individual cabins with fans, private bath and hot water are US$137/150 a single/double or US$150/163 with private jacuzzi. Two bedroom villas with kitchen rent for US$205 to US$300. Breakfast is included.

Getting There & Away

Air Tango Mar has a private airstrip to which planes can be chartered. Travelair has daily flights at 7.30 am from San José to Tambor. They also have a 3.40 pm flight daily, subject to minimum booking requirements, returning 55 minutes after departure from San José. Fares are US$45 one way, US$80 round trip. The airport is just north of the entrance to Hotel Playa Tambor.

Bus The Paquera-Montezuma bus passes through here.

CÓBANO

This small inland town is the most important community in the far south of the Península de Nicoya, though most people go on to Montezuma. There is a bank and other services.

Places to Stay & Eat

There are a few cheap sodas and basic pensiones, including *Cabinas Villa Grace*.

A couple of km north-east of Cóbano at El Cruce de La Esperanza is *La Vida Natural*, a small farm which has a couple of simple ranchos for rent at US$4 per person. One rancho sleeps three and the other sleeps eight. The owners will prepare vegan meals for guests and have a store selling vegetarian and vegan products such as granola, seaweed, medicinal herbs and natural cosmetic products. Kitchen facilities (wood-burning stoves) are available for guests.

Getting There & Away

The Paquera-Montezuma bus comes through here. A 4WD taxi to Montezuma is US$5.

MONTEZUMA

This remote little fishing village near the tip of the Península de Nicoya has good beaches, friendly residents, and several inexpensive to mid-priced hotels.

Montezuma has gained popularity over the last several years with younger gringo travellers who enjoy both the beautiful surroundings and the laid-back atmosphere – it is definitely the 'in' beach on the Costa Rican part of the 'gringo trail'. In fact, there seem to be more gringos than locals in town. Some of the more remote beaches to the north attract nude sunbathers, a custom which is not much appreciated by most of the local people, except, perhaps, some of the young machos who enjoy a leer.

Unfortunately, Montezuma's popularity has outstripped the town's resources and, although almost everyone in town seems to be engaged in the tourist business, there are not really enough rooms in the high season. In addition, the sewerage system is inadequate and there have been reports of raw sewage ending up in the ocean. Therefore swimmers are advised to avoid the beach in front of the town.

On the bright side, however, the locals are aware of the problems and are working to resolve them. Locals have started a 'Montezuma Ecological Fund' and are banding together to organise weekly beach clean-ups, place litter barrels in appropriate places and educate Montezumeños about the importance of preserving their surroundings. They are making every effort to avoid the overdevelopment so much criticised in the Manuel Antonio and Tambor areas – one can only hope that they will succeed.

Information

Electricity didn't arrive at Montezuma until the late 1980s. Until recently, there was only one telephone in town, at Chico's Bar (☎ 61 2472). This was the message phone for the whole village – and it sort of worked, some of the time. Now there is a new central phone number (☎ 61 1122) with extensions to various hotels, houses and restaurants. This new system is expanding.

There are a number of locally run information booths in the centre of town. The staff can help you find places to stay and connect you with locals who rent horses, give tours, and provide land and sea transportation (see Things to See & Do).

There are no banks, but you may be able to change dollars at either Chico's or the El Sano Banano restaurant – if they have enough colones available.

Note that Montezuma has a serious water supply problem (caused by deforestation and run-off) in the dry season. Low water pressure in the showers or water shortages are likely.

Things to See & Do

Ask at the information booths about the following. Bicycle rentals are US$7.25 per day. Horses are about US$20 a half day. Snorkelling gear is US$3.75 for half a day. Kayaks are available for US$11 a half day.

A 20 minute stroll to the south takes you to a lovely waterfall with a swimming hole, reached by taking the trail to the right just after the bridge past the Restaurant Cascada. The waterfall can be climbed, but at your own risk – a visitor was killed in a fall in 1990. (A second set of falls is found about half an hour further upriver.) There is a beautiful nature reserve a few km to the south. Lovely beaches are strung out along the coast, separated by small rocky headlands and offering great beach-combing and tidepool studying.

All-day boat excursions to Isla Tortuga are US$26 a person, but no food is provided and the boats lack canopies – bring a sun hat and sunblock. It's 90 minutes to the island, where you can swim or snorkel. There are no sodas or other facilities so bring food. Boats carrying up to four passengers are available for US$22 per hour (per boat) for fishing, snorkelling or sightseeing, but you have to bring your own gear.

Tours to Cabo Blanco are available, though most people don't bother because it's easy enough to get around yourself. Tours to other destinations may be offered if there is enough demand – lunch is rarely included, so bring your own and plenty of drinking water as well.

Places to Stay

The high season (from December to April) is a difficult time to find rooms. If you arrive on a Friday afternoon, don't expect much choice! Take whatever you can get. If you arrive midweek, first thing in the morning (which means about 9.30 am if you took the first ferry), you won't find much choice either. Wait a couple of hours for people to leave to catch the afternoon ferry. Making reservations helps – though these may not be accepted in the cheapest places and may not be honoured if you arrive late in the other places. If you have a reservation, confirm it as often as you can. Low-season discounts are common, especially in the higher priced places – high-season prices follow.

Places to Stay – bottom end

Single travellers will have a hard time finding a cheap room during the high season, as most places want to charge for a double or triple.

The cheapest accommodation is your tent – you can camp on a beach reasonably safely, though I wouldn't leave any gear inside your tent. Mischievous monkeys will remove anything that looks edible and pilfering primates will steal cameras and wallets. There is a shower in the public park behind Chico's Bar – but you have to ask several times before you can locate it. Locals are beginning to frown upon campers – the already over-stressed sewage system precludes the building of toilet facilities, and campers are soiling the beaches.

The most famous budget place is *Cabinas Karen* which consists of a white house with a couple of basic rooms near the entrance of town plus a pair of cabins with simple facilities in a private reserve 1.5 km outside town. Karen Morgenson is a charismatic and well-known local (originally from Denmark) who, along with her late Swedish husband Olof, was responsible for founding the nearby Cabo Blanco reserve in 1963, and she continues to be an avid conservationist. Her private 69 hectare preserve is open to those staying in one of her cabins. There is no electricity and bathroom facilities are outside. There is a communal kitchen. Monkeys, birds and other animals abound – it is an opportunity to almost camp in the wild yet still retain a roof over your head and a real bed. It is a 25 minute walk into town for food, beer, buses etc.

The white house in town has a couple of basic rooms. There are communal bathroom and kitchen facilities available. The problem is getting in – reservations aren't taken so you just show up and hope for the best. Usually, everything is full and there is a waiting list. Rumour has it that Doña Karen (as she is affectionately called by the locals) rents only to those travellers whom she likes – which probably makes a lot of sense. She charges anywhere between about US$5 and US$10 per person.

Pensión Jenny is quietly situated on a hill above the soccer field and has a decent view of the sea from the common porch. Rooms are basic, but clean and a fair deal for US$5.50 per person in dormitory rooms (four bunk beds) or US$11 for double rooms. All bathrooms are shared. Nearby, *Cabinas El Caracol* has bare but large rooms with communal baths for US$7.25 per person; rooms with private bath are US$17.50 a double. A cheap restaurant is attached.

Cabinas Tucan (☎ 61 1122, ext 284) is fair value for US$14.50 a room, single or double. They have an inexpensive restaurant. *Pensión Arenas* charges US$7.25 per person in shared rooms; private rooms are

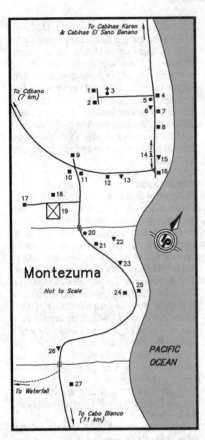

PLACES TO STAY

1 Hotel Montezuma Pacific
2 Cabinas Vilma
4 El Pargo Feliz Cabinas & Restaurant
7 Cabinas Capitan
8 Cabinas Mar y Cielo
9 Hotel La Aurora
10 El Jardín
11 Cabinas & Restaurant Tucan
12 Cabinas Karen
16 Hotel Moctezuma & Pizzería del Sol
17 Pensión Jenny
18 Cabinas & Restaurant El Caracol
21 Pensión Arenas
24 Hotel Los Mangos
25 Cabinas Lucy
27 Hotel Amor de Mar

PLACES TO EAT

4 El Pargo Feliz Restaurant & Cabinas
6 Soda Las Gemelas
11 Restaurant & Cabinas Tucan
13 El Sano Banano
15 Chico's Bar (& Public Telephone)
16 Pizzería del Sol & Hotel Moctezuma
18 Restaurant & Cabinas El Caracol
22 Restaurant El Parque
23 Restaurante La Frescura
26 Restaurant La Cascada

OTHER

3 Church
5 Abastecedor Montezuma (General Store)
14 Information Booths
19 Soccer Field
20 Guardia Civil (Police)

US$14.50/18 for singles/doubles. There's a family-run restaurant attached, and people like to camp on the beach out the front. Another cheap choice is *Pensión Lucy* (☎ 61 1222, ext 273) which charges only US$11 for an airy single or double room, and US$15.50 for a triple. The hotel overlooks the ocean.

The *Hotel Moctezuma* (☎ 61 1122, ext 258) is right in the centre and has a restaurant and popular bar with loud music competing with the nearby Chico's Bar. Light sleepers should bring earplugs if they plan on an early night. With over two dozen rooms, this is a

good place for budget travellers with no reservations to try. Clean, large rooms with fans and private bathroom cost US$14.50 a double; or US$11 in a few rooms with shared baths. Single rates are hard to get in the high season. Some triples and quads are available.

Cabinas Vilma charges US$14.50 for a single or double, is clean, quiet and offers kitchen privileges. *Cabinas Capitan* has basic but clean rooms with three beds for US$22 a triple – single travellers could try for US$11 in the high season. Their mattresses are reportedly good. The *Cabinas Mar y Cielo* (☎ 61 2472, or 61 1122, ext 261) is also clean and charges about US$18 to US$26 a double in rooms with private bath and fan. (Most rooms sleep three or four people.) The cheaper rooms are upstairs and are breezy with nice views – but the hotel has water-pressure problems during the dry season when the upstairs showers often fail. Better showers are downstairs. The hotel is trying to fix the problem – time will tell.

The *Hotel La Aurora* is a pleasant-looking vine-covered place up on the hill coming into town. Clean but ordinary rooms with private bath, fans and mosquito nets are US$26 a double (US$22 with shared bath). The *El Pargo Feliz* also has rooms with fans and private bath for US$22 to US$26 a double.

Places to Stay – middle

The quiet *Hotel Montezuma Pacific* (☎ 61 1122, ext 200; in San José, ☎/fax 22 7746) has good air-conditioned rooms with private bathrooms for US$30/40 single/double. Some rooms have fans and electric showers, and kitchen privileges are available in the low season (a small restaurant runs in the high). There are a couple of cheap rooms with shared bath for US$15 a double.

Near the entrance of town, *El Jardín* (☎ 61 2320) has fairly popular though unremarkable cabins with private bath and fans for about US$35 a double.

The new *Hotel Los Mangos* (☎ 61 1122, ext 259) is a pleasant place with a restaurant and swimming pool. Spacious rooms with fans are US$25 a double, or US$35 a double with private bath. Further south is the quiet *Hotel Amor de Mar* (☎ 61 1122, ext 262) which has pleasant grounds and a nice shorefront with a tide pool big enough to swim in. A 2nd floor balcony area overlooks the sea. There is a restaurant serving breakfasts, and maybe other meals in the high season. Good upstairs rooms with fans and shared bath are US$34 a double; downstairs rooms with fans and private bath are US$40. They also have one dormitory room with single beds at US$9 per person.

Lenny and Patricia Iacono who run the *El*

Sano Banano restaurant (☎ 61 1122, ext 272) have pleasant and attractive cabins for rent by a beach about 15 minutes walk north of town. Cabins are intriguingly shaped polygons or geodesic dome huts, many with private baths, porches and sea views. A few have shared baths, and some have refrigerators and/or private kitchens. Rates are about US$40 to US$60 depending on the cabin.

Montezuma is growing – I would expect more accommodation to open up in the next few years.

Places to Eat

Chico's Bar is the traditional place to go for a beer and a meal – the food is simple and not too expensive. A number of other places have opened in recent years – they cater to tourists and may charge 21% tax on top of the bill: ask if you are on a budget. Cheap places which recently didn't add tax include the *Restaurant Tucan, Restaurante La Frescura, Soda La Gemelas* and *Restaurant El Parque*. You can get a fish casado at these places for about US$3.50, perhaps a little less with chicken or around US$5 for a fish dinner. They don't sell alcohol, but you can bring your own. These places offer the best budget values and are very popular with young travellers – you should go by about 6 pm for the best choice of food and tables. The restaurant at *Cabinas El Caracol* is also similarly priced.

Other places which serve decent meals but are a little more expensive include *El Pargo Feliz* which serves seafood and lobster dinners, *Restaurant La Cascada* which is a quiet and pleasant place next to a stream, and the popular restaurant/bar in the *Hotel Moctezuma*. Next door to the Moctezuma is the *Pizzería del Sol* which serves slices of pizza for US$1.20 – a good snack.

The well-known and popular *El Sano Banano* restaurant serves yoghurt, juices, fruit salads and sane bananas *(sano* actually means 'healthy', but sane seems like a better transcription!) as well as full vegetarian meals and pizzas. They have a big-screen TV and show movies every night (US$2 minimum consumption). They will also prepare picnic lunches for day tours. The owners are actively involved in community affairs and are a good source of information on the area.

To make your own picnic lunches, buy supplies at the Abastecedor Montezuma. I've read reports that gringos may be overcharged in the Montezuma stores – I don't know if that's true.

Getting There & Away

The ferries from Puntarenas connect with the Paquera-Montezuma bus. Buses leave Montezuma at 5.30 am and 2 pm (plus 10 am in the dry season) for Paquera to connect with the ferries to Puntarenas. The fare is US$2.50. During the rainy season, the section to Cóbano may be impassable to 2WD. A jeep taxi between Cóbano and Montezuma is US$5. Note that the ferry leaving Puntarenas at 3 pm gets into Montezuma well after dark – not a good time to be looking for hotels in this town.

A 4WD taxi from Montezuma to Paquera costs about US$29, to Cabo Blanco about US$14.50 and to Mal País about US$25.

MAL PAÍS

This small village is on the west coast of the peninsula, about four km north of Cabo Blanco. It is reached by a poor road southwest of Cóbano – the Río Negro must be forded and high clearance or 4WD may be necessary. It can also be reached by 4WD or horseback from Montezuma using a worse road via Cabuya.

A couple of basic places to stay and eat can be found. The best known is the *Mar Azul* down on the beach which serves seafood and has a few inexpensive cabinas for rent. There are other places. Horses can be rented for the four km down to Cabo Blanco.

CABUYA

This tiny village is about nine km south of Montezuma and two km north of Cabo Blanco. An interesting feature is the local cemetery which is on Isla Cabuya, just to the south-east. The cemetery can be reached only at low tides because the (otherwise uninhabited) island is cut off from the mainland at high tide.

The *Ancla de Oro* restaurant and cabinas has simple thatched roof huts in a pleasant garden. You can stay here for US$7.25 per person. The restaurant serves decent seafood and the owner arranges local boat, horse and vehicle tours to various local sites of interest. You can rent a horse for US$18.50 a day. There is no phone, but you can leave messages at the Pulpería on ☎ 61 3234.

There are a couple of other places opening up to take some of the tourist overflow from Montezuma.

RESERVA NATURAL ABSOLUTA CABO BLANCO

This beautiful reserve encompasses 1172 hectares and includes the entire southern tip of the Península de Nicoya. The reserve was established in 1963 by Karen Morgenson and Olof Wessberg, who donated it to the Costa Rican nation several years before a park system had even been created.

Until the late 1980s, Cabo Blanco was called an 'absolute' nature reserve because no visitors were permitted. Now there are trails and visits are allowed, but the recent upsurge in the popularity of the Montezuma area has led to greater visitation than expected. Accordingly, park director Stanley Arguedas is working with founder Karen Morgensen to find ways to minimise tourist impact. This may include limiting the number of visitors on any given day, asking all visitors to attend an orientation session when they arrive, and having local guides accompany visitors on park trails. In addition, Arguedas and Morgenson are trying to buy five farms which border the park. These farms are up for sale and cover over 300 hectares of land, including some important watersheds used by the wildlife. Some US$750,000 are needed – potential donors should contact Karen Morgenson, Montezuma, Cóbano de Puntarenas, Costa Rica, for further information.

Information

Just inside the park, south of Cabuya, is a

ranger station where you pay a US$1.50 entrance fee and can obtain a trail map. The reserve is open from 8 am to 4 pm. Ask in Montezuma about current entrance requirements or restrictions.

Average annual temperatures are about 27°C and annual rainfall is some 2300 mm at the tip of the park. The easiest months for visits are from December to April – the dry season.

Camping is not permitted.

Things to Do & See

The reserve preserves an evergreen forest, a couple of attractive beaches, and a host of birds and animals. There are several km of trails, which are excellent for wildlife observation. Monkeys, squirrels, sloths, deer, agoutis and raccoons are among the more common sightings – ocelots and margays have also been recorded, but you'd have to be very lucky to see one of these elusive wild cats. Armadillos, coatis, peccaries and ant-eaters are also present.

The coastal area is known as an important nesting site of the brown booby. Some nest on the mainland, but most are found on Isla Cabo Blanco, 1.6 km south of the mainland. The island supposedly gains its name ('white cape') from the bird droppings (or guano) encrusting the rocks. Other seabirds in the area include brown pelicans and magnificent frigatebirds. The beaches at the tip of the peninsula abound in the usual marine life – starfish, sea anemones, sea urchins, conchs, lobsters, crabs and tropical fish are a few of the things to look for.

A trail leads from the ranger station south of Cabuya to the beaches at the tip of the peninsula. The hike takes a couple of hours and passes through lush forest before emerging at the coast – a great opportunity to see many different kinds of birds, ranging from parrots and trogons in the forest to pelicans and boobies on the coast. You can visit two beaches at the peninsula tip and then return by a different trail. The high point of the reserve is 375 metres, and parts of the trail are steep and strenuous.

Check with the park rangers about trails and tides. The trail joining the two beaches at the tip of the reserve may be impassable at high tide.

Getting There & Away

The reserve is about 11 km south of Montezuma by a very bad dirt road – 4WD is needed in the rainy season. Taxis with 4WD charge US$14.50 from Montezuma. Also, a daily passenger 4WD leaves Montezuma at 7 am and returns around 2 or 3 pm – the fare is US$5 per person, round trip.

Appendix I – Telephone Numbers

New Costa Rica Telephone Numbers

To change from the current six digit number to the new seven digit number, look up the six digit number in the table below. Then replace the first two digits with the three digits indicated. The last four digits do not change.

Current Numbers (Six digits)	New Numbers (Seven digits)	Current Numbers (Six digits)	New Numbers (Seven digits)
20 0000 to 20 9999	220 0000 to 220 9999	44 1000 to 44 1999	453 1000 to 453 1999
21 0000 to 21 9999	221 0000 to 221 9999	44 2000 to 44 2999	452 2000 to 452 2999
22 0000 to 22 9999	222 0000 to 222 9999	44 4000 to 44 4999	458 4000 to 458 4999
23 0000 to 23 9999	223 0000 to 223 9999	44 5000 to 44 7999	444 5000 to 444 7999
24 0000 to 24 9999	224 0000 to 224 9999	45 0000 to 45 0999	450 0000 to 450 0999
25 0000 to 25 9999	225 0000 to 225 9999	45 1000 to 45 1999	451 1000 to 451 1999
26 0000 to 26 9999	226 0000 to 226 9999	45 2000 to 45 2999	452 2000 to 452 2999
27 0000 to 27 9999	227 0000 to 227 9999	45 3000 to 45 3999	453 3000 to 453 3999
28 0000 to 28 9999	228 0000 to 228 9999	45 4000 to 45 4999	454 4000 to 454 4999
29 0000 to 29 9999	229 0000 to 229 9999	45 5000 to 45 6999	445 5000 to 445 6999
30 0000 to 30 1999	270 0000 to 270 1999	46 0000 to 46 4999	460 0000 to 460 4999
30 2000 to 30 4999	230 2000 to 230 4999	46 5000 to 46 6999	446 5000 to 446 6999
30 6000 to 30 9999	276 6000 to 276 9999	46 8000 to 46 9999	428 8000 to 428 9999
31 0000 to 31 9999	231 0000 to 231 9999	47 0000 to 47 0999	470 0000 to 470 0999
32 0000 to 32 9999	232 0000 to 232 9999	47 1000 to 47 1999	471 1000 to 471 1999
33 0000 to 33 9999	233 0000 to 233 9999	47 2000 to 47 2999	472 2000 to 472 2999
34 0000 to 34 2999	234 0000 to 234 2999	47 3000 to 47 3999	473 3000 to 473 3999
34 3000 to 34 4999	273 3000 to 273 4999	47 4000 to 47 4999	474 4000 to 474 4999
34 6000 to 34 9999	234 6000 to 234 9999	47 5000 to 47 5999	475 5000 to 475 5999
35 0000 to 35 9999	235 0000 to 235 9999	47 6000 to 47 6999	476 6000 to 476 6999
36 0000 to 36 9999	236 0000 to 236 9999	47 7000 to 47 7999	477 7000 to 477 7999
37 0000 to 37 9999	237 0000 to 237 9999	47 8000 to 47 8999	478 8000 to 478 8999
38 0000 to 38 9999	238 0000 to 238 9999	47 9000 to 47 9999	479 9000 to 479 9999
39 0000 to 39 3999	239 0000 to 239 3999	48 0000 to 48 1999	438 0000 to 438 1999
39 5000 to 39 6999	265 5000 to 265 6999	48 2000 to 48 2999	482 2000 to 482 2999
39 7000 to 39 7999	267 7000 to 267 7999	48 3000 to 48 3999	483 3000 to 483 3999
39 8000 to 39 8999	268 8000 to 268 8999	48 5000 to 48 6999	448 5000 to 448 6999
39 9000 to 39 9999	269 9000 to 269 9999	48 7000 to 48 7999	487 7000 to 487 7999
40 0000 to 40 9999	240 0000 to 240 9999	48 9000 to 48 9999	469 9000 to 469 9999
41 0000 to 41 9999	441 0000 to 441 9999	49 0000 to 49 0999	410 0000 to 410 0999
42 0000 to 42 9999	442 0000 to 442 9999	49 1000 to 49 2999	249 1000 to 249 2999
43 0000 to 43 6999	443 0000 to 443 6999	49 3000 to 49 3999	463 3000 to 463 3999
43 7000 to 43 9999	433 7000 to 433 9999	49 5000 to 49 5999	449 5000 to 449 5999
44 0000 to 44 0999	452 0000 to 452 0999	49 6000 to 49 7999	416 6000 to 416 7999

Current Numbers *(Six digits)*	New Numbers *(Seven digits)*	Current Numbers *(Six digits)*	New Numbers *(Seven digits)*
49 8000 to 49 8999	418 8000 to 418 8999	68 2000 to 68 2999	682 2000 to 682 2999
49 9000 to 49 9999	419 9000 to 419 9999	68 3000 to 68 3999	683 3000 to 683 3999
50 0000 to 50 9999	250 0000 to 250 9999	68 4000 to 68 4999	684 4000 to 684 4999
51 0000 to 51 9999	551 0000 to 551 9999	68 5000 to 68 5999	685 5000 to 685 5999
52 0000 to 52 6999	552 0000 to 552 6999	68 6000 to 68 6999	686 6000 to 686 6999
53 0000 to 53 9999	253 0000 to 253 9999	68 9000 to 68 9999	685 9000 to 685 9999
54 0000 to 54 9999	254 0000 to 254 9999	69 0000 to 69 1999	669 0000 to 669 1999
55 0000 to 55 4999	255 0000 to 255 4999	69 4000 to 69 4999	694 4000 to 694 4999
56 0000 to 56 7999	556 0000 to 556 7999	69 5000 to 69 5999	695 5000 to 695 5999
57 0000 to 57 9999	257 0000 to 257 9999	69 6000 to 69 6999	695 6000 to 695 6999
58 0000 to 58 4999	758 0000 to 758 4999	69 8000 to 69 8999	688 8000 to 688 8999
58 5000 to 58 5999	755 5000 to 755 5999	70 0000 to 70 2999	710 0000 to 710 2999
59 0000 to 59 9999	259 0000 to 259 9999	71 0000 to 71 5999	771 0000 to 771 5999
60 0000 to 60 7999	260 0000 to 260 7999	71 6000 to 71 7999	710 6000 to 710 7999
61 0000 to 61 9999	661 0000 to 661 9999	72 0000 to 72 4999	272 0000 to 272 4999
62 0000 to 62 9999	662 0000 to 662 9999	73 0000 to 73 0999	530 0000 to 530 0999
63 0000 to 63 3999	663 0000 to 663 3999	73 1000 to 73 1999	531 1000 to 531 1999
63 4000 to 63 4999	634 4000 to 634 4999	73 2000 to 73 2999	532 2000 to 532 2999
63 5000 to 63 5999	635 5000 to 635 5999	73 3000 to 73 3999	533 3000 to 533 3999
63 6000 to 63 6999	636 6000 to 636 6999	73 4000 to 73 4999	534 4000 to 534 4999
63 7000 to 63 7999	663 7000 to 663 7999	73 5000 to 73 5999	535 5000 to 535 5999
63 9000 to 63 9999	639 9000 to 639 9999	73 6000 to 73 6999	536 6000 to 536 6999
64 0000 to 64 0999	650 0000 to 650 0999	73 7000 to 73 8999	573 7000 to 573 8999
64 1000 to 64 1999	641 1000 to 641 1999	74 1000 to 74 1999	541 1000 to 541 1999
64 2000 to 64 2999	642 2000 to 642 2999	74 5000 to 74 5999	544 5000 to 544 5999
64 3000 to 64 3999	643 3000 to 643 3999	74 6000 to 74 7999	574 6000 to 574 7999
64 4000 to 64 4999	644 4000 to 644 4999	75 0000 to 75 1999	775 0000 to 775 1999
64 5000 to 64 5999	645 5000 to 645 5999	75 3000 to 75 4999	783 3000 to 783 4999
64 6000 to 64 6999	684 6000 to 684 6999	75 5000 to 75 5999	784 5000 to 784 5999
65 5000 to 65 5999	655 5000 to 655 5999	75 6000 to 75 7999	786 6000 to 786 7999
65 6000 to 65 6999	675 6000 to 675 6999	75 8000 to 75 8999	788 8000 to 788 8999
65 7000 to 65 7999	657 7000 to 657 7999	75 9000 to 75 9999	789 9000 to 789 9999
65 8000 to 65 8999	678 8000 to 678 8999	76 0000 to 76 0999	760 0000 to 760 0999
65 9000 to 65 9999	659 9000 to 659 9999	76 1000 to 76 1999	761 1000 to 761 1999
66 0000 to 66 3999	666 0000 to 666 3999	76 2000 to 76 2999	754 2000 to 754 2999
66 9000 to 66 9999	679 9000 to 679 9999	76 3000 to 76 3999	763 3000 to 763 3999
67 0000 to 67 0999	670 0000 to 670 0999	76 4000 to 76 4999	764 4000 to 764 4999
67 1000 to 67 1999	671 1000 to 671 1999	76 5000 to 76 5999	716 5000 to 716 5999
67 2000 to 67 2999	672 2000 to 672 2999	76 6000 to 76 6999	766 6000 to 766 6999
67 3000 to 67 3999	673 3000 to 673 3999	76 7000 to 76 7999	767 7000 to 767 7999
67 4000 to 67 4999	654 4000 to 654 4999	76 8000 to 76 9999	768 8000 to 768 9999
67 5000 to 67 5999	653 5000 to 653 5999	77 0000 to 77 1999	777 0000 to 777 1999
68 0000 to 68 0999	680 0000 to 680 0999	77 3000 to 77 3999	773 3000 to 773 3999
68 1000 to 68 1999	681 1000 to 681 1999	77 4000 to 77 4999	774 4000 to 774 4999

Current Numbers *(Six digits)*	New Numbers *(Seven digits)*
77 5000 to 77 5999	717 5000 to 717 5999
77 6000 to 77 6999	546 6000 to 546 6999
77 7000 to 77 7999	547 7000 to 547 7999
77 8000 to 77 8999	756 8000 to 756 8999
77 9000 to 77 9999	779 9000 to 779 9999
78 0000 to 78 1999	730 0000 to 730 1999
78 2000 to 78 2999	732 2000 to 732 2999
78 3000 to 78 3999	733 3000 to 733 3999
78 4000 to 78 4999	734 4000 to 734 4999
78 5000 to 78 5999	735 5000 to 735 5999
78 6000 to 78 6999	736 6000 to 736 6999
78 8000 to 78 8999	778 8000 to 778 8999
79 0000 to 79 9999	279 0000 to 279 9999
80 0000 to 80 9999	280 0000 to 280 9999
81 0000 to 81 9999	281 0000 to 281 9999
82 0000 to 82 9999	282 0000 to 282 9999
83 0000 to 83 9999	283 0000 to 283 9999
84 0000 to 84 9999	284 0000 to 284 9999
85 0000 to 85 9999	285 0000 to 285 9999

Current Numbers *(Six digits)*	New Numbers *(Seven digits)*
86 0000 to 86 9999	286 0000 to 286 9999
87 0000 to 87 0999	287 0000 to 287 0999
87 1000 to 87 1999	207 1000 to 207 1999
87 2000 to 87 2999	287 2000 to 287 2999
87 3000 to 87 3999	277 3000 to 277 3999
87 4000 to 87 4999	247 4000 to 247 4999
87 5000 to 87 7999	287 5000 to 287 7999
87 8000 to 87 8999	247 8000 to 247 8999
87 9000 to 87 9999	287 9000 to 287 9999
88 0000 to 88 9999	288 0000 to 288 9999
89 0000 to 89 9999	289 0000 to 289 9999
90 0000 to 90 5999	490 0000 to 490 5999
91 0000 to 91 5999	591 0000 to 591 5999
92 0000 to 92 9999	292 0000 to 292 9999
93 0000 to 93 4999	293 0000 to 293 4999
94 0000 to 94 4999	494 0000 to 494 4999
95 0000 to 95 9999	295 0000 to 295 9999
96 0000 to 96 9999	296 0000 to 296 9999
97 0000 to 97 2999	297 0000 to 297 2999
98 0000 to 98 1999	798 0000 to 798 1999

Glossary

Abastecedor – general store

Apartotel – furnished apartments available for nightly or weekly rental

ATEC –Asociación Talamanqueño de Ecotourismo y Conservación

Avenida – Avenue

Automercado – a type of supermarket

B&B – Bed & Breakfast

Boca – a snack served with a drink in a bar

Calle – Street

Campesino – small-time farmer

Cantón – sub-division of a province; county

Carreta – ox-cart

Carretera – highway

Casado – economical set meal of rice, beans, vegetables and meat or sometimes fish

Cerro – mountain peak

Coca-Cola – main San José bus terminal area

Colectivo – shared taxi, minibus

Cordillera – mountain chain

Costanera – the coastal highway

CRBBG – Costa Rican Bed & Breakfast Group

Filibuster – an American provoking military insurrections in Latin America in the 1800s

Finca – farm, ranch (especially for coffee)

Gallo Pinta – typical breakfast dish of rice mixed with black beans

ICE – Instituto Costarricense de Electricidad (phone/fax services)

ICT – Instituto Costarricense de Tourismo (Costa Rican tourist information office)

IGN – Instituto Geográfico Nacional

Joséfino – inhabitant of San José

Lago – lake

Laguna – lake, lagoon

Llanura – large plain

Mariachi – Mexican street musician

Marimba – a xylophone-like instrument with resonators beneath each bar

Mercado – market

Minimercado – small general store

Municipalidad, Municipio – town hall

Páramo – high altitude grass and shrubland

Pensión – a cheap, often family-run hotel

Pulpería – a small general store

Sabanero – Costa Rican cowboy, especially from Guanacaste Province

Soda – small café or lunch counter

SPN – Servico de Parques Nacionales (National Parks Service)

Supermercado – supermarket

Tico/tica – Costa Rican people (male/female)

Vivero – plant nursery

Index

MAPS

TEXT

Map references are in **bold** type.

THANKS

Thanks to all the following travellers and others (apologies if we've misspelt your name) who took time to write to us about their experiences in Costa Rica.

To those whose names have been omitted through oversight, apologies, your time and efforts are appreciated.

Ackman, Dan (USA); Alfaro, María (CR); Amrein, Alois Anton (CH); Arguedas, Juan Stanley (CR); Arnold-Forster, David (UK); Arthur, Dee Dee (USA); Asch, Erick (CR); Atkinson, Laurie (CR); Bak, Nettie (NL); Balen, Johan H van (NL); Barrett, Laurel (C); Becker, Martin Fischer (CR); Bell, C Vernon (CR); Benedetti, Laura & Marshall, Brad (Fr); Berkum, Robert van & Knake, Margaret (NL); Berman, Rod S (USA); Bien, Amos (CR); Bjornson, Marie (USA); Bolaños Gutiérrez, Luis A (CR); Bohmer, Robert (C); Borella, Stéphane (CH); Brady, Charlie Brinckerhoff, Joris A (CR); Brown, R L (USA); Bruno, Vikki (USA); Campbell, Mari (USA); Canossa, Alfredo (CR); Cazedessus, J Cooper (CR); Charness, Gary (USA); Coberly, Chris & Laurie (CR); Connery, Rick & Thea (C); Cook, David (USA); Cory, Cotner, Kelly (USA); Coyne, Lee & Trev (Aus); Creswell, Christine & Tony (USA); Currier, Melinda Merrill (USA); DeConcini, Dino (USA); Delapré, Pascal (C); Del Prete, Tony (USA); Dumontier, Odi (CR); Eitan & Elya (Isr); Erb, John W (CR); Esquivel, Ronald (CR); Eure, Alicia (USA); Ewasiuk, Pamela (C); Ewing, Natalie (USA); Fast, Norman (USA); Fergusen, Kyle (CR); Feteris, Maarten (NL); Fischer, Martin (CR); Fridberg, Ofer (Isr); Friedman, Steve & Paula (CR); Freundlieb, Marion (D); Galati, Randy (USA); Gámez, Aurira (CR); Garwood, Martin (UK); Gaudette, Thea (CR); Geer, Sandy (USA); Gillenkirk, Jeff (USA); Gordon, Julie (USA); Grounds, Bridget; Guido, Marlene Fallas (CR); Hamilton, G; Jaime M (CR); Hendley, Tim (USA); Hoelzli, Ursula (C); Honan, Mark (UK); Hood, Charles (USA); – thanks for extensive birding notes; Houtzager, Marianne (NL); Johnson, Ralph (USA); Kalmbach, Susan (CR); Kerr, Ronald (USA); Kimball, Marden D (USA); King, Deborah Lee (CR); Kinghorn, Sandra (CR); Lamont, Fiona (CR); Lantos, Steve (USA); Martelli, Arnold (USA); Martín, Rubén L (CR); McCreary, Jan (USA); McGorman, Owen (C); McKellar, David (C); McLaren, Marjay (USA); McMurray, Debbi (CRBBG, CR); Medill, Michael (USA); Messenger, Mary (CR); Meyer, Marietta (CH); Michaud, Herbert (CR); Milligan, Jennifer (USA); Mikuls, Melinda & Mermelstein, Suzanne (USA); Milum, Brenda ; Monjaras, Emmanuel (Mex); Morales, Romy (CR); Morse, Bertha H (USA); Moyal, Jessica & Henri (USA); Munn, Melissa (C); Navarro, Enrique Batalla (CR); O'Brien, Robert (CR); O'Mara, Joan (USA); Ossa, Tomás I de la (CR); Ostrander, Tom (USA); Parsons, Rick (USA); Pearce, Jon & Boylan, Fay (UK); Perron, Julie (USA); Piat, Marlene (USA); Pinel, Javier & Helen (USA); Preninger, Stephanie (USA); Puerini, Karen; Rabion, Mary Ann (USA); Ramos T, Juan Carlos (CR); Reilly, Sharon (USA); Robertson, Lisa J (C); Rogers, Yvonne (USA); Rojas, Michelle de (CR); Romero, César T (CR); Rusling, Tina (USA); Sacks, Marcy (USA); Salas Picado, Juan Antonio (CR); Salazar, Mauricio (ATEC, CR); Schnurpfeil, Herbert (A); Schoenherr, Mr & Mrs R J (USA); Schrager, Fran & Gary (USA); Sessions, Kitty (USA); Sherar, Nia & Ernie (USA); Sinclair, Jean (UK); Singer, Lisa (USA); Sobeck, Joseph (USA); Sotela, Mariamalia (CR); Soto Chaves, Alfredo (CR); Spinnler, René & Lüscher, Ruth (CR); Stackhouse, Cyd (USA); Stasaitis, Terry (Honduras); Stearns, Tim (USA); Stephenson, Carl & Marian (C); Stiles, Michael (CR); St John, A P (USA); Stonehouse, Duncan J (UK); Strippoli, Anthony (USA); Taines, Sarah & Gordon, Joe (USA); Tanaka, Mark (USA); Tape, Vicki (C); Taylor, Dave & Mary (C); Taylor, Simon Watson (UK); Torr, Geordie (Aus); Walthert, Bruno (USA); Webster, Andrea (UK); Weisz, Arnold (N); Westmaas, Thorwald (CR); Williamson, Harriet (USA); Wolfe, James A (CR); Woudman, Jaup (NL); Zemans, David H (C)

Aus – Australia, A – Austria, C – Canada, CH – Switzerland, CR – Costa Rica, D – Denmark, Fr – France, H – Honduras, Isr – Israel, It – Italy, Mex – Mexico, N – Norway, NL – The Netherlands, UK – United Kingdom, USA – United States of America

Keep in touch!

We love hearing from you and think you'd like to hear from us.

The Lonely Planet Newsletter covers the when, where, how and what of travel. (AND it's free!)

When...is the right time to see reindeer in Finland?
Where...can you hear the best palm-wine music in Ghana?
How...do you get from Asunción to Areguá by steam train?
What...should you leave behind to avoid hassles with customs in Iran?

To join our mailing list just contact us at any of our offices. (details below)

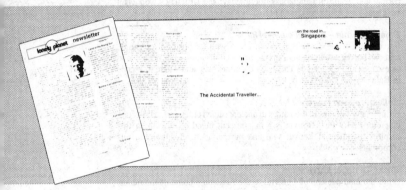

Every issue includes:

- *a letter from Lonely Planet founders Tony and Maureen Wheeler*
- *travel diary from a Lonely Planet author - find out what it's really like out on the road*
- *feature article on an important and topical travel issue*
- *a selection of recent letters from our readers*
- *the latest travel news from all over the world*
- *details on Lonely Planet's new and forthcoming releases*

Also available Lonely Planet T-shirts. 100% heavy weight cotton (S, M, L, XL)

LONELY PLANET PUBLICATIONS
Australia: PO Box 617, Hawthorn, 3122, Victoria (tel: 03-819 1877)
USA: Embarcadero West, 155 Filbert Street, Suite 251, Oakland, CA 94607 (tel: 510-893 8555)
UK: Devonshire House, 12 Barley Mow Passage, Chiswick, London W4 4PH (tel: 081-742 3161)

Guides to the Americas

Alaska – a travel survival kit
Jim DuFresne has travelled extensively through Alaska by foot, road, rail, barge and kayak. This guide has all the information you'll need to make the most of one of the world's great wilderness areas.

Argentina, Uruguay & Paraguay – a travel survival kit
This guide gives independent travellers all the essential information on three of South America's lesser known countries. Discover some of South America's most spectacular natural attractions in Argentina; friendly people and beautiful handicrafts in Paraguay; and Uruguay's wonderful beaches.

Baja California – a travel survival kit
For centuries, Mexico's Baja peninsula – with its beautiful coastline, raucous border towns and crumbling Spanish missions – has been a land of escapes and escapades. This book describes how and where to escape in Baja.

Bolivia – a travel survival kit
From lonely villages in the Andes to ancient ruined cities and the spectacular city of La Paz, Bolivia is a magnificent blend of everything that inspires travellers. Discover safe and intriguing travel options in this comprehensive guide.

Brazil – a travel survival kit
From the mad passion of Carnival to the Amazon – home of the richest and most diverse ecosystem on earth – Brazil is a country of mythical proportions. This guide has all the essential travel information.

Canada – a travel survival kit
This comprehensive guidebook has all the facts on the USA's huge neighbour – the Rocky Mountains, Niagara Falls, ultramodern Toronto, remote villages in Nova Scotia, and much more.

Central America on a shoestring
Practical information on travel in Belize, Guatemala, Costa Rica, Honduras, El Salvador, Nicaragua and Panama. A team of experienced Lonely Planet authors reveals the secrets of this culturally rich, geographically diverse and breathtakingly beautiful region.

Chile & Easter Island – a travel survival kit
Travel in Chile is easy and safe, with possibilities as varied as the countryside. This guide also gives detailed coverage of Chile's Pacific outpost, mysterious Easter Island.

Colombia – a travel survival kit
Colombia is a land of myths – from the ancient legends of El Dorado to the modern tales of Gabriel Garcia Marquez. The reality is beauty and violence, wealth and poverty, tradition and change. This guide shows how to travel independently and safely in this exotic country.

Ecuador & the Galápagos Islands – a travel survival kit
Ecuador offers a wide variety of travel experiences, from the high cordilleras to the Amazon plains – and 600 miles west, the fascinating Galápagos Islands. Everything you need to know about travelling around this enchanting country.

Hawaii – a travel survival kit
Share in the delights of this island paradise – and avoid its high prices – both on and off the beaten track. Full details on Hawaii's best-known attractions, plus plenty of uncrowded sights and activities.

La Ruta Maya: Yucatán, Guatemala & Belize – a travel survival kit
Invaluable background information on the cultural and environmental riches of La Ruta Maya (The Mayan Route), plus practical advice on how best to minimise the impact of travellers on this sensitive region.

Mexico – a travel survival kit
A unique blend of Indian and Spanish culture, fascinating history, and hospitable people, make Mexico a travellers' paradise.

Peru – a travel survival kit
The lost city of Machu Picchu, the Andean altiplano and the magnificent Amazon rainforests are just some of Peru's many attractions. All the travel facts you'll need can be found in this comprehensive guide.

South America on a shoestring
This practical guide provides concise information for budget travellers and covers South America from the Darien Gap to Tierra del Fuego. The *New York Times* dubbed the author 'the patron saint of travellers in the third world'.

Trekking in the Patagonian Andes
The first detailed guide to this region gives complete information on 28 walks, and lists a number of other possibilities extending from the Araucanía and Lake District regions of Argentina and Chile to the remote icy of South America in Tierra del Fuego.

Also available:
Brazilian phrasebook, **Latin American Spanish** phrasebook and **Quechua** phrasebook.

Lonely Planet Guidebooks

Lonely Planet guidebooks cover every accessible part of Asia as well as Australia, the Pacific, South America, Africa, the Middle East, Europe and parts of North America. There are five series: *travel survival kits*, covering a country for a range of budgets; *shoestring guides* with compact information for low-budget travel in a major region; *walking guides*; *city guides* and *phrasebooks*.

Australia & the Pacific
Australia
Bushwalking in Australia
Islands of Australia's Great Barrier Reef
Fiji
Melbourne city guide
Micronesia
New Caledonia
New Zealand
Tramping in New Zealand
Papua New Guinea
Bushwalking in Papua New Guinea
Papua New Guinea phrasebook
Rarotonga & the Cook Islands
Samoa
Solomon Islands
Sydney city guide
Tahiti & French Polynesia
Tonga
Vanuatu
Victoria

South-East Asia
Bali & Lombok
Bangkok city guide
Cambodia
Indonesia
Indonesia phrasebook
Laos
Malaysia, Singapore & Brunei
Myanmar (Burma)
Burmese phrasebook
Philippines
Pilipino phrasebook
Singapore city guide
South-East Asia on a shoestring
Thailand
Thai phrasebook
Vietnam
Vietnamese phrasebook

North-East Asia
China
Beijing city guide
Mandarin Chinese phrasebook
Hong Kong, Macau & Canton
Japan
Japanese phrasebook
Korea
Korean phrasebook
Mongolia
North-East Asia on a shoestring
Seoul city guide
Taiwan
Tibet
Tibet phrasebook
Tokyo city guide

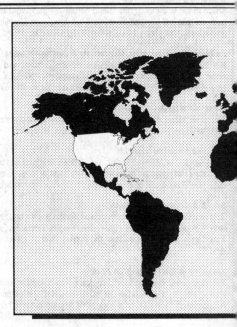

West Asia
Trekking in Turkey
Turkey
Turkish phrasebook
West Asia on a shoestring

Middle East
Arab Gulf States
Egypt & the Sudan
Arabic (Egyptian) phrasebook
Iran
Israel
Jordan & Syria
Yemen

Indian Ocean
Madagascar & Comoros
Maldives & Islands of the East Indian Ocean
Mauritius, Réunion & Seychelles

Mail Order

Lonely Planet guidebooks are distributed worldwide.They are also available by mail order from Lonely Planet, so if you have difficulty finding a title please write to us. US and Canadian residents should write to Embarcadero West, 155 Filbert St, Suite 251, Oakland CA 94607, USA ; European residents should write to Devonshire House, 12 Barley Mow Passage, Chiswick, London W4 4PH; and residents of other countries to PO Box 617, Hawthorn, Victoria 3122, Australia.

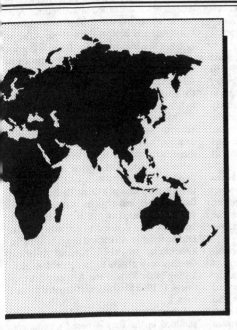

Indian Subcontinent
Bangladesh
India
Hindi/Urdu phrasebook
Trekking in the Indian Himalaya
Karakoram Highway
Kashmir, Ladakh & Zanskar
Nepal
Trekking in the Nepal Himalaya
Nepal phrasebook
Pakistan
Sri Lanka
Sri Lanka phrasebook

Africa
Africa on a shoestring
Central Africa
East Africa
Trekking in East Africa
Kenya
Swahili phrasebook
Morocco, Algeria & Tunisia
Arabic (Moroccan) phrasebook
South Africa, Lesotho & Swaziland
Zimbabwe, Botswana & Namibia
West Africa

Central America
Baja California
Central America on a shoestring
Costa Rica
La Ruta Maya
Mexico

North America
Alaska
Canada
Hawaii

Europe
Dublin city guide
Eastern Europe on a shoestring
Eastern Europe phrasebook
Finland
Hungary
Iceland, Greenland & the Faroe Islands
Ireland
Italy
Mediterranean Europe on a shoestring
Mediterranean Europe phrasebook
Poland
Scandinavian & Baltic Europe on a shoestring
Scandinavian Europe phrasebook
Switzerland
Trekking in Spain
Trekking in Greece
USSR
Russian phrasebook
Western Europe on a shoestring
Western Europe phrasebook

South America
Argentina, Uruguay & Paraguay
Bolivia
Brazil
Brazilian phrasebook
Chile & Easter Island
Colombia
Ecuador & the Galápagos Islands
Latin American Spanish phrasebook
Peru
Quechua phrasebook
South America on a shoestring
Trekking in the Patagonian Andes

The Lonely Planet Story

Lonely Planet published its first book in 1973 in response to the numerous 'How did you do it?' questions Maureen and Tony Wheeler were asked after driving, bussing, hitching, sailing and railing their way from England to Australia.

Written at a kitchen table and hand collated, trimmed and stapled, *Across Asia on the Cheap* became an instant local bestseller, inspiring thoughts of another book.

Eighteen months in South-East Asia resulted in their second guide, *South-East Asia on a shoestring*, which they put together in a backstreet Chinese hotel in Singapore in 1975. The 'yellow bible' as it quickly became known to backpackers around the world, soon became *the* guide to the region. It has sold well over half a million copies and is now in its 7th edition, still retaining its familiar yellow cover.

Today there are over 120 Lonely Planet titles in print – books that have that same adventurous approach to travel as those early guides; books that 'assume you know how to get your luggage off the carousel' as one reviewer put it.

Although Lonely Planet initially specialised in guides to Asia, they now cover most regions of the world, including the Pacific, South America, Africa, the Middle East and Europe. The list of *walking guides* and *phrasebooks* (for 'unusual' languages such as Quechua, Swahili, Nepalese and Egyptian Arabic) is also growing rapidly.

The emphasis continues to be on travel for independent travellers. Tony and Maureen still travel for several months of each year and play an active part in the writing, updating and quality control of Lonely Planet's guides.

They have been joined by over 50 authors, 54 staff – mainly editors, cartographers, & designers – at our office in Melbourne, Australia, 10 at our US office in Oakland, California and another three at our office in London to handle sales for Britain, Europe and Africa. In 1992 Lonely Planet opened an editorial office in Paris. Travellers themselves also make a valuable contribution to the guides through the feedback we receive in thousands of letters each year.

The people at Lonely Planet strongly believe that travellers can make a positive contribution to the countries they visit, both through their appreciation of the countries' culture, wildlife and natural features, and through the money they spend. In addition, the company makes a direct contribution to the countries and regions it covers. Since 1986 a percentage of the income from each book has been donated to ventures such as famine relief in Africa; aid projects in India; agricultural projects in Central America; Greenpeace's efforts to halt French nuclear testing in the Pacific and Amnesty International. In 1993 $100,000 was donated to such causes.

Lonely Planet's basic travel philosophy is summed up in Tony Wheeler's comment, 'Don't worry about whether your trip will work out. Just go!'